The Connects

DONALENE
267321

JOHN
456711

BILLIE JEAN
000100

PHYLLIS
87 3201

# LATIN POETRY

*Corot*                                                  *Museum of Fine Arts, Boston*

VERGIL AND DANTE ENTERING THE UNDERWORLD

In his epic poem, "The Divine Comedy," Dante acknowledges Vergil
as his master and guide.

# LATIN POETRY

BY

## WILBERT LESTER CARR

PROFESSOR OF LATIN
TEACHERS COLLEGE
COLUMBIA UNIVERSITY

AND

## HARRY E. WEDECK

CHAIRMAN, CLASSICAL LANGUAGES
ERASMUS HALL HIGH SCHOOL
BROOKLYN, NEW YORK

## D. C. HEATH AND COMPANY

BOSTON      NEW YORK      CHICAGO
ATLANTA      SAN FRANCISCO      DALLAS
LONDON

PRINTED IN THE UNITED STATES OF AMERICA

# PREFACE

This book is designed primarily to meet the needs of students who will read Latin poetry instead of Latin prose following two years of Latin in high school or one year in college.

*Special Features.* Some special features of the book which the authors believe will commend themselves to alert teachers and to students are the following:

1. Emphasis upon Vergil's *Aeneid*, especially Books I, II, IV, and VI. The entire text, together with comprehension questions, of Books III and V. Representative, interesting selections from various Latin poets.
2. The device of the marginal vocabulary as a ready aid to minimize the vocabulary burden.
3. Notes on the same page with the text.
4. Comprehension questions on the text.
5. Work units providing abundant teaching material and comprehensive drills based on the Latin text.
6. An appendix giving biographical material, a survey of Latin poetry, and a compendium of Latin grammar.
7. A complete Latin-English vocabulary.
8. Attractive, artistic, relevant illustrations.

Following is a more detailed description of the special features mentioned above:

*Latin Selections.* Part I consists of the complete text of Vergil's *Aeneid*, Books I–VI, with notes and marginal vocabulary on Books I, II, IV, VI — the books most commonly used for intensive study. The text of Books III and V is given entire for cross reference, sight reading, and individual assignments. Part II consists of selections from Catullus, Vergil (*Eclogues* and *Georgics*), Ovid, Horace, Phaedrus, Martial, Hadrian, Ausonius, and Claudian. The selections from Ovid are especially generous.

*The Marginal Vocabulary.* As every teacher knows, the chief difficulty in the reading of Vergil or Ovid lies in the vocabulary burden which these authors impose. The device of the marginal vocabulary — which is becoming a feature in modern foreign language texts — removes most of that burden. Every word beyond the "required" words of the first two years is explained on its first, second, and third appearance in the text. This explanation is given in the margin directly to the right or left of the word in the text, so that the student secures the needed aid with a minimum loss of time and without losing his place in the text. It has been demonstrated in the laboratory that the eye moves right and left many times more quickly than up and down. In this marginal vocabulary each "College Board" word for the third or fourth year is indicated, one star denoting its first appearance in the book, two stars the second appearance, and three stars a third appearance. All starred words are also listed in the work units for drill and mastery.

*Notes on the Text.* The authors of this book believe that notes on the text should be addressed exclusively to the student and designed to help him understand the Latin text he is reading. They also believe that the notes should be so placed as to make reference to them as accessible as possible for the student. In this book the notes are placed at the foot of the page with line references to the text.

*Comprehension Questions.* Comprehension questions are provided at frequent intervals on the entire text of Part I. Classical teachers and testing agencies, such as the College Entrance Examination Board, are placing increasing emphasis upon the use of comprehension questions as a means of testing the student's understanding of the Latin text and also of giving the student a "reading attitude" toward the printed Latin page. Experience has shown that a student may give a wrong answer to a comprehension question, but he is not likely to give a meaningless response, as students frequently do when they are asked to "translate."

*Work Units.* A series of twenty work units, based on the *Aeneid*, Books I, II, IV, and VI, offers valuable teaching material consisting of vocabulary drills, word study, metrical reading, cultural content and background, references and allusions covering a wide field of literature, figures of speech, and poetic syntax.

*The Appendix.* The Appendix provides the sort of reference material commonly found in an introduction, in addition to a complete list of the grammatical forms, syntactical uses, and figures of speech needed for reading and discussing the Latin text.

*Latin-English Vocabulary.* The book contains a Latin-English vocabulary of all the words appearing in the Latin text. All words in the College Entrance Examination Board's *Latin Word List* are indicated by an asterisk (*). Words included in the New York State Syllabus list, but not included in the College Board list, are indicated by a dagger (†).

*Illustrations.* The illustrations have been chosen for their artistic value as well as for their appositeness in helping to interpret the Latin text to which they refer.

W. L. C.<br>H. E. W.

# TABLE OF CONTENTS

v

# LIST OF ILLUSTRATIONS

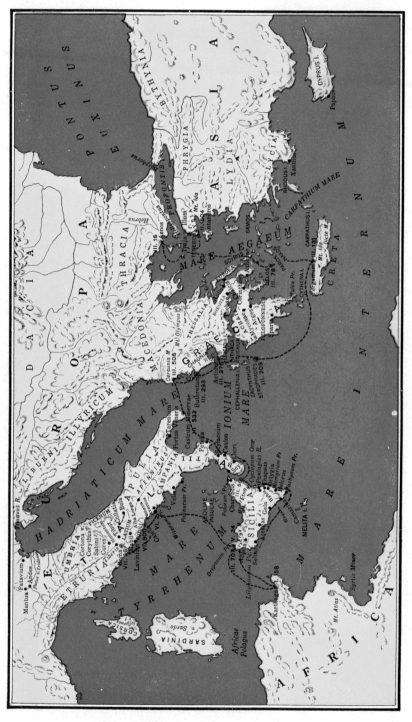

THE WANDERINGS OF AENEAS

# PART I

VERGIL'S AENEID, BOOKS I-VI

# VERGIL'S AENEID

## BOOK I

*I sing of arms and the man.*

Arma virumque canō, [Trōjae quī prīmus ab ōrīs  
Ītaliam, fātō profugus, Lāvīniaque vēnit  
lītora, multum ille et terrīs jactātus et altō  
vī superum, saevae memorem Jūnōnis ob īram,  
multa quoque et bellō passus, dum conderet urbem    5  
īnferretque deōs Latiō, genus unde Latīnum,  
Albānīque patrēs, atque altae moenia Rōmae.

*cano sing (of); *ōra shore

*fātum destiny; profugus exiled  
jactō toss (about), buffet

*superī the gods above; *saevus cruel; *memor mindful; *īra wrath  
*condō found  
īnferō bring

*moenia walls

---

**1. Arma virumque:** the general subject of the *Aeneid.* **virum:** i.e., Aeneas, the leading character in the *Aeneid.* **canō:** *I sing.* Vergil in beginning his epic poem imitates Homer, whose *Odyssey* (in Palmer's translation) begins:

Tell of the storm-tossed man, O Muse, who wandered  
long after he sacked the sacred citadel of Troy.

Later poets, in turn, followed Vergil. Compare Milton's beginning of *Paradise Lost:*

Of man's first disobedience and the fruit  
of that forbidden tree . . .  
sing, heavenly muse.

**Trōjae:** gen. modifying **ōrīs;** placed first in its clause for emphasis. For help in the metrical reading of the text see App. 23–29. Troy was a famous city in Northwestern Asia Minor; consult the map facing page 1. **2. Ītaliam:** *to Italy.* In Latin poetry the acc. without a prep. is often used to denote place whither; so **lītora** in line 3. **Ītaliam** here has the first syllable long, although it is short in prose; see App. 33. **Lāvīnia:** *Lavinian.* Aeneas founded the town of Lavinium, in Latium, naming the place after his wife Lavinia, daughter of King Latinus; see the map facing page 1. **Lāvīnia** is here pronounced in three syllables as if spelled **Lāvīnja;** see App. 32. **3. multum jactātus:** *much buffeted.* **multum:** adv. The last syllable of **multum** is elided before the first syllable of **ille,** and the second syllable of **ille** is elided before **et.** This metrical device is called *elision;* see App. 29. **ille:** i.e., Aeneas. **terrīs et altō:** in Latin poetry,

the abl. without a prep. is often used to denote place where. **altō:** *on the deep;* a noun, as often in English poetry. **4. superum:** i.e., **deōrum superōrum.** The ending –um is often used in poetry for the genitive plural of second declension nouns. **saevae . . . īram:** *on account of the mindful wrath of cruel Juno.* Throughout the *Aeneid* Juno is represented as hostile to Aeneas and the Trojans. Note that **saevae** modifies **Jūnōnis** and **memorem** modifies **īram.** This crisscross arrangement of words is called *synchysis;* see App. 22, 20. **5. multa passus:** *after much suffering (having suffered many things).* **multa:** a cognate acc. with **passus. quoque et:** read as if spelled **quoqu'et;** i.e., elide the final **e** of **quoque;** see App. 29. **passus:** perf. partic. of **patior. dum:** *until.* **conderet:** *should found;* subjunctive in a clause of anticipation; so **īnferret** in line 6. **urbem:** i.e., Lavinium. **6. deōs:** the images of the guardian gods of Troy which Aeneas took with him when he escaped from Troy. **Latiō:** *to Latium,* i.e., to Italy; see a map of ancient Italy. In poetry the dat. is often used to express place whither instead of the acc. with **ad** or **in. genus unde Latīnum:** supply **fuit.** Similarly supply **fuērunt** with **patrēs** and **moenia** in line 7. According to tradition Rome was founded in 753 B.C. from Alba Longa, which had itself been founded in 1053 B.C. by Ascanius, son of Aeneas. **7. Albānī:** *Alban,* i.e., of Alba Longa, mother city of Rome. **patrēs:** the first syllable is short here. **Patrēs** is often used in a broad sense like English *forefathers.* **atque altae:** elide and read as if spelled **atqu'altae;** see App. 29.

3

memorō tell; *nūmen divine
will; *laedō injure, thwart
*–ve or; *rēgīna queen; *volvō
(un)roll, undergo
*īnsignis distinguished; pietās
loyalty; adeō encounter
impellō drive, force; caelestis
heavenly; **īra wrath.

Mūsa, mihī causās memorā, quō nūmine laesō
quidve dolēns rēgīna deum tot volvere cāsūs
10 īnsignem pietāte virum, tot adīre labōrēs
impulerit.  Tantaene animīs caelestibus īrae?

QUESTIONS ON LINES 1–11.  1. In what line does Vergil state the
subject of his poem?  2. What was Aeneas's object in coming to
Italy?  3. From what part of what continent did Aeneas come?
4. Why did Aeneas leave his native land?  5. What divinity
was especially hostile to Aeneas?  6. What city did Aeneas
found in Italy?  7. Who founded Alba Longa?

*These are the causes of Juno's hatred.*

colōnus settler

longē far

ōstium mouth; *dīves rich;
studium pursuit; *asper
rough, fierce
*fertur is said*
posthabeō esteem less; *colō
cherish; *hīc here
**hīc here; *currus chariot

quā in any way; **fātum fate;
*sinō permit; *foveō cherish
*prōgeniēs race; *sanguis blood

*ōlim some day; *arx citadel

*hinc from this source; lātē
widely; *superbus proud

Urbs antīqua fuit (Tyriī tenuēre colōnī),
Carthāgō, Ītaliam contrā Tiberīnaque longē
ōstia, dīves opum, studiīsque asperrima bellī,
15 quam Jūnō fertur terrīs magis omnibus ūnam
posthabitā coluisse Samō: hīc illius arma,
hīc currus fuit; hoc rēgnum dea gentibus esse,
sī quā Fāta sinant, jam tum tenditque fovetque.
Prōgeniem sed enim Trōjānō ā sanguine dūcī
20 audierat, Tyriās ōlim quae verteret arcīs;
hinc populum lātē rēgem bellōque superbum

8. Mūsa: i.e., Calliope, the muse of epic poetry,
whom Vergil here invokes for inspiration.  mihī:
the final i is here long, although it is usually short.
quō nūmine laesō: (*with*) *what divine will thwarted;*
abl. abs. phrase.  9. quidve dolēns: *or grieving at
what.*  quid: cognate acc.  rēgīna deum: i.e.,
Juno, wife of Jupiter.  deum: gen. pl.  Cf. su-
perum in line 4.  tot volvere cāsūs: *to undergo
so many hazards.*  volvere: infin. depending on
impulerit.  10. pietāte: *in sense of duty* (to man
and gods).  Pietās is the distinguishing charac-
teristic of Aeneas throughout the poem.  virum:
i.e., Aeneas; subject of volvere.  11. impulerit:
subjunctive in the indirect question which begins
with quō in line 8.  Tantaene: supply sunt.  Tan-
taene animīs: elide and read as if spelled tan-
taen'animīs.  animīs: dat. of possession.
12. Tyriī: the tradition was that Phoenicians
from Tyre had colonized Carthage.  tenuēre:
tenuērunt; see App. 195, d.  13. Carthāgō: a city
in Northern Africa; see a map of the ancient world.
Ītaliam contrā longē: *far away opposite Italy.*  The
position of contrā, which in prose would precede
Ītaliam, is called *anastrophe.*  Tiberīna: *of the
Tiber,* an adj. modifying ōstia in line 14.  14. dīves
opum: *rich in resources.*  opum: gen. of specifica-

tion, a poetic usage.  studiīs bellī: *in the pursuits
of war.*  15. quam: the antecedent is Urbs Car-
thāgō.  terrīs: abl. of comparison with magis.
16. posthabitā Samō: *esteeming Samos less;* abl.
abs. phrase.  Although Juno had a famous temple
on the island of Samos, in the Aegean Sea, she pre-
ferred Carthage.  hīc: i.e., at Carthage.  There
is no elision between Samō and hīc.  This lack of
elision is called *hiatus;* see App. 30.  illius:
usually illīus.  17. hīc: the repetition of hīc at
the beginning of the second phrase is an example of
*anaphora;* see App. 22, 2.  hoc rēgnum dea genti-
bus esse ... tendit: *the goddess even then was
aiming that this should be the ruling power over the
nations;* i.e., Juno wanted Carthage to have su-
preme power.  dea: i.e., Juno.  gentibus: dat. of
reference.  18. sī quā ... sinant: *if in any way the
Fates should permit.*  The Fates were considered to
have control over even the gods.  19. Prōgeniem:
i.e., the Romans.  dūcī: *were being derived;* an
infin. in indirect statement dependent on audierat
in line 20.  20. verteret: subjunctive in a clause
of purpose.  Tyriās arcīs: *Tyrian citadels;* i.e.,
Carthage; arcīs is acc. pl.  21. hinc: i.e., Trō-
jānō ā sanguine.  lātē rēgem: *ruling widely.*
rēgem has here the force of rēgnantem.

ventūrum excidiō Libyae: sīc volvere Parcās.

Id metuēns, veterisque memor Sāturnia bellī,

prīma quod ad Trōjam prō cārīs gesserat Argīs

(necdum etiam causae īrārum saevīque dolōrēs

exciderant animō: manet altā mente repostum

jūdicium Paridis, sprētaeque injūria fōrmae,

et genus invīsum, et raptī Ganymēdis honōrēs),

hīs accēnsa super, jactātōs aequore tōtō

Trōas, relliquiās Danaum atque immītis Achillī,

arcēbat longē Latiō, multōsque per annōs

errābant, āctī Fātīs, maria omnia circum.

Tantae mōlis erat Rōmānam condere gentem.

Vix ē cōnspectū Siculae tellūris in altum

vēla dabant laetī, et spūmās salis aere ruēbant,

cum Jūnō, aeternum servāns sub pectore vulnus,

excidium destruction; **volvō (un)roll
metuō fear; **memor mindful
*cārus dear

25 necdum not yet; ***īra wrath; **saevus cruel; dolor pain
excidō fall from; repōnō store away
jūdicium judgment; *spernō despise, slight; fōrma beauty
invīsus hated; cf. *invideō envy

*accendō inflame, enrage; *super besides; jactō buffet;
30 *aequor (surface of) the sea
reliquiae those left, remnant; immītis cruel; cf. *mītis mild
*arceō keep away; longē far
*errō wander; ***fātum fate

*mōlēs mass, task; **condō found
cōnspectus sight; *tellūs land

35 *vēlum sail; *laetus happy; *spūma foam; *sal the salt sea; *ruō upheave, churn up
*aeternus everlasting; *pectus breast

---

**22. ventūrum excidiō**: read as if spelled **ventūr' excidiō**; see App. 29.   **excidiō Libyae**: for the destruction of Libya.   **excidiō**: dat. of purpose.   **Libyae**: dat. of reference.   Libya was and is a region in Northern Africa.   **sīc volvere Parcās**: that so the Fates unrolled (their scroll). The Parcae were represented by the ancients as three sisters: Clotho, who spun the threads of life, Lachesis, who measured them, and Atropos, who cut them.   **23. Id metuēns**: fearing this, i.e., fearing the destruction of Carthage and world domination by Rome.   **Sāturnia**: Saturn's daughter, here Juno.   **bellī**: i.e., the Trojan War; gen. with **memor**.   **24. prīma quod gesserat**: which she had been foremost in waging.   **ad Trōjam**: at Troy.   Ad with the acc. of the name of a city implies vicinity.   **Argīs**: Argos, in Greece, was noted for its worship of Juno.   **25. necdum etiam**: read as if spelled **necd'etiam**; see App. 29.   **īrārum**: a plural form, with singular meaning, is often used in poetry.   **26. altā mente**: literally, in her deep mind, i.e., deep in her mind; abl. of place where without a prep., as often in poetry.   Cf. **terrīs . . . et altō** in line 3.   **repostum**: a form of **repositum**, used here for metrical reasons.   **27. jūdicium Paridis**: the Judgment of Paris has been the subject of many poems and paintings and sculptures.   **sprētaeque injūria fōrmae**: and the insult to her slighted beauty.   Paris, a Trojan prince, had selected Venus as more beautiful than Juno or Minerva, the other contestants.   **28. genus invīsum**: the hated race, i.e., the Trojans.   **invīsum et**: elide and read as if spelled **invīs'et**; see App. 29.   **raptī Ganymēdis**

**honōrēs**: the honor (done) to Ganymede (who was) carried off.   **honōrēs**: a plural form with singular force; cf. **īrārum** in line 25.   Ganymede, a youthful Trojan prince, was carried off by an eagle and made cupbearer to Jupiter in place of Juno's daughter Hebe.   **29. hīs**: on account of these things.   **aequore tōtō**: abl. of place where without a prep.   **30. Trōas**: the Trojans; Greek acc. pl., object of **arcēbat** in line 31.   **relliquiās . . . Achillī**: the remnants of the Greeks and of ruthless Achilles, i.e., the Trojans who had escaped from the Greeks and from Achilles in the long drawn out Trojan War.   **relliquiās**: the poetic spelling with double l makes the first syllable long.   **Danaum**: Danaus was a legendary king of Greece; hence **Danaī**, the Greeks.   **31. arcēbat longē Latiō**: was keeping far from Latium, i.e., far from Italy.   **arcēbat**: imperf. tense, because Juno now for the seventh year was keeping the Trojans from their goal.   **32. āctī Fātīs**: driven on by the Fates; implying the helplessness of the Trojans thus destined to roam the seas.   **maria omnia circum**: another example of anastrophe; cf. **Ītaliam contrā** in line 13.   **33. Tantae mōlis**: (of) so great a task; gen. of quality in the predicate.

**34. Siculae tellūris**: of the Sicilian land; the Trojans had spent the preceding winter in Sicily and were now sailing for Italy. The story of their previous wanderings is told in Book III.   **35. vēla dabant**: were spreading their sails; supply **Trōes** as subject.   **aere**: with the bronze (prow).   **36. aeternum vulnus**: the undying wound, i.e., her hatred of the Trojans.   **sub pectore**: in her breast.

inceptum undertaking

āvertō turn aside

quippe forsooth; *vetō forbid, prevent; exūrō burn up

submergō sink; *pontus sea

noxa crime; *furia madness

rapidus swift; jaculor hurl; cf. *jaculum dart; *nūbēs cloud

disjiciō scatter; *ratis ship; *ēvertō overturn; **aequor (*surface of*) the sea

exspīrō breathe out; trānsfīgō pierce; **pectus breast; *flamma fire

*turbō whirlwind; corripiō snatch up; *scopulus crag; īnfīgō impale; *acuō sharpen

ast but; *dīvus a god; incēdō move, walk; **rēgīna queen

*soror sister; conjūnx wife

**nūmen divine power; adōrō worship

*supplex suppliant; *āra altar; impōnō place

haec sēcum: "Mēne inceptō dēsistere victam
nec posse Ītaliā Teucrōrum āvertere rēgem?
Quippe vetor Fātīs. Pallasne exūrere classem
40 Argīvum atque ipsōs potuit submergere pontō,
ūnius ob noxam et furiās Ājācis Oīleī?
Ipsa, Jovis rapidum jaculāta ē nūbibus ignem,
disjēcitque ratīs ēvertitque aequora ventīs,
illum exspīrantem trānsfīxō pectore flammās
45 turbine corripuit, scopulōque īnfīxit acūtō.

Ast ego, quae dīvum incēdō rēgīna, Jovisque
et soror et conjūnx, ūnā cum gente tot annōs
bella gerō. Et quisquam nūmen Jūnōnis adōrat
praetereā, aut supplex ārīs impōnet honōrem?"

QUESTIONS ON **12–49**. 1. Who, according to Vergil, founded Carthage? 2. What association had Juno with Carthage? 3. What had Juno heard about the destined fate of Carthage? 4. What powers had the Fates? 5. What three special reasons does Vergil mention for Juno's hatred of the Trojans? 6. Against what goddess was Juno especially resentful? Why? 7. Why did Pallas destroy Ajax and his fleet?

*Juno seeks the aid of Aeolus, god of the winds.*

*tālis such; flammō inflame; *cor heart; volūtō revolve

*nimbus storm cloud; *patria land; *furō rage

***hīc here; *vāstus vast; *āntrum cave

*luctor struggle; sonōrus roaring

*vinc(u)lum bond; *carcer prison; frēnō curb, check

50 Tālia flammātō sēcum dea corde volūtāns
nimbōrum in patriam, loca fēta furentibus Austrīs,
Aeoliam venit. Hīc vāstō rēx Aeolus antrō
luctantīs ventōs tempestātēsque sonōrās
imperiō premit, ac vinclīs et carcere frēnat.

---

**37.** haec sēcum: *to herself.* haec: object of some such word as dīxit to be supplied. Mēne... dēsistere victam?: *Shall I defeated give up my plan?;* infin. of exclamation with an acc. subject; see App. 179. inceptō: abl. of separation. **38.** Teucrōrum: *of the Teucrians,* i.e., Trojans; Teucer was one of the founders of the Trojan race. **40.** Argīvum (Argīvōrum): *of the Argives,* i.e., Greeks. pontō: *in the sea;* abl. of place where without a prep. **41.** ūnius Ājācis Oīleī: *of one man only,* Ajax, son of Oīleus. During the sack of Troy Ajax had enraged Minerva by dragging Cassandra, daughter of King Priam and priestess of Minerva, from her temple. **42.** Ipsa: i.e., Minerva. Jovis ignem: i.e., lightning. **43.** que... que: *both ...*

*and.* **44.** illum: i.e., Ajax. **45.** scopulō: dat. with the compound īnfīxit or abl. of place where. **46.** Ast: an early form of at. dīvum: dīvōrum. **47.** ūnā cum gente: i.e., with the Trojans. **49.** ārīs: dat. with the compound impōnet or abl. of place where. sacrifices. For Work Unit I, based on lines 1–49, see page 249.

**50.** sēcum: *inwardly, to herself.* corde: abl. of place where. **51.** fēta: *teeming* (with). Austrīs: *with south winds;* here refers to winds in general. **52.** Aeoliam: *Aeolia,* a group of volcanic islands north of Sicily. Aeolus: ruler over the winds. antrō: abl. of place where. **53.** luctantīs: acc. pl. agreeing with ventōs. **54.** vinclīs: an early form of vinculīs, here used for metrical reasons.

Illī indignantēs magnō cum murmure montis
circum claustra fremunt; celsā sedet Aeolus arce,
scēptra tenēns, mollitque animōs et temperat
    īrās.

Nī faciat, maria ac terrās caelumque profundum
quippe ferant rapidī sēcum, verrantque per aurās.
Sed pater omnipotēns spēluncīs abdidit ātrīs,
hoc metuēns, mōlemque et montīs īnsuper altōs
imposuit, rēgemque dedit, quī foedere certō
et premere et laxās scīret dare jussus habēnās.
Ad quem tum Jūnō supplex hīs vōcibus ūsa est:
"Aeole, namque tibī dīvum pater atque homi-
    num rēx
et mulcēre dedit flūctūs et tollere ventō,
gēns inimīca mihī Tyrrhēnum nāvigat aequor,
Īlium in Ītaliam portāns victōsque Penātīs;
incute vim ventīs submersāsque obrue puppīs,
aut age dīversōs et disjice corpora pontō.

Sunt mihi bis septem praestantī corpore nymphae,
quārum quae fōrmā pulcherrima Dēiopēa,

**55** indignor be angry; **murmur** roar, rumble
**claustrum** barrier; \*fremō roar, rage; \*celsus lofty; \*sedeō sit; \*\*arx citadel, height
\*scēptrum staff, scepter; mollīō soothe; temperō control, calm; cf. \*temperantia moderation
\*nī (nisi) if not; \*caelum sky; profundus deep, vast
quippe surely; rapidus swift; verrō sweep; \*aura air
**60** omnipotēns almighty; \*spēlunca cavern; \*āter dark
metuō fear, dread; \*\*mōlēs mass; īnsuper above
impōnō place; \*foedus agreement
laxus loose, free; \*habēna rein
\*\*supplex humble,
**65** \*\*dīvus god

\*mulceō soothe, calm; \*flūctus wave
\*\*\*aequor (*surface of*) the sea

incutiō strike into, give to; cf. \*–cutiō shake, strike; submergō sink; obruō overwhelm; \*puppis stern; ship
disjiciō scatter, disperse; \*\*pontus sea
**70** praestāns surpassing; \*nympha nymph; *see notes.*
\*pulcher beautiful

---

**55. magnō cum murmure montis:** note the repetition of **m**; an example of *alliteration;* see App. 22, 1. The sound of the phrase suggests the rumbling mountain. This harmony of sound and meaning is called *onomatopeia;* see App. 22, 14. **56. arce:** abl. of place where. **57. scēptra:** a poetic use of the plural. **animōs:** *spirits, passions.* **58. Nī** (nisi) **faciat:** *if he should not do this.* **59. ferant, verrant:** subjunctives in the conclusion of a future less vivid conditional sentence; see App. 157, 1. **60. pater omnipotēns:** i.e., Jupiter. **spēluncīs:** abl. of place where. The plural form is a poetic use. **abdidit:** the object is ventōs understood. **61–62. mōlemque et montīs imposuit:** this expression of one idea by two coördinate nouns is called *hendiadys;* see App. 22, 9. **montīs:** acc. pl. **62. rēgem:** i.e., Aeolus. **foedere certō:** *under definite agreement.* **62–63. quī et premere et laxās scīret dare habēnās:** *who would know how to check them or to give them loose reins.* **scīret:** subjunctive in a clause of characteristic. **65. tibī:** for the long i cf. mihī in line 8. **dīvum pater atque hominum rēx:** i.e., Jupiter. **dīvum:**

dīvōrum. **atque hominum:** read as if spelled atqu'ominum; see App. 29. **66. mulcēre dedit:** *granted* (the power) *to soothe.* **67. gēns inimīca:** i.e., the Trojans. **Tyrrhēnum aequor:** the Tyrrhenian Sea is that part of the Mediterranean Sea that lies north of Sicily. **68. Īlium:** *Troy.* **Penātīs:** *Penates,* gods of the household or of the state; cf. deōs in line 6. **69. incute vim ventīs:** *give might to the winds.* **ventīs:** dat. after the compound verb incute. **submersāsque obrue puppīs:** *and overwhelm the sunken ships,* i.e., sink the ships and overwhelm them. **submersās:** this anticipatory use of the perfect participle is called *prolepsis;* see App. 22, 18. **70. age dīversōs:** *scatter the men in different directions.* **pontō:** abl. of place where. **71. Sunt mihi:** i.e., *I have.* **mihi:** dat. of possession. **nymphae:** the nymphs were semi-divine maidens. **praestantī corpore:** *of surpassing beauty;* abl. of quality or description. **72. quārum ... Dēiopēa:** *one of whom, who is the most beautiful, Deiopea.* **Dēiopēa** is attracted into nom. case by **quae** instead of agreeing with **ūnam,** understood as object of **jungam.**

*cōnūbium marriage, wedlock; *stabilis firm; *proprius one's own; dicō proclaim
meritum service, good deed; **tālis such
*exigō finish, spend; **pulcher beautiful; *prōlēs progeny; *parēns parent
***rēgīna queen; *optō desire, wish
jussum command, order; capessō seize, carry out; *fās right, divine law
**scēptrum scepter

*conciliō secure, gain; *epulae banquet, feast; accumbō recline at; cf.*–cumbō lie; ***dīvus god
**nimbus storm cloud

cōnūbiō jungam stabilī propriamque dicābō,
omnīs ut tēcum meritīs prō tālibus annōs
75 exigat, et pulchrā faciat tē prōle parentem."

Aeolus haec contrā: "Tuus, ō rēgīna, quid optēs
explōrāre labor; mihi jussa capessere fās est.
Tū mihi quodcumque hoc rēgnī, tū scēptra Jovemque
conciliās, tū dās epulīs accumbere dīvum,
80 nimbōrumque facis tempestātumque potentem."

QUESTIONS ON **50–80.** 1. Why does Juno appeal to Aeolus? 2. What power has Aeolus received? From whom? 3. What does Juno ask Aeolus to do? 4. What reward does Juno promise him? 5. Why do you think Aeolus is so ready to obey Juno? 6. What Roman custom is referred to in epulīs accumbere (79)?

*Aeolus raises a storm which scatters the fleet.*

*cavus hollow; convertō reverse; *cuspis point; spear
impellō strike against; *velut just as
**ruō rush forth; **turbō whirlwind; perflō blow over; cf. *flō blow
incumbō fall upon; cf. **–cumbō lie; *sēdēs seat; depths
***ruō upturn, upheave; procella blast, gust
**vāstus huge; ***volvō roll; **flūctus wave, billow
īnsequor follow; clāmor shouting; strīdor creaking; rudēns rope
ēripiō snatch away; **nūbēs cloud; **caelum sky
***pontus sea; incubō brood over; **āter black

Haec ubi dicta, cavum conversā cuspide montem
impulit in latus; ac ventī, velut agmine factō,
quā data porta, ruunt et terrās turbine perflant.

Incubuēre marī, tōtumque ā sēdibus īmīs
85 ūnā Eurusque Notusque ruunt crēberque procellīs
Āfricus, et vāstōs volvunt ad lītora flūctūs;
īnsequitur clāmorque virum strīdorque rudentum.

Ēripiunt subitō nūbēs caelumque diemque
Teucrōrum ex oculīs; pontō nox incubat ātra.

73. cōnūbiō: read as if spelled cōnūbjō. jungam: supply tibi. propriamque dicābō: *and I shall proclaim her your very own.* 75. prōle: abl. of means. 76. haec: supply dīcit. Tuus: supply est. 78. quodcumque hoc rēgnī: supply est; *whatever of realm this is,* i.e., such realm as this is. Jovem: i.e., the favor of Jupiter. Note in lines 78 and 79 the repetition of tū in an emphatic position. This repetition is called *anaphora;* see App. 22, 2. 79. dās accumbere: *you grant* (me the right) *to recline.* The Romans reclined at their more formal meals and the gods were assumed to do likewise. epulīs: dat. with the compound verb accumbere. 80. nimbōrumque tempestātumque potentem:

*powerful over the clouds and storms.* nimbōrumque tempestātumque: objective gen. with potentem. facis: the object is mē understood. 81. dicta: supply sunt. 83. quā data porta: supply est; *where a gateway was provided.* 84. Incubuēre: Incubuērunt. The perfect tense here implies the sudden onset of the winds: *they have fallen upon the sea.* tōtum: supply mare as object of ruunt. 85. Eurus: *East Wind.* Notus: *South Wind.* –que … –que … –que: this repetition of the conjunction is called *polysyndeton;* see App. 22, 16. 87. virum: virōrum. 89. pontō: dat. with the compound verb incubat or abl. of place where.

Intonuēre polī, et crēbrīs micat ignibus aethēr,
praesentemque virīs intentant omnia mortem.
Extemplō Aenēae solvuntur frīgore membra;
ingemit, et, duplicīs tendēns ad sīdera palmās,
tālia vōce refert: "Ō terque quaterque beātī,
quīs ante ōra patrum Trōjae sub moenibus altīs
contigit oppetere! Ō Danaum fortissime gentis
Tȳdīdē! Mēne Īliacīs occumbere campīs
nōn potuisse tuāque animam hanc effundere
   dextrā,
saevus ubi Aeacidae tēlō jacet Hector, ubi ingēns
Sarpēdōn, ubi tot Simoīs correpta sub undīs
scūta virum galeāsque et fortia corpora volvit!"
Tālia jactantī strīdēns Aquilōne procella
vēlum adversa ferit, flūctūsque ad sīdera tollit:
franguntur rēmī; tum prōra āvertit et undīs
dat latus; īnsequitur cumulō praeruptus aquae
   mōns.
Hī summō in flūctū pendent, hīs unda dehīscēns
terram inter flūctūs aperit; furit aestus harēnīs.
Trīs Notus abreptās in saxa latentia torquet
(saxa vocant Italī mediīs quae in flūctibus Ārās,
dorsum immāne marī summō), trīs Eurus ab altō
in brevia et syrtīs urget (miserābile vīsū),

90 **intōnō** thunder; ***polus** sky, heaven; ***micō** flash, gleam; ***aethēr** upper air, sky
**intentō** threaten
***extemplō** immediately; ***solvō** loosen; ***frīgus** cold, chill; ***membrum** limb
**ingemō** groan; ***duplex** two; ***sīdus** star; ***palma** hand
****tālis** such; **referō** relate, say; ***ter** thrice, three times; 95 **quater** four times; ***beātus** blessed
***ōs, ōris** face; ****moenia** walls
***contingit** it befalls; **oppetō** encounter (death)
**occumbō** sink down, die; cf.
****–cumbō** lie
***anima** breath, life; **effundō** pour out

****saevus** fierce, valiant; ***jaceō** lie; ***ingēns** huge, mighty
100 **corripiō** snatch, catch up; ***unda** wave, billow
***galea** helmet ;

**jactō** throw out, utter wildly; ***strīdeō** whistle, roar; **procella** blast, gale
****vēlum** canvas, sail; ***feriō** strike; ****flūctus** wave, billow; ****sīdus** star
105 ***prōra** prow; ****unda** wave, billow
**īnsequor** follow; **cumulus** heap, mass; **praeruptus** towering
***pendeō** hang; ****unda** wave, water; **dehīscō** yawn
****furō** rage, boil; ***harēna** sand

**abripiō** snatch away; ***lateō** lie hidden; ***torqueō** twist, hurl
****āra** altar

110 **dorsum** back; reef; ***immānis** huge
**syrtis** sand bar; ***urgeō** drive; **miserābilis** pitiful

---

**90. Intonuēre: Intonuērunt. ignibus:** *lightning.*
**94. beātī:** Aeneas is addressing his former comrades who had perished in battle on the plains of Troy. Although he is the hero of the poem, Aeneas is frequently represented as weeping and lamenting. **95. quīs: quibus;** dat. with **contigit** in line 96. **96. oppetere (mortem):** *to meet death.* **Danaum: Danaōrum. 97. Tȳdīdē:** i.e., Diomedes, who wounded Aeneas in battle at Troy and would have killed him if Venus had not rescued Aeneas. **97–98. Mēne . . . potuisse:** *could I not have fallen on the plains of Ilium.* Aeneas feels that it would have been better to meet death at the hands of Diomedes than now to perish at sea. **99. Aeacidae:** i.e., Achilles, grandson of Aeacus. The suffixes **–ades, –iades, –ides** are used to form patronymics denoting descent from a father or ancestor. **Hector:** son

of Priam and bravest of the Trojans. **100. Sarpēdōn:** son of Jupiter and ally of the Trojans. **Simoīs:** a river near Troy. **correpta sub undīs:** *swept away under its waters.* **101. virum: virōrum. 102. Tālia jactantī:** *as he utters such words;* supply **Aenēae,** a dat. of reference. **102–103. strīdēns . . . ferit:** *a gale, roaring with the North Wind, strikes the sail in front.* **adversa:** qualifies **procella. 104. rēmī:** ancient ships were equipped with both oars and sails. **āvertit:** supply **sē. 105. cumulō:** *in a mass.* **106. Hī . . . his:** *Some . . . for others.* **108. Trīs (nāvīs):** object of **torquet. 109. saxa . . . Ārās:** *which rocks in the midst of the waves the Italians call Altars.* These Arae were just outside the harbor of Carthage. **110. mari:** abl. of place where. **trīs (nāvīs):** object of **urget** in line 111. **111. brevia:** *shallows.* **syrtīs:** acc. pl. **miserābile vīsū:** *pitiful to behold.* **vīsū:** supine

# 10 LATIN POETRY

**inlīdō** dash upon; *****cingō** gird, encircle; ******harēna** sand
*****fīdus** faithful

******ingēns** huge; *****vertex** top, height
******puppis** stern; ship; ******feriō** strike; **excutiō** shake off; cf. **--cutiō** shake, strike; *****prōnus** forward; *****magister** pilot
**ast** but; ******ter** thrice; **ibīdem** in the same place
******torqueō** turn, twist; **rapidus** swift; **vorō** swallow up; ******vertex** whirlpool
*****appāreō** appear; **rārus** scattered; *****nō** swim, float; *****gurges** gulf, flood; *******vāstus** huge, immense
*****tabula** plank; **gaza** treasure
**validus** strong, mighty
**grandaevus** aged, old
**laxus** loose, open; **compāgēs** joint, seam
*****imber** rain, water; **rīma** crack, fissure; **fatīscō** gape open

inlīditque vadīs, atque aggere cingit harēnae.
Ūnam, quae Lyciōs fīdumque vehēbat Orontēn,
ipsius ante oculōs ingēns ā vertice pontus
115 in puppim ferit: excutitur prōnusque magister
volvitur in caput; ast illam ter flūctus ibīdem
torquet agēns circum, et rapidus vorat aequore
     vertex;
appārent rārī nantēs in gurgite vāstō,
arma virum, tabulaeque, et Trōia gaza per undās.
120 Jam validam Īlioneī nāvem, jam fortis Achātae,
et quā vectus Abās, et quā grandaevus Alētēs,
vīcit hiems; laxīs laterum compāgibus ōmnēs
accipiunt inimīcum imbrem, rīmīsque fatīscunt.

QUESTIONS ON **81–123**. 1. What regret does Aeneas express at the onset of the storm? 2. What happens to three of Aeneas's ships? 3. What happens to three others of Aeneas's ships? 4. What happens to Orontes's ship? 5. What were the Arae?

*Neptune calms the storm.*

*****misceō** stir up; **murmur** roar, rumble
**ēmittō** send forth

*****stāgnum** still water; **refundō** upheave; **graviter** greatly; **commoveō** move, disturb
**prōspiciō** look out; **placidus** calm
**disjiciō** scatter, disperse
*******caelum** sky; *****ruīna** downfall

******lateō** lie hidden from; *****dolus** deceit
**dehinc** then, thereupon; *****for** speak, say

*******nūmen** divine will

Intereā magnō miscērī murmure pontum
125 ēmissamque hiemem sēnsit Neptūnus et īmīs
stāgna refūsa vadīs, graviter commōtus, et, altō
prōspiciēns, summā placidum caput extulit undā.
Disjectam Aenēae tōtō videt aequore classem,
flūctibus oppressōs Trōas caelīque ruīnā;
130 nec latuēre dolī frātrem Jūnōnis et īrae.
Eurum ad sē Zephyrumque vocat, dehinc tālia fātur:
"Tantane vōs generis tenuit fīdūcia vestrī?
Jam caelum terramque meō sine nūmine, ventī,

---

in ū; see App. 193. **112. vadīs:** *upon the shoals.* **113. Orontēn:** Greek acc. Orontes was leader of the Lycians who followed Aeneas. **114. ipsius:** i.e., of Aeneas. The second i of **ipsius** is here short. **116. illam:** i.e., Orontes's ship. **118. rārī nantēs:** *men swimming here and there.* **119. virum:** virōrum. **tabulae:** *planks* (of the ship). **120. Īlioneī:** the letters eī are pronounced as one long syllable by *synizesis;* see App. 32. Ilioneus and Achates were Trojan leaders. **121. et . . . Alētēs:** *and* (the ship) *in which Abas sailed and* (the ship) *in which*

the aged *Aletes* sailed. Abas and Aletes were Trojan leaders. **122. omnēs:** supply nāvēs. **126. stāgna:** *still waters.* **altō:** *over the sea;* abl. of place where. **127. summā undā:** *from the crest of the waves;* **undā** is an abl. of place whence without a prep. **128. aequore:** abl. of place where. **129. Trōas:** Greek acc. pl. **130. latuēre:** latuērunt; *lay hidden from;* the object is frātrem. **frātrem:** i.e., Neptune, brother of Juno. **131. Zephyrum:** *the West Wind.* **dehinc:** pronounced as if spelled dinc. **132. generis fīdūcia vestrī:** *confi-*

"Quos Ego —"

Neptune rebukes the winds and calms the waves.

miscēre et tantās audētis tollere mōlīs?

Quōs ego — sed mōtōs praestat compōnere flūctūs. 135

Post mihi nōn similī poenā commissa luētis.

Mātūrāte fugam, rēgīque haec dīcite vestrō:

nōn illī imperium pelagī, saevumque tridentem,

sed mihi sorte datum.  Tenet ille immānia saxa,

vestrās, Eure, domōs; illā sē jactet in aulā    140

Aeolus et clausō ventōrum carcere rēgnet."

Sīc ait, et dictō citius tumida aequora plācat,

collēctāsque fugat nūbīs sōlemque redūcit.

Cȳmothoē simul et Trītōn adnīxus acūtō

dētrūdunt nāvīs scopulō; levat ipse tridentī,    145

et vāstās aperit syrtīs et temperat aequor,

atque rotīs summās levibus perlābitur undās.

Ac velutī magnō in populō cum saepe coörta est

sēditiō, saevitque animīs ignōbile vulgus,

jamque facēs et saxa volant (furor arma ministrat), 150

tum pietāte gravem ac meritīs sī forte virum quem

cōnspexēre, silent arrēctīsque auribus astant;

ille regit dictīs animōs et pectora mulcet;

sīc cūnctus pelagī cecidit fragor, aequora postquam

prōspiciēns genitor caelōque invectus apertō    155

flectit equōs, currūque volāns dat lōra secundō.

---

**misceo** stir up; **mōlēs** mass

**compōnō** compose, calm

**commissum** misdeed; **luō** wash away, atone for

**mātūrō** hasten, speed

*pelagus sea; **tridēns** trident

*sors lot; **immānis** huge

aula court, hall

**carcer** prison; *rēgnō reign

*ajō speak; **dictum** word, speech; **citō** quickly, soon; **tumidus** swollen; *plācō calm
**fugō** put to flight; ***nūbēs cloud; **redūcō** bring back
**adnītor** strive; **acuō** sharpen

**dētrūdō** push off, dislodge; **scopulus** rock; *levō lift, raise; **tridēns** trident
**temperō** control, calm; cf. **temperantia** moderation
*rota wheel, chariot; **perlābor** glide over

**velut(ī)** just as; **coörior** arise, break out
**sēditiō** riot, uprising; *saeviō be angry; **ignōbilis** common
*fax firebrand; *volō fly; **furor** rage; **ministrō** supply
**pietās** loyalty, devotion; **meritum** service
*sileō be silent; *arrigō prick up; *auris ear; *astō stand
**dictum** word, speech; ***pectus breast; **mulceō** soothe, calm
*cūnctus whole, entire; **pelagus** sea; **fragor** uproar
**prōspiciō** look out on; *genitor sire, father; **invehō** carry, convey; **apertus** open, clear
*flectō turn, guide; **currus** chariot, car; **volō** fly, speed; **lōrum** rein

---

dence in your race; the winds were inferior deities. **134. tantās mōlis:** such masses (of waves). **135. Quōs ego —:** Neptune does not finish his threat.  This breaking off of a sentence is called *aposiopesis;* see App. 22, 4. **praestat:** it is better. **136. Post:** adv. **137. rēgī:** to your king, i.e., to Aeolus. **138. imperium, tridentem:** acc. subjects of datum (esse), an infin. in indirect statement, dependent on dīcite in line 137. **139. sorte:** Jupiter, Neptune, and Pluto had divided Saturn's realms by lot, the sea falling to Neptune. **ille:** i.e., Aeolus. **140. vestrās:** pl., referring to all the winds, although only Eurus is being directly addressed. **sē jactet:** let him flaunt himself; jussive subjunctive, as is rēgnet in line 141. **141. car-**

cere: abl. of place where. **142. dictō citius:** no sooner had he spoken than (sooner than saying). **144. Cȳmothoē:** a sea nymph. **Trītōn:** a minor sea-god, son of Neptune. **145. nāvīs:** acc. pl. **levat:** supply nāvīs as the object. **ipse:** i.e., Neptune. **147. rotīs:** with the wheels (of his chariot). **148. Ac velutī:** the ancient Greek and Roman epics abound in such similes. **149. saevit animīs:** rages with passion. **152. cōnspexēre:** cōnspexērunt. **153. ille:** i.e., the man who pacifies the crowd. **155. genitor:** i.e., Neptune. **caelō apertō:** under a clear sky. **invectus:** riding. **156. dat lōra secundō:** gives the reins to his obedient chariot. **currū:** an early dat. form.  For Work Unit II, based on lines 50–156, see page 250.

QUESTIONS ON **124–156**. 1. Whom does Neptune suspect as the cause of the storm? 2. What is Neptune's attitude toward the winds? 3. What is his message to Aeolus? 4. What divinities aid in rescuing Aeneas's ships? 5. With what does Vergil compare Neptune's pacification of the storm?

### *Aeneas with seven ships lands on the coast of Africa.*

Dēfessī Aeneadae, quae proxima lītora, cursū
contendunt petere, et Libyae vertuntur ad ōrās.
Est in sēcessū longō locus: īnsula portum
160 efficit objectū laterum, quibus omnis ab altō
frangitur inque sinūs scindit sēsē unda reductōs.
Hinc atque hinc vāstae rūpēs gemināque minantur
in caelum scopulī, quōrum sub vertice lātē
aequora tūta silent; tum silvīs scaena coruscīs
165 dēsuper, horrentīque ātrum nemus imminet umbrā.

Fronte sub adversā scopulīs pendentibus antrum,
intus aquae dulcēs, vīvōque sedīlia saxō,
nymphārum domus. Hīc fessās nōn vincula nāvīs
ūlla tenent, uncō nōn alligat ancora morsū.
170 Hūc septem Aenēās collēctīs nāvibus omnī
ex numerō subit, ac, magnō tellūris amōre
ēgressī, optātā potiuntur Trōes harēnā,
et sale tābentīs artūs in lītore pōnunt.
Ac prīmum silicī scintillam excūdit Achātēs
175 suscēpitque ignem foliīs, atque ārida circum
nūtrīmenta dedit, rapuitque in fōmite flammam.
Tum Cererem corruptam undīs Cereāliaque arma

**Glossary:** proximus nearest; **ōra shore, coast; sēcessus inlet, recess; objectus projection, barrier; *sinus fold, bay; *scindō split, divide; ***hinc from here, here; *rūpēs crag, cliff; *geminus twin, two; *minor threaten, tower; ***scopulus rock, cliff; ***vertex top, summit; lātē widely; **sileō be silent; *coruscus waving, flashing; dēsuper (from) above; *horreō bristle; cf. *abhorreō shrink from, ***āter dark; *nemus grove; *immineō overhang; *umbra shade; **pendeō hang, overhang; **antrum cave, cavern; *intus within; *dulcis sweet, fresh; sedīle seat, bench; **nympha nymph; fessus weary; **vinc(u)lum chain; *uncus hooked, curved; alligō bind; *morsus bite; fluke (of an anchor); subeō come; **tellūs land; amor love, longing; ēgredior disembark; **optō long for; ***harēna sand, beach; **sal salt, salt water; tābeō drip; *artus joint, limb; silex flint-stone; scintilla spark; excūdō strike (from); *folium leaf; āridus dry; nūtrīmentum food, fuel; fōmes tinder, kindling; **flamma flame, fire; *corrumpō ruin, spoil**

157. Aeneadae: *followers of Aeneas.* quae proxima: supply sunt. 159–160. portum efficit: *makes (it) a harbor.* 160. objectū laterum: *by the projection of the sides.* 161. inque ... reductōs: *and the water divides itself into* (i.e., divides and flows into) *the innermost bays.* 162. Hinc atque hinc: *on one side and on the other.* 166. Fronte sub adversā: *under the brow* (of the cliff) *straight ahead.* 167. vīvō sedīlia saxō: *seats of natural rock.* 168. Hīc: i.e., in this harbor. 170. septem: Aeneas had set out from the Troad with twenty ships. He now feared that the other thirteen were lost. 171. subit: *enters.* 172. Trōes: Greek nom. pl. 173. sale tābentīs: *dripping with sea water.* tābentīs: acc. pl. 174. silicī: *from flint;* dat. of separation. See App. 100, a. 175. circum: adv. 177. Cererem: *grain.* This figure of speech is called *metonymy;* see App. 22, 13 **arma:**

expediunt, fessī rērum, frūgēsque receptās
et torrēre parant flammīs et frangere saxō.

Aenēās scopulum intereā cōnscendit, et omnem 180
prōspectum lātē pelagō petit, Anthea sī quem
jactātum ventō videat Phrygiāsque birēmīs,
aut Capyn, aut celsīs in puppibus arma Caīcī,
Nāvem in cōnspectū nūllam, trīs lītore cervōs
prōspicit errantīs; hōs tōta armenta sequuntur 185
ā tergō, et longum per vallīs pāscitur agmen.
Cōnstitit hīc, arcumque manū celerīsque sagittās
corripuit, fīdus quae tēla gerēbat Achātēs,
ductōrēsque ipsōs prīmum capita alta ferentīs
cornibus arboreīs sternit, tum vulgus, et omnem 190
miscet agēns tēlīs nemora inter frondea turbam,
nec prius absistit quam septem ingentia victor
corpora fundat humī, et numerum cum nāvibus
    aequet.
Hinc portum petit, et sociōs partītur in omnīs.
Vīna bonus quae deinde cadīs onerārat Acestēs 195
lītore Trīnacriō, dederatque abeuntibus hērōs,
dīvidit, et dictīs maerentia pectora mulcet:
"Ō sociī, neque enim ignārī sumus ante malōrum,
ō passī graviōra, dabit deus hīs quoque fīnem.
Vōs et Scyllaeam rabiem penitusque sonantīs 200
accestis scopulōs, vōs et Cyclōpia saxa
expertī; revocāte animōs, maestumque timōrem

**fessus** weary, tired; **frūx** grain; **recipiō** recover
*torreō parch; ***flamma flame, fire
cōnscendō climb, mount
**prōspectus** view; **lātē** widely, far and wide; ***pelagus sea
**birēmis** bireme
**celsus** high, lofty; ***puppis stern; ship
cōnspectus sight, view; *cervus stag
prōspiciō see; **errō wander, stray; *armentum herd
*pāscō feed
*arcus bow
**corripiō** seize; **fīdus** faithful, trusty
**ductor** leader
arboreus tree-like, branching; *sternō lay low
***misceō throw into confusion; **nemus grove, forest; *turba throng, crowd
absistō stop, desist; ***ingēns huge, great
*humus ground

partior distribute

*vīnum wine; cadus jar; onerō stow away
abeō go away, depart; *hērōs hero, chief
dictum word; maereō mourn, sorrow; cf. *maeror sorrow; ***mulceō soothe, calm
*ignārus ignorant, inexperienced; malum trouble, misfortune
*rabiēs rage, fury; *penitus within; *sonō sound, roar
revocō call back, revive; *maestus sad, gloomy; timor fear

---

utensils. **178. fessī rērum:** tired of their adventures. **frūgēs receptās:** the rescued grain.
**181. pelagō:** over the sea. **181–182. Anthea sī quem videat:** if he can see any (thing of) Antheus. **183. Capyn:** Greek acc. Capys and Caïcus were Trojan leaders. **184. lītore:** abl. of place where. **187. Cōnstitit:** supply **Aenēās** as the subject. **189. ductōrēs:** i.e., the three leading stags. **ferentīs:** acc. pl. modifying **ductōrēs. 190. vulgus:** the herd; object of **sternit** understood. **192. victor:** i.e., Aeneas. **193. humī:** on the ground; locative. **numerum aequet:** i.e., Aeneas kills as many stags as he has ships. **fundat, aequet:** subjunctives in a clause of anticipation with **prius** ... **quam** in line 192. **194. sociōs ... omnīs:** dis-

tributes (the venison) among all his comrades. **195. cadīs:** abl. of place where or dat. of direction; see App. 103. **Acestēs:** a king in Sicily. **onerārat:** onerāverat. This kind of shortened pluperfect form is common. Cf. **audierat** in line 20. **Acestēs:** Acestes had been host to the Trojans in Sicily during the preceding winter. **196. lītore:** abl. of place where. **Trīnacriō:** Sicilian. **abeuntibus:** to (the Trojans) on their departure. **hērōs:** i.e., Acestes. **197. dīvidit:** distributes; understand **Aenēās** as the subject. **199. passī graviōra:** you who have suffered more severe trials (than these present ones). **200. Scyllaeam rabiem:** the fury of Scylla. **201. accestis:** shortened form of **accessistis. 202. expertī:** supply estis.

forsan perhaps; **ōlim sometime; *meminī remember
*varius different; *discrīmen crisis, danger
**sēdēs seat; home; *quiēscō become quiet
illīc there; **fās divine will, right; resurgō rise again
dūrō be hard, persevere; *-met enclitic, *emphasizing the word to which it is subjoined*

mittite; forsan et haec ōlim meminisse juvābit.

Per variōs cāsūs, per tot discrīmina rērum

205 tendimus in Latium, sēdīs ubi Fāta quiētās

ostendunt; illīc fās rēgna resurgere Trōjae.

Dūrāte, et vōsmet rēbus servāte secundīs.''

QUESTIONS ON 157–207. 1. How does Achates make a fire? 2. What sort of food do the Trojans prepare to cook? 3. Where does Aeneas go meanwhile? 4. Who accompanies Aeneas? 5. What does Aeneas hope to see? 6. What does Aeneas see? 7. How many deer does Aeneas kill? Why that number? 8. What were two great hardships that Aeneas reminds the Trojans they had already successfully encountered?

## The Trojans bewail the loss of their comrades.

referō utter, say

*vultus countenance, face; **cor heart; dolor pain, grief
accingō gird; *daps feast

tergus back, hide; dēripiō strip off; costa rib; *vīscus flesh
frūstum piece; *secō cut; verū spit, spike; *tremō quiver
aēnum bronze kettle; cf. *aēnus of bronze; locō place; ministrō tend
victus food; revocō call back, restore; *herba grass
impleō fill; *pinguis fat, rich; ferīna game, venison
eximō take away; **epulae feast, banquet; *mēnsa table, food; removeō remove
*sermō talk, discourse; *requīrō inquire about
*dubius doubtful, wavering

exaudiō hear

praecipuē especially; cf. *praecipuus chief, especial; *pius dutiful, devoted, good, loyal
*gemō bemoan, lament; *crūdēlis cruel, bitter

Tālia vōce refert, cūrīsque ingentibus aeger

spem vultū simulat, premit altum corde dolōrem.

210 Illī sē praedae accingunt dapibusque futūrīs:

tergora dēripiunt costīs et vīscera nūdant;

pars in frūsta secant veribusque trementia fīgunt,

lītore aēna locant aliī, flammāsque ministrant.

Tum victū revocant vīrīs, fūsīque per herbam

215 implentur veteris Bacchī pinguisque ferīnae.

Postquam exēmpta famēs epulīs mēnsaeque remōtae,

āmissōs longō sociōs sermōne requīrunt,

spemque metumque inter dubiī, seu vīvere crēdant

sīve extrēma patī nec jam exaudīre vocātōs.

220 Praecipuē pius Aenēās nunc ācris Orontī,

nunc Amycī cāsum gemit, et crūdēlia sēcum

fāta Lycī, fortemque Gyān, fortemque Cloanthum.

---

203. et haec: *even these* (hardships). This sentence has become famous through frequent quotation. 204. discrīmina rērum: *hazards*. 206. fās: supply est; *it is ordained* (by the Fates). rēgna Trōjae: *the realms of Troy*. rēgna: poetic pl. 207. vōsmet ... secundīs: *save yourselves for happier days*. 208. Tālia: supply verba. 209. vultū: abl. of means or of place where. premit: *represses*. corde: abl. of place where. 210. Illī: i.e., the other Trojans. 211. costīs: abl. of separation. 212. secant: the object is vīscera understood. pars, although singular, takes a plural verb. Cf.

the common English usage "a number of men were present." veribus: abl. of means. 213. lītore: abl. of place where. 214. vīrīs: acc. pl. fūsī: *stretched:* from fundō. 215. implentur: *they are filled,* i.e., they fill themselves. Bacchī, ferīnae: genitives with implentur; see App. 96. Bacchus, god of wine, here means wine itself; an example of *metonymy.* 216. exēmpta: supply est. 218. vīvere: the subject of vīvere is sociōs understood. 219. extrēma patī: *suffering the last penalty,* i.e., death. 220. pius: a characteristic epithet of Aeneas. 221–222. cāsum gemit: *bemoans the fate.*

QUESTIONS ON **208–222.** 1. How do the Trojans cook their venison? 2. What emotion does Aeneas simulate? Why? 3. After the meal, what do the Trojans discuss? 4. What lost comrades does Aeneas in particular lament?

*Venus pleads with Jupiter in behalf of the Trojans and of her son Aeneas.*

Et jam fīnis erat, cum Juppiter, aethere summō

**aethēr** heaven

dēspiciēns mare vēlivolum terrāsque jacentīs

**vēlivolus** sail-covered; **jaceō** lie outspread

lītoraque et lātōs populōs, sīc vertice caelī    225

cōnstitit, et Libyae dēfīxit lūmina rēgnīs.

**dēfīgō** fix, fasten; *lūmen light; eye

Atque illum, tālīs jactantem pectore cūrās,

trīstior et lacrimīs oculōs suffūsa nitentīs

*trīstis sad; *lacrima tear; suffundō fill, suffuse; *niteō shine, glisten

adloquitur Venus: Ō quī rēs hominumque deum-que

adloquor address, speak to

aeternīs regis imperiīs, et fulmine terrēs,    230

**aeternus** everlasting; *fulmen thunderbolt

quid meus Aenēās in tē committere tantum,

quid Trōes potuēre, quibus tot fūnera passīs

*fūnus death, disaster

cūnctus ob Ītaliam terrārum clauditur orbis?

**cūnctus** whole, entire; orbis circle; orbis terrārum world certē surely; ***ōlim sometime

Certē hinc Rōmānōs ōlim volventibus annīs,

hinc fore ductōrēs, revocātō ā sanguine Teucrī,    235

ductor leader; revocō recall, revive; **sanguis blood, race diciō power, sway

quī mare, quī terrās omnī diciōne tenērent,

pollicitus. Quae tē, genitor, sententia vertit?

**genitor** sire, father

Hōc equidem occāsum Trōjae trīstīsque ruīnās

*equidem indeed; *trīstis sad, dire; **ruīna ruin

sōlābar, fātīs contrāria fāta rependēns;

*sōlor find consolation for; contrārius opposite, opposing; rependō weigh, balance

nunc eadem fortūna virōs tot cāsibus āctōs    240

īnsequitur. Quem dās fīnem, rēx magne, labōrum?

īnsequor follow, pursue

Antēnor potuit, mediīs ēlāpsus Achīvīs,

ēlābor slip out, escape

---

Amycus, Lycus, Gyas, and Cloanthus were Trojan companions of Aeneas. **Gyān:** Greek acc. sing. **223. aethere:** abl. of place whence without a prep. **224. jacentīs:** *low-lying;* acc. pl. **225. lātōs:** *wide-spread, far-flung.* **vertice:** abl. of place where. **226. lūmina:** i.e., his eyes. **rēgnīs:** dat. of direction. **227. illum:** i.e., Jupiter. **228. lacrimīs . . . nitentīs:** *her shining eyes suffused with tears.* **oculōs:** after the perfect passive participle **suffūsa.** The construction is of Greek origin; see App. 114. **229. Ō quī:** i.e., **Ō tū quī. deum:** **deōrum. 230. regis:** 2nd person sing. present indic. of **regō;** its subject is **quī. 231. quid tantum:** *what great offense.* **232. quibus . . .**

passīs: *to whom, after they have suffered so many disasters.* **233. ob Ītaliam:** *on account of Italy;* i.e., on account of Juno's determined opposition to their ever reaching Italy. **234. hinc:** i.e., from the Trojans. **volventibus annīs:** *as the years roll by.* **235. revocātō . . . Teucrī:** *from the restored race of Teucer.* Teucer was an early king of Troy. **236. quī . . . tenērent:** relative clause of purpose. **237. pollicitus:** supply **es. 238. Hōc:** *by means of this* (promise). **239. fātīs . . . rependēns:** *balancing hostile fates with* (favorable) *fates,* i.e., trusting that the future will be favorable for the Trojans. **240. fortūna:** *fate.* **Fortūna** may mean either good or bad fortune. **242. Antēnor:** this

penetrō enter, penetrate; **si-
nus curve; bay, gulf
*fōns spring, source

Īllyricōs penetrāre sinūs, atque intima tūtus
rēgna Liburnōrum et fontem superāre Timāvī,

**ōs, ōris mouth

245 unde per ōra novem vāstō cum murmure montis

prōruptus rushing, raging; *ar-
vum land; **sonō resound
***sēdēs seat; abode; locō
place, establish

it mare prōruptum, et pelagō premit arva sonantī.
Hīc tamen ille urbem Patavī sēdīsque locāvit
Teucrōrum, et gentī nōmen dedit armaque fīxit

placidus calm, quiet; compōnō
settle; **quiēscō rest
**prōgeniēs progeny, offspring;
adnuō nod assent, promise;
cf. *nūtus a nod; ***arx cita-
del, height
īnfandus unspeakable
longē far; disjungō keep away
from; ***ōra shore
pietās dutifulness, devotion;
***scēptrum scepter; power;
repōnō put

Trōia, nunc placidā compostus pāce quiēscit;
250 nōs, tua prōgeniēs, caelī quibus adnuis arcem,
nāvibus (īnfandum!) āmissīs, ūnīus ob īram
prōdimur, atque Italīs longē disjungimur ōrīs.
Hic pietātis honōs? Sīc nōs in scēptra repōnis?"

QUESTIONS ON **223–253**. 1. What emotion does Venus show
when she addresses Jupiter? 2. Of what promise does she re-
mind him? 3. What had Antenor accomplished since the fall of
Troy? 4. With whom does she compare Antenor? 5. Against
whom particularly does Venus show resentment?

### Jupiter sends Mercury to Carthage.

subrīdeō smile; cf. *rīdeō
laugh; sator sower; creator
**vultus countenance; expres-
sion; serēnō clear, calm
*ōsculum lip; *lībō sip, touch;
kiss; nāta daughter; dehinc
then; **for speak
immōtus unmoved, unshaken
prōmittō promise

Ollī subrīdēns hominum sator atque deōrum
255 vultū quō caelum tempestātēsque serēnat
ōscula lībāvit nātae, dehinc tālia fātur:
"Parce metū, Cytherēa: manent immōta tuōrum
fāta tibī; cernēs urbem et prōmissa Lavīnī

***moenia walls; *sublīmis
high, aloft; ***sīdus star
magnanimus great-souled

moenia, sublīmemque ferēs ad sīdera caelī
260 magnanimum Aenēān, neque mē sententia vertit.

***for speak; *quandō since;
remordeō bite; worry

Hic tibi (fābor enim, quandō haec tē cūra remordet,

Trojan leader had been able to pass through the
dangers that Venus now proceeds to enumerate.
Shall Aeneas not likewise be allowed to succeed?
**ēlāpsus**: Antenor had escaped from the Greeks
at Troy, as had Aeneas. **243. Īllyricōs sinūs:**
the rugged Illyrian coast was dangerous to sailors.
**244. fontem:** *source*. **superāre:** *to pass beyond*.
**Timāvī:** the Timavus flows underground for some
miles, then emerges through several openings.
**246. mare prōruptum:** (like) *a furious sea*. **pelagō
sonantī:** *with roaring flood*. **247. ille:** i.e., An-
tenor. **Patavī:** ancient Patavium is now called
Padua. See the map facing page 1. The Roman
historian Livy was born here. **248. fīxit:** *hung
up*, i.e., dedicated them to the gods as a thank
offering. **250. tua prōgeniēs:** Venus was Jupiter's
daughter. **caelī arcem:** *the citadel of heaven*, i.e.,

deification (for Aeneas). **251. īnfandum:** *O
horror!* **ūnīus:** i.e., of Juno. **253. Hic:** supply
est. **pietātis honōs:** *the reward for his devotion*.
in scēptra: *into power*.
**254. Ollī:** *on her*; an early form of **illī**; dat.
of reference. **255. vultū:** take this with **subrī-
dēns**. **256. dehinc:** pronounced as one syllable.
**tālia:** supply verba. **257. Parce metū:** *spare
your fear*. **metū:** dat. with **parce**. **Cytherēa:**
Venus is called Cytherean because she was reared
in the Greek island of Cythera. **tuōrum:** i.e.,
of your Trojans. **258. Lavīnī:** see note on line 2.
In line 2 the first **a** is long; here it is short by
poetic license. **259. ad sīdera caelī:** i.e., Aeneas
will become a god. Cf. **caelī . . . arcem** in line
250. **260. neque . . . vertit:** Jupiter thus answers
Venus's question in line 237. **261. Hic:** i.e.,

longius et volvēns Fātōrum arcāna movēbō)
bellum ingēns geret Ītaliā, populōsque ferōcīs
contundet, mōrēsque virīs et moenia pōnet,
tertia dum Latiō rēgnantem vīderit aestās,
ternaque trānsierint Rutulīs hīberna subāctīs.
At puer Ascanius, cui nunc cognōmen Iūlō
additur (Īlus erat, dum rēs stetit Īlia rēgnō),
trīgintā magnōs volvendīs mēnsibus orbīs
imperiō explēbit, rēgnumque ab sēde Lavīnī
trānsferet, et Longam multā vī mūniet Albam.
Hīc jam ter centum tōtōs rēgnābitur annōs
gente sub Hectoreā, dōnec rēgīna sacerdōs,
Mārte gravis, geminam partū dabit Īlia prōlem.
Inde, lupae fulvō nūtrīcis tegmine laetus,
Rōmulus excipiet gentem, et Māvortia condet
moenia, Rōmānōsque suō dē nōmine dīcet.
Hīs ego nec mētās rērum nec tempora pōnō;
imperium sine fīne dedī.  Quīn aspera Jūnō,
quae mare nunc terrāsque metū caelumque fatīgat,
cōnsilia in melius referet, mēcumque fovēbit
Rōmānōs, rērum dominōs gentemque togātam.
Sīc placitum.  Veniet lūstrīs lābentibus aetās,

arcānum secret
*ferōx fierce, savage
contundō crush
265 **rēgnō rule, reign
ternī three; trānseō pass; subigō subdue
*cognōmen surname
addō add
trīgintā thirty; **orbis circle, cycle
270 expleō fill (out); complete
*albus white
***ter thrice, three times; ***rēgnō rule, reign
*dōnec until; *sacerdōs priestess
**geminus twin; partus birth; **prōlēs offspring
275 lupa she-wolf; cf. *lupus hewolf; *fulvus tawny; nūtrīx nurse; teg(i)men covering; skin; **laetus rejoicing
***condō found, establish
*mēta limit, boundary
**asper harsh, fierce
280 *fatīgō weary, tire
referō change; **foveō cherish
*dominus lord, master; *togātus toga-clad
lūstrum a period of five years; lābor slip, glide by

Aeneas. tibi: dat. of reference equivalent to some such parenthetical phrase as "I tell you." 261–262. fābor enim longius et . . . movēbō: for I shall speak more fully and unrolling the secrets of the Fates I shall reveal them. 263. bellum: this war, waged against the Rutulians under Turnus, is described in Books VII–XII of the Aeneid. 264. mōrēs: laws, institutions. virīs: to his people. 265. dum: until. Latiō: abl. of place where. rēgnantem: modifies Aenēān understood as object of vīderit. 266. ternaque . . . subāctīs: and three winter camps (i.e., three winters) shall have passed after the subjugation of the Rutulians. 267. Ascanius: Aeneas's son. Iūlō: dat. by attraction to the dat. cui. The Julian family, descended from Aeneas, the son of Venus, included Julius Caesar and Augustus, who thus claimed divine origin. 268. rēs Īlia: the Ilian (i.e., Trojan) state. rēgnō: abl. of means or of specification. 269. magnōs orbīs: great cycles (i.e., years). volvendīs mēnsibus: with its revolving months.

270–271. rēgnum trānsferet: i.e., Ascanius will move his seat of government from Lavinium to his newly founded Alba Longa. 272. rēgnābitur: used impersonally; literally, it will be reigned; the reign will endure. 273. Hectoreā: i.e., Trojan, since Hector was the son of King Priam of Troy. rēgīna sacerdōs: a royal priestess, i.e., Rhea Silvia or Ilia, daughter of King Numitor. 274. Mārte gravis: pregnant by Mars, god of war. geminam prōlem: twin offspring, i.e., Romulus and Remus. partū dabit: shall give birth to. 275. lupae nūtrīcis: i.e., of the she-wolf that nursed the twins. 276. excipiet: will inherit. Māvortia: Romulus, the founder of Rome, was the son of Mars or Mavors. 278. Hīs: to these, i.e., to the Romans. 279. Quīn: nay more. 281. in melius referet: will change for the better. 282. rērum dominōs: masters of the world. gentem togātam: the toga-clad race, i.e., the Roman nation. 283. placitum (est): it is ordained. lūstrīs lābentibus: as the years glide on.

*clārus bright; illustrious

servitium slavery, bondage;
dominor rule over
***pulcher beautiful; illustri-
ous; *orīgō source
terminō bound; *astrum star

dēmittō send down; derive

*spolium spoils, booty; onus-
tus laden
sēcūrus free from care; vōtum
vow, prayer; cf. *voveō vow
***asper rough, cruel; mītēscō
become mild; cf. **mītis
mild; *saeculum age
*cānus white, hoary
*dīrus dread, awful; compāgēs
joint, fastening; artus close-
fitted, tight
impius wicked; **intus within
**sedeō sit; **super upon;
*vinciō bind; **aēnus bra-
zen, of bronze
*nōdus knot; **fremō rage;
horridus bristling; ***ōs
mouth; *cruentus bloody
**ajō say; *gignō bear, give
birth to

hospitium hospitality, welcome;
nescius ignorant, unaware
**arceō keep away; ***volō fly;
*āēr air
rēmigium oar-like motion; *āla
wing; *citus quick, swift;
**adstō take a stand, alight
jussum order; **ferōx savage
***cor heart, feeling; ***quiēscō
become quiet
benignus kindly

cum domus Assaracī Phthīam clārāsque Mycēnās
285 servitiō premet, ac victīs dominābitur Argīs.
Nāscētur pulchrā Trōjānus orīgine Caesar,
imperium Ōceanō, fāmam quī terminet astrīs,
Jūlius, ā magnō dēmissum nōmen Iūlō.
Hunc tū ōlim caelō spoliīs Orientis onustum
290 accipiēs sēcūra; vocābitur hic quoque vōtīs.
Aspera tum positīs mītēscent saecula bellīs;
cāna Fidēs et Vesta, Remō cum frātre Quirīnus
jūra dabunt; dīrae ferrō et compāgibus artīs
claudentur bellī portae; Furor impius intus,
295 saeva sedēns super arma, et centum vīnctus aēnīs
post tergum nōdīs, fremet horridus ōre cruentō."

Haec ait, et Mājā genitum dēmittit ab altō,
ut terrae utque novae pateant Carthāginis arcēs
hospitiō Teucrīs, nē fātī nescia Dīdō
300 fīnibus arcēret. Volat ille per āera magnum
rēmigiō ālārum, ac Libyae citus adstitit ōrīs,
et jam jussa facit, pōnuntque ferōcia Poenī
corda, volente deō; in prīmīs rēgīna quiētum
accipit in Teucrōs animum mentemque benignam.

QUESTIONS ON 254–304. 1. What prophecy does Jupiter make
in reference to Aeneas? Ascanius? Romulus? Juno? Augus-
tus? 2. What mission does Jupiter give Mercury? 3. What
attitude does Dido assume toward the Trojans?

284–285. domus Assaracī . . . premet: Greece be-
came a Roman province in 146 B.C. Assaracus
was an early king of Troy, Phthia was the home
of Achilles, and Mycenae was the home of Aga-
memnon, the leader of the Greeks at Troy.
Argīs: *Argos*, i.e., the Greeks. 286. Caesar: i.e.,
Augustus. 287. terminet: subjunctive in a rela-
tive clause of purpose. 288. Jūlius: i.e., Augus-
tus. 289. ōlim: *some day*. caelō: abl. of place
where. spoliīs . . . onustum: the reference is to
Augustus's triumph over Cleopatra at Actium in
31 B.C. and his later victories in Asia Minor and
Syria. 290. hic quoque: i.e., Augustus, as well as
Aeneas, will be invoked as a god. 291. Aspera . . .
bellīs: i.e., an era of peace will dawn. 292. Vesta:
goddess of the hearth and home. Quirīnus:
Romulus's name after his deification. 293. jūra

dabunt: *will administer justice*. 294. portae: i.e.,
the doors of the temple of Janus, which Augustus
closed in 29 B.C., after many years of warfare.
Furor: the frenzy of war is personified. 295. saeva
sedēns super: note the *alliteration*. 295–296. cen-
tum . . . nōdīs: *bound behind his back with a hundred
brazen knots*, i.e., with his hands bound, etc.
297. Mājā genitum: i.e., Mercury. Mājā is
an ablative of source. 299. hospitiō Teucrīs: *in
welcome to the Trojans*. Dīdō: founder and queen
of Carthage. 300. fīnibus: abl. of separation
with arcēret; supply Teucrōs as object of arcēret.
āera: acc. sing. ōrīs: abl. of place where.
302. pōnunt: *lay aside*. Poenī: *the Carthaginians*.
303. rēgīna: i.e., Queen Dido. 304. accipit: *as-
sumes*. in Teucrōs: *toward the Trojans*. For Work
Unit III, based on lines 157–304, see page 252.

*Aeneas sets out with Achates to explore the new land
and meets Venus, disguised as a huntress.*

At pius Aenēās, per noctem plūrima volvēns,  305

ut prīmum lūx alma data est, exīre locōsque

explōrāre novōs, quās ventō accesserit ōrās,

quī teneant (nam inculta vīdēt), hominēsne feraene,

quaerere cōnstituit sociīsque exācta referre.

Classem in convexō nemorum sub rūpe cavātā,  310

arboribus clausam circum atque horrentibus um-
brīs,

occulit; ipse ūnō graditur comitātus Achātē,

bīna manū lātō crīspāns hastīlia ferrō.

Cui māter mediā sēsē tulit obvia silvā,

virginis ōs habitumque gerēns et virginis arma  315

Spartānae, vel quālis equōs Thrēissa fatīgat

Harpalycē, volucremque fugā praevertitur He-
brum:

namque umerīs dē mōre habilem suspenderat ar-
cum

vēnātrīx, dederatque comam diffundere ventīs,

nūda genū, nōdōque sinūs collēcta fluentīs.  320

Ac prior "Heus," inquit, "juvenēs, mōnstrāte,
meārum

vīdistis sī quam hīc errantem forte sorōrum,

succīnctam pharetrā, et maculōsae tegmine lyncis,

aut spūmantis aprī cursum clāmōre prementem."

---

**305** **pius** dutiful, good

*almus nurturing; kindly; **exeō**
go forth

**incultum** waste land; **fera** wild
beast
**exigō** track out, discover

**convexum** a hollow; a recess;
***nemus** grove, forest; **rū-
pēs** cliff; **cavō** hollow out
**horreō** bristle; quiver; cf.
**abhorreō** shrink from,
shudder at; **umbra** shade
**occulō** hide, conceal; *gradior**
step, proceed; *comitor** ac-
company
**crispō** brandish; wave; **hastīle**
spear-shaft, spear
*obvius** in the way, across the
path
*virgō** maiden; **habitus** ap-
pearance, dress
*quālis** what sort, as; **fatīgō**
weary, tire out
*volucer** flying, swift

*umerus** shoulder; **habilis**
easily handled; light; *sus-
pendō** suspend, hang; **ar-
cus** bow
**vēnātrīx** huntress; **coma** hair;
**diffundō** scatter, spread out
**nūdus** bare; *genū** knee; **nō-
dus** knot; ***sinus** fold
**heus** ho!; *juvenis** young man;
**mōnstrō** show

***errō** wander; **soror** sister
**succingō** gird; *pharetra** quiver;
**maculōsus** spotted; **teg(i)-
men** skin; **lynx** *a wild-cat*
**spūmō** foam, froth; **aper** wild
boar

---

**305.** plūrima volvēns: *pondering many thoughts.*
**307–308.** accesserit, teneant: subjunctives in in-
direct questions, depending on **quaerere** in line
309. **308.** vidēt: the original quantity of the e
is here retained for metrical reasons. **hominēsne
feraene:** *whether men or beasts.* **309.** exācta re-
ferre: *to report his discoveries.* **312.** ipse: i.e.,
Aeneas. **Achātē:** abl. of means with **comitātus.**
**313.** lātō ferrō: *with a broad iron point.* **314.** Cui
... silvā: *his mother came to meet him in the
heart of the forest.* **316–317.** vel ... Harpalycē:
*or like Thracian Harpalyce, who tires out horses;*

for the figure of speech here used see App. 22, 19.
**317.** praevertitur: *outstrips.* **Hebrum:** a swift
river in Thrace. **318.** dē mōre: *according to the
custom* (of hunters). **319.** vēnātrīx: *as a huntress.*
diffundere: *to toss;* infin. of purpose, a poetic
construction. **320.** genū: for the case see App.
113. nōdōque ... fluentīs: *having gathered the
flowing folds* (of her robe) *in a knot;* sinūs is the
object of **collecta** used as a middle voice; for this
use of **collecta** see App. 188. **321.** prior: i.e., she
was the first to speak. **324.** cursum prementem:
*following the trail.*

*ōrdior begin (*to speak*)

***soror sister

memorō call; ***virgō maiden; *haud not, not at all; ***vultus countenance

mortālis human; ***sonō sound; certē certainly, surely ***nympha nymph; ***sanguis blood, race

*fēlīx favorable, helpful; **levō lighten

*tandem at last; ***orbis circle; world **ignārus ignorant

***āra altar; hostia sacrificial victim

325 Sīc Venus; et Veneris contrā sīc fīlius ōrsus:
"Nūlla tuārum audīta mihī neque vīsa sorōrum,
ō quam tē memorem, virgō?; namque haud tibi vultus
mortālis, nec vōx hominem sonat: ō dea certē!
An Phoebī soror, an nymphārum sanguinis ūna?
330 Sīs fēlīx, nostrumque levēs, quaecumque, labōrem,
et quō sub caelō tandem, quibus orbis in ōrīs
jactēmur doceās; ignārī hominumque locōrumque
errāmus, ventō hūc vāstīs et flūctibus āctī;
multa tibi ante ārās nostrā cadet hostia dextrā."

QUESTIONS ON 305–334. 1. What does Aeneas decide to do at dawn? 2. Where does he hide his fleet? 3. Where does he meet Venus? 4. Who does Venus pretend to be? 5. For whom does Venus pretend to be looking? 6. Who does Aeneas think Venus is?

*Venus tells Aeneas he is near Carthage, the seat of Queen Dido's kingdom.*

**haud not, not at all; **equidem indeed, surely; *dignor deem worthy

gestō bear; **pharetra quiver

purpureus crimson, red; altē high up; sūra calf (*of the leg*); **vinciō bind; cothurnus boot, buskin intractābilis invincible

*germānus brother

ambāgēs winding; details: fastīgium top, high point

335 Tum Venus: "Haud equidem tālī mē dignor honōre;
virginibus Tyriīs mōs est gestāre pharetram
purpureōque altē sūrās vincīre cothurnō.
Pūnica rēgna vidēs, Tyriōs et Agēnoris urbem,
sed fīnēs Libycī, genus intractābile bellō.
340 Imperium Dīdō Tyriā regit urbe profecta,
germānum fugiēns. Longa est injūria, longae
ambāgēs; sed summa sequar fastīgia rērum.

---

**325.** contrā: *in his turn.* ōrsus: supply est.
**326.** audīta, vīsa: supply est. mihī: dat. of agent; see note on mihī in line 8. **327.** ō . . . memorem: *O what shall I call you?* The Romans were very scrupulous about invoking a deity by the correct name. memorem: deliberative subjunctive. tibi: supply est. **328.** nec vōx hominem sonat: *nor does your voice sound human;* hominem is a cognate acc.; see App. 115. dea certē: Aeneas is certain that she is a goddess, but he does not know which one. **329.** An: supply es. Phoebī soror: i.e., Diana. **330.** Sīs, levēs: *may you be, may you lighten;* optative subjunctives; see App. 149. quaecumque: supply es. **332.** doceās: optative subjunctive. jac-

tēmur: subjunctive in an indirect question depending on doceās. locōrumque: the e of que is elided before errāmus in the next line. This kind of elision is called *synapheia* and a line like 332 is called *hypermetric;* see App. 31. **334.** multa hostia: *many a sacrificial victim.*

**335.** honōre: abl. with dignor; see App. 126, a. **338.** Agēnoris urbem: Agenor was an ancient king of Phoenicia and, since Carthage had been founded by Phoenicians, it could properly be called Agenor's city. **339.** fīnēs: supply sunt. Libycī: *Libyan,* i.e., African. genus: loosely in apposition with fīnēs Libycī. **341.** Longa est injūria: *long is* (the story of) *her wrongs.* **342.** summa fastīgia rērum: *the main points of the tale.*

Huic conjūnx Sȳchaeus erat, dītissimus agrī
Phoenīcum, et magnō miserae dīlēctus amōre,
cui pater intāctam dederat, prīmīsque jugārat
ōminibus.  Sed rēgna Tyrī germānus habēbat
Pygmaliōn, scelere ante aliōs immānior omnīs.
Quōs inter medius vēnit furor; ille Sychaeum,
impius ante ārās atque aurī caecus amōre
clam ferrō incautum superat, sēcūrus amōrum
germānae, factumque diū cēlāvit, et aegram
multa malus simulāns vānā spē lūsit amantem.
Ipsa sed in somnīs inhumātī vēnit imāgō
conjugis, ōra modīs attollēns pallida mīrīs;
crūdēlīs ārās trājectaque pectora ferrō
nūdāvit, caecumque domūs scelus omne retēxit;
tum celerāre fugam patriāque excēdere suādet,
auxiliumque viae veterīs tellūre reclūdit
thēsaurōs, ignōtum argentī pondus et aurī.
Hīs commōta, fugam Dīdō sociōsque parābat. 360

Conveniunt quibus aut odium crūdēle tyrannī
aut metus ācer erat; nāvīs, quae forte parātae,
corripiunt, onerantque aurō; portantur avārī
Pygmaliōnis opēs pelagō; dux fēmina factī.
Dēvēnēre locōs, ubi nunc ingentia cernēs
moenia surgentemque novae Carthāginis arcem, 365
mercātīque solum, factī dē nōmine Byrsam,

**conjūnx** husband; **dīves** rich, wealthy
**dīligō** love; **amor** affection
345 **intāctus** untouched; unwedded; **jugō** join, unite
**ōmen** omen, auspices; **germānus** brother
**scelus** crime, villainy; **immānis** monstrous; cruel
**furor** madness, hatred

**impius** impious, wicked; **aurum** gold; **caecus** blind;
350 **amor** love, desire; **incautus** off guard, unsuspecting; **sēcūrus** heedless
**germāna** sister; **factum** deed; **cēlō** hide, conceal
**vānus** empty, false; **lūdō** mock, deceive; **amō** love
**somnus** sleep; **inhumātus** unburied; **imāgō** ghost
**conjūnx** husband; **attollō** lift, raise; **pallidus** pale, wan
355 **crūdēlis** cruel; **trājiciō** pierce
**caecus** blind; hidden; **scelus** crime; **retegō** disclose
**celerō** hasten; **patria** fatherland, country; **excēdō** depart; **suādeō** urge
**tellūs** earth; **reclūdō** disclose
**thēsaurus** treasure, hoard; **ignōtus** unknown; **argentum** silver; **pondus** weight; **aurum** gold
360 **commoveō** move, arouse

**conveniō** come together; **odium** hate, hatred; **crūdēlis** fierce, vengeful; **tyrannus** king, despot
**onerō** load; **aurum** gold; **avārus** covetous, greedy; cf. **avāritia** greediness
**fēmina** woman; **factum** deed, exploit
365 **dēveniō** come to, arrive at
**surgō** rise
**solum** ground, soil; **factum** deed

343. **Huic:** i.e., to Dido.  **Sȳchaeus:** deceased husband of Dido.  344. **Phoenīcum:** *of the Phoenicians.*  **miserae:** *by the wretched woman;* dat. of agent with **dīlēctus.**  The reference is to Dido.  345. **pater:** Dido's father was King Belus.  **intāctam:** modifies **eam,** understood as object of **dederat** and **jugā(ve)-rat.**  345–346. **prīmīs ōminibus:** the omens were consulted before a Roman wedding.  347. **ante:** here has the force of *than.*  348. **Quōs inter medius:** *between them,* i.e., between Pygmalion and Sychaeus.  350–351. **sēcūrus amōrum germānae:** *heedless of his sister's love* (for Sychaeus).  **amōrum:** obj. gen. depending on **sēcūrus.**  Note the poetic use of the plural.  352. **multa simulāns:** *inventing many stories.*  354. **ōra:** poetic plural; so also

**modīs mīrīs;** see App. 195, 4.  355. **crūdēlīs:** the altar is said to be cruel because it witnessed such a cruel deed.  **pectora:** i.e., Sychaeus's.  **ārās, pectora:** poetic plurals.  357. **celerāre suādet:** *urges* (her) *to hasten.*  The subject of **suādet** is Sychaeus's ghost.  In prose **suādet** would require the subjunctive.  358. **auxilium viae:** (as) *an aid for the journey.*  **auxilium** is in apposition with **thēsaurōs.**  359. **pondus:** in apposition with **thēsaurōs.**  361. **tyrannī:** i.e., Pygmalion.  362. **parātae:** supply **sunt.**  364. **dux fēmina factī:** supply **erat.**  Dido was the head of the expedition.  365. **Dēvēnēre:** **Dēvēnērunt.**  **locōs:** acc. of place whither.  367. **mercātī:** supply **sunt.**  **factī . . . Byrsam:** (called) *Byrsa from the name*

taurīnus of a bull

\*\*tandem at last

\*\*-ve *enclitic* or

taurīnō quantum possent circumdare tergō.
Sed vōs quī tandem? Quibus aut vēnistis ab ōrīs,
370 quōve tenētis iter?"

QUESTIONS ON 335–370. 1. Who was Sychaeus? Pygmalion?
2. What crime did Pygmalion commit? 3. What effect did this
crime have on Dido? 4. Why do you think Venus tells Aeneas
this story of Dido's life?

*Aeneas recounts his adventures and Venus encourages
him.*

suspīrō draw a deep breath, sigh

\*repetō repeat, retrace; \*\*orīgō beginning; pergō proceed

vacō be free; annālēs annals, story

compōnō lay to rest

\*\*auris ear

appellō drive to

\*\*\*pius dutiful, god-fearing

\*\*\*super above, beyond; \*\*\*aethēr upper air, sky

\*\*\*patria (*one's own*) country

dēnī ten; cōnscendō embark upon

mōnstrō show, point out

convellō wrench, batter; cf. \*vellō tear

\*\*ignōtus unknown; \*\*egeō be in need; dēserta waste lands; peragrō wander over

interfor interrupt; dolor grief

Quaerentī tālibus ille
suspīrāns īmōque trahēns ā pectore vōcem:
"Ō dea, sī prīmā repetēns ab orīgine pergam,
et vacet annālīs nostrōrum audīre labōrum,
ante diem clausō compōnet Vesper Olympō.
375 Nōs Trōjā antīquā, sī vestrās forte per aurīs
Trōjae nōmen iit, dīversa per aequora vectōs
forte suā Libycīs tempestās appulit ōrīs.
Sum pius Aenēās, raptōs quī ex hoste Penātīs
classe vehō mēcum, fāmā super aethera nōtus;
380 Ītaliam quaerō patriam et genus ab Jove summō.
Bis dēnīs Phrygium cōnscendī nāvibus aequor,
mātre deā mōnstrante viam, data fāta secūtus;
vix septem, convulsae undīs Eurōque, supersunt;
ipse ignōtus, egēns, Libyae dēserta peragrō,
385 Eurōpā atque Asiā pulsus." Nec plūra querentem
passa Venus mediō sīc interfāta dolōre est:

*of the act.* The Greek word **byrsa** means a bull's
hide. The Carthaginian word **bosra** means a
citadel. Hence arose the story that the settlers,
under Dido, bought from the Libyans as much
land as could be covered by a bull's hide and that
the colonists cut the hide into strips to ensure the
largest possible area of land. **369. quī:** supply **estis.**
    **370. Quaerentī:** modifies **Venerī** understood as
indirect object of **dīxit** or of **respondit** to be sup-
plied. **tālibus:** supply **vōcibus** or **verbīs. ille:**
i.e., Aeneas. **372. sī . . . pergam:** *if I should pro-
ceed starting from the very beginning;* a less vivid
condition; see App. 150, 1. **373. vacet:** (if)
*there should be time.* **374. ante . . . Olympō:** *sooner
will Olympus be closed and Evening lay the day to
rest.* Note that **compōnet,** in the conclusion of a

less vivid condition, is here future indicative, to
express the certainty of the conclusion. **376. vec-
tōs:** *having sailed;* modifies **Nōs** in line 375,
which is the object of **appulit** in line 377.
**377. forte suā:** *by its own whim.* **ōrīs:** dat. of
place whither. **379. aethera:** Greek acc. sing.
**381. Bis dēnīs nāvibus:** *with twice ten ships.*
**Phrygium aequor:** the sea near Troy, in Phrygia.
**382. mātre:** i.e., Venus. **data fāta:** *the ordained
fates.* **385. Eurōpā, Asiā:** abl. of place whence.
**Eurōpā** refers more specifically to Italy, and **Asiā**
to Troy. **385–386. Nec . . . est:** *And Venus did
not let him longer lament, but interrupted him in
the midst of his grief.* **querentem:** modifies
**Aenēān,** understood as object of **passa. plūra:**
acc. neuter pl., object of **querentem.**

"Quisquis es, haud, crēdō, invīsus caelestibus
   aurās
vītālīs carpis, Tyriam quī advēneris urbem;
perge modo, atque hinc tē rēgīnae ad līmina perfer.
Namque tibī reducīs sociōs classemque relātam    390
nūntiō et in tūtum versīs Aquilōnibus āctam,
nī frūstrā augurium vānī docuēre parentēs.

Aspice bis sēnōs laetantīs agmine cycnōs,
aetheriā quōs lāpsa plagā Jovis āles apertō
turbābat caelō; nunc terrās ōrdine longō    395
aut capere aut captās jam dēspectāre videntur:
ut reducēs illī lūdunt strīdentibus ālīs,
et coetū cīnxēre polum, cantūsque dedēre,
haud aliter puppēsque tuae pūbēsque tuōrum
aut portum tenet aut plēnō subit ōstia vēlō.    400
Perge modo, et, quā tē dūcit via, dīrige gressum."

QUESTIONS ON 370–401. 1. What excuse does Aeneas give for
not giving Venus a complete account of his adventures?
2. Where does Venus tell Aeneas to go? 3. With what prophecy
does she encourage him? 4. On what evidence does she base
this prophecy? 5. What is the "bird of Jupiter"?

*Made invisible by Venus, Aeneas and Achates enter
   Carthage.*

Dīxit, et āvertēns roseā cervīce refulsit,
ambrosiaeque comae dīvīnum vertice odōrem
spīrāvēre; pedēs vestis dēflūxit ad īmōs,
et vēra incessū patuit dea. Ille ubi mātrem    405
agnōvit, tālī fugientem est vōce secūtus:

*quisquis whoever; ***haud not, not at all; invīsus hated, hateful; cf. **invideō look askance at, envy; caelestēs heavenly beings; **aura air vītālis of life; *carpō pluck; breathe; adveniō come to pergō continue, proceed; *līmen threshold; perferō bear redux led back, restored

**nī if not, unless; *augurium soothsaying; **vānus deceitful; **parēns parent

aspiciō see, look at; sēnī six; *laetor rejoice; cycnus swan aetherius of the upper air; **lābor slip, glide; plaga region, tract; *āles bird; apertus open, clear turbō throw into confusion dēspectō look down on redux led back, restored; **lūdō play, sport; **strīdeō whir, rustle; **āla wing coetus company, flock; **cingō encircle, gird; **polus sky; cantus song, cry *pūbēs band (of men) *plēnus full; subeō go into, enter; ōstium mouth, entrance; ***vēlum canvas, sail pergō go on, proceed; gressus step

āvertō turn away; roseus rosy; *cervīx neck, shoulder; refulgeō shine, gleam ambrosius immortal; **coma hair; *dīvīnus heavenly; odor fragrance *spīrō breathe forth; dēfluō flow down incessus walk, gait *agnōscō recognize

387. Quisquis es: Venus pretends ignorance of Aeneas's identity. 387–388. aurās vītālīs carpis: *you breathe the air of life.* 388. advēneris: subjunctive in a relative clause of characteristic with the additional idea of cause. 389. perge modo: *only go on.* 391. versīs Aquilōnibus: *by a change in the winds.* 392. nī . . . parentēs: i.e., I tell you that these things will really happen, unless I have not learned how to prophesy. 393. bis sēnōs: *twice six.* agmine: *in orderly flight.* 394. plagā: abl. of place whence. Jovis āles: i.e., the eagle.

395. caelō: abl. of place where or of route. 396. capere: *to seize upon,* i.e., to alight upon. captās: supply terrās. videntur: *are seen.* 397. illī: i.e., the swans. 398. cīnxēre, dedēre: cīnxērunt, dedērunt. 399. puppēs: literally, *sterns;* by *metonymy* (see App. 22, 13) for *ships.* pūbēs tuōrum: *the young men of your company.* 402. Dīxit: supply Venus as subject. 404. spīrāvēre: spīrāvērunt. 405. patuit: *she stood revealed.* dea: note the hiatus after dea at the end of a sentence.

*totiēns so many times; falsus deceptive
***lūdō mock, delude; **imāgō form, guise

incūsō reproach, accuse; gressus step
*obscūrus dark, obscuring; **gradior step forward, proceed; **āēr air; mist; saepiō hedge in, inclose
nebula cloud; *amictus mantle contingō touch; cf. **contingit it happens, it befalls
*mōlior pile up; contrive
**sublīmis aloft; abeō go away; revīsō revisit
***laetus joyous, happy; *templum temple
tūs incense; *caleō burn, glow; *sertum wreath, garland; hālō breathe; be fragrant

sēmita path; mōnstrō show, point out
ascendō mount

**immineō overhang; aspectō gaze at; dēsuper from above
māgālia huts; *quondam once, formerly
*strepitus noise, uproar; strātum pavement
*ārdeō burn, glow; be eager

**mōlior pile up, construct; subvolvō roll up
***optō choose; *tēctum roof; house; conclūdō inclose;
*sulcus furrow
*legō gather; choose
effodiō dig out

fundāmentum foundation; locō place
***rūpēs rock; excīdō cut out; *decus beauty, decoration; cf. *dēdecus blemish
**quālis what (sort of); apis bee; rūs country; field
adultus full-grown
fētus offspring; līquēns fluid, liquid; mel honey
stīpō stuff, stow away; **dulcis sweet; distendō pack

"Quid nātum totiēns, crūdēlis tū quoque, falsīs
lūdis imāginibus? Cūr dextrae jungere dextram
nōn datur ac verās audīre et reddere vōcēs?"
410 Tālibus incūsat, gressumque ad moenia tendit.
At Venus obscūrō gradientīs āere saepsit,
et multō nebulae circum dea fūdit amictū,
cernere nē quis eōs neu quis contingere posset
mōlīrīve moram aut veniendī poscere causās.
415 Ipsa Paphum sublīmis abit, sēdīsque revīsit
laeta suās, ubi templum illī centumque Sabaeō
tūre calent ārae, sertīsque recentibus hālant.

Corripuēre viam intereā, quā sēmita mōnstrat.
Jamque ascendēbant collem, quī plūrimus ūrbī
420 imminet, adversāsque aspectat dēsuper arcis.
Mīrātur mōlem Aenēās, māgālia quondam,
mīrātur portās, strepitumque, et strāta viārum.
Īnstant ārdentēs Tyriī, pars dūcere mūrōs
mōlīrīque arcem et manibus subvolvere saxa,
425 pars optāre locum tēctō et conclūdere sulcō;
jūra magistrātūsque legunt sānctumque senātum;
hīc portūs aliī effodiunt, hīc alta theātrī
fundāmenta locant aliī, immānīsque columnās
rūpibus excīdunt, scaenīs decora alta futūrīs:
430 quālis apēs aestāte novā per flōrea rūra
exercet sub sōle labor, cum gentis adultōs
ēdūcunt fētūs, aut cum līquentia mella
stīpant, et dulcī distendunt nectare cellās,
aut onera accipiunt venientum, aut, agmine factō,

---

407. Quid: *why.* 410. Tālibus: supply vōcibus or verbīs. 411. gradientīs: *as they* (i.e., Aeneas and Achates) *proceed;* acc. pl. 415. Paphum: Paphos was a city in the island of Cyprus sacred to Venus. 416. Sabaeō: *Sabaean,* i.e., Arabian. 418. Corripuēre viam: *they sped their way.* 419. plūrimus: *in huge mass.* 423. pars: in partitive apposition with Tyriī. dūcere: complementary infin. depending on Īnstant; so also

mōlīrī and subvolvere in line 424 and similarly optāre and conclūdere in line 425. 429. scaenīs ...futūrīs: *lofty adornments for stages yet to be.* 430–436. This famous simile compares the bustling Carthaginians, building their city, with busy bees; see App. 22, 19. For another reference to bees see *Aen.* VII, 707–709. 430–431. quālis apēs exercet labor: *such toil as busies bees (what toil busies bees).*

ignāvum fūcōs pecus ā praesaepibus arcent;

fervet opus, redolentque thymō fragrantia mella.

"Ō fortūnātī, quōrum jam moenia surgunt!"

Aenēās ait, et fastīgia suspicit urbis.

Īnfert sē, saeptus nebulā (mīrābile dictū)

per mediōs, miscetque virīs, neque cernitur ūllī.

435 **ignāvus** lazy; **fūcus** drone; **praesaepe** hive; ***arceō** keep off
*ferveō boil; move briskly; redoleō smell of; thymum thyme; mel honey
**surgō rise
***ajō say; fastīgium roof; *suspiciō gaze at
īnferō bear; saepiō hedge in, wrap; nebula cloud; mīrābilis wonderful
440

QUESTIONS ON **402–440**. 1. How does Venus make Aeneas and Achates invisible? 2. For what purpose does Venus make Aeneas and Achates invisible? 3. Where do Aeneas and Achates hasten to go? 4. From what place do Aeneas and Achates get their first view of the city? 5. What are some of the activities which Aeneas observes going on in Carthage?

*Visiting the temple of Juno, Aeneas finds important events of the Trojan War pictured on the walls.*

Lūcus in urbe fuit mediā, laetissimus umbrae,

quō prīmum, jactātī undīs et turbine, Poenī

effōdēre locō signum, quod rēgia Jūnō

mōnstrārat, caput ācris equī; sīc nam fore bellō

ēgregiam et facilem vīctū per saecula gentem.

Hīc templum Jūnōnī ingēns Sīdōnia Dīdō

condēbat, dōnīs opulentum et nūmine dīvae,

aerea cui gradibus surgēbant līmina nexaeque

aere trabēs, foribus cardō strīdēbat aēnīs.

Hōc prīmum in lūcō nova rēs oblāta timōrem

lēniit, hīc prīmum Aenēās spērāre salūtem

ausus et adflīctīs melius cōnfīdere rēbus.

Namque sub ingentī lūstrat dum singula templō,

rēgīnam opperiēns, dum quae fortūna sit urbī,

artificumque manūs intrā sē operumque labōrem

*lūcus grove, wood; ***umbra shade, shadow
***turbō whirlwind, tempest

effodiō dig up; rēgius royal, regal

445 saeculum age, generation

**templum temple

*dōnum gift; cf. *dōnō present; opulentus rich
aereus brazen; *gradus step; ***surgō rise; **limen threshold; *nectō bind
*foris door; cardō hinge; ***strīdeō creak; ***aēnus of bronze, brazen

450 **lūcus grove, wood; timor fear, anxiety
lēniō soothe, calm

*adflīgō shatter

*lūstrō move over; survey; ***templum temple
opperior await

455 artifex artisan, artist

---

**435.** ignāvum pecus: in apposition with fūcōs. **437.** Ō fortūnātī: i.e., the Carthaginians. **440.** miscet virīs: *mingles with the men.* Note the poetic use of the dat. with misceō; see App. 98, *a.* ūllī: dat. of agent with cernitur. For Work Unit IV, based on lines 305–440, see p. 255.

**441.** umbrae: gen. of specification with laetissimus; a poetic use; see App. 94. **443.** effōdēre: effōdērunt. **444.** mōnstrārat: mōnstrāverat. caput: acc. in apposition with signum in line 443.

fore: futūram esse. **445.** facilem vīctū: *easy to sustain.* vīctū: supine of vīvō. **446.** Sīdōnia: *Phoenician.* **448.** aerea: bronze was a costly metal, second only to gold. cui gradibus: *on the steps of which;* cui is a dat. of reference. nexaeque: supply erant. The e of –que is elided before aere in the next line; see App. 31. **450.** timōrem: i.e., Aeneas's fear. **452.** adflīctīs rēbus: *in his fallen fortunes;* abl. or dat. with cōnfīdere. **455.** artificum manūs: *the handicraft of the*

mīrātur, videt Īliacās ex ōrdine pugnās

**vulgō** spread abroad

bellaque jam fāmā tōtum vulgāta per orbem,

**\*ambō** both

Atrīdās, Priamumque, et saevum ambōbus Achillem.

**:acrimō** weep, shed tears

Cōnstitit, et lacrimāns, "Quis jam locus," inquit, "Achātē,

**\*\*plēnus** full

460 quae regiō in terrīs nostrī nōn plēna labōris?

**\*ēn** behold!

Ēn Priamus! Sunt hīc etiam sua praemia laudī,

**\*\*lacrima** tear

sunt lacrimae rērum, et mentem mortālia tangunt.

**\*\*solvō** loose; dismiss

Solve metūs; feret haec aliquam tibi fāma salūtem."

**\*\*pāscō** feed; **\*inānis** empty

Sīc ait, atque animum pictūrā pāscit inānī,

**\*\*gemō** sigh over, lament; **largus** copious; **ūmectō** wet **bellō** make war, battle

465 multa gemēns, largōque ūmectat flūmine vultum.
Namque vidēbat utī bellantēs Pergama circum

**hāc** this way, here; **\*juventūs** youth
**hāc** this way, here; **\*\*\*currus** chariot; **cristātus** plumed
**niveus** snowy, snow-white; **tentōrium** tent

hāc fugerent Grajī, premeret Trōjāna juventūs,
hāc Phryges, īnstāret currū cristātus Achillēs.
Nec procul hinc Rhēsī niveīs tentōria vēlīs

**\*\*agnōscō** recognize; **lacrimō** weep; **\*\*somnus** sleep
**\*\*cruentus** bloody; ruthless

470 agnōscit lacrimāns, prīmō quae prōdita somnō
Tȳdīdēs multā vāstābat caede cruentus,

**\*\*ārdeō** burn, glow, be fiery; **āvertō** turn away
**gustō** taste; **\*bibō** drink

ārdentīsque āvertit equōs in castra, priusquam
pābula gustāssent Trōjae, Xanthumque bibissent.
Parte aliā fugiēns āmissīs Trōilus armīs,

**īnfēlīx** unfortunate, unlucky; **impār** unequal; **congressus** encounter; match
**\*haereō** cling; **resupīnus** supine; **\*\*inānis** empty
**lōrum** rein; **\*\*cervīx** neck, shoulder; **\*\*\*coma** hair

475 īnfēlīx puer atque impār congressus Achillī,
fertur equīs, currūque haeret resupīnus inānī,
lōra tenēns tamen; huic cervīxque comaeque trahuntur

---

artists. **intrā sē:** *inwardly, to himself.* **456. Īliacās:** *Trojan.* **ex ōrdine:** *in sequence.* **458. Atrīdās:** i.e., Agamemnon and Menelaus, Greek leaders in the Trojan War. **saevum:** Achilles was hostile to Agamemnon especially because the latter had taken from Achilles a captive maiden named Briseis. **460. plēna:** supply **est. 462. lacrimae rērum:** *tears for* (human) *affairs,* i.e., sympathy for human sorrows. **mortālia:** *human sufferings.* **465. multa gemēns:** *lamenting deeply.* **multa:** acc. pl. neuter. **466. utī:** *how;* introducing a series of indirect questions. **Pergama:** *Troy.* **467–468. hāc . . . hāc:** *here . . . elsewhere* (in the series of wall paintings). **Grajī:** *the Greeks;* pronounce as if spelled **Grajjī. 468. Phryges:**

*the Trojans;* supply **fugerent. 469. Rhēsī:** since an oracle had proclaimed Troy impregnable if Rhesus's horses should drink the waters of the Xanthus River or graze on Trojan meadows, the Greek leaders Ulysses and Diomedes slew Rhesus, a Thracian ally of the Trojans, immediately upon his arrival at Troy and drove away his horses. **470. prīmō prōdita somnō:** *betrayed by their first sleep* (at Troy). Note the alliteration of c in line 471. **471. Tȳdīdēs:** *the son of Tydeus;* i.e., Diomedes. **472. in castra:** i.e., to the Greek camp. **473. gustāssent:** gustāvissent. **474. Trōilus:** Priam's youngest son, slain by Achilles. **477. huic cervīx:** *his neck.* **huic:** dat. of reference.

per terram, et versā pulvīs īnscrībitur hastā.
Intereā ad templum nōn aequae Palladis ībant
crīnibus Īliades passīs, peplumque ferēbant
suppliciter, trīstēs et tūnsae pectora palmīs;
dīva solō fīxōs oculōs āversa tenēbat.

**\*pulvis** dust; **īnscrībō** mark;
**\*hasta** spear

480 **\*crīnis** hair; **\*pandō** spread out;
dishevel; **peplum** robe
**suppliciter** suppliantly, humbly;
**\*\*\*trīstis** sad, sorrowful;
**\*tundō** beat; **\*\*palma** palm
**\*\*solum** ground; **āversus**
turned away; unfriendly

Ter circum Īliacōs raptāverat Hectora mūrōs,
exanimumque aurō corpus vēndēbat Achillēs.
Tum vērō ingentem gemitum dat pectore ab īmō, 485
ut spolia, ut currūs utque ipsum corpus amīcī
tendentemque manūs Priamum cōnspexit inermīs.
Sē quoque prīncipibus permixtum agnōvit Achīvīs,
Ēōāsque aciēs, et nigrī Memnonis arma.
Dūcit Amāzonidum lūnātīs agmina peltīs
Penthesilēa furēns, mediīsque in mīlibus ārdet,
aurea subnectēns exsertae cingula mammae,
bellātrīx, audetque virīs concurrere virgō.

**raptō** drag

**exanimus** breathless; lifeless;
**\*vēndō** sell
**vērō** truly, indeed; **gemitus**
groan, lament
**\*\*spolium** spoils, booty

**permisceō** mingle; **\*\*\*agnōscō**
recognize
**\*niger** black, dusky

490 **lūnātus** moon-shaped, crescent;
**pelta** shield
**\*\*\*furō** rage; **\*\*\*ārdeō** burn;
be eager
**aureus** golden; **subnectō** bind
beneath; **exserō** expose; **cin-
gulum** girdle; **mamma** breast
**bellātrīx** female warrior; **con-
currō** run with; fight with

QUESTIONS ON 441–493. 1. Why do you think Aeneas weeps on observing the Trojan scenes pictured in the temple? 2. What encouragement does Aeneas get from discovering these pictures? 3. Which side did Pallas Athena favor in the Trojan War? 4. Who was Penthesilea? Memnon?

*Dido enters the temple.*

    Haec dum Dardaniō Aenēae mīranda videntur,
dum stupet, obtūtūque haeret dēfīxus in ūnō,
rēgīna ad templum, fōrmā pulcherrima Dīdō,
incessit, magnā juvenum stīpante catervā.

495 **\*stupeō** stand agape, be amazed;
**obtūtus** gaze; **\*\*haereō** cling;
**dēfīgō** fix

**incēdō** advance; **\*\*juvenis**
young man; **stīpō** crowd
around; **\*caterva** throng

---

**478. pulvīs:** the i is long here by poetic license; cf. **videt** in line 308. **versā hastā:** *with turned* (i.e., trailing) *spear.* **479. nōn aequae:** *unfriendly.* Pallas Athene was hostile to the Trojans because of the adverse judgment of Paris. **480. crīnibus passīs:** *with dishevelled hair.* Dishevelled hair was a mark of grief. **Īliades:** *Trojan women.* **481. tūnsae pectora:** *beating their breasts.* **pectora:** object of the perfect participle **tūnsae,** which here has a reflexive or middle force; see App. 114. **482. dīva:** i.e., Pallas. **solō:** *on the ground;* dat. of direction. **483. Hectora:** Greek acc. sing. **484. aurō:** abl. of price. Hector's body was sold

to Priam. **485. dat:** supply **Aenēās** as subject. **486. ut:** *as, when.* Note the repetition (*anaphora*) of **ut. spolia:** the spoils that Achilles had taken from the Trojans. **487. inermīs:** acc. pl. with **manūs. 488. prīncipibus permixtum Achīvīs:** *mingling with the Greek chiefs.* **489. Ēōās aciēs:** *Eastern battle lines.* These troops were Ethiopian allies of the Trojans and were under the command of Memnon. **nigrī:** pronounce nig–rī with both syllables long. See App. 45, a. **491. Penthesilēa:** queen of the Amazons.

    **494. Dardaniō:** *Trojan;* Dardanus was an early king of Troy. **495. obtūtūque ... ūnō:**

***quālis** what sort; as

***chorus** band of dancers

***glomerō** gather; ****pharetra** quiver

****umerus** shoulder; ****gradior** step, move; **superēmineō** tower above

****taceō** be silent; **pertemptō** test, fill; **gaudium** joy

Quālis in Eurōtae rīpīs aut per juga Cynthī
exercet Diāna chorōs, quam mīlle secūtae
500 hinc atque hinc glomerantur Oreades; illa pharetram
fert umerō, gradiēnsque deās superēminet omnīs
(Lātōnae tacitum pertemptant gaudia pectus);
tālis erat Dīdō, tālem sē laeta ferēbat
per mediōs, īnstāns operī, rēgnīsque futūrīs.

****foris** door; **testūdō** tortoise; dome

**saepiō** hedge in, surround; **solium** throne; **altē** high; **subnīxus** resting on; **resīdō** sit down

505 Tum foribus dīvae, mediā testūdine templī,
saepta armīs, soliōque altē subnīxa resēdit.

QUESTIONS ON **494–506**. 1. Where does Dido hold her court?
2. Who accompanies Dido on her entrance into the temple?
3. With whom does Vergil compare Dido? 4. Who was Latona?
5. Where is Dido's throne placed?

*A deputation from Aeneas's missing ships arrives and appeals to Dido for protection.*

****sors** lot

**concursus** throng, crowd

Jūra dabat lēgēsque virīs, operumque labōrem
partibus aequābat jūstīs aut sorte trahēbat,
cum subitō Aenēās concursū accēdere magnō
510 Anthea Sergestumque videt, fortemque Cloanthum,
Teucrōrumque aliōs, āter quōs aequore turbō

**dispellō** scatter; ****penitus** far away; **āvehō** carry away

***obstīpēscō** be amazed; **percutiō** strike; cf. ***-cutiō** shake, strike

**laetitia** gladness, joy; ***avidus** eager; **conjungō** join

**incognitus** unknown; uncertain; **turbō** disturb, perplex

***dissimulō** conceal one's feelings; ****cavus** hollow; **speculor** watch; **amiciō** envelop

**linquō** leave

****cūnctus** all; ****legō** choose

***venia** favor; **clāmor** shouting

dispulerat penitusque aliās āvexerat ōrās.
Obstipuit simul ipse, simul percussus Achātēs
laetitiāque metūque; avidī conjungere dextrās
515 ārdēbant, sed rēs animōs incognita turbat.
Dissimulant, et nūbe cavā speculantur amictī
quae fortūna virīs, classem quō lītore linquant,
quid veniant, cūnctīs nam lēctī nāvibus ībant,
ōrantēs veniam, et templum clāmōre petēbant.

---

and remains rooted in one gaze. **498–502. Quālis ... pectus:** with this extended simile compare lines 430–435. **Eurōtae:** of Eurotas, a river in Greece. **Cynthi:** of Cynthus, a mountain on the island of Delos, where Latona gave birth to Diana and Apollo. **499. exercet chorōs:** *trains her dancing bands.* **Diāna:** goddess of the hunt; the i is long here. **500. Oreades:** mountain nymphs. **illa:** i.e., Diana. **501. umerō:** abl. of place where. **502. Lātōnae:** Latona was the mother of Diana and Apollo. **503. tālis:** correlative with Quālis in line 498. **tālem ... ferēbat:** such she bore herself in her joy. **505. foribus dīvae:** *at the doors of the goddess,* i.e., before the doors of the inner room that contained the sacred image of the goddess. **foribus:** abl. of place where; so **testūdine** in line 505 and **soliō** in line 506.

**508. partibus:** *assignments.* **510. Anthea:** Greek acc. Antheus, Sergestus, and Cloanthus were Trojan leaders. **511. aequore:** *over the sea.* **512. ōrās:** acc. of place whither. **513. ipse:** i.e., Aeneas. **percussus:** supply **est. 517. fortūna:** supply **sit. 518. quid: cūr. cūnctīs lēctī nāvibus:** *delegates from all the ships.*

Postquam intrōgressī, et cōram data cōpia fandī, 520 **intrōgredior** enter; **cōram** face
to face

maximus Īlioneus placidō sīc pectore coepit :  **placidus** calm, tranquil

"Ō rēgīna, novam cui condere Juppiter urbem

jūstitiāque dedit gentīs frēnāre superbās,  **frēnō** check, restrain; **\*\*super-bus** haughty, proud

Trōes tē miserī, ventīs maria omnia vectī,

ōrāmus : prohibē īnfandōs ā nāvibus ignīs,  525 **īnfandus** unspeakable

parce piō generī, et propius rēs aspice nostrās.  **aspiciō** look at, examine

Nōn nōs aut ferrō Libycōs populāre Penātīs  **populō** ravage, plunder

vēnimus, aut raptās ad lītora vertere praedās;

nōn ea vīs animō, nec tanta superbia victīs.  **superbia** pride, haughtiness

Est locus (Hesperiam Grajī cognōmine dīcunt),  530 **\*\*cognōmen** name

terra antīqua, potēns armīs atque ūbere glaebae :  **\*ūber** fertility; **glaeba** soil

Oenōtrī coluēre virī; nunc fāma minōrēs  **\*\*colō** cultivate; inhabit

Ītaliam dīxisse ducis dē nōmine gentem.

Hic cursus fuit,

cum subitō adsurgēns flūctū nimbōsus Orīōn  535 **adsurgō** rise; **nimbōsus** stormy

in vada caeca tulit, penitusque procācibus Austrīs  **\*\*\*caecus** blind; hidden; **\*\*\*penitus** deep within; afar; **procāx** wanton, boisterous

perque undās superante salō perque invia saxa  **salum** salt sea; **invius** pathless, impassable

dispulit; hūc paucī vestrīs adnāvimus ōrīs.  **dispellō** scatter; **adnō** float to; cf. **\*\*nō** swim

Quod genus hoc hominum, quaeve hunc tam bar-
bara mōrem

permittit patria? Hospitiō prohibēmur harēnae;  540 **hospitium** hospitality

bella cient, prīmāque vetant cōnsistere terrā.  **\*cieō** stir up; **\*\*vetō** forbid

Sī genus hūmānum et mortālia temnitis arma,  **\*hūmānus** human; **mortālis** earthly; **temnō** scorn, despise

at spērāte deōs memorēs fandī atque nefandī.  **\*\*\*memor** mindful; **fandum** right; **nefandum** wrong

**520. intrōgressī:** supply **sunt. cōpia fandī:** *an opportunity of speaking.* **data:** supply **est.** **521. maximus:** *eldest.* **Īlioneus:** a Trojan leader; **eu** is here a diphthong. **placidō pectore:** as befits his age and dignity and the justice of his pleas. **524. Trōes:** in apposition with **nōs** understood as subject of **ōrāmus. maria:** best taken as an acc. of extent of space. **525. ignīs:** the Carthaginians had threatened to burn the Trojan ships, when the latter were driven ashore. **526. propius . . . nostrās:** *look more closely into our affairs.* **527. populāre:** infin. of purpose; a poetic usage. **529. vīs:** supply **est. animō, victīs:** dat. of possession. **530. Hesperiam:** *Westernland,* a poetic name for Italy. **532. Oenōtrī:** *Oenotrian;* Oenotria was in Southern Italy. **fāma:** supply

**est;** *the story is.* **minōrēs:** *descendants.* **533. ducis:** Italus, who gave his name to Italy, is said to have been chief of the Oenotrians. **534.** This line is incomplete. More than fifty lines in the *Aeneid* were left unfinished at Vergil's death. **535. Orīōn:** a constellation. **536. tulit:** supply **nōs** as object. **538. ōrīs:** dat. of direction. **539. genus:** supply **est. hoc:** here, a long syllable, as if spelled **hocc. barbara:** so characterized because the Carthaginians had not allowed the Trojans to beach their battered ships. **541. cient:** the subject understood is **hominēs** or some such word referring to the Carthaginians. **prīmā terrā:** *on the beach;* abl. of place where. **543. at:** *at least.*

Rēx erat Aenēās nōbīs, quō jūstior alter
545 nec pietāte fuit nec bellō major et armīs.

vēscor feed on; breathe;
***aura air

Quem sī Fāta virum servant, sī vēscitur aurā

aetherius of heaven; *adhūc
as yet, still; occubō lie dead
*certō strive; vie

aetheriā, neque adhūc crūdēlibus occubat umbrīs,
nōn metus, officiō nec tē certāsse priōrem

*paenitet it repents

paeniteat. Sunt et Siculīs regiōnibus urbēs

**arvum field, land; **clārus
illustrious

550 arvaque, Trojānōque ā sanguine clārus Acestēs.

quassō shake, shatter; sub-
dūcō draw up, beach
*aptō fit, fashion; *stringō
strip, trim
recipiō recover

Quassātam ventīs liceat subdūcere classem,
et silvīs aptāre trabēs, et stringere rēmōs,
sī datur Ītaliam sociīs et rēge receptō
tendere ut Ītaliam laetī Latiumque petāmus,

*sīn but if; absūmō take away,
destroy
*restō remain

555 sīn absūmpta salūs, et tē, pater optime Teucrum,
pontus habet Libyae, nec spēs jam restat Iūlī,

*fretum strait; sea

at freta Sīcaniae saltem sēdīsque parātās,

advehō bear, carry

unde hūc advectī, rēgemque petāmus Acestēn."

***fremō shout (assent)

Tālibus Īlioneus; cūnctī simul ōre fremēbant
560 Dardanidae.

QUESTIONS ON 507–560. 1. What are Aeneas's feelings when he sees Antheus and the other Trojans enter the temple? 2. Why does he remain silent? 3. What three requests does Ilioneus at once make of Dido? 4. In whose name does he make these requests? 5. What do the Trojans plan to do, if they find that Aeneas has perished in the storm?

*Dido consoles the Trojans and promises to send messengers to search for Aeneas.*

breviter briefly; dēmittō lower;
profor speak out
***solvō loose, dismiss; sē-
clūdō shut out, banish
novitās newness

Tum breviter Dīdō, vultum dēmissa, profātur:
"Solvite corde metum, Teucrī, sēclūdite cūrās.
Rēs dūra et rēgnī novitās mē tālia cōgunt

---

**546–547.** sī vēscitur aurā aetheriā: *if he breathes the air of heaven,* i.e., if he is still alive. For the case of aurā see App. 128. **547.** umbrīs: *among the shades* (of the dead); abl. of place where. **548.** nōn metus: supply nōbīs est. **548–549.** officiō . . . paeniteat: *nor would you regret that you had been the first to vie in kindly duty.* tē: object of the impersonal verb paeniteat. certāsse: certāvisse. paeniteat: potential subjunctive; see App. 150. **549.** regiōnibus: abl. of place where. **551.** liceat: *let permission be granted;* jussive subjunctive; see App. 148, *a.* **552.** silvīs: abl. of place where. **553.** sī datur: *if it is granted.* **554.** ut . . . petā-

mus: clause of purpose. **555.** absūmpta: supply est. pater: i.e., Aeneas. Teucrum: *of the Teucrians,* i.e., of the Trojans. **557–558.** at petāmus: *that at least we may seek.* Sicaniae: *of Sicily.* **558.** advectī: supply sumus. **559.** Tālibus: supply verbīs. Īlioneus: supply locūtus est. ōre fremēbant: *voiced approval.* **560.** Dardanidae: *descendants of Dardanus,* i.e., Trojans.

**561.** vultum dēmissa: *with downcast look.* vultum: direct object of the perfect participle dēmissa, which here has a reflexive or middle force; see App. 188. **563.** tālia: *such things,* i.e., the ungracious treatment of the shipwrecked Trojans.

mōlīrī, et lātē fīnīs custōde tuērī.

Quis genus Aeneadum, quis Trōjae nesciat urbem, 565

virtūtēsque, virōsque, aut tantī incendia bellī?

Nōn obtūnsa adeō gestāmus pectora Poenī,

nec tam āversus equōs Tyriā Sōl jungit ab urbe.

Seu vōs Hesperiam magnam Sāturniaque arva

sīve Erycis fīnīs rēgemque optātis Acestēn,              570

auxiliō tūtōs dīmittam, opibusque juvābō.

Vultis et hīs mēcum pariter cōnsīdere rēgnīs?

Urbem quam statuō, vestra est: subdūcite nāvīs;

Trōs Tyriusque mihī nūllō discrīmine agētur.

Atque utinam rēx ipse, Notō compulsus eōdem,      575

adforet Aenēās!  Equidem per lītora certōs

dīmittam, et Libyae lūstrāre extrēma jubēbō,

sī quibus ējectus silvīs aut urbibus errat."

***mōlior pile up; contrive

*nesciō not know

incendium conflagration

obtundō blunt, dull;  gestō bear, carry

āversus turned away; remote

***arvum field, land

dīmittō send away

pariter on equal terms

subdūcō draw up, beach

**discrīmen distinction

*utinam would that; com-pellō drive
***equidem indeed

dīmittō send out; **lūstrō trav-erse
ējiciō cast out; shipwreck

QUESTIONS ON **561–578**.  1. What explanation does Dido make for the hostile reception given the shipwrecked Trojans? 2. What does Dido promise to do for the Trojans?  3. In what statement does she indicate her freedom from prejudice? 4. What wish does she express?  5. What does she promise to do in regard to the lost Aeneas?

*Aeneas is revealed to Dido and expresses his grati-tude.*

Hīs animum arrēctī dictīs, et fortis Achātēs

et pater Aenēās jam dūdum ērumpere nūbem

ārdēbant.  Prior Aenēān compellat Achātēs:

"Nāte deā, quae nunc animō sententia surgit?

Omnia tūta vidēs, classem sociōsque receptōs.

**arrigō raise, prick up

580 jam dūdum long since; cf. *dūdum a while ago; ērumpō burst
*compellō address, speak to

recipiō recover

---

565. nesciat: *would not know;* potential subjunc-tive.  **566.** incendia: poetic pl.  **567.** Nōn ob-tūnsa . . . Poenī: *we Carthaginians are not so dull-minded* (as not to know about the Trojans).  **568.** nec . . . urbe: *nor does the Sun yoke his steeds so far from the Tyrian city,* i.e., we are not so far from civilization as not to know what goes on in the world.  **569.** Sāturnia arva: *the fields of Saturn,* i.e., Italy.  Saturn was the mythical ruler of Italy in the Golden Age.  **570.** Erycis fīnīs: *the territory of Eryx,* i.e., Sicily.  Eryx, son of Venus, had a town and a mountain in Sicily named after him.  **571.** tūtōs: supply vōs as ob-ject of dīmittam and juvābō.  **572.** rēgnīs: abl. of place where.  **573.** Urbem quam statuō: *what city I am founding,* i.e., the city which I am founding.  **574.** Tyrius: i.e., Carthaginian.  mihī: dat. of agent with agētur.  agētur: *will be treated.* **576.** adforet: adesset;  optative subjunctive. certōs: *trustworthy* (messengers).  For Work Unit V, based on lines 441–578, see p. 256.

**579.** animum arrēctī: *elated in spirit.* animum: acc. of respect; a poetic usage; see App. 113. **582.** Nāte deā: *born of a goddess.* Nāte: voc.

**absum** be lacking
**submergō** sink
**circumfundō** pour around
\*\***scindō** divide, part; **pūrgō** clear away; **apertus** open
\*\***restō** remain; \*\*\***clārus** clear, bright; **refulgeō** shine, gleam
\*\*\***umerus** shoulder; \***decōrus** lovely, comely
**caesariēs** locks; **nātus** son; **genetrīx** mother; \*\***lūmen** light; \***juventa** youth
**purpureus** crimson, bright; cf. \***purpura** purple color; **adflō** breathe upon; cf. \*\***flō** blow
**addō** add; \***ebur** ivory; \*\***decus** beauty; cf. \*\***dēdecus** blemish; \***flāvus** yellow
\*\***argentum** silver; \*\*\***-ve** or
**adloquor** speak to, address
**imprōvīsus** unforeseen, unexpected; **cōram** in person
**ēripiō** snatch from, rescue
**īnfandus** unspeakable; \***misereor** pity
**reliquiae** those left, leavings
**exhauriō** drain, exhaust; **egēnus** needy, lacking
**sociō** make sharer; cf. \***societās** fellowship; **grātēs** thanks; **persolvō** pay
\*\***quisquis** whoever; **ubīque** everywhere; anywhere
\***spargō** scatter, disperse
**respectō** give heed to
\***usquam** anywhere; **jūstitia** righteousness; \***cōnscius** aware; cf. \***cōnscientia** consciousness; **rēctum** right, virtue; cf. \***rēctē** rightly
\*\*\***saeculum** age; \*\***gignō** beget; bear; \*\*\***parēns** parent
\*\***fretum** sea; \***fluvius** river
\*\*\***lūstrō** move over; traverse; **convexum** arch; \*\*\***polus** sky; \*\*\***pāscō** feed

Ūnus abest, mediō in flūctū quem vīdimus ipsī
585 submersum; dictīs respondent cētera mātris."
Vix ea fatus erat, cum circumfūsa repente
scindit sē nūbēs, et in aethera pūrgat apertum.
Restitit Aenēās, clārāque in lūce refulsit,
ōs umerōsque deō similis, namque ipsa decōram
590 caesariem nātō genetrīx, lūmenque juventae
purpureum, et laetōs oculīs adflārat honōrēs;

quāle manūs addunt eborī decus, aut ubi flāvō
argentum Pariusve lapis circumdatur aurō.
Tum sīc rēgīnam adloquitur, cūnctīsque repente
595 imprōvīsus ait: "Cōram, quem quaeritis, adsum,
Trōius Aenēās, Libycīs ēreptus ab undīs.
Ō sōla īnfandōs Trōjae miserāta labōrēs,
quae nōs, relliquiās Danaum, terraeque marisque
omnibus exhaustōs jam cāsibus, omnium egēnōs,
600 urbe, domō sociās, grātīs persolvere dignās
nōn opis est nostrae, Dīdō, nec quidquid ubīque est
gentis Dardaniae, magnum quae sparsa per orbem.
Dī tibi, sī qua piōs respectant nūmina, sī quid
usquam jūstitia est et mēns sibi cōnscia rēctī,
605 praemia digna ferant. Quae tē tam laeta tulērunt
saecula? Quī tantī tālem genuēre parentēs?
In freta dum fluviī current, dum montibus umbrae
lūstrābunt convexa, polus dum sīdera pāscet,
semper honōs nōmenque tuum laudēsque manēbunt,

---

of perfect participle **nātus**. **deā**: abl. of source. **animō**: abl. of place where. **584. Ūnus**: i.e., Orontes, whose fate is described in lines 113-116. **585. dictīs ... mātris**: *the other events coincide with your mother's words.* Venus's prophecy occurs in lines 390-400. **587. pūrgat**: supply **sē**; *melts, vanishes.* **589. ōs umerōsque**: acc. of respect; a poetic use. **590. nātō**: dat. with the compound verb **adflā(ve)rat**. **591. laetōs honōrēs**: *joyful grace.* **593. Parius lapis**: *Parian stone*, i.e., Parian marble. The best marble came from the Greek island of Paros. **597. Ō sōla miserāta**: *O thou who alone hast pitied.* **598. relliquiās Danaum**: *those left by the Greeks.* **600. urbe, domō**: abl. of means. **601. nōn ... nostrae**: *it is not within our power.* **opis**: predicate gen. of possession. **601-602. nec ... Dardaniae**: *nor (within the power) of whatever of the Trojan race there is anywhere.* **602. sparsa**: supply **est**. **603-604. sī quid ... est**: *if justice means (is) anything anywhere.* **605. ferant**: optative subjunctive. The subject is **Dī** in line 603. **606. genuēre**: **genuērunt**. **607. montibus**: abl. of place where. **608. convexa**: *slopes;* acc. pl.

quae mē cumque vocant terrae." Sīc fātus, amīcum 610
Īlionēa petit dextrā laevāque Serestum,
post aliōs, fortemque Gyān, fortemque Cloanthum.

**laeva** left hand; cf. *****laevus** left

QUESTIONS ON **579–612**. 1. How is Aeneas revealed to Dido?
2. With what does Vergil compare Aeneas's appearance? 3. In
what manner does Aeneas address Dido? 4. What does he pray
that the gods may do? 5. How long does Aeneas say he will re-
member Dido and her kindness? 6. Which of the Trojan leaders
does Aeneas greet first?

*Dido welcomes Aeneas and the other Trojan leaders
to a banquet. Aeneas sends Achates for Asca-
nius and presents for Dido.*

Obstipuit prīmō aspectū Sīdōnia Dīdō,
cāsū deinde virī tantō, et sīc ōre locūta est:
"Quis tē, nāte deā, per tanta perīcula cāsus          615
īnsequitur? Quae vīs immānibus applicat ōrīs?
Tūne ille Aenēās, quem Dardaniō Anchīsae
alma Venus Phrygiī genuit Simoëntis ad undam?
Atque equidem Teucrum meminī Sīdōna venīre,
fīnibus expulsum patriīs, nova rēgna petentem      620
auxiliō Bēlī: genitor tum Bēlus opīmam
vāstābat Cyprum, et victor diciōne tenēbat.
Tempore jam ex illō cāsus mihi cognitus urbis
Trōjānae, nōmenque tuum, rēgēsque Pelasgī.
Ipse hostis Teucrōs īnsignī laude ferēbat,            625
sēque ortum antīquā Teucrōrum ab stirpe volēbat.
Quārē agite, ō tēctīs, juvenēs, succēdite nostrīs.
Mē quoque per multōs similis fortūna labōrēs

*****obstipēscō** be amazed; **as-
pectus** sight

**applicō** join to, drive to

*****almus** nurturing, gracious;
******gignō** bear
*****meminī** remember

**expellō** drive out, banish; **pa-
trius** father's, ancestral
******genitor** sire, father; **opīmus**
rich, fruitful
**diciō** sway, rule

*****īnsignis** distinguished

*****stirps** stock, race

**quārē** therefore; *****tēctum** roof;
house; ******juvenis** youth,
young man

**610. quae mē cumque:** i.e., **quaecumque mē.** This
separation of the parts of a compound word is
called *tmesis;* see App. 22, 22. **611. Īlionēa petit
dextrā laevāque Serestum:** this crisscross arrange-
ment of words is called *chiasmus* from the Greek
letter *chi* (χ). **Īlionēa:** Greek acc.
**614. cāsū:** *at the experiences.* **deinde:** pro-
nounce as if spelled **dinde;** an example of *synizesis.*
**616. ōrīs:** dat. of place whither. **617. Tūne (es):**
*are you?* **Dardaniō Anchīsae:** note the hiatus
between these words. This line has a spondee in
the fifth foot. **Anchīsae:** *to Anchises.* **619. Teu-
crum:** *Teucer,* son of Telamon, king of Salamis,

who was exiled by his father because he had not
brought his brother Ajax home in safety from the
Trojan War. **Sīdōna:** Greek acc.; the famous
town of Sidon was in Phoenicia, not far from Tyre.
**621. Bēlī:** Belus was a Phoenician king, father of
Dido. **622. Cyprum:** *Cyprus,* an island in the
Eastern Mediterranean. **623. cognitus:** supply
est. **624. Pelasgī:** *Pelasgian,* i.e., Greek.
**625. Ipse hostis:** *though he himself* (Teucer)
*was an enemy.* **ferēbat:** *extolled.* **626. volēbat:**
*wanted* (it believed). Teucer's mother, Hesione,
was a Trojan princess. **627. agite:** *come!* **tēctīs:**
dat. with the compound verb **succēdite.**

**\*dēmum** finally

**\*\*\*ignārus** ignorant; **malum**
evil, misfortune; **succurrō**
run to; help; **\*discō** learn
**memorō** recount; speak; **rē-
gius** royal
**\*\*\*tēctum** roof; house

**\*taurus** bull; **\*\*\*horreō** bristle;
cf. **\*\*\*abhorreō** shrink from
**sūs** swine, pig; **\*\*pinguis** fat;
**agnus** lamb
**laetitia** rejoicing

**rēgālis** royal; **splendidus** re-
splendent; cf. **\*splendor** bril-
liance; **lūxus** magnificence;
cf. **\*lūxuria** extravagance
**\*convīvium** banquet, feast
**\*ars** skill; **ostrum** crimson dye;
**\*\*\*superbus** gorgeous
**\*\*\*argentum** silver; **\*\*mēnsa**
table; **caelō** engrave
**seriēs** succession
**\*\*\*orīgō** beginning

**patrius** father's, paternal

**\*\*cārus** dear, beloved

**ēripiō** snatch, rescue; **\*\*\*ruīna**
downfall, ruin
**palla** robe, mantle; **\*rigeō** be
stiff
**circumtextus** embroidered; **cro-
ceus** yellow, saffron; **vēlā-
men** veil, robe; **acanthus**
acanthus
**ōrnātus** adornment; garment;
cf. **\*ōrnō** adorn
**inconcessus** forbidden; **\*hy-
menaeus** marriage
**mīrābilis** marvelous; **\*\*dōnum**
gift; cf. **\*\*dōnō** present
**nāta** daughter; **\*collum** neck;
**monīle** necklace
**bācātus** studded with pearls;
**\*\*duplex** double; **gemma**
jewel; **\*corōna** crown
**\*\*celerō** hasten, speed

jactātam hāc dēmum voluit cōnsistere terrā;
630 nōn ignāra malī, miserīs succurrere discō.''
Sīc memorat; simul Aenēān in rēgia dūcit
tēcta, simul dīvum templīs indīcit honōrem.
Nec minus intereā sociīs ad lītora mittit
vīgintī taurōs, magnōrum horrentia centum
635 terga suum, pinguīs centum cum mātribus agnōs,
mūnera laetitiamque diī.
At domus interior rēgālī splendida lūxū
īnstruitur, mediīsque parant convīvia tēctīs:
arte labōrātae vestēs ostrōque superbō, —
640 ingēns argentum mēnsīs, caelātaque in aurō
fortia facta patrum, seriēs longissima rērum
per tot ducta virōs antīquae ab orīgine gentis.
   Aenēās (neque enim patrius cōnsistere mentem
passus amor) rapidum ad nāvīs praemittit Achātēn,
645 Ascaniō ferat haec, ipsumque ad moenia dūcat:
omnis in Ascaniō cārī stat cūra parentis.
Mūnera praetereā Īliacīs ērepta ruīnīs
ferre jubet, pallam signīs aurōque rigentem,
et circumtextum croceō vēlāmen acanthō,
650 ōrnātūs Argīvae Helenae, quōs illa Mycēnīs,
Pergama cum peterēt inconcessōsque hymenaeōs,
extulerat, mātris Lēdae mīrābile dōnum;
praetereā scēptrum, Īlionē quod gesserat ōlim,
maxima nātārum Priamī, collōque monīle
655 bācātum, et duplicem gemmīs aurōque corōnam.
Haec celerāns, iter ad nāvīs tendēbat Achātēs.

---

**629. terrā:** abl. of place where. **630. nōn
ignāra . . . discō:** Dido can sympathize with
Aeneas because she herself has suffered. This
line, as well as the sentiment, has become pro-
verbial. **631. Aenēān:** Greek acc. **632. honō-
rem:** i.e., sacrifices. **633. Nec minus:** *and also.*
**sociīs:** *for* (Aeneas's) *companions.* **635. suum:**
gen. pl. of **sūs.** **636. diī:** early form of gen. sing.
of **diēs.** **638. tēctīs:** abl. of place where.
**641–642. seriēs . . . ducta:** *record of exploits traced.*

**644. passus:** supply *est.* **645. ferat, dūcat:**
subjunctives in loosely attached volitive clauses
of indirect command. **648. signīs:** *figures* (em-
broidered on the mantle). **650. ōrnātūs:** acc. pl.
in apposition with **pallam** and **vēlāmen.** **651. Per-
gama:** *Troy.* **inconcessōs hymenaeōs:** *forbidden
marriage* (i.e., with Paris). The last syllable of
**peterēt** is here long; cf. **vidēt** in line 308. **652. Lē-
dae:** Leda was Helen's mother. **656. Haec ce-
lerāns:** *speeding these commands.*

QUESTIONS ON **613-656.** 1. From whom did Dido first hear the story of the Trojan War? 2. Why is Dido so ready to sympathize with Aeneas? 3. By what act does Dido show her consideration for Aeneas? 4. By what act does Dido show her consideration for Aeneas's comrades left at the shore? 5. What five gifts does Aeneas tell Achates to bring for Dido? 6. Who had been the previous owner of two of these gifts?

*Venus conspires with Cupid to make Dido fall in love with Aeneas.*

At Cytherēa novās artīs, nova pectore versat

cōnsilia, ut, faciem mūtātus et ōra, Cupīdō

prō dulcī Ascaniō veniat, dōnīsque furentem

incendat rēgīnam, atque ossibus implicet ignem:  660

quippe domum timet ambiguam Tyriōsque bilin-
guīs;

ūrit atrōx Jūnō, et sub noctem cūra recursat.

Ergō hīs āligerum dictīs adfātur Amōrem:

"Nāte, meae vīrēs, mea magna potentia sōlus,

nāte, patris summī quī tēla Typhōia temnis,  665

ad tē cōnfugiō, et supplex tua nūmina poscō.

Frāter ut Aenēās pelagō tuus omnia circum

lītora jactētūr, odiīs Jūnōnis inīquae,

nōta tibi, et nostrō doluistī saepe dolōre.

Hunc Phoenissa tenet Dīdō, blandīsque morātur  670

vōcibus, et vereor quō sē Jūnōnia vertant

hospitia; haud tantō cessābit cardine rērum.

Quōcircā capere ante dolīs et cingere flammā

rēgīnam meditor, nē quō sē nūmine mūtet,

sed magnō Aenēae mēcum teneātur amōre.  675

*Marginal glosses:*

**\*\*ars** scheme; **versō** keep turning; revolve; ponder
**\*\*faciēs** form, appearance
**\*\*\*dōnum** gift; cf. **\*\*\*dōnō** present, bestow
**\*os, ossis** bone; inmost part; **\*implicō** infold, mingle
**quippe** in sooth, truly; **ambiguus** doubtful, deceitful; **bilinguis** double-tongued
**\*ūrō** burn; **\*atrōx** dark; cruel; **recursō** keep returning
**\*ergō** therefore; **\*āliger** wing-bearing, winged; **adfor** address, speak to
**potentia** power, strength
**nātus** son; **temnō** scorn, despise
**cōnfugiō** flee for help; **\*\*\*supplex** suppliant, humble
**odium** hatred
**blandus** flattering, seductive
**hospitium** hospitality; **\*cessō** hesitate; **cardō** hinge; crisis
**quōcircā** wherefore; **\*\*dolus** trick; **\*\*\*cingō** encircle
**meditor** plan

---

**657. Cytherēa:** i.e., Venus, who was born on the island of Cythera. **novās ... nova:** an example of *anaphora.* **658. faciem, ōra:** acc. of respect with **mūtātus. Cupīdō:** *Cupid,* son of Venus and god of love. **660. ossibus:** dat. with the compound verb **implicet. ignem:** *the fire* (of love). **662. ūrit atrōx Jūnō:** *cruel Juno inflames* (Venus). Throughout the *Aeneid* Juno and Venus are represented as hostile to each other, Venus aiding the Trojans and Juno constantly putting obstacles and difficulties in their way. **665. patris:** i.e., of Jupiter. **tēla Typhōia:** i.e., thunderbolts.

Typhoeus was a giant slain by Jupiter's thunderbolts. **667-668. Frāter ut Aenēās jactētūr:** *how your brother Aeneas is buffeted.* **jactētūr:** subjunctive in indirect question depending on **nōta (sunt).** The last syllable of **jactētūr** is here lengthened for metrical reasons. This lengthening is called *diastole;* see App. 33. **671-672.** Jūnōnia hospitia: Venus implies that Dido's hospitality to Aeneas was inspired by Juno. **vertant:** subjunctive in indirect question. **672. haud ... rērum:** *in such a great crisis she will not remain idle.* **675. mēcum:** *with me,* i.e., as I am held.

Quā facere id possīs nostram nunc accipe mentem.

rēgius royal; accītus summons;
***cārus beloved

Rēgius accītū cārī genitōris ad urbem

Sīdoniam puer īre parat, mea maxima cūra,

***restō remain, survive

dōna ferēns pelagō et flammīs restantia Trōjae.

sōpītus slumberous; ***somnus sleep
*sacrō consecrate; recondō hide, put away
quā in any way; ***dolus trick

680 Hunc ego, sōpītum somnō, super alta Cythēra

aut super Īdalium sacrātā sēde recondam,

nē quā scīre dolōs mediusve occurrere possit.

**faciēs form; appearance

Tū faciem illīus noctem nōn amplius ūnam

nōtus known, familiar; *induō put on, don
*gremium bosom; embrace

falle dolō, et nōtōs puerī puer indue vultūs,

685 ut, cum tē gremiō accipiet laetissima Dīdō

rēgālis royal; ***mēnsa table; latex liquid
amplexus embrace; **ōsculum kiss; ***dulcis sweet
īnspīrō breathe into; impart; *venēnum poison (of love)
genetrīx mother; ***āla wing

rēgālīs inter mēnsās laticemque Lyaeum,

cum dabit amplexūs, atque ōscula dulcia fīget,

occultum īnspīrēs ignem, fallāsque venēnō."

Pāret Amor dictīs cārae genetrīcis et ālās

*exuō lay aside, doff; gressus step, gait; *gaudeō rejoice; incēdō walk along
**membrum member, limb
inrigō diffuse; ***foveō cherish, fondle; **gremium bosom
***lūcus grove; *mollis soft, dainty; amāracus sweet marjoram
*flōs flower, blossom; adspīrō breathe on; *complector embrace

690 exuit, et gressū gaudēns incēdit Iūlī.

At Venus Ascaniō placidam per membra quiētem

inrigat, et fōtum gremiō dea tollit in altōs

Īdaliae lūcōs, ubi mollis amāracus illum

flōribus et dulcī adspīrāns complectitur umbrā.

QUESTIONS ON 657–694. 1. With what motive does Venus secretly substitute Cupid for Ascanius? 2. What fear causes Venus to do this? 3. What does Venus do meantime with Ascanius? 4. What is her purpose in so doing?

*At the banquet Dido asks Aeneas many questions about the Trojan War.*

695 Jamque ībat, dictō pārens, et dōna Cupīdō

rēgia portābat Tyriīs, duce laetus Achātē.

aulaea tapestry

Cum venit, aulaeīs jam sē rēgīna superbīs

aureus golden; sponda couch

aureā composuit spondā, mediamque locāvit;

**juventūs youth

jam pater Aenēās et jam Trōjāna juventūs

676. Quā (viā): *by what means.* possīs: subjunctive in indirect question. mentem: *plan.* 678. puer: i.e., Ascanius. 679. dōna... restantia: *bearing gifts surviving the sea and flames.* 680. Cythēra: an island off the southern tip of Greece near which Venus rose from the sea; hence Venus is frequently called Cytherea. 681. Īdalium: a town in Cyprus sacred to Venus. 682. mediusve

occurrere: *or to intervene and thwart.* 684. falle dolō: *trickily imitate.* 686. laticem Lyaeum: *Lyaean liquid,* i.e., wine. 687. fīget: *imprints (shall imprint).* 690. gressū Iūlī: *in the gait of Iulus.* 697. aulaeīs: abl. of place where. 697–698. sē composuit: *has installed herself.* 698. aureā: pronounce as two long syllables, by *synizesis.* mediamque (sē) locāvit: *and placed herself in the midst.*

conveniunt, strātōque super discumbitur ostrō.

Dant manibus famulī lymphās, Cereremque canistrīs

expediunt, tōnsīsque ferunt mantēlia villīs.

Quīnquāgintā intus famulae, quibus ōrdine longō

cūra penum struere et flammīs adolēre Penātīs;

centum aliae totidemque parēs aetāte ministrī,

quī dapibus mēnsās onerent et pōcula pōnant.

Nec nōn et Tyriī per līmina laeta frequentēs

convēnēre, torīs jussī discumbere pictīs.

Mīrantur dōna Aenēae, mīrantur Iūlum,

flagrantīsque deī vultūs, simulātaque verba,

pallamque, et pictum croceō vēlāmen acanthō.

Praecipuē īnfēlīx, pestī dēvōta futūrae,

explērī mentem nequit, ārdēscitque tuendō

Phoenissa, et pariter puerō dōnīsque movētur.

Ille ubi complexū Aenēae collōque pependit,

et magnum falsī implēvit genitōris amōrem,

rēgīnam petit. Haec oculīs, haec pectore tōtō

haeret, et interdum gremiō fovet īnscia Dīdō

īnsīdat quantus miserae deus. At memor ille

mātris Acīdaliae paulātim abolēre Sychaeum

incipit, et vīvō temptat praevertere amōre

jam prīdem residīs animōs dēsuētaque corda.

Postquam prīma quiēs epulīs mēnsaeque remōtae,

crātēras magnōs statuunt, et vīna corōnant.

---

700 **conveniō** assemble; **\*\*sternō** spread; **discumbō** recline; **ostrum** crimson (*coverlet*) **\*famulus** man-servant; **lympha** water; **canistrum** basket

**\*tondeō** trim, clip; **mantēle** napkin; **villus** nap **quīnquāgintā** fifty; **\*\*\*intus** within, inside; **famula** maid-servant **penum** food; **\*struō** pile high, 705 arrange; **adoleō** honor **minister** attendant **\*\*daps** feast, rich food; **onerō** load; **pōculum** cup, goblet **\*\*\*līmen** threshold, door; **\*frequēns** thronging, in crowds **conveniō** assemble; **\*torus** couch; **discumbō** recline; **\*pingō** paint, embroider

710 **\*flagrō** glow, burn, blaze; **\*verbum** word **\*\*pingō** paint, embroider; **croceus** yellow, saffron; **vēlāmen** veil, robe; **acanthus** acanthus **praecipuē** especially; cf. **\*\*praecipuus** chief, especial; **īnfēlīx** unfortunate, unhappy; **\*pestis** ruin; **dēvōtus** doomed **expleō** fill, satisfy; **nequeō** be unable; **ārdēscō** begin to burn **pariter** equally, alike 715 **complexus** embrace; **\*\*collum** neck; **\*\*\*pendeō** hang **falsus** pretended; **impleō** fill, satisfy

**\*\*\*haereō** cling to; **\*interdum** now and again; **\*\*\*gremium** bosom, lap **īnsīdō** sit upon, take possession 720 of **aboleō** blot out, remove **praevertō** surpass; occupy

**\*prīdem** long since; **reses** inactive, dormant; **dēsuētus** unaccustomed; cf. **\*suēscō** become accustomed **\*\*\*epulae** banquet, feast; **removeō** remove **\*crātēr** mixing bowl; **\*\*vīnum** wine; **corōnō** crown, wreathe

---

**700.** discumbitur: impersonal form of verb; *they recline.* **701.** manibus: *for the hands.* Cererem: bread; an example of *metonymy;* see App. 22, 13. **704.** cūra: *task;* supply est. **707.** Nec nōn et: *And also.* **708.** convēnēre: convēnērunt. torīs: abl. of place where. **710.** deī: i.e., of Cupid. vultūs: *countenance;* poetic plural. **712.** pestī dēvōta futūrae: *doomed to future destruction.* dēvōta agrees with Phoenissa in line 714. **713.** explērī mentem nequit: *she cannot sate her mind.*

tuendō: *with gazing* (at Aeneas). **715.** Ille: i.e., Cupid. **717.** Haec . . . haec: an example of *anaphora.* **718.** gremiō: abl. of place where. **718–719.** īnscia . . . deus: *Dido, unaware how great a god clings to her, unhappy woman.* **720.** Acīdaliae: Veneris. Sychaeum: Dido's dead husband. **722.** jam . . . corda: *her long inactive feelings and her heart grown unused* (to love). corda: poetic plural. **723.** quiēs: supply fuit. remōtae: supply sunt. **724.** vīna corōnant: *they crown the wine* (bowls

**strepitus** noise, din; **volūtō** roll

**ātrium** hall; **dēpendeō** hang
down; **lychnus** lamp; **la-
quear** panel (*of a ceiling*);
**aureus** golden
**fūnāle** taper
**gemma** gem, jewel
**merum** unmixed wine; *patera
libation bowl
*soleō be accustomed

*hospes guest; host

***meminī remember, recall

**laetitia** joy, cheer; **dator** giver,
bestower
**coetus** meeting; *celebrō
throng; cf. *celeber fre-
quented; *faveō favor
**latex** liquid; **lībō** pour out
(*as a libation*)
**summum** surface; **tenus** just to

**increpitō** challenge; cf. *crepō
rattle; **impiger** not lazy,
quick; *hauriō drain
**spūmō** foam, froth; **patera
bowl; ***plēnus full; **prōluō
drench
**procerēs** princes, lords; **cithara
harp; **crīnītus** long-haired
**personō** sound, play; **aurātus
gilded
**canō sing (of); *lūna moon
*pecus sheep, goat, cow; **im-
ber rain

**pluvius** rainy; ***geminus twin,
two

*properō hasten, hurry; *tin-
g(u)ō wet, dip
**hibernus** wintry, of winter;
**obstō** oppose, hinder
**ingeminō** redouble; *plausus
applause

725 Fit strepitus tēctīs, vōcemque per ampla volūtant
ātria; dēpendent lychnī laqueāribus aureīs
incēnsī, et noctem flammīs fūnālia vincunt.
Hīc rēgīna gravem gemmīs aurōque poposcit
implēvitque merō pateram, quam Bēlus et omnēs
730 ā Bēlō solitī; tum facta silentia tēctīs:
"Juppiter, hospitibus nam tē dare jūra loquuntur,
hunc laetum Tyriīsque diem Trōjāque profectīs
esse velīs nostrōsque hujus meminisse minōrēs.
Adsit laetitiae Bacchus dator et bona Jūnō;
735 et vōs ō coetum, Tyriī, celebrāte faventēs."

Dīxit, et in mēnsam laticum lībāvit honōrem,
prīmaque lībātō summō tenus attigit ōre;
tum Bitiae dedit increpitāns; ille impiger hausit
spūmantem pateram, et plēnō sē prōluit aurō;
740 post aliī procerēs. Cithārā crīnītus Iōpās
personat aurātā, docuit quem maximus Atlās.
Hic canit errantem lūnam, sōlisque labōrēs,
unde hominum genus et pecudēs, unde imber et
ignēs,
Arctūrum, pluviāsque Hyadas, geminōsque Tri-
ōnēs,
745 quid tantum Ōceanō properent sē tingere sōlēs
hībernī, vel quae tardīs mora noctibus obstet.
Ingeminant plausū Tyriī, Trōesque sequuntur.

---

with garlands). **725. tēctīs:** abl. of place where.
**726. laqueāribus:** abl. of place whence. **aureīs:**
pronounce as two long syllables; an example of
*synizesis.* **728. Hīc:** *At this point.* **729–
730. omnēs ā Bēlō:** *all the descendants of Belus.*
**730. solitī:** supply **sunt implēre. facta:** supply
**sunt. silentia:** poetic plural. **tēctīs:** abl. of
place where. **732. Trōjāque profectīs:** *and to
those who have set out from Troy.* **733. velīs:** *may
you grant;* optative subjunctive. **hujus:** i.e.,
**hujus diēi. 734. Adsit Bacchus:** *may Bacchus be
with us.* **735. coetum celebrāte faventēs:** *honor
this assembly graciously.* **736. laticum honōrem:**
*a liquid sacrifice,* i.e., a libation of wine. **737. lī-
bātō:** *after the libation was poured;* an impersonal

abl. abs.; see App. 131, *c.* **summō . . . ōre:** *she
touched* (the goblet) *just to the surface* (of the wine)
*with her lips.* **738. Bitiae:** *to Bitias,* a nobleman
of Dido's court. **dedit:** understand **pateram** as
object. **740. Iōpās:** a bard at Dido's court.
**741. personat:** *makes resounding music.* **Atlās:**
the giant who supported the heavens on his
shoulders. **742. Hic:** *he,* i.e., Iōpas. **labōrēs:**
*eclipses.* **743. unde:** supply **veniant. 744. Arc-
tūrum:** a star the rising and setting of which is
accompanied by stormy weather. **Hyadas:** *the
Hyades,* a constellation associated with rainy
weather. **Triōnēs:** the constellations of the Great
and Little Bears. **745–746. quid . . . hībernī:** *why
the winter suns hurry so much to dip themselves in*

Nec nōn et variō noctem sermōne trahēbat

īnfēlīx Dīdō, longumque bibēbat amōrem,

multa super Priamō rogitāns, super Hectore multa; 750

nunc, quibus Aurōrae vēnisset fīlius armīs,

nunc, quālēs Diomēdis equī, nunc, quantus Achil-
    lēs.

"Immō age, et ā prīmā dīc, hospes, orīgine nōbīs

īnsidiās," inquit, "Danaum, cāsūsque tuōrum;

errōrēsque tuōs, nam tē jam septima portat        755

omnibus errantem terrīs et flūctibus aestās."

**\*\*varius** varied; **\*\*sermō** talk, conversation
**īnfēlīx** ill-fated, unfortunate; **\*\*bibō** drink (in)
**rogitō** keep asking

**\*aurōra** dawn

**\*immō** nay rather; **\*\*hospes** guest

**error** wandering

QUESTIONS ON **695–756.** 1. Do any of the guests at the banquet recognize Cupid? 2. Who was the Roman god of hospitality? Of wine? 3. How is the bard Iōpas's music received? 4. Who was Bitias? 5. Why do you think Dido asks Aeneas so many questions about the Trojan War? 6. What does Dido finally ask Aeneas to do?

*the ocean*, i.e., why the days in winter are so short. **748. trahēbat:** *prolonged.* **751–752. nunc . . . nunc . . . nunc:** *at one moment . . . at another . . . at another.* **Aurōrae fīlius:** *the son of Aurora,* i.e., Memnon, an ally of the Trojans. **Diomēdis:** *of*

*Diomedes,* a Greek chieftain. **equī:** supply **essent. 753. Immō age:** *Nay come.* **754. cāsūs tuōrum:** *the adventures of your comrades.* **756. terrīs, flūctibus:** abl. of place where. For Work Unit VI, based on lines 579–756, see p. 258.

# BOOK II

*Aeneas begins the account of his adventures.*

conticēscō become silent; in-
tentus eager; cf. *intendō
stretch, strain
**torus cushion, banqueting
couch; **ōrdior begin
renovō renew, revive
lāmentābilis piteous, sad

ēruō overthrow

temperō refrain; cf. ***tempe-
rantia moderation; ***la-
crima tear; *ūmidus dewy
praecipitō rush headlong;
**suādeō urge

breviter briefly; suprēmus
highest; last
*quamquam although; lūctus
grief, sorrow; refugiō flee
from, shrink from

Conticuēre omnēs, intentīque ōra tenēbant.
Inde torō pater Aenēās sīc ōrsus ab altō:
"Īnfandum, rēgīna, jubēs renovāre dolōrem,
Trōjānās ut opēs et lāmentābile rēgnum
5 ēruerint Danaī, quaeque ipse miserrima vīdī,
et quōrum pars magna fuī. Quis tālia fandō
Myrmidonum Dolopumve aut dūrī mīles Ulixī
temperet ā lacrimīs? Et jam nox ūmida caelō
praecipitat, suādentque cadentia sīdera somnōs.
10 Sed sī tantus amor cāsūs cognōscere nostrōs,
et breviter Trōjae suprēmum audīre labōrem,
quamquam animus meminisse horret lūctūque re-
fūgit,
incipiam.

QUESTIONS ON LINES 1–13. 1. At whose request does Aeneas
begin the story of his adventures? 2. What three adjectives
does Aeneas use to indicate his emotions in regard to the story
which he is asked to tell? 3. What reason aside from his emo-
tions does Aeneas give for not wishing to tell the complete story
at this time?

*The Greeks feign a return home and leave behind
the Wooden Horse.*

repellō thrust back, repulse

ductor leader; ***lābor slip,
glide
īnstar likeness, size; **dīvīnus
divine; ***ars art, skill

"Frāctī bellō, Fātīsque repulsī,
ductōrēs Danaum, tot jam lābentibus annīs,
15 īnstar montis equum dīvīnā Palladis arte

---

1. Conticuēre: Conticuērunt. ōra tenēbant:
*kept gazing.* 3. renovāre: supply mē as the sub-
ject. 4. ut: *how,* introducing an indirect ques-
tion. 5. quaeque ... miserrima: et (ea) quae
miserrima vīdī: *and* (to describe) *those sad events
that I saw.* 6–8. Quis ... lacrimīs?: i.e., who
could help weeping? 7. Myrmidonum, Dolopum:
partitive genitives, depending on Quis in line 6;
the Myrmidons were Achilles's people and the

Dolopes were Thessalian Greeks. Ulixī: Ulysses
was a wily Greek leader. 8. temperet: potential
subjunctive. caelō: abl. of place whence.
10. amor: supply est.
14. tot ... annīs: this was now the tenth year
of the Trojan War. 15. īnstar montis: *like a
mountain,* i.e., as big as a mountain. Palladis:
i.e., of Minerva, goddess of the arts and of wis-
dom.

40

aedificant, sectāque intexunt abiete costās:
vōtum prō reditū simulant; ea fāma vagātur.


Hūc dēlēcta virum sortītī corpora fūrtim
inclūdunt caecō laterī, penitusque cavernās
ingentīs uterumque armātō mīlite complent.
"Est in cōnspectū Tenedos, nōtissima fāmā
īnsula, dīves opum, Priamī dum rēgna manēbant,
nunc tantum sinus et statiō male fīda carīnīs;
hūc sē prōvectī dēsertō in lītore condunt.
Nōs abiisse ratī et ventō petiisse Mycēnās.
Ergō omnis longō solvit sē Teucria lūctū:
panduntur portae; juvat īre et Dōrica castra
dēsertōsque vidēre locōs lītusque relictum.
Hīc Dolopum manus, hīc saevus tendēbat Achillēs;
classibus hīc locus; hīc aciē certāre solēbant.
Pars stupet innūptae dōnum exitiāle Minervae,
et mōlem mīrantur equī; prīmusque Thymoetēs
dūcī intrā mūrōs hortātur et arce locārī,
sīve dolō seu jam Trōjae sīc fāta ferēbant.
At Capys, et quōrum melior sententia mentī,
aut pelagō Danaum īnsidiās suspectaque dōna
praecipitāre jubent, subjectīsque ūrere flammīs,
aut terebrāre cavās uterī, et temptāre latebrās.
Scinditur incertum studia in contrāria vulgus.

**aedificō** build; **\*\*secō** cut; **intexō** interweave; cf. **\*texō** weave; **abiēs** fir wood; **costa** rib, side
**vōtum** votive offering; cf. **\*\*voveō** vow, promise solemnly; **reditus** a return
**sortior** assign by lot; **fūrtim** secretly
**inclūdō** shut in; **caverna** cavity
20 **uterus** belly, abdomen; **armō** arm; **compleō** fill
**nōtus** well-known

**\*\*\*dīves** rich

**\*tantum** only, merely; **male** badly; **\*\*\*fīdus** trustworthy, safe; **\*carīna** keel, ship
**prōvehō** bear, carry
25 **abeō** go away; **\*reor** suppose, think
**\*\*ergō** therefore; then; **lūctus** grief, mourning
**\*\*pandō** spread, open

30 **\*\*certō** strive, fight; **\*\*soleō** be accustomed
**\*\*stupeō** be amazed; **innūptus** unwed, virgin; **exitiālis** fatal, deadly

35

**\*\*suspiciō** suspect

**praecipitō** cast headlong; **subjiciō** place under; **\*\*ūrō** burn
**terebrō** bore into, pierce; **\*\*\*cavus** hollow; **uterus** belly; **latebra** hiding place
**\*\*\*scindō** split, divide; **incertus** wavering; **studium** desire; **contrārius** opposing

---

**16. sectā abiete:** *with cut fir,* i.e., with fir cut into planks; pronounce **abiete** as if spelled **abjete**. **18. Hūc:** i.e., inside the horse. **virum:** *virōrum.* **19. caecō laterī:** *within its blind* (i.e., secret) *side.* **21. Tenedos:** an island near the Trojan coast. **22. rēgna:** poetic plural. **23. male fīda:** *unsafe.* **24. condunt:** the subject is **Danaī** understood. **25. ratī:** supply **sumus**. **Mycēnās:** i.e., Greece. **26. Teucria:** *Troy.* **27. Dōrica:** *Greek.* **29. tendēbat:** supply **tentōria** (*tents*). **31. exitiāle:** *fatal* (to the Trojans). **Minervae:** Minerva, goddess of wisdom and of the arts, was hostile to the Trojans. **32. mīrantur:** plural with the col- lective subject **pars,** although **stupet** in line 31 is singular. **Thymoetēs:** a Trojan leader. **34. ferēbant:** supply **sē;** *were tending.* An oracle had foretold the fall of Troy through a child born on a certain day. As Paris, son of Priam, and also the son of Thymoetes were born on that day, Priam had Thymoetes's son put to death. **35. et quōrum . . . mentī:** *and those that had a better thought in mind.* **mentī:** dat. of possession with **erat** understood. **36. pelagō:** *into the sea;* dat. of direction. **īnsidiās:** i.e., the Wooden Horse. **38. latebrās:** pronounce **la–teb–rās** with the second syllable long and accented.

**comitor** accompany; **caterva** crowd

**dēcurrō** run down

**īnsānia** insanity, madness

**āvehō** carry away, bear away

*careō be free from, lack

**inclūdō** shut in, inclose; **lignum** wood, timber
**fabricō** build; **māchina** engine, contrivance
**inspiciō** look into

***lateō lie hidden; **error** deceit, trick
***quisquis whoever

**validus** mighty; **hasta** spear

**ferus** beast, monster; *curvus curved; **compāgēs** joint, seam; **alvus** body
**contorqueō** hurl; **tremō** tremble, quiver; **uterus** belly; **recutiō** strike
**īnsonō** resound, echo; **gemitus** groan; **caverna** cavern
**laevus left; **misguided

**impellō** drive, force; **foedō** make foul; mangle; **latebra** hiding place

---

40 "Prīmus ibi ante omnīs, magnā comitante
       catervā,
Lāocoön ārdēns summā dēcurrit ab arce,
et procul: 'Ō miserī, quae tanta īnsānia, cīvēs?
Crēditis āvectōs hostīs, aut ūlla putātis
dōna carēre dolīs Danaum? Sīc nōtus Ulixēs?
45 Aut hōc inclūsī lignō occultantur Achīvī,
aut haec in nostrōs fabricāta est māchina mūrōs,
īnspectūra domōs ventūraque dēsuper urbī,
aut aliquis latet error; equō nē crēdite, Teucrī.
Quidquid id est, timeō Danaōs et dōna ferentīs.'
50 Sīc fātus, validīs ingentem vīribus hastam
in latus inque ferī curvam compāgibus alvum
contorsit. Stetit illa tremēns, uterōque recussō,
īnsonuēre cavae gemitumque dedēre cavernae;

et, sī fāta deum, sī mēns nōn laeva fuisset,
55 impulerat ferrō Argolicās foedāre latebrās,
Trōjaque nunc stāret, Priamīque arx alta, manērēs.

QUESTIONS ON **13–56**. 1. With whose help did the Greeks build the Wooden Horse? 2. What did Thymoetes propose doing with the Wooden Horse? Capys? 3. What advice did Laocoön give the Trojans in regard to the Wooden Horse? 4. What did Laocoön do to the Wooden Horse? 5. What explanation does Aeneas give for the failure of the Trojans to follow Laocoön's advice?

*Sinon tells his story.*

*ecce lo! behold!; revinciō bind

*pāstor shepherd

***ignōtus unknown

"Ecce manūs juvenem intereā post terga revīnc-
       tum
pāstōrēs magnō ad rēgem clāmōre trahēbant
Dardanidae, quī sē ignōtum venientibus ultrō,

---

41. Lāocoön: a priest of Neptune. 42. īnsānia: supply est. 43. āvectōs: supply esse. 44. nōtus: supply est. Ulysses was well known to the Trojans for his cunning. 47. urbī: dat. of direction. 48. nē crēdite: a poetic use of the negative imperative. 49. This line has become proverbial as an expression of suspicion. et: *even.* 51. ferī: i.e., equī. 52. illa: *it,* i.e., the spear. 55. impulerat: stronger than impulisset, which would be the regular form in this contrary to fact conclusion.

The subject of **impulerat** is Lāocoön understood. Argolicās: *Argive,* i.e., Greek. foedāre: supply nōs as subject. 56. arx alta: vocative. Aeneas is here represented as addressing Priam's citadel; an example of *apostrophe;* see App. 22, 5.

57. manūs post terga revīnctum: *with his hands bound behind his back.* manūs: acc. with revīnctum; see App. 113. terga: poetic plural. 58. rēgem: i.e., Priam. 59. ignōtum: the man's name, as we later learn, was Sinon.

hoc ipsum ut strueret Trōjamque aperīret Achīvīs,   **\*\*struō** contrive

obtulerat, fīdēns animī, atque in utrumque parātus,   **fīdēns** confident

seu versāre dolōs, seu certae occumbere mortī.   **versō** keep turning over; work out; **occumbō** fall upon

Undique vīsendī studiō Trōjāna juventūs   **\*vīsō** view, look at; **studium** desire; **\*\*\*juventūs** youth

circumfūsa ruit, certantque inlūdere captō.   **circumfundō** pour around; **\*\*\*certō** vie; **inlūdō** mock

Accipe nunc Danaum īnsidiās, et crīmine ab ūnō   65 **\*crīmen** charge; guilty act

disce omnīs.   **\*\*discō** learn

Namque ut cōnspectū in mediō turbātus inermis   **cōnspectus** sight; **turbō** confuse, disturb

cōnstitit, atque oculīs Phrygia agmina circum-   **circumspiciō** look around at
    spexit,

'Heu, quae nunc tellūs,' inquit, 'quae me aequora   **\*heu** alas!
    possunt

accipere, aut quid jam miserō mihi dēnique restat,   70 **\*dēnique** finally

cui neque apud Danaōs usquam locus, et super ipsī   **\*\*usquam** anywhere

Dardanidae īnfēnsī poenās cum sanguine poscunt?'   **īnfēnsus** hostile

Quō gemitū conversī animī, compressus et omnis   **gemitus** groan, moan; **convertō** change; **comprimō** check

impetus.   Hortāmur fārī quō sanguine crētus   **\*crēscō** grow; spring

quidve ferat; memoret quae sit fīdūcia captō.   75

Ille haec dēpositā tandem formīdine fātur:   **dēpōnō** put aside; **\*\*\*tandem** at length; **\*formīdō** fear

"'Cūncta equidem tibi, rēx, fuerit quodcumque,
    fatēbor   **\*fateor** confess, acknowledge; cf. **\*profiteor** avow, profess

vēra,' inquit, 'neque mē Argolicā dē gente negābō;

hoc prīmum, nec, sī miserum Fortūna Sinōnem

fīnxit, vānum etiam mendācemque improba finget.   80 **\*\*\*fingō** make, fashion; **\*\*\*vānus** false; **mendāx** lying, deceitful; **\*improbus** base

Fandō aliquod sī forte tuās pervēnit ad aurīs   **perveniō** come; **\*\*\*auris** ear

Bēlīdae nōmen Palamēdis et incluta fāmā   **inclutus** famous, renowned

glōria, quem falsā sub prōditiōne Pelasgī   **falsus** groundless; **prōditiō** betrayal, accusation

---

**60. hoc(c) ipsum ut strueret:** *in order to contrive this very scheme;* i.e., deceive the Trojans. **strueret, aperīret:** subjunctives in a clause of purpose. **64. circumfūsa ruit:** *rushes and crowds around.* **certant:** for this use of the plural with a singular subject compare **mīrantur** in line 32. **65. Accipe:** Aeneas, while relating his adventures, is addressing Dido. **66. disce omnīs (Danaōs):** *learn about all the Greeks.* **71–72. cui . . . poscunt:** i.e., Sinon represents himself as helpless and hopeless between the hostile Trojans on one hand and the hostile Greeks on the other. **73. conversī animī:** supply **sunt;** *our feelings were changed.* **compressus:** sup-

ply **est. 74. Hortāmur (eum) fārī:** *in prose we should expect* **hortāmur ut loquātur. crētus:** supply **sit. 75. quidve ferat:** *or what* (message) *he bears.* **memoret:** subjunctive in indirect command; see App. 194, 3.

**77. rēx:** i.e., Priam. **fuerit quodcumque:** *whatever shall happen.* **79–80. nec . . . finget:** i.e., Sinon may be unfortunate, but he will not tell a falsehood. **81. Fandō:** *by hearsay.* **81–82. aliquod nomen:** *any mention.* **82. Bēlīdae Palamēdis:** Palamedes, son of Belus, was a Greek leader who was treacherously convicted of treason and executed by the Greeks.

īnsōns innocent; **indicium** evidence; *quia because; ***vetō forbid, oppose
*nex death; **cassus** lacking, deprived of; ***lūmen light; *lūgeō mourn, lament
*comes companion; cōnsanguinitās blood-kinship
pauper poor, needy
vigeō flourish, thrive

***decus glory, honor; cf. ***dēdecus disgrace
*invidia envy, malice; **pellāx** crafty, wily
superus upper, earthly

**adflīgō strike down, crush; *tenebrae darkness, gloom; lūctus grief, mourning
īnsōns innocent; **indignor** be angry at
*taceō keep silent; *dēmēns mad, foolish
patrius ancestral, native; remeō return, go back
prōmittō promise; *ultor avenger; **verbum word, speech; odium hatred
malum evil, misfortune; lābēs slip, downward step
**crīmen charge, accusation; **spargō scatter
ambiguus of double meaning; **cōnscius conscious (of guilt); cf. **cōnscientia consciousness
requiēscō rest; **dōnec until; minister servant, tool
*nēquīquam in vain, to no purpose; ingrātus unwelcome; revolvō unroll; reveal

jam dūdum long since (due); cf. **dūdum a while ago

vērō indeed, truly; scītor inquire
***scelus crime, villainy

prōsequor proceed; pavitō tremble; cf. *paveō fear; ***fingō make up, fashion

---

īnsontem īnfandō indiciō, quia bella vetābat,
85 dēmīsēre necī, nunc cassum lūmine lūgent;
illī mē comitem et cōnsanguinitāte propinquum
pauper in arma pater prīmīs hūc mīsit ab annīs.

Dum stābat rēgnō incolumis, rēgumque vigēbat
conciliīs, et nōs aliquod nōmenque decusque
90 gessimus; invidiā postquam pellācis Ulixī
(haud ignōta loquor) superīs concessit ab ōrīs,
adflīctus vītam in tenebrīs lūctūque trahēbam,
et cāsum īnsontis mēcum indignābar amīcī.
Nec tacuī dēmēns, et mē, fors sī qua tulisset,
95 sī patriōs umquam remeāssem victor ad Argōs,
prōmīsī ultōrem, et verbīs odia aspera mōvī.

Hinc mihi prīma malī lābēs, hinc semper Ulixēs
crīminibus terrēre novīs, hinc spargere vōcēs
in vulgum ambiguās, et quaerere cōnscius arma.

100 Nec requiēvit enim, dōnec, Calchante ministrō —
sed quid ego haec autem nēquīquam ingrāta revolvō,
quidve moror, sī omnīs ūnō ōrdine habētis Achīvōs,
idque audīre sat est? Jam dūdum sūmite poenās:
hoc Ithacus velit, et magnō mercentur Atrīdae.
105 "Tum vērō ārdēmus scītārī, et quaerere causās,
ignārī scelerum tantōrum artisque Pelasgae.
Prōsequitur pavitāns, et fictō pectore fātur:
"'Saepe fugam Danaī Trōjā cupiēre relictā

---

**84.** īnfandō indiciō: *on infamous evidence.* Ulysses hid money and a forged letter to Priam in Palamedes's tent.　　**85.** necī: dat. of direction. cassum lūmine: *deprived of the light* (of life). **87.** hūc: i.e., to Troy.　　**88.** stābat: the subject is Palamēdēs understood. rēgnō: abl. of place where.　　**89.** conciliīs: abl. of place where. nōs: i.e., Sinon.　　**91.** haud ignōta: *well-known facts.* superīs concessit ab ōrīs: *he passed away from the upper regions,* i.e., he died. The subject is Palamēdēs understood.　　**93.** mēcum: *in my heart.* **94.** fors . . . tulisset: *if any chance should offer.*

**96.** mōvī: *I aroused.*　　**98.** terrēre: historical infin., = terrēbat; so also spargere (*spread*) in line 98 and quaerere in line 99.　　**100.** Calchante ministrō: *with Calchas as tool.* Calchas was a Greek soothsayer. After ministrō there is a break, leaving the sentence incomplete; an example of *aposiopesis;* see note on I, 135.　　**102.** omnīs . . . Achīvōs: *you consider all Greeks of the same sort.*　　**104.** Ithacus: *the Ithacan,* i.e., Ulysses. magnō: *at a great price;* abl. of price.　　**105.** ārdēmus: *we* (Trojans) *are eager.*　　**107.** fictō pectore: *with treacherous heart.*

mōlīrī, et longō fessī discēdere bellō

(fēcissentque utinam!); saepe illōs aspera pontī    110

interclūsit hiems et terruit Auster euntīs;

praecipuē, cum jam hic trabibus contextus acernīs

stāret equus, tōtō sonuērunt aethere nimbī,

Suspēnsī Eurypylum scītantem ōrācula Phoebī

mittimus, isque adytīs haec trīstia dicta reportat: 115

*Sanguine plācāstis ventōs et virgine caesā,*

*cum prīmum Īliacās, Danaī, vēnistis ad ōrās;*

*sanguine quaerendī reditūs, animāque litandum*

*Argolicā.)* Vulgī quae vōx ut vēnit ad aurīs,

obstipuēre animī, gelidusque per īma cucurrit    120

ossa tremor, cui fāta parent, quem poscat Apollō.

Hīc Ithacus vātem magnō Calchanta tumultū

prōtrahit in mediōs; quae sint ea nūmina dīvum

flāgitat. Et mihi jam multī crūdēle canēbant

artificis scelus, et tacitī ventūra vidēbant.    125

Bis quīnōs silet ille diēs, tēctusque recūsat

prōdere vōce suā quemquam aut oppōnere mortī.

Vix tandem, magnīs Ithacī clāmōribus āctus,

compositō rumpit vōcem, et mē dēstinat ārae.

Adsēnsēre omnēs, et quae sibi quisque timēbat    130

ūnius in miserī exitium conversa tulēre.

Jamque diēs īnfanda aderat; mihi sacra parārī

et salsae frūgēs et circum tempora vittae.

Ēripuī, fateor, lētō mē, et vincula rūpī,

līmōsōque lacū per noctem obscūrus in ulvā    135

---

fessus tired, wearied; **discēdō** depart

**utinam** would that!

praecipuē especially; cf. ***praecipuus** especial; con-texō construct; cf. **texō** weave; **acernus** of maple

***nimbus** storm cloud

suspēnsus in suspense; cf. **suspendō** hang; **scītor** seek to know; **ōrāculum** oracle

adytum inner shrine, sanctuary

**plācō** placate, appease

reditus return; **anima** life; litō sacrifice

***obstipēscō** be dazed; *geli-dus** icy, cold

**os** bone, inmost part; **tremor** trembling

*vātēs** soothsayer

**prōtrahō** drag forth

*flāgitō** demand; ***canō** sing (of), prophesy

artifex contriver, schemer; ***taceō** keep silent

quīnī five; ***sileō** be silent

oppōnō expose

compositō according to agree-ment; **dēstinō** mark, destine

adsentiō assent, agree

*exitium destruction; **convertō** turn

*sacer sacred, holy

salsus salted; **frūx** grain, meal; *vitta** fillet, headband

**fateor** confess; cf. **profiteor** avow, profess; *lētum** death; ***vinc(u)lum** bond, chain

līmōsus muddy; *lacus marsh; **obscūrus** unseen; **ulva** marsh grass

---

**111. euntīs:** agrees with **eōs** understood as ob-ject of **terruit. 113. aethere:** abl. of place where. **114. Eurypylum:** *Eurypylus,* a Greek leader. **115. adytīs:** abl. of place whence. **116. virgine caesā:** the reference is to the sacrifice of Iphi-genia, daughter of Agamemnon, so that the Greeks might be able to sail, under favorable winds, to Troy. **118. litandum:** supply **est;** *expiation must be made.* **121. cui fāta parent:** *for whom the Fates are preparing* (this death). **parent:** subjunctive in indirect question depending on **cucurrit tremor**

(= *they wonder);* so also **poscat. 122. Calchanta:** Greek acc. **126. ille:** *he,* i.e., Calchas. **tēctus:** literally, *covered,* i.e., remaining in his tent. **130. Adsēnsēre: Adsēnsērunt. 131. ūnius . . . tulēre:** supply **ea** (*those dread things*) as object of **tulēre** and antecedent of **quae** in line 130. **132. diēs:** i.e., the day which Sinon pretends was set for his death. **sacra:** *the holy implements* (for the sacrifice). **parārī:** historical infin., = **parā-bantur. 134. lētō:** abl. of separation. **135. lacū:** place where.

dēlitēscō hide, lie hidden

dēlituī, dum vēla darent, sī forte dedissent.

Nec mihi jam patriam antīquam spēs ūlla videndī

nātus son; exoptō desire, long for
reposcō demand

nec dulcīs nātōs exoptātumque parentem,

quōs illī fors et poenās ob nostra reposcent

effugium flight; *culpa fault, offense; piō expiate
**superī the gods above; ***cōnscius aware; cf. ***cōnscientia consciousness **adhūc still, as yet; ***usquam anywhere
intemerātus unsullied, pure; *misereor pity
**misereor pity

140 effugia, et culpam hanc miserōrum morte piābunt.

Quod tē per superōs et cōnscia nūmina vērī,

per sī qua est quae restat adhūc mortālibus usquam

intemerāta fidēs, ōrō, miserēre labōrum

tantōrum, miserēre animī nōn digna ferentis.'

QUESTIONS ON **57–144**. 1. Who did Sinon claim to be? 2. What at first was the attitude of the Trojans toward Sinon? 3. What caused a change in their attitude? 4. Who was Calchas? 5. What, according to Sinon, did Calchas advise the Greeks to do? 6. What did Sinon "confess" he had done?

*Sinon's story is believed.*

miserēscō take pity on

145   "Hīs lacrimīs vītam damus, et miserēscimus ultrō.

manicae manacles; artus close-fitted, tight; ***levō lighten, remove

Ipse virō prīmus manicās atque arta levārī

vincla jubet Priamus, dictīsque ita fātur amīcīs:

*oblīvīscor forget

'Quisquis es, āmissōs hinc jam oblīvīscere Grajōs;

ēdisserō set forth, tell

noster eris, mihique haec ēdissere vēra rogantī.

150 Quō mōlem hanc immānis equī statuēre? Quis auctor,

māchina engine

quidve petunt? Quae relligiō aut quae māchina bellī?'

Dīxerat. Ille, dolīs īnstrūctus et arte Pelasgā,

**exuō strip, free; ***palma palm, hand
***aeternus everlasting; violābilis that can be violated
*testor call to witness; *ēnsis sword, knife; nefandus unspeakable
**vitta fillet; hostia sacrificial victim

sustulit exūtās vinclīs ad sīdera palmās:

'Vōs, aeternī ignēs, et nōn violābile vestrum

155 testor nūmen,' ait, 'vōs, ārae ēnsēsque nefandī,

quōs fūgī, vittaeque deum, quās hostia gessī:

---

**136. dum . . . dedissent:** *until they should sail, if by chance they should sail.* **darent:** subjunctive in a clause of anticipation. **dedissent:** subjunctive in a past-future clause. See App. 156, *a*. **137. spēs ūlla:** supply **est**. **139. illī:** i.e., the Greeks. **fors et:** *perhaps.* **poenās:** secondary object of **reposcent**; see App. 106, *a*. **140. culpam hanc:** i.e., Sinon's guilt. **141. tē:** i.e., Priam; **tē** is direct object of **ōrō** in line 143. **cōnscia nūmina vērī:** *the divine powers that are aware of the truth.*

**143–144. miserēre labōrum tantōrum:** *have pity on such heavy toils.* **labōrum:** gen. with **miserēre**; see App. 93, *c*. **144. animī . . . ferentis:** *a soul suffering punishments undeserved.* For Work Unit VII, based on lines 1–144 of Book II, see p. 260.

**148. hinc jam:** *from now on.* **150. Quō:** *for what purpose?* **statuēre:** statuērunt. The subject is **Danaī** understood. **auctor:** supply **est**. **152. Ille:** i.e., Sinon. **arte Pelasgā:** i.e., the art of lying.

fās mihi Grajōrum sacrāta resolvere jūra,

fās ōdisse virōs atque omnia ferre sub aurās,

sī qua tegunt, teneor patriae nec lēgibus ūllīs.

Tū modo prōmissīs maneās, servātaque servēs

Trōja fidem, sī vēra feram, sī magna rependam.

"'Omnis spēs Danaum et coeptī fīdūcia bellī

Palladis auxiliīs semper stetit.  Impius ex quō

Tȳdīdēs sed enim scelerumque inventor Ulixēs,

fātāle adgressī sacrātō āvellere templō

Palladium, caesīs summae custōdibus arcis,

corripuēre sacram effigiem, manibusque cruentīs

virgineās ausī dīvae contingere vittās,

ex illō fluere ac retrō sublāpsa referrī

spēs Danaum, frāctae vīrēs, āversa deae mēns.

Nec dubiīs ea signa dedit Trītōnia mōnstrīs.

Vix positum castrīs simulācrum: ārsēre coruscae

lūminibus flammae arrēctīs, salsusque per artūs

sūdor iit, terque ipsa solō (mīrābile dictū)

ēmicuit, parmamque ferēns hastamque trementem.

Extemplō temptanda fugā canit aequora Calchās

nec posse Argolicīs exscindī Pergama tēlīs,

ōmina nī repetant Argīs nūmenque redūcant,

quod pelagō et curvīs sēcum āvexēre carīnīs.

Et nunc quod patriās ventō petiēre Mycēnās,

arma deōsque parant comitēs, pelagōque remēnsō

imprōvīsī aderunt; ita dīgerit ōmina Calchās.

*160*
*165*
*170*
*175*
*180*

***fās** right;  ****sacrō** consecrate;  **resolvō** break
*****ōdī** hate
160 **prōmissum** a promise
**rependō** repay

**impius** impious, wicked

165 **fātālis** fateful;  ****sacrō** consecrate;  **āvellō** tear away

****sacer** holy;  **effigiēs** image;  ****cruentus** bloodstained
**virgineus** of a maiden, virgin;  **contingō** touch;  ****vitta** fillet
*****retrō** backward;  **sublābor** slip, fall
170
****dubius** doubtful, uncertain;  ***mōnstrum** omen, portent
**simulācrum** image, likeness;  ***coruscus** flashing, quivering
****arrigō** raise, uplift;  **salsus** salty;  ****artus** joint, limb
**sūdor** sweat, perspiration;  ****solum** ground, earth;
**mīrābilis** marvelous
175 **ēmicō** leap up;  **parma** shield;  ****hasta** spear;  ****tremō** tremble, quiver
****extemplō** immediately
**exscindō** tear down, destroy
***ōmen** omen;  ***nī** unless, if not;  ****repetō** seek again;  **redūcō** bring anew
****curvus** curved;  **āvehō** convey;  ****carīna** keel, ship
****comes** comrade;  **remētior** retrace
**imprōvīsus** unexpected;  **dīgerō** explain;  ****ōmen** portent

---

**157. fās:** supply est.  **158. sub aurās:** *into open view.*  **159. sī . . . tegunt:** *if they* (i.e., the Greeks) *hide any secrets.*  **160. Tū . . . maneās:** *Do you but abide by* (*in*) *your promises.*  **Tū:** i.e., Troy.  **prōmissīs:** abl. of place where.  **161. Trōja:** vocative.  **sī . . . rependam:** *if I shall make good requital.*  **163–164. ex quō sed enim:** *but indeed from the time when.*  **165–166. fātāle Palladium:** *the fateful statue of Pallas.*  An oracle had declared that Troy would survive while this statue of Pallas remained in the citadel of Troy.  Diomedes and Ulysses entered the city in disguise and carried off the statue.  **165. templō:** place whence.  **168. dīvae:** i.e., Minerva's.  **169. ex illō (tempore):** *since then.*

**fluere, referrī:** historical infinitives.  **170. frāctae:** supply sunt.  **āversa:** supply est.  **171. Trītōnia:** *Minerva.*  **172. positum:** supply erat.  **castrīs:** i.e., in the Greek camp.  **ārsēre:** ārsērunt.  **173. lūminibus arrēctīs:** *from staring eyes.*  **174. ipsa:** i.e., the goddess.  **solō:** place whence.  **178. ōmina . . . Argīs:** *unless they seek again the auspices from Argos* (i.e., from Greece).  **repetant, redūcant:** subjunctives in a subordinate clause in indirect discourse.  **179. pelagō:** abl. of route by which.  **180. petiēre:** petiērunt.  **181. deōs comitēs:** *the gods as companions.*  **pelagō remēnsō:** *after crossing the sea.*  **remēnsō:** used as passive here, although the verb is deponent.

**\*\*laedō** injure, offend

**effigiēs** image, statue; **\*nefās** impiety, guilt; **piō** alone for

**immēnsus** huge; **attollō** raise, rear

**\*rōbur** oak; timber; **\*\*\*texō** weave, join; **ēdūcō** build up

**\*violō** violate, profane

**\*\*exitium** destruction

**\*\*sīn** but if

**\*nepōs** grandson; descendant

**perjūrus** perjured

**\*domō** subdue, vanquish; **\*\*\*carīna** keel; ship

Hanc prō Palladiō monitī, prō nūmine laesō
effigiem statuēre, nefās quae trīste piāret.
185 Hanc tamen immēnsam Calchās attollere mōlem
rōboribus textīs caelōque ēdūcere jussit,
nē recipī portīs aut dūcī in moenia posset
neu populum antīquā sub relligiōne tuērī;
nam sī vestra manus violāsset dōna Minervae,
190 tum magnum exitium (quod dī prius ōmen in ipsum
convertant!) Priamī imperiō Phrygibusque futū-
rum,
sīn manibus vestrīs vestram ascendisset in urbem,
ultrō Asiam magnō Pelopēa ad moenia bellō
ventūram, et nostrōs ea fāta manēre nepōtēs.'
195 "Tālibus īnsidiīs perjūrīque arte Sinōnis
crēdita rēs, captīque dolīs lacrimīsque coāctīs,
quōs neque Tȳdīdēs nec Lārissaeus Achillēs,
nōn annī domuēre decem, nōn mīlle carīnae.

QUESTIONS ON **145–198.** 1. What questions did Priam ask Sinon? 2. What sin against Pallas had Diomedes and Ulysses committed? 3. What effect, according to Sinon, had this sin had on the fortunes of the Greeks? 4. What, according to Sinon, did Calchas say the Greeks would have to do to regain divine favor? 5. How, according to Sinon, did the Greeks try to regain the favor of Pallas? 6. Why, according to Sinon, did the Greeks make the Wooden Horse so large?

*Laocoön and his sons are slain by two sea monsters.*

**imprōvidus** unforeseeing

"Hīc aliud majus miserīs multōque tremendum
200 objicitur magis, atque imprōvida pectora turbat.

**183. prō nūmine laesō:** *for her offended divinity.* **184. nefās:** i.e., the theft of the Palladium. **186. rōboribus textīs:** *of joined timbers;* abl. of material; see App. 117, *f.* **caelō:** dat. of direction, depending on **ēdūcere.** The Greeks were ordered to build the horse so large that the Trojans could not take it into Troy and thus be able to make the horse serve as a protection in place of the Palladium which had been stolen from them. **190. ipsum:** i.e., Calchas. **191. futūrum:** supply **esse;** main verb in indirect statement, depending on **Calchas dīxit** understood. **192. ascendisset:** the subject understood is **equus.** **193. Asiam:** i.e., Troy, a Trojan army. **Pelopēa ad** moenia: *to Pelops's walls;* i.e., to Greece; Pelops was a legendary Greek king. **194. manēre:** *awaited;* the subject acc. is **ea fāta,** a poetic plural. **196. crēdita:** supply **est. 197. quōs:** supply **nōs** as antecedent of **quōs** and subject of **captī (sumus). Lārissaeus Achillēs:** *Thessalian Achilles;* Larissa was a town in Thessaly. **198. domuēre: domuērunt.** The Trojans, who had withstood Diomedes and Achilles and ten years of warfare, were now caught by Sinon's wiles. **199. majus:** read as if spelled **majjus. miserīs:** i.e., to the wretched Trojans; dat. with compound verb **objicitur.**

Lāocoön, ductus Neptūnō sorte sacerdōs,
sollemnīs taurum ingentem mactābat ad ārās.
Ecce autem geminī ā Tenedō tranquilla per alta
(horrēscō referēns) immēnsīs orbibus anguēs
incumbunt pelagō, pariterque ad lītora tendunt,     205
pectora quōrum inter flūctūs arrēcta jubaeque
sanguineae superant undās; pars cētera pontum
pōne legit, sinuatque immēnsa volūmine terga.
Fit sonitus spūmante salō, jamque arva tenēbant,
ārdentīsque oculōs suffectī sanguine et ignī     210
sībila lambēbant linguīs vibrantibus ōra.
Diffugimus, vīsū exsanguēs.  Illī agmine certō
Lāocoönta petunt, et prīmum parva duōrum
corpora nātōrum serpēns amplexus uterque
implicat, et miserōs morsū dēpāscitur artūs;     215
post ipsum auxiliō subeuntem et tēla ferentem
corripiunt, spīrīsque ligant ingentibus; et jam
bis medium amplexī, bis collō squāmea circum
terga datī superant capite et cervīcibus altīs.
Ille simul manibus tendit dīvellere nōdōs,     220
perfūsus saniē vittās ātrōque venēnō,
clāmōrēs simul horrendōs ad sīdera tollit;
quālīs mūgītūs, fūgit cum saucius āram
taurus et incertam excussit cervīce secūrim.
At geminī lāpsū dēlūbra ad summa dracōnēs     225
diffugiunt, saevaeque petunt Trītōnidis arcem,
sub pedibusque deae clipcīque sub orbe teguntur.
Tum vērō tremefacta novus per pectora cūnctīs
īnsinuat pavor, et scelus expendisse merentem

***sors lot; **sacerdōs priest

sollemnis customary; sacred;
**taurus bull; *mactō sacrifice
**ecce lo! behold!
horrēscō shudder; *anguis
snake, serpent
incumbō lie upon

juba crest; mane

sanguineus bloody, blood-red

pōne behind; ***legō choose,
pick; skim over; sinuō
wind; volūmen roll, coil
sonitus sound; spūmō foam,
froth; salum salt sea
sufficiō suffuse
sībilus hissing; lambō lick;
*lingua tongue; vibrō dart
diffugiō flee, scatter; vīsus
vision; exsanguis bloodless;
pale

serpēns serpent, snake; cf.
*serpō creep; *amplector
embrace; envelop
**implicō entwine; **morsus
bite; teeth; dēpāscor feed on;
***artus joint, limb
subeō go up, approach
spīra coil; ligō bind, tie
**amplector embrace; envelop;
***collum neck; squāmeus
scaly
***cervīx neck
dīvellō tear away; cf. **vellō
tear; ***nōdus knot; coil
perfundō drench; saniēs blood;
**venēnum poison, venom
horrendus terrifying

mūgītus bellowing; *saucius
wounded, stricken
***taurus bull; incertus uncertain; ill-aimed; *secūris ax
lāpsus gliding motion; *dēlūbrum shrine; dracō serpent
diffugiō flee

*clipeus shield, buckler

vērō truly, indeed; tremefactus
trembling, quaking
īnsinuō creep; pavor terror;
expendō pay for, atone for

---

**201.** ductus . . . sorte: *drawn by lot for Neptune.*
**204.** immēnsīs orbibus: *with huge coils.* **205.** pelagō: dat. with the compound verb incumbunt or
abl. of place where. tendunt: *make for.* **210.** ārdentīsque . . . ignī: *their blazing eyes suffused with
blood and flame.* oculōs: acc. with suffectī; see App.
114. **212.** Illī: *they,* i.e., the serpents. **213.** Lāocoönta: Greek acc. **216.** post: *afterward;* an adverb. ipsum: i.e., Laocoön. **218.** medium amplexī:

*coiling around his body.* **218–219.** bis . . . datī:
*coiling their scaly bodies around his neck.* circum
. . . datī: an example of *tmesis;* see App. 22, 22.
collō: dat. with circum datī. terga: acc. with
circum datī: see App. 106, c. **220.** Ille: i.e., Laocoön. **221.** perfūsus . . . vittās: *his fillets smeared
with blood.* vittās: acc. with perfūsus; see App.
114. **224.** cervīce: place whence. **226.** Trītōnidis: *of Minerva.* **229.** scelus . . . merentem: *de-*

***sacer** sacred, holy; **\*\*cuspis** point; spear; **\*\*rōbur** oak
***laedō** strike, injure; *scelerātus wicked, accursed; **intorqueō** hurl against
**\*\*simulācrum** image, likeness
**conclāmō** shout

230 Lāocoönta ferunt, sacrum quī cuspide rōbur
laeserit, et tergō scelerātam intorserit hastam.
Dūcendum ad sēdīs simulācrum ōrandaque dīvae
nūmina conclāmant.

QUESTIONS ON **199–233.** 1. What had Laocoön done to the Wooden Horse? 2. What made the Trojans believe that what happened to Laocoön was punishment for sacrilege? 3. What goddess seemed especially interested in the punishment of Laocoön? 4. What did the Trojans decide to do with the Wooden Horse?

*The Wooden Horse is brought into Troy, and the Greeks seize the city at night.*

***pandō** spread out, lay open

"Dīvidimus mūrōs, et moenia pandimus urbis.

**accingō** gird; **\*\*rota** wheel

235 Accingunt omnēs operī, pedibusque rotārum

**subjiciō** place under; **stuppeus** hempen
**\*\*intendō** stretch; **scandō** mount; **fātālis** fateful; **māchina** contrivance
**fētus** filled; **innūptus** unwed; **puella** girl
***fūnis** rope, cable; **contingō** touch; **\*\*gaudeō** rejoice
**\*\*minor** threaten; tower aloft; **inlābor** glide into
**inclutus** famous, renowned
**quater** four times

subjiciunt lāpsūs, et stuppea vincula collō
intendunt. Scandit fātālis māchina mūrōs,
fēta armīs. Puerī circum innūptaeque puellae
sacra canunt, fūnemque manū contingere gaudent;
240 illa subit, mediaeque mināns inlābitur urbī.
Ō patria, ō dīvum domus Īlium, et incluta bellō
moenia Dardanidum! Quater ipsō in līmine portae

**subsistō** stop, halt; **sonitus** sound; **quater** four times
**immemor** unmindful

substitit, atque uterō sonitum quater arma dedēre;
īnstāmus tamen immemorēs caecīque furōre,

**\*\*mōnstrum** monster; ***sistō** cause to stand; place
***tunc** then, at that time

245 et mōnstrum īnfēlīx sacrātā sistimus arce.
Tunc etiam fātīs aperit Cassandra futūrīs

**jussus** command

ōra, deī jussū nōn umquam crēdita Teucrīs;

**\*\*dēlūbrum** shrine, temple

nōs dēlūbra deum miserī, quibus ultimus esset

**fēstus** festal, festive; ***vēlō** cover; adorn; ***frōns** leaf; leafy bough

ille diēs, fēstā vēlāmus fronde per urbem.
250 "Vertitur intereā caelum, et ruit Ōceanō nox,

---

*servedly had paid for his crime.* **230. sacrum rōbur:** i.e., the Wooden Horse. **231. laeserit, intorserit:** subjunctives in a clause of characteristic. **tergō:** dat. with the compound verb **intorserit.** **232. sēdīs:** i.e., the citadel.
**234. Dīvidimus mūrōs:** i.e., we break open the walls. **235. Accingunt:** supply sē. **235–236. pedibusque . . . lāpsūs:** *and place rolling wheels under its feet.* **pedibus:** dat. with the compound verb **subjiciunt.** **236. collō:** place whence. **239. sacra:** *sacred hymns.* **240. illa:** i.e., the **māchina,** *the structure.* **urbī:** dat. with the compound

verb **inlābitur. 242–243. in līmine . . . substitit:** to stumble on a threshold was considered an evil omen. **243. uterō:** place whence. **245. arce:** place where. **246. Cassandra:** Priam's daughter, to whom Apollo gave the power of prophecy but whom later in revenge for unrequited love he doomed never to be believed. **247. ōra:** *lips.* **deī:** i.e., of Apollo. **Teucrīs:** dat. of agent with the passive participle **crēdita. 248. dēlūbra:** object of **vēlāmus** in line 249. **esset:** subjunctive in a relative clause of characteristic.
**250. Ōceanō:** place whence.

TAKING THE WOODEN HORSE INTO TROY

From a wall painting in Pompeii.

*Courtesy Fogg Museum of Art*

involvēns umbrā magnā terramque polumque

Myrmidonumque dolōs; fūsī per moenia Teucrī

conticuēre; sopor fessōs complectitur artūs.

Et jam Argīva phalānx īnstrūctīs nāvibus ībat

ā Tenedō, tacitae per amīca silentia lūnae    255

lītora nōta petēns, flammās cum rēgia puppis

extulerat, fātīsque deum dēfēnsus inīquīs

inclūsōs uterō Danaōs et pīnea fūrtim

laxat claustra Sinōn. Illōs patefactus ad aurās

reddit equus, laetīque cavō sē rōbore prōmunt    260

Thessandrus Sthenelusque ducēs, et dīrus Ulixēs,

dēmissum lāpsī per fūnem, Acamāsque, Thoāsque,

Pēlīdēsque Neoptolemus, prīmusque Machāōn,

et Menelāus, et ipse dolī fabricātor Epēos.

Invādunt urbem, somnō vīnōque sepultam;    265

caeduntur vigilēs, portīsque patentibus omnīs

accipiunt sociōs, atque agmina cōnscia jungunt.

**involvō** wrap, envelop

**conticēscō** become silent; ***sopor** sleep; ****complector** embrace, enfold  
**phalānx** army  
****lūna** moon

**nōtus** well-known, familiar

**inclūdō** shut in; **pīneus** of pine; **fūrtim** secretly  
*laxō loosen; **claustrum** bar, bolt; *patefaciō open  
***rōbur** oak; **prōmō** bring forth  
**dīrus** dreaded

**fūnis** rope, cable

**fabricātor** maker

**invādō** rush into; ***vīnum** wine; *sepeliō bury

QUESTIONS ON **234-267**. 1. How did the Trojans manage to get the huge Wooden Horse into the city? 2. What bad omen ought to have warned the Trojans? 3. What sounds ought to have warned the Trojans? 4. What further part did Sinon play in the capture of Troy? 5. How did he know when to play the part?

*Hector advises Aeneas in a dream to flee from Troy.*

"Tempus erat, quō prīma quiēs mortālibus aegrīs

incipit, et dōnō dīvum grātissima serpit.

In somnīs ecce ante oculōs maestissimus Hector    270

vīsus adesse mihī largōsque effundere flētūs,

raptātus bīgīs, ut quondam, āterque cruentō

pulvere, perque pedēs trājectus lōra tumentīs

****serpō** creep in

***ecce** lo! behold!; ****maestus** sad, mournful  
**largus** copious; **effundō** pour out; **flētus** weeping; tears  
**raptō** drag; **bīgae** two-horse chariot; ****quondam** once  
****pulvis** dust; **trājiciō** pierce; **lōrum** thong; *tumeō swell

---

**254. phalānx:** i.e., the fleet was in line formation. **256. flammās:** *fires;* presumably a signal to Sinon. **rēgia puppis:** *the royal ship,* i.e., the ship that carried Agamemnon. **257. extulerat:** *had raised.* The regular form in prose would be extulisset. **deum:** deōrum. **inīquīs:** *unfriendly* (i.e., to the Trojans). **258. uterō:** place where. **259. Illōs:** i.e., the Greeks. **ad aurās:** *into the open.* **260. rōbore:** place whence. **263. Neoptolemus:** son of Achilles. **prīmus:** *first of all* (though seventh in order of mention). **264. Menelāus:** brother of Agamemnon and lawful husband of Helen. **dolī:** i.e., of the Wooden Horse. **266. portīs:** abl. of route by which. **267. cōnscia:** *confederate.* For Work Unit VIII, based on lines 145–267 of Book II, see p. 262.

**271. mihī:** i.e., to Aeneas. **272. raptātus:** Achilles had dragged Hector's body thrice around the walls of Troy. **273. perque . . . tumentīs:** *his swollen feet pierced with thongs.* **lōra:** acc. with

| | |
|---|---|
| ei ah! alas! | (ei mihi, quālis erat, quantum mūtātus ab illō |
| *exuviae spoils; **induō put on | 275 Hectore, quī redit exuviās indūtus Achillī, |
| jaculor hurl; cf. **jaculum dart, javelin | vel Danaum Phrygiōs jaculātus puppibus ignīs), |
| squāleō be filthy; barba beard; concrētus matted; **crīnis hair | squālentem barbam et concrētōs sanguine crīnīs vulneraque illa gerēns, quae circum plūrima mūrōs accēpit patriōs! Ultrō flēns ipse vidēbar |
| **compellō address, speak to; ***maestus sad, mournful; exprōmō bring forth; utter | 280 compellāre virum et maestās exprōmere vōcēs: 'Ō lūx Dardaniae, spēs ō fīdissima Teucrum, quae tantae tenuēre morae? Quibus, Hector, ab ōrīs exspectāte venīs? Ut tē post multa tuōrum |
| **fūnus death; disaster; ***varius diverse, manifold aspiciō see; indignus unworthy, undeserved; *serēnus fair foedō defile, make foul | fūnera, post variōs hominumque urbisque labōrēs 285 dēfessī aspicimus! Quae causa indigna serēnōs foedāvit vultūs, aut cūr haec vulnera cernō?' Ille nihil, nec mē quaerentem vāna morātur, |
| graviter heavily, grievously | sed, graviter gemitūs īmō dē pectore dūcēns, |
| **heu alas! | 'Heu fuge, nāte deā, tēque hīs,' ait, 'ēripe flammīs. |
| *culmen top, summit | 290 Hostis habet mūrōs; ruit altō ā culmine Trōja. Sat patriae Priamōque datum; sī Pergama dextrā dēfendī possent, etiam hāc dēfēnsa fuissent. |
| *commendō entrust, commit | Sacra suōsque tibī commendat Trōja Penātīs: |
| ***comes companion | hōs cape fātōrum comitēs, hīs moenia quaere |
| pererrō wander over; **dēnique finally, at last | 295 magna, pererrātō statuēs quae dēnique pontō.' Sīc ait, et manibus vittās Vestamque potentem |
| adytum shrine, sanctuary; *penetrālis inner | aeternumque adytīs effert penetrālibus ignem. |

QUESTIONS ON 268–297. 1. How did Aeneas first learn that the Greeks had captured Troy? 2. What two great exploits of Hector are referred to in lines 274–276? 3. What appearance did Hector present to Aeneas at this time? 4. What did Hector urge Aeneas to do with the Trojan Penates?

---

trājectus; see App. 106, c. 274. ei mihi: *woe is me!* quālis erat: *what a sorrowful sight he was!* 275. exuviās indūtus: *wearing the spoils,* i.e., the armor. exuviās: acc. with indūtus; see App. 114. Hector had slain Patroclus, who had borrowed Achilles's armor. 276. puppibus: dat. of direction. Hector had set fire to several Greek ships. 278. plūrima: *so plentifully.* 279. ipse: i.e., Aeneas. 281. Dardaniae: *of Dardania,* i.e., of Troy, the city of Dardanus. Teucrum: Teucrōrum. 282. tenuēre: understand tē as object.

283. exspectāte: voc. of exspectātus. Ut: *how* (joyfully). 287. nihil: understand dīcit or respondit. quaerentem vāna: *asking vain questions.* 289. nāte deā: *goddess-born.* 291. Sat . . . datum: supply est; *enough has been given* (by you); i.e., you have done enough. 294. comitēs: *as companions.* moenia: *a city;* an example of *metonymy.* 296. Vestam: Vesta was goddess of the hearth and home. Aeneas only dreams that he receives the image of Vesta and the sacred fire from her altar.

*Aeneas is aroused from sleep and goes forth to battle.*

"Dīversō intereā miscentur moenia lūctū,
et magis atque magis, quamquam sēcrēta parentis
Anchīsae domus arboribusque obtēcta recessit, 300
clārēscunt sonitūs, armōrumque ingruit horror.
Excutior somnō, et summī fastīgia tēctī
ascēnsū superō, atque arrēctīs auribus astō,
in segetem velutī cum flamma furentibus Austrīs
incidit, aut rapidus montānō flūmine torrēns 305
sternit agrōs, sternit sata laeta boumque labōrēs,
praecipitīsque trahit silvās; stupet īnscius altō
accipiēns sonitum saxī dē vertice pāstor.
Tum vērō manifesta fidēs Danaumque patēscunt
īnsidiae. Jam Dēiphobī dedit ampla ruīnam 310
Vulcānō superante domus, jam proximus ārdet
Ūcalegōn; Sīgēa ignī freta lāta relūcent.
Exoritur clāmorque virum clangorque tubārum.
Arma āmēns capiō; nec sat ratiōnis in armīs,
sed glomerāre manum bellō et concurrere in arcem 315
cum sociīs ārdent animī; furor īraque mentem
praecipitant, pulchrumque morī succurrit in armīs.

"Ecce autem tēlīs Panthūs ēlapsus Achīvum,
Panthūs Othryadēs, arcis Phoebīque sacerdōs,
sacra manū victōsque deōs parvumque nepōtem 320
ipse trahit, cursūque āmēns ad līmina tendit.
'Quō rēs summa locō, Panthū? Quam prēndimus
    arcem?'
Vix ea fātus eram, gemitū cum tālia reddit:
'Vēnit summa diēs et inēluctābile tempus

---

**quamquam although; sēcrē- tus sequestered, retired; cf.
*sēcernō sunder, separate
obtegō cover, hide; recēdō stand back
clārēscō grow clear; sonitus sound; ingruō rush on; horror shudder; frightful din
fastīgium summit, top
ascēnsus climbing, ascent; ***astō stand
seges grain field; ***velutī as
torrēns torrent; cf. **torreō parch; boil, surge
sternō lay low; sata sown fields, crops; cf. *serō sow, plant; *bōs bull, ox, cow
*praeceps headlong; ***stupeō be dazed, stand amazed; īnscius ignorant, bewildered
**pāstor shepherd, herdsman
*manifestus clear; patēscō become disclosed

proximus next, neighboring

fretum strait, water; relūceō light up, shine
exorior arise, spring up; clangor blare; tuba trumpet
*āmēns frantic

**glomerō gather; concurrō run, rush

praecipitō throw headlong; urge on; *morior die, perish; succurrō run to, occur
ēlābor slip out, escape

**nepōs grandson

**āmēns distracted, out of one's mind

inēluctābilis inescapable

---

**299–300. sēcrēta recessit:** *stood back secluded.*
**305. flūmine:** abl. of means. **306. sternit, sternit:** note the *anaphora.* **309. fidēs:** *truth;* supply est. **310. Dēiphobī:** Deiphobus was a son of Priam and after the death of Paris married Helen. He tells his story in Book VI, lines 509–534. **dedit ruīnam:** *crashed in ruin.* **311. Vul- cānō:** *fire,* by *metonymy;* Vulcan was the god of

fire. **312. Sīgēa freta:** *the waters about Sigeum,* a promontory near Troy. **314. nec sat . . . armīs:** *nor is there enough reason for taking up arms.* **317. succurrit:** *the thought occurs* (to me).
**318–319. Panthūs:** note the repetition, which produces an effect of pity. **320. sacra:** *the sacred images.* **322. Quō . . . locō:** *How fares the state?* locō: place where. **Panthū:** Greek voc.

**translferō** carry over, transfer;
**dominor** rule, hold sway
***arduus** high; **armō** arm

**incendium** fire

**īnsultō** taunt; **bipatēns** doubly
open, wide open
***quot** how many; (as many) as

**oppositus** opposing, hostile;
***mūcrō** point; blade; ***corusco**
**ruscus** flashing, gleaming
****stringō** draw; ****nex** death,
carnage

**fremitus** uproar, din

****lūna** moon

**adglomerō** gather

**īnsānus** mad

***gener** son-in-law

**spōnsa** promised wife; **prae-**
**ceptum** warning

***cupīdō** a desire

**excēdō** depart; **adytum** shrine,
sanctuary
**succurrō** run to aid, succor

325 Dardaniae.   Fuimus Trōes, fuit Īlium et ingēns
glōria Teucrōrum, ferus omnia Juppiter Argōs
trānstulit, incēnsā Danaī dominantur in urbe.
Arduus armātōs mediīs in moenibus astāns
fundit equus, victorque Sinōn incendia miscet
330 īnsultāns.   Portīs aliī bipatentibus adsunt,
mīlia quot magnīs umquam vēnēre Mycēnīs:
obsēdēre illī tēlīs angusta viārum
oppositīs;  stat ferrī aciēs mūcrōne coruscō
stricta, parāta necī;  vix prīmī proelia temptant
335 portārum vigilēs, et caecō Mārte resistunt.'
Tālibus Othryadae dictīs et nūmine dīvum
in flammās et in arma feror, quō trīstis Erīnys,
quō fremitus vocat et sublātus ad aethera clāmor.
Addunt sē sociōs Rīpheus et maximus armīs
340 Epytus, oblātī per lūnam, Hypanisque Dymāsque,
et laterī adglomerant nostrō, juvenisque Coroebus
Mygdonidēs;  illīs ad Trōjam forte diēbus
vēnerat, īnsānō Cassandrae incēnsus amōre,
et gener auxilium Priamō Phrygibusque ferēbat,
345 īnfēlīx, quī nōn spōnsae praecepta furentis
audierit.
Quōs ubi cōnfertōs audēre in proelia vīdī,
incipiō super hīs: 'Juvenēs, fortissima frūstrā
pectora, sī vōbīs audentem extrēma cupīdō
350 certa sequī, quae sit rēbus fortūna vidētis:
excessēre omnēs adytīs ārīsque relictīs
dī, quibus imperium hoc steterat;  succurritis urbī

---

**325. Fuimus Trōes:** *we have been Trojans* (in the
past, but no longer are). **326. Argōs:** i.e., to Greece.
**330. Portīs adsunt:** *are at the gates.* **331. Mycē-**
**nīs:** place whence. **332. angusta viārum:** literally,
*the narrows of the streets,* i.e., the narrow streets.
**335. caecō Mārte:** *in blind combat;* an example
of *metonymy.* **337. Erīnys:** one of the Furies.
**338. sublātus ad aethera:** *rising heavenward.*
**aethera:** Greek acc. **339. armīs:** abl. of re-
spect. **340. oblātī per lūnam:** *borne to me*
*through the moonlight.* **341–342. Coroebus Myg-**

**donidēs:** *Coroebus, son of Mygdon;* ally of Priam
and suitor of Cassandra. **345. spōnsae:** *of his*
*betrothed,* i.e., of Cassandra. **346. audierit:** sub-
junctive in a relative causal clause. **347. audēre**
**in proelia:** *were bold for battle.* **348. incipiō super**
**hīs:** *I begin, besides, in these words.* **349. pectora:**
voc., in apposition with **juvenēs. 349–350. sī . . .**
**sequī:** *if it is your fixed desire to follow me, daring*
*the utmost dangers.* With **vōbīs** supply **est.**
**audentem:** modifies **mē** understood as object of
**sequī. rēbus:** *for our interests.* **352. quibus:** *by*

incēnsae;  moriāmur et in media arma ruāmus.

Ūna salūs victīs nūllam spērāre salūtem.'

Sīc animīs juvenum furor additus.  Inde lupī ceu 355

raptōrēs ātrā in nebulā, quōs improba ventris

exēgit caecōs rabiēs catulīque relictī

faucibus exspectant siccīs, per tēla, per hostīs

vādimus haud dubiam in mortem, mediaeque tenē-

   mus

urbis iter; nox ātra cavā circumvolat umbrā. 360

Quis clādem illīus noctis, quis fūnera fandō

explicet, aut possit lacrimīs aequāre labōrēs?

Urbs antīqua ruit multōs domināta per annōs;

plūrima perque viās sternuntur inertia passim

corpora perque domōs et rēligiōsa deōrum 365

līmina.  Nec sōlī poenās dant sanguine Teucrī:

quondam etiam victīs redit in praecordia virtūs,

victōrēsque cadunt Danaī; crūdēlis ubīque

lūctus, ubīque pavor, et plūrima mortis imāgō.

**QUESTIONS ON 298–369.** 1. With whom did Aeneas live in Troy?
2. With what sort of catastrophe does Aeneas compare the burn-
ing of Troy?  3. What objects did Panthus entrust to Aeneas?
4. What hope of safety did Aeneas hold out to his band of fol-
lowers?  5. With what does Aeneas compare his band as they
go forth?  6. Did the Greeks lose any men in the street fighting
at Troy?

*Aeneas and his companions put on Greek armor.*

  "Prīmus sē, Danaum magnā comitante catervā, 370

Androgeōs offert nōbīs, socia agmina crēdēns,

īnscius, atque ultrō verbīs compellat amīcīs:

'Festīnāte, virī.  Nam quae tam sēra morātur

sēgnitiēs?  Aliī rapiunt incēnsa feruntque

---

**Margin glosses (right column):**

**morior** die, perish

**lupus** wolf; *ceu as, just as

**raptor** plunderer; **nebula** cloud; pack; **improbus** evil, cruel; **venter** stomach; hunger **exigō** drive forth; **rabiēs** madness; **catulus** whelp
*faux throat, jaws; *siccus dry, thirsty
*vādō go, advance, rush; **dubius** doubtful, uncertain

**circumvolō** hover around

**clādēs** havoc; **fūnus** death

**explicō** unfold

**dominor** rule, hold sway

**iners** lifeless; cf. *inertia inactivity; *passim everywhere
**rēligiōsus** holy, sacred

**quondam** sometimes, at times; **praecordia** heart, breast
**ubīque** everywhere
**ubīque** everywhere; **pavor** terror, fear; **imāgō** form

**caterva** crowd, band

**īnscius** unwitting; **verbum** word; **compellō** address
**festīnō** hasten, hurry; *sērus late
**sēgnitiēs** sloth; cf. *sēgnis slow, sluggish

---

**Footnotes (bottom):**

*whose aid;* abl. of means.  **urbī:** dat. with the compound verb **succurritis.**  **353. moriāmur . . . ruāmus:** *let us die and let us rush into the midst of the battle;* an example of *hysteron proteron;* see App. 22, 10.  **354. salūs victīs:** supply **est. 355. animīs:** dat. with **additus.  356. raptōrēs:** practically an adj., *plundering, ravenous.* **359–360. mediaeque urbis iter:** *our way through the middle of the city.* **361. fūnera fandō:** note the *alliteration.* **fandō:** *in speech* (by speaking). **362. explicet, possit:** potential subjunctives. **365. corpora:** i.e., of the Trojans. **367. quondam:** *at times.* **369. lūctus:** supply **est. pavōr:** note the long o here, for metrical reasons. **plūrima imāgō:** *many a form.*

**371. Androgeōs:** a Greek who supposed Aeneas and his band were also Greeks.  **socia agmina:** (us to be) *allied forces.* **373. morātur:** under-

***celsus** high, lofty

***extemplō** at once; **respōnsum** reply
**delābor** slip, fall

**\*\*retrō** back; **reprimō** hold back, check
**imprōvīsus** unexpected; **sentis** brier; **\*\*anguis** snake
**\*\*humus** ground, earth; **\*nītor** lean on; force one's way; **\*trepidus** trembling, agitated; **refugiō** fall back
**attollō** raise, rear; **\*caerul(e)us** sea-green; **\*\*tumeō** swell
**\*secus** otherwise; **vīsus** sight; **tremefaciō** cause to tremble
**inruō** rush in; **\*dēnsus** crowded

**\*\*passim** everywhere, all about; **\*\*formīdō** fear, panic
**adspīrō** breathe on; favor

**\*exsultō** leap up; exult

**\*\*clipeus** shield, buckler; **īnsigne** mark, device
**\*\*aptō** fit; **\*\*requīrō** ask

**comāns** plumed, crested

**\*\*galea** helmet; **\*\*clipeus** shield; **īnsigne** mark, adornment; **\*\*decōrus** beautiful
***induō** put on, don; **accommodō** fit, gird; **\*\*ēnsis** sword

***spolium** booty, plunder; **armō** arm, equip
**\*\*vādō** advance; **immisceō** intermingle
**congredior** meet, encounter

**cōnserō** engage in

**diffugiō** flee

***formīdō** terror, panic

**scandō** climb, mount; **alvus** belly, body

---

375 Pergama: vōs celsīs nunc prīmum ā nāvibus ītis?

Dīxit, et extemplō (neque enim respōnsa dabantur
fīda satis) sensit mediōs dēlāpsus in hostīs.

Obstipuit, retrōque pedem cum vōce repressit,
imprōvīsum asprīs velutī quī sentibus anguem
380 pressit humī nītēns, trepidusque repente refūgit
attollentem īrās et caerula colla tumentem;
haud secus Androgeōs vīsū tremefactus abībat.

Inruimus, dēnsīs et circumfundimur armīs,
ignārōsque locī passim et formīdine captōs
385 sternimus; adspīrat prīmō fortūna labōrī.

Atque hīc successū exsultāns animīsque Coroebus
'Ō sociī, quā prīma,' inquit, 'fortūna salūtis
mōnstrat iter quāque ostendit sē dextra, sequāmur;
mūtēmus clipeōs Danaumque īnsignia nōbīs
390 aptēmus. Dolus an virtūs, quis in hoste requīrat?
Arma dabunt ipsī.' Sīc fātus, deinde comantem
Androgeī galeam clipeīque īnsigne decōrum
induitur, laterīque Argīvum accommodat ēnsem.
Hoc Rīpheus, hoc ipse Dymās omnisque juventūs
395 laeta facit; spoliīs sē quisque recentibus armat.
Vādimus immixtī Danaīs, haud nūmine nostrō,
multaque per caecam congressī proelia noctem
cōnserimus, multōs Danaum dēmittimus Orcō;
diffugiunt aliī ad nāvīs et lītora cursū
400 fīda petunt; pars ingentem formīdine turpī
scandunt rūrsus equum et nōtā conduntur in alvō.

---

stand **vōs** as object. **377. sēnsit ... hostīs:** a Greek construction, = **sēnsit mediōs sē dēlāpsum esse in hostīs. 381. attollentem:** acc. in agreement with **eum** (i.e., **anguem**) understood. **colla:** acc. of respect. Note the poetic plural. **383. circumfundimur:** literally, *we are poured around,* i.e., we encircle them. **385. labōrī:** dat. with the compound verb **adspīrat. 389. īnsignia:** i.e., decorations on the armor. **390. Dolus an virtūs:** supply **sit. requīrat:** potential subjunctive.

**391. deinde:** pronounce as two syllables; an example of *synizesis;* see App. 32. **393. induitur:** *puts on;* see App. 140, *b.* **394. hoc:** here a long syllable as if spelled **hocc. 396. immixtī Danaīs:** *mingling with the Greeks.* **haud nūmine nostrō:** *not under* (the protection of) *our own gods.* **397. per caecam noctem:** i.e., through the dark night. **398. Orcō:** dat. of direction; **Orcus** may refer either to the god of the underworld or to the underworld itself.

QUESTIONS ON **370–401**. 1. Who was the first Greek encountered by Aeneas's band? 2. How did Androgeos discover that Aeneas and his band were not Greeks? 3. What scheme did Coroebus propose? What had given him the idea? 4. How successful was Coroebus's scheme at first? 5. What did some of the Greeks do in their terror? What did others do?

*Aeneas and his party vainly try to rescue Cassandra. They go to Priam's palace.*

"Heu! Nihil invītīs fās quemquam fīdere dīvīs!
Ecce trahēbātur passīs Priamēia virgō
crīnibus ā templō Cassandra adytīsque Minervae,
ad caelum tendēns ārdentia lūmina frūstrā,    405
lūmina, nam tenerās arcēbant vincula palmās.
Nōn tulit hanc speciem furiātā mente Coroebus,
et sēsē medium injēcit peritūrus in agmen;
cōnsequimur cūnctī, et dēnsīs incurrimus armīs.
Hīc prīmum ex altō dēlūbrī culmine tēlīs    410
nostrōrum obruimur, oriturque miserrima caedēs
armōrum faciē et Grajārum errōre jubārum;
tum Danaī gemitū atque ēreptae virginis īrā
undique collēctī invādunt, ācerrimus Ājāx
et geminī Atrīdae Dolopumque exercitus omnis,    415
adversī ruptō ceu quondam turbine ventī
cōnflīgunt, Zephyrusque Notusque et laetus Eōīs
Eurus equīs; strīdunt silvae, saevitque tridentī
spūmeus atque īmō Nēreus ciet aequora fundō.
Illī etiam, sī quōs obscūrā nocte per umbram    420
fūdimus īnsidiīs tōtāque agitāvimus urbe,
appārent; prīmī clipeōs mentītaque tēla
agnōscunt, atque ōra sonō discordia signant.
Īlicet obruimur numerō, prīmusque Coroebus

***heu alas!; fīdō rely on

tener tender, frail
furiō madden, make frenzied

**dēnsus thick, compact; incurrō rush into
***dēlūbrum shrine, temple; **culmen top, roof
obruō overpower, overwhelm

***faciēs appearance; juba crest

invādō attack

**ceu just as

**saeviō rage

spūmeus foam-covered; **cieō stir up; fundus bottom, depth
***obscūrus dark, dim

*agitō drive, pursue

**appāreō appear; mentītus deceitful, lying
sonus sound; discors discordant, different; *signō mark, note; cf. *dēsignō describe
īlicet immediately; obruō overwhelm, crush

**402.** fās: supply est. dīvīs: dat. with fīdere.
**405.** lūmina: *eyes.* Note the repetition of lūmina in line 406. Cassandra could raise only her eyes, not her hands. **409.** armīs: abl. of means. **415.** geminī Atrīdae: i.e., Agamemnon and Menelaus, sons of Atreus. **416.** ruptō turbine: *when a storm bursts.* **417–418.** laetus Eōīs equīs: *re-*

*joicing in his Eastern steeds.* Note the *alliteration* by means of the s, reproducing the sounds of the storm. **419.** Nēreus: a sea-god. fundō: *place whence.* **420.** Illī: i.e., the Greeks. **421.** īnsidiīs: *by our stratagem* (of putting on Greek armor). **423.** ōra ... signant: *note our speech differing in sound.* The Greeks and the Trojans spoke dif-

**armipotēns** powerful in arms

**prōcumbō** fall, sink

**servāns** heedful, observant


**cōnfīgō** pierce

**īnfula** fillet, headband

***cinis** ashes

****testor** call to witness

***vicis** change, chance

**dīvellō** tear apart

***aevum** age, old age

425 Pēnelēī dextrā dīvae armipotentis ad āram
prōcumbit; cadit et Rīpheus, jūstissimus ūnus
quī fuit in Teucrīs et servantissimus aequī
(dīs aliter vīsum); pereunt Hypanisque Dymāsque,
cōnfīxī ā sociīs, nec tē tua plūrima, Panthū,
430 lābentem pietās nec Apollinis īnfula tēxit.
Īliacī cinerēs et flamma extrēma meōrum,
testor in occāsū vestrō nec tēla nec ūllās
vītāvisse vicēs Danaum et, sī fāta fuissent
ut caderem, meruisse manū. Dīvellimur inde,
435 Īphitus et Peliās mēcum, quōrum Īphitus aevō
jam gravior, Peliās et vulnere tardus Ulixī;
prōtinus ad sēdīs Priamī clāmōre vocātī.

QUESTIONS ON **402–437.** 1. What occurrence caused Coroebus
to forget his disguise? 2. By whom were Aeneas and his band
now attacked? 3. Who of Aeneas's band was first to fall?
4. Why does Aeneas seem to think that Ripheus's death was es-
pecially unjust? 5. What two companions did Aeneas now have
left? 6. What was the condition of each of these companions?
7. Where did Aeneas now go?

### The Greeks led by Pyrrhus attack Priam's palace.

***nusquam** nowhere


**indomitus** unrestrained

**testūdō** testudo, *military forma-
tion with overlapping shields*
***pariēs** wall; **scālae** scaling
ladder; ***postis** doorpost
****nītor** struggle upward; ****gra-
dus** step
**prēnsō** seize, grasp

"Hīc vērō ingentem pugnam, ceu cētera nusquam
bella forent, nūllī tōtā morerentur in urbe,
440 sīc Mārtem indomitum Danaōsque ad tēcta ruentīs
cernimus obsessumque āctā testūdine līmen.
Haerent parietibus scālae, postīsque sub ipsōs
nītuntur gradibus, clipeōsque ad tēla sinistrīs
prōtēctī objiciunt, prēnsant fastīgia dextrīs.
445 Dardanidae contrā turrīs ac tōta domōrum

---

ferent dialects. **ōra:** *words uttered*, by *metonymy.*
**425. dīvae armipotentis:** i.e., Minerva. **427. ser-
vantissimus aequī:** *most observant of justice.*
**428. dīs aliter vīsum:** supply **est;** *it seemed
otherwise to the gods,* i.e., although Ripheus was a
lover of justice, he did not seem to receive justice
from the gods. This phrase has become pro-
verbial. **430. Apollinis īnfula:** i.e., the fact that
Panthus was a priest of Apollo did not save him.
**431. cinerēs, flamma:** vocatives. **433. vītāvisse:**
understand **mē** as the subject. **vicēs Danaum:**

the hazardous chances at the hands of the Greeks.
**433–434. sī fāta ... manū:** *if it had been fated
that I should fall, I deserved to do so by my deeds.*
**caderem:** subjunctive in a substantive volitive
clause, depending on **fāta. 436. vulnere Ulixī:**
*because of a wound received from Ulysses.* For
Work Unit IX, based on lines 268–437 of Book II,
see p. 264.
   **438. pugnam:** object of **cernimus** in line 441.
**439. nūllī:** i.e., **ceu nūllī. 442. parietibus:** pro-
nounce as if spelled **parjetibus. 443. gradibus:**

culmina convellunt; hīs sē, quandō ultima cernunt,

extrēmā jam in morte parant dēfendere tēlīs;

aurātāsque trabēs, veterum decora illa parentum,

dēvolvunt; aliī strictīs mūcrōnibus īmās

obsēdēre forīs; hās servant agmine dēnsō.

Īnstaurātī animī rēgis succurrere tēctīs

auxiliōque levāre virōs vimque addere victīs.

"Līmen erat caecaeque forēs, et pervius ūsus

tēctōrum inter sē Priamī, postēsque relictī

ā tergō, īnfēlīx quā sē, dum rēgna manēbant,

saepius Andromachē ferre incomitāta solēbat

ad socerōs, et avō puerum Astyanacta trahēbat.

Ēvādō ad summī fastīgia culminis, unde

tēla manū miserī jactābant inrita Teucrī.

Turrim in praecipitī stantem summīsque sub astra

ēductam tēctīs, unde omnis Trōja vidērī

et Danaum solitae nāvēs et Achāica castra,

adgressī ferrō circum, quā summa labantīs

jūnctūrās tabulāta dabant, convellimus altīs

sēdibus impulimusque; ea lāpsa repente ruīnam

cum sonitū trahit, et Danaum super agmina lātē

incidit.  Ast aliī subeunt, nec saxa nec ūllum

tēlōrum intereā cessat genus.

"Vēstibulum ante ipsum prīmōque in līmine

Pyrrhus

exsultat, tēlīs et lūce coruscus aēnā;

quālis ubi in lūcem coluber, mala grāmina pāstus,

frīgida sub terrā tumidum quem brūma tegēbat,

---

***culmen top; roof; convellō tear away; **quandō when

aurātus gilded, gold-covered

dēvolvō roll down; ***stringō draw; **mūcrō point, sword

450 ***foris door; ***dēnsus thick, massed

īnstaurō renew, revive

pervius affording a passage

**postis doorpost; door

455

incomitātus unaccompanied; ***soleō be accustomed

*socer father-in-law; *avus grandfather

*ēvādō go forth

inritus useless, unavailing

460 **praeceps steep edge; **astrum star

ēdūcō build up

labō give way, yield

jūnctūra joint; tabulātum floor, story; convellō tear away

465

ast but

**cessō cease

vēstibulum entry

470 **exsultō leap up, exult

coluber snake; *grāmen grass, herb

frīgidus cold; tumidus swollen; brūma winter season

---

up the rungs (of the ladders); abl. of route.
**446. ultima:** *their last* (moments).  **451. Īnstau-
rātī . . . succurrere:** (our) *desires are renewed to give
help.*  **succurrere:** infin. depending on **animī;** so
**levāre** and **addere** in line 452; a poetic construc-
tion.
  **453–454. pervius . . . Priamī:** *a private passage
between Priam's dwellings.*  **456. Andromachē:**
wife of Hector and mother of Astyanax, men-
tioned in line 457.  **457. socerōs:** *parents-in-law,*
i.e., Priam and Hecuba.  **avō:** dat. of direction.

Astyanacta: Greek acc.  **460. Turrim:** object of
**adgressī** in line 463; cf. **convellimus** in line 464
and **impulimus** in line 465.  **461. tēctīs:** place
whence.  Trōja vidērī: understand solita est.
**462. Achāica:** *Achaean,* i.e., Greek.  **463. ferrō:**
*with iron* (tools).  **464. dabant:** *offered.*  **465. ea:**
i.e., the tower.  **467. aliī:** i.e., other Greeks.
  **469. Pyrrhus:** another name for Neoptolemus,
son of Achilles.  **471. in lūcem:** construe with
**convolvit** in line 474.  **mala grāmina:** *poisonous
herbs.*

**\*\*exuviae** skin; **nitidus** shining, sleek; **\*\*juventa** youth
**lūbricus** slippery, slimy; **con-volvō** roll, coil
**\*\*arduus** high; **\*\*lingua** tongue; **\*\*micō** dart, quiver, flash; **trisulcus** three-forked
**agitātor** driver
**armiger** armor-bearer; **\*\*pūbēs** youth

**bipennis** two-bladed ax

**perrumpō** break through; **\*\*\*postis** doorpost; door; **cardō** hinge; socket; **\*\*\*vellō** tear away
**aerātus** bronze-covered; **ex-cīdō** cut away; **cavō** hollow out; cave in
**fenestra** window, opening
**\*\*\*appāreō** appear; **ātrium** great hall; **patēscō** lie open
**penetrālia** inner rooms; cf. **\*\*penetrālis** inner, innermost

**plangor** wailing; **\*aedēs** house

**fēmineus** women's; **\*ululō** resound; **\*\*\*feriō** strike
**pavidus** frightened; cf. **\*\*paveō** be frightened
**\*\*\*amplector** embrace; **\*\*\*ōs-culum** kiss
**claustrum** bar, bolt

**sufferō** resist; **labō** give way; **ariēs** battering-ram
**jānua** door; **ēmoveō** remove; **prōcumbō** fall forward
**trucīdō** slay

**\*immittō** let in; **compleō** fill

**spūmeus** foaming; **\*amnis** river

**ēvincō** overcome; **\*\*gurges** swirling waters, flood
**cumulus** mass, pile

**\*stabulum** stable, stall; **\*\*ar-mentum** herd

**nurus** daughter-in-law

nunc, positīs novus exuviīs nitidusque juventā,
lūbrica convolvit sublātō pectore terga,
475 arduus ad sōlem, et linguīs micat ōre trisulcīs.
Ūnā ingēns Periphās et equōrum agitātor Achillis,
armiger Automedōn, ūnā omnis Scȳria pūbēs
succēdunt tēctō, et flammās ad culmina jactant.
Ipse inter prīmōs correptā dūra bipennī
480 līmina perrumpit, postīsque ā cardine vellit
aerātōs; jamque, excīsā trabe, firma cavāvit
rōbora, et ingentem lātō dedit ōre fenestram.

Appāret domus intus et ātria longa patēscunt,
appārent Priamī et veterum penetrālia rēgum,
485 armātōsque vident stantīs in līmine prīmō.
"At domus interior gemitū miserōque tumultū
miscētur, penitusque cavae plangōribus aedēs
fēmineīs ululant; ferit aurea sīdera clāmor.
Tum pavidae tēctīs mātrēs ingentibus errant,
490 amplexaeque tenent postīs, atque ōscula fīgunt.
Īnstat vī patriā Pyrrhus. Nec claustra nec ipsī
custōdēs sufferre valent; labat ariete crēbrō
jānua, et ēmōtī prōcumbunt cardine postēs.
Fit via vī; rumpunt aditūs prīmōsque trucīdant
495 immissī Danaī, et lātē loca mīlite complent:
nōn sīc, aggeribus ruptīs cum spūmeüs amnis
exiit oppositāsque ēvīcit gurgite mōlīs,
fertur in arva furēns cumulō, campōsque per omnīs
cum stabulīs armenta trahit. Vīdī ipse furentem
500 caede Neoptolemum, geminōsque in līmine Atrīdās,
vīdī Hecubam, centumque nurūs, Priamumque per
ārās

**473. positīs exuviīs:** *after shedding its skin.* **475. ōre:** place where. **477. Scȳria pūbēs:** Pyrrhus had been brought up in the island of Scyros. **478. tēctō:** dat. of direction. **479. Ipse:** i.e., Pyrrhus. **480. līmina:** *doors,* by *metonymy.* **482. dedit:** i.e., made. **485. vident:** understand **Danaī** as the subject.

**489. tēctīs:** place where. **492. ariete crēbrō:** *with frequent blows of the battering-ram;* pronounce **ariete** as if spelled **arjete. 493. cardine:** abl. of separation, depending on **ēmōtī. 501. Hecubam:** *Hecuba,* wife of King Priam. **nurūs:** Priam had fifty daughters and fifty daughters-in-law. **501–502. Priamumque . . . foedantem:** Pyrrhus's

sanguine foedantem quōs ipse sacrāverat ignīs.
Quīnquāgintā illī thalamī, spēs tanta nepōtum,
barbaricō postēs aurō spoliīsque superbī,
prōcubuēre; tenent Danaī, quā dēficit ignis.    505

**foedō** defile, pollute

**quīnquāgintā** fifty; *****thalamus** marriage chamber; ***nepōs** grandson
**barbaricus** foreign
505 **prōcumbō** fall

QUESTIONS ON **438–505.** 1. What methods were the Greeks using in their attack on Priam's palace? 2. What methods were the Trojans using in their defense of the palace? 3. For what purpose had Andromache frequently used the secret passage in Priam's palace? 4. What youthful Greek leader was prominent in the attack on the palace? To what does Aeneas compare him? 5. What were the women of the palace doing at this time? 6. What happened to the palace doors? 7. What happened to the guards inside the palace doors?

*Pyrrhus slays Priam at his very altar.*

"Forsitan et Priamī fuerint quae fāta requīrās.
Urbis utī captae cāsum convulsaque vīdit
līmina tēctōrum et medium in penetrālibus hostem,
arma diū senior dēsuēta trementibus aevō
circumdat nēquīquam umerīs, et inūtile ferrum      510
cingitur, ac dēnsōs fertur moritūrus in hostīs.
Aedibus in mediīs nūdōque sub aetheris axe
ingēns āra fuit jūxtāque veterrima laurus,
incumbēns ārae atque umbrā complexa Penātīs.
Hīc Hecuba et nātae nēquīquam altāria circum,    515
praecipitēs ātrā ceu tempestāte columbae,
condēnsae et dīvum amplexae simulācra sedēbant.

Ipsum autem sūmptīs Priamum juvenālibus armīs
ut vīdit, 'Quae mēns tam dīra, miserrime conjūnx,
impulit hīs cingī tēlīs, aut quō ruis?' inquit.      520
'Nōn tālī auxiliō nec dēfēnsōribus istīs
tempus eget; nōn, sī ipse meus nunc adforet
    Hector.

**forsitan** perhaps, perchance; ***requīrō** seek to learn, ask

**penetrālia** inner rooms; cf. ***penetrālis** inner
**senior** aged man; cf. *****senex** old; **dēsuētus** unused; cf. ****suēscō** become accustomed; ****aevum** old age
****nēquīquam** in vain; **inūtilis** useless
***morior** die, perish
****aedēs** house; **nūdus** bare, open; *****axis** axis; vault
*****jūxtā** near, near by; *****laurus** laurel tree
**incumbō** lie on, lean over; ***complector** embrace
**nāta** daughter; ***nēquīquam** in vain; *****altāria** altars
***praeceps** headlong; ***ceu** just as; **columba** dove
**condēnsus** huddled together; ***simulācrum** image; ***sedeō** sit
**juvenālis** youthful

***dīrus** dire, dreadful

**dēfēnsor** protector

****egeō** need; require

---

slaying of Priam at the altar is described in lines 526–553.
**506.** et: *also.* fuerint: subjunctive in indirect question depending on requīrās. requīrās: potential subjunctive. **507.** utī: *when.* **510.** circumdat umerīs: *he places around his shoulders.* umerīs:

dat. with the compound verb **circumdat. 511.** cingitur: *girds on.* **514.** ārae: dat. with the compound verb **incumbēns. 516.** praecipitēs: (driven) *headlong.* **517.** dīvum: divōrum. **520.** impulit: supply tē. cingī: *to gird yourself.* **521.** auxiliō, dēfēnsōribus: abl. with the verb eget. **522.** ad-

Hūc tandem concēde; haec āra tuēbitur omnīs,

**effor** speak

aut moriēre simul.' Sīc ōre effāta, recēpit

**longaevus** aged

525 ad sēsē et sacrā longaevum in sēde locāvit.

**ēlābor** slip out, escape

"Ecce autem ēlāpsus Pyrrhī dē caede Polītēs,

ūnus nātōrum Priamī, per tēla, per hostīs

**porticus** colonnade, corridor; **ātrium** atrium, great hall
**\*\*saucius** wounded; **\*īnfestus** hostile, threatening

porticibus longīs fugit, et vacua ātria lūstrat

saucius. Illum ārdēns īnfestō vulnere Pyrrhus

530 īnsequitur, jam jamque manū tenet et premit hastā.

**\*\*ēvādō** make one's way

Ut tandem ante oculōs ēvāsit et ōra parentum,

**concidō** fall, collapse

concidit, ac multō vītam cum sanguine fūdit.

**\*\*\*quamquam** although

Hīc Priamus, quamquam in mediā jam morte tenētur,

**abstineō** hold back

nōn tamen abstinuit nec vōcī īraeque pepercit.

**exclāmō** cry out; **ausum** daring deed

535 'At tibi prō scelere,' exclāmat, 'prō tālibus ausīs

dī, sī qua est caelō pietās quae tālia cūret,

**persolvō** pay in full; render; **grātēs** thanks, requital
**cōram** in person, with one's own eyes; **\*\*lētum** death

persolvant grātīs dignās, et praemia reddant

dēbita, quī nātī cōram mē cernere lētum

fēcistī, et patriōs foedāstī fūnere vultūs.

**\*\*serō** sow; beget; **mentior** falsely say

540 At nōn ille, satum quō tē mentīris, Achillēs

tālis in hoste fuit Priamō, sed jūra fidemque

**ērubēscō** blush for; respect; **exsanguis** bloodless, lifeless; **\*sepulcrum** tomb, burial

supplicis ērubuit, corpusque exsangue sepulcrō

reddidit Hectoreum, mēque in mea rēgna remīsit.'

**senior** aged man; cf. **\*\*senex** old; **imbellis** unwarlike, harmless; **\*ictus** stroke, blow; **conjiciō** hurl; **\*raucus** hoarse; ringing; **repellō** thrust back; **umbō** knob, boss
**\*\*\*ergō** therefore

Sīc fātus senior, tēlumque imbelle sine ictū

545 conjēcit, raucō quod prōtinus aere repulsum

et summō clipeī nēquīquam umbōne pependit.

Cui Pyrrhus: 'Referēs ergō haec et nūntius ībis

Pēlīdae genitōrī. Illī mea trīstia facta

**dēgener** base, degenerate; **nārrō** tell, report
**\*\*altāria** altar

dēgeneremque Neoptolemum nārrāre mementō;

550 nunc morere.' Hoc dīcēns, altāria ad ipsa trementem

---

foret: adesset. **524.** moriēre: i.e., moriēris, *you will perish.* recēpit: supply **Priamum** as object. **529.** vulnere: i.e., tēlō. **530.** jam jamque tenet: *all but grasps.* **536.** caelō: place where. cūret: subjunctive in a clause of characteristic. **537.** persolvant, reddant: optative subjunctives. **538–539.** quī mē cernere fēcistī: *who have made me behold;* a poetic construction. Prose would require fēcistī ut cernerem. **539.** foedāstī: foedā-

vistī. **540.** satum . . . mentīris: *from whom you falsely say you are sprung.* **541.** in hoste Priamō: *in the case of his enemy Priam.* **541–542.** jūra . . . ērubuit: *he respected the rights and the protection due to a suppliant.* Priam had come as a suppliant to Achilles, to ransom the dead body of his son Hector. **542.** sepulcrō: *for burial.* **545.** repulsum: supply est. **547.** Pyrrhus: supply some such verb as inquit. **548.** genitōrī: i.e., to

trāxit et in multō lāpsantem sanguine nātī,

implicuitque comam laevā, dextrāque coruscum

extulit ac laterī capulō tenus abdidit ēnsem.

Haec fīnis Priamī fātōrum, hic exitus illum

sorte tulit, Trōjam incēnsam et prōlāpsa videntem 555

Pergama, tot quondam populīs terrīsque superbum

rēgnātōrem Asiae. Jacet ingēns lītore truncus,

āvulsumque umerīs caput, et sine nōmine corpus.

**lāpsō** slip

***implicō** infold; grasp; **laeva** left hand; cf. ***laevus** left **capulus** handle, hilt; **tenus** up to, as far as; ***ēnsis** sword

**prōlābor** slip; sink; fall

***jaceō** lie; ***truncus** trunk; body **āvellō** tear away

QUESTIONS ON **506–558**. 1. What did Priam do when he saw the Greeks entering the palace? 2. Where were Hecuba and her daughters at this time? 3. With what argument did Hecuba try to restrain Priam? 4. What happened to Polites? 5. What comparison did Priam make between Achilles and Pyrrhus? 6. Where did Pyrrhus slay Priam? 7. What sort of burial was given to Priam's body?

*Aeneas sees Helen and is tempted to slay her.*

"At mē tum prīmum saevus circumstetit horror.

Obstipuī; subiit cārī genitōris imāgō,     560

ut rēgem aequaevum crūdēlī vulnere vīdī

vītam exhālantem; subiit dēserta Creūsa

et dīrepta domus et parvī cāsus Iūlī.

Respiciō, et quae sit mē circum cōpia lūstrō.

Dēseruēre omnēs dēfessī, et corpora saltū     565

ad terram mīsēre aut ignibus aegra dedēre.

Jamque adeō super ūnus eram, cum līmina Vestae

servantem et tacitam sēcrētā in sēde latentem

Tyndarida aspiciō; dant clāra incendia lūcem

errantī passimque oculōs per cūncta ferentī.     570

Illa sibi īnfestōs ēversa ob Pergama Teucrōs

**circumstō** surround; beset

**aequaevus** of equal age

**exhālō** breathe out

**respiciō** look back

**saltus** leap

***sēcernō** separate, secrete

**incendium** fire

***passim** everywhere, all about ***īnfestus** hostile; **ēvertō** overturn, destroy

---

Achilles, Pyrrhus's father. **552. coruscum:** understand **ēnsem. 553. laterī:** dat. of direction. **554. Haec:** supply **fuit.** Note that **fīnis** is here feminine. **illum.** i.e., Priam. **555. tulit:** *carried off.* **556. populīs terrīsque:** abl. of cause with **superbum** or dat. of reference with **rēgnātōrem. 557. lītore:** place where.

**560. subiit:** *came to my mind.* **genitōris:** *of my own father,* i.e., Anchises. **562. Creūsa:** daughter of Priam, wife of Aeneas, and mother of Iulus (Ascanius). **564. cōpia:** i.e., **cōpia mīlitum. 565–**

**566.** Aeneas's comrades had jumped either to the ground or into the flames. **Dēseruēre, mīsēre, dedēre: Dēseruērunt, mīsērunt, dedērunt. aegra** (corpora): i.e., weak from wounds and exhaustion. **567. super ūnus eram:** i.e., **ūnus supereram,** *I alone survived;* an example of *tmesis.* **569. Tyndarida:** Greek acc. Tyndaris is another name for Helen. **570. errantī:** modifies **mihi** understood; so **ferentī. 571. Illa:** i.e., Helen. **Teucrōs:** object of **praemetuēns** in line 573. **ēversa ob Pergama:** *on account of the overthrow of Troy.*

et poenās Danaum et dēsertī conjugis īrās

**praemetuō** dread

praemetuēns, Trōjae et patriae commūnis Erīnys,

**invīsus** hated, detested; cf.
 ***invideō look askance at
**exārdēscō** blaze up

abdiderat sēsē atque ārīs invīsa sedēbat.

575 Exārsēre ignēs animō; subit īra cadentem

**\*ulcīscor** avenge;  **\*\*scelerātus**
 guilty
**\*scīlicet** forsooth

ulcīscī patriam et scelerātās sūmere poenās.

'Scīlicet haec Spartam incolumis patriāsque My-
 cēnās

**\*pariō** bring forth;  secure;
 **\*triumphus** triumphal pro-
 cession
**conjugium** marriage; husband

aspiciet, partōque ībit rēgīna triumphō,

conjugiumque domumque, patrēs nātōsque vidē-
 bit,

**\*\*turba** throng, crowd;  ***co-
mitor** accompany;  **minister**
 attendant, servant
**\*occidō** fall;  die
**\*\*totiēns** so many times;  **sūdō**
 sweat
**memorābilis** glorious

580 Īliadum turbā et Phrygiīs comitāta ministrīs?

Occiderit ferrō Priamus?  Trōja ārserit ignī?

Dardanium totiēns sūdārit sanguine lītus?

**fēmineus** of a woman

Nōn ita; namque etsī nūllum memorābile nōmen

fēmineā in poenā est nec habet victōria laudem,

**\*exstinguō** put out,  quench;
 destroy;  **\*\*nefās** wrong; im-
 pious wretch
**expleō** fill up;  satisfy
**ultrīx** avenging;  **\*\*cinis** ashes;
 **satiō** sate, satisfy
**furiō** madden, make mad

585 exstīnxisse nefās tamen ēt sūmpsisse merentīs

laudābor poenās, animumque explēsse juvābit

ultrīcis flammae et cinerēs satiāsse meōrum.'

"Tālia jactābam et furiātā mente ferēbar,

cum mihi sē, nōn ante oculīs tam clāra, videndam

**pūrus** clear, bright;  **refulgeō**
 shine, gleam
 ***almus** dear, nurturing;  **cōn-
fiteor** confess, reveal
**caelicola** heavenly being

590 obtulit, et pūrā per noctem in lūce refulsit

alma parēns, cōnfessa deam quālisque vidērī

caelicolīs et quanta solet, dextrāque prehēnsum

**roseus** roseate; lovely;  **īnsuper**
 in addition
**indomitus** ungovernable;  **ex-
citō** arouse, stir up; cf. **\*con-
citō** stir up
**quōnam** whither

continuit, roseōque haec īnsuper addidit ōre:

'Nāte, quis indomitās tantus dolor excitat īrās?

595 Quid furis, aut quōnam nostrī tibi cūra recessit?

Nōn prius aspiciēs ubi fessum aetāte parentem

**linquō** leave

līqueris Anchīsēn, superet conjūnxne Creūsa

---

**572. conjugis:** i.e., of Menelaus.  **574. ārīs:**
abl. of place where.  **575. Exārsēre:** Exārsērunt.
**animō:** place where.  **575–576. subit īra ulcīscī:**
*the angry desire comes to me to avenge.*  **576.** ulcīscī:
infin. depending on īra; a poetic construction.
scelerātās . . . poenās: *to exact penalties for her
wickedness.*  **577–578.** Scīlicet haec aspiciet: *Will
she see, forsooth?*  **Spartam:** *Sparta,* home of
Helen and Menelaus.  **580.** turbā, ministrīs: abl.
of means with comitāta.  **581–582.** Occiderit,
ārserit, sūdārit: fut. perf. indicatives.  **583.** Nōn
ita: supply erit.  **585.** nefās: *abominable creature.*
**585–586.** merentīs poenās: *penalties from one
who deserves them.*  **586.** explēsse: explēvisse.
**587.** ultrīcis flammae: *with avenging flame;* gen.
used with explēsse.  satiāsse: satiāvisse.
   **591.** alma parēns: i.e., Venus.  cōnfessa deam:
*revealing herself as a goddess.*  **592.** caelicolīs: dat.
of agent with vidērī.  **594.** Nāte: voc.  **595.** nostrī
cūra: *concern for us.*  tibi: *I ask you;* dat. of
reference.  **597.** līqueris, superet: subjunctives in
indirect questions depending on aspiciēs.

Ascaniusque puer? Quōs omnīs undique Grajae
circum errant aciēs, et, nī mea cūra resistat,
jam flammae tulerint inimīcus et hauserit ēnsis. 600  **hauriō drain
Nōn tibi Tyndaridis faciēs invīsa Lacaenae
culpātusve Paris; dīvum inclēmentia, dīvum,   culpātus blameworthy; **in-
                   clēmentia mercilessness
hās ēvertit opēs sternitque ā culmine Trōjam.  ***ēvertō overturn, destroy
Aspice (namque omnem, quae nunc obducta tuentī obdūcō draw before
mortālīs hebetat vīsūs tibi et ūmida circum  605 hebetō blunt, dull, dim; **ūmi-
                   dus damp, moist
cālīgat, nūbem ēripiam; tū nē qua parentis  cālīgō send out a mist
jussa timē neu praeceptīs pārēre recūsā):   jussum command, behest; prae-
                   ceptum advice, precept
hīc, ubi disjectās mōlīs āvulsaque saxīs  āvellō tear away
saxa vidēs mixtōque undantem pulvere fūmum, undō rise in waves; ***pulvis
                   dust; *fūmus smoke
Neptūnus mūrōs magnōque ēmōta tridentī 610 ēmoveō move, upheave
fundāmenta quatit tōtamque ā sēdibus urbem fundāmentum  foundation,
                   base; *quatiō shake
ēruit; hīc Jūnō Scaeās saevissima portās  ēruō overthrow
prīma tenet, sociumque furēns ā nāvibus agmen
ferrō accīncta vocat.          accingō gird; arm
Jam summās arcīs Trītōnia, respice, Pallas 615 respiciō look back, look
īnsēdit, nimbō effulgēns et Gorgone saeva;  īnsīdō sit upon, occupy; efful-
                   geō gleam
ipse pater Danaīs animōs vīrīsque secundās
sufficit, ipse deōs in Dardana suscitat arma. sufficiō supply; suscitō arouse
Ēripe, nāte, fugam, fīnemque impōne labōrī. impōnō place, put
Nusquam aberō, et tūtum patriō tē līmine sistam.' 620 **nusquam nowhere; absum
Dīxerat, et spissīs noctis sē condidit umbrīs.  be absent; **sistō cause to
                   stand; set, place
Appārent dīrae faciēs inimīcaque Trōjae  spissus thick, dense
nūmina magna deum.

---

**598. Quōs omnīs:** acc. with **circum**. **601. tibi:**
*I tell you;* dat. of reference. **Lacaenae:** *Spartan.*
**602. dīvum inclēmentia, dīvum:** *the mercilessness
of the gods, aye, of the gods.* **604. omnem:** con-
strue with **nūbem** in line 606. **604–605. quae . . .
tibi:** *which now, drawn before you as you gaze,
dims mortal vision.* **tuentī:** construe with **tibi** in
line 605. **tibi:** dat. with the compound **obducta.**
**605–606. et . . . cālīgat:** *and moistly surrounds*
(you) *with darkness.* **606–607. nē timē:** neg.
imperat. **parentis:** i.e., of Venus, the speaker.
**608. saxīs:** abl. of separation, depending on
**āvulsa. 610. Neptūnus:** with Apollo's help, Nep-
tune had built the walls of Troy for Laomedon,

Priam's father; but, having been refused pay-
ment, he was now destroying them. **612. Jūnō:**
Juno's hatred for Troy and the Trojans was deep
and lasting; some of the reasons for this hatred
are given in Book I, lines 26–28. **Scaeās portās:**
*Scaean gate,* the chief gate of Troy. **613. socium
agmen:** i.e., the Greeks, with whom Juno was
allied. **616. Gorgone:** the Gorgon was a mon-
ster with snaky locks, whose head was fixed on
the shield of Athena. **617. pater:** i.e., Jupiter.
**618. in:** *against.* **620. līmine:** place where.
**622. Appārent:** *appear* (as in a vision). For Work
Unit X, based on lines 438–623 of Book II, see
p. 265.

QUESTIONS ON **559–623**. 1. What caused Aeneas suddenly to think of the possible fate of his father? 2. How many companions had Aeneas at this time? 3. Whom did Aeneas happen to see hiding in Vesta's temple? 4. What feelings did she inspire in Aeneas? 5. Who rebuked Aeneas for such feelings? 6. What did Venus suggest that Aeneas should be doing? 7. Who did Venus say were responsible for Troy's downfall? 8. What share had Neptune in the destruction of Troy? Juno? Pallas Athena?

*Aeneas returns to his home and urges Anchises to flee.*

"Tum vērō omne mihī vīsum cōnsīdere in ignīs
625 Īlium, et ex īmō vertī Neptūnia Trōja;

ac velutī summīs antīquam in montibus ornum

cum ferrō accīsam crēbrīsque bipennibus īnstant

ēruere agricolae certātim: illa usque minātur,

et, tremefacta comam, concussō vertice nūtat,

630 vulneribus dōnec paulātim ēvicta suprēmum

congemuit, trāxitque jugīs āvulsa ruīnam.

Dēscendō, ac, dūcente deō, flammam inter et hostīs

expedior; dant tēla locum, flammaeque recēdunt.

"Atque ubi jam patriae perventum ad līmina sēdis

635 antīquāsque domōs, genitor, quem tollere in altōs

optābam prīmum montīs prīmumque petēbam,

abnegat excīsā vītam prōdūcere Trōjā

exsiliumque patī. 'Vōs ō, quibus integer aevī

sanguis,' ait, 'solidaeque suō stant rōbore vīrēs,

640 vōs agitāte fugam.

Mē sī caelicolae voluissent dūcere vītam,

hās mihi servāssent sēdīs. Satis ūna superque

vīdimus excidia et captae superāvimus urbī.

**Glossary (left margin):**

ornus ash tree

accīdō cut into, hew; bipennis two-edged ax

ēruō overthrow; agricola farmer; certātim zealously; ***minor threaten

tremefaciō cause to tremble; concutiō shake; nūtō nod; cf. **nūtus a nod

***dōnec until; ēvincō overcome

congemō groan

perveniō arrive, come

abnegō refuse; excīdō cut off, destroy; prōdūcō prolong

*exsilium exile; ***aevum age

*solidus firm

**agitō pursue; hasten

caelicola heavenly being, god

excidium destruction

---

**624.** vīsum: supply est. cōnsīdere in ignīs: *to sink into flames.* **625.** Neptūnia Trōja: Neptune had helped build Troy. **628.** illa: i.e., the ash tree. **630–631.** suprēmum congemuit: *it has groaned its last.* **631.** trāxit ruīnam: *it has fallen full length.* jugīs: abl. of separation with āvulsa. **632.** Dēscendō: i.e., from the top of the palace. dūcente deō: *under divine guidance,* an ablative absolute phrase. **633.** expedior: *I extricate myself.* dant locum: *make way.* **634.** perventum: supply est: *when I reached.*

**636.** prīmum . . . prīmum: the repetition suggests the dutifulness of Aeneas toward Anchises. **638–639.** quibus integer aevī sanguis: supply est: *whose blood is unspoiled by age.* aevī: gen. with the adjective integer; see App. 94. **642–643.** Satis . . . urbī: *enough and more than enough is it that I have seen one destruction and have survived one capture of the city.* urbī: dat. with superāvimus, which here = superfuimus. Once already Troy had been captured and sacked, by Hercules, when Laomedon broke his promise to

Sīc, ō sīc positum adfātī discēdite corpus.

Ipse manū mortem inveniam; miserēbitur hostis 645

exuviāsque petet.  Facilis jactūra sepulcrī.

Jam prīdem invīsus dīvīs et inūtilis annōs

dēmoror, ex quō mē dīvum pater atque hominum rēx

fulminis adflāvit ventīs et contigit ignī.'

Tālia perstābat memorāns fīxusque manēbat.    650

Nōs contrā effūsī lacrimīs, conjūnxque Creūsa

Ascaniusque omnisque domus, nē vertere sēcum

cūncta pater fātōque urgentī incumbere vellet.

Abnegat, inceptōque et sēdibus haeret in īsdem.

Rūrsus in arma feror, mortemque miserrimus optō; 655

nam quod cōnsilium aut quae jam fortūna dabātur?

'Mēne efferre pedem, genitor, tē posse relictō

spērāstī, tantumque nefās patriō excidit ōre?

Sī nihil ex tantā superīs placet urbe relinquī,

et sedet hoc animō peritūraeque addere Trōjae    660

tēque tuōsque juvat, patet istī jānua lētō,

jamque aderit multō Priamī dē sanguine Pyrrhus,

nātum ante ōra patris, patrem quī obtruncat ad

    ārās.

Hoc erat, alma parēns, quod mē per tēla, per ignīs

ēripis, ut mediīs hostem in penetrālibus utque    665

Ascanium patremque meum jūxtāque Creūsam

alterum in alterius mactātōs sanguine cernam?

Arma, virī, ferte arma; vocat lūx ultima victōs.

---

**Glosses (right margin):**

discēdō depart

***misereor pity

***exuviae spoils; jactūra loss; **sepulcrum burial

**prīdem long since; inūtilis useless

dēmoror delay, keep waiting

**fulmen thunderbolt, lightning; adflō blow on, blast; cf. ***flō blow

perstō persist, continue

**urgeō press, pursue

abnegō refuse; inceptum purpose

***nefās impiety; excidō fall (from)

***superī gods above

jānua door; ***lētum death, destruction

obtruncō slay, kill

**jūxtā near by

**mactō slaughter

---

give him his daughter Hesione in marriage. **644. positum adfātī corpus:** *having addressed my laid-out body,* i.e., after thrice saying *valē* to my body. Anchises represents himself as already dead. **647–648. Jam prīdem annōs dēmoror:** *for long have I delayed the years,* i.e., I have already lived too long. **648. ex quō:** supply *tempore: since the time when.* **649. adflāvit:** supply **mihi.** Jupiter had struck Anchises with lightning for boasting of his marriage with Venus. **651. effūsī:** supply **sumus;** *we were dissolved.* **652–653. nē ... vellet:** (*begging) my father not to be willing to destroy everything along with himself and to add his weight to our crushing doom.* **vellet:** subjunctive

in a substantive volitive clause depending on the idea of begging implied in **effūsī (sumus),** line 251. **655. feror:** *I rush.* **657. tē relictō:** *leaving you behind.* **658. spērāstī:** spērāvistī. **tantumque ... ōre:** *and did such a horrible thought fall from a father's lips?* **660. (sī) sedet hoc animō:** *if this decision remains fixed in your mind.* **661. juvat:** supply **tē. 662. dē:** *fresh from.* **663. patris, patrem:** i.e., Priam. Note that in **patris** the first syllable is short, but in **patrem** it is long; see App. 45, a. **664. Hoc erat quod:** *Was this the reason why.* **parēns:** i.e., Venus. **667. alterum ... sanguine:** *slaughtered in each other's blood.* **668. lūx:** i.e., **diēs.**

**sinō** permit, allow; **īnstaurō** renew; **revīsō** visit again
*hodiē this day, today; **inultus** unavenged

Reddite mē Danaīs; sinite īnstaurāta revīsam
670 proelia. Numquam omnēs hodiē moriēmur inultī.'

QUESTIONS ON **624–670**. 1. Where was Aeneas when Venus appeared to him? 2. Where did he now go? 3. What reason did Anchises give for refusing to flee with Aeneas? 4. What did Anchises urge Aeneas and others to do? 5. On what occasion had Anchises previously witnessed a destruction of Troy? 6. Who joined Aeneas in urging Anchises to flee? 7. What did Aeneas decide to do when Anchises positively refused to leave the house?

*Anchises finally agrees to accompany Aeneas.*

sinistra left hand
***aptō fit

"Hinc ferrō accingor rūrsus, clipeōque sinistram
īnsertābam aptāns, mēque extrā tēcta ferēbam.
Ecce autem complexa pedēs in līmine conjūnx
haerēbat, parvumque patrī tendēbat Iūlum:
675 'Sī peritūrus abīs, et nōs rape in omnia tēcum;

***sīn but if

sīn aliquam expertus sūmptīs spem pōnis in armīs,

tūtor protect, guard

hanc prīmum tūtāre domum. Cui parvus Iūlus,
cui pater et conjūnx quondam tua dicta relinquor?'

vōciferor scream, cry out; **repleō** fill
*subitus sudden; ***mōnstrum portent

"Tālia vōciferāns, gemitū tēctum omne replēbat,
680 cum subitum dictūque oritur mīrābile mōnstrum;
namque manūs inter maestōrumque ōra parentum
ecce levis summō dē vertice vīsus Iūlī

apex point; tāctus touch; **innoxius** harmless; **mollis** soft
lambō lick
pavidus frightened; cf. ***paveō** be afraid; **trepidō** hurry;
***crīnis hair; **flagrō** blaze
restinguō extinguish; **fōns** spring; water

fundere lūmen apex, tāctūque innoxia mollīs
lambere flamma comās et circum tempora pāscī.
685 Nōs pavidī trepidāre metū, crīnemque flagrantem
excutere, et sānctōs restinguere fontibus ignīs.
At pater Anchīsēs oculōs ad sīdera laetus
extulit, et caelō palmās cum vōce tetendit:

**flectō bend, turn

'Juppiter omnipotēns, precibus sī flecteris ullīs,

**tantum only

690 aspice nōs hoc tantum, et, sī pietāte merēmur,

firmō strengthen, confirm

dā deinde auxilium, pater, atque haec ōmina firmā.'

senior old man; cf. ***senex old; **subitus sudden; fragor crash

"Vix ea fātus erat senior, subitōque fragōre

---

**671. accingor:** *I gird myself.* **674. patrī:** i.e., to Aeneas. **675. et ... omnia:** *take us too into all the dangers.* **677. tūtāre:** imperat. sing. **678. conjūnx tua dicta:** *called your wife.*
**680. dictū mīrābile:** *wonderful to relate.* **dictū:** supine in ū. **681. manūs inter:** inter manūs.

**682. levis:** modifying **apex. vīsus:** supply **est. 683. tāctū innoxia:** *harmless in touch.* **tāctū:** supine in ū. **685–686. trepidāre, excutere, restinguere:** historical infinitives. **fontibus:** i.e., **aquā. 688. caeiō:** dat. of direction. **690. hoc tantum:** *only this once.*

intonuit laevum, et dē caelō lāpsa per umbrās
stella facem dūcēns multā cum lūce cucurrit.
Illam summa super lābentem culmina tēctī                    695
signantemque viās clāram sē condere silvā
cernimus Īdaeā; tum longō līmite sulcus
dat lūcem, et lātē circum loca sulpure fūmant.
Hīc vērō victus genitor sē tollit ad aurās,
adfāturque deōs, et sānctum sīdus adōrat:
'Jam jam nūlla mora est; sequor et quā dūcitis
   adsum.
Dī patriī, servāte domum, servāte nepōtem;
vestrum hoc augurium, vestrōque in nūmine Trōja
   est.
Cēdō equidem nec, nāte, tibī comes īre recūsō.'

QUESTIONS ON **671–704**.  1. What alternative pleas did Creusa
make to Aeneas?  2. What omen appeared as Aeneas was about
to leave the house?  3. What did Aeneas and some of the others
try to do when the omen appeared?  4. What effect did the
omen have on Anchises?  5. What confirming omen induced
Anchises to accompany Aeneas?

*In the flight, Creusa disappears.*

"Dīxerat ille, et jam per moenia clārior ignis          705
audītur, propiusque aestūs incendia volvunt.
'Ergō age, cāre pater, cervīcī impōnere nostrae:
ipse subībō umerīs, nec mē labor iste gravābit.
Quō rēs cumque cadent, ūnum et commūne perī-
   clum,
ūna salūs ambōbus erit.  Mihi parvus Iūlus          710
sit comes, et longē servet vēstīgia conjūnx.
Vōs, famulī, quae dīcam animīs advertite vestrīs.

---

intonō  thunder

*stella  star;  **fax  torch, fiery
   tail

**signō  mark out, indicate;  cf.
   **dēsignō  describe
līmes  line, path;  **sulcus  fur-
   row
sulpur  brimstone;  fūmō  smoke,
   reek

700 adfor  speak to, address;  adōrō
   worship

**augurium  omen, augury

gravō  weigh down, burden

quōcumque  whithersoever

710 **ambō  both

*vēstīgium  footprint

**famulus  servant;  advertō
   turn to, heed

---

**693**. intonuit laevum: *it thundered on the left;*
a good omen.  **694**. facem dūcēns: *making a
trail of light.*  **695**. Illam: i.e., the meteor; sub-
ject of condere.  **696–697**. silvā Īdaeā: *in the
forests of Ida.*  Mt. Ida is near Troy to the south-
east.  **697**. longō limite sulcus: *the long-drawn
furrow.*  **699**. sē tollit ad aurās: *rises up.*  An-
chises is now convinced that the gods want him
to flee.  **702**. domum: *family.*  nepōtem: i.e.,
Ascanius.  **703**. vestrum: supply est.  vestrō in
nūmine: *under your divine protection.*
  **706**. aestūs: *waves of heat;*  acc. pl.  **707**. im-
pōnere: *place yourself;*  imperat. pass. with re-
flexive force.  **708**. umerīs: abl. of means.
**709**. Quō rēs cumque cadent: i.e., Quōcumque
rēs cadent; *tmesis;* see App. 22, 22.  **711**. sit,
servet: jussive subjunctives.  longē: *at a dis-
tance.*

**ēgredior** go forth; **vetustus** ancient
**\*\*\*jūxtā** close by; **cupressus** cypress tree

Est urbe ēgressīs tumulus templumque vetustum
dēsertae Cereris, jūxtāque antīqua cupressus,
715 relligiōne patrum multōs servāta per annōs;
hanc ex dīversō sēdem veniēmus in ūnam.
Tū, genitor, cape sacra manū patriōsque Penātīs;

**dīgredior** depart

mē bellō ē tantō dīgressum et caede recentī

**attrectō** touch

attrectāre nefās, dōnec mē flūmine vīvō

**abluō** wash, purify

720 abluerō.'

**subjiciō** place under; bow

Haec fātus, lātōs umerōs subjectaque colla

**\*\*fulvus** tawny; **īnsternō** spread, cover; **\*pellis** skin; **\*leō** lion

veste super fulvīque īnsternor pelle leōnis,
succēdōque onerī; dextrae sē parvus Iūlus
implicuit, sequiturque patrem nōn passibus aequīs;

**pōne** behind; **\*opācus** dark, shadowy
**\*\*\*dūdum** but now, recently; **injiciō** throw, cast
**\*\*\*glomerō** gather, mass

725 pōne subit conjūnx. Ferimur per opāca locōrum,
et mē, quem dūdum nōn ūlla injecta movēbant
tēla neque adversō glomerātī ex agmine Grajī,

**sonus** sound; **excitō** startle; cf. **\*\*concitō** stir up
**\*\*\*suspendō** hang up, suspend; make anxious; **pariter** equally

nunc omnēs terrent aurae, sonus excitat omnis
suspēnsum et pariter comitīque onerīque timentem.

**propinquō** draw near, approach

730 Jamque propinquābam portīs, omnemque vidēbar

**\*\*\*ēvādō** traverse

ēvāsisse viam, subitō cum crēber ad aurīs
vīsus adesse pedum sonitus, genitorque per umbram

**exclāmō** exclaim, shout; propinquō come near, approach

prōspiciēns, 'Nāte,' exclāmat, 'fuge, nāte; propinquant;

**\*\*\*micō** flash, gleam

ārdentīs clipeōs atque aera micantia cernō.'

**\*\*nescio** know not; **\*\*trepidus** agitated, alarmed
**cōnfundō** bewilder, confuse; **āvia** out-of-the-way places
**excēdō** depart (from)

735 Hīc mihi nesciō quod trepidō male nūmen amīcum
cōnfūsam ēripuit mentem; namque āvia cursū
dum sequor, et nōtā excēdō regiōne viārum,

---

713. urbe ēgressīs: *as you go out of the city.* ēgressīs: literally, *to those having gone out.* 716. ex dīversō: *from different directions.* The members of Aeneas's family were not to leave in one group, for fear of attracting the attention of the Greeks. 719. flūmine vīvō: *in a running stream.* 721–722. umerōs subjectaque colla super īnsternor: *I cover over my bowed shoulders and neck.* 723. succēdōque onerī: *and I take up the burden.* onerī: dat. with the compound verb succēdō. dextrae: dat. with the compound verb implicuit. 724. nōn passibus aequīs: *with unequal steps.* 725. opāca locōrum: *dark places.*

726–727. quem ... tēla: *whom but recently no hurled spears affected.* 727. adversō ... agmine: *massed in opposing lines.* 729. suspēnsum:* construe with mē in line 726; so timentem. comitī: i.e., for Ascanius. onerīque: i.e., for Anchises. 730. portīs: dat. with propinquābam. 732. vīsus: supply est. 733. propinquant: supply Danaī as subject. 734. aera: *bronze* (weapons). 735. mihi: *from me;* dat. of separation with ēripuit. nesciō quod male nūmen amīcum: *some hostile divinity.* nesciō: pronounce as if spelled nescjō; *synizesis.* 736. āvia: *bypaths.* 737. nōtā regiōne viārum: *from the known course through the*

THE FLIGHT FROM TROY

heu! miserō conjūnx fātōne ērepta Creūsa
substitit, errāvitne viā seu lassa resēdit,
incertum; nec post oculīs est reddita nostrīs;
nec prius āmissam respexī animumve reflexī
quam tumulum antīquae Cereris sēdemque sacrā-
tam
vēnimus; hīc dēmum collēctīs omnibus ūna
dēfuit et comitēs nātumque virumque fefellit.
Quem nōn incūsāvī āmēns hominumque deōrum-
que,
aut quid in ēversā vīdī crūdēlius urbe?
Ascanium Anchīsēnque patrem Teucrōsque Penātīs
commendō sociīs et curvā valle recondō;
ipse urbem repetō et cingor fulgentibus armīs;
stat cāsūs renovāre omnīs omnemque revertī
per Trōjam et rūrsus caput objectāre perīclīs.

subsistō stop; **lassus** weary, tired; **resīdō** sit down
740 **incertus** uncertain

**respiciō** look back for; **reflectō** turn back, turn

***dēmum** at last, finally

745 **incūsō** accuse, blame; ***āmēns** out of one's mind, distracted

**commendō** entrust, commit; ***curvus** winding; **recondō** put away, hide
***repetō** seek again; *fulgeō 750 gleam
**renovō** renew, repeat
**objectō** throw in the way of, expose

QUESTIONS ON **705–751**. 1. How did Aeneas arrange for the escape of Anchises? Of Ascanius? Of Creusa? Of his household servants? 2. Why did Aeneas himself not carry the Trojan Penates? 3. What frightened Aeneas as they neared the gate on the way out of the city? 4. When did Aeneas discover the loss of Creusa? 5. What did he immediately do?

*Creusa's spirit appears to Aeneas.*

"Prīncipiō mūrōs obscūraque līmina portae,
quā gressum extuleram, repetō, et vēstīgia retrō
observāta sequor per noctem et lūmine lūstrō;
horror ubīque animō, simul ipsa silentia terrent. 755
Inde domum, sī forte pedem, sī forte tulisset,
mē referō. Inruerant Danaī et tēctum omne tenē-
bant.
Īlicet ignis edāx summa ad fastīgia ventō

*prīncipium beginning

**vēstīgium footprint; ***retrō backward
observō note, observe

inruō rush in

edāx devouring

*streets.* **738.** (mihi) miserō: dat. of separation with ērepta. **740.** incertum: supply est. **741.** nec āmissam respexī: supply eam with āmissam; *nor did I, looking back, see that she was lost.* **741–742.** prius ... quam: priusquam, by *tmesis; until.* **742.** tumulum, sēdem: place whither. **743.** ūna: i.e., Creusa. **745.** deōrumque: hypermetric; see App. 31. **746.** in ēversā urbe: *in the destruction of the*

*city.* **748.** valle: place where. **749.** cingor: *I gird myself.* **750.** stat: supply mihi; *I am resolved.*
**754.** lūmine: *with my eyes.* **755.** horror: supply est. **756.** sī forte, sī forte: the rhetorical repetition suggests Aeneas's wistful, faint hope. tulisset: understand Creūsa as subject. tulisset is subjunctive in implied indirect discourse.

**exsuperō** rise above. rise high

volvitur; exsuperant flammae, furit aestus ad aurās.

760 Prōcēdō, et Priamī sēdīs arcemque revīsō.

**porticus** colonnade; **asȳlum** sanctuary

Et jam porticibus vacuīs Jūnōnis asȳlō

custōdēs lēctī Phoenīx et dīrus Ulixēs

**adservō** guard, watch; **gaza** treasure

praedam adservābant; hūc undique Trōia gaza

incēnsīs ērepta adytīs, mēnsaeque deōrum

**\*\*crātēr** mixing bowl; **\*\*solidus** massive

765 crātēresque aurō solidī, captīvaque vestis

**congerō** bring together; heap up; **pavidus** frightened

congeritur; puerī et pavidae longō ōrdine mātrēs

stant circum.

Ausus quīn etiam vōcēs jactāre per umbram

**impleō** fill

implēvī clāmōre viās, maestusque Creūsam

**ingeminō** repeat; **\*\*\*iterum** again

770 nēquīquam ingemināns iterumque iterumque vo-

cāvī.

Quaerentī et tēctīs urbis sine fīne furentī

īnfēlīx simulācrum atque ipsius umbra Creūsae

vīsa mihi ante oculōs et nōtā major imāgō.

**\*\*faux** throat

Obstipuī, steteruntque comae, et vōx faucibus

haesit.

**adfor** speak to, address; **dēmō** take away

775 Tum sīc adfārī et cūrās hīs dēmere dictīs:

**īnsānus** mad; **indulgeō** yield to, indulge in

'Quid tantum īnsānō juvat indulgēre dolōrī,

ō dulcis conjūnx? Nōn haec sine nūmine dīvum

**ēveniō** come, happen

ēveniunt, nec tē comitem hinc portāre Creūsam

**\*\*\*sinō** permit, allow; **superus** high; **rēgnātor** ruler

fās aut ille sinit superī rēgnātor Olympī.

**\*\*exsilium** exile; **\*arō** plow; sail over

780 Longa tibi exsilia, et vāstum maris aequor arandum,

et terram Hesperiam veniēs, ubi Lȳdius arva

**opīmus** rich, fertile

inter opīma virum lēnī fluit agmine Thybris.

Illīc rēs laetae rēgnumque et rēgia conjūnx

**\*\*pariō** bring forth; win; **\*\*dī-ligō** love

parta tibī; lacrimās dīlēctae pelle Creūsae.

---

**761. porticibus:** place where. **asȳlō:** in apposition with **porticibus. 764. adytīs:** abl. of separation depending on **ērepta. 766. longō ōrdine:** *in a long line.* **771. Quaerentī:** i.e., **mihi quaerentī. tēctīs:** place where. **773. vīsa:** supply **est. nōtā major imāgō:** *form larger than the form so well known.* **774. steterunt:** the penultimate syllable is here short. This shortening of a syllable for metrical reasons is called *systole.* **775. adfārī, dēmere:** historical infinitives; understand **Creūsa** or **imāgō** as subject. **776. juvat:** understand **tē**

as object. **778–779. nec . . . fās:** supply **est;** i.e., Aeneas is not permitted to take Creusa along with him. **779. rēgnātor:** i.e., Jupiter. **780. exsilia:** supply **sunt. 781–782. Lȳdius Thybris:** *Lydian Tiber;* the Etruscans through whose land the Tiber flowed were said to have come from Lydia in Asia Minor. **782. lēnī agmine:** *with gentle current.* **783. rēgia conjūnx:** i.e., Lavinia, daughter of King Latinus. **784. parta (est) tibi:** *exists for you;* i.e., awaits you. **Creūsae:** *for Creusa;* objective gen.

Nōn ego Myrmidonum sēdīs Dolopumve superbās 785
aspiciam, aut Grajīs servītum mātribus ībō,    *servī be a slave, serve
Dardanis et dīvae Veneris nurus,    nurus daughter-in-law
sed mē magna deum genetrīx hīs dētinet ōrīs.    genetrīx mother; dētineō hold, detain
Jamque valē, et nātī servā commūnis amōrem.'
Haec ubi dicta dedit, lacrimantem et multa volen- 790  lacrimō shed tears, weep
 tem
dīcere dēseruit, tenuīsque recessit in aurās.    *tenuis thin, light
Ter cōnātus ibī collō dare bracchia circum;    *bracchium arm
ter frūstrā comprēnsa manūs effūgit imāgō,    comprēndō grasp; effugiō escape
pār levibus ventīs volucrīque simillima somnō.    **volucer winged, swift

QUESTIONS ON **752–794**. 1. To what place did Aeneas first go in his effort to find Creusa? Where next? Where next? 2. What final effort did Aeneas make to find Creusa? 3. In what form did Creusa appear to Aeneas? 4. Who did Creusa say had refused to allow her to accompany Aeneas? 5. What reasons does Creusa give for this refusal? 6. What does Creusa assure Aeneas would not happen to her? 7. What was Creusa's final request of Aeneas?

*The Trojan survivors make for the mountains.*

"Sīc dēmum sociōs, cōnsūmptā nocte, revīsō.  795  ***dēmum at length, finally
Atque hīc ingentem comitum adflūxisse novōrum    adfluō flow to; come
inveniō admīrāns numerum, mātrēsque virōsque,    admīror wonder
collēctam exsiliō pūbem, miserābile vulgus.    ***exsilium exile; ***pūbēs group of young men
Undique convēnēre, animīs opibusque parātī
in quāscumque velim pelagō dēdūcere terrās.  800  dēdūcō lead forth
Jamque jugīs summae surgēbat Lūcifer Īdae
dūcēbatque diem, Danaīque obsessa tenēbant
līmina portārum, nec spēs opis ūlla dabātur.
Cessī, et sublātō montīs genitōre petīvī.

QUESTIONS ON **795–804**. 1. When did Aeneas return to his father and son? 2. Whom else did he find there? 3. What were the refugees ready to do? 4. In what general direction did Aeneas lead his band of refugees?

---

**786. servītum:** supine in –um with verb of motion. **787. Dardanis:** *a daughter (descendant) of Dardanus.* **788. genetrīx:** i.e., Cybele, the Phrygian goddess, called the Great Mother of the Gods. **ōrīs:** place where. **790. lacrimantem, volentem:** understand mē; i.e., Aeneas. **792. cōnātus:** supply **sum. collō:** dat. with **circumdare.**

**798. exsiliō:** dat. of purpose. **799. convēnēre:** convēnērunt. **parātī:** understand **īre. 800. dēdūcere:** *to lead out* (a colony). **801. Lūcifer:** *Light Bringer,* the morning star. **803. spēs opis:** *hope of relief,* i.e., relief for Troy. **804. montīs:** i.e., Mt. Ida. For Work Unit XI, based on lines 624–804 of Book II see p. 267.

# BOOK III

*The Trojans build a fleet, and sail away in search of a new home.*

"Postquam rēs Asiae Priamīque ēvertere gentem
immeritam vīsum superīs, ceciditque superbum
Īlium, et omnis humō fūmat Neptūnia Trōja,
dīversa exsilia et dēsertās quaerere terrās
5 auguriīs agimur dīvum, classemque sub ipsā
Antandrō et Phrygiae mōlīmur montibus Īdae,
incertī quō Fāta ferant, ubi sistere dētur,
contrahimusque virōs.  Vix prīma incēperat aestās
et pater Anchīsēs dare Fātīs vēla jubēbat,
10 lītora cum patriae lacrimāns portūsque relinquō
et campōs, ubi Trōja fuit.  Feror exsul in altum
cum sociīs nātōque, Penātibus et magnīs dīs.

QUESTIONS ON LINES 1–12.  1. Where did Aeneas and his fol-
lowers build their fleet?  2. In what season of the year did the
Trojans set sail?  In what general direction?  3. Do you think
that Aeneas was at this time sure of his exact destination?

*Landing in Thrace, they found a new city, but an omen compels them to continue their course.*

"Terra procul vāstīs colitur Māvortia campīs
(Thrācēs arant), ācrī quondam rēgnāta Lycurgō,
15 hospitium antīquum Trōjae sociīque Penātēs,
dum fortūna fuit.  Feror hūc, et lītore curvō
moenia prīma locō, Fātīs ingressus inīquīs,
Aeneadāsque meō nōmen dē nōmine fingō.

"Sacra Diōnaeae mātrī dīvīsque ferēbam
20 auspicibus coeptōrum operum, superōque nitentem
caelicolum rēgī mactābam in lītore taurum.
Forte fuit jūxtā tumulus, quō cornea summō

74

virgulta et dēnsīs hastīlibus horrida myrtus./
Accessī, viridemque ab humō convellere silvam
cōnātus, rāmīs tegerem ut frondentibus ārās,            25
horrendum et dictū videō mīrābile mōnstrum;
nam, quae prīma solō ruptīs rādīcibus arbōs
vellitur, huic ātrō līquuntur sanguine guttae
et terram tābō maculant.  Mihi frīgidus horror
membra quatit, gelidusque coit formīdine sanguis. 30
Rūrsus et alterius lentum convellere vīmen
īnsequor et causās penitus temptāre latentīs;
āter et alterius sequitur dē cortice sanguis.
Multa movēns animō, nymphās venerābar agrestīs
Grādīvumque patrem, Geticīs quī praesidet arvīs, 35
rīte secundārent vīsūs ōmenque levārent.
Tertia sed postquam majōre hastīlia nīsū
adgredior genibusque adversae obluctor harēnae
(ēloquar an sileam?), gemitus lacrimābilis īmō
audītur tumulō, et vōx reddita fertur ad aurīs:      40
'Quid miserum, Aenēā, lacerās?  Jam parce se-
      pultō,
parce piās scelerāre manūs.  Nōn mē tibi Trōja
externum tulit aut cruor hic dē stīpite mānat.
Heu!  Fuge crūdēlīs terrās, fuge lītus avārum,
nam Polydōrus ego.  Hīc cōnfīxum ferrea tēxit      45
tēlōrum seges et jaculīs incrēvit acūtīs.'
Tum vērō ancipitī mentem formīdine pressus
obstipuī, steteruntque comae, et vōx faucibus
      haesit.
Hunc Polydōrum aurī quondam cum pondere
      magnō
īnfēlīx Priamus fūrtim mandārat alendum           50
Thrēiciō rēgī, cum jam diffīderet armīs
Dardaniae, cingīque urbem obsidiōne vidēret.
Ille, ut opēs frāctae Teucrum et fortūna recessit,
rēs Agamemnoniās victrīciaque arma secūtus

55 fās omne abrumpit; Polydōrum obtruncat, et aurō
vī potitur.  Quid nōn mortālia pectora cōgis,
aurī sacra famēs!  Postquam pavor ossa relīquit,
dēlēctōs populī ad procerēs prīmumque parentem
mōnstra deum referō, et quae sit sententia poscō.
60 Omnibus īdem animus, scelerātā excēdere terrā,
linquī pollūtum hospitium et dare classibus Aus-
    trōs.

Ergō īnstaurāmus Polydōrō fūnus, et ingēns
aggeritur tumulō tellūs; stant Mānibus ārae,
caeruleīs maestae vittīs ātrāque cupressō,
65 et circum Īliades crīnem dē mōre solūtae;
īnferimus tepidō spūmantia cymbia lacte
sanguinis et sacrī paterās, animamque sepulcrō
condimus, et magnā suprēmum vōce ciēmus.

QUESTIONS ON **13–68**.  1. What name did Aeneas give to his
city in Thrace?  2. To whom did Aeneas offer a sacrifice?
3. What occurrence in connection with this sacrifice frightened
Aeneas?  4. Who was Polydorus?  5. What warning did Poly-
dorus's spirit give Aeneas?  6. What did the Trojans now decide
to do?  7. What ceremony did the Trojans perform before leav-
ing Thrace?

*The Trojans go on to Delos, to consult the oracle.*
*They then sail to Crete.*

"Inde, ubi prīma fidēs pelagō plācātaque ventī
70 dant maria, et lēnis crepitāns vocat Auster in al-
    tum,
dēdūcunt sociī nāvīs et lītora complent.
Prōvehimur portū, terraeque urbēsque recēdunt.
Sacra marī colitur mediō grātissima tellūs
Nēreïdum mātrī et Neptūnō Aegaeō,
75 quam pius Arcitenēns ōrās et lītora circum
errantem Myconō ē celsā Gyarōque revīnxit,
immōtamque colī dedit et contemnere ventōs.
Hūc feror; haec fessōs tūtō placidissima portū
accipit.  Ēgressī, venerāmur Apollinis urbem.

Rēx Anius, rēx īdem hominum Phoebīque sacerdōs, 80
vittīs et sacrā redimītus tempora laurō,
occurrit. Veterem Anchīsēn agnōscit amīcum;
jungimus hospitiō dextrās et tēcta subīmus.
   "Templa deī saxō venerābar strūcta vetustō:
'Dā propriam, Thymbraee, domum; dā moenia 85
   fessīs
et genus et mānsūram urbem; servā altera Trōjae
Pergama, relliquiās Danaum atque immītis Achillī.
Quem sequimur, quōve īre jubēs? ubi pōnere sēdīs?
Dā, pater, augurium atque animīs inlābere nostrīs.'
Vix ea fātus eram: tremere omnia vīsa repente, 90
līminaquē laurusque deī, tōtusque movērī
mōns circum et mūgīre adytīs cortīna reclūsīs.
Submissī petimus terram, et vōx fertur ad aurīs:
'Dardanidae dūrī, quae vōs ā stirpe parentum
prīma tulit tellūs, eadem vōs ūbere laetō 95
accipiet reducīs. Antīquam exquīrite mātrem.
Hīc domus Aenēae cūnctīs dominābitur ōrīs
et nātī nātōrum et quī nāscentur ab illīs.'
Haec Phoebus; mixtōque ingēns exorta tumultū
laetitia, et cūnctī quae sint ea moenia quaerunt, 100
quō Phoebus vocet errantīs jubeatque revertī.
Tum genitor, veterum volvēns monumenta virō-
   rum,
'Audīte, ō procerēs,' ait, 'et spēs discite vestrās.
Crēta Jovis magnī mediō jacet īnsula pontō,
mōns Īdaeus ubi et gentis cūnābula nostrae. 105
Centum urbēs habitant magnās, ūberrima rēgna,
maximus unde pater, sī rīte audīta recordor,
Teucrus Rhoetēās prīmum est advectus ad ōrās,
optāvitque locum rēgnō. Nōndum Īlium et arcēs
Pergameae steterant; habitābant vallibus īmīs. 110
Hinc māter cultrīx Cybelae Corybantiaque aera
Īdaeumque nemus, hinc fīda silentia sacrīs

et jūnctī currum dominae subiēre leōnēs.

Ergō agite, et dīvum dūcunt quā jussa sequāmur;

115 plācēmus ventōs, et Gnōsia regna petāmus.

Nec longō distant cursū; modo Juppiter adsit,

tertia lūx classem Crētaeīs sistet in ōrīs.'

Sīc fātus, meritōs ārīs mactāvit honōrēs,

taurum Neptūnō, taurum tibi, pulcher Apollō.

120 nigram Hiemī pecudem, Zephyrīs fēlīcibus albam.

"Fāma volat pulsum rēgnīs cessisse paternīs

Īdomenēa ducem, dēsertaque lītora Crētae,

hoste vacāre domōs sēdīsque astāre relictās.

Linquimus Ortygiae portūs, pelagōque volāmus,

125 bacchātamque jugīs Naxon viridemque Donȳsam,

Ōlearon niveamque Paron, sparsāsque per aequor

Cycladas, et crēbrīs legimus freta concita terrīs.

Nauticus exoritur variō certāmine clāmor;

hortantur sociī Crētam proavōsque petāmus.

130 Prōsequitur surgēns ā puppī ventus euntīs,

et tandem antīquīs Cūrētum adlābimur ōrīs.

QUESTIONS ON **69–131**. 1. Where did the Trojans next land?
2. Who gave the Trojans a friendly welcome? 3. To whom did
Aeneas make his prayer? 4. For what did Aeneas pray?
5. What instructions did Aeneas receive from the god? 6. How
did Anchises interpret these instructions? 7. To what gods did
Anchises offer sacrifice before the Trojans sailed from Delos?

*A pestilence compels them to leave Crete and seek
"Hesperia."*

"Ergō avidus mūrōs optātae mōlior urbis,

Pergameamque vocō, et laetam cognōmine gentem

hortor amāre focōs arcemque attollere tēctīs.

135 Jamque ferē siccō subductae lītore puppēs;

cōnūbiīs arvīsque novīs operāta juventūs;

jūra domōsque dabam, subitō cum tābida membrīs

corruptō caelī tractū miserandaque vēnit

arboribusque satīsque luēs et lētifer annus.

140 Linquēbant dulcīs animās aut aegra trahēbant

corpora; tum sterilīs exūrere Sīrius agrōs;
ārēbant herbae, et vīctum seges aegra negābat.
Rūrsus ad ōrāclum Ortygiae Phoebumque remēnsō
hortātur pater īre marī, veniamque precārī,
quam fessīs fīnem rēbus ferat, unde labōrum      145
temptāre auxilium jubeat, quō vertere cursūs.
   "Nox erat, et terrīs animālia somnus habēbat;
effigiēs sacrae dīvum Phrygiīque Penātēs,
quōs mēcum ā Trōjā mediīsque ex ignibus urbis
extuleram, vīsī ante oculōs astāre jacentis,      150
in somnīs multō manifestī lūmine, quā sē
plēna per īnsertās fundēbat lūna fenestrās.
Tum sīc adfārī, et cūrās hīs dēmere dictīs:
'Quod tibi dēlātō Ortygiam dictūrus Apollō est,
hīc canit, et tua nōs, ēn, ultrō ad līmina mittit.      155
Nōs, tē Dardaniā incēnsā tuaque arma secūtī,
nōs, tumidum sub tē permēnsī classibus aequor,
īdem ventūrōs tollēmus in astra nepōtēs
imperiumque urbī dabimus; tū moenia magnīs
magna parā longumque fugae nē linque labōrem.      160
Mūtandae sēdēs; nōn haec tibi lītora suāsit
Dēlius aut Crētae jussit cōnsīdere Apollō.
Est locus (Hesperiam Grajī cognōmine dīcunt),
terra antīqua, potēns armīs atque ūbere glaebae:
Oenōtrī coluēre virī; nunc fāma minōrēs      165
Ītaliam dīxisse ducis dē nōmine gentem.
Hae nōbīs propriae sēdēs, hinc Dardanus ortus
Īasiusque pater, genus ā quō prīncipe nostrum.
Surge age, et haec laetus longaevō dicta parentī
haud dubitanda refer: Corythum terrāsque re-170
      quīrat
Ausoniās. Dictaea negat tibi Juppiter arva.'
Tālibus attonitus vīsīs et vōce deōrum
(nec sopor illud erat, sed cōram agnōscere vultūs
vēlātāsque comās praesentiaque ōra vidēbar;

175 tum gelidus tōtō mānābat corpore sūdor),
corripiō ē strātīs corpus, tendōque supīnās
ad caelum cum vōce manūs, et mūnera lībō
intemerāta focīs. Perfectō laetus honōre
Anchīsēn faciō certum remque ōrdine pandō.
180 Agnōvit prōlem ambiguam geminōsque parentīs,
sēque novō veterum dēceptum errōre locōrum.
Tum memorat: 'Nāte, Īliacīs exercite fātīs,
sōla mihī tālīs cāsūs Cassandra canēbat;
nunc repetō haec generī portendere dēbita nostrō
185 et saepe Hesperiam, saepe Ītala rēgna vocāre.
Sed quis ad Hesperiae ventūrōs lītora Teucrōs
crēderet, aut quem tum vātēs Cassandra movēret?
Cēdāmus Phoebō, et monitī meliōra sequāmur.'
Sīc ait, et cūnctī dictō pārēmus ovantēs.
190 Hanc quoque dēserimus sēdem, paucīsque relictīs
vēla damus, vāstumque cavā trabe currimus ae-
quor.

QUESTIONS ON **132–191**. 1. What name did Aeneas give to the
city which he founded in Crete? 2. What disasters overtook the
Trojans in Crete? 3. What did Anchises urge Aeneas to do in
this crisis? 4. From what source did Aeneas receive instruc-
tions? 5. In what land was Aeneas now definitely told to es-
tablish his new city? 6. Whose earlier prophecy did Anchises
now recall? 7. Why had Anchises ignored that earlier prophecy?

*A storm drives the Trojans to the Strophades, home
of the Harpies.*

"Postquam altum tenuēre ratēs, nec jam amplius
ūllae
appārent terrae, caelum undique et undique pon-
tus,
tum mihi caeruleus suprā caput astitit imber,
195 noctem hiememque ferēns, et inhorruit unda tene-
brīs.
Continuō ventī volvunt mare, magnaque surgunt
aequora; dispersī jactāmur gurgite vāstō.

Involvēre diem nimbī, et nox ūmida caelum
abstulit; ingeminant abruptīs nūbibus ignēs.
Excutimur cursū, et caecīs errāmus in undīs.  200
Ipse diem noctemque negat discernere caelō
nec meminisse viae mediā Palinūrus in undā.
Trīs adeō incertōs caecā cālīgine sōlēs
errāmus pelagō, totidem sine sīdere noctīs;
quārtō terra diē prīmum sē attollere tandem  205
vīsa, aperīre procul montīs ac volvere fūmum.
Vēla cadunt, rēmīs īnsurgimus; haud mora, nautae
adnīxī torquent spūmās et caerula verrunt.
Servātum ex undīs Strophadum mē lītora prīmum
accipiunt. Strophades Grajō stant nōmine dictae 210
īnsulae Ioniō in magnō, quās dīra Celaenō
Harpyiaeque colunt aliae, Phīnēia postquam
clausa domus mēnsāsque metū līquēre priōrēs.
Trīstius haud illīs mōnstrum, nec saevior ūlla
pestis et īra deum Stygiīs sēsē extulit undīs.  215
Virgineī volucrum vultūs, foedissima ventris
prōluviēs, uncaeque manūs, et pallida semper
ōra famē.

"Hūc ubi dēlātī portūs intrāvimus, ecce
laeta boum passim campīs armenta vidēmus  220
caprigenumque pecus, nūllō custōde, per herbās.
Inruimus ferrō, et dīvōs ipsumque vocāmus
in partem praedamque Jovem; tum lītore curvō
exstruimusque torōs dapibusque epulāmur opīmīs.
At subitae horrificō lāpsū dē montibus adsunt  225
Harpyiae, et magnīs quatiunt clangōribus ālās,
dīripiuntque dapēs, contāctūque omnia foedant
immundō; tum vōx taetrum dīra inter odōrem.
"Rūrsum in sēcessū longō sub rūpe cavātā
arboribus clausā circum atque horrentibus umbrīs 230
īnstruimus mēnsās, ārīsque repōnimus ignem;

rūrsum ex dīversō caelī caecīsque latebrīs
turba sonāns praedam pedibus circumvolat uncīs,
polluit ōre dapēs.  Sociīs tunc arma capessant
235 ēdīcō et dīrā bellum cum gente gerendum.
Haud secus ac jussī faciunt, tēctōsque per herbam
dispōnunt ēnsīs et scūta latentia condunt.
Ergō, ubi dēlāpsae sonitum per curva dedēre
lītora, dat signum speculā Mīsēnus ab altā
240 aere cavō; invādunt sociī et nova proelia temptant,
obscēnās pelagī ferrō foedāre volucrīs;
sed neque vim plūmīs ūllam nec vulnera tergō
accipiunt, celerīque fugā sub sīdera lāpsae
sēmēsam praedam et vēstīgia foeda relinquunt.
245 Ūna in praecelsā cōnsēdit rūpe Celaenō,
īnfēlīx vātēs, rumpitque hanc pectore vōcem:
'Bellum etiam prō caede boum strātīsque juven-
cīs,
Lāomedontiadae, bellumne īnferre parātis
et patriō Harpyiās īnsontīs pellere rēgnō?
250 Accipite ergō animīs atque haec mea fīgite dicta,
quae Phoebō pater omnipotēns, mihi Phoebus
Apollō
praedīxit, vōbīs Furiārum ego maxima pandō.
Ītaliam cursū petitis, ventīsque vocātīs
ībitis Ītaliam, portūsque intrāre licēbit:
255 sed nōn ante datam cingētis moenibus urbem
quam vōs dīra famēs nostraeque injūria caedis
ambēsās subigat mālīs absūmere mēnsās.'
Dīxit, et in silvam, pinnīs ablāta, refūgit.

QUESTIONS ON **192–258**.  1. What misfortune overtook the Tro-
jans soon after they sailed from Crete?  2. How long did the
Trojans sail blindly over the sea?  3. Where did the Trojans
next land?   4. On what did the Trojans prepare to feast?
5. Who interrupted the Trojans' feast?  How many times?
6. What terrifying prophecy did Celaeno make?  7. From whom
did Celaeno say she had received her information?

*The Trojans leave the Strophades.   They arrive at
Actium and celebrate "the Trojan Games."*

"At sociīs subitā gelidus formīdine sanguis
dēriguit; cecidēre animī, nec jam amplius armīs,   260
sed vōtīs precibusque jubent exposcere pācem,
sīve deae seu sint dīrae obscēnaeque volucrēs,
et pater Anchīsēs, passīs dē lītore palmīs,
nūmina magna vocat meritōsque indīcit honōrēs:
'Dī, prohibēte minās; dī, tālem āvertite cāsum,   265
et placidī servāte piōs!'   Tum lītore fūnem
dēripere excussōsque jubet laxāre rudentīs.
Tendunt vēla Notī; fugimus spūmantibus undīs,
quā cursum ventusque gubernātorque vocābat.
Jam mediō appāret flūctū nemorōsa Zacynthos   270
Dūlichiumque Samēque et Nēritos ardua saxīs;
effugimus scopulōs Ithacae, Lāertia rēgna,
et terram altrīcem saevī exsecrāmur Ulixī;
mox et Leucātae nimbōsa cacūmina montis
et formīdātus nautīs aperītur Apollō.   275
Hunc petimus fessī, et parvae succēdimus urbī;
ancora dē prōrā jacitur, stant lītore puppēs.
Ergō, īnspērātā tandem tellūre potītī,
lūstrāmurque Jovī vōtīsque incendimus ārās,
Actiaque Īliacīs celebrāmus lītora lūdīs.   280
Exercent patriās oleō lābente palaestrās
nūdātī sociī; juvat ēvāsisse tot urbīs
Argolicās mediōsque fugam tenuisse per hostīs.
Intereā magnum sōl circumvolvitur annum,
et glaciālis hiems Aquilōnibus asperat undās;   285
aere cavō clipeum, magnī gestāmen Abantis,
postibus adversīs fīgō et rem carmine signō:
*Aenēās haec dē Danaīs victōribus arma.*

QUESTIONS ON **259–288**.   1. What did Anchises do in an effort
to prevent the fulfillment of Celaeno's prophecy?   2. What
orders did Anchises give the Trojans?   3. In what general direc-

tion did the Trojans now sail? 4. In what way did the Trojans show their hatred of Ulysses? 5. At what time of the year did the Trojans sail from Actium? 6. What trophy did Aeneas set up before leaving Actium?

### The Trojans sail to Buthrotum, where Aeneas meets Andromache.

"Linquere tum portūs jubeō et cōnsīdere trāns-
 trīs;
290 certātim sociī feriunt mare et aequora verrunt.
Prōtinus āeriās Phaeācum abscondimus arcīs,
lītoraque Ēpīrī legimus, portūque subīmus
Chāoniō, et celsam Būthrōtī accēdimus urbem.
 "Hīc incrēdibilis rērum fāma occupat aurīs,
295 Prīamidēn Helenum Grajās rēgnāre per urbīs,
conjugiō Aeacidae Pyrrhī scēptrīsque potītum,
et patriō Andromachēn iterum cessisse marītō.
Obstipuī, mīrōque incēnsum pectus amōre
compellāre virum et cāsūs cognōscere tantōs.
300 Prōgredior portū, classīs et lītora linquēns,
sollemnīs cum forte dapēs et trīstia dōna
ante urbem in lūcō falsī Simoëntis ad undam
lībābat cinerī Andromachē, Mānīsque vocābat
Hectoreum ad tumulum, viridī quem caespite inā-
 nem
305 et geminās, causam lacrimīs, sacrāverat ārās.
Ut mē cōnspexit venientem et Trōia circum
arma āmēns vīdit, magnīs exterrita mōnstrīs
dēriguit vīsū in mediō, calor ossa relīquit;
lābitur, et longō vix tandem tempore fātur:
310 'Vērane tē faciēs, vērus mihi nūntius adfers,
nāte deā? Vīvisne, aut, sī lūx alma recessit,
Hector ubi est?' Dīxit, lacrimāsque effūdit, et
 omnem
implēvit clāmōre locum. Vix pauca furentī
subjiciō, et rārīs turbātus vōcibus hīscō:

'Vīvō equidem, vītamque extrēma per omnia dūcō; 315
nē dubitā; nam vēra vidēs.
Heu! Quis tē cāsus dējectam conjuge tantō
excipit, aut quae digna satis fortūna revīsit?
Hectoris Andromachē Pyrrhīn cōnūbia servās?'
Dējēcit vultum, et dēmissā vōce locūta est:        320
'Ō fēlīx ūna ante aliās Priamēia virgō,
hostīlem ad tumulum Trōjae sub moenibus altīs
jussa morī, quae sortītūs nōn pertulit ūllōs,
nec victōris erī tetigit captīva cubīle!
Nōs, patriā incēnsā, dīversa per aequora vectae   325
stirpis Achillēae fastūs juvenemque superbum
servitiō ēnīxae tulimus; quī deinde, secūtus
Lēdaeam Hermionēn Lacedaemoniōsque hyme-
        naeōs,
mē famulō famulamque Helenō trānsmīsit haben-
        dam.
Ast illum, ēreptae magnō īnflammātus amōre     330
conjugis et scelerum furiīs agitātus, Orestēs
excipit incautum patriāsque obtruncat ad ārās.
Morte Neoptolemī rēgnōrum reddita cessit
pars Helenō, quī Chāoniōs cognōmine campōs
Chāoniamque omnem Trōjānō ā Chāone dīxit,   335
Pergamaque Īliacamque jugīs hanc addidit ar-
        cem.
Sed tibi quī cursum ventī, quae Fāta dedēre,
aut quisnam ignārum nostrīs deus appulit ōrīs?
Quid puer Ascanius? Superatne et vēscitur aurā,
quem tibi jam Trōjā —                                   340
Ecqua tamen puerō est āmissae cūra parentis?
Ecquid in antīquam virtūtem animōsque virīlīs
et pater Aenēās et avunculus excitat Hector?'

QUESTIONS ON **289–343**. 1. What strange story did the Trojans
hear on landing at Buthrotum? 2. What was Andromache doing
when Aeneas saw her? 3. What did Andromache do when she

saw Aeneas?  4. What did Andromache think she was seeing?
5. What indignities had Andromache suffered since the fall of
Troy?  6. What had finally happened to Pyrrhus?  7. Why had
Helenus called his new kingdom Chaonia?  8. What relation
was Ascanius to Hector?

### King Helenus receives the Trojans.

"Tālia fundēbat lacrimāns, longōsque ciēbat
345 incassum flētūs, cum sēsē ā moenibus hērōs
Prīamidēs multīs Helenus comitantibus adfert,
agnōscitque suōs, laetusque ad līmina dūcit,
et multum lacrimās verba inter singula fundit.
Prōcēdō, et parvam Trōjam simulātaque magnīs
350 Pergama et ārentem Xanthī cognōmine rīvum
agnōscō, Scaeaeque amplector līmina portae.
Nec nōn et Teucrī sociā simul urbe fruuntur.
Illōs porticibus rēx accipiēbat in amplīs;
aulāī mediō lībābant pōcula Bacchī
355 impositīs aurō dapibus, paterāsque tenēbant.
"Jamque diēs alterque diēs prōcessit, et aurae
vēla vocant, tumidōque īnflātur carbasus Austrō.
Hīs vātem adgredior dictīs, ac tālia quaesō:
'Trōjugena, interpres dīvum, quī nūmina Phoebī,
360 quī tripodas, Clariī laurūs, quī sīdera sentīs
et volucrum linguās et praepetis ōmina pinnae,
fāre age (namque omnem cursum mihi prōspera
dīxit
relligiō, et cūnctī suāsērunt nūmine dīvī
Ītaliam petere et terrās temptāre repostās;
365 sōla novum dictūque nefās Harpyia Celaenō
prōdigium canit, et trīstīs dēnūntiat īrās
obscēnamque famem): quae prīma perīcula vītō,
quidve sequēns tantōs possim superāre labōrēs?'

QUESTIONS ON **344–368**. 1. What city had Helenus used as a
model in laying out his city?  2. What was Helenus's attitude
toward Aeneas and his followers?  3. From what god had Hel-
enus received his gift of prophecy?  4. What threatened hard-
ship did Aeneas ask Helenus to help him avoid?

*King Helenus advises Aeneas in regard to the rest*
*of his journey.*

"Hīc Helenus, caesīs prīmum dē mōre juvencīs,
exōrat pācem dīvum vittāsque resolvit       370
sacrātī capitis, mēque ad tua līmina, Phoebe,
ipse manū multō suspēnsum nūmine dūcit,
atque haec deinde canit dīvīnō ex ōre sacerdōs:
'Nāte deā; nam tē majōribus īre per altum
auspiciīs manifesta fidēs (sīc fāta deum rēx     375
sortītur volvitque vicēs, is vertitur ōrdō),
pauca tibi ē multīs, quō tūtior hospita lūstrēs
aequora, et Ausoniō possīs cōnsīdere portū,
expediam dictīs; prohibent nam cētera Parcae
scīre Helenum, fārīque vetat Sāturnia Jūnō.     380
Prīncipiō Ītaliam, quam tū jam rēre propinquam
vīcīnōsque, ignāre, parās invādere portūs,
longa procul longīs via dīvidit invia terrīs.
Ante et Trīnacriā lentandus rēmus in undā,
et salis Ausoniī lūstrandum nāvibus aequor,     385
īnfernīque lacūs Aeaeaeque īnsula Circae
quam tūtā possīs urbem compōnere terrā.
Signa tibī dīcam, tū condita mente tenētō.
Cum tibi sollicitō sēcrētī ad flūminis undam
lītoreīs ingēns inventa sub īlicibus sūs,     390
trīgintā capitum fētūs ēnīxa, jacēbit,
alba, solō recubāns, albī circum ūbera nātī,
is locus urbis erit, requiēs ea certa labōrum.
Nec tū mēnsārum morsūs horrēsce futūrōs;
Fāta viam invenient, aderitque vocātus Apollō.     395
Hās autem terrās Italīque hanc lītoris ōram,
proxima quae nostrī perfunditur aequoris aestū,
effuge; cūncta malīs habitantur moenia Grajīs.
Hīc et Nāryciī posuērunt moenia Locrī,
et Sallentīnōs obsēdit mīlite campōs     400

Lyctius Īdomeneus; hīc illa ducis Meliboeī
parva Philoctētae subnīxa Petēlia mūrō.
Quīn, ubi trānsmissae steterint trāns aequora
    classēs,
et, positīs ārīs, jam vōta in lītore solvēs,
405 purpureō vēlāre comās adopertus amictū,
nē qua inter sānctōs ignīs in honōre deōrum
hostīlis faciēs occurrat et ōmina turbet.
Hunc sociī mōrem sacrōrum, hunc ipse tenētō;
hāc castī maneant in relligiōne nepōtēs.
410 Ast, ubi dīgressum Siculae tē admōverit ōrae
ventus, et angustī rārēscent claustra Pelōrī,
laeva tibī tellūs et longō laeva petantur
aequora circuitū; dextrum fuge lītus et undās.
Haec loca vī quondam et vāstā convulsa ruīnā
415 (tantum aevī longinqua valet mūtāre vetustās)
dissiluisse ferunt, cum prōtinus utraque tellūs
ūna foret; vēnit mediō vī pontus, et undīs
Hesperium Siculō latus abscidit, arvaque et urbīs
lītore dīductās angustō interluit aestū.
420 Dextrum Scylla latus, laevum implācāta Charybdis
obsidet, atque īmō barathrī ter gurgite vāstōs
sorbet in abruptum flūctūs, rūrsusque sub aurās
ērigit alternōs, et sīdera verberat undā.
At Scyllam caecīs cohibet spēlunca latebrīs
425 ōra exsertantem et nāvīs in saxa trahentem.
⟋ Prīma hominis faciēs et pulchrō pectore virgō
pūbe tenus, postrēma immānī corpore pistrīx,
delphīnum caudās uterō commissa lupōrum.
Praestat Trīnacriī mētās lūstrāre Pachȳnī
430 cessantem longōs et circumflectere cursūs,
quam semel īnfōrmem vāstō vīdisse sub antrō
Scyllam et caeruleīs canibus resonantia saxa.
Praetereā, sī qua est Helenō prūdentia vātī,
sī qua fidēs, animum sī vērīs implet Apollō,

ūnum illud tibi, nāte deā, prōque omnibus ūnum  435
praedīcam, et repetēns iterumque iterumque monē-
    bō:
Jūnōnis magnae prīmum prece nūmen adōrā,
Jūnōnī cane vōta libēns, dominamque potentem
supplicibus superā dōnīs; sīc dēnique victor
Trīnacriā fīnīs Italōs mittēre relictā.          440
Hūc ubi dēlātus Cūmaeam accesseris urbem
dīvīnōsque lacūs et Averna sonantia silvīs,
īnsānam vātem aspiciēs, quae rūpe sub īmā
fāta canit foliīsque notās et nōmina mandat.
Quaecumque in foliīs dēscrīpsit carmina virgō,   445
dīgerit in numerum atque antrō sēclūsa relinquit;
illa manent immōta locīs neque ab ōrdine cēdunt:
vērum eadem, versō tenuis cum cardine ventus
impulit et tenerās turbāvit jānua frondēs,
numquam deinde cavō volitantia prēndere saxō     450
nec revocāre sitūs aut jungere carmina cūrat;
incōnsultī abeunt sēdemque ōdēre Sibyllae.
Hīc tibi nē qua morae fuerint dispendia tantī,
quamvīs increpitent sociī et vī cursus in altum
vēla vocet possīsque sinūs implēre secundōs,     455
quīn adeās vātem, precibusque ōrācula poscās
ipsa canat, vōcemque volēns atque ōra resolvat.
Illa tibi Ītaliae populōs ventūraque bella
et quō quemque modō fugiāsque ferāsque labōrem
expediet, cursūsque dabit venerāta secundōs.     460
Haec sunt quae nostrā liceat tē vōce monērī.
Vāde age, et ingentem factīs fer ad aethera Trō-
    jam.'

QUESTIONS ON **369–462**.  1. To what place did Helenus first
conduct Aeneas?  2. Under whose auspices did Helenus say
Aeneas was making his way over the sea?  3. On which coast of
Italy did Helenus tell Aeneas he must found his city?  4. What
assurance did Helenus give Aeneas about having to "eat his
plate"?  5. What reasons did Helenus give Aeneas for avoiding
the eastern coast of Italy?  6. What reasons did Helenus give

Aeneas for sailing around Sicily? 7. To what goddess did Helenus especially advise Aeneas to make prayers and offer sacrifices? 8. What priestess did Helenus urge Aeneas to consult on reaching Cumae? 9. In what form did Helenus urge Aeneas to insist on receiving his response from the Sibyl?

### The Trojans sail from Buthrotum and land on the eastern coast of Italy.

"Quae postquam vātēs sīc ōre effātus amīcō est,
dōna dehinc auro gravia sectōque elephantō
465 imperat ad nāvīs ferrī, stīpatque carīnīs
ingēns argentum Dōdōnaeōsque lebētas,
lōrīcam cōnsertam hāmīs aurōque trilīcem,
et cōnum īnsignis galeae cristāsque comantīs,
arma Neoptolemī. Sunt et sua dōna parentī.
470 Addit equōs additque ducēs;
rēmigium supplet, sociōs simul īnstruit armīs.
"Intereā classem vēlīs aptāre jubēbat
Anchīsēs, fieret ventō mora nē qua ferentī.
Quem Phoebī interpres multō compellat honōre:
475 'Conjugiō, Anchīsē, Veneris dignāte superbō,
cūra deum, bis Pergameīs ērepte ruīnīs,
ecce tibi Ausoniae tellūs; hanc arripe vēlīs.
Et tamen hanc pelagō praeterlābāre necesse est;
Ausoniae pars illa procul quam pandit Apollō.
480 Vāde,' ait, 'ō fēlīx nātī pietāte. Quid ultrā
prōvehor, et fandō surgentīs dēmoror Austrōs?'
Nec minus Andromachē dīgressū maesta suprēmō
fert pictūrātās aurī subtēmine vestīs
et Phrygiam Ascaniō chlamydem, nec cēdit honōre.
485 textilibusque onerat dōnīs ac tālia fātur:
'Accipe et haec, manuum tibi quae monumenta
meārum
sint, puer, et longum Andromachae testentur
amōrem,
conjugis Hectoreae. Cape dōna extrēma tuōrum,

ō mihi sōla meī super Astyanactis imāgō.
Sīc oculōs, sīc ille manūs, sīc ōra ferēbat, 490
et nunc aequālī tēcum pūbēsceret aevō.'
Hōs ego dīgrediēns lacrimīs adfābar obortīs:
'Vīvite fēlīcēs, quibus est fortūna perācta
jam sua; nōs alia ex aliīs in fāta vocāmur.
Vōbīs parta quiēs; nūllum maris aequor arandum, 495
arva neque Ausoniae semper cēdentia retrō
quaerenda.  Effigiem Xanthī Trōjamque vidētis,
quam vestrae fēcēre manūs meliōribus, optō,
auspiciīs, et quae fuerit minus obvia Grajīs.
Sī quandō Thybrim vīcīnaque Thybridis arva 500
intrārō, gentīque meae data moenia cernam,
cognātās urbīs ōlim populōsque propinquōs
Ēpīrō, Hesperiā, quibus īdem Dardanus auctor
atque īdem cāsūs, ūnam faciēmus utramque
Trōjam animīs; maneat nostrōs ea cūra nepōtēs.' 505
  "Prōvehimur pelagō vīcīna Ceraunia jūxtā,
unde iter Ītaliam cursusque brevissimus undīs.
Sōl ruit intereā, et montēs umbrantur opācī.
Sternimur optātae gremiō tellūris ad undam,
sortītī rēmōs, passimque in lītore siccō 510
corpora cūrāmus; fessōs sopor inrigat artūs.
Necdum orbem medium Nox Hōrīs ācta subībat:
haud sēgnis strātō surgit Palinūrus et omnīs
explōrat ventōs, atque auribus āera captat;
sīdera cūncta notat tacitō lābentia caelō, 515
Arctūrum pluviāsque Hyadas geminōsque Triōnēs,
armātumque aurō circumspicit Ōrīona.
Postquam cūncta videt caelō cōnstāre serēnō,
dat clārum ē puppī signum; nōs castra movēmus,
temptāmusque viam, et vēlōrum pandimus ālās. 520
Jamque rubēscēbat stellīs Aurōra fugātīs,
cum procul obscūrōs collīs humilemque vidēmus
Ītaliam.  Ītaliam prīmus conclāmat Achātēs,

Ītaliam laetō sociī clāmōre salūtant.

525 Tum pater Anchīsēs magnum crātēra corōnā
induit, implēvitque merō, dīvōsque vocāvit,
stāns celsā in puppī:
'Dī maris et terrae tempestātumque potentēs,
ferte viam ventō facilem et spīrāte secundī!'

530 Crēbrēscunt optātae aurae, portusque patēscit
jam propior, templumque appāret in arce Minervae.
Vēla legunt sociī, et prōrās ad lītora torquent.
Portus ab Eurōō flūctū curvātus in arcum;
objectae salsā spūmant aspargine cautēs;

535 ipse latet; geminō dēmittunt bracchia mūrō
turrītī scopulī, refugitque ab lītore templum.
Quattuor hīc, prīmum ōmen, equōs in grāmine vīdī
tondentīs campum lātē, candōre nivālī.
Et pater Anchīsēs: 'Bellum, ō terra hospita, por-
tās;

540 bellō armantur equī, bellum haec armenta minan-
tur.
Sed tamen īdem ōlim currū succēdere suētī
quadrupedēs et frēna jugō concordia ferre;
spēs et pācis,' ait. Tum nūmina sāncta precāmur
Palladis armisonae, quae prīma accēpit ovantīs,

545 et capita ante ārās Phrygiō vēlāmur amictū
praeceptīsque Helenī, dederat quae maxima, rīte
Jūnōnī Argīvae jussōs adolēmus honōrēs.

QUESTIONS ON **463–547**. 1. What presents did Helenus give
Aeneas at his departure? 2. With what additional men and
equipment did Helenus provide Aeneas? 3. What presents did
Andromache give Ascanius? 4. Why did Ascanius and Asty-
anax resemble each other in appearance? 5. In what ways did
Aeneas say that Helenus and Andromache were more fortunate
than he? 6. Where did the Trojans land the next evening after
they sailed from Buthrotum? 7. At about what time of day did
the Trojans sail from Ceraunia? 8. At about what time of
day did the Trojans come in sight of Italy? 9. What did the
Trojans see on the shore which Anchises interpreted as a good
omen? 10. To whom did the Trojans offer prayer on first land-
ing on Italian soil? To whom next?

*The Trojans continue their journey and land in Sicily near Mt. Etna.*

"Haud mora, continuō, perfectīs ōrdine vōtīs,
cornua vēlātārum obvertimus antemnārum,
Grajugenumque domōs suspectaque linquimus 550
arva.
Hinc sinus Herculeī, sī vēra est fāma, Tarentī
cernitur; attollit sē dīva Lacīnia contrā
Caulōnisque arcēs et nāvifragum Scylacēum.
Tum procul ē flūctū Trīnacria cernitur Aetna,
et gemitum ingentem pelagī pulsātaque saxa       555
audīmus longē frāctāsque ad lītora vōcēs,
exsultantque vada, atque aestū miscentur harēnae.
Et pater Anchīsēs: 'Nīmīrum haec illa Charybdis;
hōs Helenus scopulōs, haec saxa horrenda canēbat.
Ēripite, ō sociī, pariterque īnsurgite rēmīs.'       560
Haud minus ac jussī faciunt, prīmusque rudentem
contorsit laevās prōram Palinūrus ad undās;
laevam cūncta cohors rēmīs ventīsque petīvit.
Tollimur in caelum curvātō gurgite, et īdem
subductā ad Mānīs īmōs dēsēdimus undā;       565
ter scopulī clāmōrem inter cava saxa dedēre,
ter spūmam ēlīsam et rōrantia vīdimus astra.
Intereā fessōs ventus cum sōle relīquit,
ignārīque viae Cyclōpum adlābimur ōrīs.
"Portus ab accessū ventōrum immōtus et ingēns 570
ipse; sed horrificīs jūxtā tonat Aetna ruīnīs,
interdumque ātram prōrumpit ad aethera nūbem,
turbine fūmantem piceō et candente favīllā,
attollitque globōs flammārum et sīdera lambit,
interdum scopulōs āvulsaque vīscera montis       575
ērigit ērūctāns, liquefactaque saxa sub aurās
cum gemitū glomerat, fundōque exaestuat īmō.
Fāma est Enceladī sēmūstum fulmine corpus

urgērī mōle hāc, ingentemque īnsuper Aetnam
580 impositam ruptīs flammam exspīrāre camīnīs,
et, fessum quotiēns mūtet latus, intremere omnem
murmure Trīnacriam et caelum subtexere fūmō.
Noctem illam, tēctī silvīs, immānia mōnstra
perferimus, nec quae sonitum det causa vidēmus,
585 nam neque erant astrōrum ignēs nec lūcidus aethrā
sīdereā polus, obscūrō sed nūbila caelō,
et lūnam in nimbō nox intempesta tenēbat.

QUESTIONS ON 548–587. 1. How did Anchises discover the Trojan ships were near Charybdis? 2. What change did Palinurus at once make in his course? 3. At what time of day did the Trojans land on the coast of Sicily? 4. What unusual sights and sounds terrified the Trojans that night? 5. Who was Enceladus?

*The Trojans rescue a Greek, who had been abandoned by Ulysses.*

"Postera jamque diēs prīmō surgēbat Eōō,
ūmentemque Aurōra polō dīmōverat umbram,
590 cum subitō ē silvīs maciē cōnfecta suprēmā
ignōtī nova fōrma virī miserandaque cultū
prōcēdit, supplexque manūs ad lītora tendit.
Respicimus. Dīra inluviēs, immissaque barba,
cōnsertum tegumen spīnīs; at cētera Grajus
595 et quondam patriīs ad Trōjam missus in armīs.
Isque ubi Dardaniōs habitūs et Trōia vīdit
arma procul, paulum aspectū conterritus haesit
continuitque gradum; mox sēsē ad lītora praeceps
cum flētū precibusque tulit: 'Per sīdera testor,
600 per superōs atque hoc caelī spīrābile lūmen,
tollite mē, Teucrī; quāscumque abdūcite terrās;
hoc sat erit. Sciō mē Danaīs ē classibus ūnum,
et bellō Īliacōs fateor petiisse Penātīs;
prō quō, sī sceleris tanta est injūria nostrī,
605 spargite mē in flūctūs vāstōque immergite pontō;
sī pereō, hominum manibus periisse juvābit.'

Dīxerat, et genua amplexus genibusque volūtāns
haerēbat.  Quī sit fārī, quō sanguine crētus
hortāmur, quae deinde agitet fortūna fatērī.
Ipse pater dextram Anchīsēs, haud multa morātus, 610
dat juvenī, atque animum praesentī pignore firmat.
Ille haec, dēpositā tandem formīdine, fātur:
'Sum patriā ex Ithacā, comes īnfēlīcis Ulixī,
nōmine Achaemenidēs, Trōjam genitōre Adamastō
paupere (mānsissetque utinam fortūna!) profectus. 615
Hīc mē, dum trepidī crūdēlia līmina linquunt,
immemorēs sociī vāstō Cyclōpis in antrō
dēseruēre.  Domus saniē dapibusque cruentīs,
intus opāca, ingēns.  Ipse arduus altaque pulsat
sīdera (dī, tālem terrīs āvertite pestem!),          620
nec vīsū facilis nec dictū adfābilis ūllī;
vīsceribus miserōrum et sanguine vēscitur ātrō.
Vīdī egomet, duo dē numerō cum corpora nostrō
prēnsa manū magnā, mediō resupīnus in antrō,
frangeret ad saxum, saniēque aspersa natārent      625
līmina: vīdī ātrō cum membra fluentia tābō
manderet, et tepidī tremerent sub dentibus artūs;
haud impūne quidem, nec tālia passus Ulixēs
oblītusve suī est Ithacus discrīmine tantō.
Nam simul, explētus dapibus vīnōque sepultus,      630
cervīcem īnflexam posuit, jacuitque per antrum
immēnsus, saniem ērūctāns et frūsta cruentō
per somnum commixta merō, nōs magna precātī
nūmina sortītīque vicēs ūnā undique circum
fundimur, et tēlō lūmen terebrāmus acūtō           635
ingēns, quod torvā sōlum sub fronte latēbat,
Argolicī clipeī aut Phoebēae lampadis īnstar,
et tandem laetī sociōrum ulcīscimur umbrās.
Sed fugite, ō miserī, fugite atque ab lītore fūnem
rumpite;                                           640
nam quālis quantusque cavō Polyphēmus in antrō

lānigerās claudit pecudēs atque ūbera pressat,
centum aliī curva haec habitant ad lītora vulgō
īnfandī Cyclōpes, et altīs montibus errant.
645 Tertia jam lūnae sē cornua lūmine complent,
cum vītam in silvīs inter dēserta ferārum
lustra domōsque trahō, vāstōsque ab rūpe Cyclō-
pas
prōspiciō, sonitumque pedum vōcemque tremēscō;
vīctum īnfēlīcem, bācās lapidōsaque corna,
650 dant rāmī, et vulsīs pāscunt rādīcibus herbae.
Omnia conlūstrāns, hanc prīmum ad lītora classem
prōspexī venientem.  Huic mē, quaecumque fuis-
set,
addīxī; satis est gentem effūgisse nefandam.
Vōs animam hanc potius quōcumque absūmite
lētō.'

**QUESTIONS ON 588–654.** 1. Who was Achaemenides?  2. What did Achaemenides first ask the Trojans to do with him?  3. What did he ask them to do if they could not grant his first request? Why?  4. How tall did Achaemenides say the Cyclops was? 5. What feast of the Cyclops did Achaemenides report having witnessed?  6. What punishment had Ulysses inflicted on the Cyclops?  7. What was the Cyclops's name?  8. Why did Achaemenides urge the Trojans to flee from this region?  9. How long before Aeneas's arrival had Ulysses left the island?

### The Trojans flee from the Cyclopes.

655 "Vix ea fātus erat, summō cum monte vidēmus
ipsum inter pecudēs vāstā sē mōle moventem
pāstōrem Polyphēmum et lītora nōta petentem,
mōnstrum horrendum, īnforme, ingēns, cui lūmen
adēmptum.
Trunca manū pīnus regit et vēstīgia firmat;
660 lānigerae comitantur ovēs; ea sōla voluptās
sōlāmenque malī.
Postquam altōs tetigit flūctūs et ad aequora vēnit,
lūminis effossī fluidum lavit inde cruōrem,
dentibus īnfrendēns gemitū, graditurque per aequor

jam medium, necdum flūctus latera ardua tīnxit. 665
Nōs procul inde fugam trepidī celerāre, receptō
supplice sīc meritō, tacitīque incīdere fūnem,
verrimus et prōnī certantibus aequora rēmīs.
Sēnsit, et ad sonitum vōcis vēstīgia torsit,
vērum ubi nūlla datur dextrā adfectāre potestās 670
nec potis Ioniōs flūctūs aequāre sequendō,
clāmōrem immēnsum tollit, quō pontus et omnēs
contremuēre undae, penitusque exterrita tellūs
Italiae, curvīsque immūgiit Aetna cavernīs.
At genus ē silvīs Cyclōpum et montibus altīs 675
excītum ruit ad portūs, et lītora complent.
Cernimus astantīs nēquīquam lūmine torvō
Aetnaeōs frātrēs, caelō capita alta ferentīs,
concilium horrendum; quālēs cum vertice celsō
āeriae quercūs aut cōniferae cyparissī 680
cōnstiterunt, silva alta Jovis lūcusve Diānae.
Praecipitīs metus ācer agit quōcumque rudentīs
excutere et ventīs intendere vēla secundīs.
Contrā jussa monent Helenī Scyllam atque Cha-
    rybdim
inter, utramque viam lētī discrīmine parvō, 685
nī teneant cursūs; certum est dare lintea retrō.
Ecce autem Boreās angustā ab sēde Pelōrī
missus adest; vīvō praetervehor ōstia saxō
Pantagiae, Megarōsque sinūs, Thapsumque jacen-
    tem.
Tālia mōnstrābat relegēns errāta retrōrsus 690
lītora Achaemenidēs, comes īnfēlīcis Ulixī.

QUESTIONS ON 655–691. 1. What was Polyphemus's occupa-
tion? 2. Why did Polyphemus wade into the sea? 3. How did
Polyphemus discover the presence of the Trojans? 4. What did
Polyphemus first try to do? 5. What did he do next? 6. What
resulted from Polyphemus's shouting? 7. In what direction did
the Trojans in their terror think first of sailing? 8. Why did
they decide to sail in the opposite direction?

*The Trojans sail to Drepanum, where Anchises dies.*

"Sīcaniō praetenta sinū jacet īnsula contrā
Plēmyrium undōsum; nōmen dīxēre priōrēs
Ortygiam. Alphēum fāma est hūc Ēlidis amnem
695 occultās ēgisse viās subter mare, quī nunc
ōre, Arethūsa, tuō Siculīs cōnfunditur undīs.
Jussī nūmina magna locī venerāmur, et inde
exsuperō praepingue solum stāgnantis Helōrī.
Hinc altās cautīs prōjectaque saxa Pachȳnī
700 rādimus, et Fātīs numquam concessa movērī
appāret Camarīna procul, campīque Gelōī,
immānisque Gelā fluviī cognōmine dicta.
Arduus inde Acragās ostentat maxima longē
moenia, magnanimum quondam generātor equō-
    rum,
705 tēque datīs linquō ventīs, palmōsa Selīnūs,
et vada dūra legō saxīs Lilybēia caecīs.
Hinc Drepanī mē portus et inlaetābilis ōra
accipit. Hīc, pelagī tot tempestātibus āctus,
heu, genitōrem, omnis cūrae cāsūsque levāmen,
710 āmittō Anchīsēn; hīc mē, pater optime, fessum
dēseris, heu, tantīs nēquīquam ērepte perīclīs!
Nec vātēs Helenus, cum multa horrenda monēret,
hōs mihi praedīxit lūctūs, nōn dīra Celaenō.
Hic labor extrēmus, longārum haec mēta viārum;
715 hinc mē dīgressum vestrīs deus appulit ōrīs."

Sīc pater Aenēās intentīs omnibus ūnus
fāta renārrābat dīvum cursūsque docēbat.
Conticuit tandem, factōque hīc fīne quiēvit.

QUESTIONS ON **692–718**. 1. Who or what was Arethusa? 2. Who
or what was Alpheus? 3. Along what coast of Sicily did the
Trojans next sail? 4. Where was Drepanum? 5. At what line
of what book of the *Aeneid* is the beginning of Aeneas's story
which ends at line 715 of Book III?

# BOOK IV

*Dido reveals to Anna her love for Aeneas.*

At rēgīna, gravī jam dūdum saucia cūrā,
vulnus alit vēnīs, et caecō carpitur ignī.
Multa virī virtūs animō multusque recursat
√ gentis honōs; haerent īnfīxī pectore vultūs
verbaque, nec placidam membrīs dat cūra quiētem. 5
√ Postera Phoebēā lūstrābat lampade terrās
ūmentemque Aurōra polō dīmōverat umbram,
cum sīc ūnanimam adloquitur male sāna sorōrem:
"Anna soror, quae mē suspēnsam īnsomnia terrent!
Quis novus hic nostrīs successit sēdibus hospes, 10
quem sēsē ōre ferēns, quam fortī pectore et armīs!
Crēdō equidem, nec vāna fidēs, genus esse deōrum.
Dēgenerīs animōs timor arguit. Heu, quibus ille
jactātus fātīs! Quae bella exhausta canēbat!
Sī mihi nōn animō fīxum immōtumque sedēret, 15
nē cui mē vinclō vellem sociāre jugālī,
postquam prīmus amor dēceptam morte fefellit;
sī nōn pertaesum thalamī taedaeque fuisset,
huic ūnī forsan potuī succumbere culpae;

Anna, fatēbor enim, miserī post fāta Sychaeī 20
conjugis et sparsōs frāternā caede Penātīs,
sōlus hic īnflexit sēnsūs animumque labantem
impulit. Agnōscō veteris vēstīgia flammae.

***saucius wounded; stricken

vēna vein; **carpō pluck; consume

recursō recur

īnfīgō fix (in)

***membrum limb

lampas torch

ūmēns moist; **aurōra dawn; dīmoveō remove
ūnanimus of one heart, sympathizing; adloquor speak to, address; male badly, scarcely
īnsomnium dream
***hospes guest

dēgener base, ignoble; timor fear, cowardice; arguō prove; cf. *argūmentum evidence
exhauriō drain; undergo
immōtus immovable, unchangeable
sociō ally, unite; jugālis matrimonial, of marriage
dēcipiō deceive

pertaedet (it) wearies; **thalamus room, bridal room; *taeda bridal torch
forsan perhaps, perchance; succumbō yield to; **culpa weakness, fault

***fateor confess; cf. ***profiteor avow, profess
**spargō scatter, spatter; frāternus of a brother
īnflectō bend; sway; sēnsus feeling; labō yield
***vēstīgium footprint; trace

---

1. cūrā: i.e., amōre. 3. virī: i.e., of Aeneas. animō: dat. of direction. 4. pectore: abl. with haerent. 6. Phoebēā lampade: *with Phoebus's torch*, i.e., with the sun's rays. 10. Quis . . . hospes: *What a stranger guest this has entered our home!* 11. quem . . . ferēns: *how distinguished his appearance!* quam . . . armīs!: *how bravehearted and valiant!* 12. fidēs: supply est. 13. Dēgenerīs . . . arguit: *Fear proves souls base.*

14. jactātus: supply est. 15. Sī . . . sedēret: *If it were not my fixed and unchangeable resolve.* 18. pertaesum fuisset: understand mē as object. thalamī, taedae: gen. with pertaesum fuisset; see App. 93, c. 19. potuī succumbere: *I might have yielded.* culpae: i.e., to the "weakness" of falling in love with Aeneas. 21. frāternā caede: the reference is to the murder of Sychaeus by Dido's brother Pygmalion. 22. hic: i.e., Aeneas.

99

**dehīscō** yawn, open

Sed mihi vel tellūs optem prius īma dehīscat

**\*\*\*fulmen** thunderbolt, lightning
**\*palleō** be pale; **profundus** deep, profound
**\*ante** . . . **quam** sooner . . . than, before; **\*pudor** self-respect, modesty; **\*\*violō** do violence to; **resolvō** loosen; disregard
**\*auferō** bear off, take away; **\*\*\*sepulcrum** tomb, grave
**effor** speak; **obortus** rising, starting

25 vel pater omnipotēns adigat mē fulmine ad umbrās,
pallentīs umbrās Erebī noctemque profundam,
ante, pudor, quam tē violō aut tua jūra resolvō.
Ille meōs, prīmus quī mē sibi jūnxit, amōrēs
abstulit: ille habeat sēcum servetque sepulcrō."
30 Sic effāta, sinum lacrimīs implēvit obortīs.

QUESTIONS ON LINES 1–30. 1. Why does Dido think that Aeneas must be of divine origin? 2. Why is Dido ashamed to admit her feelings toward Aeneas? 3. Who was Sychaeus? What happened to him?

### Dido's love for Aeneas increases.

**\*\*\*dīligō** love

Anna refert: "Ō lūce magis dīlēcta sorōrī,

**maereō** grieve, sorrow; cf. **\*\*maeror** sorrow; **\*\*\*carpō** pluck; waste; **\*\*\*juventa** youth
**\*\*\*cinis** ashes; **\*mānēs** spirit of the dead; **\*\*sepeliō** bury
**\*\*\*flectō** bend, move; **marītus** husband; suitor

sōlane perpetuā maerēns carpēre juventā,
nec dulcīs nātōs Veneris nec praemia nōris?
Id cinerem aut Mānīs crēdis cūrāre sepultōs?
35 Estō: aegram nūllī quondam flexēre marītī,
nōn Libyae, nōn ante Tyrō; dēspectus Iarbās

**\*\*triumphus** triumph, victory

ductōrēsque aliī, quōs Āfrica, terra triumphīs

**pugnō** fight against; resist

dīves, alit. Placitōne etiam pugnābis amōrī?
Nec venit in mentem quōrum cōnsēderis arvīs?

**īnsuperābilis** unconquerable

40 Hinc Gaetūlae urbēs, genus īnsuperābile bellō,

**īnfrēnus** unbridled; **inhospitus** inhospitable; wild
**sitis** thirst; drought

et Numidae īnfrēnī cingunt et inhospita Syrtis;
hinc dēserta sitī regiō lātēque furentēs
Barcaeī. Quid bella Tyrō surgentia dīcam

**\*\*\*germānus** brother; **\*minae** threats
**auspex** augur; guide; **\*\*reor** think, believe

germānīque minās?
45 Dīs equidem auspicibus reor et Jūnōne secundā
hunc cursum Īliacās ventō tenuisse carīnās.

---

**25. pater:** i.e., Jupiter. **26. umbrās Erebī:** *the shades of Erebus*, i.e., of the underworld. **27. ante:** repeats **prius** in line 24. **28. Ille:** i.e., Sychaeus. **amōrēs:** poetic plural. **29. habeat:** understand **meōs amōrēs** as object. **habeat** is a jussive subjunctive, as is **servet**. **sepulcrō:** place where. **31. lūce:** i.e., **vītā**. **sorōrī:** *by your sister*, i.e., by Anna; dat. of agent with the pass. partic. **dīlēcta**. **32. carpēre:** **carpēris:** *will you waste yourself away;* reflexive. **34. Id:** i.e., Dido's decision not to remarry. **Mānīs:** *the spirit of the dead*, i.e., Sychaeus's spirit. **35. Estō:** *So be*

*it*. **36. Libyae:** locative. **Tyrō:** abl. of place where, instead of the usual locative. **dēspectus:** supply **est. Iarbās:** an African prince, one of Dido's suitors. **38. Placitōne . . . amōrī:** *Will you fight even against an acceptable love?* **39. arvīs:** place where. **40–43. Gaetūlae urbēs, Numidae, Barcaeī:** the Gaetulians, Numidians, and Barcaeans were fierce African peoples. **41. cingunt:** understand **tē** as object. **43. Tyrō:** place whence. **44. germānī:** i.e., of Pygmalion. **45. Jūnōne secundā:** *with Juno's favor;* Juno was the protectress of Carthage.

Quam tū urbem, soror, hanc cernēs, quae surgere
   rēgna
conjugiō tālī!  Teucrum comitantibus armīs
Pūnica sē quantīs attollet glōria rēbus!
Tū modo posce deōs veniam, sacrīsque litātīs
indulgē hospitiō, causāsque innecte morandī,
dum pelagō dēsaevit hiems et aquōsus Orīōn,
quassātaeque ratēs, dum nōn tractābile caelum."
   Hīs dictīs incēnsum animum īnflammāvit amōre,
spemque dedit dubiae mentī, solvitque pudōrem.
Prīncipiō dēlūbra adeunt, pācemque per ārās
exquīrunt; mactant lēctās dē mōre bidentīs
lēgiferae Cererī Phoebōque patrīque Lyaeō,
Jūnōnī ante omnīs, cui vincla jugālia cūrae;
ipsa tenēns dextrā pateram pulcherrima Dīdō
candentis vaccae media inter cornua fundit,
aut ante ōra deum pinguīs spatiātur ad ārās,
īnstauratque diem dōnīs, pecudumque reclūsīs
pectoribūs inhiāns spīrantia cōnsulit exta.
Heu, vātum ignārae mentēs!  Quid vōta furentem,
quid dēlūbra juvant?  Ēst mollīs flamma medullās
intereā, et tacitum vīvit sub pectore vulnus.
Ūritur īnfēlīx Dīdō, tōtāque vagātur
urbe furēns, quālis conjectā cerva sagittā,
quam procul incautam nemora inter Crēsia fīxit
pāstor, agēns tēlīs, līquitque volātile ferrum
nescius; illa fugā silvās saltūsque peragrat

conjugium marriage

50 **venia favor; litō offer
indulgeō yield to; innectō weave, contrive
dēsaeviō rage furiously; aquōsus watery, rainy
quassō shatter; **ratis boat, ship; tractābilis manageable; gracious

55 **pudor sense of shame
**prīncipium beginning; adeō go to, visit
exquīrō earnestly seek for; ***mactō sacrifice; bidēns sheep
lēgifer law-bringing, law-giving
jugālis of marriage

60 ***patera libation bowl
*candeō shine, be white; vacca heifer
***pinguis fat, rich; spatior walk back and forth
īnstaurō renew; **pecus animal; reclūdō open up
inhiō gape at; pore over; cf. *hiō gape; **spīrō breathe; quiver; exta vitals
65 **vātēs prophet; vōtum a vow, prayer; cf. ***voveō vow
*edō eat, consume; ***mollis soft; medulla marrow

***ūrō burn, torment

conjiciō throw, cast; cerva deer, doe
70 incautus unsuspecting

***pāstor shepherd; linquō leave behind; volātilis winged
nescius not knowing; saltus woodland; peragrō wander through

**47–48. Quam . . . tālī!:** *What a great city, Sister, you will see this become, what a great realm arise, through such a marriage!* **49. quantīs rēbus:** *by what great exploits.* **50. sacrīs litātīs:** *after offering acceptable sacrifice.* **52. Orīōn:** associated with rainy weather. **53. quassātae:** supply sunt.
**56. adeunt:** the subject is **Dīdō et Anna** understood. **57. bidentīs:** *sheep;* properly **bidēns** refers to a sheep with two permanent teeth, i.e., in its second year. **58. lēgiferae Cererī:** Ceres is called *law-giving* because agriculture is associated with stabilized society. **59. cui . . . cūrae:** *whose concern is the bonds of matrimony;* supply sunt. **cui:** dat. of reference. **cūrae:** dat. of purpose. **61. fundit:** understand **vīnum** as object. **62. ōra deum:** i.e., the statue of the gods. **65. vātum:** i.e., of the priests who, ignorant of future woes for Dido, assist her with the sacrifices. **65–66. Quid . . . juvant?:** *Of what avail are vows and shrines to one who is madly in love?* **66. Ēst:** pres. indic. of edō. **flamma:** i.e., the fire of love. **69. urbe:** place where. **70. Crēsia:** *Cretan.* **71. agēns tēlīs:** *pursuing with his darts.* **72. illa:** i.e., cerva.

lētālis deadly; *harundō reed; arrow

ostentō show, display

effor speak; resistō stop

**convīvium feast, banquet

***iterum again, anew; **dēmēns insane
exposcō demand, ask; nārrō tell
dīgredior go away, depart; vicissim in turn
***suādeō urge, invite

maereō grieve, mourn; cf. ***maeror grief; strātum coverlet, couch
incubō lie upon

dētineō hold

adsurgō rise

prōpugnāculum battlement, defense
**minae threats, menaces

Dictaeōs: haeret laterī lētālis harundō.
Nunc media Aenēān sēcum per moenia ducit,
75 Sīdoniāsque ostentat opēs urbemque parātam:
incipit effārī, mediāque in vōce resistit;
nunc eadem, lābente diē, convīvia quaerit,
Īliacōsque iterum dēmēns audīre labōrēs
exposcit, pendetque iterum nārrantis ab ōre.
80 Post, ubi dīgressī, lūmenque obscūra vicissim
lūna premit, suādentque cadentia sīdera somnōs,
sōla domō maeret vacuā, strātīsque relictīs
incubat. Illum absēns absentem auditque videt-
que,
aut gremiō Ascanium, genitōris imāgine capta,
85 dētinet, īnfandum sī fallere possit amōrem.
Nōn coeptae adsurgunt turrēs, nōn arma juventūs
exercet, portūsve aut prōpugnācula bellō
tūta parant; pendent opera interrupta, minaeque
mūrōrum ingentēs, aequātaque māchina caelō.

QUESTIONS ON **31–89**. 1. What are two of Anna's arguments in favor of Dido's marrying Aeneas? 2. What reasons for delaying at Carthage does Anna suggest to Dido she can offer to Aeneas? 3. Why was it especially appropriate for Dido to sacrifice to Juno? 4. To what does Vergil compare Dido in her love-stricken state? 5. What effect on building operations at Carthage has Dido's love for Aeneas?

*Juno craftily proposes a union between Aeneas and Dido.*

persentiō perceive clearly; **pestis plague; destruction
obstō withstand, resist

90    Quam simul ac tālī persēnsit peste tenērī
cāra Jovis conjūnx nec fāmam obstāre furōrī,
tālibus adgreditur Venerem Sāturnia dictīs:
"Ēgregiam vērō laudem et spolia ampla refertis

---

73. **Dictaeōs**: *of Dicte*, a mountain in Crete. 77. **lābente diē**: *as the day slips away.* 79. **nārrantis ab ōre**: *on the words of the speaker.* 80. **dīgressī**: supply *sunt.* 82. **domō**: place where. **relictīs**: *abandoned* (by Aeneas). 84. **genitōris . . . capta**: *attracted by his likeness to his father.* 87. **bellō**: *for war;* dat. of purpose.

88–89. **minaeque mūrōrum**: literally, *threats of walls,* i.e., *looming walls.* 89. **aequātaque . . . caelō**: *and the* (military) *engines high as heaven.* 90. **Quam**: = Dīdōnem; subject of **tenērī**. **peste**: i.e., by her passion for Aeneas. 91. **cāra . . . conjūnx**: i.e., Juno. **nec . . . furōrī**: *and that* (regard for) *her reputation did not withstand her*

tūque puerque tuus;  magnum et memorābile nū-
   men,
ūna dolō dīvum sī fēmina victa duōrum est.
Nec mē adeō fallit veritam tē moenia nostra
suspectās habuisse domōs Carthāginis altae.
Sed quis erit modus, aut quō nunc certāmine tantō?
Quīn potius pācem aeternam pāctosque hymenaeōs
exercēmus?  Habēs tōtā quod mente petīstī:
ārdet amāns Dīdō trāxitque per ossa furōrem.
Commūnem hunc ergō populum paribusque regā-
   mus
auspiciīs; liceat Phrygiō servīre marītō
dōtālīsque tuae Tyriōs permittere dextrae."
   Ollī (sēnsit enim simulātā mente locūtam,
quō rēgnum Ītaliae Libycās āverteret ōrās)
sīc contrā est ingressa Venus: "Quis tālia dēmēns
abnuat, aut tēcum mālit contendere bellō?
Sī modo, quod memorās, factum fortūna sequātur!
Sed Fātīs incerta feror, sī Juppiter ūnam
esse velit Tyriīs urbem Trōjāque profectīs,
miscērīve probet populōs aut foedera jungī.
Tū conjūnx, tibi fās animum temptāre precandō.
Perge: sequar. Tum sīc excēpit rēgia Jūnō:
"Mēcum erit iste labor.  Nunc quā ratiōne quod
   īnstat
cōnfierī possit paucīs, adverte, docēbō.
Vēnātum Aenēās ūnāque miserrima Dīdō

**Marginal glosses:**

memorābilis memorable, glorious

95 **fēmina woman

***suspiciō mistrust

*certāmen contest, strife

*potius rather; pacīscor agree upon; cf. *pactum compact, agreement;  **hymenaeus marriage

100

**amō love;  ***os, ossis bone, marrow

*auspicium auspices, authority; **serviō serve;  marītus husband

dōtālis as dowry

105

ingredior enter; begin;  ***dēmēns insane, mad

abnuō refuse (by nod)

110

probō approve;  **foedus alliance, pact

*precor pray, entreat; cf. *dēprecor avert by prayer

115

cōnfiō be done;  advertō turn (the mind) to, notice

*vēnor hunt

---

madness.  **94. puer:** i.e., Cupid.  **nūmen:** (display of) *divine power;* supply est.  **95. ūna fēmina:** i.e, Dido.  **97. suspectās:** *under suspicion.*  **98. modus:** *limit,* i.e., to the hostility between Venus and Juno.  **quō:** understand some verb like **prōgrediēmur.  99–100. Quīn potius exercēmus?:** *Why don't we rather arrange?*  **102–103. paribus auspiciīs:** *with equal authority.* Juno proposes an alliance with Venus so that they will jointly direct the united Carthaginians and the Trojans.  **103. liceat (Dīdōnī):** *let it be permitted to Dido.*  **liceat:** jussive subjunctive.  **104. dōtālīsque ... dextrae:** *and to deliver the*

*Carthaginian people as a dowry to your hands.*  **105. Ollī:** *to her;* an early form of illī.  **106. ōrās:** place whither.  **107. contrā est ingressa Venus:** *Venus proceeded* (to say) *in answer.*  **109. Sī . . . sequātur!:** *If only good fortune accompany the deed that you mention!* i.e., bringing about the marriage of Aeneas and Dido.  **111. Trōjāque profectīs:** *and for those who set out from Troy,* i.e., for the Trojans.  **113. conjūnx:** supply es.  **fās:** supply est.  **animum temptāre:** *to test his feelings.*  **115. labor:** i.e., the task of securing Jupiter's consent to the plan.  **quod īnstat:** *this urgent task.*  **117. Vēnātum:** supine in

**cràstinus** of tomorrow; **ortus** rising
*****radius** ray; **retegō** uncover, reveal
**nigrāns** black, dark; **grandō** hail
**trepidō** hurry to and fro; **saltus** woodland, glade; **indāgō** circle (*of nets, dogs, etc.*)
**dēsuper** from above; **īnfundō** pour; **tonitrus** thunder; ***cieō** stir up
****opācus** dark
****spēlunca** cave, grotto
**dēveniō** come to, arrive at

****cōnūbium** wedlock; ****stabilis** lasting; ****proprius** one's very own; **dicō** proclaim
*****hymenaeus** marriage; **adversor** oppose
**adnuō** nod assent; cf. *****nūtus** nod; ****rīdeō** laugh

in nemus īre parant, ubi prīmōs cràstinus ortūs
extulerit Tītān radiīsque retēxerit orbem.
120 Hīs ego nigrantem commixtā grandine nimbum,
dum trepidant ālae saltūsque indāgine cingunt,
dēsuper īnfundam, et tonitrū caelum omne ciēbō.
Diffugient comitēs, et nocte tegentur opācā;
spēluncam Dīdō dux et Trōjānus eandem
125 dēvenient. Aderō, et, tua sī mihi certa voluntās,
cōnūbiō jungam stabilī propriamque dicābō;
hic Hymenaeus erit." Nōn adversāta petentī
adnuit, atque dolīs rīsit Cytherēa repertīs.

QUESTIONS ON **90–128**. 1. Of what unfairness does Juno accuse Venus in her dealings with Dido? 2. What proposal does Juno make to Venus? 3. What motive does Venus think has led Juno to make this proposal? 4. Whom does Juno promise to consult about the proposed alliance? 5. In what way does Juno plan to bring Aeneas and Dido together under romantic circumstances?

*Dido and Aeneas while out hunting are driven by a storm into a lonely cave.*

*****aurōra** dawn

**jubar** light; **exorior** rise, appear
**rēte** net; **rārus** wide-meshed; **plaga** net, snare; **vēnābulum** hunting spear
**odōrus** keen-scented; *****canis** dog, hound
*****thalamus** bed-chamber; *****cūnctor** linger, delay
**ostrum** crimson; *****īnsignis** conspicuous
**sonipēs** prancing steed; *****frēnum** bit; *****ferōx** fiery, spirited; **mandō** champ
**prōgredior** advance; **stīpō** press around, crowd
*****pingō** paint, embroider; **chlamys** cloak, mantle; **limbus** border
**nōdō** knot, bind

Ōceanum intereā surgēns Aurōra relīquit.
130 It portīs jubare exortō dēlēcta juventūs;
rētia rāra, plagae, lātō vēnābula ferrō
Massȳlīque ruunt equitēs et odōra canum vīs.
Rēgīnam thalamō cūnctantem ad līmina prīmī
Poenōrum exspectant, ostrōque īnsignis et aurō
135 stat sonipēs ac frēna ferōx spūmantia mandit.

Tandem prōgreditur, magnā stīpante catervā,
Sīdoniam pictō chlamydem circumdata limbō,
cui pharetra ex aurō, crīnēs nōdantur in aurum,

---

–um depending on **īre**. **118–119**. cràstinus Tītān: *tomorrow's sun.* **120**. Hīs: *over them;* dat. with the compound verb **īnfundam** in line 122. **121**. ālae: *beaters* (of game). **124**. spēluncam: place whither. **125**. voluntās: *consent;* supply erit. **126**. jungam: understand eōs as object. dicābō: understand eam as object. **127**. Nōn adversāta petentī: *not opposing her* (i.e., Juno's) *request.* petentī: agrees with eī understood.

**130**. portīs: abl. of route. **132**. Massȳlī: *of the Massyli,* a people of Northern Africa. canum vīs: *pack of hounds.* **133**. thalamō: place where. **136**. prōgreditur: understand Dīdō as subject. **137**. Sīdoniam . . . limbō: *wrapped in a Sidonian robe with an embroidered border.* chlamydem: acc. with circumdata; see App. 106, *c.* **138**. pharetra: supply est. crīnēs . . . in aurum: *her hair is knotted into a gold* (clasp).

aurea purpuream subnectit fībula vestem.

Nec nōn et Phrygiī comitēs et laetus Iūlus    140

incēdunt; ipse ante aliōs pulcherrimus omnīs

īnfert sē socium Aenēās atque agmina jungit.

Quālis ubi hībernam Lyciam Xanthīque fluenta

dēserit, ac Dēlum māternam invīsit Apollō

īnstauratque chorōs, mixtīque altāria circum    145

Crētesque Dryopesque fremunt pictīque Agathyrsī;

ipse jugīs Cynthī graditur mollīque fluentem

fronde premit crīnem fingēns atque implicat aurō,

tēla sonant umerīs; haud illō sēgnior ībat

Aenēās, tantum ēgregiō decus ēnitet ōre.    150

Postquam altōs ventum in montīs atque invia lustra,

ecce ferae saxī dējectae vertice caprae

dēcurrēre jugīs; aliā dē parte patentīs

trānsmittunt cursū campōs, atque agmina cervī

pulverulenta fugā glomerant, montīsque relinquunt.  155

At puer Ascanius mediīs in vallibus ācrī

gaudet equō, jamque hōs cursū, jam praeterit illōs,

spūmantemque darī pecora inter inertia vōtīs

optat aprum, aut fulvum dēscendere monte leōnem.

Intereā magnō miscērī murmure caelum    160

incipit; īnsequitur commixtā grandine nimbus,

et Tyriī comitēs passim et Trōjāna juventūs

Dardaniusque nepōs Veneris dīversa per agrōs

tēcta metū petiēre; ruunt dē montibus amnēs.

Spēluncam Dīdō dux et Trōjānus eandem    165

dēveniunt. Prīma et Tellūs et prōnuba Jūnō

dant signum; fulsēre ignēs et cōnscius aethēr

---

purpureus crimson; cf. **purpura** purple color; **subnectō** fasten; **fībula** brooch, clasp

**īnferō** bring on, present

**hībernus** wintry; **fluentum** stream, river
**māternus** of one's mother; **invīsō** visit
**chorus** band of dancers; ***altāria** altar

***frōns** leaf, garland

***sēgnis** sluggish

**ēniteō** shine out

**invius** pathless; **lustrum** haunt, lair
**dējiciō** hurl down, dislodge; **capra** she-goat
**dēcurrō** run down

**trānsmittō** send across, cross; ***cervus** stag, deer
**pulverulentus** dusty

***gaudeō** delight, rejoice; *praetereō** pass by, outstrip
**iners** spiritless; cf. ***inertia** inactivity
**aper** wild boar; ***fulvus** tawny, yellow; ***leō** lion

**grandō** hail

***amnis** river, torrent

***spēlunca** cave, grotto

**dēveniō** come to, arrive at; **prōnuba** bride's attendant
***fulgeō** flash

---

**140. Nec nōn et:** *and furthermore.* **142. agmina jungit:** *joins his columns* (with Dido's). **143. hībernam Lyciam:** *his winter home in Lycia.* **144. Dēlum:** *Delos,* an island in the Aegean Sea, birthplace of Apollo. **146. Crētes, Dryopes, Agathyrsī:** peoples of Crete, Northern Greece, and Scythia, respectively. **147. ipse:** i.e., Apollo. **148. fronde:** i.e., with a laurel wreath. **149. illō:** abl. of comparison. **151. ventum:** supply **est:** *they came.* **153. dēcurrēre: dēcurrērunt. 154.** (sē) trānsmittunt: *they cross.* **160. magnō miscērī murmure:** alliteration. **163. nepōs:** i.e., Ascanius. **165.** same as line 124. **167. dant signum:** *give the signal* (for the wedding). Note the supernatural attendants at this wedding. **ignēs:** *flashes of lightning.* **167–168. cōnscius . . . cōnūbiīs:** *Heaven was a witness to the marriage.*

***cōnūbium wedlock, marriage; **ululō howl, scream

fūrtīvus stolen, secret; meditor have in mind
conjugium marriage; praetexō cover, conceal; ***culpa fault, guilt

*vēlōx swift

mōbilitās movement; vigeō be strong, thrive; adquīrō acquire, gain
*mox soon, presently
ingredior walk; *nūbila clouds

inrītō vex, provoke

perhibeō present; say

prōgignō bring forth, bear; pernīx agile, quick
horrendus terrible, dire; **quot how many, (as many) as; plūma feather

subter beneath

***lingua tongue; subrigō raise

medium middle

dēclīnō droop, close

territō frighten

cōnūbiīs, summōque ululārunt vertice nymphae.
Ille diēs prīmus lētī prīmusque malōrum
170 causa fuit; neque enim speciē fāmāve movētur,
nec jam fūrtīvum Dīdō meditātur amōrem:
conjugium vocat; hōc praetexit nōmine culpam.

QUESTIONS ON 129–172. 1. What features of Dido's dress and equipment does Vergil mention? 2. In what respects does Vergil compare Aeneas to Apollo? 3. What part does Ascanius take in the hunt? 4. About how old do you think Aeneas was at this time? 5. After the meeting in the cave was Dido more secretive or less secretive about her love for Aeneas? 6. Does Vergil say that Aeneas now considered himself married to Dido?

*Iarbas hears about Dido's love for Aeneas and begs Jupiter to help him.*

Extemplō Libyae magnās it Fāma per urbīs,
Fāma, malum quā nōn aliud vēlōcius ūllum.
175 Mōbilitāte viget vīrīsque adquīrit eundō;
parva metū prīmō, mox sēsē attollit in aurās,
ingrediturque solō, et caput inter nūbila condit.
Illam Terra parēns, īrā inrītāta deōrum,
extrēmam, ut perhibent, Coeō Enceladōque sorōrem
180 prōgenuit, pedibus celerem et pernīcibus ālīs,
mōnstrum horrendum, ingēns, cui, quot sunt corpore plūmae,
tot vigilēs oculī subter (mīrābile dictū),
tot linguae, totidem ōra sonant, tot subrigit aurīs.
Nocte volat caelī mediō terraeque per umbram,
185 strīdēns, nec dulcī dēclīnat lūmina somnō;
lūce sedet custōs aut summī culmine tēctī
turribus aut altīs, et magnās territat urbīs,

---

168. summō vertice: *from the mountain top.* For Work Unit XII, based on lines 1–172 of Book IV, see p. 269.
   174. nōn: supply est. 177. solō: *place where.* 178. īrā inrītāta deōrum: *vexed with anger at the gods.* The gods had slain Earth's children, the Titans; in revenge, Earth bore giants, among whom were Fama and Enceladus; Coeus was a Titan. 181–183. cui ... aurīs: *who has as many*

*watchful eyes under* (her wings) *as she has feathers on her body* (*strange to tell*) *and as many clattering tongues, as many babbling mouths, as many pricked up ears.* 184. caelī ... terraeque: *between heaven and earth.* mediō: *place where.* 185. lūmina: i.e., eyes. 186. lūce sedet custōs: *by day she sits a sentinel;* such an implied comparison is called a *metaphor;* see App. 22, 12. culmine: *place where.* 187. turribus: *place where.*

tam fictī prāvīque tenāx quam nūntia vērī.

Haec tum multiplicī populōs sermōne replēbat

gaudēns, et pariter facta atque īnfecta canēbat: 190

vēnisse Aenēān Trōjānō sanguine crētum,

cui sē pulchra virō dignētur jungere Dīdō;

nunc hiemem inter sē lūxū, quam longa, fovēre,

rēgnōrum immemorēs, turpīque cupīdine captōs.

Haec passim dea foeda virum diffundit in ōra. 195

Prōtinus ad rēgem cursūs dētorquet Iarbān,

incenditque animum dictīs atque aggerat īrās.

Hic, Hammōne satus raptā Garamantide nym-
    phā,

templa Jovī centum lātīs immānia rēgnīs,

centum ārās posuit, vigilemque sacrāverat ignem, 200

excubiās dīvum aeternās, pecudumque cruōre

pingue solum, et variīs flōrentia līmina sertīs.

Isque, āmēns animī, et rūmōre accēnsus amārō,

dīcitur ante ārās media inter nūmina dīvum

multa Jovem manibus supplex ōrāsse supīnīs: 205

"Juppiter omnipotēns, cui nunc Maurūsia pictīs

gēns epulāta torīs Lēnaeum lībat honōrem,

aspicis haec, an tē, genitor, cum fulmina torquēs,

nēquīquam horrēmus, caecīque in nūbibus ignēs

terrificant animōs et inānia murmura miscent? 210

Fēmina, quae nostrīs errāns in fīnibus urbem

exiguam pretiō posuit, cui lītus arandum

cuique locī lēgēs dedimus, cōnūbia nostra

reppulit, ac dominum Aenēān in rēgna recēpit.

---

**fictus** made up, false; **prāvus** wrong, perverse; **tenāx** tenacious; **nūntia** messenger
**multiplex** manifold, varied;
***sermō** talk; **repleō** fill
**īnfectus** not done
***crēscō** grow; spring, be born

***dignor** deem worthy, condescend
**lūxus** luxury, excess; cf. ***lūxuria** extravagance
**immemor** unmindful, forgetful;
**cupīdō** desire, love
*foedus** foul; **diffundō** pour

**dētorqueō** turn

**aggerō** heap up; increase

****serō** sow; beget

**excubiae** guard, sentry; ****pecus** animal (of the flock)
*flōreō** blossom, bloom; ****sertum** wreath, garland
**accendō** inflame; **amārus** bitter

**supīnus** upturned

**epulor** feast; ****torus** banqueting couch
****torqueō** twist; hurl

**terrificō** terrify; ****inānis** vain, useless
****fēmina** woman

*pretium** price; ***arō** plow, till

**repellō** thrust back, spurn;
**dominus** master, lord

---

**189. Haec:** i.e., Fama. **191. vēnisse:** infinitive in indirect statement, depending on **canēbat.** **192. virō:** *as husband.* **193. nunc . . . fovēre:** *they were passionately caressing each other the whole winter long.* So Fama falsely reported; presumably Aeneas remained in Carthage only a few weeks at most. **hiemem:** extent of time. **longa:** supply sit. **195. Haec:** acc. neuter pl., object of diffundit. **dea:** i.e., Fāma. **virum:** virōrum.

**198. Hammōne satus:** *begotten of Hammon,* a god of the Libyans, identified by the Romans

with Jupiter. **Garamantide:** *African.* **199. rēgnīs:** place where. **202. solum:** supply **erat.** **203. animī:** *in mind;* a locative. **204. media . . . dīvum:** *in the midst of the divine presence of the gods.* **205. multa:** *many* (favors); secondary object of ōrāsse. **206. Maurūsia:** *Moorish.* **207. Lēnaeum honōrem:** *Bacchic honor,* i.e., an offering of wine. **211. Fēmina:** i.e., Dido. **212. pretiō:** *at a price.* Dido had had to buy the site of Carthage. **213. locī lēgēs:** *conditions of tenure.*

LATIN POETRY

108

**sēmivir** unmanly, effeminate;
**\*comitātus** retinue

**mentum** chin; **mitra** head-dress, cap; **\*madeō** be wet, drip

**subnectō** tie under

215 Et nunc ille Paris, cum sēmivirō comitātū,
Maeoniā mentum mitrā crīnemque madentem
subnexus, raptō potitur: nōs mūnera templīs
quippe tuīs ferimus fāmamque fovēmus inānem."

QUESTIONS ON **173–218.** 1. What characteristics of Fama does Vergil mention? 2. How many eyes has Fama? How many ears? How many tongues? 3. What favors does Iarbas say he has shown Dido? 4. What offer does Iarbas say Dido rejected? 5. With whom does Iarbas compare Aeneas? Why? 6. By what expression does Iarbas indicate his lack of faith in Jupiter?

*Jupiter sends Mercury to Carthage, to remind Aeneas of Italy and his duty to Ascanius.*

Tālibus ōrantem dictīs ārāsque tenentem
220 audiit omnipotēns, oculōsque ad moenia torsit

**\*\*oblīvīscor** forget; **amāns** lover; cf. **\*\*\*amō** love

rēgia et oblītōs fāmae meliōris amantīs.
Tum sīc Mercurium adloquitūr, ac tālia mandat:

**\*\*\*vādō** go; **\*pinna** feather; wing

"Vāde age, nāte, vocā Zephyrōs, et lābere pinnīs,
Dardaniumque ducem, Tyriā Carthāgine quī nunc
225 exspectat Fātīsque datās nōn respicit urbīs,
adloquere, et celerīs dēfer mea dicta per aurās.
Nōn illum nōbīs genetrīx pulcherrima tālem

**ideō** for this reason; **\*vindicō** claim; defend
**gravidus** heavy, pregnant

prōmīsit, Grajumque ideō bis vindicat armīs,
sed fore quī gravidam imperiīs bellōque frementem
230 Italiam regeret, genus altō ā sanguine Teucrī
prōderet, ac tōtum sub lēgēs mitteret orbem.

**\*\*\*accendō** fire; arouse

Sī nūlla accendit tantārum glōria rērum,
nec super ipse suā mōlītur laude labōrem,
Ascaniōne pater Rōmānās invidet arcīs?

---

**215. Paris:** Aeneas is called a Paris because he has stolen Dido from Iarbas, just as Paris had stolen Helen from Menelaus. **216–217. Maeoniā...subnexus:** *with a Lydian cap tied under his chin and his locks dripping* (with perfume). **mentum, crīnem:** acc. with **subnexus;** see App. 114. **217. raptō:** *the plunder,* i.e., Dido; abl. with **potitur. 218. fāmam inānem:** *an empty name.* **220. moenia:** i.e., the walls of Carthage. **221. fāmae:** gen. used with **oblītōs. 222. Mercurium:** *Mercury,* messenger of the gods. **adloquitūr:** the final syllable is here long. **223. lābere:**

imperat. **224.** ducem: object of **adloquere** in line 226. **Carthāgine:** locative. **228. Grajumque ...armīs:** *nor for this purpose did she save him twice from the weapons of the Greeks.* Venus saved Aeneas when he fought with Diomedes (see Book I, lines 96–98) and again when Troy fell (see Book II, lines 632–633). **230. regeret:** subjunctive in a clause of characteristic; so **prōderet** and **mitteret** in line 231. In lines 229–231 Vergil alludes to the greatness of Rome in his own time under the Emperor Augustus. **234. Ascaniō:** dat. used with **invidet.** The Idea is that by delaying

Quid struit, aut quā spē inimīcā in gente morātur 235
nec prōlem Ausoniam et Lāvīnia respicit arva?
Nāviget! Haec summa est, hic nostrī nūntius estō."
  Dīxerat. Ille patris magnī pārēre parābat
imperiō, et prīmum pedibus tālāria nectit
aurea, quae sublīmem ālīs sīve aequora suprā 240
seu terram rapidō pariter cum flāmine portant.
Tum virgam capit; hāc animās ille ēvocat Orcō
pallentīs, aliās sub Tartara trīstia mittit,
dat somnōs adimitque, et lūmina morte resignat.
Illā frētus, agit ventōs, et turbida trānat 245
nūbila. Jamque volāns apicem et latera ardua cernit
Atlantis dūrī, caelum quī vertice fulcit,
Atlantis, cīnctum adsiduē cui nūbibus ātrīs
pīniferum caput et ventō pulsātur et imbrī;
nix umerōs īnfūsa tegit; tum flūmina mentō 250
praecipitant senis, et glaciē riget horrida barba.
Hīc prīmum paribus nītēns Cyllēnius ālīs
cōnstitit; hinc tōtō praeceps sē corpore ad undās
mīsit, avī similis, quae circum lītora, circum
piscōsōs scopulōs humilis volat aequora jūxtā. 255
Haud aliter terrās inter caelumque volābat
lītus harēnōsum ad Libyae ventōsque secābat
māternō veniēns ab avō Cyllēnia prōlēs.
Ut prīmum ālātīs tetigit māgālia plantīs,
Aenēān fundantem arcīs ac tēcta novantem 260
cōnspicit. Atque illī stellātus iāspide fulvā
ēnsis erat, Tyriōque ārdēbat mūrice laena
dēmissa ex umerīs, dīves quae mūnera Dīdō
fēcerat, et tenuī tēlās discrēverat aurō.

*struō heap up; contrive
***prōlēs offspring

tālāria winged sandals; **nectō tie, bind
***sublīmis aloft
flāmen wind
*virga twig; wand; ***anima soul, spirit; ēvocō call forth, summon
**palleō be pale
*adimō take away; resignō unseal
*frētus relying on; turbidus disordered, tumbling; trānō swim across; fly over; cf. ***nō swim
**nūbila clouds; apex peak, summit; ***arduus steep
fulciō prop up, support
adsiduē unceasingly
pīnifer pine-bearing; cf. *pīnus pine tree; *pulsō beat, lash; ***imber rain
*nix snow; īnfundō pour upon; mentum chin
glaciēs ice; **rigeō be stiff; horridus bristling; barba beard
***nītor support oneself by, poise on
*avis bird
piscōsus fish-haunted; scopulus rock, cliff
harēnōsus sandy; ***secō cut through, cleave
māternus maternal; **avus grandfather
ālātus winged; māgālia huts; planta sole of the foot, foot
fundō lay foundation for; novō make new, build
stellātus starred, studded; iāspis jasper
mūrex crimson; laena cloak, mantle
**tenuis thin, fine-drawn; tēla web, cloth; discernō divide; interweave

in Carthage Aeneas seems to begrudge Ascanius his heritage in Italy. 235. spē: note the hiatus. 237. hic ... estō: *let this be our message.* nostrī: gen. pl. of ego. estō: imperat. 3rd pers. 238. Ille: i.e., Mercury. 242. virgam: i.e., the caduceus, a wand entwined with serpents. 243. Tartara: *the underworld.* 244. lūmina: i.e., oculōs. 248–249. cīnctum ... caput: *whose pine-bearing summit is ever girt with black clouds.* 250. mentō: place whence. 252. Cyllēnius: *Mercury,* who was born on Mount Cyllene. 258. māternō veniēns ab avō: i.e., from Mt. Atlas. Mercury's mother was Maja, daughter of Atlas. 261. illī: i.e., Aeneas; dat. of possession.

**continuō** at once, without delay; **invādō** rush upon, assail
**fundāmentum** a foundation; **uxōrius** excessively devoted to one's wife
**exstruō** build

**rēgnātor** ruler

**mandātum** command, injunction
**terō** waste, idle away; *ōtium leisure

**hērēs** heir

***tenuis** thin, unsubstantial; **ēvānēscō** vanish, fade away

265 Continuō invādit: "Tū nunc Carthāginis altae
fundāmenta locās pulchramque uxōrius urbem
exstruis, heu, rēgnī rērumque oblīte tuārum?
Ipse deum tibi mē clārō dēmittit Olympō
rēgnātor, caelum et terrās quī nūmine torquet;
270 ipse haec ferre jubet celerīs mandāta per aurās.
Quid struis, aut quā spē Libycīs teris ōtia terrīs?
Sī tē nūlla movet tantārum glōria rērum,
nec super ipse tuā mōlīris laude labōrem,
Ascanium surgentem et spēs hērēdis Iūlī
275 respice, cui rēgnum Ītaliae Rōmānaque tellūs
dēbentur." Tālī Cyllēnius ōre locūtus
mortālīs vīsūs mediō sermōne relīquit,
et procul in tenuem ex oculīs ēvānuit auram.

QUESTIONS ON **219-278**. 1. To whom does Jupiter send Mercury? 2. What questions does Jupiter ask Mercury in regard to Aeneas? 3. What order does Jupiter tell Mercury to give to Aeneas? 4. What was Mercury's flying equipment? 5. What did Mercury carry in his hand? 6. Where does Mercury stop on his way to Carthage? 7. What was Aeneas doing when Mercury arrived in Carthage? How was he dressed?

*Aeneas secretly prepares to leave Carthage. Dido, on discovering the plan, reproaches him bitterly.*

**aspectus** sight; **obmūtēscō** be mute, stand speechless
***faux** throat

*attonō thunder at; astound; **monitus** warning
**ambiō** go around, get around

**adfātus** speech; **exōrdium** beginning

**versō** keep turning

**alternō** waver, hesitate

At vērō Aenēās aspectū obmūtuit āmēns,
280 arrēctaeque horrōre comae, et vōx faucibus haesit.
Ārdet abīre fugā dulcīsque relinquere terrās,
attonitus tantō monitū imperiōque deōrum.
Heu! Quid agat? Quō nunc rēgīnam ambīre furentem
audeat adfātū? Quae prīma exōrdia sūmat?
285 Atque animum nunc hūc celerem, nunc dīvidit illūc,
in partīsque rapit variās, perque omnia versat.
Haec alternantī potior sententia vīsa est:

---

**267. oblīte:** *forgetful;* vocative of **oblītus. 271. terrīs:** place where. **277. sermōne:** place where. **281. dulcīs terrās:** i.e., Carthaginian territory. **283. Quid agat?:** *What shall he do?;* deliberative subjunctive; so **audeat** and **sūmat** in line 284.

**284. Quae sūmat?:** *What beginning shall he make?* **285-286. Atque ... versat:** *And he sends his swift mind hither and thither and hurries it on in different directions and turns it to all kinds of plans.* **287. alternantī:** *wavering;* agrees with **eī** under-

Mnēsthea Sergestumque vocat fortemque Serestum,
classem aptent tacitī sociōsque ad lītora cōgant,
arma parent, et quae rēbus sit causa novandīs
dissimulent; sēsē intereā, quandō optima Dīdō
nesciat et tantōs rumpī nōn spēret amōrēs,
temptātūrum aditūs, et quae mollissima fandī
tempora, quis rēbus dexter modus. Ōcius omnēs
imperiō laetī pārent et jussa facessunt.

At rēgīna dolōs (quis fallere possit amantem?)
praesēnsit, mōtūsque excēpit prīma futūrōs,
omnia tūta timēns; eadem impia Fāma furentī
dētulit armārī classem cursumque parārī.
Saevit inops animī, tōtamque incēnsa per urbem
bacchātur, quālis commōtīs excita sacrīs
Thyias, ubi audītō stimulant trietērica Bacchō
orgia, nocturnusque vocat clāmōre Cithaerōn.
Tandem hīs Aenēān compellat vōcibus ultrō:

"Dissimulāre etiam spērāstī, perfide, tantum
posse nefās, tacitusque meā dēcēdere terrā?
Nec tē noster amor nec tē data dextera quondam
nec moritūra tenet crūdēlī fūnere Dīdō?
Quīn etiam hībernō mōlīris sīdere classem,
et mediīs properās Aquilōnibus īre per altum,
crūdēlis? Quid? Sī nōn arva aliēna domōsque
ignōtās peterēs et Trōja antīqua manēret,
Trōja per undōsum peterētur classibus aequor?
Mēne fugis? Per ego hās lacrimās dextramque
    tuam tē
(quandō aliud mihi jam miserae nihil ipsa relīquī), 315

290 **novō** renew

**\*\*dissimulō** hide, conceal;
  **\*\*\*quandō** when; since, because

**ōcius** (more) swiftly; cf. **\*ōcior** swifter, swift
295 **facessō** do with zeal

**praesentiō** foresee, detect

300 **\*\*\*saeviō** rage, rave; **inops** helpless, bereft
  **bacchor** rush wildly; **commoveō** move, shake; **exciō** excite, rouse; cf. **\*\*\*concitō** stir up
  **stimulō** spur on, goad; **trietēricus** biennial
  **orgia** mystic rites; **nocturnus** of the night; by night
305 **\*\*\*dissimulō** dissemble, hide, conceal; **perfidus** faithless, false
  **dēcēdō** go away, depart

**hībernus** of winter, wintry
310 **\*\*properō** hasten, hurry

**undōsus** billowy

---

stood. **289. aptent**; subjunctive in indirect command depending on **vocat**. So **cōgant** in line 289, **parent** in line 290, and **dissimulent** in line 291. **290. rēbus novandīs**: *for making new plans*. **293. temptātūrum**: supply **esse**; infinitive in an indirect statement, depending on **vocat**. **293–294. quae ... tempora**: *what moments are most propitious for speaking*; supply **sint**. **294. quis ... modus**: *what way is favorable for his interests*; supply **sit**.

**298. furenti**: *to the frenzied* (queen). **300. inops animī**: *bereft of reason*. **302. Thyias**: *a Bacchante*, a woman worshipper of Bacchus, pronounced as if spelled Tyjjas. **audītō Bacchō**: *after the Bacchus cry has been heard*. **stimulant**: understand **illam** as object. **303. vocat**: understand **illam** as object. **Cithaerōn**: a mountain in Greece. **309. Quīn etiam**: *nay, even*. **314. ego**: subject of **ōrō** in line 319. **tē**: object of **ōrō** in line 319.

per cōnūbia nostra, per inceptōs hymenaeōs,
sī bene quid dē tē meruī, fuit aut tibi quicquam
dulce meum, miserēre domūs lābentis, et istam,

***adhūc** still, yet; ***exuō** put off, lay aside·

ōrō, sī quis adhūc precibus locus, exue mentem.

**tyrannus** ruler, despot

320 Tē propter Libycae gentēs Nomadumque tyrannī

***ōdī** hate; **īnfēnsus** hostile

ōdēre, īnfēnsī Tyriī; tē propter eundem

***exstinguō** blot out; ***pudor** shame; sense of shame; **adeō** go to, reach **moribundus** ready to die

extīnctus pudor et quā sōlā sīdera adībam
fāma prior. Cui mē moribundam dēseris, hospes,
hoc sōlum nōmen quoniam dē conjuge restat?

325 Quid moror?  An mea Pygmaliōn dum moenia frāter

**dēstruō** destroy

dēstruat, aut captam dūcat Gaetūlus Iarbās?
Saltem sī qua mihī dē tē suscepta fuisset

**subolēs** offspring, child; **parvulus** little; **aula** hall; palace

ante fugam subolēs, sī quis mihi parvulus aulā
lūderet Aenēās, quī tē tamen ōre referret,

330 nōn equidem omnīnō capta ac dēserta vidērer."

QUESTIONS ON 279–330.  1. What effect does Mercury's message have on Aeneas?  2. What orders does Aeneas give three of his captains?  3. What difficult task does Aeneas say he himself intends to undertake meantime?  4. How does Vergil say Dido learned of Aeneas's preparations for departure?  5. What arguments does Dido use in her appeal to Aeneas to delay his departure?  6. What two men does Dido especially fear if Aeneas deserts her now?  Why in each case?

*Aeneas tries to excuse his conduct and declares that he is following the decree of fate.*

**monitum** warning, admonition

Dīxerat.  Ille Jovis monitīs immōta tenēbat

**obnītor** strive, struggle

lūmina, et obnīxus cūram sub corde premēbat.
Tandem pauca refert: "Ego tē, quae plūrima fandō
ēnumerāre valēs, numquam, rēgīna, negābō

**prōmereor** deserve well; **piget** (it) displeases, (it) irks

335 prōmeritam, nec mē meminisse pigēbit Elissae,

---

318. miserēre: *imperat.* 318–319. istam exue mentem: *put aside your intention.* 319. locus: supply *est.* 320. Tē propter: i.e., propter tē. This inversion is called *anastrophe.* Nomadum: *of the Numidians.* 321. ōdēre: ōdērunt; understand mē as object. īnfēnsī: supply sunt. Dido suggests that her own people, as well as the neighboring tribes, resent Aeneas's presence. 322. quā

... adībam: *through which alone I was gaining immortality.* 324. dē conjuge: *from* (the name of) *husband.* 325. An (moror): *am I waiting.* For Work Unit XIII, based on lines 173–330 of Book IV, see p. 270.

332. lūmina: i.e., oculōs. 335. prōmeritam (esse): *that you have deserved* (well of me). Elissae: gen. with meminisse; Elissa was an-

dum memor ipse meī, dum spīritus hōs regit artūs.

Prō rē pauca loquar.   Neque ego hanc abscondere
    fūrtō

spērāvī (nē finge) fugam, nec conjugis umquam

praetendī taedās, aut haec in foedera vēnī.

Mē sī Fāta meīs paterentur dūcere vītam                    340

auspiciīs et sponte meā compōnere cūrās,

urbem Trōjānam prīmum dulcīsque meōrum

relliquiās colerem, Priamī tēcta alta manērent,

et recidīva manū posuissem Pergama victīs.

Sed nunc Ītaliam magnam Grȳnēus Apollō,                   345

Ītaliam Lyciae jussēre capessere sortēs;

hic amor, haec patria est.   Sī tē Carthāginis arcēs

Phoenissam Libycaeque aspectus dētinet urbis,

quae tandem Ausoniā Teucrōs cōnsīdere terrā

invidia est?   Et nōs fās extera quaerere rēgna.         350

Mē patris Anchīsae, quotiēns ūmentibus umbrīs

nox operit terrās, quotiēns astra ignea surgunt,

admonet in somnīs et turbida terret imāgō;

mē puer Ascanius capitisque injūria cārī,

quem rēgnō Hesperiae fraudō et fātālibus arvīs.         355

Nunc etiam interpres dīvum, Jove missus ab ipsō

(testor utrumque caput) celerīs mandāta per aurās

dētulit; ipse deum manifestō in lūmine vīdī

intrantem mūrōs, vōcemque hīs auribus hausī.

Dēsine mēque tuīs incendere tēque querēlīs;             360

Ītaliam nōn sponte sequor."

**spīritus** breath, breath of life

**abscondō** hide; **\*fūrtum** stealth

**praetendō** hold out; proffer; **\*\*taeda** torch, bridal torch; marriage; **\*\*\*foedus** alliance, agreement **\*\*auspicium** auspices, authority

**reliquiae** remains; **\*\*\*colō** cherish; care for **recidīvus** revived; new

**capessō** seize, strive to reach

**aspectus** sight; **dētineō** hold

**\*\*invidia** envy, jealousy; **\*exterus** outer, foreign **\*quotiēns** how often; (as often) as; **ūmēns** moist, dewy **operiō** cover; **\*\*quotiēns** how often; (as often) as; **\*\*\*astrum** star; **igneus** fiery, flaming **\*admoneō** warn, admonish; **turbidus** troubled **fraudō** cheat, rob; **fātālis** fated, destined **interpres** go-between, messenger **\*\*\*testor** call to witness, swear by; **mandātum** command **\*\*manifestus** clear

**\*intrō** enter; **\*\*\*hauriō** drink in **dēsinō** cease; **\*querēla** complaint

QUESTIONS ON **331–361**.   1. What two statements does Aeneas make in acknowledgment of Dido's services to him?   2. What does Aeneas deny intending to do?   3. Who besides Mercury

---

other name for Dido.   **336. memor:** supply sum. **337. Prō rē:** *In defense of my conduct.*   **338. nē finge:** poetic negative imperative.   **338–339. nec . . . vēnī:** *nor have I ever held out* (to you) *the rite of marriage nor have I entered into such a covenant;* i.e., Aeneas disclaims having married Dido or having had any intention of doing so.   **344. et . . . victīs:** *and with my own hand I should have built a second Troy for the defeated* (Trojans).

**345. Grȳnēus:** *Grynean, of Grynia,* where there was a temple to Apollo.   **350. fās:** supply est. **351. patris Anchīsae:** gen. depending on imāgō in line 353.   **354. mē:** supply some verb like **admonet. capitisque injūria cārī:** *and the wrong done to his dear life.* Apparently Aeneas has taken Mercury's words (272–276) to heart.   **356. interpres dīvum:** i.e., Mercury.   **357. testor utrumque caput:** *I swear by my life and yours.*

does Aeneas say has admonished him to leave Carthage?
4. What does Aeneas say would now be the situation if he were
allowed to live in accordance with his own wishes? 5. In what
four words does Aeneas deny responsibility for continuing his
journey to Italy?

*After a violent scene, Dido rushes away, beside her-*
*self with grief.*

āversus hostile

pererrō wander over; survey

profor speak

Tālia dīcentem jam dūdum āversa tuētur,

hūc illūc volvēns oculōs tōtumque pererrat

lūminibus tacitīs, et sīc accēnsa profātur:

365 "Nec tibi dīva parēns, generis nec Dardanus auc-
tor,

perfidus faithless, false; cautēs rock

admoveō move to; **ūber ud- der, breast; tigris tigress

reservō keep back

perfide, sed dūrīs genuit tē cautibus horrēns

Caucasus, Hyrcānaeque admōrunt ūbera tigrēs.

Nam quid dissimulō, aut quae mē ad majōra re-
servō?

flētus weeping; ingemō groan, show sorrow

**miseror pity

Num flētū ingemuit nostrō? Num lūmina flexit?

370 Num lacrimās victus dedit, aut miserātus aman-
tem est?

anteferō place before

Quae quibus anteferam? Jam jam nec maxima
Jūnō

nec Sāturnius haec oculīs pater aspicit aequīs.

***nusquam nowhere; ējiciō cast out; shipwreck; ***egeō be in want, lack

Nusquam tūta fidēs. Ējectum lītore, egentem

excēpī, et rēgnī dēmēns in parte locāvī;

375 āmissam classem, sociōs ā morte redūxī.

**furia rage, fury; augur prophet

Heu! Furiīs incēnsa feror! Nunc augur Apollō,

nunc Lyciae sortēs, nunc et Jove missus ab ipsō

interpres go-between, messen- ger

**scīlicet forsooth

interpres dīvum fert horrida jussa per aurās.

Scīlicet is superīs labor est, ea cūra quiētōs

refellō refute

380 sollicitat. Neque tē teneō neque dicta refellō;

---

**363-364. tōtum ... tacitīs:** *she surveys Aeneas from head to foot with expressionless eyes.* **365. tibi:** supply **est. 366. perfide:** a vocative. **cautibus:** place where. **367. Caucasus:** a mountain range in Asia. **Hyrcānae:** *Hyrcanian, of the Hyrcani,* a tribe on the Caspian Sea. **admōrunt (admō-vērunt) ūbera:** *suckled.* **368. majōra:** *greater* (wrongs). **369. ingemuit, flexit:** the subject is Aeneas. Dido uses the third person contemp-

tuously. **371. Quae quibus anteferam?:** literally, *What shall I prefer to what?* i.e., What shall I mention first? **372. Sāturnius pater:** i.e., Jupiter. **373. Nusquam:** supply **est. Ējectum:** supply **eum. lītore:** place where. **376. Furiīs:** *by the Furies;* dat. of agent. **379. quiētōs:** understand **deōs.** Dido is sarcastic in suggesting that the gods might be interested in so despicable a creature as Aeneas.

Ī, sequere Ītaliam, ventīs pete rēgna per undās.
Spērō equidem mediīs, sī quid pia nūmina possunt,
supplicia hausūrum scopulīs, et nōmine Dīdō
saepe vocātūrum.  Sequar ātrīs ignibus absēns,      **absēns** absent; left behind
et, cum frīgida mors animā sēdūxerit artūs,      385 **frīgidus** cold; **sēdūcō** take away, separate
omnibus umbra locīs aderō.  Dabis, improbe,      ***improbus** wicked, base
      poenās.
Audiam, et haec Mānīs veniet mihi fāma sub īmōs."      **mānēs** spirits of the dead; underworld
Hīs medium dictīs sermōnem abrumpit, et aurās
aegra fugit, sēque ex oculīs āvertit et aufert,      **auferō** bear away
linquēns multa metū cūnctantem et multa volen-390 **cūnctor** delay, hesitate
      tem
dīcere.  Suscipiunt famulae, conlāpsaque membra      **famula** maidservant; **conlābor** fall; swoon
marmoreō referunt thalamō strātīsque repōnunt.      **marmoreus** of marble; **strātum** bed, couch; **repōnō** place

QUESTIONS ON **362–392.** 1. Whom does Dido directly address in lines 365–367? Whom in lines 369–370? 2. In what ways does Dido remind Aeneas that she has helped him and the Trojans? 3. Do you think Dido believed Aeneas's statement about Mercury's orders to leave Carthage? 4. Why do you think Dido tells Aeneas to go? 5. What does she say she hopes will happen to him on the voyage? 6. What happens to Dido as a result of her violent outburst?

*Dido sends Anna to plead with Aeneas.*

At pius Aenēās, quamquam lēnīre dolentem      **lēniō** soothe, calm
sōlandō cupit et dictīs āvertere cūrās,      **sōlor** console, comfort
multa gemēns magnōque animum labefactus amōre 395 ***gemō** groan, lament; **labefaciō** shake
jussa tamen dīvum exsequitur, classemque revīsit.      **exsequor** follow out, execute
Tum vērō Teucrī incumbunt, et lītore celsās
dēdūcunt tōtō nāvīs.  Natat ūncta carīna,      **dēdūcō** bring down, launch; **natō** swim, float; **unguō** smear (*with pitch*)
frondentīsque ferunt rēmōs et rōbora silvīs      **frondēns** leafy
īnfabricāta fugae studiō.      400 **īnfabricātus** unfashioned, rough
Migrantīs cernās tōtāque ex urbe ruentīs;      **migrō** depart

**383. scopulīs:** place where. **Dīdō:** Greek acc. **384. ātrīs ignibus:** *with black torches* (like a Fury). **386. umbra:** *as a shade.* The thought is that Dido will constantly haunt Aeneas, in life and after her death. **387. haec fāma:** literally, *this report,* i.e., the report of this (punishment of yours). **388–389. aurās fugit:** *flees the air,* i.e., she flees indoors. **392. thalamō:** dat. of direction. **strātīs:** dat. of place whither or abl. of place where. **393. dolentem:** understand eam. **395. animum labefactus:** *shaken in spirit.* **399. silvīs:** place whence. **401. cernās:** *you may see;* potential subjunctive.

**formīca** ant; **far** spelt, *a kind of grain;* **acervus** heap, pile
**populō** plunder

\*\***niger** black; \*\***herba** grass

**convectō** carry along, convey; **callis** path; **grandis** great, huge; **trūdō** push along; shove
**obnītor** struggle, strain
**castīgō** chastise, punish; **sēmita** path; \*\***ferveō** boil; be alive
**sēnsus** feelings, emotion
**fervō** be hot; be alive

\*\***precor** pray, entreat; cf. \*\***dēprecor** avert by prayer
**submittō** subject

**inexpertus** untried

\*\*\***properō** hasten, make haste

**carbasus** sail

\***nauta** sailor, seaman; \*\*\***corōna** wreath, garland

**perferō** bear, endure

**exsequor** follow out; perform; **perfidus** false, faithless
**arcānus** hidden, secret; **sēnsus** thought, feeling

**exscindō** tear down, destroy

\*\*\***mānēs** spirits of the dead; soul; **revellō** tear away, desecrate

ac velut ingentem formīcae farris acervum
cum populant, hiemis memorēs, tēctōque repōnunt:
it nigrum campīs agmen, praedamque per herbās
405 convectant calle angustō; pars grandia trūdunt
obnīxae frūmenta umerīs, pars agmina cōgunt
castīgantque morās; opere omnis sēmita fervet.
Quis tibi tum, Dīdō, cernentī tālia sēnsus,
quōsve dabās gemitūs, cum lītora fervere lātē
410 prōspicerēs arce ex summā, tōtumque vidērēs
miscērī ante oculōs tantīs clāmōribus aequor!
Improbe amor, quid nōn mortālia pectora cōgis!
Īre iterum in lacrimās, iterum temptāre precandō
cōgitur et supplex animōs submittere amōrī,
415 nē quid inexpertum frūstrā moritūra relinquat.
"Anna, vidēs tōtō properārī lītore circum:
undique convēnēre; vocat jam carbasus aurās,
puppibus et laetī nautae imposuēre corōnās.
Hunc ego sī potuī tantum spērāre dolōrem,
420 et perferre, soror, poterō. Miserae hoc tamen ūnum
exsequere, Anna, mihī; sōlam nam perfidus ille
tē colere, arcānōs etiam tibi crēdere sēnsūs,
sōla virī mollīs aditūs et tempora nōrās.
Ī, soror, atque hostem supplex adfāre superbum.
425 Nōn ego cum Danaīs Trōjānam exscindere gentem
Aulide jūrāvī, classemve ad Pergama mīsī,
nec patris Anchīsae cinerem Mānīsve revellī:
cūr mea dicta negat dūrās dēmittere in aurīs?
Quō ruit? Extrēmum hoc miserae det mūnus
amantī;
430 exspectet facilemque fugam ventōsque ferentīs.

---

403. **tēctō:** place where. 404. **it:** the subject is **agmen,** which, in line 405, has a plural verb, **convectant. campīs:** abl. of route. 406. **agmina cōgunt:** *keep the ranks close.* 408. **Quis tibi sēnsus:** supply **erat.** 413. **temptāre:** understand **Aenēān** as object. 414. **animōs:** her proud spirit. 416. **properārī:** *there is bustle.* The verb is here used impersonally. 418. **corōnās:** sailors

decked their ships with garlands on leaving a port. 420. **Miserae:** construe with **mihī** in line 421. 422. **colere, crēdere:** historical infinitives. 423. **tempora:** *suitable moments.* **nōrās:** **nōverās.** 426. **Aulide:** *at Aulis,* the port from which the Greek fleet sailed to attack Troy. 429. **det:** jussive subjunctive; so **exspectet** in line 430. 430. **ferentīs:** *favorable.*

Nōn jam conjugium antīquum, quod prōdidit, ōrō,

nec pulchrō ut Latiō careat rēgnumque relinquat;  **careō** be without

tempus ināne petō, requiem spatiumque furōrī,  **requiēs** rest, respite

dum mea mē victam doceat fortūna dolēre.

Extrēmam hanc ōrō veniam (miserēre sorōris),  435 ***venia** favor

quam mihi cum dederit, cumulātam morte remit-  **cumulō** heap up, augment
   tam."

QUESTIONS ON **393–436**. 1. What does Aeneas now wish to do?
What does he do? 2. Do you think the word *pius* in line 393 is
an appropriate term to apply to Aeneas at this point of the
story? 3. What preparation for sailing do the Trojans make?
4. To what does Vergil compare the Trojans busy with their
preparations? 5. What reason does Dido give for sending Anna
to intercede for her? 6. What final favor does Dido, through
Anna, ask of Aeneas?

*Dido, alarmed by strange omens and dreams, resolves
   on death.*

Tālibus ōrābat, tālīsque miserrima flētūs  **flētus** weeping, tearful plea

fertque refertque soror.  Sed nūllīs ille movētur

flētibus, aut vōcēs ūllās tractābilis audit;  **tractābilis** manageable, yield-
   ing

Fāta obstant, placidāsque virī deus obstruit aurīs. 440 **obstō** oppose; **obstruō** block up;
   stop

Ac velut annōsō validam cum rōbore quercum  **annōsus** full of years, old;
   **validus** strong, sturdy; **quer-
   cus** oak tree

Alpīnī Boreae nunc hinc nunc flātibus illinc  **flātus** blast; **illinc** from that
   side

ēruere inter sē certant; it strīdor, et altae  **strīdor** creaking

cōnsternunt terram concussō stīpite frondēs;  **cōnsternō** strew; **concutiō** shake
   violently; **stīpes** stock, trunk;
   ***frōns** leaf, foliage

ipsa haeret scopulīs, et quantum vertice ad aurās 445

aetheriās, tantum rādīce in Tartara tendit:  **aetherius** of heaven, heavenly;
   *rādīx root

haud secus adsiduīs hinc atque hinc vōcibus hērōs  **secus** otherwise, differently;
   *adsiduus constant, unceas-
   ing; **hērōs** hero

tunditur, et magnō persentit pectore cūrās:  **tundō** beat upon, assail; **per-
   sentiō** feel deeply

mēns immōta manet; lacrimae volvuntur inānēs.

Tum vērō īnfēlīx, Fātīs exterrita, Dīdō  450 **exterreō** frighten, terrify

mortem ōrat; taedet caelī convexa tuērī.  **taedet** (it) wearies; **convexum**
   arch, vault

Quō magis inceptum peragat lūcemque relinquat,  **inceptum** undertaking; **peragō**
   go through with, finish

---

**432. Latiō:** abl. depending on **careat. careat:**
in a substantive volitive clause depending on **ōrō;**
so **relinquat. 433. tempus ināne:** *a brief respite.*
**436. quam ... remittam:** *which, when he grants it
to me, I shall repay in full measure by my death.*

**438. fertque refertque:** *bears and bears again*
(to Aeneas). **442. Boreae:** *North Wind.* **443.** it
**strīdor:** *a roar goes forth.* **445. ipsa:** i.e., **quercus.**
**449. inānēs:** *in vain.*
**452. Quō ... peragat:** a clause of purpose.

**tūricremus** incense-burning

**horrendus** frightful, awful; **la-tex** liquid; wine; **nigrēscō** grow black
**obscēnus** foul;   ill-omened;
**\*cruor** blood
**vīsum** sight, portent
**\*marmor** marble

**vellus** wool, wool fillet; **niveus** snowy, snow-white; **fēstus** festal; **revinciō** bind, wreathe
**exaudiō** hear

**fērālis** funereal, mournful; **\*car-men** song, note; **būbō** owl

**\*\*\*vātēs** soothsayer; **praedic-tum** prophecy
**terribilis** terrifying,   awful;
**monitus** warning; **horrificō** terrify

**incomitātus** unaccompanied

**\*\*\*duplex** double, two

**\*\*\*agitō** drive, pursue

**\*\*\*fax** torch, firebrand; **ser-pēns** serpent; cf. **\*\*\*serpō** creep, crawl
**ultrīx** avenging

vīdit, tūricremīs cum dōna impōneret ārīs,
(horrendum dictū) laticēs nigrēscere sacrōs,
455 fūsaque in obscēnum sē vertere vīna cruōrem.
Hoc vīsum nūllī, nōn ipsī effāta sorōrī.
Praetereā fuit in tēctīs dē marmore templum
conjugis antīquī, mīrō quod honōre colēbat,
velleribus niveīs et fēstā fronde revīnctum;
460 hinc exaudīrī vōcēs et verba vocantis
vīsa virī, nox cum terrās obscūra tenēret,
sōlaque culminibus fērālī carmine būbō
saepe querī et longās in flētum dūcere vōcēs;
multaque praetereā vātum praedicta priōrum
465 terribilī monitū horrificant.  Agit ipse furentem
in somnīs ferus Aenēās, semperque relinquī
sōla sibī, semper longam incomitāta vidētur
īre viam, et Tyriōs dēsertā quaerere terrā,
Eumenidum velutī dēmēns videt agmina Pentheus,
470 et sōlem geminum et duplicīs sē ostendere Thēbās,
aut Agamemnonius scaenīs agitātur Orestēs,
armātam facibus mātrem et serpentibus ātrīs
cum fugit, ultrīcēsque sedent in līmine Dīrae.

QUESTIONS ON **437–473**.  1.  Why is Aeneas not moved by Anna's pleas?  2.  To what does Vergil compare Aeneas?  3.  What strange sights and sounds terrify Dido?  4.  What bad dreams further terrify her?

*Dido bids Anna build a funeral pyre, on which she says she intends to burn everything that might remind her of Aeneas.*

**concipiō** take on; **\*\*\*furia** mad-ness, frenzy; **ēvincō** over-come

Ergō ubi concēpit furiās ēvicta dolōre,
475 dēcrēvitque morī, tempus sēcum ipsa modumque
exigit, et, maestam dictīs adgressa sorōrem,

---

**456. nūllī:** *to no one.* **effāta:** supply est. **457. tem-plum:** *a chapel.* **458. conjugis antīquī:** i.e., ded-icated to Sychaeus. **460. hinc:** i.e., from the chapel. **461. vīsa:** supply sunt. **462. culminibus:** place where. **463. querī:** supply vīsa est. **469. Eume-nidum:** *of the Furies.* **Pentheus:** a mad king of

Thebes. **471. scaenīs agitātur:** *is driven over the stage.* The story of Orestes was a favorite dramatic subject. **Orestēs:** Agamemnon's son, pursued by the Furies because he had murdered his mother, Cly-temnestra. **473. Dīrae:** *the Furies.* For Work Unit XIV, based on lines 331–473 of Book IV, see p. 272.

cōnsilium vultū tegit, ac spem fronte serēnat:
"Invēnī, germāna, viam (grātāre sorōrī),
quae mihi reddat eum vel eō mē solvat amantem.
Ōceanī fīnem jūxtā sōlemque cadentem                    480
ultimus Aethiopum locus est, ubi maximus Atlās
axem umerō torquet, stellīs ārdentibus aptum;
hinc mihi Massȳlae gentis mōnstrāta sacerdōs,
Hesperidum templī custōs epulāsque dracōnī
quae dabat et sacrōs servābat in arbore rāmōs,          485
spargēns ūmida mella sopōriferumque papāver.
Haec sē carminibus prōmittit solvere mentīs,
quās velit, ast aliīs dūrās immittere cūrās,
sistere aquam fluviīs et vertere sīdera retrō,
nocturnōsque movet Mānīs; mūgīre vidēbis               490
sub pedibus terram et dēscendere montibus ornōs.
Testor, cāra, deōs et tē, germāna, tuumque
dulce caput magicās invītam accingier artīs.
Tū sēcrēta pyram tēctō interiōre sub aurās
ērige, et arma virī, thalamō quae fīxa relīquit        495
impius, exuviāsque omnīs lectumque jugālem,
quō periī, superimpōnās; abolēre nefandī
cūncta virī monumenta juvat, mōnstratque sacer-
dōs."
Haec effāta silet; pallor simul occupat ōra.
Nōn tamen Anna novīs praetexere fūnera sacrīs          500
germānam crēdit, nec tantōs mente furōrēs
concipit, aut graviōra timet quam morte Sychaeī.
Ergō jussa parat.

QUESTIONS ON **474–503**. 1. What has Dido now resolved to do
with herself? 2. What two possible results does Dido tell Anna
she hopes to attain by magic rites? 3. By whose aid does Dido

serēnō make bright; feign

grātor congratulate

**axis sky; **stella star; *ap-
tus fitted, studded
***sacerdōs priestess

dracō serpent, dragon

*rāmus branch, bough

***ūmidus liquid, dewy; me!
honey; sopōrifer sleep-bring-
ing; papāver poppy; poppy
juice
**carmen song; incantation
**immittō send upon
***sistō stop, halt; **fluvius
river
nocturnus of the night; **mū-
giō rumble
ornus ash tree

sēcrētus in secret; cf. ***sē-
cernō separate, set apart;
pyra funeral pile, pyre
*ērigō erect, raise
lectus bed; jugālis marriage,
nuptial
superimpōnō place thereon;
aboleō destroy; nefandus un-
speakable; accursed
*monumentum reminder

pallor paleness

praetexō conceal, disguise

concipiō conceive, imagine

---

**478.** grātāre: imperative. **479.** eō: *from him.*
**481.** Aethiopum: *of the Ethiopians.* **482.** umerō:
abl. of means. **483.** mōnstrāta: supply **est.**
**484.** Hesperidum: *of the Hesperides,* the maidens
who guarded the Golden Apples. **487.** Haec:
i.e., the priestess. solvere: *to free* (from cares).
**490.** nocturnōs Mānīs: *the ghosts of night.*

**493.** magicās ... artīs: *that unwillingly I gird on
the arts of magic.* accingier: an early form of
the passive infin. **497.** superimpōnās: jussive
subjunctive with force of an imperative.
**498.** juvat: *it pleases;* understand mē. **501.** fu-
rōrēs: *frenzy.* i.e., on Dido's part. **502.** morte:
abl. of time.

tell her sister she expects to carry out these magic rites? What
examples does Dido report of this person's magic power? 4. What
does Dido order built? Where?

### Dido and the priestess perform certain magic rites in vain. Dido laments her fate.

**pyra** funeral pile, pyre

At rēgīna, pyrā penetrālī in sēde sub aurās

**\*\*ērigō** erect, raise; **\*\*\*taeda** 505 ērēctā, ingentī taedīs atque īlice sectā,
pine fagot; **\*ilex** holm-oak, evergreen
**\*\*\*intendō** stretch; festoon;      intenditque locum sertīs et fronde corōnat
**\*\*\*sertum** wreath, garland; **corōnō** encircle, wreathe      fūnereā; super exuviās ēnsemque relictum
**fūnereus** funereal
**effigiēs** effigy, image      effigiemque torō locat, haud ignāra futūrī.

Stant ārae circum, et crīnīs effūsa sacerdōs

**\*tonō** thunder out, invoke      510 ter centum tonat ōre deōs, Erebumque, Chaosque,

**tergeminus** three-bodied      tergeminamque Hecatēn, tria virginis ōra Diānae.

**\*\*\*fōns** spring, lake, river      Sparserat et laticēs simulātōs fontis Avernī,

**falx** sickle, pruning-knife; **metō** reap, cut      falcibus et messae ad lūnam quaeruntur aēnīs
**pūbēns** full-grown; **\*\*\*herba** grass, herb; **\*\*\*niger** black;      pūbentēs herbae, nigrī cum lacte venēnī;
**lac** milk; milky juice; 515 quaeritur et nāscentis equī dē fronte revulsus
**\*\*\*venēnum** poison
**revellō** tear away      et mātrī praereptus amor.
**praeripiō** snatch
**mola** meal, ground spelt      Ipsa molā manibusque piīs altāria jūxtā,

**recingō** ungird, loosen      ūnum exūta pedem vinclīs, in veste recīnctā,

testātur moritūra deōs et cōnscia fātī

520 sīdera; tum, sī quod nōn aequō foedere amantīs

**\*\*\*precor** pray; beg for; cf. **\*\*\*dēprecor** avert by prayer      cūrae nūmen habet jūstumque memorque, precātur.
**\*\*sopor** sleep, slumber

Nox erat, et placidum carpēbant fessa sopōrem

corpora per terrās, silvaeque et saeva quiērant

aequora, cum mediō volvuntur sīdera lāpsū,

**volucris** winged creature, bird; 525 cum tacet omnis ager, pecudēs pictaeque volucrēs,
cf. **\*\*\*volucer** winged, flying

---

**508. effigiem:** i.e., of Aeneas. **torō:** place
where. **509. crīnīs effūsa:** *with dishevelled locks.*
crīnīs: acc. with **effūsa**; see App. 114. **510. tonat**
ōre deōs: *she thunderously invokes the gods.*
Chaos: a deity of the underworld; Greek acc.
**511. tria Diānae:** Diana was a goddess with
threefold attributes. She was Luna in heaven,
Diana on earth, Hecate in the underworld. In
this threefold capacity she was invoked in magic
rites. **512. fontis Avernī:** of *Lake Avernus,* the
traditional entrance to the underworld. **513. ad
lūnam:** *by moonlight.* The night was considered
propitious for magic. **515. nāscentis equī:** *of a*

colt at birth. **516. amor:** *a love charm.* It was
thought that at birth a colt had a sort of tumor
on its forehead. This was considered a powerful
love charm, but it had to be secured before the
mother of the colt bit it off. **517. Ipsa:** i.e.,
Dido. **518. ūnum . . . vinclīs:** *with one foot out
of its fetters,* i.e., with one foot bare of sandal.
**pedem:** acc. with **exūta**; see App. 114. **520–
521. sī . . . habet:** *whatever divine power cares for
those who love on unequal terms,* i.e., those whose
love is not returned, as in Dido's case. **cūrae:**
dat. of purpose.
**523. quiērant: quiēverant.**

quaeque lacūs lātē liquidōs quaeque aspera dūmīs
rūra tenent, somnō positae sub nocte silentī.
Lēnībant cūrās et corda oblīta labōrum.
At nōn īnfēlīx animī Phoenissa nec umquam
solvitur in somnōs oculīsve aut pectore noctem      530
accipit; ingeminant cūrae, rūrsusque resurgēns
saevit amor, magnōque īrārum flūctuat aestū.
Sīc adeō īnsistit, sēcumque ita corde volūtat:
"Ēn quid agō? Rūrsusne procōs inrīsa priōrēs
experiar, Nomadumque petam cōnūbia supplex,      535
quōs ego sim totiēns jam dēdignāta marītōs?
Īliacās igitur classīs atque ultima Teucrum
jussa sequar? Quiane auxiliō juvat ante levātōs,
et bene apud memorīs veteris stat grātia factī?
Quis mē autem (fac velle) sinet ratibusve superbīs      540
invīsam accipiet? Nescīs, heu! perdita, necdum
Lāomedontēae sentīs perjūria gentis?
Quid tum? Sōla fugā nautās comitābor ovantīs,
an Tyriīs omnīque manū stīpāta meōrum
īnferar, et, quōs Sīdoniā vix urbe revellī,      545
rūrsus agam pelagō, et ventīs dare vēla jubēbō?
Quīn morere, ut merita es, ferrōque āverte dolōrem.
Tū lacrimīs ēvicta meīs, tū prīma furentem
hīs, germāna, malīs onerās, atque objicis hostī.
Nōn licuit thalamī expertem sine crīmine vītam      550
dēgere, mōre ferae, tālīs nec tangere cūrās!
Nōn servāta fidēs cinerī prōmissa Sychaeō!"
Tantōs illa suō rumpēbat pectore questūs.

**lacus lake; liquidus fluid: limpid; dūmus bramble; thicket
rūs country; field
lēniō soothe, calm; ***oblīvīscor forget

ingeminō redouble; resurgō rise again
flūctuō toss, surge

īnsistō press on, persist; volūtō keep turning, reflect
**ēn lo!; procus suitor; inrīdeō laugh at, mock

***totiēns so many times; dēdignor disdain, scorn; marītus husband; suitor
*igitur therefore
**quia because

***ratis raft; ship

***nesciō not know; *perdō destroy; necdum and not yet
perjūrium treachery
**nauta sailor; *ovō rejoice, exult

545 revellō tear away

550 expers without part in, free from; ***crīmen guilt, reproach
dēgō spend, pass; fera wild beast

questus lamentation

526. que ... que: both ... and. 527. somnō positae: lying in slumber. 528. Lēnībant: Lēniēbant. 529. īnfēlīx animī: sad at heart. animī: locative. Phoenissa: understand cūrās lēnībat. 534. quid agō?: what am I to do? 535. experiar, petam: deliberative questions. 536. marītōs: as husbands. 538-539. Quiane ... factī?: (Shall I follow the Trojans) because they are pleased to have been helped before by me and because gratitude for a past good deed lingers in their mindful hearts? 540. fac velle: suppose I want to. fac: imperative. 541. perdita: lost one; Dido is addressing herself. 542. Lāomedontēae gentis: of Laomedon's race; Laomedon, Priam's father, was a notorious breaker of promises. 544. Tyriīs ... meōrum: attended by my Tyrians and the whole band of my subjects. 545. īnferar: shall I fling myself (upon them)? 547. Quīn morere: Nay, die; imperat. 548. furentem: i.e., mē furentem. 549. germāna: voc.; Dido rebukes the absent Anna for having encouraged her love for Aeneas. 550. thalamī expertem: free from marriage. 552. servāta: supply est.

QUESTIONS ON **504–553**. 1. What objects does Dido place on
the pyre? 2. What materials does the priestess use in her magic
rites? 3. What part does Dido perform in the magic rites?
4. What other possible solutions of her difficulties occur to Dido
in the night, which are rejected one by one? 5. Whom does
Dido unjustly blame for her present unbearable situation?
6. What promise does Dido now wish she had kept?

### *Mercury again appears to Aeneas, who now hastens to sail away.*

Aenēās celsā in puppī, jam certus eundī,

555 carpēbat somnōs, rēbus jam rīte parātīs.

Huic sē fōrma deī vultū redeuntis eōdem

obtulit in somnīs, rūrsusque ita vīsa monēre est,

omnia Mercuriō similis, vōcemque colōremque

et crīnīs flāvōs et membra decōra juventā:

560 "Nāte deā, potes hōc sub cāsū dūcere somnōs,

nec quae tē circum stent deinde perīcula cernis,

dēmēns, nec zephyrōs audīs spīrāre secundōs?

Illa dolōs dīrumque nefās in pectore versat,

certa morī, variōque īrārum flūctuat aestū.

565 Nōn fugis hinc praeceps, dum praecipitāre potes-
tās?

Jam mare turbārī trabibus saevāsque vidēbis

conlūcēre facēs, jam fervere lītora flammīs,

sī tē hīs attigerit terrīs Aurōra morantem.

Heia age, rumpe morās!  Varium et mūtābile sem-
per

570 fēmina."  Sīc fātus, noctī sē immiscuit ātrae.

Tum vērō Aenēās, subitīs exterritus umbrīs,

corripit ē somnō corpus sociōsque fatīgat:

"Praecipitēs vigilāte, virī, et cōnsīdite trānstrīs;

solvite vēla citī.  Deus aethere missus ab altō

575 festīnāre fugam tortōsque incīdere fūnīs

---

**Glossary (margin):**

*rīte* duly

*color* color, complexion

**flāvus** auburn, golden; ***decōrus** beautiful

*flūctuō* toss, surge

*conlūceō* gleam; *fervō* glow

*heia* away!; *mūtābilis* changeable, fickle

*immisceō* mingle with

***subitus** sudden, unexpected; *exterreō* startle, alarm
***fatīgō** tire out; importune

*vigilō awake; *trānstrum* rowing bench
**citus** quick

*festīnō* hurry, hasten; *incīdō* cut; ***fūnis** rope, cable

---

**556.** deī: i.e., Mercury.  **558.** omnia ... similis:
*like Mercury in all respects.*  omnia: acc. of respect.  So vōcem, colōrem, crīnīs, and membra.
colōremque: a hypermetric line.  **560.** potes ...
somnōs: *can you continue your sleep at such a*
crisis?  **563.** Illa: i.e., Dido.  **564.** certa morī:
*resolved to die;* an infinitive dependent on an adjective is a poetic construction.  **565.** potestās:
supply est.  **570.** fēmina: supply est.
**571.** umbrīs: *vision.*

ecce iterum stimulat.  Sequimur tē, sāncte deōrum,

quisquis es, imperiōque iterum pārēmus ovantēs.

Adsīs ō placidusque juvēs, et sīdera caelō

dextra ferās."  Dīxit, vāgīnāque ēripit ēnsem

fulmineum, strictōque ferit retinācula ferrō.

Īdem omnīs simul ārdor habet: rapiuntque ruunt-
    que;

lītora dēseruēre, latet sub classibus aequor,

adnīxī torquent spūmās, et caerula verrunt.

**stimulō** spur on, urge

**\*\*ovō** rejoice

**vāgīna** sheath, scabbard

580 **fulmineus** flashing;  **retināculum** cable, hawser
**ārdor** zeal

**adnītor** strive;  **\*\*spūma** foam;  **caerula** sea; cf. **\*\*caerul(e)us** deep blue, sea-green;  **verrō** sweep, sweep over

QUESTIONS ON **554–583.**  1. Where is Aeneas when Mercury again appears to him?  What is he doing?  2. What reason does Mercury give Aeneas for immediate flight?  3. What does Aeneas do at once as a result of the vision?  4. What two words in Aeneas's prayer indicate that he is not sure what god has appeared to him?  5. Do the Trojans first use sails or oars in their departure from Carthage?

*From the palace Dido beholds the departure of Aeneas.*
    *She prays the gods to punish him and his de-*
    *scendants.*

Et jam prīma novō spargēbat lūmine terrās

Tīthōnī croceum linquēns Aurōra cubīle.

Rēgīna, ē speculīs ut prīmum albēscere lūcem

vīdit et aequātīs classem prōcēdere vēlīs,

lītoraque et vacuōs sēnsit sine rēmige portūs,

terque quaterque manū pectus percussa decōrum,

flāventīsque abscissa comās, "Prō Juppiter! Ībit

hic," ait, "et nostrīs inlūserit advena rēgnīs?

Nōn arma expedient tōtāque ex urbe sequentur,

dēripientque ratīs aliī nāvālibus?  Īte,

ferte citī flammās, date tēla, impellite rēmōs!

Quid loquor aut ubi sum?  Quae mentem īnsānia

    mūtat?

Īnfēlīx Dīdō, nunc tē facta impia tangunt?

585 **croceus** yellow;  **cubīle** couch, bed
**specula** watch tower;  **albēscō** grow white
**prōcēdō** go forth, proceed

**rēmex** oarsman, rower

**percutiō** strike, beat

590 **flāvēns** yellow, golden;  **abscindō** tear;  **prō** O! Ah!
**inlūdō** make sport of, mock;  **advena** stranger

**dēripiō** snatch;  **nāvāle** shipyard, dock
**\*\*\*citus** quick

595

**576. sāncte deōrum:** *holy god.*  **deōrum:** partitive gen.  **578–579. sīdera dextra:** *favorable stars;* i.e., propitious weather.

    **585. Tīthōnī:** *of Tithonus,* husband of the goddess Aurora.  **589. pectus:** acc. with percussa;

see App. 114.  So **comās** in line 590.  **591. rēgnīs:** dat. with the compound verb **inlūserit;** poetic plural.  **592. expedient:** understand **Poenī** as subject.  **595. Quid . . . sum:** Dido realizes that such commands would be useless.

**\*decet** (it) is fitting; **\*\*\*ēn lo!** see!

**abripiō** seize, snatch; **dīvellō** tear apart
**absūmō** destroy

**epulor** feast upon

**\*vērum** but; **anceps** doubtful

**metuō** fear, dread

**forus** gangway

**\*\*\*exstinguō** destroy, blot out; **\*\*–met** *enclitic, emphasizing the word to which it is subjoined*
**interpres** go-between, agent

**nocturnus** of the night; **trivium** junction of three roads, crossroads; **\*\*\*ululō** howl; salute with shouts
**ultrīx** avenging
**meritus** due; **advertō** turn (to)

**adnō** sail to

**\*terminus** goal

**\*vexō** harass

**extorris** exiled, banished; **complexus** embrace
**implōrō** beg for; **indignus** shameful

**\*fruor** enjoy; cf. **\*fructus** enjoyment; produce
**inhumātus** unburied

**\*\*stirps** stock, stem; race

Tum decuit, cum scēptra dabās. Ēn dextra fidēsque,
quem sēcum patriōs ajunt portāre Penātīs,
quem subiisse umerīs cōnfectum aetāte parentem!
600 Nōn potuī abreptum dīvellere corpus et undīs
spargere? Nōn sociōs, nōn ipsum absūmere ferrō
Ascanium patriīsque epulandum pōnere mēnsīs?
Vērum anceps pugnae fuerat fortūna. Fuisset:
quem metuī moritūra? Facēs in castra tulissem
605 implēssemque forōs flammīs, nātumque patremque
cum genere exstīnxem, mēmet super ipsa dedissem.
Sōl, quī terrārum flammīs opera omnia lūstrās,
tūque, hārum interpres cūrārum et cōnscia Jūnō,
nocturnīsque Hecatē triviīs ululāta per urbīs,
610 et Dīrae ultrīcēs, et dī morientis Elissae,
accipite haec, meritumque malīs advertite nūmen,
et nostrās audīte precēs. Sī tangere portūs
īnfandum caput ac terrīs adnāre necesse est,
et sīc fāta Jovis poscunt, hic terminus haeret;
615 at bellō audācis populī vexātus et armīs,
fīnibus extorris, complexū āvulsus Iūlī,
auxilium implōret, videatque indigna suōrum
fūnera; nec, cum sē sub lēgēs pācis inīquae
trādiderit, rēgnō aut optātā lūce fruātur,
620 sed cadat ante diem mediāque inhumātus harēnā.
Haec precor, hanc vōcem extrēmam cum sanguine
fundō.
Tum vōs, ō Tyriī, stirpem et genus omne futūrum
exercēte odiīs, cinerīque haec mittite nostrō
mūnera. Nūllus amor populīs nec foedera suntō;

---

**597. dabās:** i.e., to Aeneas. **dextra fidēsque:** understand ejus; i.e., Aeneas's. **601. absūmere:** supply potuī. **602. epulandum:** *to be feasted on.* **603. Fuisset:** *Granted it had been so;* jussive subjunctive. **604. castra:** i.e., of the Trojans. **tulissem:** *I should have hurled.* **606. genere:** i.e., the Trojan race. **exstīnxem:** exstīnxissem. **mēmet dedissem:** *I should have hurled myself* (into the fire). **611. meritumque**

... **nūmen:** *turn* (to me) *your divine favor that I have deserved by my misfortunes.* **613. īnfandum caput:** *the cursed head* (i.e., Aeneas). **615. audācis populī:** the Rutulians, with whom the Trojans came into conflict after reaching Italy. **617. implōret:** subjunctive in a wish. **620. inhumātus:** supply jaceat. **621–624.** This prophecy refers to the conflicts between Romans and Carthaginians, known as the Punic Wars. **624. populīs:**

DIDO LAMENTING

exoriāre aliquis nostrīs ex ossibus ultor,

quī face Dardaniōs ferrōque sequāre colōnōs,

nunc, ōlim, quōcumque dabunt sē tempore vīrēs;

lītora lītoribus contrāria, flūctibus undās

imprecor, arma armīs; pugnent ipsīque nepōtēs-
que."

625 **exorior** arise, spring up; **\*\*ultor**
avenger
**\*\*colōnus** settler, colonist

**contrārius** opposite, opposed

**imprecor** invoke, pray for;
**pugnō** fight, battle

QUESTIONS ON **584–629**. 1. When Dido sees the Trojans sailing away, what orders does she at first think of giving to her fleet? 2. Why does she not give these orders? 3. What does Dido say she might have done to Aeneas? To Ascanius? To the Trojan camp? To the Trojan fleet? To herself? 4. To whom does Dido pray for vengeance on Aeneas? 5. What misfortune does Dido pray may come to Aeneas? 6. What misfortune does Dido pray may come to the Romans? 7. Whom does Vergil presumably have in mind as the *ultor* of line 625?

*Mounting the pyre, Dido stabs herself with Aeneas's sword.*

Haec ait, et partīs animum versābat in omnīs, 630

invīsam quaerēns quam prīmum abrumpere lūcem.

Tum breviter Barcēn nūtrīcem adfāta Sychaeī

(namque suam patriā antīquā cinis āter habēbat):

"Annam, cāra mihī nūtrīx, hūc siste sorōrem;

dīc corpus properet fluviālī spargere lymphā

et pecudēs sēcum et mōnstrāta piācula dūcat;

sīc veniat, tūque ipsa piā tege tempora vittā;

sacra Jovī Stygiō, quae rīte incepta parāvī,

perficere est animus, fīnemque impōnere cūrīs,

Dardaniīque rogum capitis permittere flammae." 640

Sīc ait. Illa gradum studiō celerābat anīlem.

At trepida et coeptīs immānibus effera Dīdō,

**breviter** briefly; **nūtrīx** nurse

635 **fluviālis** from a river; **lympha** water
**piāculum** sin-offering, sacrifice

**\*\*rīte** duly

640 **rogus** funeral pyre

**\*\*\*gradus** step; **\*\*\*celerō** quicken, hasten; **anīlis** of an old woman
**\*\*\*trepidus** trembling; **coeptum** undertaking; **efferus** wild, frenzied

i.e., the Romans and the Carthaginians. **suntō:** imperat. pl. of **sum**. **625. exoriāre:** exoriāris: a second person singular subjunctive with the force of an imperative. Hannibal arose as avenger and invaded Italy in 218 B.C. **626. sequāre:** sequāris; subjunctive in a relative clause of purpose. For Work Unit XV, based on lines 474–629 of Book IV, see p. 274.

**633. suam:** *her own nurse*. **patriā:** place where.

**635. properet:** subjunctive in an indirect command. So **dūcat** in line 636. **638. Jovī Stygiō:** *to Stygian Jove;* i.e., to Pluto; the Styx was a river in Hades. **639. est animus:** *it is my resolve.* **640. Dardaniīque ... capitis:** *the pyre of the Trojan,* i.e., the pyre on which Dido had placed an image of Aeneas. Note that throughout this passage Dido does not mention Aeneas by name. **641. Illa:** i.e., Barce.

sanguineus bloodshot; *macula spot
interfundō pour between; suffuse; gena cheek; pallidus pale, pallid
inrumpō rush into
cōnscendō climb, mount; furibundus frantic, frenzied; rogus funeral pyre; reclūdō unsheathe
cubīle couch

sanguineam volvēns aciem, maculīsque trementīs
interfūsa genās, et pallida morte futūrā,
645 interiōra domūs inrumpit līmina, et altōs
cōnscendit furibunda rogōs, ēnsemque reclūdit
Dardanium, nōn hōs quaesītum mūnus in ūsūs.
Hīc, postquam Īliacās vestīs nōtumque cubīle
cōnspexit, paulum lacrimīs et mente morāta
650 incubuitque torō dīxitque novissima verba:
"Dulcēs exuviae, dum Fāta deusque sinēbat,

exsolvō release, free

accipite hanc animam, mēque hīs exsolvite cūrīs.

peragō finish

Vīxī, et quem dederat cursum fortūna perēgī,
et nunc magna meī sub terrās ībit imāgō.

*praeclārus splendid, renowned
**ulcīscor avenge, punish
**fēlīx happy, fortunate; nimium too; cf. *nimius too great, excessive; ***tantum only
imprimō press; inultus unavenged

655 Urbem praeclāram statuī, mea moenia vīdī,
ulta virum poenās inimīcō ā frātre recēpī,
fēlīx, heu! nimium fēlīx, sī lītora tantum
numquam Dardaniae tetigissent nostra carīnae!"
Dīxit, et, ōs impressa torō, "Moriēmur inultae,
660 sed moriāmur," ait; "sīc, sīc juvat īre sub umbrās.
Hauriat hunc oculīs ignem crudēlis ab altō
Dardanus, et nostrae sēcum ferat ōmina mortis."
Dīxerat, atque illam media inter tālia ferrō

conlābor sink, fall; **cruor blood

conlāpsam aspiciunt comitēs, ēnsemque cruōre
665 spūmantem sparsāsque manūs. It clāmor ad alta

concutiō shake; agitate; bacchor run wildly
lāmentum lamentation; fēmineus of women; ululātus wail, shriek
resonō resound; plangor beating of the breast; wailing
***immittō let in

ātria; concussam bacchātur Fāma per urbem.
Lāmentīs gemitūque et fēmineō ululātū
tēcta fremunt, resonat magnīs plangōribus aethēr,
nōn aliter quam sī immissīs ruat hostibus omnis
670 Carthāgō, aut antīqua Tyros, flammaeque furentēs
culmina perque hominum volvantur perque deōrum.

---

643. aciem: *eyes.*   643–644. maculīsque ... genās: *her trembling cheeks suffused with spots.*
649. mente: *in thought.*   656. ulta virum: *avenging my husband,* i.e., Sychaeus.   poenās recēpī: *I exacted punishment* (by carrying away Pygmalion's wealth).   657. sī tantum: *if only.*   659. ōs ... torō: *pressing her mouth to the couch.*   662. Dardanus: *the Dardanian,* i.e., Aeneas.   667. fēmineō ululātū: *note the hiatus.*   669. quam sī: *than* (would be the case) *if.*

*Anna appears, too late to save her sister.   Juno*
*performs a last service for Dido.*

Audiit exanimis trepidōque exterrita cursū

unguibus ōra soror foedāns et pectora pugnīs

per mediōs ruit, ac morientem nōmine clāmat:

"Hoc illud, germāna, fuit?  Mē fraude petēbās?   675

Hoc rogus iste mihi, hoc ignēs āraeque parābant?

Quid prīmum dēserta querar?  Comitemne sorōrem

sprēvistī moriēns?  Eadem mē ad fāta vocāssēs!

Īdem ambās ferrō dolor atque eadem hōra tulisset.

Hīs etiam strūxī manibus patriōsque vocāvī       680

vōce deōs, sīc tē ut positā crudēlis abessem!

Exstīnxtī tē mēque, soror, populumque patrēsque

Sīdoniōs urbemque tuam.  Date vulnera lymphīs

abluam, et, extrēmus sī quis super hālitus errat,

ōre legam."  Sīc fāta, gradūs ēvāserat altōs,      685

sēmianimemque sinū germānam amplexa fovēbat

cum gemitū, atque ātrōs siccābat veste cruōrēs.

Illa gravīs oculōs cōnāta attollere rūrsus

dēficit; īnfīxum strīdit sub pectore vulnus.

Ter sēsē attollēns cubitōque adnīxa levāvit;      690

ter revolūta torō est, oculīsque errantibus altō

quaesīvit caelō lūcem, ingemuitque repertā.

Tum Jūnō omnipotēns, longum miserāta dolōrem

difficilīsque obitūs, Īrim dēmīsit Olympō,

**exanimis** breathless; unnerved; **exterreō** terrify, frighten
*****unguis** finger-nail; **pugnus** fist

*****fraus** deceit

**rogus** funeral pyre

******spernō** scorn

*******ambō** both

**absum** be away, be wanting

**abluō** wash; cleanse; **hālitus** breath

**sēmianimis** half-alive; dying

**siccō** dry; stanch; *******cruor** blood

**īnfīgō** fix; implant

**cubitum** elbow; **adnītor** lean on

**revolvō** roll back

**ingemō** groan

**omnipotēns** all-mighty, all-powerful; *******miseror** pity **obitus** death

**678. Eadem ... vocāssēs:** *You should have called me to* (share) *the same death.* **679. tulisset:** *should have carried off.* **680. strūxī:** *did I build up* (your pyre). **682. Exstīnxtī: Exstīnxistī. 683– 684. Date abluam:** *suffer me to wash* (*give that I wash*). **685. ōre legam:** *catch with my lips.* It was a Roman custom for someone to catch in his

mouth the last breath of a dying relative. **686. sēmianimemque:** pronounce as if spelled **sēmianimemque**; see App. 32. **688. Illa:** i.e., Dido. **689. strīdit:** *gurgles.* **692. caelō:** place where **repertā** (lūce): abl. abs. phrase.

**694. Īrim:** *Iris,* goddess of the rainbow and messenger of Juno.

**\*\*luctor** struggle; bind; entwine; loosen, sever
**\*\*\*nectō** **resolvō**
**\*\*\*quia** because; **meritus** deserved, just
**\*\*\*flāvus** yellow, golden
**\*\*\*auferō** take away, remove; **\*damnō** condemn, consign
**rōscidus** dewy; **\*\*pinna** feather; wing
**color** color, tint
**dēvolō** fly down

695 quae luctantem animam nexōsque resolveret artūs.
Nam quia nec fātō meritā nec morte perībat,
sed misera ante diem subitōque accēnsa furōre,
nōndum illī flāvum Prōserpina vertice crīnem
abstulerat, Stygiōque caput damnāverat Orcō.
700 Ergō Īris croceīs per caelum rōscida pinnīs
mīlle trahēns variōs adversō sōle colōrēs
dēvolat, et suprā caput adstitit. "Hunc ego Dītī
sacrum jussa ferō, tēque istō corpore solvō."
Sīc ait, et dextrā crīnem secat; omnis et ūnā

**dīlābor** slip away, disappear; **calor** heat, warmth

705 dīlāpsus calor, atque in ventōs vīta recessit.

QUESTIONS ON 672–705. 1. How does Anna learn of Dido's act? 2. For what does Anna reproach Dido? 3. For what does Anna reproach herself? 4. What does Dido now do? 5. Why, according to Vergil, is Dido's death so long delayed? 6. What last service does Juno, through Iris, render to Dido?

---

**698. Prōserpina:** queen of the underworld. **699. abstulerat:** a lock of hair was plucked from the head of a dying person as a symbol of sacrifice to the gods of the underworld. **702. Hunc:** supply **crīnem. Dītī:** *to Dis,* i.e., to Pluto, god of the underworld. **705. dīlāpsus:** supply **est.** For Work Unit XVI, based on lines 630–705 of Book IV, see p. 276.

# BOOK V

*Aeneas, sailing toward Italy, is forced by a storm to
   land in Sicily.*

Intereā medium Aenēās jam classe tenēbat,
certus iter, flūctūsque ātrōs Aquilōne secābat,
moenia respiciēns, quae jam īnfēlīcis Elissae
conlūcent flammīs. Quae tantum accenderit ignem
causa latet; dūrī magnō sed amōre dolōrēs          5
pollūtō nōtumque furēns quid fēmina possit
trīste per augurium Teucrōrum pectora dūcunt.
Ut pelagus tenuēre ratēs, nec jam amplius ūlla
occurrit tellūs, maria undique et undique caelum,
ollī caeruleus suprā caput astitit imber,          10
noctem hiememque ferēns, et inhorruit unda tene-
     brīs.
Ipse gubernātor puppī Palinūrus ab altā:
"Heu! Quianam tantī cīnxērunt aethera nimbī,
quidve, pater Neptūne, parās?" Sīc deinde locū-
     tus
colligere arma jubet validīsque incumbere rēmīs,   15
oblīquatque sinūs in ventum, ac tālia fātur:
"Magnanime Aenēā, nōn, sī mihi Juppiter auctor
spondeat, hōc spērem Ītaliam contingere caelō.
Mūtātī trānsversa fremunt et Vespere ab ātrō
cōnsurgunt ventī, atque in nūbem cōgitur āēr;      20
nec nōs obnītī contrā nec tendere tantum
sufficimus. Superat quoniam fortūna, sequāmur,
quōque vocat vertāmus iter. Nec lītora longē
fīda reor frāterna Erycis portūsque Sicānōs,
sī modo rīte memor servāta remētior astra."        25
Tum pius Aenēās: "Equidem sīc poscere ventōs

jam dūdum et frūstrā cernō tē tendere contrā.
Flecte viam vēlīs.  An sit mihi grātior ūlla,
quōve magis fessās optem dēmittere nāvīs
30 quam quae Dardanium tellūs mihi servat Acestēn,
et patris Anchīsae gremiō complectitur ossa?"
Haec ubi dicta, petunt portūs, et vēla secundī
intendunt Zephyrī; fertur cita gurgite classis,
et tandem laetī nōtae advertuntur harēnae.
35      At procul ex celsō mīrātus vertice montis
adventum sociāsque ratīs occurrit Acestēs,
horridus in jaculīs et pelle Libystidis ursae,
Trōia Crīnīsō conceptum flūmine māter
quem genuit.  Veterum nōn immemor ille paren-
            tum,
40 grātātur reducīs, et gazā laetus agrestī
excipit, ac fessōs opibus sōlātur amīcīs.

QUESTIONS ON LINES 1–41.  1. From what port has Aeneas just
sailed?  2. What do the Trojans suspect is the cause of the fire
which they view from the sea?  3. Who is Palinurus?  4. What
orders does Palinurus give the sailors?  Why?  5. What advice
does Palinurus give Aeneas?  With what results?  6. Who meets
the Trojans when they land at Drepanum?

*Aeneas announces funeral games at Drepanum in
memory of Anchises.*

Postera cum prīmō stellās Oriente fugārat
clāra diēs, sociōs in coetum lītore ab omnī
advocat Aenēās tumulīque ex aggere fātur:
45 "Dardanidae magnī, genus altō ā sanguine dīvum,
annuus exāctīs complētur mēnsibus orbis,
ex quō relliquiās dīvīnīque ossa parentis
condidimus terrā, maestāsque sacrāvimus ārās.
Jamque diēs, nisi fallor, adest, quem semper acer-
            bum,
50 semper honōrātum (sīc, dī, voluistis) habēbō.
Hunc ego Gaetūlīs agerem sī Syrtibus exsul,
Argolicōve marī dēprēnsus et urbe Mycēnae,

annua vōta tamen sollemnīsque ōrdine pompās
exsequerer, strueremque suīs altāria dōnīs.
Nunc ultrō ad cinerēs ipsīus et ossa parentis      55
(haud equidem sine mente, reor, sine nūmine dī-
      vum)
adsumus, et portūs dēlātī intrāmus amīcōs.
Ergō agite, et laetum cūnctī celebrēmus honōrem;
poscāmus ventōs, atque haec mē sacra quotannīs
urbe velit positā templīs sibi ferre dicātīs.      60
Bīna boum vōbīs Trōjā generātus Acestēs
dat numerō capita in nāvīs; adhibēte Penātīs
et patriōs epulīs et quōs colit hospes Acestēs.
Praetereā, sī nōna diem mortālibus almum
Aurōra extulerit radiīsque retēxerit orbem,      65
prīma citae Teucrīs pōnam certāmina classis;
quīque pedum cursū valet, et quī vīribus audāx
aut jaculō incēdit melior levibusque sagittīs,
seu crūdō fīdit pugnam committere caestū,
cūnctī adsint, meritaeque exspectent praemia pal-  70
      mae.
Ōre favēte omnēs, et cingite tempora rāmīs."

QUESTIONS ON **42–71.** 1. How long after Anchises's death do the
Trojans now land at Drepanum? 2. In what festivities do the
Trojans at once participate? 3. What four contests does Aeneas
announce for the funeral games? 4. How soon are these games
to be held?

*Aeneas offers sacrifices at Anchises's tomb.*

Sīc fātus, vēlat māternā tempora myrtō.
Hoc Helymus facit, hoc aevī mātūrus Acestēs,
hoc puer Ascanius, sequitur quōs cētera pūbēs.
Ille ē conciliō multīs cum mīlibus ībat      75
ad tumulum, magnā medius comitante catervā.
Hīc duo rīte merō lībāns carchēsia Bacchō
fundit humī, duo lacte novō, duo sanguine sacrō,
purpureōsque jacit flōrēs, ac tālia fātur:

80 "Salvē, sāncte parēns, iterum salvēte, receptī
nēquīquam cinerēs, animaeque umbraeque pa-
ternae!
Nōn licuit fīnīs Italōs fātāliaque arva
nec tēcum Ausonium, quīcumque est, quaerere
Thybrim."
Dīxerat haec, adytīs cum lūbricus anguis ab īmīs
85 septem ingēns gȳrōs, septēna volūmina trāxit,
amplexus placidē tumulum lāpsusque per ārās,
caeruleae cui terga notae maculōsus et aurō
squāmam incendēbat fulgor, ceu nūbibus arcus
mīlle jacit variōs adversō sōle colōrēs.
90 Obstipuit vīsū Aenēās. Ille, agmine longō
tandem inter paterās et lēvia pōcula serpēns,
lībāvitque dapēs rūrsusque innoxius īmō
successit tumulō, et dēpāsta altāria līquit.
Hōc magis inceptōs genitōrī īnstaurat honōrēs,
95 incertus geniumne locī famulumne parentis
esse putet; caedit bīnās dē mōre bidentīs
atque suēs, totidem nigrantīs terga juvencōs,
vīnaque fundēbat paterīs, animamque vocābat
Anchīsae magnī Mānīsque Acheronte remissōs.
100 Nec nōn et sociī, quae cuique est cōpia, laetī
dōna ferunt; onerant ārās mactantque juvencōs;
ōrdine aēna locant aliī, fūsīque per herbam
subjiciunt veribus prūnās, et vīscera torrent.

QUESTIONS ON **72–103**. 1. What offerings does Aeneas make at
the tomb of Anchises? 2. To whom does Aeneas address his
prayer? 3. What sight convinces Aeneas that his prayer has
been favorably received? 4. What further sacrifices does Aeneas
now make? 5. What do the Trojans do with the meat of the
animals slain in sacrifice?

*Cloanthus wins the boat race.*

Exspectāta diēs aderat, nōnamque serēnā
105 Aurōram Phaëthontis equī jam lūce vehēbant,
fāmaque fīnitimōs et clārī nōmen Acestae

excierat; laetō complēbant lītora coetū
vīsūrī Aeneadās, pars et certāre parātī.
Mūnera prīncipiō ante oculōs circōque locantur
in mediō, sacrī tripodes, viridēsque corōnae,     110
et palmae, pretium victōribus, armaque, et ostrō
perfūsae vestēs, argentī aurīque talentum,
et tuba commissōs mediō canit aggere lūdōs.
    Prīma parēs ineunt gravibus certāmina rēmīs
quattuor ex omnī dēlēctae classe carīnae.     115
Vēlōcem Mnēstheus agit ācrī rēmige Pristim,
mox Italus Mnēstheus, genus ā quō nōmine
    Memmī,
ingentemque Gyās ingentī mōle Chimaeram,
urbis opus, triplicī pūbēs quam Dardana versū
impellunt (ternō cōnsurgunt ōrdine rēmī),     120
Sergestusque, domus tenet ā quō Sergia nōmen,
Centaurō invehitur magnā, Scyllāque Cloanthus
caeruleā, genus unde tibī, Rōmāne Cluentī.
    Est procul in pelagō saxum spūmantia contrā
lītora, quod tumidīs submersum tunditur ōlim     125
flūctibus, hībernī condunt ubi sīdera Caurī;
tranquillō silet, immōtāque attollitur undā
campus et aprīcīs statiō grātissima mergīs.
Hīc viridem Aenēās frondentī ex īlice mētam
cōnstituit signum nautīs pater, unde revertī     130
scīrent et longōs ubi circumflectere cursūs.
Tum loca sorte legunt, ipsīque in puppibus aurō
ductōrēs longē effulgent ostrōque decōrī;
cētera pōpuleā vēlātur fronde juventūs,
nūdātōsque umerōs oleō perfūsa nitēscit.     135
Cōnsīdunt trānstrīs, intentaque bracchia rēmīs;
intentī exspectant signum, exsultantiaque haurit
corda pavor pulsāns laudumque arrēcta cupīdō.
Inde, ubi clāra dedit sonitum tuba, fīnibus omnēs,
haud mora, prōsiluēre suīs; ferit aethera clāmor     140

nauticus, adductīs spūmant freta versa lacertīs;
īnfindunt pariter sulcōs, tōtumque dehīscit
convūlsum rēmīs rōstrīsque tridentibus aequor;
nōn tam praecipitēs bijugō certāmine campum
145 corripuēre ruuntque effūsī carcere currūs,
nec sīc immissīs aurīgae undantia lōra
concussēre jugīs, prōnīque in verbera pendent.
Tum plausū fremitūque virum studiīsque faventum
cōnsonat omne nemus, vōcemque inclūsa volūtant
150 lītora; pulsātī collēs clāmōre resultant.
Effugit ante aliōs, prīmīsque ēlābitur undīs
turbam inter fremitumque Gyās, quem deinde
        Cloanthus
cōnsequitur, melior rēmīs, sed pondere pīnus
tarda tenet; post hōs aequō discrīmine Pristis
155 Centaurusque locum tendunt superāre priōrem;
et nunc Pristis habet, nunc victam praeterit ingēns
Centaurus, nunc ūnā ambae jūnctīsque feruntur
frontibus, et longā sulcant vada salsa carīnā.
Jamque propinquābant scopulō mētamque tenē-
        bant,
160 cum prīnceps mediōque Gyās in gurgite victor
rēctōrem nāvis compellat vōce Menoetēn:
"Quō tantum mihi dexter abīs? Hūc dīrige gres-
        sum;
lītus amā, et laevās stringat sine palmula cautīs.
Altum aliī teneant." Dīxit, sed caeca Menoetēs
165 saxa timēns prōram pelagī dētorquet ad undās.
"Quō dīversus abīs?" iterum "Pete saxa, Me-
        noetē!"
cum clāmōre Gyās revocābat, et ecce Cloanthum
respicit īnstantem tergō et propiōra tenentem.
Ille inter nāvemque Gyae scopulōsque sonantīs
170 rādit iter laevum interior, subitōque priōrem
praeterit, et mētīs tenet aequora tūta relictīs.

Tum vērō exārsit juvenī dolor ossibus ingēns,
nec lacrimīs caruēre genae, sēgnemque Menoetēn,
oblītus decorisque suī sociumque salūtis,
in mare praecipitem puppī dēturbat ab altā;      175
ipse gubernāclō rēctor subit, ipse magister
hortāturque virōs clāvumque ad lītora torquet.
At gravis, ut fundō vix tandem redditus īmō est,
jam senior madidāque fluēns in veste Menoetēs
summa petit scopulī, siccāque in rūpe resēdit.      180
Illum et lābentem Teucrī et rīsēre natantem
et salsōs rīdent revomentem pectore flūctūs.
Hīc laeta extrēmīs spēs est accēnsa duōbus,
Sergestō Mnēstheīque, Gyān superāre morantem.
Sergestus capit ante locum, scopulōque propinquat, 185
nec tōtā tamen ille prior praeëunte carīnā,
parte prior; partem rōstrō premit aemula Pristis.
At mediā sociōs incēdēns nāve per ipsōs
hortātur Mnēstheus: "Nunc, nunc īnsurgite rē-
      mīs,
Hectoreī sociī, Trōjae quōs sorte suprēmā      190
dēlēgī comitēs; nunc illās prōmite vīrīs,
nunc animōs, quibus in Gaetūlīs Syrtibus ūsī
Īoniōque marī Maleaeque sequācibus undīs.
Nōn jam prīma petō Mnēstheus, neque vincere
      certō
(quamquam ō! sed superent, quibus hoc, Neptūne, 195
      dedistī);
extrēmōs pudeat rediisse: hoc vincite, cīvēs,
et prohibēte nefās." Ollī certāmine summō
prōcumbunt; vāstīs tremit ictibus aerea puppis,
subtrahiturque solum; tum crēber anhēlitus artūs
āridaque ōra quatit, sūdor fluit undique rīvīs.      200
Adtulit ipse virīs optātum cāsus honōrem;
namque, furēns animī dum prōram ad saxa subur-
      get

interior, spatiōque subit Sergestus inīquō,
īnfēlīx saxīs in prōcurrentibus haesit;
205 concussae cautēs, et acūtō in mūrice rēmī
obnīxī crepuēre, inlīsaque prōra pependit.
Cōnsurgunt nautae, et magnō clāmōre morantur,
ferrātāsque trudēs et acūtā cuspide contōs
expediunt, frāctōsque legunt in gurgite rēmōs.
210 At laetus Mnēstheus successūque ācrior ipsō
agmine rēmōrum celerī ventīsque vocātīs
prōna petit maria et pelagō dēcurrit apertō.
Quālis spēluncā subitō commōta columba,
cui domus et dulcēs latebrōsō in pūmice nīdī,
215 fertur in arva volāns, plausumque exterrita pinnīs
dat tēctō ingentem, mox āere lāpsa quiētō
rādit iter liquidum celerīs neque commovet ālās,
sīc Mnēstheus, sīc ipsa fugā secat ultima Pristis
aequora, sīc illam fert impetus ipse volantem;
220 et prīmum in scopulō luctantem dēserit altō
Sergestum brevibusque vadīs, frūstrāque vocantem
auxilia, et frāctīs discentem currere rēmīs;
inde Gyān ipsamque ingentī mōle Chimaeram
cōnsequitur; cēdit, quoniam spoliāta magistrō est.
225 Sōlus jamque ipsō superest in fīne Cloanthus,
quem petit, et summīs adnīxus vīribus urget.
Tum vērō ingeminat clāmor, cūnctīque sequentem
īnstīgant studiīs, resonatque fragōribus aethēr.
Hī proprium decus et partum indignantur honōrem
230 nī teneant vītamque volunt prō laude pacīscī,
hōs successus alit: possunt, quia posse videntur.
Et fors aequātīs cēpissent praemia rōstrīs,
nī palmās pontō tendēns utrāsque Cloanthus
fūdissetque precēs dīvōsque in vōta vocāsset:
235 "Dī, quibus imperium est pelagī, quōrum aequora
currō,
vōbīs laetus ego hōc candentem in lītore taurum

cōnstituam ante ārās, vōtī reus, extaque salsōs
prōjiciam in flūctūs, et vīna liquentia fundam."
Dīxit, eumque īmīs sub flūctibus audiit omnis
Nēreidum Phorcīque chorus Panopēaque virgō,          240
et pater ipse manū magnā Portūnus euntem
impulit; illa Notō citius volucrīque sagittā
ad terram fugit, et portū sē condidit altō.
Tum satus Anchīsā, cūnctīs ex mōre vocātīs,
victōrem magnā praecōnis vōce Cloanthum          245
dēclārat, viridīque advēlat tempora laurō,
mūneraque in nāvīs ternōs optāre juvencōs
vīnaque et argentī magnum dat ferre talentum.
Ipsīs praecipuōs ductōribus addit honōrēs:
victōrī chlamydem aurātam, quam plūrima circum 250
purpura maeandrō duplicī Meliboea cucurrit
intextusque puer frondōsā rēgius Īdā
vēlōcīs jaculō cervōs cursūque fatīgat
ācer, anhēlantī similis, quem praepes ab Īdā
sublīmem pedibus rapuit Jovis armiger uncīs;          255
longaevī palmās nēquīquam ad sīdera tendunt
custōdēs, saevitque canum lātrātus in aurās.
At quī deinde locum tenuit virtūte secundum,
lēvibus huic hāmīs consertam aurōque trilīcem
lōrīcam, quam Dēmoleō dētrāxerat ipse          260
victor apud rapidum Simoënta sub Īliō altō,
dōnat habēre virō, decus et tūtāmen in armīs.
Vix illam famulī Phēgeus Sagarisque ferēbant
multiplicem cōnīxī umerīs: indūtus at ōlim
Dēmoleos cursū pālantīs Trōas agēbat.          265
Tertia dōna facit geminōs ex aere lebētas,
cymbiaque argentō perfecta, atque aspera signīs.
Jamque adeō dōnātī omnēs opibusque superbī
pūniceīs ībant ēvīnctī tempora taenīs,
cum, saevō ē scopulō multā vix arte revulsus,          270
āmissīs rēmīs, atque ōrdine dēbilis ūnō,

inrīsam sine honōre ratem Sergestus agēbat.

Quālis saepe viae dēprēnsus in aggere serpēns,

aerea quem oblīquum rota trānsiit, aut gravis ictū

275 sēminecem līquit saxō lacerumque viātor;

nēquīquam longōs fugiēns dat corpore tortūs,

parte ferōx, ārdēnsque oculīs, et sībila colla

arduus attollēns; pars vulnere clauda retentat

nīxantem nōdīs sēque in sua membra plicantem:

280 tālī rēmigiō nāvis sē tarda movēbat;

vēla facit tamen, et plēnīs subit ōstia vēlīs.

Sergestum Aenēās prōmissō mūnere dōnat,

servātam ob nāvem laetus sociōsque reductōs;

ollī serva datur, operum haud ignāra Minervae,

285 Crēssa genus, Pholoē, geminīque sub ūbere nātī.

QUESTIONS ON **104–285**. 1. Who besides the Trojans attend the funeral games? 2. What prizes does Aeneas display? 3. What is the name of each of the captains who enter the boat race and what is the name of his boat? 4. What course are the boats to follow? 5. To what does Vergil compare the boats as they get off to a quick start? 6. Which boat takes the lead at first? 7. Which boats struggle for third place? 8. Which boat is leading as they approach the turn? 9. What orders does Gyas give his helmsman? 10. Why does the helmsman not obey these orders? 11. What does Gyas now do? 12. Which boat gains the lead at the turn? How? 13. What happens to Sergestus's boat at the turn? Why? 14. What is Mnestheus's only remaining hope at the turn? 15. By whose aid does Cloanthus win the race? 16. What prize does Cloanthus receive? 17. What prize does Mnestheus receive? 18. What prize does Gyas receive? 19. To what does Vergil compare Sergestus's disabled boat as it comes to the shore? 20. What prize does Sergestus receive?

*Euryalus wins the foot race.*

Hōc pius Aenēās missō certāmine tendit

grāmineum in campum, quem collibus undique

curvīs

cingēbant silvae, mediāque in valle theātrī

circus erat; quō sē multīs cum mīlibus hērōs

290 cōnsessum in medium tulit, exstrūctōque resēdit.

Hīc, quī forte velint rapidō contendere cursū

invītat pretiīs animōs, et praemia pōnit.

Undique conveniunt Teucrī mixtīque Sicānī,
Nīsus et Euryalus prīmī,
Euryalus fōrmā īnsignis viridīque juventā,                  295
Nīsus amōre piō puerī;  quōs deinde secūtus
rēgius ēgregiā Priamī de stirpe Diōrēs;
hunc Salius simul et Patrōn, quōrum alter Acarnān
alter ab Arcadiō Tegeaeae sanguine gentis;
tum duo Trīnacriī juvenēs, Helymus Panopēsque, 300
adsuētī silvīs, comitēs seniōris Acestae;
multī praetereā, quōs fāma obscūra recondit.
Aenēās quibus in mediīs sīc deinde locūtus:
"Accipite haec animīs, laetāsque advertite mentīs.
Nēmō ex hōc numerō mihi nōn dōnātus abībit.          305
Gnōsia bīna dabō lēvātō lūcida ferrō
spīcula caelātamque argentō ferre bipennem;
omnibus hīc erit ūnus honōs.  Trēs praemia prīmī
accipient, flāvāque caput nectentur olīvā.
Prīmus equum phalerīs īnsignem victor habētō;      310
alter Amāzoniam pharetram plēnamque sagittīs
Thrēiciīs, lātō quam circum amplectitur aurō
balteus, et teretī subnectit fībula gemmā,
tertius Argolicā hāc galeā contentus abītō."
Haec ubi dicta, locum capiunt, signōque repente  315
corripiunt spatia audītō, līmenque relinquunt,
effūsī nimbō similēs;  simul ultima signant.
Prīmus abit, longēque ante omnia corpora Nīsus
ēmicat, et ventīs et fulminis ōcior ālīs;
proximus huic, longō sed proximus intervallō,           320
īnsequitur Salius;  spatiō post deinde relictō
tertius Euryalus;
Euryalumque Helymus sequitur;  quō deinde sub
     ipsō
ecce volat calcemque terit jam calce Diōrēs,
incumbēns umerō, spatia et sī plūra supersint,       325
trānseat ēlāpsus prior, ambiguumve relinquat.

Jamque ferē spatiō extrēmō fessīque sub ipsam
fīnem adventābant, lēvī cum sanguine Nīsus
lābitur īnfēlīx, caesīs ut forte juvencīs
330 fūsus humum viridīsque super madefēcerat herbās:
hīc juvenis jam victor ovāns vēstīgia pressō
haud tenuit titubāta solō, sed prōnus in ipsō
concidit immundōque fimō sacrōque cruōre;
nōn tamen Euryalī, nōn ille oblītus amōrum,
335 nam sēsē opposuit Saliō per lūbrica surgēns;
ille autem spissā jacuit revolūtus harēnā.
Ēmicat Euryalus, et, mūnere victor amīcī,
prīma tenet, plausūque volat fremitūque secundō;
post Helymus subit, et, nunc tertia palma, Diōrēs.
340 Hīc tōtum caveae consessum ingentis et ōra
prīma patrum magnīs Salius clāmōribus implet,
ēreptumque dolō reddī sibi poscit honōrem.
Tūtātur favor Euryalum, lacrimaeque decōrae,
grātior et pulchrō veniēns in corpore virtūs;
345 adjuvat et magnā prōclāmat vōce Diōrēs,
quī subiit palmae frūstrāque ad praemia vēnit
ultima, sī prīmī Saliō reddantur honōrēs.
Tum pater Aenēās "Vestra," inquit, "mūnera vō-
bīs
certa manent, puerī, et palmam movet ōrdine
nēmō;
350 mē liceat cāsūs miserārī īnsontis amīcī."
Sīc fātus, tergum Gaetūlī immāne leōnis
dat Saliō, villīs onerōsum atque unguibus aureīs.
Hīc Nīsus "Sī tanta," inquit, "sunt praemia victīs,
et tē lāpsōrum miseret, quae mūnera Nīsō
355 digna dabis, prīmam meruī quī laude corōnam,
nī mē, quae Salium, fortūna inimīca tulisset?",
et simul hīs dictīs faciem ostentābat et ūdō
turpia membra fimō. Rīsit pater optimus ollī,
et clipeum efferrī jussit, Didymāonis artīs,

Neptūnī sacrō Danaīs dē poste refīxum;     360
hōc juvenem ēgregium praestantī mūnere dōnat.

QUESTIONS ON **286–361.** 1. What two Trojan youths first appear for the foot race? 2. Which is older, Nisus or Euryalus? 3. What special prize does Aeneas offer for first place in the foot race? For second place? For third place? 4. What reward is every contestant to receive? 5. Who gets off to the best start? Who is second? Who is third? 6. What happens to Nisus close to the finish? 7. How does Nisus help Euryalus to win the race? 8. Who wins second place? 9. Who wins third place? 10. What claim does Salius loudly make? 11. Which contestant opposed Salius's claim? Why? 12. How does Aeneas settle the dispute? 13. What claim does Nisus now make? With what success?

*Entellus wins the boxing match.*

    Post ubi cōnfectī cursūs et dōna perēgit,
"Nunc, sī cui virtūs animusque in pectore prae-
       sēns,
adsit, et ēvīnctīs attollat bracchia palmīs."
Sīc ait, et geminum pugnae prōpōnit honōrem,     365
victōrī vēlātum aurō vittīsque juvencum,
ēnsem atque īnsignem galeam sōlācia victō.
Nec mora: continuō vāstīs cum vīribus effert
ōra Darēs, magnōque virum sē murmure tollit,
sōlus quī Paridem solitus contendere contrā,     370
īdemque ad tumulum, quō maximus occubat Hec-
       tor,
victōrem Būtēn, immānī corpore quī sē
Bebryciā veniēns Amycī dē gente ferēbat,
perculit, et fulvā moribundum extendit harēnā;
tālis prīma Darēs caput altum in proelia tollit,     375
ostenditque umerōs lātōs, alternaque jactat
bracchia prōtendēns, et verberat ictibus aurās.
Quaeritur huic alius; nec quisquam ex agmine
       tantō
audet adīre virum manibusque indūcere caestūs.
Ergō, alacris cūnctōsque putāns excēdere palmā,     380
Aenēae stetit ante pedēs, nec plūra morātus

tum laevā taurum cornū tenet, atque ita fātur:
"Nāte deā, sī nēmō audet sē crēdere pugnae,
quae fīnis standī? Quō mē decet usque tenērī?
385 Dūcere dōna jubē." Cūnctī simul ōre fremēbant
Dardanidae reddīque virō prōmissa jubēbant.

Hīc gravis Entellum dictīs castīgat Acestēs,
proximus ut viridante torō cōnsēderat herbae:
"Entelle, hērōum quondam fortissime frūstrā,
390 tantane tam patiēns nūllō certāmine tollī
dōna sinēs? Ubi nunc nōbīs deus ille magister
nēquīquam memorātus Eryx? Ubi fāma per om-
nem
Trīnacriam et spolia illa tuīs pendentia tēctīs?"
Ille sub haec: "Nōn laudis amor nec glōria cessit
395 pulsa metū, sed enim gelidus tardante senectā
sanguis hebet, frīgentque effētae in corpore vīrēs.
Sī mihi, quae quondam fuerat quāque improbus
iste
exsultat fīdēns, sī nunc foret illa juventās,
haud equidem pretiō inductus pulchrōque juvencō
400 vēnissem, nec dōna moror." Sīc deinde locūtus
in medium geminōs immānī pondere caestūs
prōjēcit, quibus ācer Eryx in proelia suētus
ferre manum dūrōque intendere bracchia tergō.
Obstipuēre animī; tantōrum ingentia septem
405 terga boum plumbō īnsūtō ferrōque rigēbant.
Ante omnīs stupet ipse Darēs longēque recūsat,
magnanimusque Anchīsiadēs et pondus et ipsa
hūc illūc vinclōrum immēnsa volūmina versat.
Tum senior tālīs referēbat pectore vōcēs:
410 "Quid sī quis caestūs ipsīus et Herculis arma
vīdisset trīstemque hōc ipsō in lītore pugnam?
Haec germānus Eryx quondam tuus arma gerēbat
(sanguine cernis adhūc sparsōque īnfecta cerebrō),
hīs magnum Alcīdēn contrā stetit, hīs ego suētus,

dum melior vīrīs sanguis dabat, aemula necdum    415
temporibus geminīs cānēbat sparsa senectūs.
Sed sī nostra Darēs haec Trōius arma recūsat,
idque piō sedet Aenēae, probat auctor Acestēs,
aequēmus pugnās.  Erycis tibi terga remittō
(solve metūs), et tū Trōjānōs exue caestūs."         420
Haec fātus, duplicem ex umerīs rejēcit amictum,
et magnōs membrōrum artūs, magna ossa lacertōs-
    que
exuit, atque ingēns mediā cōnsistit harēnā.
Tum satus Anchīsā caestūs pater extulit aequōs,
et paribus palmās ambōrum innexuit armīs.          425
Cōnstitit in digitōs extemplō arrēctus uterque,
bracchiaque ad superās interritus extulit aurās.
Abdūxēre retrō longē capita ardua ab ictū,
immiscentque manūs manibus, pugnamque laces-
    sunt,
ille pedum melior mōtū frētusque juventā,          430
hic membrīs et mōle valēns, sed tarda trementī
genua labant, vāstōs quatit aeger anhēlitus artūs.
Multa virī nēquīquam inter sē vulnera jactant,
multa cavō laterī ingeminant, et pectora vāstōs
dant sonitūs, erratque aurīs et tempora circum     435
crēbra manus, dūrō crepitant sub vulnere mālae.
Stat gravis Entellus, nīsūque immōtus eōdem
corpore tēla modo atque oculīs vigilantibus exit;
ille, velut celsam oppugnat quī mōlibus urbem,
aut montāna sedet circum castella sub armīs,       440
nunc hōs, nunc illōs aditūs omnemque pererrat
arte locum, et variīs adsultibus inritus urget.
Ostendit dextram īnsurgēns Entellus, et altē
extulit: ille ictum venientem ā vertice vēlōx
praevīdit, celerīque ēlāpsus corpore cessit;        445
Entellus vīrīs in ventum effūdit, et ultrō
ipse gravis graviterque ad terram pondere vāstō

concidit, ut quondam cava concidit aut Ery-
    manthō
aut Īdā in magnā rādīcibus ēruta pīnus.
450 Cōnsurgunt studiīs Teucrī et Trīnacria pūbēs;
it clāmor caelō, prīmusque accurrit Acestēs
aequaevumque ab humō miserāns attollit amīcum.
At nōn tardātus cāsū neque territus hērōs
ācrior ad pugnam redit ac vim suscitat īra;
455 tum pudor incendit vīrīs et cōnscia virtūs,
praecipitemque Darēn ārdēns agit aequore tōtō,
nunc dextrā ingeminān̄s ictūs, nunc ille sinistrā.
Nec mora nec requiēs; quam multā grandine nimbī
culminibus crepitant, sīc dēnsīs ictibus hērōs
460 crēber utrāque manū pulsat versatque Darēta.
Tum pater Aenēās prōcēdere longius īrās
et saevīre animīs Entellum haud passus acerbīs,
sed fīnem imposuit pugnae fessumque Darēta
ēripuit, mulcēns dictīs, ac tālia fātur:
465 "Īnfēlīx, quae tanta animum dēmentia cēpit?
Nōn vīrīs aliās conversaque nūmina sentīs?
Cēde deō." Dīxitque et proelia vōce dirēmit.
Ast illum fīdī aequālēs genua aegra trahentem
jactantemque utrōque caput crassumque cruōrem
470 ōre ējectantem mixtōsque in sanguine dentīs
dūcunt ad nāvīs, galeamque ēnsemque vocātī
accipiunt, palmam Entellō taurumque relinquunt.
Hic, victor, superāns animīs, taurōque superbus,
"Nāte deā, vōsque haec," inquit, "cognōscite,
    Teucrī,
475 et mihi quae fuerint juvenālī in corpore vīrēs,
et quā servētis revocātum ā morte Darēta."
Dīxit, et adversī contrā stetit ōra juvencī,
quī dōnum astābat pugnae, dūrōsque reductā
lībrāvit dextrā media inter cornua caestūs,
480 arduus, effrāctōque inlīsit in ossa cerebrō;

sternitur, exanimisque tremēns prōcumbit humī
   bōs.

Ille super tālīs effundit pectore vōcēs:
"Hanc tibi, Eryx, meliōrem animam prō morte
   Darētis

persolvō; hīc victor caestūs artemque repōnō."

QUESTIONS ON **362–484**. 1. What is to be the reward for the
winner of the boxing match? 2. What is to be the reward of the
loser? 3. Who first appears for the boxing match? 4. What
request does Dares soon make of Aeneas? On what basis?
5. What finally causes Entellus to enter the contest? To what
people does he belong? 6. With what are Entellus's "boxing
gloves" loaded? 7. From whom has Entellus received his
"boxing gloves"? 8. What relation was Eryx to Aeneas?
9. What concession in the matter of "gloves" does Entellus
make to Dares? 10. What advantage does Dares have over
Entellus? 11. What advantage does Entellus have over Dares?
12. What style of boxing does Entellus adopt? What style
does Dares adopt? 13. Which is first to go down? How does
this happen? 14. What effect does his fall have on Entellus?
15. Who stops the contest? Why? 16. In what way does En-
tellus now further demonstrate his strength? 17. To whom does
Entellus give the credit for his victory?

*Acestes wins the archery contest.*

   Prōtinus Aenēās celerī certāre sagittā       **485**
invītat quī forte velint, et praemia pōnit,
ingentīque manū mālum dē nāve Serestī
ērigit, et volucrem trājectō in fūne columbam,
quō tendant ferrum, mālō suspendit ab altō.
Convēnēre virī, dējectamque aerea sortem       **490**
accēpit galea; et prīmus clāmōre secundō
Hyrtacidae ante omnīs exit locus Hippocoöntis,
quem modo nāvālī Mnēstheus certāmine victor
cōnsequitur, viridī Mnēstheus ēvīnctus olīvā;
tertius Eurytiōn, tuus, ō clārissime, frāter,      **495**
Pandare, quī quondam, jussus cōnfundere foedus,
in mediōs tēlum torsistī prīmus Achīvōs;
extrēmus galeāque īmā subsēdit Acestēs,
ausus et ipse manū juvenum temptāre labōrem.
Tum validīs flexōs incurvant vīribus arcūs      **500**

prō sē quisque virī, et dēprōmunt tēla pharetrīs,
prīmaque per caelum nervō strīdente sagitta
Hyrtacidae juvenis volucrīs dīverberat aurās,
et venit adversīque īnfīgitur arbore mālī;
505 intremuit mālus, timuitque exterrita pinnīs
āles, et ingentī sonuērunt omnia plausū.
Post ācer Mnēstheus adductō cōnstitit arcū,
alta petēns, pariterque oculōs tēlumque tetendit,
ast ipsam miserandus avem contingere ferrō
510 nōn valuit; nōdōs et vincula līnea rūpit,
quīs innexa pedem mālō pendēbat ab altō:
illa Notōs atque ātra volāns in nūbila fūgit.
Tum rapidus jam dūdum arcū contenta parātō
tēla tenēns frātrem Eurytiōn in vōta vocāvit,
515 jam vacuō laetam caelō speculātus et ālīs
plaudentem nigrā fīgit sub nūbe columbam;
dēcidit exanimis, vītamque relīquit in astrīs
aetheriīs, fīxamque refert dēlāpsa sagittam.
Āmissā sōlus palmā superābat Acestēs,
520 quī tamen āeriās tēlum contorsit in aurās
ostentāns artemque patēr arcumque sonantem.
Hīc oculīs subitum objicitur magnōque futūrum
auguriō mōnstrum (docuit post exitus ingēns,
sēraque terrificī cecinērunt ōmina vātēs);
525 namque volāns liquidīs in nūbibus ārsit harundō,
signāvitque viam flammīs, tenuīsque recessit
cōnsūmpta in ventōs, caelō ceu saepe refīxa
trānscurrunt crīnemque volantia sīdera dūcunt.
Attonitīs haesēre animīs, superōsque precātī
530 Trīnacriī Teucrīque virī; nec maximus ōmen
abnuit Aenēās, sed laetum amplexus Acestēn
mūneribus cumulat magnīs, ac tālia fātur:
"Sūme, pater; nam tē voluit rēx magnus Olympī
tālibus auspiciīs exsortem dūcere honōrem;
535 ipsius Anchīsae longaevī hoc mūnus habēbis,

crātēra impressum signīs, quem Thrācius ōlim
Anchīsae genitōrī in magnō mūnere Cisseus
ferre suī dederat monumentum et pignus amōris."
Sīc fātus, cingit viridantī tempora laurō,
et prīmum ante omnīs victōrem appellat Acestēn. 540
Nec bonus Eurytiōn praelātō invīdit honōrī,
quamvīs sōlus avem caelō dējēcit ab altō;
proximus ingreditur dōnīs quī vincula rūpit,
extrēmus volucrī quī fīxit harundine mālum.

QUESTIONS ON **485–544**. 1. What is the target in the archery
contest? Where is it placed? 2. In what way do the contestants
determine the order in which they are to shoot? 3. Who gets
the first position? The last? 4. What is the result of the first
shot? 5. What is the result of the second shot? 6. What is the
result of the third shot? With whose divine aid? 7. What hap-
pened to Acestes's arrow? 8. What prize does Acestes receive?
Eurytion? Mnestheus? Hippocoön?

*Ascanius participates in the equestrian games.*

At pater Aenēās, nōndum certāmine missō,      545
custōdem ad sēsē comitemque impūbis Iūlī
Ēpytidēn vocat, et fīdam sīc fātur ad aurem:
"Vāde age, et Ascaniō, sī jam puerīle parātum
agmen habet sēcum, cursūsque īnstrūxit equōrum,
dūcat avō turmās, et sēsē ostendat in armīs,      550
dīc," ait. Ipse omnem longō dēcēdere circō
īnfūsum populum et campōs jubet esse patentīs.
Incēdunt puerī, pariterque ante ōra parentum
frēnātīs lūcent in equīs, quōs omnis euntīs
Trīnacriae mīrāta fremit Trōjaeque juventūs.      555
Omnibus in mōrem tōnsā coma pressa corōnā;
cornea bīna ferunt praefīxa hastīlia ferrō,
pars lēvīs umerō pharetrās; it pectore summō
flexilis obtortī per collum circulus aurī.
Trēs equitum numerō turmae, ternīque vagantur 560
ductōrēs; puerī bis sēnī quemque secūtī
agmine partītō fulgent paribusque magistrīs.

Ūna aciēs juvenum dūcit quam parvus ovantem
nōmen avī referēns Priamus, tua clāra, Polītē,
565 prōgeniēs, auctūra Italōs, quem Thrācius albīs
portat equus bicolor maculīs, vēstīgia prīmī
alba pedis frontemque ostentāns arduus albam;
alter Atys, genus unde Atiī dūxēre Latīnī,
parvus Atys puerōque puer dīlēctus Iūlō;
570 extrēmus fōrmāque ante omnīs pulcher Iūlus
Sīdoniō est invectus equō, quem candida Dīdō
esse suī dederat monumentum et pignus amōris.
Cētera Trīnacriīs pūbēs seniōris Acestae
fertur equīs.
575    Excipiunt plausū pavidōs, gaudentque tuentēs
Dardanidae, veterumque agnōscunt ōra parentum.
Postquam omnem laetī cōnsessum oculōsque suō-
    rum
lūstrāvēre in equīs, signum clāmōre parātīs
Ēpytidēs longē dedit, īnsonuitque flagellō.
580 Ollī discurrēre parēs, atque agmina ternī
dīductīs solvēre chorīs, rūrsusque vocātī
convertēre viās, īnfestaque tēla tulēre;
inde aliōs ineunt cursūs aliōsque recursūs,
adversī spatiīs, alternōsque orbibus orbīs
585 impediunt, pugnaeque cient simulācra sub armīs,
et nunc terga fugā nūdant, nunc spīcula vertunt
īnfēnsī, factā pariter nunc pāce feruntur.
Ut quondam Crētā fertur Labyrinthus in altā
parietibus textum caecīs iter ancipitemque
590 mīlle viīs habuisse dolum, quā signa sequendī
falleret indēprēnsus et inremeābilis error;
haud aliō Teucrum nātī vēstīgia cursū
impediunt, texuntque fugās et proelia lūdō,
delphīnum similēs quī per maria ūmida nandō
595 Carpathium Libycumque secant, lūduntque per
    undās.

Hunc mōrem cursūs atque haec certāmina prīmus
Ascanius, Longam mūrīs cum cingeret Albam,
rettulit, et prīscōs docuit celebrāre Latīnōs,
quō puer ipse modō, sēcum quō Trōia pūbēs;
Albānī docuēre suōs; hinc maxima porrō          600
accēpit Rōma et patrium servāvit honōrem,
Trōjaque nunc puerī, Trōjānum dīcitur agmen.
Hāc celebrāta tenus sānctō certāmina patrī.

QUESTIONS ON **545-603**.  1. What surprise event does Aeneas
now introduce?  2. What does each boy wear on his head?
Around his neck?  3. What arms do part of the boys carry?
What arms do the rest of the boys carry?  4. How many boys
participate in these maneuvers?  5. Who are the three leaders?
6. From whom did Ascanius get his horse?  7. From whom did
the other boys get their horses?  8. To what does Vergil compare
the intricate movements which the boys execute?

*The Trojan women set fire to the ships.*

   Hīc prīmum Fortūna fidem mūtāta novāvit.
Dum variīs tumulō referunt sollemnia lūdīs,          605
Īrim dē caelō mīsit Sāturnia Jūnō
Īliacam ad classem, ventōsque adspīrat euntī,
multa movēns, necdum antīquum saturāta dolō-
      rem.
Illa viam celerāns per mīlle colōribus arcum,
nūllī vīsa, citō dēcurrit trāmite virgō.          610
Cōnspicit ingentem concursum, et lītora lūstrat,
dēsertōsque videt portūs classemque relictam.
At procul in sōlā sēcrētae Trōades actā
āmissum Anchīsēn flēbant, cūnctaeque profundum
pontum aspectābant flentēs.  Heu, tot vada fessīs 615
et tantum superesse maris, vōx omnibus ūna.
Urbem ōrant; taedet pelagī perferre labōrem.
Ergō inter mediās sēsē haud ignāra nocendī
conjicit, et faciemque deae vestemque repōnit;
fit Beroē, Tmariī conjūnx longaeva Doryclī,          620
cui genus et quondam nōmen nātīque fuissent,

ac sīc Dardanidum mediam sē mātribus īnfert.
"Ō miserae, quās nōn manus," inquit, "Achāica
  bellō
trāxerit ad lētum patriae sub moenibus!  Ō gēns
625 īnfēlīx, cui tē exitiō Fortūna reservat?
Septima post Trōjae excidium jam vertitur aestās,
cum freta, cum terrās omnīs, tot inhospita saxa
sīderaque ēmēnsae ferimur, dum per mare magnum
Ītaliam sequimur fugientem, et volvimur undīs.
630 Hīc Erycis fīnēs frāternī atque hospes Acestēs.
Quis prohibet mūrōs jacere et dare cīvibus urbem?
Ō patria, et raptī nēquīquam ex hoste Penātēs,
nūllane jam Trōjae dīcentur moenia?  Nusquam
Hectoreōs amnīs, Xanthum et Simoënta, vidēbō?
635 Quīn agite, et mēcum īnfaustās exūrite puppīs!
Nam mihi Cassandrae per somnum vātis imāgō
ārdentīs dare vīsa facēs: 'Hīc quaerite Trōjam,
hīc domus est,' inquit, 'vōbīs.' Jam tempus agī rēs,
nec tantīs mora prōdigiīs.  Ēn quattuor ārae
640 Neptūnō; deus ipse facēs animumque ministrat."
Haec memorāns, prīma īnfēnsum vī corripit ignem,
sublātāque procul dextrā cōnīxa coruscat
et jacit.  Arrēctae mentēs stupefactaque corda
Īliadum.  Hīc ūna ē multīs, quae maxima nātū,
645 Pyrgō, tot Priamī nātōrum rēgia nūtrīx:
"Nōn Beroē vōbīs, nōn haec Rhoetēia, mātrēs,
est Dōryclī conjūnx; dīvīnī signa decōris
ārdentīsque notāte oculōs.  Quī spīritus illī,
quī vultus vōcisque sonus vel gressus euntī!
650 Ipsa egomet dūdum Beroēn dīgressa relīquī,
aegram, indignantem, tālī quod sōla carēret
mūnere nec meritōs Anchīsae īnferret honōrēs."
Haec effāta.
At mātrēs prīmō ancipitēs oculīsque malignīs
655 ambiguae spectāre ratīs miserum inter amōrem

praesentis terrae fātīsque vocantia rēgna;
cum dea sē paribus per caelum sustulit ālīs,
ingentemque fugā secuit sub nūbibus arcum.
Tum vērō attonitae mōnstrīs āctaeque furōre
conclāmant, rapiuntque focīs penetrālibus ignem;660
pars spoliant ārās, frondem ac virgulta facēsque
conjiciunt. Furit immissīs Vulcānus habēnīs
trānstra per et rēmōs et pictās abiete puppīs.

QUESTIONS ON **604–663**. 1. What are the Trojan women doing
while the games are in progress? 2. Whom does Juno send down
from heaven to the Trojan camp? 3. Whose form does Iris as-
sume? 4. What does Iris urge the women to do? 5. What
reason does Iris give the Trojan women for doing this? 6. What
does Iris herself now do? 7. Who exposes Iris as an impostor?
With what proofs? 8. Where does Iris now go? 9. What do
the Trojan women now do? With what results?

*A miraculous rainstorm saves most of the ships.*

Nūntius Anchīsae ad tumulum cuneōsque theātrī
incēnsās perfert nāvīs Eumēlus, et ipsī                665
respiciunt ātrō in nimbō volitāre favīllam.
Prīmus et Ascanius, cursūs ut laetus equestrīs
dūcēbat, sīc ācer equō turbāta petīvit
castra, nec exanimēs possunt retinēre magistrī.
"Quis furor iste novus? Quō nunc, quō tenditis,"670
      inquit,
"heu! miserae cīvēs? Nōn hostem inimīcaque
      castra
Argīvum, vestrās spēs ūritis. Ēn, ego vester
Ascanius!" Galeam ante pedēs prōjēcit inānem,
quā lūdō indūtus bellī simulācra ciēbat.
Accelerat simul Aenēās, simul agmina Teucrum.   675
Ast illae dīversa metū per lītora passim
diffugiunt, silvāsque et sīcubi concava fūrtim
saxa petunt; piget inceptī lūcisque, suōsque
mūtātae agnōscunt, excussaque pectore Jūnō est.
Sed nōn idcircō flammae atque incendia vīrīs      680

indomitās posuēre;　ūdō sub rōbore vīvit
stuppa, vomēns tardum fūmum, lentusque carīnās
ēst vapor, et tōtō dēscendit corpore pestis,
nec vīrēs hērōum īnfūsaque flūmina prōsunt.
685 Tum pius Aenēās umerīs abscindere vestem
auxiliōque vocāre deōs et tendere palmās:
"Juppiter omnipotēns, sī nōndum exōsus ad ūnum
Trōjānōs, sī quid pietās antīqua labōrēs
respicit hūmānōs, dā flammam ēvādere classī
690 nunc, pater, et tenuīs Teucrum rēs ēripe lētō;
vel tū, quod superest, īnfestō fulmine mortī,
sī mereor, dēmitte, tuāque hīc obrue dextrā."
Vix haec ēdiderat, cum effūsīs imbribus ātra
tempestās sine mōre furit, tonitrūque tremēscunt
695 ardua terrārum et campī;　ruit aethere tōtō
turbidus imber aquā dēnsīsque nigerrimus Austrīs,
implenturque super puppēs, sēmūsta madēscunt
rōbora, restīnctus dōnec vapor omnis, et omnēs
quattuor āmissīs servātae ā peste carīnae.

QUESTIONS ON **664–699**.　1. How do the Trojan men learn about
the fire?　2. Who from the scene of the games first reaches
the shore?　3. How does he get there?　4. Who next arrives
at the shore?　5. What do the women do?　6. What do the men
try to do?　7. What does Aeneas do at this crisis?　What was the
result?　8. How many ships are found to be a total loss?

*Aeneas sails for Cumae, leaving some of the Trojans
in Sicily.*

700　At pater Aenēās, cāsū concussus acerbō,
nunc hūc ingentīs, nunc illūc pectore cūrās
mūtābat versāns, Siculīsne resīderet arvīs,
oblītus fātōrum, Italāsne capesseret ōrās.
Tum senior Nautēs, ūnum Trītōnia Pallas
705 quem docuit, multāque īnsignem reddidit arte
(hāc respōnsa dabat, vel quae portenderet īra
magna deum vel quae Fātōrum posceret ōrdō),
isque hīs Aenēān sōlātus vōcibus īnfit:

"Nāte deā, quō Fāta trahunt retrahuntque, se-
    quāmur:
quidquid erit, superanda omnis fortūna ferendō est. 710
Est tibi Dardanius dīvīnae stirpis Acestēs;
hunc cape cōnsiliīs socium et conjunge volentem:
huic trāde, āmissīs superant quī nāvibus et quōs
pertaesum magnī inceptī rērumque tuārum est,
longaevōsque senēs, ac fessās aequore mātrēs,     715
et quidquid tēcum invalidum metuēnsque perīclī
    est
dēlige, et hīs habeant terrīs sine moenia fessī;
urbem appellābunt permissō nōmine Acestam."
    Tālibus incēnsus dictīs seniōris amīcī,
tum vērō in cūrās animō dīdūcitur omnīs.           720
Et nox ātra polum bīgīs subvecta tenēbat;
vīsa dehinc caelō faciēs dēlāpsa parentis
Anchīsae subitō tālīs effundere vōcēs:
"Nāte, mihī vītā quondam, dum vīta manēbat,
cāre magis, nāte Īliacīs exercite fātīs,            725
imperiō Jovis hūc veniō, quī classibus ignem
dēpulit, et caelō tandem miserātus ab altō est.
Cōnsiliīs pārē quae nunc pulcherrima Nautēs
dat senior; lēctōs juvenēs, fortissima corda,
dēfer in Ītaliam; gēns dūra atque aspera cultū     730
dēbellanda tibī Latiō est.   Dītis tamen ante
īnfernās accēde domōs, et Averna per alta
congressūs pete, nāte, meōs; nōn mē impia namque
Tartara habent, trīstēs umbrae, sed amoena piō-
    rum
concilia Ēlysiumque colō.  Hūc casta Sibylla       735
nigrārum multō pecudum tē sanguine dūcet.
Tum genus omne tuum et quae dentur moenia
    discēs.
Jamque valē; torquet mediōs nox ūmida cursūs,
et mē saevus equīs Oriēns adflāvit anhēlīs."

740 Dīxerat, et tenuīs fūgit ceu fūmus in aurās.

Aenēās "Quō deinde ruis, quō prōripis," inquit,

"quem fugis, aut quis tē nostrīs complexibus ar-
cet?"

Haec memorāns, cinerem et sōpītōs suscitat ignīs,

Pergameumque Larem et cānae penetrālia Vestae

745 farre piō et plēnā supplex venerātur acerrā.

Extemplō sociōs prīmumque arcessit Acestēn,

et Jovis imperium et cārī praecepta parentis

ēdocet, et quae nunc animō sententia cōnstet.

Haud mora cōnsiliīs, nec jussa recūsat Acestēs.

750 Trānscrībunt urbī mātrēs, populumque volentem

dēpōnunt, animōs nīl magnae laudis egentīs.

Ipsī trānstra novant, flammīsque ambēsa repōnunt

rōbora nāvigiīs, aptant rēmōsque rudentīsque,

exiguī numerō, sed bellō vīvida virtūs.

755 Intereā Aenēās urbem dēsignat arātrō,

sortīturque domōs; hoc Īlium et haec loca Trōjam

esse jubet. Gaudet rēgnō Trōjānus Acestēs,

indīcitque forum, et patribus dat jūra vocātīs.

Tum vīcīna astrīs Erycīnō in vertice sēdēs

760 fundātur Venerī Īdaliae, tumulōque sacerdōs

ac lūcus lātē sacer additur Anchīsēō.

Jamque diēs epulāta novem gēns omnis, et ārīs

factus honōs; placidī strāvērunt aequora ventī,

crēber et adspīrāns rūrsus vocat Auster in altum.

765 Exoritur prōcurva ingēns per lītora flētus;

complexī inter sē noctemque diemque morantur.

Ipsae jam mātrēs, ipsī quibus aspera quondam

vīsa maris faciēs et nōn tolerābile nōmen

īre volunt omnemque fugae perferre labōrem.

770 Quōs bonus Aenēās dictīs sōlātur amīcīs,

et cōnsanguineō lacrimāns commendat Acestae.

Trīs Erycī vitulōs et Tempestātibus agnam

caedere deinde jubet solvīque ex ōrdine fūnem.

Ipse, caput tōnsae foliīs ēvīnctus olīvae,
stāns procul in prōrā pateram tenet, extaque salsōs 775
prōjicit in flūctūs, ac vīna liquentia fundit.
Prōsequitur surgēns ā puppī ventus euntīs;
certātim sociī feriunt mare et aequora verrunt.

QUESTIONS ON **700–778**. 1. What change of plans does Aeneas
now consider? 2. What advice does Nautes give Aeneas?
3. What vision appears to Aeneas at night? 4. What advice
does the vision give Aeneas for the immediate future? 5. What
place does the vision tell Aeneas to visit before undertaking the
conquest that awaits him in Italy? 6. Who is to be Aeneas's
guide on this journey? 7. What does Aeneas do as soon as the
vision disappears? 8. To whom does Aeneas report the advice
of the vision? 9. What division of the Trojans do Aeneas and
Acestes now make? 10. What provision do Aeneas and Acestes
make for those Trojans who prefer to settle in Sicily? 11. What
delays Aeneas's departure? 12. To what deities does Aeneas
offer sacrifice before he sails from Sicily?

*Neptune calms the sea at Venus's bidding.*

At Venus intereā Neptūnum, exercita cūrīs,
adloquitur, tālīsque effundit pectore questūs:     780
"Jūnōnis gravis īra nec exsaturābile pectus
cōgunt mē, Neptūne, precēs dēscendere in omnīs,
quam nec longa diēs pietās nec mītigat ūlla,
nec Jovis imperiō Fātīsque īnfrācta quiēscit.
Nōn mediā dē gente Phrygum exēdisse nefandīs    785
urbem odiīs satis est nec poenam trāxe per omnem;
relliquiās Trōjae, cinerēs atque ossa perēmptae,
īnsequitur. Causās tantī sciat illa furōris.
Ipse mihī nūper Libycīs tū testis in undīs
quam mōlem subitō excierit; maria omnia caelō    790
miscuit, Aeoliīs nēquīquam frēta procellīs,
in rēgnīs hoc ausa tuīs.
Per scelus ecce etiam Trōjānīs mātribus āctīs
exussit foedē puppīs, et classe subēgit
āmissā sociōs ignōtae linquere terrae.     795
Quod superest, ōrō, liceat dare tūta per undās
vēla tibī, liceat Laurentem attingere Thybrim,

sī concessa petō, sī dant ea moenia Parcae."

Tum Sāturnius haec domitor maris ēdidit altī:

800 "Fas omne est, Cytherēa, meīs tē fīdere rēgnīs,
unde genus dūcis. Meruī quoque; saepe furōrēs
compressī et rabiem tantam caelīque marisque.
Nec minor in terrīs (Xanthum Simoëntaque testor)
Aenēae mihi cūra tuī. Cum Trōia Achillēs
805 exanimāta sequēns impingeret agmina mūrīs,
mīlia multa daret lētō, gemerentque replētī
amnēs, nec reperīre viam atque ēvolvere posset
in mare sē Xanthus, Pēlīdae tunc ego fortī
congressum Aenēān nec dīs nec vīribus aequīs
810 nūbe cavā rapuī, cuperem cum vertere ab īmō
strūcta meīs manibus perjūrae moenia Trōjae.
Nunc quoque mēns eadem perstat mihi; pelle
    timōrem.
Tūtus quōs optās portūs accēdet Avernī.
Ūnus erit tantum, āmissum quem gurgite quaerēs;
815 ūnum prō multīs dabitur caput."

Hīs ubi laeta deae permulsit pectora dictīs,
jungit equōs aurō genitor, spūmantiaque addit
frēna ferīs, manibusque omnīs effundit habēnās.
Caeruleō per summa levis volat aequora currū:
820 subsīdunt undae, tumidumque sub axe tonantī
sternitur aequor aquīs; fugiunt vāstō aethere nimbī.
Tum variae comitum faciēs, immānia cētē,
et senior Glaucī chorus, Īnōusque Palaemōn,
Trītōnesque citī, Phorcīque exercitus omnis;
825 laeva tenet Thetis, et Melitē, Panopēaque virgō,
Nīsaeē, Spīōque, Thalīaque, Cȳmodocēque.

QUESTIONS ON **779–826.** 1. What steps does Venus now take to insure a safe voyage for Aeneas? 2. For what misfortunes to the Trojans does Venus blame Juno? 3. On what previous occasions has Neptune been of service to Aeneas? 4. At what price does Neptune now agree to bring Aeneas safe to Italy? 5. What does Neptune now do to insure a calm sea? 6. Who was Thetis?

*Palinurus falls overboard, and Aeneas guides the*
   *fleet to Cumae.*

Hīc patris Aenēae suspēnsam blanda vicissim
gaudia pertemptant mentem; jubet ōcius omnīs
attollī mālōs, intendī bracchia vēlīs.
Ūnā omnēs fēcēre pedem, pariterque sinistrōs,          830
nunc dextrōs solvēre sinūs; ūnā ardua torquent
cornua dētorquentque; ferunt sua flāmina classem.
Prīnceps ante omnīs dēnsum Palinūrus agēbat
agmen; ad hunc aliī cursum contendere jussī.
Jamque ferē mediam caelī nox ūmida mētam             835
contigerat, placidā laxābant membra quiēte,
sub rēmīs fūsī per dūra sedīlia nautae;
cum levis aetheriīs dēlāpsus Somnus ab astrīs
āera dīmōvit tenebrōsum, et dispulit umbrās,
tē, Palinūre, petēns, tibi somnia trīstia portāns      840
īnsontī, puppīque deus cōnsēdit in altā,
Phorbantī similis, funditque hās ōre loquēlās:
"Īasidē Palinūre, ferunt ipsa aequora classem;
aequātae spīrant aurae; datur hōra quiētī:
pōne caput, fessōsque oculōs fūrāre labōrī;            845
ipse ego paulisper prō tē tua mūnera inībō."
Cui vix attollēns Palinūrus lūmina fātur:
"Mēne salis placidī vultum flūctūsque quiētōs
ignōrāre jubēs? Mēne huic cōnfīdere mōnstrō?
Aenēān crēdam (quid enim?) fallācibus aurīs,          850
et caelī totiēns dēceptus fraude serēnī?"
Tālia dicta dabat, clāvumque adfīxus et haerēns
nusquam āmittēbāt, oculōsque sub astra tenēbat.
Ecce deus rāmum Lēthaeō rōre madentem
vīque sopōrātum Stygiā super utraque quassat           855
tempora, cūnctantīque natantia lūmina solvit.
Vix prīmōs inopīna quiēs laxāverat artūs,
et super incumbēns cum puppis parte revulsā

cumque gubernāclō liquidās prōjēcit in undās
860 praecipitem, ac sociōs nēquīquam saepe vocantem;
ipse volāns tenuīs sē sustulit āles ad aurās.
Currit iter tūtum nōn sētius aequore classis,
prōmissīsque patris Neptūnī interrita fertur.

Jamque adeō scopulōs Sīrēnum advecta subībat,
865 difficilīs quondam, multōrumque ossibus albōs
(tum rauca adsiduō longē sale saxa sonābant),
cum pater āmissō fluitantem errāre magistrō
sēnsit, et ipse ratem nocturnīs rēxit in undīs,
multa gemēns, cāsūque animum concussus amīcī:
870 "Ō nimium caelō et pelagō cōnfīse serēnō,
nūdus in ignōtā, Palinūre, jacēbis harēnā."

QUESTIONS ON **827–871**. 1. What does Aeneas do to speed his
ships? 2. Who is pilot of Aeneas's flagship? 3. Who appears
to Palinurus? In what guise? 4. What does Somnus urge Pa-
linurus to do? Why? 5. How much trust in the sea does Pali-
nurus's reply indicate? 6. What magic power does Somnus
employ against Palinurus? 7. What does Somnus now do to
Palinurus? 8. What causes Aeneas to take over the task of
piloting his ship? 9. What fate does Aeneas assume has over-
taken Palinurus? 10. Why did the ancients consider death at
sea a much worse fate than death on land?

# BOOK VI

*The Trojans land at Cumae and Aeneas visits the temple of Apollo.*

Sīc fātur lacrimāns, classīque immittit habēnās,
et tandem Euboïcīs Cūmārum adlābitur ōrīs.
Obvertunt pelagō prōrās; tum dente tenācī
ancora fundābat nāvīs, et lītora curvae
praetexunt puppēs.  Juvenum manus ēmicat ār- 5
dēns
lītus in Hesperium; quaerit pars sēmina flammae
abstrūsa in vēnīs silicis, pars dēnsa ferārum
tēcta rapit silvās, inventaque flūmina mōnstrat.
At pius Aenēās arcīs, quibus altus Apollō
praesidet, horrendaeque procul sēcrēta Sibyllae, 10
antrum immāne, petit, magnam cui mentem ani-
mumque
Dēlius īnspīrat vātēs, aperitque futūra.
Jam subeunt Triviae lūcōs atque aurea tēcta.
Daedalus, ut fāma est, fugiēns Mīnōia rēgna,
praepetibus pinnīs ausus sē crēdere caelō, 15
īnsuētum per iter gelidās ēnāvit ad Arctōs,
Chalcidicāque levis tandem super adstitit arce.
Redditus hīs prīmum terrīs tibi, Phoebe, sacrāvit
rēmigium ālārum, posuitque immānia templa.
In foribus lētum Androgeō: tum pendere poenās 20

**habēna** rein

**adlābor** glide to

**obvertō** turn toward; **prōra**
prow; **dēns** tooth; fluke (*of
an anchor*); **tenāx** tenacious,
holding fast
**fundō** make secure
**praetexō** fringe, border; **ēmicō**
dart forth

**sēmen** seed

**abstrūdō** hide away; **vēna** vein;
**silex** stone, flint; **fera** wild
beast

**praesideō** preside over; **sēcrē-
tum** retreat, haunt
**antrum** cave, cavern

**īnspīrō** breathe into; inspire

**praepes** swift, flying; **pinna**
feather, wing
**īnsuētus** unfamiliar, strange;
cf. **suēscō** become ac-
customed; **gelidus** icy,
cold; **ēnō** swim forth, fly

**rēmigium** oarage

---

**1. Sīc fātur lacrimāns:** Aeneas had just been
lamenting the drowning of Palinurus, as described
at the end of Book V. **2. Euboïcīs:** *Euboean, of
Euboea.* **Cūmārum:** *of Cumae,* a city on the coast
of Campania in Italy, founded by colonists from
Euboea, in Chalcis. **ōrīs:** dat. of direction. **10. Si-
byllae:** *of the Sibyl,* a famous prophetess at Cumae.
**11–12. magnam ... vātēs:** *in whom the Delian
prophet inspires a lofty mind and spirit.* **12. Dēlius**

vātēs: i.e., Apollo, who was born on the island of
Delos.
**14. Daedalus:** a famous craftsman and the first
aviator. **Mīnōia:** *of Minos,* King of Crete.
**16. Arctōs:** the constellations of the Bears, i.e.,
the North. **17. Chalcidicā:** *Chalcidian,* i.e.,
Euboean. **20. Androgeō:** Greek gen. Androgeos,
son of King Minos, had been murdered by the
Athenians. As punishment, Minos compelled the

septēnī seven (each); quotan-
nīs each year, annually
urna urn, vase

suppōnō place under; mate
with; **fūrtum craft; stealth
biförmis two-formed

īnsum be present; **monumen-
tum memorial, memento
inextrīcābilis unsolvable

ambāgēs winding, intricacy

fīlum thread

effingō fashion, represent

perlegō scan, examine

spectāculum sight, spectacle

*grex flock, herd; intāctus un-
touched, unbroken; *juven-
cus bullock
bidēns sheep

Cecropidae jussī (miserum!) septēna quotannīs
corpora nātōrum; stat ductīs sortibus urna.
Contrā ēlāta marī respondet Gnōsia tellūs;
hīc crūdēlis amor taurī, suppostaque fūrtō
25 Pāsiphaē, mixtumque genus, prōlēsque biförmis
Mīnōtaurus inest, Veneris monumenta nefandae;
hīc labor ille domūs et inextrīcābilis error,
magnum rēgīnae sed enim miserātus amōrem
Daedalus ipse dolōs tēctī ambāgīsque resolvit,
30 caeca regēns fīlō vēstīgia. Tū quoque magnam
partem opere in tantō, sineret dolor, Īcare, habērēs;
bis cōnātus erat cāsūs effingere in aurō,
bis patriae cecidēre manūs. Quīn prōtinus omnia
perlegerent oculīs, nī jam praemissus Achātēs
35 adforet atque unā Phoebī Triviaeque sacerdōs,
Dēiphobē Glaucī, fātur quae tālia rēgī:
"Nōn hoc ista sibī tempus spectācula poscit;
nunc grege dē intāctō septem mactāre juvencōs
praestiterit, totidem lēctās dē mōre bidentīs."
40 Tālibus adfāta Aenēān (nec sacra morantur
jussa virī), Teucrōs vocat alta in templa sacerdōs.

QUESTIONS ON LINES 1–41. 1. What does one group of Trojans
do as soon as they land at Cumae? What does another group
do? 2. What does Aeneas do? 3. What scenes from the The-
seus story are engraved on the double doors of the temple?
4. What other scene did Daedalus try to engrave on these doors?
5. Why could he not complete the task? 6. Who recalls Aeneas
from the contemplation of these scenes? To perform what task?
7. Had Aeneas come alone to the temple? 8. Whom had
Aeneas sent ahead?

Athenians to sacrifice to the Minotaur seven
youths and seven maidens annually. 21. Cecro-
pidae: *descendants of Cecrops,* fabled founder of
Athens. 23. ēlāta marī: *rising out of the sea.*
Gnōsia: *of Gnosus,* a city in Crete. 24. crūdēlis
amor taurī: *tragic love for a bull.* suppostaque
fūrtō: *and secretly mated* (with a bull). 25. Pāsi-
phaē: wife of Minos and mother of the Minotaur,
a monster half bull and half man. 26. Veneris:
i.e., amōris. 27. labor ille domūs: i.e., the
Labyrinth, built by Daedalus to house the Mino-
taur. error: *the maze,* i.e., the Labyrinth. 28. rē-

gīnae: the princess Ariadne, who fell in love with
the Athenian youth, Theseus, and persuaded Dae-
dalus to give him the clue to the Labyrinth.
30. vēstīgia: (Theseus's) *steps.* 31. sineret dolor:
supply sī. Īcare: *Icarus,* son of Daedalus.
32. cāsūs: *the fall* (of Icarus). 33. patriae: adj.
modifying manūs. omnia: here a dissyllable, by
*synizesis.* 34. perlegerent: *they would have ex-
amined.* 36. Glaucī: (daughter) *of Glaucus.*
39. praestiterit: *it would be better;* potential sub-
junctive; see App. 150. 40. sacra: *sacrifices:* ob-
ject of morantur.

The Cumaean Sibyl and Verses of Vergil

*Aeneas prays to Apollo to end the Trojans' wan-
derings.*

Excīsum Euboïcae latus ingēns rūpis in antrum,
quō lātī dūcunt aditūs centum, ōstia centum,                    **ōstium** mouth, entrance
unde ruunt totidem vōcēs, respōnsa Sibyllae.
Ventum erat ad līmen, cum virgō "Poscere fāta   45
tempus," ait, "deus, ecce, deus!"  Cui tālia fantī
ante forīs subitō nōn vultus, nōn color ūnus,
nōn cōmptae mānsēre comae, sed pectus anhēlum,        **cōmō** arrange; **anhēlus** pant-
                                                          ing, heaving
et rabiē fera corda tument, majorque vidērī              ***rabiēs** madness,   frenzy;
                                                         ***tumeō** swell
nec mortāle sonāns, adflāta est nūmine quandō   50   **adflō** breathe upon, inspire
jam propiōre deī.  "Cessās in vōta precēsque,        ***cessō** pause, hesitate
Trōs," ait, "Aenēā, cessās?  Neque enim ante de-      **dehīscō** yawn, gape open
hīscent
attonitae magna ōra domūs."  Et, tālia fāta,         **attonō** thunder at;  strike
                                                          with awe
conticuit.  Gelidus Teucrīs per dūra cucurrit        **conticēscō** become   silent;
                                                         ***gelidus** icy
ossa tremor, funditque precēs rēx pectore ab īmō :55 **tremor** shudder
"Phoebe, gravīs Trōjae semper miserāte labōrēs,
Dardana quī Paridis dīrēxtī tēla manūsque
corpus in Aeacidae, magnās obeuntia terrās           *obeō** envelop, surround
tot maria intrāvī duce tē, penitusque repostās       **intrō** enter
Massȳlum gentīs, praetentaque Syrtibus arva;     60  **praetendō** stretch before, ex-
jam tandem Ītaliae fugientis prēndimus ōrās :           tend to
hāc Trōjāna tenus fuerit fortūna secūta.             **hāctenus** thus far
Vōs quoque Pergameae jam fās est parcere gentī,
dīque deaeque omnēs, quibus obstitit Īlium et in-
gēns
glōria Dardaniae.  Tūque, ō sānctissima vātēs,   65
praescia ventūrī, dā (nōn indēbita poscō            **praescius** having foreknowl-
                                                        edge; **indēbitus** not due, not
                                                        owed

---

**45. Ventum erat:** *They had come.* **45–46. Pos-
cere fāta tempus:** (it is) *time to ask for the oracles.*
**47. ūnus:** *the same.* **48. pectus:** supply est. **49–
50. majorque . . . sonāns:** *she is greater in ap-
pearance and her voice does not sound human.*
**51. Cessās in vōta:** *Do you hesitate* (to turn)
*to your vows?* **53. fāta:** *having spoken.* **55. rēx:**
Aeneas. **56. miserāte:** *thou who hast pitied;* voc.

of the participle. **57. dīrēxtī: dīrēxistī.** Apollo
had guided the arrow shot by Paris into Achilles's
heel. **62. hāc . . . secūta:** *thus far* (and no
farther) *let Trojan ill luck have followed* (us), i.e.,
let our misfortunes now cease. **hāc . . . tenus:** an
example of *tmesis;* see App. 22, 22. **64. dīque . . .
omnēs:** especially Juno and Minerva. **66–67. dā
cōnsīdere Teucrōs:** *grant the Trojans to settle.*

rēgna meīs fātīs) Latiō cōnsīdere Teucrōs
errantīsque deōs agitātaque nūmina Trōjae.

***solidus massive; **marmor marble

Tum Phoebō et Triviae solidō de marmorc tem-
plum

fēstus festal, festival

70 īnstituam fēstōsque diēs dē nōmine Phoebī.

penetrālia sanctuary

Tē quoque magna manent rēgnīs penetrālia nostrīs;

arcānus secret

hīc ego namque tuās sortīs arcānaque fāta
dicta meae gentī pōnam, lēctōsque sacrābō,

**folium leaf; ***carmen song, verse; prophecy
lūdibrium sport, plaything

alma, virōs.  Foliīs tantum nē carmina mandā,

75 nē turbāta volent rapidīs lūdibria ventīs;
ipsa canās ōrō." Fīnem dedit ōre loquendī.

QUESTIONS ON 42–76. 1. What physical changes does the Sibyl undergo when she comes to the entrance of the cave-like inner room of the temple? 2. Whom does Aeneas first address in his prayer? 3. What favor does he ask of the god? 4. What honors does Aeneas promise the god if his prayer is answered? 5. What honors does Aeneas promise the Sibyl? 6. In what form does Aeneas ask the Sibyl to deliver her prophecy? 7. What was her usual method?

*The Sibyl tells Aeneas that war awaits him in Italy.*

At Phoebī nōndum patiēns, immānis in antrō

bacchor rave

bacchātur vātēs, magnum sī pectore possit
excussisse deum; tantō magis ille fatīgat

rabidus raving, frenzied;
**domō tame, subdue

80 ōs rabidum, fera corda domāns, fingitque pre-
mendō.

Ōstia jamque domūs patuēre ingentia centum
sponte suā, vātisque ferunt respōnsa per aurās:

dēfungor go through with; finish

"Ō tandem magnīs pelagī dēfūncte perīclīs
(sed terrae graviōra manent), in rēgna Lavīnī
85 Dardanidae venient (mitte hanc dē pectore cūram),

---

68. deōs: i.e., the Trojan Penates. 69–70. Tum ... Phoebī: there is an allusion here to the temple of Apollo and the temple of Diana, built by Augustus at Rome, and to the *Lūdī Apollinārēs*, held annually in honor of Apollo. 71. Tē: i.e., the Sibyl, whose written prophecies, known as the Sibylline books, were kept in the temple of Apollo. rēgnīs: *in my kingdom*. 73–74. lēctōs virōs: these men (*quīndecimvirī sacrīs faciundīs*) guarded and interpreted the Sibylline oracles. 74. nē ...

mandā: negative imperative. The Sibyl commonly wrote her prophecies on leaves, which the winds were likely to blow away or disarrange. 75. rapidīs ... ventīs: *the sport of swift breezes.* 76. ipsa canās: *that thou thyself speak.*

77. Phoebī patiēns: *yielding to Phoebus.* immānis: *wild*(ly). 81. patuēre: patuērunt. 83. dēfūncte: *thou who hast experienced;* voc. of the participle. 84. graviōra: understand perīcula.

sed nōn et vēnisse volent.  Bella, horrida bella,
et Thybrim multō spūmantem sanguine cernō.
Nōn Simoīs tibi nec Xanthus nec Dōrica castra
dēfuerint; alius Latiō jam partus Achillēs,        ***pariō  bring forth
nātus et ipse deā; nec Teucrīs addita Jūnō        90
usquam aberit, cum tū supplex in rēbus egēnīs      egēnus needy; humble
quās gentīs Italum aut quās nōn ōrāveris urbīs!
Causa malī tantī conjūnx iterum hospita Teucrīs    hospitus strange, foreign
externīque iterum thalamī.                         *externus outside, foreign
Tū nē cēde malīs, sed contrā audentior ītō         95
quam tua tē fortūna sinet.  Via prīma salūtis,
quod minimē rēris, Grajā pandētur ab urbe."        ***reor think, suppose

QUESTIONS ON 77–97.  1. Does the Sibyl yield at once to Apollo's
influence?  2. What favorable prediction does the Sibyl make
for Aeneas?  3. Of what unfavorable events does the Sibyl warn
Aeneas?  4. What does the Sibyl tell Aeneas to do in view
of these unfavorable predictions?  5. From what unexpected
source does the Sibyl tell Aeneas he will receive help?

*The Sibyl tells Aeneas how to reach the spirit of
Anchises in the underworld.*

Tālibus ex adytō dictīs Cūmaea Sibylla
horrendās canit ambāgīs, antrōque remūgit,         ambāgēs winding;  mystery;
                                                     remūgiō resound
obscūrīs vēra involvēns; ea frēna furentī          100 involvō roll up, infold; **frē-
                                                     num rein
concutit, et stimulōs sub pectore vertit Apollō.    *stimulus spur
Ut prīmum cessit furor et rabida ōra quiērunt,     rabidus raving, frenzied
incipit Aenēās hērōs: "Nōn ūlla labōrum,           ***hērōs hero
ō virgō, nova mī faciēs inopīnave surgit;          inopīnus unexpected
omnia praecēpī, atque animō mēcum ante perēgī. 105 peragō go over
Ūnum ōrō: quandō hīc īnfernī jānua rēgis           īnfernus of the underworld;
                                                     jānua door, entrance
dīcitur et tenebrōsa palūs Acheronte refūsō,       tenebrōsus shadowy, dark; re-
                                                     fundō overflow
īre ad cōnspectum cārī genitōris et ōra

89. dēfuerint: fut. perf.  alius Achillēs: i.e.,   riage" of Helen had been the cause of the Trojan
Turnus, with whom Aeneas came into conflict       War.  95. ītō: future imperat. of eō.  97. quod
on his arrival in Italy.  92. Italum: Italōrum.    ... rēris: (a thing) *which you little think*.  Grajā
ōrāveris: fut. perf.  93. Causa: supply erit.      urbe: i.e., from Evander's city, Pallanteum, which
conjūnx: i.e., Lavinia, previously betrothed to    was later the site of Rome.
Turnus, but promised to Aeneas by her father,         104. mī: mihi.  106. īnfernī rēgis: i.e., of
King Latinus.  iterum: just as the "foreign mar-   Pluto.  107. palūs Acheronte refūsō: *pool*

**\*\*contingit** (it) befalls, (it) happens

**\*\*\*minae** threats, menaces

**invalidus** weak, feeble; **ultrā** beyond; **senecta** old age

**mandātum** order, command

**\*\*frētus** relying on; **cithara** cither, lute; **fidēs** strings (of a musical instrument); **canōrus** tuneful
**\*alternus** alternating; **redimō** redeem, ransom

**\*\*\*ōrdior** begin

**dēscēnsus** descent

**superus** upper

**ēvehō** carry up

**circumveniō** encircle

**\*\*\*cupīdō** desire

**innō** swim; sail across; **\*\*\*lacus** lake
**īnsānus** mad; **indulgeō** yield to, indulge in

contingat; doceās iter, et sacra ōstia pandās.

110 Illum ego per flammās et mīlle sequentia tēla
ēripuī hīs umerīs, mediōque ex hoste recēpī;
ille meum comitātus iter maria omnia mēcum,
atque omnīs pelagīque minās caelīque ferēbat,
invalidus, vīrīs ultrā sortemque senectae.

115 Quīn ut tē supplex peterem et tua līmina adīrem
īdem ōrāns mandāta dabat. Gnātīque patrisque,
alma, precor, miserēre (potes namque omnia, nec tē
nēquīquam lūcīs Hecatē praefēcit Avernīs).
Sī potuit Mānīs arcessere conjugis Orpheus,

120 Thrēiciā frētus citharā fidibusque canōrīs,
sī frātrem Pollūx alternā morte redēmit,
itque reditque viam totiēns (quid Thēsea magnum,
quid memorem Alcīdēn?); et mī genus ab Jove
summō."

Tālibus ōrābat dictīs, ārāsque tenēbat,

125 cum sīc ōrsa loquī vātēs: "Sate sanguine dīvum,
Trōs Anchīsiadē, facilis dēscēnsus Avernō;
noctīs atque diēs patet ātrī jānua Dītis;
sed revocāre gradum superāsque ēvādere ad aurās,
hoc opus, hic labor est. Paucī, quōs aequus amāvit

130 Juppiter, aut ārdēns ēvexit ad aethera virtūs,
dīs genitī, potuēre. Tenent media omnia silvae,
Cōcȳtosque sinū lābēns circumvenit ātrō.
Quod sī tantus amor mentī, sī tanta cupīdō
bis Stygiōs innāre lacūs, bis nigra vidēre

135 Tartara, et īnsānō juvat indulgēre labōrī,

(formed) *by the overflow of the Acheron.* **109. contingat:** jussive subj.; so **doceās** and **pandās.**
**114. vīrīs ultrā:** an example of *anastrophe.*
**116. Gnātīque patrisque:** gen. used with **miserēre** in line 117. **119. Orpheus:** a famous musician who attempted to rescue his wife Eurydice from the underworld. **120. Thrēiciā:** *Thracian.*
**121. Pollūx:** brother of Castor, in whose stead he spent every other day in the underworld.
**122. Thēsea:** *Theseus,* a famous hero who accompanied Pirithoüs to the underworld. **123. quid**

**memorem:** *why should I mention?* **Alcīdēn:** i.e., Hercules. **et mī (est):** *I too have.*
**125. ōrsa:** supply est. **Sate:** *thou who art descended;* voc. of the participle. **126. Anchīsiadē:** *son of Anchises,* i.e., Aeneas; the reference is especially appropriate here, since Aeneas is seeking admission to Hades in order to see his father. **Avernō:** dat. of direction. **131. dīs genitī:** *born of the gods.* **132. Cōcȳtos:** a river in Hades. **134. bis:** i.e., now, while alive, and again after death.

accipe quae peragenda prius.  Latet arbore opācā
aureus et foliīs et lentō vīmine rāmus,
Jūnōnī īnfernae dictus sacer; hunc tegit omnis
lūcus, et obscūrīs claudunt convallibus umbrae.
Sed nōn ante datur tellūris operta subīre
auricomōs quam quī dēcerpserit arbore fētūs.
Hoc sibi pulchra suum ferrī Prōserpina mūnus
īnstituit; prīmō āvulsō nōn dēficit alter
aureus, et similī frondēscit virga metallō.
Ergō altē vēstīgā oculīs, et rīte repertum
carpe manū, namque ipse volēns facilisque sequētur,
sī tē Fāta vocant; aliter nōn vīribus ūllīs
vincere nec dūrō poteris convellere ferrō.
Praetereā jacet exanimum tibi corpus amīcī
(heu! nescīs), tōtamque incestat fūnere classem,
dum cōnsulta petis, nostrōque in līmine pendēs;
sēdibus hunc refer ante suīs, et conde sepulcrō.
Dūc nigrās pecudēs; ea prīma piācula suntō.
Sīc dēmum lūcōs Stygis et rēgna invia vīvīs
aspiciēs." Dīxit, pressōque obmūtuit ōre.

***opācus overshadowed, obscure
***folium leaf; *lentus pliant; clinging; vīmen stem; **rāmus branch, bough
īnfernus of the underworld
convallis valley

140 **ante ... quam sooner ... than, i.e., before; opertum secret place
auricomus golden-tressed; dēcerpō pluck; fētus offspring; bough

frondēscō put forth leaves; **virga twig, branch; metallum metal
145 altē high, aloft; vēstīgō search; ***rīte duly

exanimus lifeless
150 incestō defile, pollute
*cōnsultum counsel, advice

piāculum expiatory offering
invius inaccessible
155 obmūtēscō become silent, be mute

QUESTIONS ON 98-155.  1. What special petition does Aeneas now address to the Sibyl? 2. To what occasion does Aeneas refer in lines 110-111? 3. At whose command has Aeneas come to consult the Sibyl? 4. For what purpose did Orpheus descend alive into the underworld? Pollux? Theseus? Hercules? 5. Does the Sibyl say it is hard or easy to descend into the underworld? To return? 6. What does the Sibyl tell Aeneas to take with him as a gift to Proserpina? 7. Where is Aeneas to look for this gift? 8. What important duty does the Sibyl tell Aeneas he must at once perform?

*Aeneas finds the body of Misenus.*

Aenēās maestō dēfīxus lūmina vultū
ingreditur, linquēns antrum, caecōsque volūtat
ēventūs animō sēcum.  Cui fīdus Achātēs

dēfīgō fasten, fix
ingredior walk along
ēventus occurrence

136. peragenda: supply sint.  arbore: place where.  138. Jūnōnī īnfernae: i.e., to Proserpina.  140-141. ante quam quī: *before one.*  143. prīmō: supply rāmō.  149. jacet: *lies* (unburied).  149. amīcī: i.e., of Misenus.  152. sē-  dibus suīs: *to his proper place.*  153. suntō: *let them be;* 3rd pers. pl. imperative.  155. pressō ōre: *with lips closed.*  156. dēfīxus lūmina: *with downcast eyes.*  lūmina: acc. with dēfīxus; see App. 114.

it comes, et paribus cūrīs vēstīgia fīgit.

160 Multa inter sēsē variō sermōne serēbant,

quem socium exanimem vātēs, quod corpus hu-
  mandum

dīceret. Atque illī Mīsēnum in lītore siccō,

ut vēnēre, vident indignā morte perēmptum,

Mīsēnum Aeolidēn, quō nōn praestantior alter

165 aere ciēre virōs Mārtemque accendere cantū.

Hectoris hic magnī fuerat comes, Hectora circum

et lituō pugnās īnsignis obībat et hastā;

postquam illum vītā victor spoliāvit Achillēs,

Dardaniō Aenēae sēsē fortissimus hērōs

170 addiderat socium, nōn īnferiōra secūtus.

Sed tum, forte cavā dum personat aequora conchā,

dēmēns, et cantū vocat in certāmina dīvōs,

aemulus exceptum Trītōn, sī crēdere dignum est,

inter saxa virum spūmōsā immerserat undā.

175 Ergō omnēs magnō circum clāmōre fremēbant,

praecipuē pius Aenēās. Tum jussa Sibyllae,

haud mora, festīnant flentēs, āramque sepulcrī

congerere arboribus caelōque ēdūcere certant.

Ītur in antīquam silvam, stabula alta ferārum;

180 prōcumbunt piceae, sonat icta secūribus īlex,

fraxineaeque trabēs cuneīs et fissile rōbur

scinditur, advolvunt ingentīs montibus ornōs.

Nec nōn Aenēās opera inter tālia prīmus

hortātur sociōs, paribusque accingitur armīs.

**Side glosses (left margin):**

serō interweave; discuss

exanimis lifeless; humō cover with earth, bury

**siccus dry

indignus undeserved; perimō take away, destroy
praestāns outstanding, pre-eminent
cantus song; peal

lituus trumpet; **obeō go to meet, face
*spoliō plunder, rob

personō cause to resound, make ring; concha sea-shell; trumpet
cantus song, trumpet-blowing; **certāmen contest
aemulus envious
spūmōsus foaming; immergō plunge

festīnō hasten, speed

congerō pile up, build

**stabulum standing-place, abode, haunt
picea pitch-pine tree; īcō strike; cf. **ictus stroke, blow; **secūris ax; **īlex holm-oak
fraxineus of the ash tree; cuneus wedge; fissilis easily split
advolvō roll in; ornus ash tree

QUESTIONS ON 156–184. 1. What great Trojan hero did Misenus once serve? In what double capacity? 2. When did Misenus become an attendant of Aeneas? 3. By what foolish challenge has Misenus just caused his own death? 4. What do Aeneas

162. Mīsēnum: *Misenus*, a Trojan trumpeter. 164. praestantior: supply erat. 165. ciēre, accendere: infinitives used with praestantior; see App. 177. 166. Hectora: Greek acc. 168. illum: i.e., Hector. vītā: abl. of separation with spoliō. 170. nōn īnferiōra secūtus: *following no meaner fortunes;* i.e., Aeneas was no less a leader than Hector. 172. dēmēns: Misenus was mad to

challenge Triton, a god. 173. exceptum: *caught,* agreeing with virum (i.e., Misenus) in line 174. 174. undā: place where. 177. haud mora: supply est. āram sepulcrī: *the funeral pyre.* 178. caelō: dat. of direction. 179. Ītur: *They go;* impersonal use of verb. 182. montibus: place whence. 184. accingitur: *girds himself.*

and the other Trojans now hasten to construct? 5. Where do they go for material?

*Aeneas, guided by two doves, finds the Golden Bough.*

Atque haec ipse suō trīstī cum corde volūtat, 185
aspectāns silvam immēnsam, et sīc forte precātur:
"Sī nunc sē nōbīs ille aureus arbore rāmus
ostendat nemore in tantō, quandō omnia vērē
heu! nimium dē tē vātēs, Mīsēne, locūta est!"
Vix ea fātus erat, geminae cum forte columbae 190
ipsa sub ōra virī caelō vēnēre volantēs,
et viridī sēdēre solō. Tum maximus hērōs
māternās agnōscit avīs, laetusque precātur:
"Este ducēs ō, sī qua via est, cursumque per aurās
dīrigite in lūcōs, ubi pinguem dīves opācat 195
rāmus humum. Tūque ō dubiīs nē dēfice rēbus,
dīva parēns." Sīc effātus, vēstīgia pressit
observāns quae signa ferant, quō tendere pergant.
Pāscentēs illae tantum prōdīre volandō,
quantum aciē possent oculī servāre sequentum. 200
Inde, ubi vēnēre ad faucīs grave olentis Avernī,
tollunt sē celerēs, liquidumque per āera lāpsae
sēdibus optātīs geminā super arbore sīdunt,
discolor unde aurī per rāmōs aura refulsit.
Quāle solet silvīs brūmālī frīgore viscum
fronde virēre novā, quod nōn sua sēminat arbōs,
et croceō fētū teretīs circumdare truncōs,
tālis erat speciēs aurī frondentis opācā
īlice, sīc lēnī crepitābat brattea ventō.
Corripit Aenēās extemplō, avidusque refringit 210
cūnctantem, et vātis portat sub tēcta Sibyllae.

aspectō look at, gaze at

***rāmus branch, bough

vērē truly

nimium too much, too; cf.
**nimius too great, excessive
columba dove

*viridis green

māternus mother's; **avis bird

opācō shade

***humus ground, earth

prōdeō go forward

oleō smell

**liquidus clear, limpid; ***āer
air
*sīdō sit, settle

discolor of different color

brūmālis of winter; **frīgus
cold; viscum mistletoe
vireō be green, grow; sēminō
produce
fētus offspring; growth; teres
smooth; rounded; **truncus
trunk
frondēns leafy
***īlex holm-oak; crepitō
rustle; cf. **crepō rattle;
brattea metal leaf
**avidus eager; refringō break
off
***cūnctor delay, linger

---

187. arbore: place where. 188–189. quando
. . . est: since the Sibyl's words proved true of
Misenus. Aeneas hopes they will be true of the
Golden Bough. 193. māternās avīs: i.e., doves,
which were sacred to Venus. 196. dubiīs nē dēfice
rēbus: *do not fail my wavering fortunes.* 198. fe-
rant: understand avēs as subject. 199. prōdīre:
historical infinitive. 200. quantum      sequentum:

*as the eyes of those following could keep them in sight.*
201. grave olentis: *foul-smelling.* 203. gemina:
*double-natured,* i.e., partly green and partly golden.
204. discolor aurī aura: *the different-colored radi-
ance of gold.* 211. cūnctantem: *clinging;* modi-
fies rāmum understood as object of refringit. For
Work Unit XVII, based on lines 1–211 of Book
VI, see p. 277.

QUESTIONS ON **185–211**. 1. Of what other task is Aeneas think-
ing as he helps build the funeral pyre for Misenus? 2. Why does
Aeneas believe that the two doves which he sees have been sent
by Venus? 3. By what actions do the doves show Aeneas that
they are trying to guide him? 4. Where do the doves finally
alight? 5. Does Aeneas have any difficulty in removing the
Golden Bough from its tree? 6. Where does Aeneas now take
the Golden Bough?

*The Trojans perform funeral rites for Misenus.*

**ingrātus** ungrateful, unheeding;
**suprēma** last rites
**\*\*\*prīncipium** beginning

**pyra** funeral pyre

**intexō** intertwine; **fērālis** fu-
nereal; **cupressus** cypress
**decorō** adorn; **\*\*\*fulgeō** gleam,
shine
**calidus** warm; cf. **\*\*caleō** be hot,
glow; **undō** surge, seethe
**lavō** wash, bathe; **frīgēns** cold;
**unguō** anoint
**dēfleō** weep over, lament

**vēlāmen** garment; covering

**conjiciō** cast, throw; **feretrum**
bier
**ministerium** service

**congerō** pile up; **cremō** burn,
cremate
**tūreus** of incense; **\*\*\*daps**
feast, food; **crātēr** bowl;
**olīvum** olive oil
**conlābor** fall in, sink
**bibulus** thirsty; **lavō** wash,
drench; **favīlla** ashes, embers
**cadus** jar, urn

**pūrus** pure, clear; **circumferō**
bear around; encircle
**rōs** dew; spray; **\*\*\*fēlīx** lucky;
fruitful; **olīva** olive tree

**tuba** trumpet

Nec minus intereā Mīsēnum in lītore Teucrī
flēbant, et cinerī ingrātō suprēma ferēbant.
Prīncipiō pinguem taedīs et rōbore sectō
215 ingentem strūxēre pyram, cui frondibus ātrīs
intexunt latera, et fērālīs ante cupressōs
cōnstituunt, decorantque super fulgentibus armīs.
Pars calidōs laticēs et aēna undantia flammīs
expediunt, corpusque lavant frīgentis et unguunt.
220 Fit gemitus. Tum membra torō dēflēta repōnunt,
purpureāsque super vestīs, vēlāmina nōta,
conjiciunt. Pars ingentī subiēre feretrō,
trīste ministerium, et subjectam mōre parentum
āversī tenuēre facem. Congesta cremantur
225 tūrea dōna, dapēs, fūsō crātēres olīvō.
Postquam conlāpsī cinerēs et flamma quiēvit,
relliquiās vīnō et bibulam lāvēre favīllam,
ossaque lēcta cadō tēxit Corynaeus aēnō.
Īdem ter sociōs pūrā circumtulit undā,
230 spargēns rōre levī, et rāmō fēlīcis olīvae
lūstrāvitque virōs dīxitque novissima verba.
At pius Aenēās ingentī mōle sepulcrum
impōnit, suaque arma virō, rēmumque tubamque,
monte sub āeriō, quī nunc Mīsēnus ab illō
235 dīcitur, aeternumque tenet per saecula nōmen.

---

**213. suprēma ferēbant:** *paid the last respects.*
**215–216. cui latera:** *whose sides.* **219. frīgentis:**
(of Misenus), *cold in death.* **222. subiēre:** *carried*
(*went beneath*). **223. mōre parentum:** *according
to ancestral custom.* **228. cadō:** place where.

**Corynaeus:** a Trojan priest. **231. verba:** *words*
(of farewell). **232. ingentī mōle:** *of huge bulk.*
**234. Mīsēnus:** so called in Vergil's day; it is
now called Punta di Miseno. **ab illō:** *from him,*
i.e., from the man Misenus.

1. In what sad task are the Trojans meantime engaged?  2. What do the Trojans do after Misenus's body has been burned to ashes?  3. Who performs the rites of purification for the Trojans?  4. What does Aeneas place on Misenus's burial mound?  5. What name is given to the promontory which overhangs Misenus's burial mound?

*Aeneas and the Sibyl sacrifice to the gods of the underworld.*

Hīs āctīs, properē exsequitur praecepta Sibyllae.
Spēlunca alta fuit vāstōque immānis hiātū,
scrūpea, tūta lacū nigrō nemorumque tenebrīs,
quam super haud ūllae poterant impūne volantēs
tendere iter pinnīs: tālis sēsē hālitus ātrīs
faucibus effundēns supera ad convexa ferēbat,
unde locum Grajī dīxērunt nōmine Aornon.
Quattuor hīc prīmum nigrantīs terga juvencōs
cōnstituit, frontīque invergit vīna sacerdōs,
et summās carpēns media inter cornua saetās
ignibus impōnit sacrīs, lībāmina prīma,
vōce vocāns Hecatēn, caelōque Erebōque potentem.
Suppōnunt aliī cultrōs, tepidumque cruōrem
suscipiunt paterīs.  Ipse ātrī velleris agnam
Aenēās mātrī Eumenidum magnaeque sorōrī
ēnse ferit, sterilemque tibī, Prōserpina, vaccam.
Tum Stygiō rēgī nocturnās incohat ārās,
et solida impōnit taurōrum vīscera flammīs,
pingue super oleum īnfundēns ārdentibus extīs.
Ecce autem prīmī sub lūmina sōlis et ortūs
sub pedibus mūgīre solum et juga coepta movērī
silvārum, vīsaeque canēs ululāre per umbram,
adventante deā.  "Procul ō, procul este, profānī,"

**exsequor** follow out, execute; **praeceptum** bidding, command
**hiātus** opening, yawning mouth
**scrūpeus** stony, rugged; **\*\*tenebrae** darkness, shadows
**impūne** without punishment, safely
240 **hālitus** exhalation, breath

**nigrāns** black
**invergō** empty, pour upon
245 **saeta** bristle, hair
**lībāmen** offering, sacrifice

**suppōnō** place beneath, apply; **culter** knife; **tepidus** lukewarm, warm; cf. **\*tepeō** be lukewarm
250 **vellus** fleece; **agna** ewe-lamb
**sterilis** barren, sterile; **vacca** heifer
**incohō** begin; build
**\*\*vīscus** flesh
**oleum** olive oil, oil; **īnfundō** pour on; **exta** entrails, vitals
255 **ortus** rising
**\*\*mūgiō** rumble; bellow
**\*\*canis** dog
**adventō** draw near; **profānus** uninitiated

**242. Aornon:** *Aornos*, a Greek word meaning "birdless."  The Roman name was **Avernus**. **243. nigrantīs terga:** *black-backed*. **terga:** acc. of respect. **247. caelōque Erebōque:** place where. **250. mātrī Eumenidum;** i.e., to Night. **sorōrī:** i.e., to Earth. **252. Stygiō rēgī:** i.e., to Pluto.

**nocturnās:** these sacrifices were performed at night. **253. solida vīscera:** *whole carcasses.* **255. prīmī . . . ortūs:** *just before the first rays and the rising of the sun.* **256. coepta:** supply **sunt. 257. vīsae:** supply **sunt. 258. deā:** i.e., Hecate. **profānī:** i.e., Aeneas's companions.

**conclāmō** exclaim, cry out;
**absistō** depart, withdraw
**vāgīna** scabbard, sheath

conclāmat vātēs, "tōtōque absistite lūcō,
260 tūque invāde viam, vāgīnāque ēripe ferrum:
nunc animīs opus, Aenēā, nunc pectore firmō."
Tantum effāta, furēns antrō sē immīsit apertō;
ille ducem haud timidīs vādentem passibus aequat.

QUESTIONS ON **236–263**. 1. To what task does Aeneas now de-
vote his attention? 2. What animals are now sacrificed in
Aeneas's behalf? Of what color? Why of this color? 3. What
three animals does Aeneas himself sacrifice? 4. To what divin-
ities does he sacrifice each? 5. What interrupts these sacred
rites? At about what time of the day or night? 6. What orders
does the Sibyl now give to Aeneas's companions? To Aeneas
himself? 7. What does the Sibyl now do? 8. What does Aeneas
now do?

*Aeneas begins his journey through the underworld.*
*He sees strange shapes at the entrance.*

Dī, quibus imperium est animārum, umbraeque
silentēs,
265 et Chaos, et Phlegethōn, loca nocte tacentia lātē,
sit mihi fās audīta loquī, sit nūmine vestrō

**cālīgō** mist, darkness; ***mergō**
plunge

pandere rēs altā terrā et cālīgine mersās.
Ībant obscūrī, sōlā sub nocte, per umbram
perque domōs Dītis vacuās, et inānia rēgna;

**malignus** ill-disposed; scanty

270 quāle per incertam lūnam sub lūce malignā
est iter in silvīs, ubi caelum condidit umbrā
Juppiter, et rēbus nox abstulit ātra colōrem.

**vēstibulum** entrance

Vēstibulum ante ipsum prīmīsque in faucibus Orcī

**cubīle** couch, bed

Lūctus et ultrīcēs posuēre cubīlia Cūrae,

*****palleō** be pale; ***habitō**
dwell; ***morbus** disease; ***se-**
**nectūs** old age
**malesuādus** evil-counseling;
**egestās** want, poverty;
**terribilis** frightful
**cōnsanguineus** kinsman; *****so-**
**por** sleep
**gaudium** joy, pleasure; **morti-**
**fer** death-bringing
**ferreus** of iron

275 pallentēsque habitant Morbī, trīstisque Senectūs,
et Metus, et malesuāda Famēs, ac turpis Egestās,
terribilēs vīsū fōrmae, Lētumque Labōsque,
tum cōnsanguineus Lētī Sopor, et mala mentis
Gaudia, mortiferumque adversō in līmine Bellum,
280 ferreīque Eumenidum thalamī, et Discordia dē-
mēns,

---

**261.** animīs opus: supply **est**; *there is need of*
*courage.* **262.** antrō: dat. of direction.
   **265.** Phlegethōn: a river of fire in the under-
world. **266.** sit mihi fās: *may I be permitted.*
sit: optative subjunctive.
   **280.** ferreī: read as two syllables, by *synizesis.*

vīpereum crīnem vittīs innexa cruentīs.

In mediō rāmōs annōsaque bracchia pandit
ulmus opāca, ingēns, quam sēdem Somnia vulgō
vāna tenēre ferunt, foliīsque sub omnibus haerent,
multaque praetereā variārum mōnstra ferārum,     285
Centaurī in foribus stabulant, Scyllaeque bifōrmēs,
et centumgeminus Briareus, ac bēlua Lernae
horrendum strīdēns, flammīsque armāta Chimaera,
Gorgones, Harpyiaeque, et fōrma tricorporis um-
     brae.
Corripit hīc subitā trepidus formīdine ferrum     290
Aenēās, strictamque aciem venientibus offert,
et, nī docta comes tenuīs sine corpore vītās
admoneat volitāre cavā sub imāgine fōrmae,
inruat, et frūstrā ferrō dīverberet umbrās.

**vīpereus** snaky, of snakes; **innectō** wreathe, entwine
**medium** middle, center; **annō- sus** aged; **\*\*bracchium** arm
**ulmus** elm tree; **somnium** dream; **vulgō** commonly

**stabulō** have one's stable; **bi- fōrmis** two-formed
**centumgeminus** hundredfold, hundred-handed; **bēlua** beast

**tricorpor** three-bodied

**\*\*admoneō** warn, admonish; **volitō** fly about, flit about
**inruō** attack; **dīverberō** strike asunder, cleave

QUESTIONS ON **264–294**. 1. To what gods does Vergil offer a prayer at this point in his poem? 2. For what does Vergil pray? 3. To what does Vergil compare the semi-darkness of the under- world? 4. What monstrous creatures does Aeneas encounter? 5. What does Aeneas do when he encounters these creatures?

*Aeneas sees Charon. The Sibyl explains Charon's duties.*

Hinc via Tartareī quae fert Acherontis ad undās. 295
Turbidus hīc caenō vāstāque vorāgine gurges
aestuat, atque omnem Cōcȳtō ēructat harēnam.
Portitor hās horrendus aquās et flūmina servat
terribilī squālōre Charōn, cui plūrima mentō
cānitiēs inculta jacet, stant lūmina flammā,          300
sordidus ex umerīs nōdō dēpendet amictus.

**turbidus** thick, turbid; **caenum** mud, mire; **vorāgō** whirlpool; **\*\*\*gurges** flood, water
**aestuō** seethe, surge; **ēructō** belch out
**portitor** ferryman
**squālor** filth; **mentum** chin

**cānitiēs** grayness; gray beard; **incultus** uncared for, unkempt
**sordidus** dirty, filthy; **dēpendeō** hang down; **\*\*amictus** cloak, mantle

**281. vīpereum . . . cruentīs:** *her snaky locks en- twined with bloody fillets.* **283. Somnia:** subject acc. of **tenēre**. **284. haerent:** understand **Somnia** as subject. **286. Centaurī:** monsters half man and half horse. **Scyllae:** monsters half woman and half dolphin. **287. Briareus:** a hundred-handed giant. **Lernae:** *of Lerna*, a marsh famous as the haunt of the Hydra. **288. horrendum strīdēns:** *hissing horribly.* **Chimaera:** a fire-breathing monster with a lion's head and a serpent's tail.

**289. Harpyiae:** *Harpies*, foul birds with women's faces. **fōrma . . . umbrae:** i.e., Geryon, a three- bodied giant. **292. docta comes:** i.e., the Sibyl. **vītās:** *spirits.* **293. cavā . . . fōrmae:** *under a hollow pretence of form.*
     **295. via:** supply **est**. **Acherontis:** *of Acheron,* a river in Hades. **297. Cōcȳtō:** dat. of direction. **299. Charōn:** the ferryman on the river Styx. **cui mentō:** *on whose chin.* **300. stant . . . flammā:** *his staring eyes are aflame.*

contus pole, punt-pole; **subigō** push along; **ministrō** tend
ferrūgineus rust-colored; **subvectō** carry; **cumba** boat
crūdus hardy, robust; **\*\*viridis** green; vigorous; **\*\*senectūs** old age
**\*\*\*turba** throng, crowd;
dēfungor have done with, finish

magnanimus great-souled; **innūptus** unwed; **puella** girl

**\*\*\*frīgus** cold

**\*\*\*avis** bird

fugō put to flight; **aprīcus** sunny
trānsmittō send across; cross

nāvita boatman, ferryman

submoveō remove, drive away

concursus gathering, throng; **\*\*\*amnis** river

**\*\*discrīmen** distinction

līvidus dark, leaden-hued; **verrō** sweep, sweep over
longaevus aged

generō beget

**\*\*stāgnum** pool, lake

inops helpless; **inhumātus** unburied

portitor ferryman; **\*\*\*sepeliō** bury
**\*\*raucus** hoarse, deep-sounding; **fluentum** stream

volitō fly, flit

Ipse ratem contō subigit, vēlīsque ministrat,
et ferrūgineā subvectat corpora cumbā,
jam senior, sed crūda deō viridisque senectūs.
305 Hūc omnis turba ad rīpās effūsa ruēbat,
mātrēs, atque virī, dēfūnctaque corpora vītā
magnanimum hērōum, puerī innūptaeque puellae,
impositīque rogīs juvenēs ante ōra parentum;
quam multa in silvīs autumnī frīgore prīmō
310 lāpsa cadunt folia, aut ad terram gurgite ab altō
quam multae glomerantur avēs, ubi frīgidus annus
trāns pontum fugat, et terrīs immittit aprīcīs.
Stābant ōrantēs prīmī trānsmittere cursum,
tendēbantque manūs rīpae ulteriōris amōre;
315 nāvita sed trīstis nunc hōs, nunc accipit illōs,
ast aliōs longē submōtōs arcet harēnā.
Aenēās (mīrātus enim mōtusque tumultū)
"Dīc," ait, "ō virgō, quid vult concursus ad
     amnem,
quidve petunt animae, vel quō discrīmine rīpās
320 hae linquunt, illae rēmīs vada līvida verrunt?"
Ollī sīc breviter fāta est longaeva sacerdōs:
"Anchīsā generāte, deum certissima prōlēs,
Cōcȳtī stāgna alta vidēs, Stygiamque palūdem,
dī cūjus jūrāre timent et fallere nūmen.
325 Haec omnis, quam cernis, inops inhumātaque turba
     est;
portitor ille Charōn; hī, quōs vehit unda, sepultī;
nec rīpās datur horrendās et rauca fluenta
trānsportāre prius quam sēdibus ossa quiērunt.
Centum errant annōs, volitantque haec lītora cir-
     cum;

---

**304. deō:** dat. of possession. **313. trānsmittere:** infin. with ōrantēs; a poetic usage. **315. nāvita:** i.e., Charon. **322. Anchīsā generāte:** *begotten of Anchises*, i.e., son of Anchises; **generāte** is voc. **324. dī ... nūmen:** *by whose divine power the* gods fear to swear and be false. **326. sepultī:** supply **sunt**. **327. nec datur:** *nor is it allowed* (to Charon). **rīpās, fluenta:** secondary objects of **trānsportāre**. **328. trānsportāre:** understand animās as direct object. **sēdibus:** *in the tomb.*

tum dēmum admissī stāgna exoptāta revīsunt."     330 ***stāgnum deep water, pool;
Cōnstitit Anchīsā satus, et vēstīgia pressit,              exoptō long for, desire
multa putāns, sortemque animī miserātus inīquam.
Cernit ibī maestōs et mortis honōre carentīs                ***careō be without, lack
Leucaspim, et Lyciae ductōrem classis Orontēn,
quōs simul ā Trōjā ventōsa per aequora vectōs     335 ventōsus windy, stormy
obruit Auster, aquā involvēns nāvemque virōsque.      involvō envelop; engulf

QUESTIONS ON **295–336**.   1. What four descriptive adjectives
does Vergil use in lines 298–301 to picture Charon's appearance?
2. To what does Vergil compare the throng of spirits that beg
Charon to ferry them across the River Styx?   3. What spirits
does Charon refuse to ferry across the Styx?   4. What do the
spirits of the unburied have to do?   For how long?   5. Whose
spirits does Aeneas now recognize?

*Aeneas meets the spirit of Palinurus.*

Ecce gubernātor sēsē Palinūrus agēbat,                  gubernātor pilot, steersman
quī Libycō nūper cursū, dum sīdera servat,              *nūper recently
exciderat puppī mediīs effūsus in undīs.                excidō fall from
Hunc ubi vix multā maestum cognōvit in umbrā, 340
sīc prior adloquitur: "Quis tē, Palinūre, deōrum
ēripuit nōbīs, mediōque sub aequore mersit?            **mergō sink
Dīc age; namque mihī, fallāx haud ante repertus,       fallāx deceitful, false
hōc ūnō respōnsō animum dēlūsit Apollō,                dēlūdō deceive
quī fore tē pontō incolumem fīnīsque canēbat       345
ventūrum Ausoniōs.   Ēn, haec prōmissa fidēs est?"
Ille autem: "Neque tē Phoebī cortīna fefellit,          cortīna caldron; oracle
dux Anchīsiadē, nec mē deus aequore mersit;            ***mergō sink
namque gubernāclum multā vī forte revulsum,            gubernāclum tiller, rudder
cui datus haerēbam custōs cursūsque regēbam,        350
praecipitāns trāxī mēcum.   Maria aspera jūrō
nōn ūllum prō mē tantum cēpisse timōrem
quam tua nē spoliāta armīs, excussa magistrō,          **spoliō rob, strip; **magister
                                                       master; pilot

**334.** Leucaspim: *Leucaspis*, a Trojan lost at sea        the caldron or tripod which served as a seat for
and hence unburied.   Orontēn: Orontes had been       the priestess of Apollo.   **349.** gubernāclum: obj.
lost at sea; see Book I, 113–119.                      of trāxī in line 351.   **350.** datus custōs: *assigned*
**337.** sēsē agēbat: *was going by.*   Palinūrus:    *as its keeper.*   **351.** Maria aspera jūrō: *I swear*
pilot of Aeneas's ship who fell overboard; see        *by the rough seas.*   **352.** cēpisse: understand mē
Book V, 854–860.   **343.** mihī: dat. of agent with  as object.   **353–354.** tua nē dēficeret nāvis: *that*
repertus.   **345.** pontō: place where.   **347.** cortīna: *your ship would fail you;* a clause of fearing.

dēficeret tantīs nāvis surgentibus undīs.

355 Trīs Notus hībernās immēnsa per aequora noctīs
vexit mē violentus aquā; vix lūmine quārtō
prōspexī Ītaliam summā sublīmis ab undā.

**adnō** swim to

Paulātim adnābam terrae; jam tūta tenēbam,

**madidus** wet, drenched; **gravō** weigh down

nī gēns crūdēlis madidā cum veste gravātum

**prēnsō** grasp, catch at; **\*\*un-cus** hooked, bent

360 prēnsantemque uncīs manibus capita aspera montis
ferrō invāsisset, praedamque ignāra putāsset.
Nunc mē flūctus habet, versantque in lītore ventī.

**\*jūcundus** pleasant

Quod tē per caelī jūcundum lūmen et aurās,
per genitōrem ōrō, per spēs surgentis Iūlī,

**invictus** unconquered, invincible
**injiciō** cast upon

365 ēripe mē hīs, invicte, malīs: aut tū mihi terram
injice (namque potes) portūsque requīre Velīnōs;

**creātrīx** mother; cf. **\*creō** bring forth, create

aut tū, sī qua via est, sī quam tibi dīva creātrīx
ostendit (neque enim, crēdō, sine nūmine dīvum

**innō** swim

flūmina tanta parās Stygiamque innāre palūdem),

370 dā dextram miserō et tēcum mē tolle per undās,
sēdibus ut saltem placidīs in morte quiēscam."
Tālia fātus erat, coepit cum tālia vātēs:
"Unde haec, ō Palinūre, tibi tam dīra cupīdō?
Tū Stygiās inhumātus aquās amnemque sevērum

**injussus** unbidden, uninvited

375 Eumenidum aspiciēs, rīpamve injussus adībis?

**\*\*dēsinō** cease

Dēsine fāta deum flectī spērāre precandō;

**sōlācium** solace, comfort

sed cape dicta memor, dūrī sōlācia cāsūs;
nam tua fīnitimī longē lātēque per urbīs,

**prōdigium** portent, sign; **caelestis** celestial, from heaven; **piō** appease
**sollemne** holy offering

prōdigiīs āctī caelestibus, ossa piābunt,

380 et statuent tumulum, et tumulō sollemnia mittent,
aeternumque locus Palinūrī nōmen habēbit."

**ēmoveō** remove; **parumper** for a little while
**\*\*\*cognōmen** name

Hīs dictīs cūrae ēmōtae, pulsusque parumper
corde dolor trīstī; gaudet cognōmine terrae.

QUESTIONS ON **337–383.** 1. Whose spirit does Aeneas now address? 2. What details of Palinurus's death does Aeneas now

---

356. lūmine: diē. 359-360. gravātum, prēnsantemque: participles depending on mē understood as object of invāsisset. 360. capita montis: the edges of a crag. 363. Quod: wherefore. 366. Velīnōs: of Velia, a town on the coast of Lucania in Southern Italy. 367. dīva creātrīx: i.e., Venus. 374. amnem: the Cocytus. 378. fīnitimī: i.e., the Lucanians. 381. Palinūrī nōmen: there is at the present day a cape near Velia called Punta di Palinuro.

learn? 3. What two alternate requests does Palinurus make of Aeneas? 4. What consoling promise does the Sibyl make Palinurus? 5. What does the Sibyl remind Palinurus is impossible for him?

## Aeneas and the Sibyl cross the Styx. The Sibyl quiets Cerberus.

Ergō iter inceptum peragunt, fluviōque propin-
quant.

***fluvius river; propinquō approach

Nāvita quōs jam inde ut Stygiā prōspexit ab undā 385

nāvita ferryman

per tacitum nemus īre pedemque advertere rīpae,

sīc prior adgreditur dictīs, atque increpat ultrō:

increpō rebuke; cf. ***crepō rattle, crash

"Quisquis es, armātus quī nostra ad flūmina tendis,

fāre age quid veniās jam istinc, et comprime gressum.

istinc from there; comprimō hold back, check

Umbrārum hic locus est, somnī noctisque sopōrae; 390

sopōrus drowsy

corpora vīva nefās Stygiā vectāre carīnā.

vectō carry

Nec vērō Alcīdēn mē sum laetātus euntem

**laetor be happy

accēpisse lacū, nec Thēsea Pīrithoümque,

dīs quamquam genitī atque invictī vīribus essent.

invictus unconquerable, invincible

Tartareum ille manū custōdem in vincla petīvit 395

ipsius ā soliō rēgis, trāxitque trementem;

solium throne

hī dominam Dītis thalamō dēdūcere adortī."

domina mistress, queen; dēdūcō lead away, abduct

Quae contrā breviter fāta est Amphrȳsia vātēs:

"Nūllae hīc īnsidiae tālēs (absiste movērī),

absistō cease

nec vim tēla ferunt; licet ingēns jānitor antrō 400

jānitor doorkeeper

aeternum lātrāns exsanguīs terreat umbrās,

lātrō bark, howl; exsanguis bloodless, pale

casta licet patruī servet Prōserpina līmen.

*castus pure, chaste; patruus paternal uncle

Trōius Aenēās, pietāte īnsignis et armīs,

ad genitōrem īmās Erebī dēscendit ad umbrās.

Sī tē nūlla movet tantae pietātis imāgō, 405

at rāmum hunc" (aperit rāmum, quī veste latēbat)

---

**389. fāre istinc:** *speak from where you are.* **391. nefās:** supply est. **392. Alcīdēn:** *Hercules,* who carried off Cerberus. **393. lacū:** *on my waters.* **Thēsea:** Greek acc. **Pīrithoüm:** *Pirithoüs,* a Greek hero who in company with Theseus tried to abduct Proserpina. **395. ille:** i.e., Hercules. **manū:** *with* (violent) *hands.* **custōdem:** i.e., Cerberus. **in vincla petīvit:** *sought* (to lead) *into chains.* **396. rēgis:** i.e., of Pluto. **397. do-minam:** i.e., Proserpina. **398. Amphrȳsia vātēs:** i.e., the Sibyl. **400-401. licet ingēns jānitor terreat:** *let the huge gatekeeper terrify;* the clause ingēns...umbrās is the subject of licet. **401. aeter-num lātrāns:** *ever barking.* **402. patruī:** i.e., of Pluto; Proserpina was the daughter of Ceres, who was a sister of Pluto.

**tumidus** surging, swelling; **re-sīdō** sink, subside
**admīror** marvel at; **venerābilis** revered, holy; cf. *veneror worship
***virga** branch, twig

"agnōscās." Tumida ex īrā tum corda resīdunt,
nec plūra hīs. Ille, admīrāns venerābile dōnum
fātālis virgae longō post tempore vīsum,
410 caeruleam advertit puppim, rīpaeque propinquat.
Inde aliās animās, quae per juga longa sedēbant,

**dēturbō** drive away; **laxō** free, clear; **forus** gangway; **alveus** hollow vessel; boat **pondus** weight; **cumba** boat **sūtilis** sewed, seamy; **rīmōsus** full of cracks, leaky

dēturbat, laxatque forōs; simul accipit alveō
ingentem Aenēān. Gemuit sub pondere cumba
sūtilis, et multam accēpit rīmōsa palūdem.
415 Tandem trāns fluvium incolumīs vātemque virum-
        que

**īnfōrmis** shapeless; **līmus** slime, mud; **glaucus** grayish; **ulva** sedge, water grass
**lātrātus** bark, barking; **trifaux** three-throated
**personō** cause to resound, make echo; **recubō** recline, lie
**coluber** snake, serpent
**sopōrātus** drowsy; soporific; **medicō** drug; **frūx** grain, meal; **offa** cake
**rabidus** fierce, raging; **guttur** throat, gullet

īnfōrmī līmō glaucāque expōnit in ulvā.
Cerberus haec ingēns lātrātū rēgna trifaucī
personat, adversō recubāns immānis in antrō.
Cui vātēs, horrēre vidēns jam colla colubrīs,
420 melle sopōrātam et medicātīs frūgibus offam
objicit. Ille, famē rabidā tria guttura pandēns,
corripit objectam atque immānia terga resolvit,

**extendō** stretch

fūsus humī, tōtōque ingēns extenditur antrō.
Occupat Aenēās aditum, custōde sepultō,

**inremeābilis** irretraceable

425 ēvāditque celer rīpam inremeābilis undae.

**continuō** at once, immediately; **vāgītus** crying, wailing

Continuō audītae vōcēs, vāgītus et ingēns,
īnfantumque animae flentēs in līmine prīmō,

**exsors** without lot in, not sharing in; ***ūber** breast
*acerbus bitter, cruel

quōs dulcis vītae exsortīs et ab ūbere raptōs
abstulit ātra diēs, et fūnere mersit acerbō.

**damnō** condemn

430 Hōs jūxtā falsō damnātī crīmine mortis.

*jūdex judge

Nec vērō hae sine sorte datae, sine jūdice, sēdēs;

**quaesītor** examiner, inquisitor; **urna** urn, vase
***discō** learn, learn about

quaesītor Mīnōs urnam movet: ille silentum
conciliumque vocat vītāsque et crīmina discit.

**proximus** next, nearest

Proxima deinde tenent maestī loca quī sibi lētum

**perōdī** hate

435 īnsontēs peperēre manū, lūcemque perōsī

---

**407. agnōscās:** *acknowledge.* **408. nec plūra:** supply dicta sunt. **dōnum:** for Proserpina. **409. tempore:** abl. of degree of difference with the adverb post. **412. alveō:** two syllables here, by *synizesis.* **417. Cerberus:** the three-headed watchdog of Hades. **419. horrēre . . . colubrīs:** *seeing his neck now bristling with snakes.* **424. sepultō:** *buried* (in sleep).

**426. audītae:** supply sunt. **428. vītae exsortīs:** *bereft of life.* **431. datae:** supply sunt. **432-433. Mīnōs:** a semi-legendary king of Crete, who after his death was made a judge of the shades in the underworld. **silentum concilium:** *a council of the silent ones,* i.e., of the dead. For Work Unit XVIII, based on lines 212–439 of Book VI, see p. 279.

prōjēcēre animās.  Quam vellent aethere in altō
nunc et pauperiem et dūrōs perferre labōrēs!
Fās obstat, trīstīque palūs inamābilis undā
alligat, et noviēns Styx interfūsa coërcet.

**pauperiēs** poverty;  **perferō** bear, endure
**inamābilis** unlovely, hateful

**noviēns** nine times;  **interfundō** pour between;  **coërceō** restrain

QUESTIONS ON **384–439**.  1. What does Charon command Aeneas
to do?  2. What exceptions does Charon admit having made in
the past to his rule not to ferry living men across the Styx?
3. What assurance does the Sibyl give Charon in regard to Aeneas's intentions?  4. What does the Sibyl further do to convince
Charon of Aeneas's right to cross the Styx?  5. What happens
to Charon's boat when Aeneas and the Sibyl step aboard?  6. In
what way does the Sibyl quiet Cerberus?  7. What three groups
of spirits can cross the Styx but can gain admission only to the
portals of the underworld?


*Aeneas visits the Fields of Mourning.*

Nec procul hinc partem fūsī mōnstrantur in 440
    omnem
Lūgentēs Campī; sīc illōs nōmine dīcunt.

\**lūgeō** mourn

Hīc, quōs dūrus amor crūdēlī tābe perēdit
sēcrētī cēlant callēs, et myrtea circum
silva tegit; cūrae nōn ipsā in morte relinquunt.

**tābēs** wasting away;  sorrow; **peredō** eat up, consume
**cēlō** conceal;  **callis** path, walk; **myrteus** of myrtle

Hīs Phaedram Procrimque locīs maestamque Eri- 445
    phȳlēn,
crūdēlis nātī mōnstrantem vulnera cernit,
Euadnēnque, et Pāsiphaēn; hīs Lāodamīa
it comes, et juvenis quondam, nunc fēmina Cae-
    neus
rūrsus et in veterem Fātō revolūta figūram.

**revolvō** change,  transform; **figūra** form, shape

Inter quās Phoenissa recēns ā vulnere Dīdō        450
errābat silvā in magnā.  Quam Trōius hērōs
ut prīmum jūxtā stetit agnōvitque per umbram
obscūram, quālem prīmō quī surgere mēnse
aut videt aut vīdisse putat per nūbila lūnam,

\*\**nūbila** clouds

dēmīsit lacrimās, dulcīque adfātus amōre est:        455

---

**445. Phaedram:** *Phaedra*, wife of Theseus, who
killed herself because of her unrequited love for
her stepson.  **Procrim:** *Procris*, accidentally killed
by her husband.  **Eriphȳlēn:** *Eriphyle*, slain by her
son.  **447. Euadnēn:** *Euadne*, who threw herself
on her husband's funeral pyre.  **Lāodamīa:** widow
of Protesilaus, who killed herself that she might
be with her husband in the underworld.
**448. Caeneus:** a maiden changed by Apollo to
a man and then changed back to a maiden.

"Īnfēlīx Dīdō, vērus mihi nūntius ergō

vēnerat exstīnctam ferrōque extrēma secūtam?

Fūneris heu tibi causa fuī?  Per sīdera jūrō,

per superōs, et sī qua fidēs tellūre sub īmā est,

460 invītus, rēgīna, tuō dē lītore cessī,

sed mē jussa deum, quae nunc hās īre per umbrās,

**sentus** thorny, rough;  **situs**
neglect;  **profundus** deep
**queō** be able

per loca senta sitū cōgunt noctemque profundam,

imperiīs ēgēre suīs;  nec crēdere quīvī

**discessus** departure

hunc tantum tibi mē discessū ferre dolōrem.

**subtrahō** draw away, withdraw 465 Siste gradum, tēque aspectū nē subtrahe nostrō.

Quem fugis?  Extrēmum fātō, quod tē adloquor,

hoc est."

**\*torvus** glaring, fierce

Tālibus Aenēās ārdentem et torva tuentem

lēnībat dictīs animum, lacrimāsque ciēbat.

Illa solō fīxōs oculōs āversa tenēbat,

470 nec magis inceptō vultum sermōne movētur

**silex** flint;  **cautēs** cliff, rock

quam sī dūra silex aut stet Marpēsia cautēs.

**refugiō** flee away

Tandem corripuit sēsē, atque inimīca refūgit

**umbrifer** shade-bearing, shady

in nemus umbriferum, conjūnx ubi prīstinus illī

respondet cūrīs aequatque Sychaeus amōrem.

475 Nec minus Aenēās, cāsū concussus inīquō,

**prōsequor** pursue, follow after

prōsequitur lacrimīs longē, et miserātur euntem.

QUESTIONS ON **440–476**.  1. What group of spirits inhabit the
Mourning Fields?  2. Whose spirit does Aeneas there address?
3. What act of his does Aeneas try to excuse?  4. What answer
does Dido make to Aeneas?  5. To whom does Dido flee?

*Aeneas sees various Trojan heroes, among them
Deïphobus.*

Inde datum mōlītur iter.  Jamque arva tenēbant

**frequentō** throng; frequent

ultima, quae bellō clārī sēcrēta frequentant.

---

**457. exstīnctam:** (tē) exstīnctam (esse).  **extrēma
secūtam:** *went to all lengths.*  **459. et . . . est:**
*and by whatever good faith there is in the lower
world.*  **464. tibi mē ferre:** *that I was bringing
upon you.*  **466. Extrēmum . . . est:** *this word that
I speak to you is by fate the last.*  **467. ārdentem,
tuentem:** depend on **animum.  torva tuentem:**

*gazing grimly.*  **torva:** neut. acc., with force of an
adverb.  **468. lēnībat:** lēniēbat;  conative im-
perfect; see App. 137, 2, *a.*  **470. vultum:** acc.
of respect.  **471. Marpēsia:** *of Marpesus,* a moun-
tain in the island of Paros famous for its marble.
**473–474. illī . . . cūrīs:** *matches her with his sorrows.*
**475. cāsū:** i.e., by Dido's fate.

Hīc illī occurrit Tȳdeus, hīc inclutus armīs

Parthenopaeus, et Adrastī pallentis imāgō,    480

hīc multum fletī ad superōs bellōque cadūcī

Dardanidae, quōs ille omnīs longō ōrdine cernēns

ingemuit, Glaucumque, Medontaque, Thersilo-
     chumque,

trīs Antēnoridās, Cererīque sacrum Polyboetēn,

Īdaeumque, etiam currūs, etiam arma tenentem.   485

Circumstant animae dextrā laevāque frequentēs.

Nec vīdisse semel satis est; juvat usque morārī

et cōnferre gradum et veniendī discere causās.

At Danaum procerēs Agamemnoniaeque pha-
     langes,

ut vīdēre virum fulgentiaque arma per umbrās,    490

ingentī trepidāre metū; pars vertere terga,

ceu quondam petiēre ratīs, pars tollere vōcem

exiguam; inceptus clāmor frūstrātur hiantīs.

    Atque hīc Prīamidēn laniātum corpore tōtō

Dēiphobum videt et lacerum crūdēliter ōra,    495

ōra, manūsque ambās, populātaque tempora raptīs

auribus, et truncās inhonestō vulnere nārīs.

Vix adeō agnōvit pavitantem ac dīra tegentem

supplicia et nōtīs compellat vōcibus ultrō:

"Dēiphobe armipotēns, genus altō ā sanguine   500
     Teucrī,

quis tam crūdēlīs optāvit sūmere poenās?

Cui tantum dē tē licuit? Mihi fāma suprēmā

nocte tulit fessum vāstā tē caede Pelasgum

prōcubuisse super cōnfūsae strāgis acervum.

Tunc egomet tumulum Rhoetēō in lītore inānem   505

cōnstituī, et magnā Mānīs ter vōce vocāvī.

Nōmen et arma locum servant; tē, amīce, nequīvī

---

**inclutus** renowned, famous

**cadūcus** fallen, slain

**circumstō** stand around, sur-
round; **\*\*frequēns** in crowds,
thronging
**semel** only once
**cōnferō** bring together; match

**procerēs** chiefs; **phalānx** pha-
lanx, battalion

**trepidō** rush to and fro; be
agitated

**frūstror** deceive, cheat; **\*\*hiō**
gape, open the mouth
**laniō** mangle, mutilate

**lacer** torn, mangled; **crūdēliter**
cruelly
**populō** despoil, ravish

**truncus** mutilated; **inhonestus**
shameful; **nārēs** nostrils,
nose
**pavitō** tremble

**armipotēns** mighty in arms

**suprēmus** last, final

**strāgēs** carnage; **acervus** heap,
pile
**\*\*tunc** at that time, then;
**\*\*\*-met** *enclitic, emphasizing
the word to which it is sub-
joined*
**nequeō** be unable

---

**479-480. Tȳdeus, Parthenopaeus:** early Greek
heroes in the war against Thebes. Tydeus was
the father of Diomedes. **Adrastī:** *of Adrastus*, an
Argive king. **481. ad superōs:** i.e., among men.

**493. hiantīs:** *their gaping mouths (them gaping).*
**505. Rhoetēō:** *of Rhoetum*, a promontory near
Troy. **507. Nōmen:** i.e., an inscription bearing
your name. **tē, amīce:** semi-hiatus; see App. 30. *a.*

cōnspicere et patriā dēcēdēns pōnere terrā."
Ad quae Prīamidēs: "Nihil ō tibi, amīce, relictum;
510 omnia Dēiphobō solvistī et fūneris umbrīs.

**exitiālis** ruinous, baneful

***monumentum** memorial

**gaudium** joy, pleasure

**nimium** too much, too well; cf.
***nimius** too great, excessive

**saltus** leap, bound

**adferō** bring; **alvus** belly

***chorus** dance; **euhāns** shouting "Euhoë"; **orgia** revels

Sed mē fāta mea et scelus exitiāle Lacaenae
hīs mersēre malīs; illa haec monumenta relīquit.
Namque ut suprēmam falsa inter gaudia noctem
ēgerimus nōstī, et nimium meminisse necesse est.
515 Cum fātālis equus saltū super ardua vēnit
Pergama, et armātum peditem gravis adtulit alvō,
illa, chorum simulāns, euhantīs orgia circum
dūcēbat Phrygiās; flammam media ipsa tenēbat
ingentem, et summā Danaōs ex arce vocābat.
520 Tum mē, cōnfectum cūrīs somnōque gravātum,
īnfēlīx habuit thalamus, pressitque jacentem
dulcis et alta quiēs placidaeque simillima mortī.

**āmoveō** remove; **subdūcō** draw from under

Ēgregia intereā conjūnx arma omnia tēctīs
āmovet, et fīdum capitī subdūxerat ēnsem;
525 intrā tēcta vocat Menelāum et līmina pandit,

***scīlicet** forsooth

scīlicet id magnum spērāns fore mūnus amantī,
et fāmam exstinguī veterum sīc posse malōrum.

**inrumpō** break into

Quid moror? Inrumpunt thalamō; comes additur
ūnā

**hortātor** inciter, counselor

**reposcō** ask for

**vicissim** in turn

**adferō** bring

**monitus** warning, admonition

hortātor scelerum Aeolidēs. Dī, tālia Grajīs
530 īnstaurāte, piō sī poenās ōre reposcō.
Sed tē quī vīvum cāsūs, age, fāre vicissim
adtulerint. Pelagīne venīs errōribus āctus
an monitū dīvum, an quae tē fortūna fatīgat,
ut trīstīs sine sōle domōs, loca turbida, adīrēs?"

***vicis** change, interchange;
**quadrīgae** four-horse chariot

**trājiciō** throw across; cross;
***axis** axis of the heaven, sky

535 Hāc vice sermōnum roseīs Aurōra quadrīgīs
jam medium aetheriō cursū trājēcerat axem,
et fors omne datum traherent per tālia tempus,

509. **tibi:** *by you.* 510. **fūneris umbrīs:** *to the spirit of the dead.* 511. **Lacaenae:** i.e., of Helen. 513. **ut:** *how.* 514. **nimium necesse est:** *there is too much reason.* 517–518. **illa . . . Phrygiās:** *she, feigning a solemn dance, led around the Phrygian women celebrating orgies with cries of Bacchus.*

524. **capitī:** *from under my head;* i.e., pillow; dat. of separation. 526. **amantī:** *for her lover;* i.e., for Menelaus. 529. **Aeolidēs:** *descendant of Aeolus,* i.e., Ulysses.

535–536. **roseīs . . . axem:** i.e., it was now midday in the upper world.

sed comes admonuit breviterque adfāta Sibylla est:

"Nox ruit, Aeneā; nōs flendō dūcimus hōrās.

Hīc locus est, partīs ubi sē via findit in ambās:

dextera quae Dītis magnī sub moenia tendit,

hāc iter Ēlysium nōbīs, at laeva malōrum

exercet poenās et ad impia Tartara mittit."

Dēiphobus contrā: "Nē saevī, magna sacerdōs;

discēdam, explēbō numerum, reddarque tenebrīs.

Ī decus, ī, nostrum; meliōribus ūtere fātīs."

Tantum effātus, et in verbō vēstīgia pressit.

**QUESTIONS ON 477–547.** 1. What group of spirits does Aeneas now visit? 2. What do the spirits of the Trojan heroes do when they see Aeneas? 3. What do the spirits of the Greek heroes do when they see Aeneas? 4. Whose spirit does Aeneas scarcely recognize? 5. What did Aeneas hear had happened to Deiphobus on the night of the fall of Troy? 6. What had actually happened to him? 7. What time of day or night is it at this point in Aeneas's journey through the underworld? 8. What does the Sibyl imply that Aeneas should do? 9. To what part of the underworld does the Sibyl tell Aeneas the road to the right leads? The road to the left?

*The Sibyl tells Aeneas about Tartarus.*

Respicit Aenēās subitō, et sub rūpe sinistrā

moenia lāta videt triplicī circumdata mūrō,

quae rapidus flammīs ambit torrentibus amnis,

Tartareus Phlegethōn, torquetque sonantia saxa.

Porta adversa ingēns solidōque adamante colum-

nae,

vīs ut nūlla virum, nōn ipsī exscindere ferrō

caelicolae valeant; stat ferrea turris ad aurās,

Tīsiphonēque sedēns, pallā succīncta cruentā,

vēstibulum exsomnis servat noctīsque diēsque.

Hinc exaudīrī gemitūs, et saeva sonāre

verbera, tum strīdor ferrī tractaeque catēnae.

**Side glosses:**

***admoneō** warn

540 **findō** split, divide

**hāc** on this side, here

545 **discēdō** depart; ***tenebrae** shadows, darkness

**triplex** triple

550 **ambiō** surround, encircle; ***torreō** parch

**adamās** adamant; **columna** pillar, column

**exscindō** tear out, destroy

**caelicola** heaven dweller, god; **ferreus** of iron

555 **palla** robe; **succingō** gird, clothe

**vēstibulum** fore-court, entrance; **exsomnis** sleepless **exaudiō** hear clearly

***verber** lash, blow; **strīdor** clanking, rattling; **catēna** chain, fetter

**539. Nox ruit:** i.e., night will soon be here. **541. dextera:** modifies **quae**, but logically belongs with **hāc** (**viā**) in line 542. **542. iter:** supply **est**. **Ēlysium:** place whither. **547. in verbō:** *as he spoke.*

**552. Porta:** supply **est. columnae:** supply **sunt. 553. virum:** virōrum. **555. Tīsiphonē:** one of the Furies. **557. exaudīrī, sonāre:** historical infinitives.

***strepitus** noise

Cōnstitit Aenēās, strepitūque exterritus haesit.

560 "Quae scelerum faciēs, ō virgō, effāre, quibusve

***urgeō** urge on; pursue;
**plangor** wailing

urgentur poenīs?  Quis tantus plangor ad aurās?"

Tum vātēs sic ōrsa loquī: "Dux inclute Teucrum,

**castus** pure, innocent;
***scelerātus** unholy, accursed; **īnsistō** stand on, set
one's foot on

nūllī fās castō scelerātum īnsistere līmen,

sed mē, cum lūcīs Hecatē praefēcit Avernīs,

565 ipsa deum poenās docuit perque omnia dūxit.

Gnōsius haec Rhadamanthus habet dūrissima rēgna

**castīgō** chastise, punish; **subigō**
compel
***fūrtum** theft, deceit;  ***laetor** rejoice, delight
**sērus** late;  **piāculum** atonement; sin
**continuō** at once;  **sōns** guilty;
**flagellum** whip, lash
**quatiō** shake; lash;  **īnsultō**
leap on;  **torvus** savage
**intentō** stretch out; brandish;
***anguis** snake, serpent
**horrisonus** harsh-sounding,
grating
**custōdia** guard, sentry

castīgatque, auditque dolōs subigitque fatērī

quae quis apud superōs, fūrtō laetātus inānī,

distulit in sēram commissa piācula mortem.

570 Continuō sontīs ultrīx accīncta flagellō

Tīsiphonē quatit īnsultāns, torvōsque sinistrā

intentāns anguīs vocat agmina saeva sorōrum.

Tum dēmum horrisonō strīdentēs cardine sacrae

panduntur portae.  Cernis custōdia quālis

575 vēstibulō sedeat, faciēs quae līmina servet?

**quīnquāgintā** fifty;  **hiātus**
yawning mouth;  **hydra** water
serpent

Quīnquāgintā ātrīs immānis hiātibus hydra

saevior intus habet sēdem.  Tum Tartarus ipse

bis patet in praeceps tantum tenditque sub umbrās

**suspectus** view (*upward*)

quantus ad aetherium caelī suspectus Olympum.

580 Hīc genus antīquum Terrae, Tītānia pūbēs,

**dējiciō** hurl down;  **fundus**
bottom, depth

fulmine dējectī fundō volvuntur in īmō.

Hīc et Alōīdās geminōs immānia vīdī

**rescindō** tear down

corpora, quī manibus magnum rescindere caelum

**dētrūdō** thrust down

adgressī superīsque Jovem dētrūdere rēgnīs.

585 Vīdī et crūdēlīs dantem Salmōnea poenās,

dum flammās Jovis et sonitūs imitātur Olympī.

**invehō** carry, bear;  **lampas**
torch;  **quassō** shake violently, brandish

Quattuor hic invectus equīs et lampada quassāns,

---

**560.** faciēs: supply *sunt*.    **561.** plangor: supply *venit*.    **565.** deum poenās: *the punishments imposed by the gods*.    **566.** Rhadamanthus: brother of Minos; after death he was made an executer of sentences in Hades.    **568-569.** quae ... mortem: *the crimes expiation for which anyone among mortals, rejoicing in vain concealment, has postponed until death's late hour*.    **574.** custōdia:

i.e., Tisiphone.    **579.** quantus ... Olympum: *as is the upward view of the sky to heavenly Olympus*.    **581.** dējectī: masculine plural, but referring to Tītānia pūbēs.    **582.** Alōīdās: *sons of Aloeus*.    **585.** Salmōnea: *Salmoneus*, king of Elis who sought to imitate the thunder and lightning of Jupiter. Greek acc.    **587.** hic: here a long syllable as if spelled hicc.

per Grajum populōs mediaeque per Ēlidis urbem
ībat, ovāns, dīvumque sibī poscēbat honōrem,
dēmēns, quī nimbōs et nōn imitābile fulmen
aere et cornipedum pulsū simulāret equōrum;
at pater omnipotēns dēnsa inter nūbila tēlum
contorsit, nōn ille facēs nec fūmea taedīs
lūmina, praecipitemque immānī turbine adēgit.
Nec nōn et Tityon, Terrae omniparentis alumnum, 595
cernere erat, per tōta novem cui jūgera corpus
porrigitur, rōstrōque immānis vultur obuncō
immortāle jecur tondēns fēcundaque poenīs
vīscera rīmāturque epulīs habitatque sub altō
pectore, nec fibrīs requiēs datur ūlla renātīs. 600
Quid memorem Lapithās, Ixīona, Pīrithoümque,
quōs super ātra silex jam jam lāpsūra cadentīque
imminet adsimilis? Lūcent geniālibus altīs
aurea fulcra torīs, epulaeque ante ōra parātae
rēgificō lūxū; Furiārum maxima jūxtā 605
accubat, et manibus prohibet contingere mēnsās,
exsurgitque facem attollēns, atque intonat ōre.
Hīc, quibus invīsī frātrēs, dum vīta manēbat,
pulsātusve parēns, et fraus innexa clientī,
aut quī dīvitiīs sōlī incubuēre repertīs 610
nec partem posuēre suīs, quae maxima turba est,
quīque ob adulterium caesī, quīque arma secūtī
impia nec veritī dominōrum fallere dextrās,
inclūsī poenam exspectant. Nē quaere docērī
quam poenam, aut quae fōrma virōs fortūnave 615
    merset.
Saxum ingēns volvunt aliī, radiīsque rotārum
districtī pendent; sedet aeternumque sedēbit

***ovō exult, rejoice

590 imitābilis imitable

cornipēs horn-footed, hoofed; pulsus beat, pounding

contorqueō whirl, hurl; fūmeus smoky

595 omniparēns all-producing; alumnus foster child, son

jūgerum measure of land, about half an acre

*porrigō stretch; *rōstrum beak; obuncus hooked

jecur liver; **tondeō clip close; feed on; fēcundus prolific

***vīscus vitals, flesh; rīmor split open; **habitō dwell

600 fibra fiber; entrails; requiēs rest, respite; renāscor be re-born, be renewed

***immineō tower aloft; threaten; adsimilis like; *lūceō shine; geniālis festive

fulcrum support; headrest of a couch

605 rēgificus regal, royal; lūxus splendor; cf. ***lūxuria extravagance

accubō recline

exsurgō rise up; intonō thunder

**pulsō strike, beat; **fraus fraud, deceit; innectō weave, contrive

610 *dīvitiae riches, wealth; incubō brood over

adulterium adultery

***dominus master, lord

615 mersō overwhelm

**radius spoke (of a wheel); ***rota wheel
distringō stretch out

---

**591. simulāret:** for the mood see App. 162, a.
**593. ille:** i.e., Jupiter. **595. Tityon:** *Tityos,* a giant slain by Apollo for the crime of assaulting Latona. **596. cernere erat:** *it was possible to see.* **601. Lapithās:** *the Lapithae,* a tribe in Northern Greece famous for its battle

with the Centaurs. **Ixīona:** *Ixion,* king of the Lapithae. **602.** a hypermetric line; see App. 31. **605. maxima:** *the oldest.* **608. Hīc:** supply **sunt.** **613. dominōrum dextrās:** *the pledges to their masters.* **615. poenam:** supply **exspectent.** **fōrma:** *type* (of punishment). **616. aliī:** e.g.,

īnfēlīx Thēseus, Phlegyāsque miserrimus omnīs
admonet, et magnā testātur vōce per umbrās:

620 "Discite jūstitiam monitī et nōn temnere dīvōs."

Vēndidit hic aurō patriam dominumque potentem
imposuit; fīxit lēgēs pretiō atque refīxit;

hic thalamum invāsit nātae vetitōsque hymenaeōs:
ausī omnēs immāne nefās ausōque potītī.

625 Nōn, mihi sī linguae centum sint ōraque centum,
ferrea vōx, omnīs scelerum comprēndere fōrmās,
omnia poenārum percurrere nōmina possim."

temnō scorn

**vēndō sell

**pretium price, bribe; refīgō unfasten; unmake

ferreus of iron; comprēndō grasp; sum up
percurrō run through

QUESTIONS ON 548–627. 1. What sort of stream surrounds Tartarus? 2. What goddess guards the entrance of Tartarus? 3. From whom had the Sibyl received her information about Tartarus? When?

### Aeneas and the Sibyl visit Elysium.

Haec ubi dicta dedit Phoebī longaeva sacerdōs,
"Sed jam age, carpe viam, et susceptum perfice
mūnus;

630 accelerēmus," ait; "Cyclōpum ēducta camīnīs
moenia cōnspiciō atque adversō fornice portās,
haec ubi nōs praecepta jubent dēpōnere dōna."

Dīxerat, et pariter gressī per opāca viārum
corripiunt spatium medium, foribusque propin-
quant.

635 Occupat Aenēās aditum, corpusque recentī
spargit aquā, rāmumque adversō in līmine fīgit.

Hīs dēmum exāctīs, perfectō mūnere dīvae,
dēvēnēre locōs laetōs, et amoena virecta
fortūnātōrum nemorum sēdīsque beātās.

640 Largior hīc campōs aethēr et lūmine vestit
purpureō, sōlemque suum, sua sīdera nōrunt.

Pars in grāmineīs exercent membra palaestrīs,

longaevus aged

accelerō hasten; camīnus forge
fornix arch

amoenus pleasant; virectum grassy spot
fortūnātus blessed, blissful; **beātus happy, blessed
largus abundant; vestiō clothe

grāmineus grassy; cf. **grāmen grass; palaestra wrestling-place

---

Sisyphus. **618. Phlegyās:** a king of the Lapithae who set fire to a temple of Apollo. **624. ausōque potītī:** *and succeeded in their daring.*

**630. Cyclōpum ēducta camīnīs:** *built by the forges of the Cyclopes.* **632. dōna:** i.e., the Golden Bough.

contendunt lūdō, et fulvā luctantur harēnā;

pars pedibus plaudunt choreās et carmina dīcunt;

nec nōn Thrēicius longā cum veste sacerdōs 645

obloquitur numerīs septem discrīmina vōcum,

jamque eadem digitīs, jam pectine pulsat eburnō.

Hīc genus antīquum Teucrī, pulcherrima prōlēs,

magnanimī hērōes, nātī meliōribus annīs,

Īlusque Assaracusque et Trōjae Dardanus auctor. 650

Arma procul currūsque virum mīrātur inānīs;

stant terrā dēfīxae hastae, passimque solūtī

per campum pāscuntur equī: quae grātia currum

armōrumque fuit vīvīs, quae cūra nitentīs

pāscere equōs, eadem sequitur tellūre repostōs. 655

Cōnspicit ecce aliōs dextrā laevāque per herbam

vēscentīs, laetumque chorō paeāna canentīs

inter odōrātum laurī nemus, unde supernē

plūrimus Ēridanī per silvam volvitur amnis.

Hīc manus ob patriam pugnandō vulnera passī, 660

quīque sacerdōtēs castī, dum vīta manēbat,

quīque piī vātēs et Phoebō digna locūtī,

inventās aut quī vītam excoluēre per artīs

quīque suī memorēs aliquōs fēcēre merendō;

omnibus hīs niveā cinguntur tempora vittā. 665

Quōs circumfūsōs sīc est adfāta Sibylla,

Mūsaeum ante omnīs (medium nam plūrima turba

hunc habet, atque umerīs exstantem suspicit altīs):

"Dīcite, fēlīcēs animae, tūque, optime vātēs,

quae regiō Anchīsēn, quis habet locus? Illius ergō 670

vēnimus et magnōs Erebī trānāvimus amnīs."

Atque huic respōnsum paucīs ita reddidit hērōs:

"Nūllī certa domus; lūcīs habitāmus opācīs,

*lūdus sport, play; ***luctor wrestle, struggle

plaudō beat, beat time to; chorea dance

obloquor sound in accord

*digitus finger; pecten pick; ***pulsō strike, beat; eburnus of ivory

magnanimus great-souled

**niteō shine, be sleek

vēscor feed, eat; paeān hymn (to Apollo)
**laurus laurel tree; supernē in the world above

pugnō fight

***castus pure, holy

excolō cultivate, enrich

niveus snowy, snow-white

exstō stand out; tower

trānō swim, voyage across

***habitō dwell

---

**645. Thrēicius sacerdōs:** i.e., Orpheus, the famous Thracian poet and singer, belonging to pre-Homeric days. **646. obloquitur ... vōcum:** he plays, *responsive to their measures, the seven different notes.* The reference is to the seven-stringed lyre. **653. grātia currum:** *delight in their chariots.* **currum:** gen. pl. **659. Ēridanī:** *of the Po,* a river in Northern Italy. **660. manus passī:** *a group* (of men) *who have suffered.* **667. Mūsaeum:** *Musaeus,* a Thracian bard. **669. vātēs:** i.e., Musaeus. **Illius ergō:** *on his account.* **673. domus:** supply **est.**

prātum meadow; rīvus stream

rīpārumque torōs et prāta recentia rīvīs
675 incolimus. Sed vōs, sī fert ita corde voluntās,

trāmes path

hoc superātc jugum, et facilī jam trāmite sistam."

***niteō shine

Dīxit, et ante tulit gressum, campōsque nitentīs

ostentō show; dehinc hence, from this point; cacūmen summit

dēsuper ostentat; dehinc summa cacūmina lin-
quunt.

QUESTIONS ON **628–678.** 1. Where do Aeneas and the Sibyl now go? 2. What does Aeneas leave at the doorway of Pluto's palace? For whom? 3. To what part of the underworld do Aeneas and the Sibyl now go? 4. What spirits inhabit Elysium? 5. What does Aeneas find the spirits doing? 6. Who tells the Sibyl where to find Anchises?

*Aeneas at last meets Anchises.*

convallis valley; vireō be green

At pater Anchīsēs penitus convalle virentī
680 inclūsās animās superumque ad lūmen itūrās

recolō think over

lūstrābat studiō recolēns, omnemque suōrum

recēnseō review

forte recēnsēbat numerum cārōsque nepōtēs,
fātaque fortūnāsque virum mōrēsque manūsque.

***grāmen grass

Isque ubi tendentem adversum per grāmina vīdit
685 Aenēān, alacris palmās utrāsque tetendit,

gena cheek

effūsaeque genīs lacrimae, et vōx excidit ōre:

exspectō await, hope for

"Vēnistī tandem, tuaque exspectāta parentī
vīcit iter dūrum pietās? Datur ōra tuērī,
nāte, tua et nōtās audīre et reddere vōcēs?
690 Sīc equidem dūcēbam animō rēbarque futūrum,

dīnumerō count

tempora dīnumerāns, nec mē mea cūra fefellit.
Quās ego tē terrās et quanta per aequora vectum
accipiō, quantīs jactātum, nāte, perīclīs!
Quam metuī, nē quid Libyae tibi rēgna nocērent!"
695 Ille autem: "Tua mē, genitor, tua trīstis imāgō
saepius occurrēns haec līmina tendere adēgit.

***sal salt; sea

Stant sale Tyrrhēnō classēs. Dā jungere dextram,

amplexus embrace; subtrahō withdraw

dā, genitor, tēque amplexū nē subtrahe nostrō."

---

**677. ante tulit gressum:** *stepped on ahead.*
**678. dehinc:** one syllable, by *synizesis.* For Work Unit XIX, based on lines 440–678 of Book VI, see p. 282.

**686. effūsae:** supply sunt. **687. parentī:** dat. of agent with **exspectāta.** **688. Datur:** *is it granted.* **696. tendere:** understand **mē** as subject.

Sīc memorāns, largō flētū simul ōra rigābat.

**rigō** wet, bedew

Ter cōnātus ibī collō dare bracchia circum,

700 ***bracchium** arm

ter frūstrā comprēnsa manūs effūgit imāgō,

**comprēndō** seize, grasp; **effugiō** flee, escape

pār levibus ventīs volucrīque simillima somnō.

QUESTIONS ON **679–702.** 1. What is Anchises doing when Aeneas and the Sibyl appear? 2. Which of the three is first to speak? 3. Does Anchises seem to know about Aeneas's recent experiences on earth? 4. Why does Aeneas not embrace his father?

*Anchises tells Aeneas about the nature of the human soul.*

Intereā videt Aenēās in valle reductā

sēclūsum nemus, et virgulta sonantia silvae,

**sēclūdō** shut off, seclude; **virgultum** thicket, copse

Lēthaeumque domōs placidās quī praenatat amnem.

705 **praenatō** swim before; glide by

Hunc circum innumerae gentēs populīque volābant,

ac velut in prātīs ubi apēs aestāte serēnā

**prātum** meadow; **apis** bee; **serēnus** bright

flōribus īnsīdunt variīs et candida circum

**flōs** blossom; **īnsīdō** settle on; **candidus** shining, white

līlia funduntur, strepit omnis murmure campus.

**līlium** lily; **strepō** hum, resound

Horrēscit vīsū subitō, causāsque requīrit

710 **horrēscō** shudder; be thrilled

īnscius Aenēās, quae sint ea flūmina porrō,

**porrō** yonder

quīve virī tantō complērint agmine rīpās.

**compleō** fill

Tum pater Anchīsēs: "Animae, quibus altera Fātō

corpora dēbentur, Lēthaeī ad flūminis undam

sēcūrōs laticēs et longa oblīvia pōtant.

715 **sēcūrus** without care; carereleasing; **oblīvium** forgetfulness, oblivion; **pōtō** drink (of), quaff

Hās equidem memorāre tibi atque ostendere cōram,

jam prīdem hanc prōlem cupiō ēnumerāre meōrum,

***prīdem** long since; **ēnumerō** count over

quō magis Ītaliā mēcum laetēre repertā."

"Ō pater, anne aliquās ad caelum hinc īre putandum est

sublīmīs animās iterumque ad tarda revertī      720

corpora? Quae lūcis miserīs tam dīra cupīdō?"

"Dīcam equidem, nec tē suspēnsum, nāte, tenēbō,"

suscipit Anchīsēs, atque ōrdine singula pandit.

**700–702.** These lines occur also in Book II, 792–794.   *other bodies are destined by fate.* **719. caelum:** *the upper air,* i.e., the world of men. **721. Quae . . .** **705. Lēthaeum:** *of Lethe,* the river of forgetfulness. **713–714. quibus . . . dēbentur:** *for whom*   **cupīdō:** supply *est;* i.e., Can any soul desire to live again on earth?

liquēns watery, liquid

**lūceō shine

**spīritus breath; soul

marmoreus of marble, glassy

igneus fiery

**sēmen seed; noxius harmful

terrēnus of earth, earth-born;
  hebetō make dull, blunt;
  moribundus ready to die,
  mortal

dispiciō see, discern; ***carcer
  prison

funditus completely, utterly

corporeus of the body, corpo-
  real; ***pestis plague, taint
concrēscō grow together; ino-
  lēscō become ingrained in

expendō pay; suffer

īnficiō put in; ēluō wash out;
  exūrō burn out
exinde next, then

concrēscō grow together, be-
  come ingrained; eximō re-
  move; lābēs stain, taint
simplex unmixed, unpolluted

immemor unmindful, forgetful

"Prīncipiō caelum ac terrās campōsque liquentīs
725 lūcentemque globum lūnae Tītāniaque astra
spīritus intus alit, tōtamque īnfūsa per artūs
mēns agitat mōlem, et magnō sē corpore miscet.
Inde hominum pecudumque genus, vītaeque volan-
      tum,
et quae marmoreō fert mōnstra sub aequore pon-
      tus.
730 Igneus est ollīs vigor et caelestis orīgō
sēminibus, quantum nōn noxia corpora tardant
terrēnīque hebetant artūs moribundaque membra.
Hinc metuunt cupiuntque, dolent gaudentque, ne-
      que aurās
dispiciunt, clausae tenebrīs et carcere caecō.
735 Quīn et suprēmō cum lūmine vīta relīquit,
nōn tamen omne malum miserīs nec funditus omnēs
corporeae excēdunt pestēs, penitusque necesse est
multa diū concrēta modīs inolēscere mīrīs.
Ergō exercentur poenīs, veterumque malōrum
740 supplicia expendunt. Aliae panduntur inānīs
suspēnsae ad ventōs, aliīs sub gurgite vāstō
īnfectum ēluitur scelus aut exūritur ignī.
Quisque suōs patimur Mānīs. Exinde per amplum
mittimur Ēlysium, et paucī laeta arva tenēmus,
745 dōnec longa diēs perfectō temporis orbe
concrētam exēmit lābem, pūrumque relinquit
aetherium sēnsum atque aurāī simplicis ignem;
hās omnīs, ubi mīlle rotam volvēre per annōs,
Lēthaeum ad fluvium deus ēvocat agmine magnō,
750 scīlicet immemorēs supera ut convexa revīsant
rūrsus, et incipiant in corpora velle revertī."

---

**725. Tītānia astra:** i.e., the sun. **728. genus:**
supply **est. 731. quantum . . . tardant:** *so far as
harmful bodies do not hamper* (these souls).
**733. metuunt:** understand **animae** as subject.
**734. carcere:** i.e., in the body. **736. miserīs:**
*from poor mortals;* dat. of separation. **740. Aliae:**
supply **animae. 742. īnfectum scelus:** *the guilty
stain.* **744. Ēlysium:** the abode of the blessed
in the underworld. **745. diēs:** *time.* **747. aurāī:**
gen. sing. **748. rotam:** *the wheel* (of time).
**748. hās omnīs:** *all these* (other souls), i.e., all
except the **paucī** mentioned in line 744.

QUESTIONS ON **703–751.** 1. To what does Vergil compare the throng of souls who gather at the banks of the River Lethe? 2. What effect does the water of Lethe have on those who drink it? 3. What does Anchises tell Aeneas pervades sky, earth, sea, sun, and moon? 4. What does Anchises say produces men and beasts? 5. Why does every human soul have to be purified after it has left the body? 6. What methods of cleansing does Anchises mention? 7. Where are a few of the souls allowed to remain after being purified? 8. What happens to most of the souls after being purified?

*Anchises shows Aeneas the future descendants of the Trojans and foretells the greatness of Rome.*

Dīxerat Anchīsēs, nātumque ūnāque Sibyllam
conventūs trahit in mediōs turbamque sonantem,     **conventus** meeting, assembly
et tumulum capit, unde omnīs longō ōrdine posset
adversōs legere et venientum discere vultūs.     755
"Nunc age, Dardaniam prōlem quae deinde sequā-
     tur
glōria, quī maneant Italā dē gente nepōtēs,
inlūstrīs animās nostrumque in nōmen itūrās     **inlūstris** famous, illustrious
expediam dictīs, et tē tua fāta docēbō.
Ille (vidēs?) pūrā juvenis quī nītitur hastā,     760
proxima sorte tenet lūcis loca, prīmus ad aurās
aetheriās Italō commixtus sanguine surget,
Silvius, Albānum nōmen, tua postuma prōlēs,
quem tibi longaevō sērum Lāvīnia conjūnx     ***sērus** late
ēdūcet silvīs, rēgem rēgumque parentem,     765
unde genus Longā nostrum dominābitur Albā.     **albus** white
Proximus ille Procās, Trōjānae glōria gentis,
et Capys, et Numitōr, et quī tē nōmine reddet,
Silvius Aenēās, pariter pietāte vel armīs
ēgregius, sī umquam rēgnandam accēperit Albam. 770
Quī juvenēs! Quantās ostentant, aspice, vīrīs

**756. deinde:** two syllables, by *synizesis.* **758. itūrās:** *destined to assume.* **760. pūrā hastā:** i.e., on a headless spear. Such a spear was awarded for heroic military conduct. **762. Italō sanguine:** i.e., with the blood of Lavinia. **763. Silvius:** late-born son of Aeneas and Lavinia.

**766. Longā Albā:** *at Alba Longa,* the mother city of Rome. **767–769. Procās, Capys, Numitōr, Silvius Aenēās:** kings at Alba Longa. **770. umquam:** Silvius is said to have been kept from his rightful throne for fifty years. **772. cīvīlī quercū:** i.e., with the *corōna cīvica,* the wreath of oak

**umbrō** shade, shadow; **\*cīvīlis** civic; **quercus** oak, oak wreath

atque umbrāta gerunt cīvīlī tempora quercū!

Hī tibi Nōmentum et Gabiōs urbemque Fidēnam,

hī Collātīnās impōnent montibus arcīs,

775 Pōmetiōs, Castrumque Inuī, Bōlamque, Coram-
que:

haec tum nōmina erunt, nunc sunt sine nōmine
terrae.

**\*\*\*avus** grandfather

Quīn et avō comitem sēsē Māvortius addet

Rōmulus, Assaracī quem sanguinis Īlia māter

**\*crista** crest, plume

ēdūcet. Viden, ut geminae stant vertice cristae,

**\*\*\*signō** mark; cf. **\*\*\*dēsignō** designate, describe

**\*\*\*auspicium** auspices, authority

780 et pater ipse suō superum jam signat honōre?

Ēn hujus, nāte, auspiciīs illa incluta Rōma

imperium terrīs, animōs aequābit Olympō,

septemque ūna sibī mūrō circumdabit arcīs,

fēlīx prōle virum; quālis Berecyntia māter

**invehō** carry, convey; **turrītus** crowned with towers

**partus** offspring; birth

785 invehitur currū Phrygiās turrīta per urbīs,

laeta deum partū, centum complexa nepōtēs,

omnīs caelicolās, omnīs supera alta tenentīs.

"Hūc geminās nunc flecte aciēs, hanc aspice gen-
tem

Rōmānōsque tuōs; hīc Caesar et omnis Iūlī

**\*\*\*prōgeniēs** progeny, race

790 prōgeniēs, magnum caelī ventūra sub axem.

Hīc vir, hic est tibi quem prōmittī saepius audīs,

Augustus Caesar, dīvī genus, aurea condet

saecula quī rūrsus Latiō rēgnāta per arva

Sāturnō quondam; super et Garamantas et Indōs

**prōferō** carry forward, extend

795 prōferet imperium; jacet extrā sīdera tellūs,

**caelifer** heaven-bearing

extrā annī sōlisque viās, ubi caelifer Atlās

**\*\*\*stella** star; **\*\*aptus** fitted, studded

axem umerō torquet, stellīs ārdentibus aptum.

---

leaves awarded to a Roman soldier for saving a Roman in battle. **773. Hī:** supply **condent. Nōmentum,** etc.: towns in Central Italy. **777. avō:** i.e., to Numitor. **779. Viden: Vidēsne. 780. pater:** i.e., Mars. **superum:** *in* (of) *the world above.* **suō honōre:** *with his fitting honor,* i.e., with the double-crested helmet, emblem of Mars. **784. Berecyntia:** *of Berecyntus,* a mountain in Phrygia, sacred to Cybele, the Great

Mother of the gods. **787. supera alta tenentīs:** *dwelling in the lofty heaven.*
**788. aciēs: oculōs. 792. dīvī genus:** *son of the deified* (Julius Caesar). **794. Sāturnō:** *by Saturn,* an ancient Italian god; dat. of agent with **rēgnāta. Garamantas:** *the Garmantes,* an African tribe. **Indōs:** *the inhabitants of India.* **795. sīdera:** *the stars,* i.e., the twelve signs of the Zodiac.

Hujus in adventum jam nunc et Caspia rēgna
respōnsīs horrent dīvum, et Maeōtia tellūs,
et septemgeminī turbant trepida ōstia Nīlī.
Nec vērō Alcīdēs tantum tellūris obīvit,
fīxerit aeripedem cervam licet, atque Erymanthī
pācārit nemora, et Lernam tremefēcerit arcū,
nec quī pampineīs victor juga flectit habēnīs,
Līber, agēns celsō Nȳsae dē vertice tigrīs.
Et dubitāmus adhūc virtūtem extendere factīs,
aut metus Ausoniā prohibet cōnsistere terrā?
   "Quis procul ille autem rāmīs īnsignis olīvae,
sacra ferēns?  Nōscō crīnīs incānaque menta
rēgis Rōmānī, prīmam quī lēgibus urbem
fundābit, Curibus parvīs et paupere terrā
missus in imperium magnum.  Cui deinde subībit
ōtia quī rumpet patriae residīsque movēbit
Tullus in arma virōs et jam dēsuēta triumphīs
agmina.  Quem jūxtā sequitur jactantior Ancus,
nunc quoque jam nimium gaudēns populāribus
   aurīs.
Vīs et Tarquiniōs rēgēs animamque superbam
ultōris Brūtī fascīsque vidēre receptōs?
Cōnsulis imperium hic prīmus saevāsque secūrīs
accipiet, nātōsque pater nova bella moventīs
ad poenam pulchrā prō lībertāte vocābit,
īnfēlīx, utcumque ferent ea facta minōrēs;
vincet amor patriae laudumque immēnsa cupīdō.

adventus approach

800 septemgeminus seven-mouthed, sevenfold
***obeō traverse, pass over

aeripēs bronze-footed;  cerva deer

pampineus made of vine shoots; ***habēna rein
805 tigris tiger

incānus hoary, gray

810

fundō found, establish; pauper poor, humble

**ōtium quiet, peace;  reses inactive, sluggish
dēsuētus unaccustomed; ***triumphus triumphal procession
815 jactāns boastful

populāris of the people, popular

***ultor avenger

***secūris ax

820

utcumque however, in whatever way

---

798. in: *in expectation of.*   jam nunc: *even now.*   Caspia: *Caspian, of the Caspian Sea.*
799. Maeōtia: *Scythian.*   801. Alcīdēs: i.e., Hercules.   802. cervam: Hercules killed the bronze-footed deer of Arcadia.   Erymanthī: he also killed the wild boar of Erymanthus.   803. pācārit: pācāverit.   Lernam: Hercules also killed the hydra of Lerna.   805. Līber: i.e., Bacchus.   Nȳsae: *of Nysa,* a mountain in India, fabled birthplace of Bacchus.
808. ille: i.e., Numa Pompilius, second king of Rome.   811. Curibus: *from Cures,* a Sabine town.   814. Tullus: third king of Rome.

815. Ancus: fourth king of Rome.   817. Tarquiniōs: the fifth and seventh kings of Rome were named Tarquin.   818. fascīs receptōs: *the recovery of the rods.*   Brutus, one of the first two consuls of Rome, took over for the newly established republic these symbols of kingly authority.   819. saevās secūrīs: the axes, each in a bundle of fasces, were symbols of sovereign power.   820. nātōs: Brutus as consul executed his two sons, who had plotted for the restoration of monarchy.   822. īnfēlīx: the poet thus expresses his pity for Brutus.   utcumque . . . minōrēs: *however posterity may extol that deed.*

Quīn Deciōs, Drūsōsque procul, saevumque secūrī
825 aspice Torquātum, et referentem signa Camillum.
Illae autem, paribus quās fulgere cernis in armīs,

**concors** of one heart, harmonious; cf. ***concordia** harmony

concordēs animae nunc et dum nocte premuntur,
heu! quantum inter sē bellum, sī lūmina vītae

**strāgēs** slaughter, carnage

attigerint, quantās aciēs strāgemque ciēbunt,

****socer** father-in-law

830 aggeribus socer Alpīnīs atque arce Monoecī

****gener** son-in-law

dēscendēns, gener adversīs īnstrūctus Eōīs!

**adsuēscō** make familiar

Nē, puerī, nē tanta animīs adsuēscite bella,
neu patriae validās in vīscera vertite vīrīs!
Tūque prior, tū parce, genus quī dūcis Olympō,
835 prōjice tēla manū, sanguis meus!

**triumphō** conquer

"Ille triumphātā Capitōlia ad alta Corinthō
victor aget currum, caesīs īnsignis Achīvīs;
ēruet ille Argōs, Agamemnoniāsque Mycēnās,

**armipotēns** mighty in arms

ipsumque Aeacidēn, genus armipotentis Achillī,

*****ulcīscor** avenge; **temerō**
desecrate

840 ultus avōs Trōjae, templa et temerāta Minervae.
Quis tē, magne Catō, tacitum aut tē, Cosse, relinquat?
Quis Gracchī genus aut geminōs, duo fulmina bellī,

**clādēs** ruin; scourge

Scīpiadās, clādem Libyae, parvōque potentem

*****sulcus** furrow

Fabricium, vel tē, sulcō, Serrāne, serentem?
845 Quō fessum rapitis, Fabiī? Tū Maximus ille es,
ūnus quī nōbīs cūnctandō restituis rem!

---

**824–825. Deciōs** et al.: early Roman heroes; see general vocabulary. **827. animae:** i.e., Pompey and Caesar. **830. aggeribus Alpīnīs:** *from the barriers of the Alps.* **socer:** i.e., Caesar, whose daughter Julia married Pompey. **Monoecī:** of *Monoecus*, a town of Northern Italy. **831. Eōīs: with Eastern troops.** Pompey's forces in the Civil War were recruited largely from Greece and Asia Minor. **834. Tū, genus quī dūcis Olympō:** i.e., Caesar, descendant of Anchises and Venus. **836. Ille:** i.e., Lucius Mummius, who captured the famous Greek city of Corinth in 146 B.C. **Capitōlia:** *the Capitol,* the southwest summit of the Capitoline Hill in Rome. **838. ille:** i.e., Lucius Aemilius Paulus, who conquered Perseus, king of Macedonia. **839. Aeacidēn:** i.e., Perseus, who claimed descent from Achilles, and therefore from Aeacus. **840. templa:** the reference is to the stealing of the Palladium and the abduction of Cassandra by the Greeks. **841. Catō:** i.e., Cato the Elder, famous for his high moral standards. **Cosse:** *Cossus,* Roman consul in 428 B.C. **relinquat:** potential subjunctive. **842. Gracchī:** *of Gracchus,* a name borne by a distinguished Roman family. **843. Scīpiadās:** *sons of Scipio,* i.e., Africanus Major and Africanus Minor. **clādem Libyae:** *the scourge of Libya.* **844. Fabricium:** *Fabricius,* a Roman hero famous for his honor and fidelity. **Serrāne:** i.e., Regulus Serranus, a Roman general in the First Punic War. **845. fessum:** depends on **mē** understood. **Maximus:** i.e., Quintus Fabius Maximus Cunctator, whose policy of delay helped to defeat Hannibal. **846. rem:** i.e., **rem pūblicam.** Line 846 is modeled on a verse of the early Roman poet Ennius.

Excūdent aliī spīrantia mollius aera

(crēdō equidem), vīvōs dūcent dē marmore vultūs,

ōrābunt causās melius, caelīque meātūs

dēscrībent radiō, et surgentia sīdera dīcent:        850

tū regere imperiō populōs, Rōmāne, mementō

(hae tibi erunt artēs), pācisque impōnere mōrem,

parcere subjectīs, et dēbellāre superbōs."

**excūdō** strike out, hammer out; ***spīrō*** breathe; **molliter** softly, delicately
***marmor** marble
**meātus** motion, course

**dēscrībō** trace; ***radius** rod, measuring rod

**dēbellō** fight down, crush

QUESTIONS ON **752–853.** 1. What souls are now made to pass in review before Anchises and Aeneas? 2. Whose soul is first in the line? 3. Who, according to Roman tradition, was Procas? Capys? Numitor? Silvius Aeneas? 4. Who, according to Roman tradition, was the father of Romulus? 5. Who was Romulus's mother? His grandfather? 6. Whom does Anchises point out as the greatest of Aeneas's descendants? 7. To what Greek hero does Anchises compare Augustus in the extent of earth covered in his various exploits? To what god? 8. Which of the traditional kings of Rome does Anchises now point out to Aeneas? 9. Who, according to Roman tradition, was the first consul? 10. To whom does Vergil make Anchises appeal in lines 834–835? To try to prevent what? 11. Why would the Roman conquests prophesied in lines 836–840 especially appeal to Aeneas? 12. In what arts does Anchises concede the Greeks will excel the Romans? 13. In what arts does Anchises say the Romans will excel?

*Anchises laments the early death of young Marcellus.*

Sīc pater Anchīsēs, atque haec mīrantibus addit:

"Aspice, ut īnsignis spoliīs Mārcellus opīmīs        855

ingreditur, victorque virōs superēminet omnīs.

Hic rem Rōmānam magnō turbante tumultū

sistet, eques sternet Poenōs, Gallumque rebellem,

tertiaque arma patrī suspendet capta Quirīnō."

Atque hīc Aenēās (ūnā namque īre vidēbat        860

ēgregium fōrmā juvenem et fulgentibus armīs,

sed frōns laeta parum et dējectō lūmina vultū):

"Quis, pater, ille, virum quī sīc comitātur euntem?

**opīmus** rich

**superēmineō** tower above

**rebellis** rebellious

***parum** too little

***comitor** accompany

---

**847. aliī:** especially the Greeks.   **848. crēdō equidem:** *I quite admit.*   **850. dīcent:** *will name.*
**854. mīrantibus:** depends on **eīs** understood.
**855. spoliīs opīmīs:** the *spolia opīma* were the spoils won by a Roman leader in hand-to-hand fight with the leader of the enemy.   **Mārcellus:**

Roman consul in 222 B.C.   **857. tumultū:** the reference is to the Gallic revolt, crushed by Marcellus during his consulship.   **858. Poenōs:** Marcellus defeated Hannibal and his Carthaginian invaders in the Second Punic War.
**862. lūmina:** oculī.   **863. ille:** i.e., Marcellus,

**\*\*\*stirps** stock

**circā** around, about; likeness; majesty

**circumvolō** fly about, hover around

**obortus** rising, starting

**ultrā** beyond, longer

**propāgō** race, progeny

**\*\*\*proprius** one's own, lasting

**praeterlābor** glide by

**alumnus** child, nursling

**prīscus** old-time, ancient; **invictus** invincible
**impūne** with impunity

**\*\*obvius** across the path

**\*fodiō** dig; **calcar** spur; **armus** flank, side (*of a horse*)
**quā** in any way

**\*\*\*flōs** flower, blossom

**accumulō** heap high; honor; **fungor** perform

Fīlius anne aliquis magnā dē stirpe nepōtum?
**instar** 865 Quis strepitus circā comitum! Quantum īnstar in ipsō!

Sed nox ātra caput trīstī circumvolat umbrā."
Tum pater Anchīsēs lacrimīs ingressus obortīs:
"Ō gnāte, ingentem lūctum nē quaere tuōrum.
Ostendent terrīs hunc tantum Fāta, neque ultrā
870 esse sinent. Nimium vōbīs Rōmāna propāgō
vīsa potēns, superī, propria haec sī dōna fuissent.
Quantōs ille virum magnam Māvortis ad urbem
campus aget gemitūs, vel quae, Tiberīne, vidēbis
fūnera, cum tumulum praeterlābēre recentem!
875 Nec puer Īliacā quisquam dē gente Latīnōs
in tantum spē tollet avōs, nec Rōmula quondam
ūllō sē tantum tellūs jactābit alumnō.
Heu! pietās! heu! prīsca fidēs invictaque bellō
dextera! Nōn illī sē quisquam impūne tulisset
880 obvius armātō, seu cum pedes īret in hostem,
seu spūmantis equī foderet calcāribus armōs.
Heu! miserande puer, sī quā fāta aspera rumpās,
tū Mārcellus eris! Manibus date līlia plēnīs
purpureōs spargam flōrēs, animamque nepōtis
885 hīs saltem accumulem dōnīs, et fungar inānī mūnere."

QUESTIONS ON **854–886**. 1. What future taker of the *spolia opīma* does Anchises now point out? Who accompanies him?
2. What blood relation was young Marcellus to Augustus?
3. What other relation was young Marcellus to Augustus?
4. What relation does Anchises assume toward young Marcellus?
5. Why was the early death of young Marcellus the source of so great sorrow to Augustus?

son of Augustus's sister Octavia. Augustus had adopted young Marcellus in 25 B.C. and in the same year Marcellus had married Augustus's daughter Julia. Augustus had undoubtedly destined him for his successor. Marcellus died in 23 B.C., in his twentieth year. **virum:** i.e., the elder Marcellus, already mentioned. **869. tantum:** *only.* **869–870. ultrā esse:** *to live longer.* **871. vīsa:** supply *esse.* **dōna:** i.e., Marcellus. **872. Māvortis urbem:** *city of Mars,* i.e.,

Rome. **873. campus:** i.e., the Campus Martius, on the banks of the Tiber. **874. tumulum:** Marcellus's remains were placed in a mausoleum which had been built by Augustus in 27 B.C. **877. sē tantum jactābit:** *will pride itself so much.* **883. date:** i.e., **sinite,** *permit.* **884. spargam:** subjunctive in a substantive volitive clause depending on **date;** so **accumulem** and **fungar** in line 885. **flōrēs:** in apposition with **līlia,** which is the object of **spargam.**

*Anchises tells Aeneas of what awaits him in Italy.*
*Aeneas returns to the upper world and sails to*
*Latium.*

     Sīc tōtā passim regiōne vagantur
āeris in campīs lātīs, atque omnia lūstrant.
Quae postquam Anchīsēs nātum per singula dūxit,
incenditque animum fāmae venientis amōre,
exin bella virō memorat quae deinde gerenda,     890 **exin** then, next
Laurentīsque docet populōs, urbemque Latīnī,
et quō quemque modō fugiatque feratque labōrem.
     Sunt geminae somnī portae, quārum altera fertur
cornea, quā vērīs facilis datur exitus umbrīs,     **corneus** of horn
altera candentī perfecta nitēns elephantō,     895 **\*\*candeō** be white, shine; **ele-phantus** elephant; ivory
sed falsa ad caelum mittunt īnsomnia Mānēs.     **īnsomnium** dream
Hīs ubi tum nātum Anchīsēs ūnāque Sibyllam
prōsequitur dictīs, portāque ēmittit eburnā,     **prōsequor** follow; **ēmittō** send forth; **eburnus** of ivory
ille viam secat ad nāvīs sociōsque revīsit.
Tum sē ad Cajētae rēctō fert lītore portum.     900 **rēctus** straight, direct; cf. **\*\*rēctē** properly, suitably
Ancora dē prōrā jacitur; stant lītore puppēs.     **\*\*\*prōra** prow

QUESTIONS ON **886–901**. 1. What effect do you think this preview of the greatness of Rome would have on Aeneas? 2. What special information does Anchises give Aeneas concerning the immediate future? 3. What do you think Vergil meant to signify by having Aeneas depart from the underworld by the ivory door? 4. About how long does Vergil represent Aeneas as having been in the underworld? 5. Where do the Trojans next land after sailing from Cumae?

---

**890. gerenda:** supply **erunt. 891. Laurentīs:** *of Laurentum,* a town in Latium. **Latīnī:** *of Latinus,* king of Laurentum and father of Lavinia, Aeneas's Italian wife.
**898. portā eburnā:** *by the ivory gate.* The Romans believed that dreams after midnight were true. Vergil, by making Aeneas return to earth by the gate of false dreams implies that he left the underworld before midnight. For the time

when he entered the underworld see lines 255 and 535–539. **900. Cajētae:** *of Cajeta,* a coast town about forty miles northwest of Cumae. Aeneas's final landing in Italy on the bank of the Tiber is described at the beginning of Book VII. **rēctō lītore:** *straight along the coast;* abl. of route. **901.** This line is identical with line 277 in Book III. For Work Unit XX, based on lines 679–901 of Book VI, see p. 285.

# PART II

SELECTIONS FROM VARIOUS LATIN POETS

# CATULLUS

Diānae sumus in fidē
puellae et puerī integrī:               **puella** girl
Diānam puerī integrī
puellaeque canāmus.


Ō Lātōnia, maximī                       5
magna prōgeniēs Jovis,
quam māter prope Dēliam
dēposīvit olīvam,                       **dēpōnō** bring forth, bear; **olīva**
                                        olive tree


montium domina ut forēs                 **domina** mistress, ruler
silvārumque virentium                   10 **vireō** be green
saltuumque reconditōrum                 **saltus** woodland
amniumque sonantum.


Tū cursū, dea, mēnstruō                 **mēnstruus** monthly
mētiēns iter annuum,                    *\*mētior* measure;  **annuus**
                                            yearly, the year's
rūstica agricolae bonīs                 15 **rūsticus** rural; **agricola** farmer
tēcta frūgibus explēs.


Sīs quōcumque tibi placet
sāncta nōmine, Rōmulīque,
antīquē ut solita es, bona              **antīquē** of old
sospitēs ope gentem.                    20 **sospitō** protect, preserve

---

**Selection I.** This hymn was written by Catullus to be sung, in alternate stanzas, by boys and girls at some festival of Diana. For the meter see App. 35, 3. For a brief biography of Catullus see App. 16. **1. in fidē:** *under the protection.* **5. Lātōnia:** *daughter of Latona,* i.e., Diana. **7–8. Dēliam olīvam:** *the olive tree on the island* *of Delos,* where Diana was born. **dēposīvit:** perfect, as if from **dēposīnō,** an early form of **dēpōnō.** **11. reconditōrum:** elide with **amnium** in the next line. **17–18. Sīs ... nōmine:** *Be hallowed, by whatever name pleases you.* **18–20. Rōmulī gentem:** i.e., the Romans. **19. bona:** agrees with **tū** understood as subject of **sospitēs.**

# 200 LATIN POETRY

## SELECTION II. AN INVITATION TO DINNER

cēnō dine
\*\*faveō favor, be well-disposed
adferō bring
cēna dinner; candidus radiant; pretty
cachinnus laughter
venustus lovely, charming
cēnō dine
sacculus purse; arānea spider web, cobweb
merus pure, sheer
suāvis pleasant, agreeable; ēle-gāns fine, elegant
unguentum ointment, perfume

olfaciō smell

nāsus nose

Cēnābis bene, mī Fabulle, apud mē
paucīs, sī tibi dī favent, diēbus,
sī tēcum attuleris bonam atque magnam
cēnam, nōn sine candidā puellā
et vīnō et sale et omnibus cachinnīs.     5
Haec sī, inquam, attuleris, venuste noster,
cēnābis bene: nam tuī Catullī
plēnus sacculus est arāneārum.
Sed contrā accipiēs merōs amōrēs
seu quid suāvius ēlegantiusve est:     10
nam unguentum dabō, quod meae puellae
dōnārunt Venerēs Cupīdinēsque,
quod tū cum olfaciēs, deōs rogābis,
tōtum ut tē faciant, Fabulle, nāsum.

## SELECTION III. LET US LIVE AND LOVE

\*sevērus strict
aestimō value, rate; as a small Roman coin
\*\*occidō fall, set
semel once; \*\*\*occidō fall, set
dormiō sleep, spend in sleep

Vīvāmus, mea Lesbia, atque amēmus,
rūmōrēsque senum sevēriōrum
omnēs ūnius aestimēmus assis.
Sōlēs occidere et redīre possunt:
nōbīs cum semel occidit brevis lūx,     5
nox est perpetua ūna dormienda.

## SELECTION IV. HAIL AND FAREWELL

advenīo come; inferiae funeral rites

mūtus silent

Multās per gentēs et multa per aequora vectus
adveniō hās miserās, frāter, ad īnferiās,
ut tē postrēmō dōnārem mūnere mortis
et mūtam nēquīquam adloquerer cinerem,

---

SELECTION II. For the meter see App. 35, 4.
1. Fabulle: *Fabullus*, a friend of Catullus.
9. merōs amōrēs: *sheer joy.* 10. seu ... est: *or whatever is more charming and exquisite.*
SELECTION III. For the meter see App. 35, 4. This poem, of which the first part only is here given, is one of the most lyrical love songs ever written and has been imitated by many modern

poets. 1. Lesbia: Catullus's sweetheart, to whom he addressed several of his lyric poems. 3. omnēs: agrees with rumōrēs in line 2. ūnius ... assis: *let us value at one cent.*
SELECTION IV. For the meter see App. 35, 1.
2. frāter: Catullus's brother died young, and was buried in the Troad. Catullus later made a pilgrimage to the tomb. 4. mūtam cinerem:

MELIBOEUS AND TITYRUS

From a woodcut in an edition of Vergil's Eclogues published by
Grüninger in Strassburg in 1502.

quandoquidem fortūna mihī tētē abstulit ipsum,  5
heu miser indignē frāter adēmpte mihī.

**adimō** snatch away

Nunc tamen intereā haec, prīscō quae mōre paren-
tum

**prīscus** old

trādita sunt trīstī mūnere ad īnferiās,

**īnferiae** funeral rites

accipe frāternō multum mānantia flētū,

**mānō** drip, be wet

atque in perpetuum, frāter, avē atque valē.  10  **aveō** be well


# VERGIL

## SELECTION I. MELIBOEUS AND TITYRUS

*Meliboeus:*

Tītyre, tū patulae recubāns sub tegmine fāgī
silvestrem tenuī mūsam meditāris avēnā,
nōs patriae fīnīs et dulcia linquimus arva.
Nōs patriam fugimus, tū, Tītyre, lentus in umbrā
fōrmōsam resonāre docēs Amaryllida silvās.

**patulus** spreading; **recubō** lie at ease, recline; **tegmen** cover; **fāgus** beech tree **silvestris** rustic, woodland; **mūsa** song; **meditor** practice; **avēna** reed pipe **lentus** lingering

5  **fōrmōsus** beautiful, comely; **resonō** reëcho, resound


*Tītyrus:*

Ō Meliboee, deus nōbīs haec ōtia fēcit,
namque erit ille mihī semper deus, illius āram
saepe tener nostrīs ab ovīlibus imbuet agnus.
Ille meās errāre bovēs, ut cernis, et ipsum
lūdere quae vellem calamō permīsit agrestī.

***ōtium** ease, leisure

**tener** tender; **ovīle** sheepfold; **imbuō** tinge, stain; **agnus** lamb **bōs** cow

10  **calamus** reed; pipe; **agrestis** rustic


*Meliboeus:*

Nōn equidem invideō, mīror magis; undique tōtīs
usque adeō turbātur agrīs.
Sed tamen iste deus quī sit dā, Tītyre, nōbīs.

---

*silent ashes.* **5.** tētē: tē.  **6.** adēmpte: voc. with frāter. **7.** haec: i.e., Catullus's offerings. **10.** avē atque valē: the formula of farewell to the dead.

SELECTION I. This selection is a dialogue between two shepherds, Meliboeus and Tityrus. Meliboeus has been driven from his farm; Tityrus has been more fortunate. Vergil is here alluding

to conditions after the battle of Philippi, when demobilized veterans of Octavian were rewarded with lands confiscated from Italian farmers. The passage is abridged from Vergil's *Eclogues* I. See App. 4 and 5. **5.** Amaryllida: *Amaryllis*, a girl's name; Greek acc. **6.** deus: i.e., Octavian. **9.** ipsum: i.e., mē ipsum. **13.** dā: *tell*.

*Tītyrus:*

Urbem quam dīcunt Rōmam, Meliboee, putāvī
15 stultus ego huic nostrae similem, quō saepe solēmus
pāstōrēs ovium tenerōs dēpellere fētūs.
Sīc canibus catulōs similīs, sīc mātribus haedōs
nōram, sīc parvīs compōnere magna solēbam.
Vērum haec tantum aliās inter caput extulit urbīs
20 quantum lenta solent inter vīburna cupressī.

*Meliboeus:*

Et quae tanta fuit Rōmam tibi causa videndī?

*Tītyrus:*

Hīc illum vīdī juvenem, Meliboee, quotannīs
bis sēnōs cui nostra diēs altāria fūmant,
hīc mihi respōnsum prīmus dedit ille petentī:
25 "Pāscite ut ante bovēs, puerī; submittite taurōs."

*Meliboeus:*

Fortūnāte senex! Ergō tua rūra manēbunt,
et tibi magna satis, quamvīs lapis omnia nūdus
līmōsōque palūs obdūcat pāscua juncō.
Nōn īnsuēta gravīs temptābunt pābula fētās,
30 nec mala vīcīnī pecoris contāgia laedent.
Fortūnāte senex! Hīc inter flūmina nōta
et fontīs sacrōs frīgus captābis opācum.
Hinc tibi, quae semper, vīcīnō ab līmite saepēs,
Hyblaeīs apibus flōrem dēpāsta salictī,
35 saepe levī somnum suādēbit inīre susurrō;
hinc altā sub rūpe canet frondātor ad aurās;
nec tamen intereā raucae, tua cūra, palumbēs
nec gemere āeriā cessābit turtur ab ulmō.

---

**Glossary (left margin):**

*stultus dull, foolish

ovis sheep; tener tender, young; dēpellō drive
***canis dog; catulus young animal, puppy; haedus young goat, kid

**vērum but

***lentus pliant, bending; vīburnum low tree or shrub; cupressus cypress tree

quotannīs yearly, each year

sēnī six; fūmō smoke

***bōs cow; submittō bring up, rear

rūs field; country

*quamvīs however much; nūdus bare
līmōsus slimy; obdūcō cover, overspread; pāscuum pasture; juncus rush
īnsuētus unfamiliar, strange; fēta ewe, mother-sheep
vīcīnus neighboring; contāgium contact; contagion

captō seek eagerly; woo

vīcīnus neighboring; līmes cross-path, boundary; saepēs hedge
apis bee; dēpāscor feed on; salictum willow tree
susurrus murmur, humming
frondātor foliage-gatherer

***raucus deep-sounding; cooing; palumbēs wood pigeon
āerius airy, lofty; turtur turtle-dove; ulmus elm tree

---

**22.** juvenem: presumably Octavian, who restored Tityrus's farm to him. **33.** quae semper: *as it has always done.* **34.** Hyblaeīs apibus: *by Hyblean bees;* Hybla is a mountain in Sicily abounding in flowers — and bees. flōrem . . . salictī: *with its willow blossom fed on.* flōrem: acc. of respect. dēpāsta depends on saepes. **37.** tua cūra: *your delight;* in appos. with palumbēs.

quandoquidem fortūna mihī tētē abstulit ipsum,   5
heu miser indignē frāter adēmpte mihī.

\*\*adimō snatch away

Nunc tamen intereā haec, prīscō quae mōre paren-
tum

prīscus old

trādita sunt trīstī mūnere ad īnferiās,
accipe frāternō multum mānantia flētū,
atque in perpetuum, frāter, avē atque valē.   10

īnferiae funeral rites

mānō drip, be wet

aveō be well

## VERGIL

### SELECTION I. MELIBOEUS AND TITYRUS

*Meliboeus:*

Tītyre, tū patulae recubāns sub tegmine fāgī
silvestrem tenuī mūsam meditāris avēnā,
nōs patriae fīnīs et dulcia linquimus arva.
Nōs patriam fugimus, tū, Tītyre, lentus in umbrā
fōrmōsam resonāre docēs Amaryllida silvās.

patulus spreading; recubō lie at ease, recline; tegmen cover; fāgus beech tree
silvestris rustic, woodland; mūsa song; meditor practice; avēna reed pipe
\*\*lentus lingering

5 fōrmōsus beautiful, comely; resonō reëcho, resound

*Tītyrus:*

Ō Meliboee, deus nōbīs haec ōtia fēcit,
namque erit ille mihī semper deus, illius āram
saepe tener nostrīs ab ovīlibus imbuet agnus.
Ille meās errāre bovēs, ut cernis, et ipsum
lūdere quae vellem calamō permīsit agrestī.

\*\*\*ōtium ease, leisure

tener tender; ovīle sheepfold; imbuō tinge, stain; agnus lamb
\*\*bōs cow
10 calamus reed; pipe; \*agrestis rustic

*Meliboeus:*

Nōn equidem invideō, mīror magis; undique tōtīs
usque adeō turbātur agrīs.
Sed tamen iste deus quī sit dā, Tītyre, nōbīs.

---

*silent ashes.* **5.** tētē: tē.   **6.** adēmpte: voc. with fräter.   **7.** haec: i.e., Catullus's offerings.   **10.** avē atque valē: the formula of farewell to the dead.
SELECTION I.   This selection is a dialogue between two shepherds, Meliboeus and Tityrus. Meliboeus has been driven from his farm; Tityrus has been more fortunate. Vergil is here alluding

to conditions after the battle of Philippi, when demobilized veterans of Octavian were rewarded with lands confiscated from Italian farmers. The passage is abridged from Vergil's *Eclogues* I. See App. 4 and 5.   **5.** Amaryllida: *Amaryllis*, a girl's name; Greek acc.   **6.** deus: i.e., Octavian.   **9.** ipsum: i.e., mē ipsum.   **13.** dā: *tell.*

*Tītyrus:*

Urbem quam dīcunt Rōmam, Meliboee, putāvī

15 stultus ego huic nostrae similem, quō saepe solēmus

pāstōrēs ovium tenerōs dēpellere fētūs.

Sīc canibus catulōs similīs, sīc mātribus haedōs

nōram, sīc parvīs compōnere magna solēbam.

Vērum haec tantum aliās inter caput extulit urbīs

20 quantum lenta solent inter vīburna cupressī.

*Meliboeus:*

Et quae tanta fuit Rōmam tibi causa videndī?

*Tītyrus:*

Hīc illum vīdī juvencm, Meliboee, quotannīs

bis sēnōs cui nostra diēs altāria fūmant,

hīc mihi respōnsum prīmus dedit ille petentī:

25 "Pāscite ut ante bovēs, puerī; submittite taurōs."

*Meliboeus:*

Fortūnāte senex! Ergō tua rūra manēbunt,

et tibi magna satis, quamvīs lapis omnia nūdus

līmōsōque palūs obdūcat pāscua juncō.

Nōn īnsuēta gravīs temptābunt pābula fētās,

30 nec mala vīcīnī pecoris contāgia laedent.

Fortūnāte senex! Hīc inter flūmina nōta

et fontīs sacrōs frīgus captābis opācum.

Hinc tibi, quae semper, vīcīnō ab līmite saepēs,

Hyblaeīs apibus flōrem dēpāsta salictī,

35 saepe levī somnum suādēbit inīre susurrō;

hinc altā sub rūpe canet frondātor ad aurās;

nec tamen intereā raucae, tua cūra, palumbēs

nec gemere āeriā cessābit turtur ab ulmō.

---

**Glossary (left margin):**

*stultus dull, foolish

ovis sheep; tener tender, young; dēpellō drive
***canis dog; catulus young animal, puppy; haedus young goat, kid

**vērum but

***lentus pliant, bending; vīburnum low tree or shrub; cupressus cypress tree

quotannīs yearly, each year

sēnī six; fūmō smoke

***bōs cow; submittō bring up, rear

rūs field; country

*quamvīs however much; nūdus bare
līmōsus slimy; obdūcō cover, overspread; pāscuum pasture; juncus rush
īnsuētus unfamiliar, strange; fēta ewe, mother-sheep
vīcīnus neighboring; contāgium contact; contagion

captō seek eagerly; woo

vīcīnus neighboring; līmes cross-path, boundary; saepēs hedge
apis bee; dēpāscor feed on; salictum willow tree
susurrus murmur, humming
frondātor foliage-gatherer

***raucus deep-sounding; cooing; palumbēs wood pigeon
āerius airy, lofty; turtur turtledove; ulmus elm tree

---

**22. juvenem:** presumably Octavian, who restored Tityrus's farm to him. **33. quae semper:** *as it has always done.* **34. Hyblaeīs apibus:** *by Hyblean bees;* Hybla is a mountain in Sicily abounding in flowers — and bees. **flōrem . . . salictī:** *with its willow blossom fed on.* **flōrem:** acc. of respect. **dēpāsta** depends on **saepes**. **37. tua cūra:** *your delight;* in appos. with **palumbēs**.

*Tītyrus:*

Ante levēs ergō pāscentur in aequore cervī
et freta dēstituent nūdōs in lītore piscīs 40
quam nostrō illīus lābātur pectore vultus.

*Meliboeus:*

At nōs hinc aliī sitientīs ībimus Āfrōs,
pars Scythiam et rapidum Crētae veniēmus Oaxēn,
et penitus tōtō dīvīsōs orbe Britannōs.
Impius haec tam culta novālia mīles habēbit? 45
Barbarus hās segetēs? Ēn quō discordia cīvīs
prōdūxit miserōs! Hīs nōs cōnsēvimus agrōs!
Īnsere nunc, Meliboee, pirōs, pōne ōrdine vītīs.
Īte meae, quondam fēlīx pecus, īte capellae.
Nōn ego vōs posthāc viridī prōjectus in antrō 50
dūmōsā pendēre procul dē rūpe vidēbō;
carmina nūlla canam; nōn mē pāscente, capellae,
flōrentem cytisum et salicēs carpētis amārās.

*Tītyrus:*

Hic tamen hanc mēcum poterās requiēscere noctem
fronde super viridī; sunt nōbīs mītia pōma, 55
castaneae mollēs et pressī cōpia lactis.
Et jam summa procul vīllārum culmina fūmant,
majōrēsque cadunt altīs dē montibus umbrae.

***cervus stag, deer

sitiō be thirsty

novāle fallow land

seges grain field

prōdūcō lead, bring; cōnserō sow, plant
īnserō graft; pirus pear tree; vītis grapevine
capella she-goat

posthāc hereafter, henceforth; ***viridis verdant
dūmōsus bushy

capella she-goat

**flōreō bloom, blossom; cytisus clover; salix willow tree; amārus bitter

requiēscō rest

***mītis mellow, ripe; pōmum fruit; apple
castanea chestnut; lac milk

*vīlla farmhouse; fūmō smoke

SELECTION II. ORPHEUS AND EURYDICE

*Orpheus mourns for Eurydice.*

Ipse, cavā sōlāns aegrum testūdine amōrem,
tē, dulcis conjūnx, tē sōlō in lītore sēcum,

***sōlor solace, console; testūdo tortoise-shell: lyre

39. Ante: *sooner.* 41. nostrō . . . vultus: i.e., than I shall forget him. illīus: i.e., Octavian's. 43. pars: *some* (of us). Oaxēn: *to the Oaxes,* a river in Crete. 46. Barbarus: i.e., a Gaul or some other barbarian who had been in Octavian's army; supply habēbit from preceding sentence. quō: *to what a point.* 54. poterās: *you could.* 56. pressī lactis: i.e., of cheese.

SELECTION II. This passage is taken from the fourth book of Vergil's *Georgics.* See App. 4 and 5. 1. Ipse: i.e., Orpheus, who by the charm of his music almost succeeded in bringing back his dead bride from the underworld. He failed because he disobeyed Pluto's command not to look back at her until they reached the upper world. 2. conjūnx: i.e., Eurydice.

**dēcēdō** depart

**cālīgō** be gloomy

**tremendus** dread, awful

**nescius** not knowing how; \*\***hūmānus** human, of men; **mānsuēscō** grow soft, soften; cf. \***mānsuētūdō** mildness

**vesper** evening

**dēfungor** have done with, finish

**līmus** slime, mire, mud; **dēfōrmis** unsightly, ugly; \*\***harundō** reed
**inamābilis** unlovely, hateful
**adligō** bind, confine; **noviēns** nine times; **interfundō** flow between; **coërceō** restrain

**implectō** entwine, twist into

**inhiō** gape

**pōne** after, behind

**incautus** incautious, heedless; **dēmentia** madness
**ignōscō** pardon, forgive

**immītis** harsh, relentless; **tyrannus** tyrant
**fragor** crash, roar

tē veniente diē, tē dēcēdente canēbat.
Taenariās etiam faucīs, alta ōstia Dītis,
5 et cālīgantem nigrā formīdine lūcum
ingressus, Mānīsque adiit rēgemque tremendum,
nesciaque hūmānīs precibus mānsuēscere corda.
At cantū commōtae Erebī dē sēdibus īmīs
umbrae ībant tenuēs simulācraque lūce carentum,
10 quam multa in foliīs avium sē mīlia condunt,
vesper ubi aut hībernus agit dē montibus imber,
mātrēs, atque virī dēfūnctaque corpora vītā
magnanimum hērōum, puerī innūptaeque puellae,
impositīque rogīs juvenēs ante ōra parentum,
15 quōs circum līmus niger et dēfōrmis harundō
Cōcȳtī tardāque palūs inamābilis undā
adligat, et noviēns Styx interfūsa coërcet.

*Orpheus descends to Hades to bring back Eurydice,
but fails.*

Quīn ipsae stupuēre domūs, atque intima Lētī
Tartara, caeruleōsque implexae crīnibus anguēs
20 Eumenidēs, tenuitque inhiāns tria Cerberus ōra,
atque Ixīoniī ventō rota cōnstitit orbis.
Jamque pedem referēns cāsūs ēvāserat omnīs,
redditaque Eurydicē superās veriēbat ad aurās,
pōne sequēns (namque hanc dederat Prōserpina
lēgem),
25 cum subita incautum dēmentia cēpit amantem,
ignōscenda quidem, scīrent sī ignōscere Mānēs:
restitit, Eurydicēnque suam, jam lūce sub ipsā,
immemor heu! victusque animī respexit. Ibi omnis
effūsus labor, atque immītis rupta tyrannī
30 foedera, terque fragor stāgnī est audītus Avernī.

---

**4. Taenariās:** *of Taenarus,* a promontory in Greece on which was a grotto leading to the underworld. **6. rēgem:** i.e., Pluto, god of the underworld. **7. corda:** (Pluto's) *heart.* **10. quam multa avium mīlia:** *as many as the thousands of birds that.*

**12–14.** These same lines occur in the *Aeneid,* Book VI, 306–308. **21. Ixīoniī rota orbis:** *the rotation of Ixion's wheel.* **28. victus animī:** *vanquished in purpose.* **29. effūsus:** supply **est. rupta:** supply **sunt.**

ORPHEUS AND EURYDICE

Illa "Quis et mē," inquit, "miseram et tē perdidit,     **perdō destroy
   Orpheu,
quis tantus furor? Ēn iterum crūdēlia retrō
fāta vocant, conditque natantia lūmina somnus.     natō swim
Jamque valē; feror ingentī circumdata nocte,
invalidāsque tibī tendēns, heu! nōn tua, palmās!"  35 invalidus powerless
Dīxit, et ex oculīs subitō ceu fūmus in aurās     **fūmus smoke
commixtus tenuīs fūgit dīversa, neque illum
prēnsantem nequīquam umbrās et multa volentem    prēnsō grasp at
dīcere praetereā vīdit, nec portitor Orcī     portitor ferryman
amplius objectam passus trānsīre palūdem.  40 trānseō cross, pass
Quid faceret? Quō sē raptā bis conjuge ferret?
Quō flētū Mānīs, quae nūmina vōce movēret?
Illa quidem Stygiā nābat jam frīgida cumbā.     cumba boat, skiff

*In despair Orpheus wanders widely and is finally
torn to pieces by frenzied Bacchantes.*

Septem illum tōtōs perhibent ex ōrdine mēnsīs    perhibeō say
rūpe sub āeriā dēsertī ad Strȳmonis undam  45 āerius lofty
flēvisse et gelidīs haec ēvolvisse sub antrīs,    ēvolvō unroll, recount
mulcentem tigrīs et agentem carmine quercūs,    tigris tiger; quercus oak tree
quālis pōpuleā maerēns philomēla sub umbrā    pōpuleus of the poplar tree; philomēla nightingale
āmissōs queritur fētūs, quōs dūrus arātor    arātor plowman
observāns nīdō implūmīs dētrāxit; at illa  50 observō note, espy; nīdus nest; implūmis unfledged; dētrahō draw away; steal
flet noctem, rāmōque sedēns miserābile carmen    miserābilis mournful, piteous
integrat, et maestīs lātē loca questibus implet.    integrō begin anew, renew; questus plaint, lamentation
Nūlla Venus, nōn ūllī animum flexēre hymenaeī.
Sōlus Hyperboreās glaciēs, Tanaimque nivālem,    glaciēs ice; nivālis snowy
arvaque Rīphaeīs numquam viduāta pruīnīs  55 viduō deprive; pruīna frost
lūstrābat, raptam Eurydicēn atque inrita Dītis    inritus useless
dōna querēns, sprētae Ciconum quō mūnere mātrēs    ***spernō spurn, scorn

---

**29. tyrannī:** i.e., of Pluto. **31. Orpheu:** voc. **35. nōn tua:** *not your wife* (now). **37. dīversa:** *in a different direction* (from Orpheus); depends on **illa** understood as subject of **Dīxit** and **fūgit. 39. portitor Orcī:** i.e., Charon. **43. Illa:** i.e., Eurydice.

**45. Strȳmonis:** *of the Strymon,* a river in Macedonia. **46. haec ēvolvisse:** *to have recounted these misfortunes.* **53. Venus:** i.e., love. **54. Hyperboreās:** *Northern.* **Tanaim:** *Tanais,* a river in Scythia. **55. Rīphaeīs:** *of Riphaei,* a mountain range in Scythia. **57. Ciconum:** *of the*

orgia revels

discerpō tear to pieces

marmoreus marble-like

ā! ah! alas!

inter sacra deum nocturnīque orgia Bacchī
discerptum lātōs juvenem sparsēre per agrōs.
60 Tum quoque marmoreā caput ā cervīce revulsum
gurgite cum mediō portāns Oeagrius Hebrus
volveret, Eurydicēn vōx ipsa et frīgida lingua
ā! miseram Eurydicēn animā fugiente vocābat,
Eurydicēn tōtō referēbant flūmine rīpae.

## OVID

### SELECTION I. THE FOUR AGES

*First was the Golden Age.*

vindex avenger, punisher

rēctum right, virtue

mināx threatening

**jūdex judge; vindex defender, protector
peregrīnus foreign; **vīsō visit

***liquidus flowing; **pīnus pine tree

tuba trumpet; dīrēctus straight

***galea helmet

immūnis free from; rāstrum hoe; intāctus untouched
vōmer plowshare

*contentus satisfied, content; *creō make, create
arbuteus of the arbutus tree; frāga strawberries
vēr spring; **tepeō be warm

    Aurea prīma sata est aetās, quae vindice nūllō,
sponte suā, sine lēge fidem rēctumque colēbat.
Poena metusque aberant, nec verba minacia fīxō
aere legēbantur, nec supplex turba timēbat
5 jūdicis ōra suī, sed erant sine vindice tūtī.
Nōndum caesa suīs, peregrīnum ut vīseret orbem,
montibus in liquidās pīnus dēscenderat undās,
nūllaque mortālēs praeter sua lītora nōrant.
Nōndum praecipitēs cingēbant oppida fossae;
10 nōn tuba dīrēctī, nōn aeris cornua flexī,
nōn galeae, nōn ēnsis erat; sine mīlitis ūsū
mollia sēcūrae peragēbant ōtia gentēs.
Ipsa quoque immūnis rāstrōque intācta nec ūllīs
saucia vōmeribus per sē dabat omnia tellūs;
15 contentīque cibīs nūllō cōgente creātīs
arbuteōs fētūs montānaque frāga legēbant.
Vēr erat aeternum, placidīque tepentibus aurīs

---

*Cicones,* a people of Thrace.  **quō mūnere:** *by this tribute* (to Eurydice).  **61. Oeagrius:** *of Oeagrus,* father of Orpheus.  **64. referēbant:** *reëchoed.*
    SELECTION I. This selection is abridged from Ovid's *Metamorphoses* I, 1–162. See App. 17. **1. Aurea aetās:** *the Golden Age,* the early, ideal stage of human happiness. **prīma sata est:** *was sown first,* i.e., came first. **vindice nūllō:** *without any avenger,* i.e., there were no law courts, because

men acted justly. **3–4. nec . . . legēbantur:** i.e., there were no bronze tablets of laws listing penalties for crimes. **6. caesa:** modifies **pīnus. 7. montibus:** place whence. **8. nōrant:** nōverant. **10. tuba dīrēctī (aeris):** *a trumpet of straight bronze.* **12. peragēbant ōtia:** *spent a leisured life.* **15. contentī:** understand **hominēs. cibīs . . . creātīs:** *with foods produced at no man's compulsion,* i.e., with uncultivated foods.

mulcēbant zephyrī nātōs sine sēmine flōrēs.

Mox etiam frūgēs tellūs inarāta ferēbat,

nec renovātus ager gravidīs cānēbat aristīs; 20

flūmina jam lactis, jam flūmina nectaris ībant,

flāvaque dē viridī stīllābant īlice mella.

***sēmen seed

**mox soon, presently; inarā- tus unplowed

renovō make new; cultivate; gravidus heavy; cāneō be white; arista ear of grain

lac milk; nectar *the drink of the gods*

stīllō drop, drip

*Next came the Silver Age.*

Postquam, Sāturnō tenebrōsa in Tartara missō,

sub Jove mundus erat, subiit argentea prōlēs,

aurō dēterior, fulvō pretiōsior aere. 25

Juppiter antīquī contrāxit tempora vēris,

perque hiemēs aestūsque et inaequālēs autumnōs

et breve vēr, spatiīs exēgit quattuor annum.

Tum prīmum siccīs āēr fervōribus ustus

canduit, et ventīs glaciēs adstricta pependit. 30

Tum prīmum subiēre domūs. Domūs antra fuērunt

et dēnsī fruticēs et vīnctae cortice virgae.

Sēmina tum prīmum longīs Cereālia sulcīs

obruta sunt, pressīque jugō gemuēre juvencī.

tenebrōsus dark, gloomy

mundus world; argenteus of silver

dēterior worse, less good; pre- tiōsus valuable

contrahō draw together; les- sen; vēr spring

inaequālis unequal

vēr spring

***siccus dry, parched; fervor heat

***candeō glow; glaciēs ice; adstringō contract; congeal

frutex shrub, bush; ***vinciō bind; cortex bark (*of a tree*)

**juvencus bullock

*Then came the Bronze and Iron Ages.*

Tertia post illam successit aēnea prōlēs, 35

saevior ingeniīs et ad horrida prōmptior arma,

nōn scelerāta tamen. Dē dūrō est ultima ferrō.

Prōtinus inrūpit vēnae pejōris in aevum

omne nefās. Fūgēre pudor vērumque fidēsque.

In quōrum subiēre locum fraudēsque dolīque 40

īnsidiaeque et vīs et amor scelerātus habendī.

Vēla dabant ventīs, neque adhūc bene nōverat illōs

nāvita; quaeque diū steterant in montibus altīs,

fluctibus īgnōtīs īnsultāvēre carīnae.

ingenium nature, character; horridus terrible, frightful; prōmptus ready, inclined

inrumpō break in, burst in; vēna vein

***fraus deceit

nāvita sailor, seaman

īnsultō dance upon

---

**28. spatiīs . . . annum:** *he finished the year with four divisions;* i.e., he divided the year into four seasons. **33. Sēmina Cereālia:** *seeds of grain.* **36. ingeniīs:** *in temperament.* **37. Dē:** (com- posed) *of.* **ūltima:** supply **aetās. 38. vēnae pejōris:** *of worse vein,* i.e., *of worse quality.* **39. omne nefās:** *every crime.* **43. quae steterant:** *which had stood* (as trees).

**cautus** careful; **limes** boundary-line; **mensor** measurer, surveyor
**seges** crop, harvest; **alimenta** food

**recondo** hide away; **admoveo** move to

**effodio** dig out, dig up; **inritamentum** incitement, inducement

**prodeo** come forward, appear

45 Commūnemque prius, ceu lūmina sōlis et aurās,
cautus humum longō signāvit līmite mēnsor.
Nec tantum segetēs alimentaque dēbita dīves
pōscēbātur humus, sed itum est in vīscera terrae;
quāsque recondiderat Stygiīsque admōverat umbrīs,
50 effodiuntur opēs, inrītāmenta malōrum.
Jamque nocēns ferrum ferrōque nocentius aurum
prōdierat.

*War and other calamities followed.*

**sanguineus** bloody; **crepito** rattle; cf. **\*\*crepo** rattle
**raptum** booty, plunder

**\*\*\*socer** father-in-law; **\*\*\*gener** son-in-law
**\*\*\*exitium** destruction, ruin

**inquiro** inquire

**\*\*madeo** be wet, drip

Prōdit Bellum, quod pugnat utrōque,
sanguineāque manū crepitantia concutit arma.
Vīvitur ex raptō. Nōn hospes ab hospite tūtus,
55 nōn socer ā generō; frātrum quoque grātia rāra est;
imminet exitiō vir conjugis, illa marītī;
fīlius ante diem patriōs inquīrit in annōs.
Victa jacet pietās; et Virgō caede madentēs,
ūltima caelestum, terrās Astraea relīquit.
60 Nēve foret terrīs sēcūrior arduus aethēr,
adfectāsse ferunt rēgnum caeleste Gigantās,
altaque congestōs strūxisse ad sidera montēs.

**perfringo** crash through

Tum pater omnipotēns missō perfrēgit Olympum
fulmine et excussit subjectō Pēliō Ossam.
65 Obruta mōle suā cum corpora dīra jacērent,

**perfundo** drench

perfūsam multō nātōrum sanguine Terram

**immadesco** become wet; **calidus** warm; cf. **\*\*\*caleo** be warm; **animo** make alive, quicken

immaduisse ferunt calidumque animāsse cruōrem,
et, nē nūlla suae stirpis monumenta manērent,

---

**45. Commūnem ... aurās:** i.e., the land had formerly been as free as sun and air. **47. segetēs alimentaque dēbita:** retained secondary object of pōscēbātur. **48. itum est:** *men went;* impers. **49. quāsque:** supply opēs. recondiderat: the subject understood is terra. **50. inrītāmenta:** in appos. with opēs.
**54. Vīvitur:** impers.; cf. itum est in line 48. hospes: *guest.* hospite: *host.* tūtus: supply est. **57. inquīrit:** i.e., the son consults fortune-tellers

to find out the probable date of his father's death. **58–59. Virgō Astraea:** goddess of justice; seeing the wickedness of mankind, she left the earth, becoming the constellation Virgo. **60. Nēve foret aethēr:** *and that heaven might not be.* foret: esset. **63. pater omnipotēns:** i.e., Jupiter. **64. Pēliō, Ossam:** Pelion and Ossa were mountains in Thessaly. Pronounce Peliō as two long syllables by *synizesis.* **66. nātōrum:** the Giants were the sons of Earth. **67. ferunt:** *they say.*

in faciem vertisse hominum. Sed et illa propāgō
contemptrīx superum saevaeque avidissima caedis 70
et violenta fuit; scīrēs ē sanguine nātōs.

**propāgō** offspring, progeny
**contemptrīx** scornful; ***avidus**
greedy
**violentus** impetuous

## SELECTION II. THE FLOOD

*The rains descend.*

Prōtinus Aeoliīs Aquilōnem claudit in antrīs,
et quaecumque fugant inductās flāmina nūbēs,
ēmittitque Notum. Madidīs Notus ēvolat ālīs,
terribilem piceā tēctus cālīgine vultum:
barba gravis nimbīs, cānīs fluit unda capillīs, 5
fronte sedent nebulae, rōrant pinnaeque sinūsque.
Utque manū lātē pendentia nūbila pressit,
fit fragor, inclūsī funduntur ab aethere nimbī.

**fugō** chase away; **indūcō** lead
in, gather; **flāmen** blast
**ēmittō** send forth; **madidus**
dripping; **ēvolō** fly forth
**piceus** pitchy, pitch-black; **cā-
līgō** mist, fog
5 **barba** beard; **cānus** white;
**capillus** hair
**rōrō** drip, be wet

*Neptune sends forth the flood.*

Nec caelō contenta suō est Jovis ira, sed illum
caeruleus frāter juvat auxiliāribus undīs. 10
Convocat hic amnēs; quī postquam tēcta tyrannī
intrāvēre suī, "Nōn est hortāmine longō
nunc," ait, "ūtendum; vīrēs effundite vestrās;
sīc opus est; aperīte domōs, ac mōle remōtā
flūminibus vestrīs tōtās immittite habēnās." 15
Jusserat; hī redeunt, ac fontibus ōra relaxant,
et dēfrēnātō volvuntur in aequora cursū.
Ipse tridente suō terram percussit; at illa
intremuit mōtūque viās patefēcit aquārum.
Exspatiāta ruunt per apertōs flūmina campōs. 20
Jamque mare et tellūs nūllum discrīmen habēbant;
omnia pontus erant; deërant quoque lītora pontō.

**contentus** satisfied
10 **auxiliāris** strengthening
**convocō** call together
**hortāmen** appeal, plea

**relaxō** unbar, loose

**dēfrēnātus** unbridled, unre-
strained
**percutiō** strike

**intremō** tremble, quiver;
**patefaciō** open up
20 **exspatior** spread out

---

**69. vertisse:** understand **cruōrem** as the object.
SELECTION II. In this description of a universal
flood, taken from *Metamorphoses* I, 262–292, the
similarities to the biblical account are very strik-
ing. **1. claudit:** the subject understood is **Juppiter.**

**2. inductās:** *spread* (over the earth). **4. tēctus
vultum:** *with his face covered.* **vultum:** accus. of
respect. **5. unda: aqua. 6. fronte:** place where.
**10. caeruleus frāter:** i.e., Neptune. **11. hic:**
i.e., Neptune. Read **hic** as if spelled **hicc.**

## Selection III. Deucalion and Pyrrha

*Only two mortals survive the flood.*

Sēparat Āoniōs Oetaeīs Phōcis ab arvīs.

Mōns ibi verticibus petit arduus astra duōbus,

nōmine Parnāsus, superantque cacūmina nūbīs.

Hīc ubi Deucaliōn — nam cētera tēxerat aequor —

5 cum cōnsorte torī parvā rate vectus adhaesit,

Cōrycidās nymphās et nūmina montis adōrant.

Nōn illō melior quisquam nec amantior aequī

vir fuit aut illā metuentior ūlla deōrum.

Juppiter ut liquidīs stāgnāre palūdibus orbem

10 et superesse virum dē tot modo mīlibus ūnum

et superesse videt dē tot modo mīlibus ūnam,

innocuōs ambō, cultōrēs nūminis ambō,

nūbila disjēcit, nimbīsque Aquilōne remōtīs,

et caelō terrās ostendit et aethera terrīs.

15 Flūmina subsīdunt, collēsque exīre videntur.

Surgit humus, crēscunt loca dēcrēscentibus undīs,

postque diem longam nūdāta cacūmina silvae

ostendunt, līmumque tenent in fronde relictum.

*Deucalion and Pyrrha go to the temple of Themis.*

Redditus orbis erat.    Quem postquam vīdit inānem,

20 Deucaliōn lacrimīs ita Pyrrham adfātur obortīs:

"Ō soror, ō conjūnx, ō fēmina sōla superstes,

nunc genus in nōbīs restat mortāle duōbus

(sīc vīsum superīs) hominumque exempla manē-

mus!"

Dīxerat, et flēbant; placuit caeleste precārī

**Glossary (margin):**

cacūmen top, peak

cōnsors sharer; adhaereō cling

adōrō worship

stāgnō be overflowed

innocuus harmless, innocent; cultor worshiper

subsīdō settle down, subside

***crēscō enlarge, increase; dē-crēscō grow less, decrease
cacūmen top

līmus mud, slime

oborior rise

superstes surviving

*exemplum example

---

**Selection III.** This story of Deucalion and Pyrrha, taken from *Metamorphoses* I, 312–414, in some respects resembles the biblical story of Noah and his Ark. **1. Āoniōs:** *the Boeotians.* **Oetaeīs:** *of Oeta*, a mountain in Southern Thessaly. **Phōcis:** a mountainous country between Boeotia and Thessaly. **3. Parnāsus:** *Parnassus*, a mountain in Thessaly. **5. cum cōnsorte torī:** i.e., with his wife. **6. Cōrycidās:** *Corycian*, i.e., belonging to the Corycian cave on Parnassus. **8. metuentior deōrum:** *more god-fearing.* **15. videntur:** *are seen.*

**21. soror:** here *cousin.* **23. vīsum:** supply **est.**

nūmen et auxilium per sacrās quaerere sortīs.     25
Ut templī tetigēre gradūs, prōcumbit uterque
prōnus humī, gelidōque pavēns dedit ōscula saxō,          **pronus** on one's face, prone
atque ita "Sī precibus," dīxērunt, "nūmina jūstīs
victa remollēscunt, sī flectitur īra deōrum,              **remollēscō** soften
dīc, Themi, quā generis damnum reparābile nostrī 30      **damnum** loss, destruction; **reparābilis** able to be repaired
arte sit, et mersīs fer opem, mītissima, rēbus!"

*Their prayers are answered by an oracle, which*
    *Deucalion interprets.*

Mōta dea est sortemque dedit:"Discēdite templō,
et vēlāte caput, cīnctāsque resolvite vestīs,            **vēlō** veil, cover
ossaque post tergum magnae jactāte parentis!"
Obstipuēre diū, rumpitque silentia vōce          35
Pyrrha prior, jussīsque deae pārēre recūsat,
detque sibī veniam pavidō rogat ōre, pavetque
laedere jactātīs māternās ossibus umbrās.
Intereā repetunt caecīs obscūra latebrīs                 ***latebra** hiding place; riddle
verba datae sortis sēcum inter sēque volūtant.   40
Inde Promēthīdēs placidīs Epimēthida dictīs
mulcet, et "Aut fallāx," ait, "est sollertia nōbīs,      **fallāx** deceitful; **sollertia** cleverness
aut pia sunt nūllumque nefās ōrācula suādent.            **ōrāculum** oracle
'Magna parēns' terra est: lapidēs in corpore terrae
'ossa' reor dīcī: jacere hōs post terga jubēmur."  45
Conjugis auguriō quamquam Tītānia mōta est,             ***augurium** augury, interpretation
spēs tamen in dubiō est: adeō caelestibus ambō
diffīdunt monitīs.  Sed quid temptāre nocēbit?           **diffīdō** distrust; **monitum** warning; command
Discēdunt, vēlantque caput, tunicāsque recingunt,        ***vēlō** veil, cover; **tunica** tunic; **recingō** ungird, loose
et jussōs lapidēs sua post vēstigia mittunt.     50

*A new race is created.*

Saxa (quis hoc crēdat, nisi sit prō teste vetus-         **vetustās** antiquity, lapse of time
    tās?)

---

30. Themi: voc.   30–31. quā arte: quō modō.
31. mersīs rēbus: *to our tragic condition.*
    38. jactātīs ossibus: *by throwing* (her) *bones.*
39–40. repetunt sēcum: *they seek in their minds.*

41. Promēthīdēs: *son of Prometheus,* i.e., Deucalion.  Epimēthida: *daughter of Epimetheus;* i.e., Pyrrha.  Greek acc.   46. Tītānia: *daughter of a Titan,* i.e., Pyrrha.

dūritiēs hardness; **rigor** stiff-
  ness, rigidity
**molliō** make soft, soften

pōnere dūritiem coepēre suumque rigōrem,

mollīrīque morā, mollītaque dūcere fōrmam;

inque brevī spatiō, superōrum nūmine, saxa

55 missa virī manibus faciem trāxēre virōrum,

**reparō** restore

et dē fēmineō reparāta est fēmina jactū.

## SELECTION IV. DAEDALUS AND ICARUS

*Daedalus invents wings in order to escape from Crete.*

**perōdī** hate, abhor

**nātālis** native

Daedalus intereā, Crētēn longumque perōsus

exsilium, tāctusque locī nātālis amōre,

clausus erat pelagō. "Terrās licet," inquit, "et
         undās

**obstruō** block; **certē** certainly,
  surely; **illāc** (by) that way
**\*\*possideō** hold, possess

obstruat, at caelum certē patet; ībimus illāc.

5 Omnia possideat: nōn possidet āera Mīnōs."

**dīmittō** send, let go

Dīxit, et ignōtās animum dīmittit in artēs,

**novō** make new, change

nātūramque novat, nam pōnit in ōrdine pinnās,

ā minimā coeptās, longam breviōre sequente,

**clīvus** slope

ut clīvō crēvisse putēs.

**līnum** thread; **cēra wax**

10 Tum līnō mediās et cērīs adligat īmās,

**curvāmen** curve

atque ita compositās parvō curvāmine flectit,

**imitor** imitate

ut vērās imitētur avēs. Puer Īcarus ūnā

**\*tractō** handle

stābat et, ignārus sua sē tractāre perīcla,

**captō** catch at; **plūma** feather;
  **pollex** thumb; **cēra** wax
**molliō** soften; **lūsus** sport, play

captābat plūmās, flāvam modo pollice cēram

15 mollībat, lūsūque suō mīrābile patris

impediēbat opus.

*Daedalus teaches his son Icarus how to fly.*

**coeptum** undertaking

Postquam manus ultima coeptīs

**opifex** artisan; **lībrō** balance

imposita est, geminās opifex lībrāvit in ālās

---

**52. coepēre: coepērunt. 53. dūcere fōrmam:**
*to take shape.* **55. trāxēre:** *assumed.* **56. fēmina:**
*womankind.*
SELECTION IV. This story of Daedalus is taken
from *Metamorphoses* VIII, 183–235. The problem
of flying was of interest to man long before our
own days. It is noteworthy that Leonardo da
Vinci, whom we think of primarily as a great
sculptor and painter, made many elaborate experi-

ments in flying. **2. locī nātālis:** i.e., for Athens,
from which he had been banished for slaying his
nephew Perdix. **3–4. licet obstruat:** *though he*
(Minos) *block.* Minos had refused to allow Dae-
dalus to leave Crete by land or sea. **6. animum
dīmittit:** *turns his mind.* **9. clīvō crēvisse:** *that
they had grown on a slope.* **12. vērās avēs:** i.e.,
real wings.
    **16. manus ultima:** *the finishing touch.*

Daedalus and Icarus

ipse suum corpus, mōtāque pependit in aurā.

Īnstruit et nātum, "Mediō" que "ut līmite currās,

Īcare," ait, "moneō nē, sī dēmissior ībis,          20

unda gravet pinnās, sī celsior, ignis adūrat.

Inter utrumque volā."

Inter opus monitūsque genae maduēre senīlēs,

et patriae tremuēre manūs; dedit ōscula nātō

(nōn iterum repetenda) suō, pinnīsque levātus    25

ante volat comitīque timet, velut āles, ab altō

quae teneram prōlem prōdūxit in āera nīdō,

hortāturque sequī damnōsāsque ērudit artēs,

et movet ipse suās et nātī respicit ālās.

*Icarus flies too high and loses his wings.*

          Et jam Jūnōnia laevā          30

parte Samos fuerant Dēlosque Parosque relictae,

dextra Lebinthus erat fēcundaque melle Calymnē,

cum puer audācī coepit gaudēre volātū

dēseruitque ducem, caelīque cupīdine tāctus,

altius ēgit iter; rapidī vīcīnia sōlis             35

mollit odōrātās, pinnārum vincula, cērās.

Tābuerant cērae. Nūdōs quatit ille lacertōs,

rēmigiōque carēns nōn ūllas percipit aurās;

ōraque caeruleā patrium clāmantia nōmen

excipiuntur aquā quae nōmen trāxit ab illō.       40

At pater īnfēlīx, nec jam pater, "Īcare," dīxit,

"Īcare," dīxit, "ubi es? Quā tē regiōne re-

    quīram?"

"Īcare," dīcēbat. Pinnās aspexit in undīs,

dēvōvitque suās artēs, corpusque sepulcrō

condidit.                                          45

**gravō** weigh down; **adūrō** set fire to, scorch

**gena** cheek; **madēscō** grow wet; **senīlis** old man's

**\*\*āles** winged creature, bird

**prōdūcō** lead forth; **nīdus** nest

**damnōsus** causing loss, destructive; **ērudiō** teach

**fēcundus** rich, prolific

**volātus** flight

**vīcīnia** nearness

**odōrātus** fragrant; **cēra** wax

**tābēscō** melt; **\*\*\*quatiō** shake, flap; **\*lacertus** arm
**rēmigium** oars; **percipiō** catch

**dēvoveō** curse

---

**26. ab altō:** construe with **nīdō** in the next line. **32. dextra:** predicate adj. agreeing with **Lebinthus** and also with **Calymnē. Lebinthus, Calymnē:** small islands off the coast of Asia Minor. **33. puer:** i.e., Icarus. **39. caeruleā:** construe with **aquā** in the next line. **40. quae ... illō:** i.e., that part of the Aegean Sea into which Icarus fell was named the Icarian Sea. **44. suās artēs:** i.e., the skill that had enabled him to create the wings which had now caused the death of his son. **corpus:** i.e., the body of Icarus.

## Selection V. Philemon and Baucis

*Jupiter and Mercury visit the earth and find welcome in one humble home.*

**cādūcifer** caduceus-bearing

**requiēs** rest

**sera** bar (*for a door*)

**stipula** stalk, straw; **canna** reed; **palūstris** of the marsh
**anus** old woman; **parilis** equal

**juvenālis** youthful, of youth

**cōnsenēscō** grow old together; **casa** cottage; **paupertās** poverty, humble circumstances

**rēfert** it makes a difference; **illīc** there; ***famulus** servant

Juppiter hūc speciē mortālī cumque parente
vēnit Atlantiadēs positīs cādūcifer ālīs.
Mīlle domōs adiēre, locum requiemque petentēs;
mīlle domōs clausēre serae: tamen ūna recēpit,
5 parva quidem, stipulīs et cannā tēcta palūstrī,
sed pia Baucis anus parilīque aetāte Philēmōn
illā sunt annīs jūnctī juvenālibus, illā
cōnsenuēre casā paupertātemque fatendō
effēcēre levem nec inīquā mente ferendō.
10 Nec rēfert dominōs illīc famulōsne requīrās:
tōta domus duo sunt, īdem pārentque jubentque.

*Philemon and Baucis hasten to prepare a meal for their unexpected guests.*

**parcus** frugal

**submittō** lower

**relevō** rest; **sedīle** seat, chair

**superinjiciō** throw upon; **textum** cloth; **rudis** coarse; **sēdulus** attentive
**focus** fireplace; **tepidus** warm; cf. ***tepeō** be warm; **dīmoveō** push aside
**suscitō** rouse up, rekindle; ***hesternus** of yesterday; **cortex** bark
**nūtriō** nurse, feed; **anīlis** of an old woman

**multifidus** finely split; **rāmāle** twig, chip; **āridus** dry
**admoveō** place near

**riguus** well-watered; **hortus** garden
**truncō** cut off, strip; **holus** vegetable; cabbage

Ergō ubi caelicolae parcōs tetigēre penātēs
submissōque humilēs intrārunt vertice postēs,
membra senex positō jussit relevāre sedīlī,
15 quō superinjēcit textum rude sēdula Baucis.

Inque focō tepidum cinerem dīmōvit et ignēs
suscitat hesternōs foliīsque et cortice siccō
nūtrit et ad flammās animā prōdūcit anīlī;

multifidāsque facēs rāmāliaque ārida tēctō
20 dētulit et minuit parvōque admōvit aēnō,
quodque suus conjūnx riguō conlēgerat hortō,
truncat holus foliīs.

---

**Selection V.** This story is taken from *Metamorphoses* VIII, 626–719. The gods Jupiter and Mercury, wandering over the earth disguised as men, and seeking shelter, are welcomed into a humble cottage and offered a simple meal. **1. hūc:** to Phrygia, where Philemon and Baucis lived.

**cumque: et cum. cum parente:** i.e., with Jupiter. **2. Atlantiadēs:** *descendant of Atlas,* i.e., Mercury. **9. nec . . . ferendō:** *and by enduring it with a contented spirit.* **11. domus:** *household.* **12. penātēs:** *home,* by *metonymy.* **19. tēctō:** *from the garret.* **20. aēnō:** dat. of direction.

Intereā mediās fallunt sermōnibus hōrās.
Accubuēre deī.
Pōnitur hīc bicolor sincērae bāca Minervae
conditaque in liquidā corna autumnālia faece
intibaque et rādīx et lactis massa coāctī
ōvaque nōn ācrī leviter versāta favīllā.
Parva mora est, epulāsque focī mīsēre calentēs,
nec longae rūrsus referuntur vīna senectae
dantque locum mēnsīs paulum sēducta secundīs.
Hīc nux, hīc mixta est rūgōsīs Cārica palmīs
et dē purpureīs conlēctae vītibus ūvae;
candidus in mediō favus est. Super omnia vultūs
accessēre bonī nec iners pauperque voluntās.

*Jupiter and Mercury reveal their identity.*

Intereā totiēns haustum crātēra replērī
sponte suā per sēque vident succrēscere vīna.
Attonitī novitāte pavent manibusque supīnīs
concipiunt Baucisque precēs timidusque Philēmōn
et veniam dapibus nūllīsque parātibus ōrant.
Ūnicus ānser erat, minimae custōdia vīllae,
quem dīs hospitibus dominī mactāre parābant.
Ille celer pinnā tardōs aetāte fatīgat
ēlūditque diū tandemque est vīsus ad ipsōs
cōnfūgisse deōs. Superī vetuēre necārī,
"Dī" -que "sumus, meritāsque luet vīcīnia poenās
impia," dīxērunt. "Vōbīs immūnibus hujus
esse malī dabitur. Modo vestra relinquite tēcta
ac nostrōs comitāte gradūs et in ardua montis
īte simul." Pārent ambō baculīsque levātī
nītuntur longō vēstīgia pōnere clīvō.

---

accumbō recline (*at table*)

25 bicolor two-colored; sincērus pure, chaste; bāca berry
cornum cornel-cherry; autumnālis of autumn; faex brine
intibum endive; **rādīx root; radish; massa mass, curd
ōvum egg; leviter lightly; favīlla ashes

30 senecta age

sēdūcō lead aside, put aside

nux nut; rūgōsus wrinkled

vītis vine; ūva bunch of grapes

candidus white; favus honeycomb
35 pauper poor

repleō refill

succrēscō grow

novitās strangeness; supīnus upturned
concipiō begin

40 parātus preparation

ūnicus one and only; ānser gander; custōdia guardian; **vīlla farmhouse

*ēlūdō elude, evade

45 cōnfugiō flee for refuge

luō pay; vīcīnia vicinity, neighborhood
immūnis free from, exempt from

50 baculum staff, walking stick

clīvus slope, hillside

---

**25. bicolor bāca:** i.e., the olive, which when unripe is green, but becomes black when ripe. **27. lactis massa coāctī:** i.e., cheese. **30. nec longae senectae:** *of no old vintage.* **31. mēnsīs secundīs:** *for the dessert.* **paulum sēducta:** *put a little aside.* **32. Cārica (fīcus):** *Carian fig.* **pal-** **mīs:** *with dates.* **35. nec ... voluntās:** *and active and abundant goodwill.* **36. crātēra:** Greek acc. **47–48. Vōbīs ... dabitur:** *To you it will be granted to be free from this misfortune.* **49. in ardua montis:** *to the top of the hill.*

*Jupiter and Mercury offer to grant Philemon and*
*Baucis any boon they may ask.*

Flexēre oculōs et mersa palūde
cētera prōspiciunt, tantum sua tēcta manēre.
Dumque ea mīrantur, dum dēflent fāta suōrum,
55 illa vetus dominīs etiam casa parva duōbus
vertitur in templum; furcās subiēre columnae
caelātaeque forēs aurātaque tēcta videntur.
Tālia tum placidō Sāturnius ēdidit ōre:
"Dīcite, jūste senex, et fēmina conjuge jūstō
60 digna, quid optētis." Cum Baucide pauca locūtus
jūdicium superīs aperit commūne Philēmōn:
"Esse sacerdōtēs dēlūbraque vestra tuērī
poscimus: et quoniam concordēs ēgimus annōs,
auferat hōra duōs eadem, nec conjugis umquam
65 busta meae videam neu sim tumulandus ab illā."

*Philemon and Baucis's wishes are fulfilled.*

Vōta fidēs sequitur. Templī tūtēla fuēre
dōnec vīta data est. Annīs aevōque solūtī
ante gradūs sacrōs cum stārent forte locīque
nārrārent cāsūs, frondēre Philēmona Baucis,
70 Baucida cōnspexit senior frondēre Philēmōn.
Jamque super geminōs crēscente cacūmine vultūs,
mūtua, dum licuit, reddēbant dicta "Valē" -que
"Ō conjūnx," dīxēre simul, simul abdita tēxit
ōra frutex.

SELECTION VI. ATALANTA

*Atalanta announces terms to her suitors.*

Territa sorte deī per opācās innuba silvās
vīvit et īnstantem turbam violenta procōrum

---

**dēfleō** weep over

**casa** cottage

**furca** fork, forked pole; **columna** column, pillar
**caelō** engrave

**ēdō** give forth, utter

**jūdicium** judgment, decision

**concors** harmonious, in concord; cf. **\*\*concordia** harmony

**bustum** funeral pile; **tumulō** entomb, bury

**tūtēla** guardianship; guardians

**nārrō** tell, relate; **frondeō** put forth leaves
**frondeō** put forth leaves

**mūtuus** mutual, in exchange

**frutex** growth of foliage

**innubus** unwed, unmarried

**violentus** untamed; **procus** suitor

---

55. dominīs: dat. of reference. 58. Sāturnius: *son of Saturn,* i.e., Jupiter. 61. jūdicium commūne: *their joint decision.*
66. fidēs: *fulfillment.* 67. aevō solūtī: *worn out by age.* 68–69. locī cāsūs: *the incidents of the place.*
SELECTION VI. This story is taken from *Metamorphoses* X, 567–680. Atalanta was a beautiful

P. P. Rubens

Jupiter and Mercury at the House of Philemon and Baucis

George Barrie Sons

condiciōne fugat. "Nec sum potienda, nisi," inquit,
"victa prius cursū. Pedibus contendite mēcum.
Praemia vēlōcī conjūnx thalamīque dabuntur; 5 **vēlōx swift
mors pretium tardīs. Ea lēx certāminis estō." ***pretium price, prize; ***certāmen contest
Illa quidem immītis; sed (tanta potentia fōrmae immītis cruel, inhuman; potentia power
est)
vēnit ad hanc lēgem temerāria turba procōrum. temerārius rash; procus suitor

*Hippomenes, a spectator, becomes a contestant.*

Sēderat Hippomenēs cursūs spectātor inīquī
et "Petitur cuiquam per tanta perīcula conjūnx?" 10
dīxerat ac nimiōs juvenum damnārat amōrēs. ***damnō condemn
Laudandō concipit ignēs
et nē quis juvenum currat vēlōcius optat vēlōciter swiftly
invidiāque timet. "Sed cūr certāminis hujus ***invidia envy, jealousy
intemptāta mihī fortūna relinquitur?" inquit. 15 intemptātus untried
"Audentēs deus ipse juvat." Dum tālia sēcum
exigit Hippomenēs, passū volat ālite virgō. ***āles winged
Aura refert ablāta citīs tālāria plantīs, tālāria hem of a robe; planta sole of the foot, foot
inque puellārī corpus candōre rubōrem puellāris girlish, maidenly; candor whiteness; rubor flush; cf. *rubeō be red, blush
trāxerat, haud aliter quam cum super ātria vēlum 20
candida purpureum simulātās īnficit umbrās. īnficiō make, cast
Dum notat haec hospes, dēcursa novissima mēta *notō note, notice; dēcurrō run out; **mēta goal, course
est,
et tegitur fēstā victrīx Atalanta corōnā. victrīx victress; ***corōna crown, garland
Dant gemitum victī penduntque ex foedere poenās.
Nōn tamen ēventū juvenis dēterritus hōrum 25 ēventus outcome; dēterreō deter
cōnstitit in mediō, vultūque in virgine fīxō,
"Quid facilem titulum superandō quaeris inertēs? titulus title, fame
Mēcum cōnfer," ait. "Seu mē fortūna potentem cōnferō match, contend

girl who said she would marry no man who could not beat her in a foot race. Although many made the attempt, they all failed, and were put to death. Finally a noble and handsome youth named Hippomenes fell in love with Atalanta and challenged her to a race. **1. sorte deī:** *by the oracle of the god.* Apollo had warned Atalanta against marriage. **2. vīvit:** supply **Atalanta** as subject. **5. thalamī:** *marriage.* **6. Ea ... estō:** *Let this be the stipulation for the contest.* **7. immītis:** supply **erat. 8. ad hanc lēgem:** *to* (meet) *this stipulation.* **12. Laudandō:** the object is **Atalantam** understood. **16–17. sēcum exigit:** *thinks over to himself.* **25. juvenis:** subject of **cōnstitit.**

**indignor** deem it unworthy

fēcerit, ā tantō nōn indignābere vincī.

**pronepōs** great-grandson

**citrā** this side of, less than

**memorābilis** memorable

30 Namque mihī genitor Megareus Onchēstius, illī
est Neptūnus avus, pronepōs ego rēgis aquārum,
nec virtūs citrā genus est; seu vincar, habēbis,
Hippomenē victō, magnum et memorābile nōmen."

*Atalanta falls in love with Hippomenes.*

Tālia dīcentem mollī Schoenēia vultū
35 aspicit, et dubitat superārī an vincere mālit.

**fōrmōsus** handsome

Atque ita "Quis deus hunc fōrmōsīs," inquit,
"inīquus

***perdō** destroy

***jūdex** judge

perdere vult cāraeque jubet discrīmine vītae
conjugium petere hoc? Nōn sum, mē jūdice, tantī.
Nec fōrma tangor (poteram tamen hāc quoque
tangī),
40 sed quod adhūc puer est: nōn mē movet ipse, sed
aetās.

**īnsum** be in; **interritus** un-afraid

**aequoreus** of the sea; **numerō** number, reckon

Quid quod inest virtūs et mēns interrita lētī?
Quid quod ab aequoreā numerātur orīgine quārtus?
Quid quod amat tantīque putat cōnūbia nostra,
ut pereat, sī mē fors illī dūra negārit?
45 Dum licet, hospes, abī thalamōsque relinque
cruentōs.

**nūbō** marry

***sapiēns** wise

**perimō** destroy; slay

Conjugium crūdēle meum est: tibi nūbere nūlla
nōlet, et optārī potes ā sapiente puellā.
Cūr tamen est mihi cūra tuī, tot jam ante perēmptīs?
Occidet hic igitur, voluit quia vīvere mēcum,
50 indignamque necem pretium patiētur amōris?

***nex** death

***utinam** *sign of a wish*

***vēlōx** swift

**virgineus** maidenly; **puerīlis** boyish

Sed nōn culpa mea est. Utinam dēsistere vellēs,
aut, quoniam es dēmēns, utinam vēlōcior essēs!
Ā! quam virgineus puerīlī vultus in ōre est!

---

**30. Megareus:** father of Hippomenes. **Onchēstius:** *of Onchestas,* a city in Boeotia.
**34. Schoenēia:** *daughter of Schoeneus,* i.e., Atalanta. **36. fōrmōsīs:** dat. with inīquus. **37. dis-** crīmine: *at the risk.* **39. fōrma:** i.e., Hippomenes's beauty. **41. Quid quod:** *What of the fact that.* **42. quārtus:** Hippomenes is the fourth in line of descent from Neptune.

Ā! miser Hippomenē, nōllem tibi vīsa fuissem!
Vīvere dignus erās."                                 55

*Hippomenes appeals to Venus for help.*

Jam solitōs poscunt cursūs populusque paterque,
cum mē sollicitā prōlēs Neptūnia vōce            sollicitus anxious
invocat Hippomenēs "Cytherēa" -que "com-        invocō call upon; comprecor
  precor ausīs                                     pray; ausum daring at-
                                                   tempt
adsit," ait, "nostrīs, et, quōs dedit, adjuvet ignēs."  adjuvō aid
Dētulit aura precēs ad mē nōn invida blandās,   60  invidus  envious, grudging;
                                                   blandus persuasive
mōtaque sum, fateor, nec opis mora longa dabātur.
Est ager (indigenae Tamasēum nōmine dīcunt),      indigena native
tellūris Cypriae pars optima, quam mihi prīscī    prīscus ancient, of old
sacrāvēre senēs templīsque accēdere dōtem         dōs dowry, endowment
hanc jussēre meīs.  Mediō nitet arbor in arvō,  65
fulva comās, fulvō rāmīs crepitantibus aurō.      crepitō rattle; cf. ***crepō
                                                   rattle
Hinc tria forte meā veniēns dēcerpta ferēbam      dēcerpō pluck, pick
aurea pōma manū, nūllīque videnda nisi ipsī,      pōmum apple
Hippomenēn adiī docuīque quis ūsus in illīs.

*Hippomenes wins the race — and a bride.*

Signa tubae dederant, cum carcere prōnus uterque 70  ***prōnus  bending  forward,
                                                     headlong
ēmicat et summam celerī pede lībat harēnam.        ēmicō dart forth
Posse putēs illōs siccō freta rādere passū        rādō scrape, skim
et segetis cānae stantēs percurrere aristās.       ***cānus white; percurrō run
                                                     along; arista head of grain
Adjiciunt animōs juvenī clāmorque favorque         adjiciō add; favor applause
verbaque dīcentum:   "Nunc, nunc incumbere 75
  tempus,
Hippomenē, properā!  Nunc vīribus ūtere tōtīs.
Pelle moram.  Vincēs."  Dubium, Megarēius hērōs
gaudeat an virgō magis hīs Schoenēia dictīs.

---

**54. nōllem ... fuissem:** *I wish you had not seen me.*   **64. accēdere dōtem:** *to be added as a gift.*
  **56. pater:** i.e., Atalanta's father.  **57. mē:** i.e.,   **66. fulva comās:** *with golden foliage.* comās: acc.
Venus, who is represented as telling the story.   of respect.  **69. Hippomenēn:** Greek acc.
**prōlēs Neptūnia:** i.e., descendant of Neptune,   **72. freta rādere:** *to graze the sea.*  **75. tempus:**
i.e., Hippomenes.  **59. ignēs:** *the fires* (of love).   supply est.  **77. Dubium:** supply est.  **Megarēius:**
**62. Tamasēum:** *of Tamasus,* a city in Cyprus.   *son of Megareus,* i.e., Hippomenes.

***quotiēns** how often; **trānseō** pass

**āridus** dry; **lassus** weary; **anhēlitus** breath

***mēta** goal; ***dēnique** finally

**arboreus** of a tree

**nitidus** shining

**dēclīnō** bend, turn aside; **volūbilis** rolling

**praetereō** go past; pass; **resonō** resound, echo; **spectāculum** show; grandstand; **plausus** applause

**corrigō** remedy

**jactus** throw; **remoror** delay

Ō quotiēns, cum jam posset trānsīre, morāta est!
80 Āridus ē lassō veniēbat anhēlitus ōre,
mētaque erat longē. Tum dēnique dē tribus ūnum
fētibus arboreīs prōlēs Neptūnia mīsit.
Obstipuit virgō nitidīque cupīdine pōmī
dēclīnat cursūs aurumque volūbile tollit.
85 Praeterit Hippomenēs; resonant spectācula plausū.
Illa moram celerī cessātaque tempora cursū
corrigit atque iterum juvenem post terga relinquit;
et rūrsus pōmī jactū remorāta secundī
cōnsequitur trānsitque virum. Pars ultima cursūs
90 restābat. "Nunc," inquit, "ades, dea mūneris
auctor."

**tardē** slowly, tardily

**oblīquus** sidelong; **juvenāliter** with youthful strength

**adjiciō** add; ***pondus** weight; **mālum** apple

**gravitās** weight

***praetereō** pass

Inque latus campī, quō tardius illa redīret,
jēcit ab oblīquō nitidum juvenāliter aurum.
An peteret, virgō vīsa est dubitāre: coēgī
tollere et adjēcī sublātō pondera mālō
95 impediīque oneris pariter gravitāte morāque.
Nēve meus sermō cursū sit tardior ipsō,
praeterita est virgō; dūxit sua praemia victor.

SELECTION VII. PYRAMUS AND THISBE

*Pyramus and Thisbe fall in love, but their parents forbid their marriage.*

**praeferō** prefer

**contiguus** adjoining

**coctilis** baked; of brick

**nōtitia** acquaintance; **vīcinia** propinquity

**coeō** come together, unite

Pȳramus et Thisbē, juvenum pulcherrimus alter,
altera quās Oriēns habuit praelāta puellīs,
contiguās tenuēre domōs, ubi dīcitur altam
coctilibus mūrīs cīnxisse Semīramis urbem.
5 Nōtitiam prīmōsque gradūs vīcinia fēcit;
tempore crēvit amor. Taedae quoque jūre coīssent,

---

84. cursūs: obj. of dēclīnat. 86. cessāta tempora: *the time lost.* 90. ades: *help* (me). auctor: i.e., Venus. 92. ab oblīquō: *sidewise,* i.e., off the race course. 93. coēgī: Venus is represented as telling this whole story. 94. adjēcī ... mālō: i.e., Venus made the apple heavier. 96. Nēve ... ipsō: i.e., to

cut a long story short. 97. dūxit: the verb here has a double meaning: Hippomenes carried off (the reward) and he married Atalanta (in mātrimōnium dūxit).

SELECTION VII. This selection, taken from *Metamorphoses* IV, 55–166, tells the tragic love story

sed vetuēre patrēs; quod nōn potuēre vetāre,

ex aequō captīs ārdēbant mentibus ambō.

Cōnscius omnis abest; nūtū signīsque loquuntur,

quōque magis tegitur, tēctus magis aestuat ignis. 10   **aestuō** burn

Fissus erat tenuī rīmā, quam dūxerat ōlim,    **findō** split, cleave; **rīma** crack, chink

cum fieret, pariēs domuī commūnis utrīque.    **\*\*pariēs** partition wall

*Pyramus and Thisbe find a way to communicate*
*with each other.*

Id vitium, nūllī per saecula longa notātum    **vitium** flaw; crack; **\*\*notō** note, notice

(quid nōn sentit amor?) prīmī vīdistis amantēs,

et vōcis fēcistis iter, tūtaeque per illud    15

murmure blanditiae minimō trānsīre solēbant.    **blanditiae** endearments

Saepe, ubi cōnstiterant hinc Thisbē, Pȳramus illinc,   **illinc** on that side

inque vicēs fuerat captātus anhēlitus ōris,    **\*\*\*vicis** turn; **captō** catch; **anhēlitus** breath

"Invide," dīcēbant, "pariēs, quid amantibus ob-   **invidus** envious, grudging; **\*\*\*pariēs** wall

stās?

Nec sumus ingrātī; tibi nōs dēbēre fatēmur,    20

quod datus est verbīs ad amīcās trānsitus aurīs."   **trānsitus** passage

Tālia dīversā nēquīquam sēde locūtī,

sub noctem dīxēre "Valē."

*They plan a secret meeting.*

Postera nocturnōs aurōra remōverat ignīs,

sōlque pruīnōsās radiīs siccāverat herbās;    25  **siccō** dry up

ad solitum coiēre locum. Tum, murmure parvō   **coeō** come together, meet

multa prius questī, statuunt ut nocte silentī

fallere custōdēs foribusque excēdere temptent,

cumque domō exierint, urbis quoque tēcta relin-

quant;

nēve sit errandum lātō spatiantibus arvō    30  **spatior** wander about

of Pyramus and Thisbe. Shakespeare presents the tale dramatically in his *Midsummer Night's Dream*. **4. Semiramis:** a mythical queen of Assyria and builder of the walls of Babylon. **urbem:** i.e., Babylon. **6. Taedae jūre:** *in lawful wedlock.* **8. ex aequō:** *equally.* **11. Fissus erat:** the subject is **pariēs** in line 12. **11–12. quam** dūxerat ōlim pariēs: *which once the wall had produced.*
**18. inque ... ōris:** *and in turn they had caught each other's breath.*
**24. nocturnōs ignīs:** i.e., the stars. **30. nēve ... arvō:** *and in order that they may not go astray, wandering about in the wide fields.*

bustum tomb

über fruitful, abounding

mōrus mulberry tree; conter-
minus close (to)
**pactum agreement; tardē
slowly

conveniant ad busta Ninī, lateantque sub umbrā
arboris. Arbor ibī, niveīs ūberrima pōmīs,
ardua mōrus erat, gelidō contermina fontī.
Pacta placent, et lūx tardē discēdere vīsa est;
35 praecipitātur aquīs, et aquīs nox exit ab īsdem.

*Thisbe arrives first at the trysting place and is
frightened away by a lioness.*

callidus clever

adoperiō cover

perveniō arrive

leaena lioness; oblinō smear;
rictus jaw
sitis thirst; vīcīnus neighbor-
ing

Callida per tenebrās, versātō cardine, Thisbē
ēgreditur, fallitque suōs, adopertaque vultum
pervenit ad tumulum dictāque sub arbore sēdit;
audācem faciēbat amor. Venit ecce recentī
40 caede leaena boum spūmantīs oblita rictūs,
dēpositūra sitim vīcīnī fontis in undā.
Quam procul ad lūnae radiōs Babylōnia Thisbē
vīdit, et obscūrum trepidō pede fūgit in antrum;
dumque fugit, tergō vēlāmina lāpsa relīquit.

sitis thirst; compescō restrain;
quench

cruentō make bloody; laniō
tear, mangle; ***amictus
robe, mantle

45 Ut lea saeva sitim multā compescuit undā,
dum redit in silvās, inventōs forte sine ipsā
ōre cruentātō tenuīs laniāvit amictūs.

*Pyramus, supposing Thisbe to be dead, stabs himself.*

sērō late

expallēscō turn pale

**tinguō wet, stain

perimō take away; destroy

Sērius ēgressus, vēstīgia vīdit in altō
pulvere certa ferae tōtōque expalluit ōre
50 Pyramus. Ut vērō vestem quoque sanguine tīnetam
repperit, "Ūna duōs," inquit, "nox perdet aman-
tīs,
ē quibus illa fuit longā dignissima vītā.
Nostra nocēns anima est. Ego tē, miseranda,
perēmī,
in loca plēna metūs quī jussī nocte venīrēs,
55 nec prior hūc vēnī. Nostrum dīvellite corpus,

---

**31. Ninī:** *of Ninus.* Ninus was an ancient king
of Babylon.
**37. adoperta vultum:** *with her face veiled.*
**40.** spūmantīs oblita rictūs: *with frothing jaws*

*smeared.* **44. tergō lāpsa:** *that had slipped off her
back.* **46. ipsā:** i.e., Thisbe.
**53. Nostra ... est:** *Mine is the guilty soul.*
**54. jussī venīrēs:** in prose, jussī tē venīre.

et scelerāta ferō cōnsūmite vīscera morsū,  ***morsus bite; teeth
ō quīcumque sub hāc habitātis rūpe, leōnēs!  ***leō lion
Sed timidī est optāre necem." Vēlāmina Thisbēs
tollit, et ad pactae sēcum fert arboris umbram.  pacīscor agree upon
"Accipe nunc," inquit, "nostrī quoque sanguinis 60
    haustūs!"
Quōque erat accīnctus, dēmīsit in īlia ferrum.  īlia loins
Nec mora; ferventī moriēns ē vulnere trāxit,
et jacuit resupīnus humō.  resupīnus on one's back

*Thisbe returns to find Pyramus dying and she slays
    herself with Pyramus's sword.*

   Ecce, metū nōndum positō, nē fallat amantem,
illa redit, juvenemque oculīs animōque requīrit.  65
Dum dubitat, tremibunda videt pulsāre cruentum  tremibundus trembling
membra solum, retrōque pedem tulit.
Sed, postquam remorāta suōs cognōvit amōrēs,
percutit indignōs clārō plangōre lacertōs,  **lacertus arm
et laniāta comās amplexaque corpus amātum  70 laniō tear
vulnera supplēvit lacrimīs, flētumque cruōrī  suppleō fill
miscuit, et, gelidīs in vultibus ōscula fīgēns,
"Pȳrame," clāmāvit, "quis tē mihi cāsus adēmit?  ***adimō take away
Pȳrame, respondē! Tua tē cārissima Thisbē
nōminat; exaudī, vultūsque attolle jacentīs!"  75 nōminō call
Ad nōmen Thisbēs oculōs jam morte gravātōs
Pȳramus ērēxit, vīsāque recondidit illā.  ***ērigō raise
Quae postquam vestemque suam cognōvit et ēnse
vīdit ebur vacuum, "Tua tē manus," inquit,  **ebur ivory
    "amorque
perdidit, īnfēlīx! Est et mihi fortis in ūnum  80
hoc manus; est et amor: dabit hic in vulnera vīrēs.
Persequar exstīnctum lētīque miserrima dīcar  persequor follow

58. timidī est: *it is the part of a coward.* 62. trāxit: the object is **ferrum** understood.
   68. suōs amōrēs: *her lover.* 73. quis cāsus: *what mischance* 75. jacentīs: *drooping.* 76. This-bēs: a Greek gen. 79. ebur: *the ivory* (scabbard). 80–81. in ūnum hoc: *for this same purpose.* 82. exstīnctum: modifies tē understood as object of persequar.

causa comesque tuī.

Ō multum miserī, meus illīusque parentēs,

85 ut, quōs certus amor, quōs hōra novissima jūnxit,

compōnī tumulō nōn invideātis eōdem.

At tū quae rāmīs arbor miserābile corpus

nunc tegis ūnīus, mox es tēctūra duōrum,

signa tenē caedis, pullōsque et lūctibus aptōs

90 semper habē fētūs, geminī monumenta cruōris."

Dīxit, et aptātō pectus mūcrōne sub īmum

incubuit ferrō, quod adhūc ā caede tepēbat.

Vōta tamen tetigēre deōs, tetigēre parentīs,

nam color in pōmō est, ubi permātūruit, āter,

95 quodque rogīs superest ūnā requiēscit in urnā.

**mox** soon

**pullus** dark-colored; ***aptus** suited

***mūcrō** point, blade

**permātūrēscō** ripen

**requiēscō** rest

## SELECTION VIII. NIOBE

*Niobe foolishly boasts of her superiority to the goddess Latona.*

Ecce, venit comitum Niobē celeberrima turbā,

et, quantum īra sinit, fōrmōsa, movēnsque decōrō

cum capite immissōs umerum per utrumque capil-

lōs.

Cōnstitit, utque oculōs circumtulit alta superbōs,

5 "Quis furor, audītōs," inquit, "praepōnere vīsīs

caelestīs, aut cūr colitur Lātōna per ārās,

nūmen adhūc sine tūre meum est? Mihi Tantalus

auctor,

cui licuit sōlī superōrum tangere mēnsās;

Plēiadum soror est genetrīx mea; maximus Atlās

10 est avus, aetherium quī fert cervīcibus axem;

*celeber frequented, sur-rounded

fōrmōsus beautiful

**capillus hair

circumferō cast around

praepōnō place before, prefer

tūs incense

95. **quodque rogīs superest:** *and what remains from their pyres;* i.e., their ashes.

SELECTION VIII. This story is taken from *Metamorphoses* VI, 165–312. Niobe, queen of Thebes and proud mother of seven sons and seven daughters, uttered blasphemy against the goddess Latona and as a punishment her children were

destroyed and she herself was turned to stone. 3. **immissōs:** *hanging down.* 4. **alta:** *disdainfully.* 5. **furor:** supply est. 7. **Tantalus:** father of Niobe and son of Jupiter. He was punished in the underworld for insulting the gods. 9. **Plēiadum:** *of the Pleiades,* seven daughters of Atlas who were changed into a constellation.

LATONA AND THE DAUGHTERS OF NIOBE
From a wall painting in Herculaneum.

Juppiter alter avus; socerō quoque glōrior illō.  **glōrior** boast of, take pride in

Mē gentēs metuunt Phrygiae, mē rēgia Cadmī  **rēgia** royal palace

sub dominā est, fidibusque meī commissa marītī  **domina** mistress

moenia cum populīs ā mēque virōque reguntur.

In quamcumque domūs advertī lūmina partem,  15

immēnsae spectantur opēs. Accēdit eōdem

digna deā faciēs. Hūc nātās adjice septem,  **adjiciō** add

et totidem juvenīs, et mox generōsque nurūsque.  **nurus** daughter-in-law

Quaerite nunc habeat quam nostra superbia cau-  **superbia** pride

    sam;

nesciō quōque audēte satam Tītānida Coeō  20

Lātōnam praeferre mihī.

Nec caelō nec humō nec aquīs dea vestra recepta

    est;

exsul erat mundī, dōnec, miserāta vagantem,  **exsul** exile; **mundus** world

'Hospita tū terrīs errās, ego,' dīxit, 'in undīs,'  **hospita** stranger

īnstabilemque locum Dēlos dedit.  25  **īnstabilis** unstable, unsteady

Major sum quam cui possit Fortūna nocēre.

Īte (satis prō prōle sacrī est) laurumque capillīs  \*\*\***laurus** laurel, laurel wreath; \*\*\***capillus** hair

pōnite." Dēpōnunt, īnfectaque sacra relinquunt;  **infectus** not done, uncompleted

quodque licet, tacitō venerantur murmure nūmen.  \*\***veneror** worship

*Latona in anger asks Apollo and Diana to avenge her.*

    Indignāta dea est, summōque in vertice Cynthī  30

tālibus est dictīs geminā cum prōle locūta:

"Ēn ego, vestra parēns, vōbīs animōsa creātīs,  **animōsus** spirited, proud; \*\***creō** produce

et, nisi Jūnōnī, nūllī cessūra deārum,

an dea sim dubitor, perque omnia saecula cultīs

---

**genetrīx:** i.e., Dione, one of the Hyades, who were sisters of the Pleiades. **11. Juppiter:** supply **est. socerō illō:** i.e., in Jupiter, father of Amphion, Niobe's husband. **12. mē:** abl. with **sub** in line 13. **Cadmī:** *of Cadmus,* founder of Thebes. **13. fidibus commissa:** *built by the lyre.* **16–17. Accēdit . . . faciēs:** *In addition to this, I have a face worthy of a goddess.* **20–21. nesciō . . . mihī:** *and dare to prefer to me Latona, daughter of a Titan, sprung from Coeus, whoever he is.*

**23. miserāta:** modifies **Dēlos,** which is subject of **dīxit** as well as of **dedit.** Delos, a wanderer on the sea, took pity on Latona, a wanderer on the earth. **24. ego:** supply **errō. 27. satis . . . est:** *there is enough sacrificing for* (Latona's) *offspring* (Apollo and Diana). **28. pōnite:** *lay aside.* **31. geminā cum prōle:** *with her twin offspring,* i.e., with Apollo and Diana. **32. vōbīs . . . creātīs:** *proud of having borne you.* **34. cultīs:** modifies **ārīs** in line 35.

<sub>35</sub>arceor, ō nātī, nisi vōs succurritis, ārīs.

Nec dolor hic sōlus: dīrō convīcia factō

Tantalis adjēcit vōsque est postpōnere nātīs

ausa suīs, et mē (quod in ipsam recidat!) orbam

dīxit, et exhibuit linguam scelerāta paternam."

<sub>40</sub>Adjectūra precēs erat hīs Lātōna relātīs:

"Dēsine," Phoebus ait; "poenae mora longa que-

rēla est."

Dīxit idem Phoebē, celerīque per āera lāpsū

contigerant tēctī Cadmēida nūbibus arcem.

Plānus erat lātēque patēns prope moenia campus.

. . . . . . . . . . .

*Niobe, grief-stricken at the loss of her seven sons,*
*still boasts of her seven daughters.*

45 Heu! quantum haec Niobē Niobē distābat ab illā,

quae modo Lātōīs populum submōverat ārīs,

et mediam tulerat gressūs resupīna per urbem,

invidiōsa suīs, at nunc miseranda vel hostī!

Corporibus gelidīs incumbit et ōrdine nūllō

<sub>50</sub>ōscula dispēnsat nātōs suprēma per omnīs.

Ā quibus ad caelum līventia bracchia tollēns,

"Pāscere, crūdēlis, nostrō, Lātōna, dolōre,

pāscere," ait, "satiāque meō tua pectora lūctū,

corque ferum satiā," dīxit; "per fūnera septem

<sub>55</sub>efferor. Exsultā, victrīxque, inimīca, triumphā!

Cūr autem victrīx? Miserae mihi plūra supersunt

quam tibi fēlīcī; post tot quoque fūnera vincō."

---

**Margin glosses:**

convīcium wrangling, abusive word
postpōnō place after
recidō fall back; orbus childless
exhibeō display; paternus of one's father
***dēsinō cease; **querēla complaint
lāpsus glide; descent
*plānus level
distō differ
submoveō drive away
resupīnus with head thrown back, haughty
invidiōsus envied
dispēnsō dispense
līvēns dark, livid
satiō satiate, feed full
***exsultō exult; victrīx victress

---

**35.** ārīs: abl. with **arceor**. **36.** sōlus: supply est. **37.** Tantalis: *daughter of Tantalus*, i.e., Niobe. **38.** quod . . . recidat: *and may it fall upon her!* Read recidat as if spelled reccidat. **39.** linguam paternam: i.e., Niobe had spoken as boastfully as had her father Tantalus, when he revealed the secrets of the gods. **41.** poenae . . . est: *your long complaint only delays punishment.* **42.** Phoebē: *Diana.* **43.** Cadmēida: *Cadmean*, i.e., Theban; Greek acc., modifying **arcem**. **44.** Plānus . . .

campus: In the passage that follows in the original text Ovid describes how Apollo slew with his arrows the seven sons of Niobe, who were engaged in various sports on the plain just outside the city walls, and how her husband slew himself for grief.
**46.** Lātōīs ārīs: *from Latona's altars.* **52.** Pāscere: *feast yourself;* passive imperative with reflexive force. **55.** efferor: *I am carried out* (for burial).

*Diana slays Niobe's seven daughters.*

Dīxerat, et sonuit contentō nervus ab arcū,
quī praeter Niobēn ūnam conterruit omnīs;
illa malō est audāx. Stābant cum vestibus ātrīs 60
ante torōs frātrum dēmissō crīne sorōrēs,
ē quibus ūna, trahēns haerentia vīscere tēla,
impositō frātrī moribunda relanguit ōre;
altera, sōlārī miseram cōnāta parentem,
conticuit subitō, duplicātaque vulnere caecō est, 65
ōraque compressit, nisi postquam spīritus ībat.
Haec frūstrā fugiēns conlābitur; illa sorōrī
immoritur; latet haec, illam trepidāre vidērēs,
sexque datīs lētō dīversaque vulnera passīs
ultima restābat, quam tōtō corpore māter, 70
tōtā veste tegēns, "Ūnam minimamque relinque!
Dē multīs minimam poscō," clāmāvit, "et ūnam,"
dumque rogat, prō quā rogat, occidit. Orba resēdit
exanimīs inter nātōs nātāsque virumque.

**contentus** tight-drawn; *nervus string, bowstring
**conterreō** frighten, alarm

**moribundus** dying; **relanguēscō** grow faint, collapse

**duplicō** bend double

**comprimō** press together, close;
***spīritus** breath, soul

**immorior** die upon

**orbus** bereaved, childless
**exanimis** lifeless, dead

*Niobe is turned into stone but forever weeps.*

Dēriguitque malīs; nūllōs movet aura capillōs, 75
in vultū color est sine sanguine, lūmina maestīs
stant immōta genīs; nihil est in imāgine vīvum.
Flet tamen, et, validī circumdata turbine ventī,
in patriam rapta est; ibi fīxa cacūmine montis
līquitur, et lacrimās etiam nunc marmora mānant. 80

**dērigēscō** grow rigid, stiffen

**līquor** melt, dissolve; **mānō** drop, shed

## SELECTION IX. PHAËTHON

*The palace of the Sun is described.*

Rēgia Sōlis erat sublīmibus alta columnīs;
argentī biforēs radiābant lūmine valvae.

**rēgia** royal palace

**biforis** double; **radiō** shine, gleam; **valva** door

---

**58. arcū:** i.e., Diana's bow. **66. nisi . . . ībat:** *except after her breath left her* (body). **68. vidērēs:** *one might have seen.* **69. sex:** understand **fīliābus.** **79. patriam:** i.e., Lydia.

SELECTION IX. This story is taken, in an abridged form, from *Metamorphoses* II, 1–328. Phaëthon sets out to visit his father, the Sun, who receives him kindly and offers him any gift

illīc there
caelō carve, engrave

Māteriam superābat opus, nam Mulciber illīc
aequora caelārat mediās cingentia terrās,
5 terrārumque orbem, caelumque quod imminet orbī.
Terra virōs urbīsque gerit, silvāsque, ferāsque,
flūminaque, et nymphās, et cētera nūmina rūris.
Haec super imposita est caelī fulgentis imāgō,
signaque sex foribus dextrīs, totidemque sinistrīs.

*Phaëthon comes to the palace and asks permission to drive the chariot of the Sun.*

acclīvis sloping, ascending

10 Quō simul acclīvī Clymenēia līmite prōlēs
vēnit, et intrāvit dubitātī tēcta parentis,
prōtinus ad patriōs sua fert vēstīgia vultūs,

propior nearer

cōnsistitque procul, neque enim propiōra ferēbat
lūmina; purpureā vēlātus veste sedēbat

solium throne; ***lūceō gleam; smaragdus emerald

15 in soliō Phoebus, clārīs lūcente smaragdīs.
Ā dextrā laevāque Diēs et Mēnsis et Annus
Saeculaque et, positae spatiīs aeqūalibus, Hōrae;

***flōreō blossom
spīceus of ears of grain

Vērque novum stābat cīnctum flōrente corōnā,
stābat nūda Aestās et spīcea serta gerēbat,

calcō tread, tread out; sordidus dirty, stained; ūva bunch of grapes
glaciālis icy; hirsūtus shaggy
novitās newness, strangeness

20 stābat et Autumnus calcātīs sordidus ūvīs,
et glaciālis Hiems, cānōs hirsūta capillōs.
Ipse locō medius rērum novitāte paventem
Sōl oculīs juvenem, quibus aspicit omnia, vīdit,
"Quae" -que "viae tibi causa? Quid hāc," ait,
"arce petīstī,

īnfitior deny, repudiate
mundus world

25 prōgeniēs, Phaëthōn, haud īnfitianda parentī?"
Ille refert, "Ō lūx immēnsī pūblica mundī,
Phoebe pater, sī dās ūsum mihi nōminis hujus,

*pignus pledge; propāgō progeny, offspring

pignora dā, genitor, per quae tua vēra propāgō

that Phaëthon may choose. Phaëthon asks permission to drive the chariot of the Sun for one day and the results are tragic. **3. opus:** *the craftsmanship.* **Mulciber:** another name for Vulcan. **4. caelārat: caelāverat. 8. Haec super:** *above these,* i.e., on the upper part of the door and above the representations of scenes on the earth. **9. signa:** the twelve signs of the zodiac: aries, taurus, gemini, cancer, leo, virgo, libra, scorpius, arcitenens, caper, amphora, pisces. **10. Clymenēia:** *of Clymene,* Phaëthon's mother. **11. dubitātī:** Phaëthon had come to find out whether the Sun was really his father. **17. spatiīs aequālibus:** *at equal distances* (apart). **22. locō medius:** in locō mediō. **24. causa:** supply est. **26. pūblica:** *common.*

crēdar, et hunc animīs errōrem dētrahe nostrīs!''
Dīxerat; at genitor circum caput omne micantīs 30
dēposuit radiōs, propiusque accēdere jussit,
amplexūque datō, "Nec tū meus esse negārī
dignus es, et Clymenē vērōs,'' ait, "ēdidit ortūs;
quōque minus dubitēs, quodvīs pete mūnus, ut
     illud
mē tribuente ferās!''                                             35
Vix bene dēsierat, currūs rogat ille paternōs,
inque diem ālipedum jūs et moderāmen equōrum.

*dētrahō draw off, take away*

*amplexus embrace*

*ēdō give out, declare; ortus rising, origin*
*\*quīvīs any (you wish)*

*paternus of one's father, paternal*
*ālipēs wing-footed; moderāmen control*

### The Sun tries to dissuade Phaëthon.

Paenituit jūrāsse patrem, quī, terque quaterque
concutiēns inlūstre caput, "Temerāria,'' dīxit,
"vōx mea facta tuā est. Utinam prōmissa licēret 40
nōn dare! Cōnfiteor, sōlum hoc tibi, nāte, negā-
     rem.
Dissuādēre licet: nōn est tua tūta voluntās!
Magna petis, Phaëthōn, et quae nec vīribus istīs
mūnera conveniant nec tam puerīlibus annīs.
Sors tua mortālis: nōn est mortāle quod optās!  45
          Vāstī quoque rēctor Olympī,
quī fera terribilī jaculātur fulmina dextrā,
nōn aget hōs currūs: et quid Jove majus habēmus?
Ardua prīma via est et quā vix māne recentēs
ēnītuntur equī; mediō est altissima caelō.  50
Ultima prōna via est, et eget moderāmine certō.
Finge datōs currūs. Quid agēs? Poterisne rotātīs
obvius īre polīs, nē tē citus auferat axis?
Nec tibi quadrupedīs animōsōs ignibus illīs,
quōs in pectore habent, quōs ōre et nāribus efflant, 55
in prōmptū regere est; vix mē patiuntur, ubi ācrēs

*\*\*paenitet it repents*

*\*\*inlūstris bright, lustrous; temerārius rash*

*cōnfiteor confess*

*dissuādeō dissuade*

*puerīlis boyish, youthful*

*rēctor ruler*

*māne in the morning*
*ēnītor struggle up*
*moderāmen control*
*rotō whirl*
*\*\*\*obvius in the way of; obvius īre go to meet*
*animōsus spirited*
*nāris nostril; efflō blow forth, breathe out*
*in prōmptū easy*

---

**36. dēsierat:** *had he ceased* (speaking). **37. in diem:** *for a day.*
   **45.** mortālis: supply est. **46. quoque:** *even.*
rēctor Olympī: i.e., Jupiter. **52–53. Poterisne**

. . . **axis?:** *Will you be able to go contrary to the whirling heavens without letting the swift chariot carry you off?* **54–56. Nec tibi in prōmptū regere est:** *Nor is it easy for you to control.*

incalēscō grow hot; **repugnō**
fight against, oppose
***caveō** beware; **corrigō** change

**circumspiciō** look about at

**repulsa** refusal

***dēprecor** pray to be delivered
from

**blandus** persuasive, coaxing;
****lacertus** arm

**sapienter** wisely; cf. ***sapiēns**
wise

**repugnō** oppose

**prōpositum** purpose; ****flagrō**
burn, be afire

**tēmō** pole (*of a chariot*)

**curvātūra** curve; **argenteus** of
silver

**vigil** wakeful, awake; **nitidus**
shining; ****patefaciō** open
**rosa** rose

**medicāmen** drug, ointment

**praesāgus** foreboding

**sollicitus** anxious; **suspīrium**
sigh
**monitum** warning

****stimulus** goad

**inhibeō** check, hold back

incaluēre animī, cervīxque repugnat habēnīs.
Nāte, cavē, dum rēsque sinit, tua corrige vōta!
Dēnique quidquid habet dīves circumspice mun-
        dus,
60 ēque tot ac tantīs caelī terraeque marisque
posce bonīs aliquid: nūllam patiēre repulsam!
Dēprecor hoc ūnum, quod vērō nōmine poena,
nōn honor, est; poenam, Phaëthōn, prō mūnere
        poscis.
Quid mea colla tenēs blandīs, ignāre, lacertīs?
65 Nē dubitā; dabitur (Stygiās jūrāvimus undās),
quodcumque optāris; sed tū sapientius optā!"

*The Sun reluctantly grants Phaëthon's request and*
*gives him careful directions.*

Fīnierat monitūs. Dictīs tamen ille repugnat,
prōpositumque premit, flagratque cupīdine currūs.
Ergō, quā licuit, genitor cūnctātus ad altōs
70 dēdūcit juvenem, Vulcānia mūnera, currūs.
Aureus axis erat, tēmō aureus, aurea summae
curvātūra rotae, radiōrum argenteus ōrdō.
Dumque ea magnanimus Phaëthōn mīrātur opusque
perspicit, ecce vigil nitidō patefēcit ab ortū
75 purpureās Aurōra forīs et plēna rosārum
ātria; diffugiunt stellae, quārum agmina cōgit
Lūcifer, et caelī statiōne novissimus exit.
Tum pater ōra suī sacrō medicāmine nātī
contigit et rapidae fēcit patientia flammae,
80 imposuitque comae radiōs, praesāgaque lūctūs
pectore sollicitō repetēns suspīria dīxit:
"Sī potes hīs saltem monitīs pārēre parentis,
parce, puer, stimulīs, et fortius ūtere lōrīs!
Sponte suā properant: labor est inhibēre volentīs.

---

**60–61. ēque bonīs:** *and from the good things.*
**64. Quid:** *why.* **66. optāris:** optāveris.
**67. ille:** i.e., Phaëthon. **74. ab ortū:** *in the east.*

**76–77. quārum . . . Lūcifer:** *and Lucifer brings up*
*the rear.* **79. patientia:** *able to endure;* modifies
ōra in line 78.

Utque ferant aequōs et caelum et terra calōrēs,          85 **calor** heat
nec preme nec summum mōlīre per aethera currum!
Altius ēgressus, caelestia tēcta cremābis,                **cremō** burn
īnferius terrās: mediō tūtissimus ībis.                   **īnferius** too low
Inter utrumque tenē! Fortūnae cētera mandō.
Dum loquor, Hesperiō positās in lītore mētās             90
ūmida nox tetigit; nōn est mora lībera nōbīs.
Corripe lōra manū — vel, sī mūtābile pectus              **mūtābilis** capable of change
est tibi, cōnsiliīs, nōn curribus, ūtere nostrīs!''

*Phaëthon soon loses control of the horses.*

   Occupat ille levem juvenālī corpore currum,          **juvenālis** youthful
statque super, manibusque datās contingere ha- 95
    bēnās
gaudet et invītō grātīs agit inde parentī.               **invītus** unwilling
Intereā volucrēs Pyroīs et Eōus et Aethōn,
Sōlis equī, quārtusque Phlegōn hinnītibus aurās          **hinnītus** neighing
flammiferīs implent, pedibusque repāgula pulsant.        **flammifer** flame-bearing; **re-**
        **pāgula** fastenings; bars
               Ruunt, trītumque relinquunt   100 **terō** rub, wear down, beat
quadrijugī spatium, nec quō prius ōrdine currunt.        **quadrijugī** four-horse team
Ipse pavet, nec quā commissās flectat habēnās
nec scit quā sit iter, nec, sī sciat, imperet illīs.
Tum prīmum radiīs gelidī caluēre Triōnēs.
Ut vērō summō dispexit ab aethere terrās                 105 **dispiciō** see
īnfēlīx Phaëthōn penitus penitusque patentīs,
palluit, et subitō genua intremuēre timōre,              **pallēscō** turn pale; **\*\*genū**
        knee; **intremō** tremble
suntque oculīs tenebrae per tantum lūmen obortae,
et jam māllet equōs numquam tetigisse paternōs,
jam cognōsse genus piget et valuisse rogandō.            110 **piget** it is a matter of regret
Quid faciat? Multum caelī post terga relictum,
ante oculōs plūs est! Animō mētītur utrumque,            **\*\*mētior** measure
quidque agat ignārus stupet, et nec frēna remittit,      **\*\*\*frēnum** rein
nec retinēre valet, nec nōmina nōvit equōrum.            **retineō** hold in check

---

**94. ille:** i.e., Phaëthon. **96. grātīs agit:** *gives*    ran. **102. quā** (viā): *how;* abl. of manner. **103. quā**
*thanks.* **101. nec . . . currunt:** i.e., the horses do   (viā): *which way;* abl. of route. **110. genus:** *his*
not run in the same course in which they formerly   *origin,* i.e., the fact that the Sun is his father.

**exspatior** swerve from the ¹¹⁵Exspatiantur equī, nūllōque inhibente per aurās
track; **inhibeō** check, hold
back                                    ignōtae regiōnis eunt, quāque impetus ēgit,

                                        hāc sine lēge ruunt, altōque sub aethere fīxīs

**incursō** run into; **āvius** out of    incursant stellīs, rapiuntque per āvia currum,
the way
**dēclīvis** downward                     et modo summa petunt, modo per dēclīve viāsque

**propior** nearer                       ¹²⁰praecipitīs spatiō terrae propiōre feruntur.

*The chariot of the Sun gets too near the earth and
    sets it on fire.*

Parva queror: magnae pereunt cum moenibus
    urbēs,

cumque suīs tōtās populīs incendia gentīs

in cinerem vertunt; silvae cum montibus ārdent.

Tum vērō Phaëthōn cūnctīs ē partibus orbem

¹²⁵aspicit accēnsum, nec tantōs sustinet aestūs.

**piceus** pitchy; **cālīgō** darkness   Quōque eat, aut ubi sit, piceā cālīgine tēctus

**arbitrium** choice, will; **raptō**    nescit et arbitriō volucrum raptātur equōrum.
hurry along
**dissiliō** burst open; **penetrō**     Dissilit omne solum, penetratque in Tartara rīmīs
enter; **rīma** crack
**īnfernus** of the underworld           lūmen, et īnfernum terret cum conjuge rēgem;

**contrahō** draw together, lessen ¹³⁰et mare contrahitur, siccaeque est campus harēnae

                                        quod modo pontus erat, quōsque altum tēxerat
                                            aequor,

***exsistō** stand out, arise            exsistunt montēs et sparsās Cycladas augent.

*Mother Earth appeals to Jupiter.*

Alma tamen Tellūs sacrā sīc vōce locūta est:

"Sī placet hoc, meruīque, quid ō tua fulmina ces-
    sant,

¹³⁵summe deum? Liceat peritūrae vīribus ignis

**clādēs** disaster                      igne perīre tuō, clādemque auctōre levāre!

Quod sī nec frātris nec tē mea grātia tangit,

at caelī miserēre tuī! Circumspice utrumque,

---

**116. quāque (viā):** *and wherever.*   **117. hāc (viā).**       **135. summe deum:** i.e., Jupiter. **135–136. Li-**
**121. Parva:** *minor calamities.*  **129. cum con-**            **ceat ... tuō:** *Let me, if destined to die by the might*
juge rēgem: i.e., Pluto and Proserpina. **132. Cy-**             *of fire, perish by your lightning.* **peritūrae:** agrees
cladas: *the Cyclades,* a group of islands in the               with **mihi** understood with **liceat. 136. auctōre:**
Aegean Sea.                                                      supply tē. **137. frātris:** i.e., of Neptune.

fūmat uterque polus.  Quōs sī vitiāverit ignis,
ātria vestra ruent.  Atlās ēn ipse labōrat,                    140
vixque suīs umerīs candentem sustinet axem.
Sī freta, sī terrae pereunt, sī rēgia caelī,
in chaos antīquum cōnfundimur.  Ēripe flammīs
sī quid adhūc superest, et rērum cōnsule summae!''

*Jupiter strikes Phaëthon with a thunderbolt and he*
  *falls into the River Po.*

   At pater omnipotēns, superōs testātus et ipsum 145
quī dederat currūs, nisi opem ferat, omnia fātō
interitūra gravī, summam petit arduus arcem,
unde solet nūbīs lātīs indūcere terrīs,
unde movet tonitrūs, vibrātaque fulmina jactat;
sed neque quās posset terrīs indūcere nūbīs              150
tunc habuit nec quōs caelō dīmitteret imbrīs.
Intonat, et dextrā lībrātum fulmen ab aure
mīsit in aurīgam, pariterque animāque rotīsque
expulit, et saevīs compescuit ignibus ignīs.
Cōnsternantur equī, et saltū in contrāria factō       155
colla jugō ēripiunt, abruptaque lōra relinquunt.
At Phaëthōn, rutilōs flammā populante capillōs,
volvitur in praeceps, longōque per āera tractū
fertur, ut interdum dē caelō stella serēnō,
etsī nōn cecidit, potuit cecidisse vidērī.                    160
Quem procul ā patriā dīversō maximus orbe
excipit Ēridanus, fūmantiaque abluit ōra;
Nāides Hesperiae trifidā fūmantia flammā
corpora dant tumulō;  signant quoque carmine
  saxum:

*Hīc situs est Phaëthōn currūs aurīga paternī.*          165
*Quem sī nōn tenuit, magnīs tamen excidit ausīs.*

vitiō spoil, injure

rēgia royal palace

chaos chaos, confusion; cōnfundō mingle together

intereō perish

indūcō bring

tonitrus thunder; vibrō brandish
indūcō bring

dīmittō send

lībrō balance

aurīga charioteer

expellō drive out; compescō quell, quench
cōnsternō strike with terror; saltus leap
abrumpō break

rutilus red, auburn

tractus course, path

**interdum sometimes; ***serēnus clear

abluō wash

trifidus three-cleft, forked

aurīga charioteer

---

**144. rērum ... summae:** *have regard for the universe itself.*
**145. ipsum:** i.e., the Sun. **153–154. pariterque ... expulit:** *and both struck him dead and threw him from the chariot.* **155. in contrāria:** *in op-* posite directions. **161. dīversō orbe:** *in a remote region.* **163. Nāides:** *Naiads*, water nymphs. **164. corpora:** poetic plural. **166. Quem:** i.e., the chariot. **magnīs excidit ausīs:** *he failed in a mighty venture (he fell from great deeds of daring).*

# HORACE

## SELECTION I. A PRAYER FOR VERGIL'S SAFETY

dīva goddess
lūcidus bright

obstringō bind up, confine

5

dīmidium half

triplex triple, threefold

circā around; fragilis frail; 10
trux wild, fierce

dēcertō struggle

arbiter judge; ruler, lord     15

natō swim

īnfāmis of ill report, notorious 20

abscindō tear asunder, separate

prūdēns foreseeing, wise; dis-
sociābilis incompatible

trānsiliō leap across

Sīc tē dīva potēns Cyprī,
  sīc frātrēs Helenae, lūcida sīdera,
ventōrumque regat pater
  obstrictīs aliīs praeter Iāpyga,
nāvis, quae tibi crēditum
  dēbēs Vergilium fīnibus Atticīs,
reddās incolumem precor
  et servēs anĭmae dīmidium meae.

Illī rōbur et aes triplex
  circā pectus erat, quī fragilem trucī
commīsit pelagō ratem
  prīmus, nec timuit praecipitem Āfricum
dēcertantem Aquilōnibus
  nec trīstis Hyadās nec rabiem Notī,
quō nōn arbiter Hadriae
  major, tollere seu pōnere vult freta.

Quem mortis timuit gradum,
  quī siccīs oculīs mōnstra natantia,
quī vīdit mare turbidum et
  īnfāmīs scopulōs, Acroceraunia?
Nēquīquam deus abscidit
  prūdēns Ōceanō dissociābilī
terrās, sī tamen impiae
  nōn tangenda ratēs trānsiliunt vada.

SELECTION I. Horace's *Odes* I, 3, 1–24. See App. 17 and 35,. 6. The poet Vergil has sailed for Greece and Horace fears for his friend's safety. The poem is addressed to the ship. **1. tē:** obj. of **regat. dīva:** i.e., Venus. **potēns Cyprī:** *ruler over Cyprus;* Cyprus was closely associated with the worship of Venus. **2. frātrēs Helenae:** i.e., Castor and Pollux, who formed the constellation called Gemini. **3. ventōrum pater:** i.e., Aeolus. **4. ob**strictīs . . . **Iāpyga:** *all the others except Iapyx being kept imprisoned.* This wind blew from Southeastern Italy toward Greece. **5. crēditum:** *intrusted.* **6. Atticīs:** *of Athens,* i.e., of Greece. **15. Hadriae:** *of the Adriatic,* the sea that lies between Italy and Greece. **16. tollere . . . freta:** *whether he wills to raise or calm the seas.* **20. Acroceraunia:** a dangerous promontory forming the northwestern extremity of Epirus.

BUST OF HORACE

## SELECTION II. THE GOLDEN MEAN

Rēctius vīvēs, Licinī, neque altum
semper urgendō neque, dum procellās
cautus horrēscis, nimium premendō
  lītus inīquum.

***rēctē* properly

**procella** gust, blast

**cautus** careful, wary; **horrēscō** shudder at, fear

Auream quisquis mediocritātem
dīligit, tūtus caret obsolētī
sordibus tēctī, caret invidendā
  sōbrius aulā.

5 **mediocritās** mean, middle ground
**obsolētus** old, run-down

**sordēs** filth, squalor

**sōbrius** sober, moderate; **aula** palace

Saepius ventīs agitātur ingēns
pīnus et celsae graviōre cāsū
dēcidunt turrēs feriuntque summōs
  fulgura montīs.

10 ***pīnus** pine tree

**dēcidō** fall

**fulgur** lightning

Sperat īnfestīs, metuit secundīs
alteram sortem bene praeparātum
pectus. Īnfōrmīs hiemēs redūcit
  Juppiter, īdem

***īnfestus** unsafe, dangerous

**praeparō** prepare, make ready beforehand
15 **infōrmis** hideous, horrid

submovet. Nōn, sī male nunc, et ōlim
sīc erit: quondam citharā tacentem
suscitat Mūsam neque semper arcum
  tendit Apollō.

**submoveō** remove

**cithara** lute, lyre

**suscitō** arouse

20

Rēbus angustīs animōsus atque
fortis appārē; sapienter īdem
contrahēs ventō nimium secundō
  turgida vēla.

**animōsus** spirited, courageous

**sapienter** wisely; cf. ***sapiēns** wise
**contrahō** draw in, reef

**turgidus** distended, swollen

---

SELECTION II. Horace's *Odes* II, 10. For the meter see App. 35, 2. The present ode is one of Horace's most finished poems. It consists of a defense of Horace's favorite doctrine of the "golden mean," that is, of moderation in all things. **1–2. Licinī:** *Licinius*, a friend of Horace. In 23 B.C. Licinius was a colleague of Augustus in the consulship. **altum urgendō:** *by pressing out to sea.* **3–4. nimium . . . inīquum:** *by hugging too* closely the dangerous shore. **7. sordibus:** abl. with caret. **7–8. invidendā aulā:** i.e., moderation will save a man from becoming the victim of envy as the lord of a palatial mansion. **13. infestīs (rēbus):** *in adversity (in adverse circumstances).* **secundīs (rēbus):** *in prosperity (in favorable circumstances).* **14. alteram sortem:** *a different lot.* **21. Rēbus angustīs:** *in times of stress;* cf. **infestīs (rēbus)** and **secundīs (rēbus)** in line 13.

## Selection III. The Ship of State

**fortiter** boldly, manfully

Ō nāvis, referent in mare tē novī
flūctūs! Ō quid agis? Fortiter occupā
portum! Nōnne vidēs ut
nūdum rēmigiō latus

**mālus** mast

**antemna** sailyard

**dūrō** endure, withstand

**imperiōsus** imperious, domineering

**linteum** linen cloth; sail

**fīlia** daughter

**inūtilis** useless, profitless

**fīdō** trust

**lūdibrium** sport, jest; **\*\*caveō** take care, beware

**\*\*nūper** recently; **sollicitus** apprehensive; **taedium** loathing, disgust
**dēsīderium** heart's desire

5    et mālus celerī saucius Āfricō
antemnaeque gemant, ac sine fūnibus
vix dūrāre carīnae
possint imperiōsius

aequor? Nōn tibi sunt integra lintea,
10    nōn dī, quōs iterum pressa vocēs mālō.
Quamvīs Pontica pīnus,
silvae fīlia nōbilis,

Jactēs et genus et nōmen inūtile,
nīl pīctīs timidus nāvita puppibus
15    fīdit. Tū, nisi ventīs
dēbēs lūdibrium, cavē.

Nūper sollicitum quae mihi taedium,
nunc dēsīderium cūraque nōn levis,
interfūsa nitentīs
20    vītēs aequora Cycladās.

## Selection IV. Horace's Monument

**perennis** lasting

**situs** situation; structure

**edāx** devouring; **impotēns** unbridled, unrestrained

Exēgī monumentum aere perennius
rēgālīque sitū pȳramidum altius,
quod nōn imber edāx, nōn Aquilō impotēns

---

Selection III. Horace's *Odes* I, 14. For the meter see App. 35, 7. **1. nāvis:** *ship* (of state). **2. flūctūs:** i.e., billows of a threatened civil war. **occupā:** *make for.* **4. nūdum rēmigiō:** *stripped of oars.* **10. dī:** i.e., images of the gods placed in the stern. **11. Pontica:** *of Pontus,* a region on the Black Sea famous for its pines and shipbuilding. **15–16. ventīs dēbēs lūdibrium:** *you are to be the sport of the winds.* **17. quae taedium:** tū quae taedium erās. Horace as a young man had been opposed to and disgusted with Augustus's government of Rome but later became a supporter of Augustus and a distinguished member of the court circle. **18. dēsīderium:** tū quae dēsīderium es. **20. Cycladās:** secondary object of interfūsa.

Selection IV. Horace's *Odes* III, 30. For the meter see App. 35, 5.

possit dīruere aut innumerābilis

annōrum seriēs et fuga temporum.

Nōn omnis moriar, multaque pars meī

vītābit Libitīnam; usque ego posterā

crēscam laude recēns, dum Capitōlium

scandet cum tacitā virgine pontifex.

Dīcar, quā violēns obstrepit Aufidus

et quā pauper aquae Daunus agrestium

rēgnāvit populōrum, ex humilī potēns

prīnceps Aeolium carmen ad Italōs

dēdūxisse modōs. Sūme superbiam

quaesītam meritīs et mihi Delphicā

laurō cinge volēns, Melpomenē, comam.

dīruō destroy

5 seriēs succession, course

scandō climb, mount; **pontifex** high priest

10 **violēns** impetuous; **obstrepō** roar, resound
**\*\*agrestis** rustic

**superbia** pride

15 **meritum** merit

### SELECTION V. INTEGER VĪTAE

Integer vītae scelerisque pūrus

nōn eget Maurīs jaculīs neque arcū

nec venēnātīs gravidā sagittīs,

Fusce, pharetrā,

sīve per Syrtīs iter aestuōsās,

sīve factūrus per inhospitālem

Caucasum vel quae loca fābulōsus

lambit Hydaspēs.

Namque mē silvā lupus in Sabīnā,

dum meam cantō Lalagēn et ultrā

terminum cūrīs vagor expedītīs,

fūgit inermem,

**\*\*\*jaculum** dart, javelin

**venēnō** poison, make poisonous; **gravidus** heavy, loaded

5 **aestuōsus** summer-like, sweltering
**inhospitālis** inhospitable

**fābulōsus** celebrated in story

**lambō** lick; wash

**\*\*\*lupus** wolf

10 **cantō** sing of; **ultrā** beyond

**\*\*terminus** boundary

---

**7. Libitīnam:** *Libitina,* the goddess of burial, hence funeral pyre. **10. Aufidus:** a river in Apulia near Horace's birthplace. **10–14. Dīcar prīnceps dēdūxisse:** *I shall be spoken of as having been the first to adapt.* **11. pauper aquae:** *poor in water.* **12. populōrum:** gen. depending on **rēgnāvit,** a Greek usage. **ex humilī potēns:** a reference to Horace's humble origin. **14. Sūme superbiam:** *Take honorable pride.* **15. quaesītam meritīs:** *won by your merits.* **Delphicā:** the laurel was sacred to Apollo, whose oracle was at Delphi. **16. Melpomenē:** muse of lyric poetry.

SELECTION V. Horace's *Odes* I, 22. For the meter see App. 35, 2. This is one of the best known of Horace's odes. It is to be found in most college songbooks. **1. Integer ... pūrus:** *He who is of blameless life and free from guilt.* **vītae:** gen. with **Integer. sceleris:** gen. with **pūrus. 2. Maurīs:** *Moorish.* **4. Fusce:** *Fuscus,* a friend of Horace. **8. Hydaspēs:** a river in the northwestern part of India. **9. Sabīnā:** *Sabine.* **10. Lalagēn:** *Lalage,* a girl's name. **11. cūrīs expedītīs:** *with care thrown off.* **12. inermem:** (though) *unarmed;* modifies **mē** in line 9.

<table>
<tr><td>

**portentum** monstrosity; **mīli-**
**tāris** soldier-producing
**aesculētum** oak forest

**generō** beget, produce     15

</td><td>

quāle portentum neque mīlitāris
Daunias lātīs alit aesculētīs
nec Jubae tellūs generat, leōnum
    ārida nūtrīx.

</td></tr>
<tr><td>

**piger** lazy, sluggish; barren

**aestīvus** of summer; **recreō** re-
   fresh

    20

</td><td>

Pōne mē pigrīs ubi nūlla campīs
arbor aestīvā recreātur aurā,
quod latus mundī nebulae malusque
    Juppiter urget;

</td></tr>
</table>

pōne sub currū nimium propinquī
sōlis in terrā domibus negātā:
dulce rīdentem Lalagēn amābō,
    dulce loquentem.

## Selection VI. A Moneylender Turns Farmer — Almost

<table>
<tr><td>

**\*\*\*beātus** blessed, fortunate

</td><td>

"Beātus ille quī procul negōtiīs,
    ut prīsca gēns mortālium,
paterna rūra bōbus exercet suīs,

</td></tr>
<tr><td>

**faenus** interest, money lending

**excitō** rouse up, call forth;  5
   **classicum** battle-signal (*on
   the trumpet*); **trux** harsh
**īrātus** angry; cf. **\*īrāscor** be-
   come angry

</td><td>

    solūtus omnī faenore,
neque excitātur classicō mīles trucī,
    neque horret īrātum mare,
forumque vītat et superba cīvium
    potentiōrum līmina.

</td></tr>
<tr><td>

**adultus** grown-up; **vītis** vine

**marītō** wed     10

**\*\*\*mūgiō** low

**prōspectō** gaze upon; **\*\*grex**
   flock, herd
**falx** sickle, pruning knife; **am-**
   **putō** cut off
**īnserō** graft on

</td><td>

Ergō aut adulta vītium propāgine
    altās marītat pōpulōs,
aut in reductā valle mūgientium
    prōspectat errantīs gregēs,
inūtilīsve falce rāmōs amputāns
    fēlīciōrēs īnserit,

</td></tr>
</table>

---

**14. Daunias:** *land of Daunus*, mythical king of Apulia. **15. Jubae:** *of Juba*, king of the Numidians in Africa. **19. malus:** *unkindly.* **20. urget:** *broods over.*

Selection VI. Horace's *Epodes* 2, slightly abridged. See App. 17 and 35, 8. **2.** ut . . .

**mortālium:** i.e., as men lived in the Golden Age. **5. mīles:** *as a soldier.* **7. forum:** the center of public and private business in a Roman town. **7–8. superba līmina:** the reference is to the sa-lūtātiō, the morning call of clients on their patron. **11. mūgientium:** *of lowing* (cattle).

aut pressa pūrīs mella condit amphorīs,

aut tondet īnfirmās ovīs.

Vel, cum decōrum mītibus pōmīs caput

Autumnus agrīs extulit,

ut gaudet īnsitīva dēcerpēns pira

certantem et ūvam purpurae!

Libet jacēre modo sub antīquā īlice,

modo in tenācī grāmine.

Lābuntur altīs interim rīpīs aquae,

queruntur in silvīs avēs,

fontēsque lymphīs obstrepunt mānantibus,

somnōs quod invītet levīs.

At cum tonantis annus hībernus Jovis

imbrīs nivīsque comparat,

aut trūdit acrīs hinc et hinc multā cane

aprōs in obstantīs plagās,

aut amite lēvī rāra tendit rētia,

turdīs edācibus dolōs,

pavidumque leporem et advenam laqueō gruem

jūcunda captat praemia.

Quis nōn malārum, quās amor cūrās habet,

haec inter oblīvīscitur?

Quod sī pudīca mulier in partem juvet

domum atque dulcīs līberōs,

Sabīna quālis aut perusta sōlibus

pernīcis uxor Apulī,

sacrum vetustīs exstruat lignīs focum

lassī sub adventum virī,

claudēnsque textīs crātibus laetum pecus

distenta siccet ūbera,

et horna dulcī vīna prōmēns dōliō

dapēs inēmptās adparet,

---

**15** amphora storage jar

***tondeō shear; īnfirmus weak; docile; ovis sheep

īnsitīvus grafted; dēcerpō pick; pirum pear

**20** ūva bunch of grapes; ***purpura purple color

libet it is pleasing

tenāx clinging, matted

**25** lympha water; obstrepō murmur; mānō drop, drip

invītō invite

**tonō thunder

**nix snow; comparō make ready

trūdō push, drive

**30** aper wild boar; plaga net

ames net-pole; *lēvis smooth; rārus wide-meshed; rēte net

turdus thrush; edāx greedy

lepus hare; advena stranger, migrant; laqueus noose, snare; grus crane

**jūcundus pleasing

**35**

pudīcus modest, virtuous

perustus sunburned, tanned

**40** pernīx nimble, agile

vetustus old, well-seasoned; exstruō pile; lignum wood; focus fireplace

lassus weary; adventus coming, arrival

crātis wickerwork

distentus distended, full; siccō make dry, milk dry

**45** hornus this year's; prōmō bring forth; dōlium jar

inēmptus unbought; adparō prepare

---

**18.** agrīs: *above the fields.* **19.** ut: *how.* **20.** certantem . . . purpurae: *and the grape vying with purple;* purpurae is dat. **32.** dolōs: *snares;* in appos. with rētia. **37.** in partem juvet: *should*    help for her part to care for. **39.** Sabīna: *a Sabine woman.* Roman writers frequently refer to the Sabines as ideals of domestic virtue. **40.** Apulī: *of an Apulian.*

conchȳlium shellfish, oyster

rhombus flatfish, turbot; scarus
scar, *a kind of fish*

ovis sheep

vōmer plowshare; invertō in-
vert

faenerātor moneylender

rūsticus farmer

*Īdūs Ides, *mid-month day*

*Kalendae Kalends, *first day of*
*the month*

      nōn mē Lucrīna jūverint conchȳlia
      magisve rhombus aut scarī.
      Hās inter epulās ut juvat pāstās ovīs
50     vidēre properantis domum,
      vidēre fessōs vōmerem inversum bovēs
      collō trahentīs languidō!"
      Haec ubi locūtus faenerātor Alfius,
      jam jam futūrus rūsticus,
55     omnem redēgit Īdibus pecūniam,
      quaerit Kalendīs pōnere.

## PHAEDRUS

### Selection I. Don't Be Deceived by Flattery

subdolus deceitful

paenitentia repentance

fenestra window; corvus crow;
cāseus cheese

comedō eat

vulpēs fox

corvus crow; nitor brightness,
sheen

decor beauty

**stultus foolish, stupid

cāseus cheese; celeriter quickly

dolōsus tricky; vulpēs fox;
**dēns tooth

corvus crow; dēcipiō deceive;
stupor stupidity

      Quī sē laudārī gaudet verbīs subdolīs,
      sērā dat poenās turpēs paenitentiā.
      Cum dē fenestrā corvus raptum cāseum
      comēsse vellet, celsā residēns arbore,
5     vulpēs hunc vīdit; deinde sīc coepit loquī:
      "Ō quī tuārum, corve, pinnārum est nitor!
      Quantum decōris corpore et vultū geris!
      Sī vōcem habērēs, nūlla prior āles foret."
      At ille stultus, dum vult vōcem ostendere,
10   ēmīsit ōre cāseum, quem celeriter
      dolōsa vulpēs avidīs rapuit dentibus.
      Tum dēmum ingemuit corvī dēceptus stupor.

### Selection II. Greed Brings Its Own Downfall

meritō deservedly; *appetō
seek

carō meat

      Āmittit meritō proprium quī aliēnum appetit.
      Canis per flūmen carnem dum ferret natāns,

---

**47. Lucrīna:** *of Lucrinus,* a lake on the coast of Campania. **55. redēgit:** *called in.* **55–56. Īdibus, Kalendīs:** the Ides and Kalends were the days on which the Romans settled business accounts. **56. pōnere:** *to place* (as a loan).
Selection I. Phaedrus's *Fables* I, 13. See

App. 17 and 35, 9. **1–2.** These lines contain the moral of the fable. **6. quī nitor:** *what brilliance!* **7. geris:** *you display.* **8. prior:** *superior.* **foret: esset.** **9. ille:** i.e., the crow.
Selection II. Phaedrus's *Fables* I, 4. **1.** This line contains the moral. **2. Canis:** subject of

lymphārum in speculō vīdit simulācrum suum,
aliamque praedam ab aliō cane ferrī putāns
ēripere voluit; vērum dēcepta aviditās,
et, quem tenēbat, ōre dīmīsit cibum,
nec, quem petēbat, potuit adeō attingere.

**speculum** mirror

5 ***vērum** but; **dēcipiō** deceive;
**aviditās** greediness

## Selection III. Suspect Unexpected Generosity

Repente līberālis stultīs grātus est,
vērum perītīs inritōs tendit dolōs.
Nocturnus cum fūr pānem mīsisset canī,
objectō temptāns an cibō possit capī:
"Heus," inquit, "linguam vīs meam praeclūdere,
nē lātrem prō rē dominī? Multum falleris.
Namque ista subita mē jubet benignitās
vigilāre, faciās nē meā culpā lucrum."

**līberālis** generous, liberal;
***stultus** foolish, stupid
**inritus** to no avail

**fūr** thief; **pānis** bread

5 **heus!** ho!; **praeclūdō** shut up,
stop
**lātrō** bark

**benignitās** kindness

**vigilō** be awake, be on guard;
**lucrum** gain

## Selection IV. Ambition Comes to a Bad End

Inops, potentem dum vult imitārī, perit.
In prātō quondam rāna cōnspexit bovem
et tācta invidiā tantae magnitūdinis
rūgōsam īnflāvit pellem; tum nātōs suōs
interrogāvit, an bove esset lātior.
Illī negārunt. Rūrsus intendit cutem
majōre nīsū, et similī quaesīvit modō,
quis major esset. Illī dīxērunt bovem.
Novissimē indignāta dum vult validius
īnflāre sēsē, ruptō jacuit corpore.

**inops** poor; **imitor** imitate

**prātum** meadow; **rāna** frog

**magnitūdō** size

**rūgōsus** wrinkled; **īnflō** blow
into, inflate; ***pellis** skin,
5 hide
**interrogō** ask
**cutis** skin

**nīsus** effort

**validē** strongly

10 **īnflō** blow into, inflate

---

**ferret. dum:** *while.* In prose we should expect
to find **cum ferret** or **dum ferēbat. 5. dēcepta:**
supply **est.**
SELECTION III. Phaedrus's *Fables* I, 23. The
moral of the fable is stated in the first two lines.
**1. Repente līberālis:** *a person unexpectedly gen-
erous.* **stultīs:** (only) *to fools.* **5. inquit:** under-
stand **canis** as the subject. **6. prō rē dominī:**

*in the interests of my master.* **Multum falleris:**
*You are greatly mistaken.* **8. vigilāre:** *to be awake,*
i.e., *to be on my guard.*
SELECTION IV. Phaedrus's *Fables* I, 24. The
moral of the fable is stated in the first line.
**6. Illī negārunt:** *they said 'No.'* **9. Novissimē:**
*at last.* **9-10. vult validius īnflāre sēsē:** *means
to blow herself up more.*

# MARTIAL

## SELECTION I. EPITAPH ON A LITTLE SLAVE GIRL

***commendō** hand over; commend; **dēliciae** pet
**parvulus** very small

**prōdigiōsus** marvellous, prodigious
**brūma** winter

**lascīvus** playful, frolicsome; **patrōnus** protector, patron
**blaesus** lisping; **garriō** chatter

**rigidus** stiff, hard; **caespes** sod

Hanc tibi, Fronto pater, genetrīx Flaccilla, puellam
  ōscula commendō dēliciāsque meās,
parvula nē nigrās horrēscat Erōtion umbrās
  ōraque Tartareī prōdigiōsa canis.
5 Implētūra fuit sextae modo frīgora brūmae,
  vīxisset totidem nī minus illa diēs.
Inter tam veterēs lūdat lascīva patrōnōs
  et nōmen blaesō garriat ōre meum.
Mollia nōn rigidus caespes tegat ossa; nec illī,
10   terra, gravis fuerīs: nōn fuit illa tibi.

## SELECTION II. TOMORROW NEVER COMES

**crās** tomorrow

**numquid** at all (*in a question implying a negative answer*)

**emō** buy

****hodiē** today

**sapiō** be wise; **heri** yesterday

Crās tē vīctūrum, crās dīcis, Postume, semper.
  Dīc mihi, crās istud, Postume, quando venit?
Quam longē crās istud, ubi est? aut unde petendum?
  Numquid apud Parthōs Armeniōsque latet?
5 Jam crās istud habet Priamī vel Nestoris annōs.
  Crās istud quantī, dīc mihi, posset emī?
Crās vīvēs? Hodiē jam vīvere, Postume, sērum est:
  ille sapit, quisquis, Postume, vīxit heri.

## SELECTION III. I DO NOT LOVE THEE, DR. FELL

**quārē** why

Nōn amo tē, Sabidī, nec possum dīcere quārē:
  hoc tantum possum dīcere: nōn amo tē.

---

SELECTION I. Martial's *Epigrams* V, 34. See App. 19 and 35, 1. **1. Fronto, Flaccilla:** Martial's father and mother, already gone to the underworld. **3. Erōtion:** Martial's little slave girl who has just died. **4. Tartareī canis:** i.e., Cerberus, the dog that guards the entrance to the underworld. **5. Implētūra fuit:** *she would have completed.* **sextae frīgora brūmae:** *the sixth winter.* **6. totidem:** i.e., six. **7. patrōnōs:** i.e., Martial's parents. **9–10. nec ... fuerīs:** *nor rest heavy on her, O earth.* The usual formula

on a tombstone was **S.T.T.L.** (sit tibi **terra levis**), *may the earth rest lightly on you.*
SELECTION II. Martial's *Epigrams* V, 58. **1. vīctūrum:** from **vīvō. Postume:** *Postumus,* a friend of Martial. **2. crās istud:** *that tomorrow of yours.* **3. longē:** supply **est. 4. Parthōs:** *the Parthians,* a remote tribe in Asia. **5. habet annōs:** i.e., is as old as. **Priamī, Nestoris:** proverbially old men. **6. quantī:** *at what price.*
SELECTION III. Martial's *Epigrams* I, 32. **1. amo:** the final **o** is shortened for metrical-

## SELECTION IV. NOW, AELIA, YOU MAY COUGH ALL YOU LIKE

Sī meminī, fuerant tibi quattuor, Aelia, dentēs:

expulit ūna duōs tussis et ūna duōs.

Jam sēcūra potes tōtīs tussīre diēbus:

nīl istīc quod agat tertia tussis habet.

***dēns tooth

expellō drive out, eject; tussis cough

tussiō cough

istīc there

## SELECTION V. WHAT'S IN A NAME?

Nūper erat medicus, nunc est vespillō Diaulus:

quod vespillō facit, fēcerat et medicus.

***nūper recently; medicus physician; vespillō undertaker

vespillō undertaker; medicus physician

## SELECTION VI. TO A LEGACY HUNTER

Mūnera quod senibus viduīsque ingentia mittis,

vīs tē mūnificum, Gargiliāne, vocem?

Sordidius nihil, nihil est tē spurcius ūnō,

quī potes īnsidiās dōna vocāre tuās:

sīc avidīs fallāx indulget piscibus hāmus,

callida sīc stultās dēcipit esca ferās.

Quid sit largīrī, quid sit dōnāre docēbō,

sī nescis: dōnā, Gargiliāne, mihi.

viduus bereft (of wife or husband)

mūnificus benevolent, generous

sordidus sordid, base; spurcus dirty, foul

5 fallāx tricky, deceitful; piscis fish; hāmus hook

callidus clever; esca food, bait

*largior be lavish

## SELECTION VII. FEAR OF RECIPROCITY

Cūr nōn mittō meōs tibi, Pontiliāne, libellōs?

Nē mihi tū mittās, Pontiliāne, tuōs.

libellus book

## SELECTION VIII. A CONGENIAL TABLE COMPANION

Nōn cēnat sine aprō noster, Tite, Caeciliānus.

bellum convīvam Caeciliānus habet.

cēnō dine

bellus handsome, agreeable; convīva dinner-companion

---

reasons; so in **amo** in line 2. **Sabidī:** *Sabidius,* a man who was obviously *not* one of Martial's friends.

SELECTION IV. Martial's *Epigrams* I, 19. **1. Aelia:** a woman's name. **2. expulit . . . duōs:** i.e., the two coughs made her four teeth drop out. **4. nīl . . . habet:** *there is nothing that further coughing can do.*

SELECTION V. Martial's *Epigrams* I, 47. **1. Diaulus:** a man's name. **2. fēcerat et medicus:** *he also had done as a doctor.*

SELECTION VI. Martial's *Epigrams* IV, 56.

**2. vīs tē vocem:** *do you want me to call you.* **Gargiliāne:** *Gargilianus,* a man's name. **4. īnsidiās:** *stratagems* (for securing legacies). Martial's wrath is frequently directed toward legacy hunters who are disgustingly attentive to rich and childless old men and women.

SELECTION VII. Martial's *Epigrams* VII, 3. **1. Pontiliāne:** *Pontilianus,* a would-be writer.

SELECTION VIII. Martial's *Epigrams* VII, 59. **1. Tite:** *Titus,* a friend of Martial. **Caeciliānus:** a man whose table manners Martial obviously did not admire.

## Selection IX. A Candid Widow

inscrībō inscribe

potis able; **simplex** frank, honest

Īnscrīpsit tumulīs septem scelerāta virōrum
"sē fēcisse" Chloē. Quid pote simplicius?

# HADRIAN

## To His Soul

animula soul, spirit; **vagulus** wandering; **blandulus** charming

Animula vágula blandula,
hospés comésque córporis,
quae nunc abībis in loca
pallidula rígida núdula,
nec, út solés, dabís jocós!

pallidulus pale; **rigidus** stiff, rigid; **nūdulus** naked

jocus jest, joke      5

# AUSONIUS

## "Grow Old Along With Me"

Uxor, vīvāmusque ut vīximus et teneāmus
nōmina quae prīmō sūmpsimus in thalamō:
nec ferat ūlla diēs ut commūtēmur in aevō,
quīn tibi sim juvenis, tūque puella mihi.
5 Nestore sim quamvīs prōvectior aemulaque annīs
vincās Cūmānam tū quoque Dēiphobēn,
nōs ignōrēmus quid sit mātūra senectūs.
Scīre aevī meritum, nōn numerāre decet.

commūtō change

prōvectus advanced (*in years*); **aemulus** rivalling

numerō count; **\*\*decet** it is fitting

---

SELECTION IX. Martial's *Epigrams* IX, 15.
**1. septem virōrum:** *of her seven husbands.* **2. sē fēcisse:** *that she had made (done) this.* **Chloē:** a woman's name. **pote:** supply est.
HADRIAN. This little poem was written by the Emperor Hadrian, whose reign extended from A.D. 117 to 138. **1.** Note the diminutives in –ula, suggesting frailty. **4.** These adjectives modify Animula in line 1. **5. nec dabis jocōs:** *nor will you crack your jokes.*
AUSONIUS. Decimus Magnus Ausonius, the au-

thor of this selection, was born in Gaul about A.D. 310. He was a prolific writer and exercised himself in epigrams, descriptive pieces, and novel metrical fantasies. For the meter see App. 35, 1. **2. nōmina:** i.e., the names of endearment. **3. ferat faciat. 4. quīn tibi sim juvenis:** *so that I shall not seem to you a young man.* **5. Nestore:** the supreme example of old age among the Greeks and Romans. **6. Dēiphobēn:** the Cumaean Sibyl's name. **8. aevī meritum:** *the value of the years.*

# CLAUDIAN

### The Warrior and the Poet

Major Scīpiadēs, Italīs quī sōlus ab ōrīs
in proprium vertit Pūnica bella caput,
nōn sine Pīeriīs exercuit artibus arma:
semper erat vātum maxima cūra ducī.
Gaudet enim virtūs testīs sibi jungere Mūsās;   5
carmen amat, quisquis carmine digna gerit.
Ergō seu patriīs prīmaevus manibus ultor
subderet Hispānum lēgibus Ōceanum,
seu Tyriās certā fractūrus cuspide vīrīs
īnferret Libycō signa tremenda marī,   10
haerēbat doctus laterī castrīsque solēbat
omnibus in mediās Ennius īre tubās.
Illī post lituōs peditēs favēre canentī
laudāvitque novā caede cruentus eques.
Cumque triumphāret geminā Carthāgine victā   15
(hanc vindex patrī vīcerat, hanc patriae),
cum longī Libyam tandem post fūnera bellī
ante suās maestam cōgeret īre rotās,
advexit reducēs sēcum Victōria Mūsās
et sertum vātī Mārtia laurus erat.   20

*prīmaevus* youthful

*subdō* subdue

*\*\*\*cuspis* point, spear

*doctus* learned, lettered

*lituus* trumpet; *\*\*\*faveō* favor, applaud

*triumphō* celebrate a triumph

*vindex* avenger

*advehō* conduct, convey; *redux* returned, safe

CLAUDIAN. Claudius Claudianus, a contemporary of Ausonius, was a Greek who later attached himself to the court of the Emperor Honorius. He died about A.D. 408. For the meter see App. 35, 1. **1. Major Scīpiadēs:** P. Cornelius Scipio Africanus, the Roman general who conquered Carthage in the Second Punic War. **3. Pīeriīs artibus:** i.e., the arts of poetry; Pieria, a region in Macedonia, was sacred to the Muses. **4. ducī:** i.e., to Scipio. **5. testīs:** *as witnesses;* agrees with **Mūsās. 7. patriīs manibus:** i.e., with ability like his father's. **prīmaevus ultor:** Scipio when barely 24 succeeded to the command of his father's army in Spain when the latter was defeated and slain in 210 B.C., and by his subsequent victories avenged his father's death. **9. Tyriās vīrīs:** *the might of Carthage.* Carthage had been settled by Tyrians. **10. Libycō marī:** *to the Libyan Sea,* near Carthage; Scipio "carried the war into Africa."

**11. doctus:** modifies **Ennius** in the next line; *doctus* is a common epithet for poets. **12. Ennius:** an early Latin poet. **13. Illī;** i.e., Ennius. **canentī:** *as he chanted;* agrees with **Illī. favēre:** historical infinitive, the subject being **peditēs. 13–14. peditēs, eques:** i.e., the common soldiers as well as the general loved to hear Ennius read his poems. **15. triumphāret:** understand **Scīpiō** as the subject. **geminā Carthāgine:** i.e., New Carthage in Spain, old Carthage in Africa. **16. vindex patrī:** *as avenger of his father;* Scipio's father had been killed in Spain. **patriae:** i.e., **vindex patriae:** *as avenger of his country;* Italy had suffered severely in the Second Punic War. **17. Libyam:** i.e., Carthaginians, by *metonymy.* **18. ante suās īre rotās:** i.e., Carthaginian captives were forced to march before his triumphal chariot. **20. sertum vātī:** *a garland for the poet,* i.e., for Ennius. **Mārtia laurus:** *Mars's laurel,* i.e., the

**concidō** fall

**recursus** return, recurrence

Noster Scīpiadēs Stilichō, quō concidit alter  
Hannibal antīquō saevior Hannibale,  
tē mihi post quīntōs annōrum, Rōma, recursūs  
reddidit et vōtīs jussit adesse suīs.

victor's crown won in war. **21. Stilichō:** Roman general under the emperor Honorius. **quō:** *through whom,* i.e., by whose valor. **21–22. alter Hannibal:** i.e., Gildo, who had raised a revolt in Africa but had been suppressed by Stilicho in A.D. 398. **22. antīquō Hannibale:** *than the early Hannibal,* famous Carthaginian enemy of Rome

in the Second Punic War. **24. reddidit:** the subject is **Stilichō.** Claudianus had accompanied Stilicho on his successful campaign in Africa and was now returning to Rome to share in Stilicho's triumph. **vōtīs suīs:** *at the fulfillment of his vows;* dat. with **adesse;** understand **mē** as subject of **adesse.**

# WORK UNITS

# WORK UNITS

## WORK UNIT I
### (Based on *Aen.* I, 1–49)

1. Copy lines 3, 5, 7, 8, 16, and 30, indicate all elisions, and indicate below each syllable the quantity of that syllable. For help in doing this work see App. 24, 25, and 29.

2. Scan orally lines 1–7. For help in doing this work see App. 26.

3. Practice reading lines 1–7 aloud. Be sure to preserve an even march (4–4) rhythm, using a metronome or tapping with a pencil if necessary, to avoid falling into a waltz (3–4) rhythm. Remember that in reading Latin poetry quantity, or time, is the important thing and that the word or verse accent may for all practical purposes be disregarded.

4. Who or what was each of the following?

| | | |
|---|---|---|
| Achilles (a·kĭl′ēz) | Helen | Pallas (pălʹås) |
| Agamemnon | Juno | Paris |
| Alba Longa | Jupiter | Saturnia |
| Ascanius (ăs·kā′nĭ-ŭs) | Latium (lā′shi·um) | Tiber |
| Carthage | Lavinia | Troy |
| Dido (dī′dō) | Libya (lib′ĭ·å) | Venus (vē′nŭs) |
| Ganymede (găn′ĭ·mēd) | Menelaus (měn′ė-lā′ŭs) | |

5. Find in lines 1–49 a word, phrase, or sentence with which you can connect each of the following quotations:

> In heav'nly spirits could such perverseness dwell?
>
> Milton, *Paradise Lost*, 6, 788.

> That fixed decree, at silent work which wills
>
>         \*     \*     \*     \*     \*
>
> By wordless edict; having none to bid,
> None to forbid; for this is past all gods,
> Immutable, unspeakable, supreme.
>
> Edwin Arnold, *The Light of Asia*, 6, 573, 577–579.

249

And godlike Ganymede, most beautiful
Of men; the gods beheld and caught him up
To heaven, so beautiful was he, to pour
The wine to Jove, and ever dwell with them.

Homer, Iliad, 20, 293–296 (Bryant's translation).

Those three fatall Sisters, whose sad hands
Doo weave the direfull threads of destinie
And in their wrath breake off the vitall bands.

Edmund Spenser, Daphnaid, 16–18.

Minerva, child of Jove, who loves too well
Fierce war and mingling combat, and the fame
Of glorious deeds.

Shelley, Homer's Hymn to Venus, 10–12.

Troy flamed in burning gold, and o'er the throne
'Arms and the man' in golden ciphers shone.

Pope, The Temple of Fame, 208–209.

6. Memorize lines 1–7.

7. Find in lines 1–11 an example of each of the following:
   (1) an accusative without a preposition to express place whither
   (2) an ablative without a preposition to express place where
   (3) a dative of possession
   (4) an accusative used as subject of an infinitive
   (5) an ablative absolute phrase
   (6) a dative used to express place whither
   (7) an imperative
   (8) a subjunctive in a clause of anticipation
   (9) a subjunctive in an indirect question
   (10) a vocative

## WORK UNIT II

### (Based on *Aen.* I, 50–156)

1. Make sure that you know the meaning of each of the following Latin words [1]:

| | | | | |
|---|---|---|---|---|
| acuō | dīvus | īra | pontus | tabula |
| aequor | fātum | mōlēs | prōnus | tālis |
| caelum | flō | nūbēs | rēgīna | unda |
| conciliō | flūctus | nūmen | ruō | vāstus |
| –cumbō | hīc | pectus | saevus | volvō |

[1] All these words are in the College Entrance Examination Board's *Latin Word List* for the third or fourth year. Each has already appeared at least once in this book, and most of them three or more times.

2. Be prepared to explain the meaning of each of the italicized words in the following sentences and to show its etymological connection with some Latin word in the list on page 250.

(1) "There is a *divinity* that shapes our ends."

(2) The mayor made a *conciliatory* speech to the strikers.

(3) Prices of farm products have *fluctuated* rather violently during recent years.

(4) As the policeman entered the room, he saw a *recumbent* figure *prone* on the floor.

(5) We could see before us a *vast* expanse of *undulating* prairie which had recently been *devastated* by fire.

(6) True democracy *involves equal* opportunity for all.

3. Copy lines 50, 51, 53, 55, and 58, indicate all elisions, and indicate the quantity of each syllable. See App. 25–29. Note that there are many more long syllables than short. In line 53, for example, there are only two short syllables, namely, in the fifth foot. The same is true of line 55.

4. Scan orally lines 60–64. See App. 26.

5. Who or what was each of the following?

Achates (á·kā′tēz)  Eurus (ū′rŭs)  Notus (nō′tŭs)
Aeolus (ē′ó·lŭs)  Hector  Sarpedon (sär·pē′dŏn)
Africus  Ilioneus (ĭl·ī′·ó·nūs)  Triton (trī′tŏn)
Aquilo (ăk′wĭ·lō)  Neptune  Zephyrus (zĕf′ĭ·rŭs)
Diomedes (dī′ó·mē′dēz)

6. Find in lines 50–156 a word, phrase, or sentence with which you can connect each of the following quotations:

Or hear old Triton blow his wreathèd horn.

Wordsworth, *The World Is Too Much With Us*, 14.

The breezes broke the fountain's glass,
And woke aeolian melodies.

Thomas Bailey Aldrich, *Pampinea*, 42–43.

Father eternal, thine is to decree;
Mine both in heav'n and earth, to do thy will.

Milton, *Paradise Lost*, 10, 68–69.

Will all great Neptune's ocean wash this blood
Clean from my hand?

Shakespeare, *Macbeth*, 2, 2, 60–61.

For him hath Kronion made the warder of winds, and still
At his command are they stayed from blowing, are roused at his will.

Homer, Odyssey, 10, 21–22 (Way's translation).

And the East-wind and South rushed forth, and the West-wind bitter and fell,
And the blast from the skies of the north came rolling a vast sea-swell.

Homer, Odyssey, 5, 293–294 (Way's translation).

> While oft in whirls the mad tornado flies,
> Mingling the ravag'd landscape with the skies.

Goldsmith, The Deserted Village, 357–358.

> Thou frownest, and old Aeolus thy foe
> Skulks to his cavern, 'mid the gruff complaint
> Of all his rebel tempests.

Keats, Endymion, 3, 951–953.

7. Find in lines 55–80 an example of each of the following:
    (1) an ablative of place where without a preposition
    (2) alliteration
    (3) onomatopoeia
    (4) a subjunctive clause of purpose
    (5) a dative dependent on an adjective
    (6) an ablative of quality or description
    (7) synizesis
    (8) a genitive plural of a second declension noun in *–um*
    (9) an ablative with a special deponent verb
    (10) anaphora

## WORK UNIT III

### (Based on *Aen.* I, 157–304)

1. Make sure that you know the meaning of each of the following Latin words.[1]

| | | | | |
|---|---|---|---|---|
| arx | flamma | mītis | pulcher | sēdēs |
| asper | for, fārī | moenia (*pl.*) | puppis | sīdus |
| āter | harēna | mulceō | quiēscō | ter |
| cānus | hinc | ōlim | rēgnō | togātus |
| condō | ingēns | ōra | scēptrum | vertex |
| cor | mēta | ōs, ōris | scopulus | volō, –āre |
| corrumpō | misceō | pelagus | | |

[1] See footnote on page 250.

2. Find in the list on page 252 a word which is etymologically connected with each of the following English words, and be prepared to explain the connection in meaning:

| | | |
|---|---|---|
| acquiesce | incorruptible | mitigate |
| arena | ineffable | reign |
| encourage | inflammatory | vertical |
| exasperate | miscellaneous | volatile |

3. Copy lines 157, 159, 162, 163, and 165, and indicate the scansion of each line. Note that in lines 157, 159, 163, and 165 the fifth foot consists of a dactylic word and the sixth foot consists of a spondaic word. You will find that about a third of the lines in the *Aeneid* end in this way.

4. Scan orally lines 174–179.

5. Who or what was each of the following?

| | | |
|---|---|---|
| Acestes (*a·sĕs'tēz*) | Mercury | Romulus (rŏm'ū·lŭs) |
| Ceres (sē'rēz) | Mycenae (mĭ·sē'nē) | Scylla (sĭl'*a*) |
| Cyclops (sī'klŏps) | Remus (rē'mŭs) | Teucer (tū'sēr) |
| Iulus (ĭ·ū'lŭs) *little Trojan* | Rhea Silvia (rē'*a*) | Vesta |
| Mars | | |

6. Using App. 2–6 for reference, be prepared to tell how each of the following is connected with the life of Vergil: *p. 289*

| | | | |
|---|---|---|---|
| Andes | Eclogues | Mantua | Octavian |
| Augustus | Georgics | Maro | Philippi (fĭl·ip'ī) |
| Brundisium | Horace | Milan | Publius |
| Cremona | Maecenas (mē·sē'năs) | Naples | |

7. When was Vergil born? When did he die? In what year did he publish his *Eclogues?* His *Georgics?* When did Vergil begin work on the *Aeneid?* Who was responsible for the publication of the *Aeneid?*

8. Find in lines 157–304 a word, phrase, or sentence which you can connect with each of the following quotations:

> As when, on Ceres' sacred floor, the swain
> Spreads the wide fan to clear the golden grain.
>> Homer, *Iliad*, 5, 611–612 (Pope's translation).

> And here and there two crags, like turrets high,
> Point forth a port to all that sail thereby:
> The quiet seas below lie safe and still;
> The green wood like a garland grows aloft:
> Sweet caves within, cool shades and waters shrill,
> Where lie the nymphs on moss and ivy soft.
>> Tasso, *Jerusalem Delivered*, 15, 335–340 (Fairfax's translation).

He shall ascend
The throne hereditary, and bound his reign
With earth's wide bounds, his glory with the heaven's.

Milton, Paradise Lost, 12, 369–371.

But a sceptre over the Trojans the might of Aeneas shall sway,
Yea, and his children's children, the men of an unborn day.

Homer, Iliad, 20, 307–308 (Way's translation).

The troubled river knew them,
　And smoothed his yellow foam,
And gently rocked the cradle
　That bore the fate of Rome.
The ravening she-wolf knew them,
　And licked them o'er and o'er,
And gave them of her own fierce milk,
　Rich with raw flesh and gore.

Macaulay, The Prophecy of Capys, 33–40.

Thou wast not made for lucre,
　For pleasure or for rest;
Thou that art sprung from the war-god's loins,
　And hast tugged at the she-wolf's breast.
From sunrise unto sunset
　All earth shall hear thy fame:
A glorious city thou shalt build,
　And call it by thy name:
And there, unquenched through ages,
　Like Vesta's sacred fire,
Shall live the spirit of thy nurse,
　The spirit of thy sire.

Macaulay, The Prophecy of Capys, 121–132.

Foot-feather'd Mercury appear'd sublime
Beyond the tall tree tops.

Keats, Endymion, 4, 331–332.

See where the child of Heaven, with wingèd feet,
Runs down the slanted sunlight of the dawn.

Shelley, Prometheus Unbound, 1, 437–438.

9. Find in the lines indicated an example of each of the following:

(1) metonymy (174–179)
(2) a dative of separation (174–179)
(3) a genitive depending on an adjective (174–179)
(4) a dative with a special verb (257–266)
(5) a dative of reference (257–266)
(6) an ablative of place where without a preposition (257–266)
(7) an ablative absolute phrase (257–266)
(8) an ablative of source (291–301)
(9) an ablative of separation (291–301)
(10) personification (291–301)
(11) alliteration (291–301)
(12) a clause of purpose (291–301)

## WORK  UNIT  IV

(Based on *Aen*. I, 305–440)

1. Make sure that you know the meaning of each of the following Latin words:

| | | | | | |
|---|---|---|---|---|---|
| aethēr | √avāritia | immānis | optō | √sanguis | tellūs |
| ajō | √crūdēlis | laetus | orbis | sinus | vēlum |
| √āles | √errō | √lūdō | √patria | √sonō | √vinciō |
| āra | genū | nemus | √pius | soror | virgō |
| √arceō | haud | nympha | rūpēs | √super | vultus |
| aurum | | | | | |

2. Try to find another Latin word etymologically connected with each of the checked words in the above list.

3. Copy lines 305–313, 332, and 405, and indicate the scansion.

4. Who or what was each of the following?

Cyprus (sī′prŭs)          Phoebus (fē′bŭs)          Phrygia (frĭj′ĭ·ȧ)
Olympus (ȯ·lĭm′pŭs)          Phoenicia (fē·nĭ′shĭ·ȧ)          Tyre (tīr)

5. Find in lines 305–440 a word, phrase, or sentence with which you can connect each of the following quotations:

> O goddess (for such I take thee to be),
> For neither doth thy face terrestrial show,
> Nor voice sound mortal.

> Spenser, *The Faerie Queene*, 2, 3, 290–292.

Then rose Odysseus to go to the town, but Athene's care
Made round about him to flow a veil of misty air,
Lest any Phaeacian should meet him, as nigh to the city he came,
And with scoffing words should greet him, and ask of his nation and name.

Homer, Odyssey, 7, 15–18 (Way's translation).

As bees
In spring time, when the sun with Taurus rides,
Pour forth their populous youth about the hive
In clusters.

Milton, Paradise Lost, 1, 768–771.

Sabaean odors from the spicy shore
Of Araby the blest.

Milton, Paradise Lost, 4, 162–163.

The bird of Jove, stooped from his airy tour,
Two birds of gayest plume before him drove.

Milton, Paradise Lost, 11, 185–186.

Most sure, the goddess
On whom these airs attend! Vouchsafe my prayer
May know if you remain upon this island.

Shakespeare, Tempest, 1, 2, 422–424.

6. Find in the lines indicated an example of each of the following:
(1) simile (315–320)
(2) an accusative of specification (315–320)
(3) an infinitive used to express purpose (315–320)
(4) a perfect passive participle used in the middle or reflexive sense (315–320)
(5) synapheia (330–334)
(6) a subjunctive in a wish or prayer (330–334)
(7) a subjunctive in an indirect question (330–334)
(8) a genitive depending on an adjective (330–334)

## WORK UNIT V

### (Based on *Aen.* I, 441–578)

1. Make sure that you know the meaning of each of the following Latin words:

| | | | | |
|---|---|---|---|---|
| aēnus | coma | √furō | penitus | √surgō |
| agnōscō | cūnctus | √gradior | pharetra | √templum |
| √ārdeō | currus | √hūmānus | √quālis | trīstis |
| arvum | –cutiō | √memor | √solvō | turbō, –inis |
| aura | equidem | mōlior | √strīdeō | √umbra |
| caecus | fremō | √paenitet | | |

2. Try to find an English word etymologically connected with each of the checked words in the list on page 256.

3. Copy lines 445, 448, 451, 458, 485, 486, 521, and 574, and indicate the scansion.

4. Who or what was each of the following?

| | | |
|---|---|---|
| Auster (ôs'tēr) | Memnon (mĕm'nŏn) | Troilus (trō'ĭ·lŭs) |
| Dardanus (där'da·nŭs) | Pergama (pûr'ga·ma) | Ulysses (ů·lĭs'ēz) |
| Diana (dī·ā'na or dī·ă'na) | Priam (prī'ăm) | Xanthus (zăn'thŭs) |
| Hesperia (hĕs·pē'rĭ·a) | Rhesus (rē'sŭs) | |

5. Find in lines 441–578 a word, phrase, or sentence with which you can connect each of the following quotations:

> For who can match Achilles?  He who can,
> Must yet be more than hero, more than man.
>
> Homer, *Iliad*, 23, 933–934 (Pope's translation).

To NEVILLE CHAMBERLAIN (September 15, 1938)

> As Priam to Achilles for his son,
> So you into the night, divinely led,
> To ask that young men's bodies not yet dead,
> Be given from the battle not begun.
>
> John Masefield.

> The Virgilian cry,
> The sense of tears in mortal things.
>
> Matthew Arnold, *Geist's Grave*, 15–16.

> Such as Diana by the shady shore
> Of swift Eurotas, or on Cynthus greene.
>
> Spenser, *The Faerie Queene*, 2, 3, 271–272.

> Yet tears to human suffering are due;
> And mortal hopes defeated and o'erthrown
> Are mourned by man.
>
> Wordsworth, *Laodamia*, 164–166.

6. Find in the lines indicated an example of each of the following:

(1) a dative of reference (446–449)
(2) a hypermetric line (446–449)
(3) an ablative of place where without a preposition (446–449)
(4) alliteration (469–478)

(5) an ablative of quality or description (469–478)

(6) a subjunctive in a clause of anticipation (469–478)

(7) a dative of reference (469–478)

(8) a short vowel made long by poetic license (469–478)

(9) a patronymic (469–478)

# WORK UNIT VI
### (Based on *Aen.* I, 579–756)

1. Make sure that you know the meaning of each of the following Latin words:

| | | | | |
|---|---|---|---|---|
| abhorreō | dōnō | haereō | meminī | ruīna |
| āla | dōnum | horreō | mēnsa | saeculum |
| argentum | dulcis | ignārus | orīgō | societās |
| ātrōx | ebur | immō | ōrnō | somnus |
| bibō | epulae | interdum | parēns | splendor |
| cārus | faveō | intus | pāscō | superbus |
| celeber | foveō | juvenis | pendeō | supplex |
| celebrō | geminus | lībō | plausus | tēctum |
| cingō | genitor | līmen | plēnus | tingō |
| clārus | gignō | lūcus | polus | umerus |
| dolus | gremium | lūstrō | restō | –ve |

2. Be prepared to explain the meaning of each of the italicized words in the following sentences and to show its etymological connection with some word in the above list.

(1) The Celts were not the *aborigines* of ancient Gaul.

(2) Close *association* among nations naturally leads to a sense of *interdependence*.

(3) Many *pastors* believe that *secular* education alone is not sufficient if we are to avoid an increase in *juvenile* delinquency.

(4) *Atrocities* seem to be *inherent* in warfare, and it does not seem possible that they can be *eliminated*.

(5) For many years my friend suffered from *insomnia*.

(6) The palace seemed to me *ornate* rather than *splendid*.

(7) The *donor declared* that this gift was only *preliminary* to larger *donations*, but he refused to *clarify* that statement.

(8) Dardanus was *progenitor* of the Trojan race.

(9)           "The arts of pleasure in despotic courts
              I spurn *abhorrent*."

(10)          "To bow and sue for grace
              With *suppliant* knee."

(11)                        "A clime
              Where life and rapture flow in *plenitude* sublime."

(12)          "And starry *Gemini* hang like glorious crowns
              Over Orion's grave low in the west."

(13)          "So barren sands *imbibe* the showers."

(14)          "And now abideth faith, hope, *charity*."

3. Without referring to the text, rearrange the words in each of the following sentences so that it will be a dactylic hexameter verse. As a first step in doing this work indicate, below the Latin word, the quantity of each syllable.

(1) Omnia tūta vidēs, receptōs sociōsque classem.

(2) Semper honōs laudēsque nōmenque tuum manēbunt.

(3) Nōn ignāra malī miserīs discō succurrere.

(4) Tyriī plausū ingeminant, Trōesque sequuntur.

4. Who or what was each of the following?

| | | |
|---|---|---|
| Anchises (ăn·kī′sēz) | Bacchus (băk′ŭs) | Ilione (il·ī′ŏ·nē) |
| Amor (ā′mor) | Belus (bē′lŭs) | Leda (lē′dȧ) |
| Atlas | Cupid | Oceanus (ȯ·sē′ȧ·nŭs) |
| Aurora (ȯ·rō′rȧ) | Cytherea (sĭth′ĕr·ē′ȧ) | |

5. Find in lines 579–756 a word, phrase, or sentence with which you can connect each of the following quotations:

> Not great Aeneas stood in plainer day,
> When, the dark mantling mist dissolv'd away,
> He to the Tyrians show'd his sudden face,
> Shining with all his goddess mother's grace:
> For she herself had made his countenance bright,
> Breath'd honor on his eyes, and her own purple light.
>
> Dryden, *Britannia Rediviva*, 128–133.

> A fellow-feeling makes one wondrous kind.
>
> Garrick, *Prologue (spoken on quitting the stage)*, 4.

> Bacchus, that first from out the purple grape,
> Crushed the sweet poison of misusèd wine.
>
> Milton, *Comus*, 1, 46–47.

Through scudding drifts the rainy Hyades
Vext the dim sea.

Tennyson, *Ulysses*, 10–11.

A daughter of the gods, divinely tall
And most divinely fair.

Tennyson, *Dream of Fair Women*, 87–88.

The bloom of young Desire and purple light of Love.

Gray, *Progress of Poesy*, 41.

As heav'n with stars, the roof with jewels glows,
And ever-living lamps depend in rows.

Pope, *The Temple of Fame*, 143–144.

6. Find in the lines indicated an example of each of the following:
   (1) an ablative of source (579–583)
   (2) an accusative of respect (579–583)
   (3) an ablative of place where without a preposition (579–583)
   (4) a predicate genitive (597–606)
   (5) a participle in the vocative case (597–606)
   (6) a subjective genitive (597–606)
   (7) a genitive depending on an adjective (597–606)
   (8) a partitive genitive (597–606)
   (9) a subjunctive expressing a wish or prayer (597–606)
   (10) synizesis (613–618)
   (11) hiatus (613–618)
   (12) diaeresis (613–618)  *2 dots ver 2ⁿᵈ vowel*

7. Memorize lines 574, 609, and 630.  *look over*

## WORK UNIT VII
### (Based on *Aen.* II, 1–144)

1. Make sure that you know the meaning of each of the following Latin words:

| | | | | |
|---|---|---|---|---|
| adflīgō | decus | juventūs | plācō | temperantia |
| ars | dēdecus | lābor, –ī | praecipuus | usquam |
| auris | dīves | lacrima | quisquis | utinam |
| canō | dīvīnus | latebra | scelus | vānus |
| cavus | fīdus | lateō | scindō | vetō |
| certō, –āre | fingō | lūmen | sileō | vinculum |
| cōnscientia | flāgitō | nimbus | taceō | vīsō |
| cōnscius | ignōtus | obstipēscō | tandem | |

2. Find in the list on page 260 a word which is etymologically connected with each of the following English words, and be prepared to explain the connection in meaning:

| | | | | |
|---|---|---|---|---|
| affliction | conscience | implacable | lapse | tacit |
| artifice | fictitious | incantation | latent | unconscious |
| aural | fidelity | indecorous | rescind | vanity |
| concave | illuminate | lacrimal | | |

3. Without referring to the text, rearrange the words in each of the following sentences so that it will be a dactylic hexameter verse.

(1) Conticuēre omnēs, intentīque tenēbant ōra.

(2) Īnfandum, rēgīna, dolōrem renovāre jubēs.

(3) Hīc manus Dolopum, hīc saevus Achillēs tendēbat.

(4) Quidquid id est, Danaōs et dōna ferentīs timeō.

4. Who or what was each of the following?

| | | |
|---|---|---|
| Calchas (kăl′kăs) | Ithaca | Minerva |
| Iphigenia (ĭf′ĭ·jĕ·nī′ȧ) | Laocoön (lȧ·ŏk′ŏ·ŏn) | Sinon |

5. Find in lines 1–144 a word, phrase, or sentence that you can connect with each of the following quotations:

> Speak, Rome's dear friend: as erst our ancestor,
> When with his solemn tongue he did discourse
> To love-sick Dido's sad attending ear
> The story of that baleful burning night,
> When subtle Greeks surprised King Priam's Troy:
> Tell us what Sinon hath bewitch'd our ears,
> Or who hath brought the fatal engine in
> That gives our Troy, our Rome, the civil wound.
>
> Shakespeare, *Titus Andronicus*, 5, 3, **80–87**.

> [Adam] amazed
> Astonied stood and blank, while horror chill
> Ran through his veins, and all his joynts relax'd.
>
> Milton, *Paradise Lost*, 9, **889–891**.

> Thou wilt that I renew
> The desperate grief, which wrings my heart already
> To think of only, ere I speak of it.
>
> Dante, *Inferno*, 33, 4–6 (Longfellow's translation).

6. Find in the lines indicated each of the following:

  (1) a future active participle used to express purpose (45–56)
  (2) **nē** used with an imperative (45–56)
  (3) alliteration (45–56)
  (4) apostrophe (45–56)
  (5) a contrary to fact condition (45–56)
  (6) a contrary to fact conclusion (45–56)
  (7) two vocatives (45–56)
  (8) three historical infinitives (97–104)
  (9) anaphora (97–104)
 (10) aposiopesis (97–104)
 (11) an imperative (97–104)
 (12) two potential subjunctives (97–104)

7. Memorize line 49.

# WORK UNIT VIII
### (Based on *Aen.* II, 145–267)

1. Make sure that you know the meaning of each of the following Latin words:

| | | | | | |
|---|---|---|---|---|---|
| aeternus | cruentus | legō | ōmen | sacer | texō |
| arrigō | cuspis | levō | palma | sacrō | tremō |
| artus, –ūs | exitium | morsus | pandō | solum | vēlō |
| carīna | fās | nī | patefaciō | sors | vīnum |
| cervīx | hasta | nōdus | rōbur | taurus | vitta |
| collum | laedō | | | | |

2. Find in the above list a word which is etymologically connected with each of the following English words and be prepared to explain the connection in meaning:

| | | | | |
|---|---|---|---|---|
| articulation | consecrate | legible | revelation | texture |
| assortment | elevate | Minotaur | robust | tremendous |
| collar | elision | morsel | sorcerer | vinegar |
| collide | erect | remorse | | |

3. Without referring to the text, rearrange the words in each of the following sentences so that it will be a dactylic hexameter verse:

  (1) Hīs lacrimīs vītam damus et ultrō miserēscimus.

  (2) Ille simul manibus tendit nōdōs dīvellere.

  (3) Mūrōs dīvidimus et moenia urbis pandimus.

4. Who or what was each of the following?

| | | |
|---|---|---|
| Argos | Neoptolemus | Tritonia |
| Cassandra (kă·săn'drá) | Palladium (pă·lā'dĭ·ŭm) | Tydides (tĭ·dī'dēz) |
| Ilium (ĭl'ĭ·um) | Pelops (pē'lŏps) | |

5. Find in lines 145–267 a word, phrase, or sentence that you can connect with each of the following quotations:

> Vain
> The struggle; vain, against the coiling strain
> And gripe, and deepening of the dragon's grasp,
> The old man's clench; the long envenom'd chain
> Rivets the living links, — the enormous asp
> Enforces pang on pang, and stifles gasp on gasp.
>
> Byron, *Childe Harold*, 4, 1435–1440.

> Sinon's weeping
> Did scandal many a holy tear.
>
> Shakespeare, *Cymbeline* 3, 4, 61–62.

> Thus Satan talking to his nearest mate,
> With head uplift above the wave, and eyes
> That sparkling blaz'd; his other parts besides
> Prone on the flood, extended long and large,
> Lay floating many a rood.
>
> Milton, *Paradise Lost*, 1, 192–196.

> Was this the face that launch'd a thousand ships
> And burnt the topless towers of Ilium?
>
> Marlowe, *Doctor Faustus*, 14, 92–93.

> He who planned
> To take the towered city of Troy-land
>
> *        *        *        *        *
>
> With woven wiles he stole the Trojan town
> Which ten years battle could not batter down.
>
> Stephen Phillips, *Ulysses*, Prologue, 7–8, 11–12

6. Find in the lines indicated each of the following:

(1) a subjunctive with the force of an imperative (154–161)
(2) apostrophe (154–161)
(3) anaphora (154–161)
(4) a vocative (154–161)

(5) an ablative of place where without a preposition (154–161)

(6) a dative of reference (228–237)

(7) a Greek accusative form (228–237)

(8) a relative clause of characteristic (228–237)

(9) a dative with a compound verb (228–237)

(10) an ablative of place whence (228–237)

(11) a dative of agent with a perfect passive participle (246–249)

(12) a relative clause of characteristic (246–249)

## WORK UNIT IX

### (Based on *Aen.* II, 268–437)

1. Make sure that you know the meaning of each of the following Latin words:

| | | | | |
|---|---|---|---|---|
| astō | coruscus | √faciēs | √induō | quondam |
| √bōs | dēlūbrum | formīdō | √jaculum | √spolium |
| caterva | dēnique | fretum | √lūna | sternō |
| celsus | √dubius | √fūnus | lupus | √stupeō |
| clipeus | ecce | galea | maestus | √varius |
| comes | √exigō | heu | nex | velut |
| compellō, –āre | extemplō | √imāgō | √obscūrus | √verbum |

2. Try to find an English word etymologically connected with each of the checked words in the above list.

3. What is the literal meaning of the Latin phrase *Glōria in excelsīs Deō?* From what Latin word does *Australia* take its name?

4. Who or what was each of the following?

| | | |
|---|---|---|
| Androgeos (ăn·drō′jĕ·ŏs) | Deïphobus (dĕ·if′ŏ·bŭs) | Orcus |
| Coroebus (kŏ·rē′bŭs) | Nereus (nēr′ūs) | Panthus |
| Dardania (där·dā′nĭ·a) | | |

5. Find in lines 268–437 a word, phrase, or sentence with which you can connect each of the following quotations:

> It was the time, when rest, soft sliding downe
> From heaven's hight into men's heavy eyes,
> In the forgetfulnes of sleepe doth drowne
> The carefull thoughts of mortall miseries.
>
> Spenser, *Visions of Bellay*, 1–4.

Like a great water-flood, that tombling low
From the high mountaines, threates to overflow
With suddein fury all the fertile playne.

Spenser, The Faerie Queene, 2, 11, 157–159.

Awaits alike th' inevitable hour.

Gray, Elegy, 35.

6. Find in the lines indicated an example of each of the following:

  (1) an ablative of separation (289–297)
  (2) a condition contrary to fact (289–297)
  (3) personification (289–297)
  (4) metonymy (289–297)
  (5) an ablative of place whence without a preposition (289–297)
  (6) simile (302–313)
  (7) alliteration (302–313)
  (8) anaphora (302–313)
  (9) metonymy (302–313)
 (10) a dative with a compound verb (351–362)
 (11) a dative of reference (351–362)
 (12) a hortatory subjunctive (351–362)
 (13) simile (351–362)
 (14) a deliberative question (351–362)

7. Memorize line 354.

## WORK UNIT X

### (Based on *Aen.* II, 438–623)

1. Make sure that you know the meaning of each of the following Latin words:

| | | | | | |
|---|---|---|---|---|---|
| aedēs | complector | exsultō | jaceō | ōsculum | quamquam |
| almus | culmen | feriō | laevus | pariēs | requīrō |
| amplector | dēnsus | foris | morior | passim | sedeō |
| appāreō | dīrus | fūmus | mūcrō | penetrālis | simulācrum |
| armentum | ēnsis | implicō | nepōs | postis | soleō |
| ceu | ergō | īnfestus | nēquīquam | praeceps | stringō |
| comitor | ēvertō | invideō | occidō | pulvis | vellō |

2. Explain the meaning of each of the italicized words in the following sentences and be prepared to show its etymological connection with one of the Latin words in the above list.

(1) The rules are quite *stringent* on that point.

(2) The ancients believed that the *immortals* constantly *interfered* with human affairs.

(3) This sort of stone *pulverizes* easily.

(4) The Parthenon and *adjacent* buildings were magnificent *edifices*.

(5) At the first *session* of the convention a speaker made an *invidious* reference to his opponent which almost *precipitated* a riot.

(6) The alumni were urged to honor and support their *alma* mater.

(7) Hector visited Aeneas in the form of an *apparition*.

(8) International relations are becoming more and more *complex*.

(9) A *concomitant* of ingratitude is hardheartedness, which is likely to *culminate* in an *insolent* disregard for the rights of others.

(10) "His bosom swelled with *exultation*."

(11) "No rich *perfumes* refresh the fruitful field."

(12) "The meeting boughs and *implicated* leaves."

(13) "Highest woods *impenetrable* to star or sunlight." ✓

3. Who or what was each of the following?

Andromache (ăn·drŏm'á·kē)     Gorgon            Pyrrhus (pǐr'ŭs)
Astyanax (ăs·tī'á·năks)        Hecuba (hĕk'ū·bá)   Sparta
Creusa (crē·ū'sá)              Polites (pŏ·lī'tēz)

4. Find in lines 438–623 a word, phrase, or sentence with which you can connect each of the following quotations:

He fell, and deadly pale,
Groan'd out his soul with gushing blood effus'd.

Milton, *Paradise Lost*, 11, 446–447.

What new Gorgon's head
Have you beheld, that you are all turn'd statues?

Fletcher, *Queen of Corinth*, 5, 2, 118–119.

What was that snaky-headed Gorgon shield
That wise Minerva wore?

Milton, *Comus*, 446–447.

I had great beauty; ask thou not my name:
No one can be more wise than destiny.
Many drew swords and died. Where'er I came
I brought calamity.

Tennyson, *Dream of Fair Women*, 93–96.

5. What words other than *Trōja* does Vergil use to refer to Troy?

6. Find in the lines indicated an example of each of the following:
   (1) simile (491–502)
   (2) synizesis (491–502)
   (3) diaeresis (491–502)
   (4) anaphora (491–502)
   (5) two datives of place whither (547–553)
   (6) two imperatives (547–553)
   (7) a dative with a compound verb (588–607)
   (8) a dative of agent (588–607)
   (9) indirect question (588–607)
   (10) a dative of reference (588–607)
   (11) a negative imperative (588–607)
   (12) a dative with a special verb (588–607)

## WORK UNIT XI
### (Based on *Aen.* II, 624–804)

1. Make sure that you know the meaning of each of the following Latin words:

| | | | |
|---|---|---|---|
| aevum | dūdum | jūxtā | pūbēs |
| āmēns | ēvādō | lētum | repetō |
| aptō | exsilium | micō | retrō |
| augurium | exuviae | minor, –ārī | senior |
| commendō | famulus | misereor | sīn |
| crīnis | flagrō | mōnstrum | sinō |
| curvus | flō | nefās | superī |
| dēmum | glomerō | paveō | suspendō |
| dōnec | hodiē | pellis | tantum (*adv.*) |

2. Find in the following list an English word that is etymologically connected with a word in the above list and be prepared to explain the connection in meaning:

| | | | |
|---|---|---|---|
| aptitude | exile | mental | promenade |
| commiseration | flagrant | nefarious | recommend |
| conglomerate | inflate | pelt | retrospect |
| crinoline | juxtaposition | petition | sir |
| evasion | menace | primeval | |

3. Who or what was each of the following?

Laomedon (lă·ŏm′ĕ·dŏn)     Ida     Cybele (sĭb′ĕ·lē)     Lucifer (lū′sĭ·fēr)

4. Find in lines 624–804 a word, phrase, or sentence with which you can connect each of the following quotations:

I, as Aeneas, our great ancestor,
Did from the flames of Troy upon his shoulder
The old Anchises bear, so from the waves of Tiber
Did I the tired Caesar.
            Shakespeare, *Julius Caesar*, 1, 2, 112–115.

Springing forward thrice I essayed in my clasp my beloved to hold;
From mine hands did she thrice take flight like a shadow or dream of the night.
            Homer, *Odyssey*, 11, 204–205 (Way's translation).

And Priam's wail is heard no more
   By windy Ilion's sea-built walls;
Nor great Achilles, stained with gore,
   Shouts, "O ye Gods! 'tis Hector falls!"
On Ida's mount is the shining snow,
   But Jove has gone from its brow away,
And red on the plains the poppies grow
   Where the Greek and the Trojan fought that day.
            Edna Dean Proctor, *Heroes*, 9–16.

As the morning-star
Beckons the sun from the Eoan wave.
            Shelley, *Ode to Liberty*, 257–258.

5. By what names other than *Trōes* does Vergil refer to the Trojans?

6. By what names other than *Grajī* does Vergil refer to the Greeks?

7. What Roman deity was associated with each of the following?

| agriculture | love | prophecy | war | wine |
| dawn | marriage | sea | winds | wisdom |
| lightning | | | | |

8. What grammatical construction or figure of speech is illustrated by each of the following?

(1) ac velutī . . . ruīnam (626–631)
(2) jugīs (631)
(3) dūcente deō (632)
(4) vōs (638)
(5) aevī (638)
(6) voluissent (641)
(7) sepulcrī (646)
(8) vellet (653)
(9) dictū (680)
(10) caelō (688)
(11) Quō rēs cumque (709)
(12) mē (718)
(13) onerī (723)
(14) comitī (729)
(15) portīs (730)
(16) mihi (735)
(17) hominum (745)
(18) nōtā (773)
(19) collō (792)
(20) exsiliō (798)

## WORK UNIT XII
(Based on *Aen.* IV, 1–172)

1. Make sure that you know the meaning of each of the following Latin words:

| | | | | | |
|---|---|---|---|---|---|
| altāria (*pl.*) | √dēmēns | harundō | membrum | √praetereō | √stabilis |
| argūmentum | dīligō | √hospes | mollis | √profiteor | √suādeō |
| aurōra | edō | hymenaeus | √nūtus | √purpura | √suspiciō |
| carpō | fateor | inertia | os, ossis | rīdeō | thalamus |
| cervus | √ferōx | √īnsignis | √pactum | saucius | ūrō |
| cieō | flectō | iterum | √pāstor | sēgnis | √vēnor |
| cinis | fulmen | √juventa | patera | sepulcrum | vēstīgium |
| √cōnūbium | fulvus | leō | pingō | √serviō | violō |
| √convīvium | gaudeō | mactō | pinguis | spargō | √voveō |
| √culpa | germānus | √maeror | potius | spēlunca | |

2. Try to find another Latin word etymologically connected with each of the checked words in the above list.

3. Who or what was each of the following?

| | | |
|---|---|---|
| Anna | Erebus (ĕr'ĕ·bŭs) | Orion (ô·rī'ŏn) |
| Cynthus (sĭn'thŭs) | Iärbas (ĭ·är'băs) | Pygmalion (pĭg·mā'lĭ·ŏn) |
| Delos (dē'lŏs) | | |

4. Find in lines 1–172 a word, phrase, or sentence with which you can connect each of the following quotations:

> I was a stricken deer, that left the herd
> Long since; with many an arrow deep infix'd
> My panting side was charged, when I withdrew,
> To seek a tranquil death in distant shades.
>
> Cowper, *The Task*, 3, 108–111.

> Haply, in cavern harboured, at mid-day,
> Grateful as that to which Aeneas fled
> With Dido, when the tempest raged above,
> The faithful witness to their secret love.
>
> Ariosto, *Orlando Furioso*, 19, 277–280 (Rose's translation).

> Like to rosy-born Aurora,
> Glowing freshly into view.
>
> George Meredith, *Daphne*, 49–50.

5. Be prepared to explain the use of each of the following words, phrases, or clauses:

| | |
|---|---|
| (1) fortī pectore (11) | (11) Tyrō (43) |
| (2) sī . . . sedēret (15) | (12) cui (59) |
| (3) animō (15) | (13) cūrae (59) |
| (4) thalamī (18) | (14) regāmus (102) |
| (5) dehīscat (24) | (15) liceat (103) |
| (6) servet (29) | (16) āverteret (106) |
| (7) lūce (31) | (17) ōrās (106) |
| (8) sorōrī (31) | (18) vēnātum (117) |
| (9) Libyae (36) | (19) illō (149) |
| (10) Tyrō (36) | |

# WORK UNIT XIII
(Based on *Aen.* IV, 173–330)

1. Make sure that you know the meaning of each of the following Latin words:

| | | | | |
|---|---|---|---|---|
| √accendō | √dignor | √lingua | pīnus | serō, satus |
| adhūc | √dissimulō | madeō | prōlēs | √struō |
| adimō | exuō | mox | pudor | √sublīmis |
| √amō | faux | nītor, –ī | quandō | tenuis |
| √anima | √fēmina | nix | √quot | √torqueō |
| √arduus | √flōreō | nō | √rigeō | torus |
| √arō | foedus (*adj.*) | ōcior | saeviō | √vādō |
| √comitātus | imber | pecus | √secō | √vēlōx |
| √concitō | √inānis | | √sermō | √vindicō |
| √crēscō | | | | |

2. Try to find an English word etymologically connected with each of the checked words in the above list and be prepared to explain the connection in meaning.

3. Who or what was each of the following?

Fama                    Hammon                    Nomad

4. Find in lines 173–330 a word, phrase, or sentence with which you can connect each of the following quotations:

> The woman that thou will'd us entertain
> Where, straying in our borders up and down,
> She crav'd a hide of ground to build a town, —
> With whom we did divide both laws and land.

Marlowe and Nash, *The Tragedie of Dido,
Queen of Carthage,* 4, 46–49.

Dance, like a Bacchanal, from rock to rock,
Tossing her frantic thyrsus wide and high!

Wordsworth, Duddon Sonnets, 13–14.

A shape comes now,
Stretching on high from his right hand
A serpent-cinctured wand.

Shelley, Prometheus Unbound, 1, 322–324.

Like Maia's son he stood.

Milton, Paradise Lost, 5, 285.

In his hand
He tooke Caduceus, his snakie wand,
With which the damned ghosts he governeth,
And furies rules, and Tartare tempereth.
With that he causeth sleep to seize the eyes,
And feare the harts of all his enemyes;
And, when him list, an universall night
Throughout the world he makes on everie wight.

Spenser, Mother Hubbard's Tale, 1291–1298.

With Atlantean shoulders fit to bear
The weight of mightiest monarchies.

Milton, Paradise Lost, 11, 306–307.

5. Be prepared to explain the use of each of the following words:

| | | |
|---|---|---|
| (1) deōrum (178) | (12) animī (203) | (23) mentō (250) |
| (2) cui (181) | (13) dīvum (204) | (24) avī (254) |
| (3) dictū (182) | (14) pretiō (212) | (25) illī (261) |
| (4) lūce (186) | (15) raptō (217) | (26) deōrum (282) |
| (5) culmine (186) | (16) fāmae (221) | (27) agat (283) |
| (6) vēnisse (191) | (17) lābere (223) | (28) dissimulent (291) |
| (7) sanguine (191) | (18) Carthāgine (224) | (29) nesciat (292) |
| (8) hiemem (193) | (19) mitteret (231) | (30) peterēs (312) |
| (9) rēgnōrum (194) | (20) naviget (237) | (31) peterētur (313) |
| (10) virum (195) | (21) imperiō (239) | (32) dēstruat (326) |
| (11) Hammōne (198) | (22) cui (248) | (33) vidērer (330) |

## WORK UNIT XIV
### (Based on *Aen.* IV, 331–473)

1. Make sure that you know the meaning of each of the following Latin words:

| | | | | |
|---|---|---|---|---|
| agitō | exterus | hauriō | properō | sōlor |
| astrum | fax | improbus | querēla | testor |
| colō | ferveō | invidia | quotiēns | tundō |
| corōna | foedus, –eris | mānēs | rādīx | vātēs |
| duplex | frōns, frondis | manifestus | secus | venia |
| egeō | gemō | nusquam | serpō | |

2. Be prepared to explain the meaning of each of the italicized words in the following sentences and to show its etymological connection with some Latin word in the above list:

(1) Professional *agitators* soon had the *colonists* deeply stirred about the postponement of the King's *coronation*, and the government was forced to issue a *manifesto*.

(2) It is the *fervent* prayer of all that the new *federation* may succeed in *eradicating* many of the present evils.

(3) This *corollary* is concerned with *obtuse* angles only.

(4) I am sending you a *duplicate* of my recent letter.

(5) *Fronds* are very attractive decorative material.

(6) What is the *quotient* of twelve divided by four?

(7) "Against such cruelties with inward *consolations* recompensed."

(8) "Without *exterior* help sustained."

(9) "A decrepit, *exhausted* old man of fifty-five."

(10) "Enmity can scarcely be more annoying than *querulous*, jealous, exacting fondness."

(11) "So they do nothing, 'tis a *venial* slip."

(12) "Thy shape like his, and color *serpentine*."

3. Who or what was each of the following?

Aulis (ô'lĭs)  
Caucasus (kô'kà·sŭs)

Elissa (ē·lĭs'à)  
Orestes (ō·rĕs'tēz)

4. Find in lines 331–473 a word, phrase, or sentence with which you can connect each of the following quotations:

> And lofty cedars as far upward shoot,
> As to the nether heavens they drive the root.
>
> Dryden, *Eleanora*, 93–94.

> The mad sea-waves thee bare, some tigress wild
> On Caucasus' cold crags nurs'd thee apart.
>
> Tasso, *Jerusalem Delivered*, 16, 443–444
> (Fairfax's translation).

> Go cruel, go; go with such peace, such rest,
> Such joy, such comfort, as thou leav'st me here:
> My angry soul, discharg'd from this weak breast,
> Shall haunt thee ever, and attend thee near,
> And fury-like, in snakes and fire-brands drest,
> Shall aye torment thee, whom it late held dear.
>
> Tasso, *Jerusalem Delivered*, 16, 58–63
> (Fairfax's translation).

> The moping owl does to the moon complain
> Of such as, wand'ring near her secret bow'r,
> Molest her ancient solitary reign.
>
> Gray, *Elegy*, 10–12.

5. Memorize line 361.

6. Be prepared to explain the use of each of the following words or phrases:

(1) tē (333)
(2) Elissae (335)
(3) meī (336)
(4) nē finge (338)
(5) paterentur (340)
(6) posuissem (344)
(7) victīs (344)
(8) capitis (354)
(9) quae (371)
(10) quibus (371)
(11) anteferam (371)
(12) rēgnī (374)
(13) superīs (379)
(14) sequere (381)

(15) hausūrum (383)
(16) scopulīs (383)
(17) Dīdō (383)
(18) cūnctantem (390)
(19) thalamō (392)
(20) strātīs (392)
(21) silvīs (399)
(22) cernās (401)
(23) hiemis (403)
(24) campīs (404)
(25) prōspicerēs (410)
(26) aequor (411)
(27) relinquat (415)

(28) colere (422)
(29) adfāre (424)
(30) Aulide (426)
(31) det (429)
(32) amantī (429)
(33) Latiō (432)
(34) careat (432)
(35) furōrī (433)
(36) doceat (434)
(37) quantum (445)
(38) exaudīrī (460)
(39) viam (468)
(40) sōlem (470)

## WORK UNIT XV
### (Based on *Aen.* IV, 474–629)

1. Make sure that you know the meaning of each of the following Latin words:

| | | | | | |
|---|---|---|---|---|---|
| citus | ērigō | furiae (*pl.*) | oblīvīscor | sistō | ululō |
| colōnus | exstinguō | herba | perdō | spūma | ūmidus |
| crīmen | fatīgō | igitur | precor | subitus | venēnum |
| decet | fōns | intendō | ratis | taeda | vērum |
| decōrus | frūctus | nauta | sacerdōs | terminus | vexō |
| dēprecor | fruor | nesciō | sēcernō | tonō | vigilō |
| ēn! | fūnis | niger | sertum | totiēns | volucer |

2. Find in the above list a word which is etymologically connected with each of the following English words, and be prepared to explain the connection in meaning.

| | | | | | |
|---|---|---|---|---|---|
| astound | deprecate | humid | intense | spume | very |
| consist | erect | imprecation | intention | tendency | vexation |
| criminal | font | indefatigable | nice | terminal | vigil |
| decent | fruition | infuriate | sacerdotal | venom | volatile |
| decorous | herbage | insert | secrete | | |

3. Who or what was each of the following?

Avernus     Hannibal     Hecate (hěk′a·tě)     Tithonus (tǐ·thō′nǔs)

4. Find in lines 474–629 a word, phrase, or sentence with which you can connect each of the following quotations:

My lord, you know what Virgil sings —
Woman is various and most mutable.
>     Tennyson, *Queen Mary*, 3, 6, 77–78.

And we fairies, that do run
By the triple Hecate's team.
>     Shakespeare, *Midsummer Night's Dream*, 5, 1, 368–369.

All was the night's; and in her silent reign
No sound the rest of nature did invade.
>     Dryden, *Annus Mirabilis*, 864–865.

Even so the gentle Tyrian Dame,
When neither Grief nor Love prevail,
Saw the dear object of her flame,
Th' ingrateful Trojan, hoist his sail.
>     Cowley, *The Heart Fled Again*, 7–10.

And from mine ashes, let a Conqueror rise,
That may revenge this treason to a Queene.

Marlowe and Nash, *The Tragedie of Dido,*
*Queen of Carthage,* 5, 305–306.

She found no rest, and ever fail'd to draw
The quiet night into her blood.

Tennyson, *The Marriage of Geraint,* 531–532.

5. What words other than *nāvis* does Vergil use to refer to a ship?

6. What words other than *mare* does Vergil use to refer to the sea?

7. Be prepared to explain the use of each of the following words or clauses:

| | | |
|---|---|---|
| (1) grātāre (478) | (15) cūrae (521) | (28) morī (564) |
| (2) sorōrī (478) | (16) labōrum (528) | (29) potestās (565) |
| (3) quae . . . eum (479) | (17) animī (529) | (30) attigerit (568) |
| (4) sacerdōs (483) | (18) experiar (535) | (31) noctī (570) |
| (5) accingier (493) | (19) fac (540) | (32) deōrum (576) |
| (6) tēctō (494) | (20) perjūria (542) | (33) Adsīs (578) |
| (7) morte (502) | (21) morere (547) | (34) tulissem (604) |
| (8) jussa (503) | (22) hostī (549) | (35) malīs (611) |
| (9) taedīs (505) | (23) eundī (554) | (36) terrīs (613) |
| (10) futūrī (508) | (24) omnia (558) | (37) implōret (617) |
| (11) crīnīs (509) | (25) Mercuriō (558) | (38) harēnā (620) |
| (12) mātrī (516) | (26) vōcem (558) | (39) suntō (624) |
| (13) pedem (518) | (27) quae . . . perīcula (561) | (40) sequāre (626) |
| (14) vinclīs (518) | | |

8. Be prepared to give the name of the figure of speech or metrical peculiarity illustrated by each of the following:

(1) movet Mānīs; mugīre (490)

(2) pecudēs pictaeque volucrēs (525)

(3) lacūs lātē liquidōs (526)

(4) omnia . . . juventā (558–559)

(5) imprecor . . . nepōtēsque (629)

## WORK UNIT XVI

### (Based on *Aen.* IV, 630–705)

1. Make sure that you know the meaning of each of the following Latin words:

| | | | | |
|---|---|---|---|---|
| ambō | flāvus | √macula | √praeclārus | tantum (*adv.*) |
| √auferō | √gradus | √miseror | quia | √trepidus |
| √celerō | √immittō | nectō | spernō | unguis |
| √cruor | | | | |

2. Try to find another Latin word etymologically connected with each of the checked words in the above list.

3. Who or what was each of the following?

Dis (dĭs)       Pluto (plū′tŏ)            Styx (stĭks)

Iris (ī′rĭs)     Proserpina (prŏ·sûr′pĭ·n*a*)

4. Find in lines 630–705 a word, phrase, or sentence with which you can connect each of the following quotations:

The soul delighted on each accent dwells, —
Enraptur'd dwells, — not daring to respire,
The while he tells of grief around a funeral pyre.

Keats, Ode to Apollo, 15–17.

And while yet aught remains, with mournful lips,
The last faint breath of life devoutly sips.

Ariosto, Orlando Furioso, 24, 655–656<br>(Rose's translation).

Hail, many color'd messenger, that ne'er
Dost disobey the wife of Jupiter.

Shakespeare, Tempest, 4, 1, 76–77.

Iris there with humid bow,
Waters the odorous banks, that blow
Flowers of more mingled hew
Than her purfl'd scarf can shew.

Milton, Comus, 991–994.

Dreaming, I see her climb on a funeral pyre
And burn her soul to ashes in love's fire.

Virginia T. McCormick, "Dido," in<br>Poetry (Nov., 1926), p. 81.

"Thus — thus — the soul flies out and dies in the air."
With that he drove the knife into his side.

Tennyson, Lucretius, 273–274.

5. Be prepared to explain the use of each of the following words or clauses:

(1) Barcēn (632)
(2) patriā (633)
(3) dīc (635)
(4) properet (635)
(5) cūrīs (639)
(6) torō (650)
(7) cūrīs (652)
(8) meī (654)
(9) tetigissent (658)
(10) moriāmur (660)
(11) Hauriat (661)
(12) Olympō (694)
(13) quae . . . artūs (695)
(14) corpore (703)

6. Be prepared to give the name of the metrical peculiarity illustrated by each of the following:

(1) fēmineō ululātū (667)          (2) sēmianimemque (686)

## WORK UNIT XVII
### (Based on *Aen.* VI, 1–211)

1. Make sure that you know the meaning of each of the following Latin words:

| | | | | |
|---|---|---|---|---|
| √āēr | √contingit | √gelidus | √liquidus | √rīte |
| √alternus | cūnctor | √grex | minae | siccus |
| antequam | √cupīdō | √hērōs | √opācus | √sīdō |
| antrum | √dēns | humus | ōrdior | √solidus |
| attonō | domō | ictus | √pariō | √stabulum |
| √avidus | √externus | īlex | √pinna | √stimulus |
| carmen | √folium | √intrō | √rabiēs | suēscō |
| certāmen | frēnum | √lacus | √rāmus | √truncus |
| √cessō | frētus | lentus | reor | √tumeō |
| √cōnsultum | | | | |

2. Try to find an English word etymologically connected with each of the checked words in the above list.

3. Who or what was each of the following?

Ariadne (ăr'ĭ·ăd'nē)
Castor
Cocytus (kŏ·sī'tŭs)
Cumae (cū'mē)
Daedalus (dĕd'á·lŭs)
Icarus (ĭk'á·rŭs)

Minos (mī'nŏs)
Minotaur (mĭn'ŏ·tôr)
Misenus (mĭ·sē'nŭs)
Orpheus (ôr'fūs)
Palinurus (păl·ĭ·nū'rŭs)

Pollux (pŏl'ŭks)
Sibyl (sĭb'ĭl)
Theseus (thē'sūs)
Trivia (trĭv'ĭ·á)
Turnus

4. Find in lines 1–211 a word, phrase, or sentence with which you can connect each of the following quotations:

Long is the way
And hard, that out of Hell leads up to light.

Milton, *Paradise Lost*, 2, 432–433.

Abhorrèd Styx, the flood of deadly hate,
Sad Acheron of sorrow, black and deep;
Cocytus, nam'd of lamentation loud
Heard on the rueful stream.

Milton, *Paradise Lost*, 2, 577–580.

Light among the vanish'd ages; star that gildest yet this phantom shore;
Golden branch amid the shadows, kings and realms that pass to rise no more.

Tennyson, *To Vergil*, 13–14.

He who died
For soaring too audacious in the sun
When that same treacherous wax began to run.

Keats, *Endymion*, 4, 441–443.

By the dim echoes of old Triton's horn.

Keats, *Endymion*, 1, 206.

Or bid the soul of Orpheus sing
Such notes as, warbled to the string,
Drew iron tears down Pluto's cheek,
And made Hell grant what Love did seek.

Milton, *Il Penseroso*, 105–108.

Her countenance brightens — and her eye expands;
Her bosom heaves and spreads, her stature grows.

Wordsworth, *Laodamia*, 10–11.

There lived and flourished long ago, in famous Athens town,
One Daedalus, a carpenter of genius and renown;
'Twas he who with an auger taught mechanics how to bore, —
An art which the philosophers monopolized before.

J. G. Saxe, *Travesties: Icarus*, 5–8.

From thy dear lips a clearer note is born
Than ever Triton blew from wreathèd horn!

O. W. Holmes, *The Chambered Nautilus*, 24–25.

5. Be prepared to explain the use of each of the following words, phrases, or clauses:

| | | |
|---|---|---|
| (1) ōrīs (2) | (16) fuerit (62) | (31) Gnātī (116) |
| (2) quibus (9) | (17) gentī (63) | (32) lūcīs (118) |
| (3) antrum (11) | (18) quibus (64) | (33) memorem (123) |
| (4) cui (11) | (19) fātīs (67) | (34) mī (123) |
| (5) rēgna (14) | (20) rēgnīs (71) | (35) Avernō (126) |
| (6) tibi (18) | (21) nē . . . ventīs (75) | (36) dīs (131) |
| (7) Androgeō (20) | (22) canās (76) | (37) similī metallō (144) |
| (8) habērēs (31) | (23) Phoebī (77) | (38) suntō (153) |
| (9) patriae (33) | (24) sponte suā (82) | (39) lūmina (156) |
| (10) perlegerent (34) | (25) dēfūncte (83) | (40) dīceret (162) |
| (11) adforet (35) | (26) ītō (95) | (41) caelō (178) |
| (12) cui (46) | (27) labōrum (103) | (42) montibus (182) |
| (13) fāta (53) | (28) mī (104) | (43) ferant (198) |
| (14) Teucrīs (54) | (29) contingat (109) | (44) īlice (209) |
| (15) miserāte (56) | (30) ut . . . peterem (115) | |

6. Be prepared to name the figure of speech or metrical peculiarity illustrated by each of the following:

    (1) omnia (33)            (3) quandō . . . locūta est (188–189)

    (2) hāc . . . tenus (62)     (4) quāle . . . truncōs (205–207)

7. Memorize line 126.

# WORK UNIT XVIII

## (Based on *Aen.* VI, 212–439)

1. Make sure that you know the meaning of each of the following Latin words:

| | | | | |
|---|---|---|---|---|
| acerbus | creō, –āre | fulgeō | mūgiō | spoliō |
| amictus | crepō | gurges | nūper | stāgnum |
| amnis | damnō | jūcundus | palleō | tepeō |
| avis | daps | jūdex | pondus | turba |
| caeruleus | dēsinō | juvencus | prīncipium | ūber |
| caleō | discō | laxō | raucus | uncus |
| canis | discrīmen | magister | senectūs | veneror |
| careō | fēlīx | mergō | sepeliō | virga |
| cognōmen | fluvius | morbus | sopor | viridis |
| crātēr | frīgus | | | |

2. Be prepared to explain the meaning of each of the italicized words in the following sentences and to show its etymological connection with some Latin word in the above list.

(1) Long *immersed* in business cares, with little time for *relaxation* or *recreation*, he finally came to take a *morbid* view of life.

(2) The sight *appalled* the stoutest heart.

(3) The wolf belongs to the *canine* family.

(4) The people are sometimes not very *discriminating* in their *nominations* for even the most important *magistracies*.

(5) The teacher made a *judicious* use of *carets* in revising the pupil's report.

(6) Although already an octogenarian, he showed no signs of *senile* weakness.

(7) "Lincolnshire may be termed the *aviary* of England."

(8)                 "Blue, blue, as if that sky let fall
                    A flower from its *cerulean* wall."

(9) "*Condemn* the fault and not the actor of it."

(10) "Our own *felicity* we make or find."

(11)               "Night's candles are burnt out and *jocund* day
                    Stands tip-toe on the misty mountain tops."

(12) "The *sepulcher* hath oped his *ponderous* and marble jaws."

(13) "And seemed to *venerate* the sacred shade."

3. Who or what was each of the following?

Acheron (ăk'ĕr·ŏn)          Cerberus (sûr'bĕr·ŭs)      Hercules
Alcides (ăl·sī'dēz)          Charon (kā'rŏn)            Orontes (ŏ·rŏn'tēz)
Anchisiades (ăn·kĭ·sī'à·dēz)

4. Find in lines 212–439 a word, phrase, or sentence with which you can connect each of the following quotations:

When in the down I sink my head,
Sleep, Death's twin-brother, times my breath;
Sleep, Death's twin-brother, knows not death,
Nor can I dream of thee as dead.

Tennyson, *In Memoriam*, 1269–1272.

And lo! toward us coming in a boat,
An old man with the whitened hair of age.

Dante, *Inferno*, 3, 82–83 (Johnson's translation).

Nor leaves by so great numbers fall away,
When winter nips them with his new-come frosts.

Tasso, *Jerusalem Delivered*, 9, 525–526 (Fairfax's translation).

But hasting straight unto the bank apace,
With hollow call unto the rout he cried,
To swerve apart, and give the goddess place.

\* \* \* \* \*

And forth we launch full fraughted to the brink;
When, with the unwonted weight, the rusty keel
Began to crack, as if the same should sink.

> Sackville, *Induction*, 485–487, 491–493.

And Cerberus, a cruel and strange beast,
From out his triple throat barks like a dog
Over the people that are there submerged.

> Dante, *Inferno*, 6, 13–15 (Johnson's translation).

O think how to his latest day,
When Death, just hovering, claim'd his prey,
With Palinure's unalter'd mood,
Firm at his dangerous post he stood;
Each call for needful rest repell'd;
With dying hand the rudder held,
Till, in his fall with fateful sway,
The steerage of the realm gave way!

> Scott, *Marmion*, Introduction to Canto I, 109–116.

This huge convex of fire,
Outrageous to devour, immures us round
Ninefold.

> Milton, *Paradise Lost*, 2, 434–436.

As heedless fowls that take their per'lous flight
Over that bane of birds, Averno lake,
Do drop down dead.

> Henry More, *Cupid's Conflict*, 67–69.

The darksome river
Of Styx, not passable to souls returning,
Enclosing you in thrice three wards forever.

> Spenser, *Ruins of Rome*, 201–203.

And thou, who standest there, thou living soul,
Depart from these, the dead.

> Dante, *Inferno*, 3, 88–89 (Johnson's translation).

5. Be prepared to explain the use of each of the following words, phrases, or clauses:

| | | |
|---|---|---|
| (1) cui (215) | (16) venientibus (291) | (31) mihi (365) |
| (2) frīgentis (219) | (17) cui (299) | (32) terram (365) |
| (3) feretrō (222) | (18) mentō (299) | (33) quiēscam (371) |
| (4) mōre (223) | (19) deō (304) | (34) precandō (376) |
| (5) ingentī mōle (232) | (20) rīpae (314) | (35) tumulō (380) |
| (6) virō (233) | (21) Ollī (321) | (36) corde (383) |
| (7) Mīsēnus (234) | (22) Anchīsā (322) | (37) quid veniās (389) |
| (8) frontī (244) | (23) rīpās (327) | (38) Alcīdēn (392) |
| (9) ātrī velleris (249) | (24) sēdibus (328) | (39) agnōscās (407) |
| (10) mātrī (250) | (25) annōs (329) | (40) tempore (409) |
| (11) adventante deā (258) | (26) honōre (333) | (41) humī (423) |
| (12) lūcō (259) | (27) nōbīs (342) | (42) antrō (423) |
| (13) animīs (261) | (28) mihī (343) | (43) custōde sepultō (424) |
| (14) sit (266) | (29) tua nē ... undīs (354) | (44) vītae (428) |
| (15) crīnem (281) | (30) invāsisset (361) | |

6. Be prepared to name the figure of speech or metrical peculiarity illustrated by each of the following:

(1) quāle ... colōrem (270–272)      (4) ferreīque (280)

(2) Lūctus (274)      (5) quam ... aprīcīs (309–312)

(3) Senectūs (275)      (6) alveō (412)

# WORK UNIT XIX

## (Based on *Aen.* VI, 440–678)

1. Make sure that you know the meaning of each of the following Latin words:

| | | | | |
|---|---|---|---|---|
| admoneō | frequēns | lūgeō | pretium | tondeō |
| anguis | fūrtum | lūxuria | pulsō | torreō |
| axis | habitō | −met | quatiō | torvus |
| beātus | hiō | monumentum | rōstrum | tunc |
| castus | immineō | nimius | rota | urgeō |
| chorus | laetor | niteō | scelerātus | vēndō |
| digitus | laurus | nūbila | scīlicet | verber |
| dīvitiae | luctor | ovō | strepitus | vicis |
| dominus | lūdus | porrigō | tenebrae | vīscus |
| fraus | | | | |

2. Find in the list on page 282 a word which is etymologically connected with each of the following English words, and be prepared to explain the connection in meaning:

| | | | | |
|---|---|---|---|---|
| admonition | don (*noun*) | inhabitant | ovation | torrid |
| beatitude | furtive | interlude | pulsation | urgent |
| caste | hiatus | laureate | reluctant | vendor |
| chastize | imminent | lugubrious | reverberate | vicar |
| defraud | infrequent | luxuriant | rotation | viscous |
| depreciate | | | | |

3. Who or what was each of the following?

Elysium (ē·lĭzh'ĭ·ŭm)   Rhadamanthus (răd'a·măn'thŭs)   Tisiphone (tĭ·sĭf'ō·nē)
Musaeus (mū·zē'ŭs)   Salmoneus (săl·mō'nūs)   Tityos (tĭt'ĭ·ŏs)
Phlegethon (flĕg'ĕ·thŏn)   Tartarus (tär'ta·rŭs)   Tydeus (tī'dūs)
Pirithoüs (Pĭr·ĭ'thō·ŭs)

4. Find in lines 440–678 a word, phrase, or sentence with which you can connect each of the following quotations:

Saw him as one that hath seen or hath thought he hath seen
The moon, when the month is young, through mist-veils floating between.

> Apollonius Rhodius, *Argonautica*, 4, 1479–1480
> (Way's translation).

The sheeted dead
Did squeak and gibber in the Roman streets.

> Shakespeare, *Hamlet*, 1, 1, 115–116.

At last appear
Hell bounds, high reaching to the horrid roof,
And thrice threefold the gates; three folds were brass,
Three iron, three of adamantine rock,
Impenetrable, impaled with circling fire,
Yet unconsumed.  Before the gates there sat
On either side a formidable shape.

> Milton, *Paradise Lost*, 2, 643–649.

Shrieks of woe,
Sullen moans,
Hollow groans
And cries of tortured ghosts!

> Pope, *Ode for Music on Saint Cecilia's Day*, 59–62.

As far remov'd from God and light of Heav'n
As from the centre thrice to the utmost pole.

> Milton, *Paradise Lost*, 1, 73–74.

Still fly, plunge deeper in the bowering wood!
Averse, as Dido did with gesture stern
From her false friend's approach in Hades turn,
Wave us away, and keep thy solitude!

Matthew Arnold, *The Scholar Gypsy*, 207–210.

With useless endeavor,
Forever, forever,
Is Sisyphus rolling
His stone up the mountain!

Longfellow, *The Masque of Pandora*, 283–286.

An ampler ether, a diviner air,
And fields invested with purpureal gleams;
Climes which the sun, who sheds the brightest day
Earth knows, is all unworthy to survey.

Wordsworth, *Laodamia*, 105–108.

5. Be prepared to explain the use of each of the following words, phrases, or clauses:

(1) dulcī amōre (455)
(2) mihi (456)
(3) deum (461)
(4) solō (469)
(5) cūrīs (474)
(6) euntem (476)
(7) armīs (479)
(8) nocte (503)
(9) tibi (509)
(10) ēgerimus (514)
(11) mortī (522)
(12) capitī (524)
(13) scelerum (529)
(14) adīrēs (534)

(15) traherent (537)
(16) fātīs (546)
(17) adamante (552)
(18) valeant (554)
(19) diēs (556)
(20) exaudīrī (557)
(21) Teucrum (562)
(22) lūcīs (564)
(23) deum (565)
(24) Salmōnea (585)
(25) quī . . . equōrum (590–591)
(26) memorem (601)
(27) lāpsūra (602)

(28) dominōrum (613)
(29) merset (615)
(30) aurō (621)
(31) ausō (624)
(32) sint (625)
(33) possim (627)
(34) locōs (638)
(35) annīs (649)
(36) currum (653)
(37) suī (664)
(38) nūllī (673)
(39) lūcīs (673)
(40) trāmite (676)

6. Be prepared to name the figure of speech or metrical peculiarity illustrated by each of the following:

(1) quālem . . . lūnam (453–454)
(2) tē, amīce, nequīvī (507)
(3) quōs super (602)

(4) quōs . . . cadentīque (602)
(5) dehinc (678)

## WORK UNIT XX

(Based on *Aen*. VI, 679–901)

1. Make sure that you know the meaning of each of the following Latin words:

| | | | |
|---|---|---|---|
| albus | √dēsignō | parum | sērus |
| √aptus | flōs | pestis | √signō |
| arcus | fodiō | prīdem | socer |
| √auspicium | gener | √prōgeniēs | √spīritus |
| avus | grāmen | proprius | spīrō |
| bracchium | habēna | prōra | stella |
| √candeō | inlūstris | radius | stirps |
| carcer | √lūceō | √rēctē | sulcus |
| √cīvīlis | marmor | sal | triumphus |
| √comitor | √obeō | secūris | √ulcīscor |
| √concordia | √obvius | sēmen | ultor |
| crista | ōtium | serēnus | |

2. Find another Latin word that is etymologically connected with each of the checked words in the above list.

3. Who or what was each of the following?

| | | | | |
|---|---|---|---|---|
| Ancus | Camillus | Lethe (lē′thē) | Numa | Tarquin |
| Brutus | Laurentum | Marcellus | Saturn | Tullus |

4. Find in lines 679–901 a word, phrase, or sentence with which you can connect each of the following quotations:

> To spare his subjects yet to quell the proud.
>
> Ben Johnson, *Hue and Cry after Cupid*, 125.

> Millions and millions on these banks he views,
> Thick as the stars of night or morning dews,
> As thick as bees o'er vernal blossoms fly.
>
> Pope, *The Dunciad*, 3, 31–33.

> Far off from these a slow and silent stream,
> Lethe the river of oblivion roules
> Her waterie labyrinth, whereof who drinks,
> Forthwith his former state and being forgets,
> Forgets both joy and grief, pleasure and pain.
>
> Milton, *Paradise Lost*, 2, 582–586.

A sense sublime
Of something far more deeply interfused,

\* \* \* \* \*

A motion and a spirit, that impels
All thinking things, all objects of all thought,
And rolls through all things.

Wordsworth, *Lines Composed a Few Miles Above
Tintern Abbey*, 95–96, 100–102.

Such harmony is in immortal souls;
But whilst this muddy vesture of decay
Doth grossly close it in, we cannot hear it.

Shakespeare, *The Merchant of Venice*, 5, 1, 63–65.

Anchises look'd not with so pleas'd face,
In numbering o'er his future Roman race,
And marshalling the heroes of his name,
As, in their order, next to light they came.

Dryden, *Eleonora*, 197–200.

This, this is he foretold by ancient rhymes,
Th' Augustus born to bring Saturnian times.

Pope, *The Dunciad*, 3, 319–320.

For portals twain for the flitting of bodiless dreams there be,
And the one is fashioned of horn, and the other of ivory.
Now every dream through the ivory dead-smooth-sawn that flies
Is a dream that shall not be fulfilled, and it bringeth a tale of lies.
But they that come up to the earth through the horn-gate's polished sheen
Fail never, but bring to pass whatsoever the dreamer hath seen.

Homer, *Odyssey*, 19, 562–567 (Way's translation).

5. Be prepared to explain the use of each of the following words or clauses:

| | | |
|---|---|---|
| (1) parentī (687) | (9) ollīs (730) | (17) sulcō (844) |
| (2) nē . . . nocērent (694) | (10) aurāī (747) | (18) subjectīs (853) |
| (3) collō (700) | (11) Longā Albā (766) | (19) patrī (859) |
| (4) ventīs (702) | (12) Latiō (793) | (20) rumpās (882) |
| (5) complērint (712) | (13) Sāturnō (794) | (21) fugiat (892) |
| (6) laetēre (718) | (14) aurīs (816) | (22) portā (898) |
| (7) lūcis (721) | (15) patriae (823) | (23) lītore (900) |
| (8) miserīs (721) | (16) relinquat (841) | (24) lītore (901) |

6. Memorize lines 847–853.

# APPENDIX

# APPENDIX

## LIFE OF VERGIL

**1.** Publius Vergilius Maro is not only the greatest Roman poet, but one of the outstanding universal poets as well. His reputation was already established in his lifetime, and for the past 2000 years his poetry, particularly his long epic poem, the *Aeneid*, has been read and studied in every civilized country. Most of the information that we have about Vergil's life is derived from a biography of the poet written by Donatus, a grammarian of the fourth century A.D., who in turn made use of a biography written by Suetonius more than a century after Vergil's death.

**2.** Publius Vergilius Maro was born on October 15, 70 B.C., in the village of Andes (modern Pietole) near Mantua, in a peaceful rural community. Vergil's parents, though of humble origin, managed to send their son to study first at Mantua, then at Cremona, then at Milan, and later at Rome and Naples where he continued to pursue his rhetorical, philosophical, and mathematical interests. As he was physically delicate and of halting speech, he took little or no part in public life.

**3.** After the battle of Philippi (42 B.C.) the farm of Vergil's father was confiscated and assigned, along with other confiscated land, to the veteran soldiers of Octavian and Antony. With the help of friends, notably Maecenas, Vergil secured compensation for the land that had been seized. Vergil later introduced the poet Horace to Maecenas, and this literary and intellectual triumvirate endured for the rest of Vergil's life. Vergil received from Maecenas a home in Rome but he seems to have spent most of his later years at Naples, studying and writing.

**4.** After completing and publishing the *Eclogues* in 37 B.C., Vergil began work on the *Georgics*. He spent seven years in the composition of this poem, and at intervals went traveling, possibly as far as Greece. The *Georgics* were published in 29 B.C. and Vergil then began his final work, the *Aeneid*, spending the last ten years of his life on this epic. In 23 B.C. Vergil read parts of the *Aeneid* to Augustus and his sister Octavia. In 19 B.C. Vergil had completed the first draft of this great poem, although he himself was not satisfied with it and intended to revise it. With this purpose in mind, he set out for Greece. At Athens he met Augustus, who persuaded him to return to Italy. During the return voyage Vergil fell ill and died at Brundisium on September 21, 19 B.C. He was buried at Naples. On his tomb was inscribed:

> Mantua mē genuit; Calabrī rapuēre; tenet nunc
> Parthenopē. Cecinī pāscua, rūra, ducēs.
>
> Mantua was my birthplace; Calabria saw my
> death; now Naples holds me. I have sung of
> pastures, fields, and heroes.

**5.** In the list of Vergil's writings, mentioned in the inscription on his tomb, **pāscua** obviously refers to the *Eclogues,* a collection of ten pastoral poems, many of them written in imitation of the Greek pastoral poet Theocritus. The **rūra** in the inscription refers to the *Georgics,* a didactic poem on farming, which was written at the suggestion of Maecenas in the hope of reviving the old Roman interest in agricultural pursuits. This poem consists of four books dealing respectively with the culture of the fields, the cultivation of trees and vines, the breeding of cattle, and the care of bees. The **ducēs** in the inscription refers, of course, to the *Aeneid,* an epic poem of twelve books (see sections 7–11). No mention is made in the inscription of the so-called *Minor Poems* commonly attributed to Vergil.

**6.**　　　COMMONLY ACCEPTED DATES IN THE LIFE OF VERGIL

70 B.C. Vergil is born on October 15.

58 B.C. Vergil begins his studies at Cremona.

55 B.C. Vergil assumes the toga virilis.

54 B.C. Vergil studies at Milan.

53 B.C. Vergil begins his studies at Rome.

50 B.C. Vergil begins his studies at Naples.

43 B.C. Vergil begins work on the *Eclogues.*

41 B.C. Vergil's family estate is confiscated.

40 B.C. Vergil is compensated for his lost estate.

37 B.C. Vergil publishes the *Eclogues* and begins the *Georgics.*

29 B.C. Vergil publishes the *Georgics* and begins the *Aeneid.*

19 B.C. Vergil goes to Greece, returns to Brundisium, and dies there on September 21.

## THE *AENEID*

**7.** The *Aeneid,* an epic poem in twelve books, recounts the adventures of Aeneas, the traditional founder of the Roman race. Vergil's purpose in writing this poem was to glorify Rome by portraying its origins in a series of vivid, dramatic scenes of struggle, shipwreck, wanderings, and conquest; to proclaim Rome's destined future glory in a series of prophetic visions; to summon the Roman people, exhausted by civil strife, to a worshipful respect for their new Empire and their first Emperor, to a reverence for the old gods, and to a restoration of the simple lives and sturdy virtues of their forefathers.

**8.** The tradition is that Vergil wrote the *Aeneid* not consecutively, but by episodes, as the mood seized him. At any rate, the poem, as it was given to the public after Vergil's death, shows a number of inconsistencies and some fifty incomplete lines. Vergil realized that the epic was not in final shape, and before his death he asked that the poem be burned. However, through the intervention of Augustus, the *Aeneid* was saved for posterity. While Vergil was still engaged in writing the first draft of the *Aeneid,* the poet Propertius announced that a poem greater than Homer's *Iliad* was in preparation:

> Cēdite, Rōmānī scrīptōrēs; cēdite, Graī;
> nescio quid maius nāscitur Īliade.

> Give way, ye Roman authors; give way, ye Greeks;
> something greater than the *Iliad* is coming to birth.

**9.** A comparison between the *Aeneid* and the *Iliad* is appropriate, because both in phraseology and in style Vergil imitated Homer's epic poems, the *Iliad* and the *Odyssey.* The first six books of the *Aeneid* may be compared with the *Odyssey;* the last six books with the *Iliad.* The story of Troy had also been used by other Greek poets — the Cyclic Poets, so called because they treated the cycle of stories dealing with Troy. To this group of poets Vergil was indebted as well as to Homer. Vergil also made use of the old Roman epics of Naevius and Ennius. Naevius, in his *Bellum Punicum,* had treated the First Punic War. Ennius, in his *Annales,* had traced the history of Rome from the days of Aeneas onward. But Vergil, although he borrowed matter and literary devices from other poets, fused what he took from them into a new organic whole. The beauty of his language, the dignity of his rhythm, the sweep and the vastness of the poem itself, embellished with the poet's own meditations on life, made the *Aeneid* a model for later poets, both Roman and foreign. Of Latin epic poems, Lucan's *Pharsalia,* Statius's *Thebais* and *Achilleis,* Valerius Flaccus's *Argonautica,* and Silius Italicus's *Punica* are all crowded with Vergilian imitations and reminiscences. The Italian poet Dante, in his *Divine Comedy,* took Vergil as his "master and guide." Ariosto's *Orlando Furioso* and Tasso's *Jerusalem Delivered,* both Italian epics, were also influenced by the *Aeneid.* Milton's *Paradise Lost* is filled with echoes of Vergil's style and vocabulary. Other English poets and dramatists, such as Chaucer, Spenser, Shakespeare, Marlowe, Tennyson, and Swinburne, found inspiration and substance in Vergil's *Aeneid.*

**10.** In the Middle Ages Vergil had grown into a legend, and the poet himself became associated with the magical arts, with prophecy, and even with the Christian religion. The fourth *Eclogue,* in fact, was long considered as a Messianic prophecy. The name of the poet, too, began to be written Virgilius, the explanation being that the name was associated with *virga,* the wand used by medieval magicians. Vergil's own thoughts, embedded in the *Aeneid,* are of such universal application that to the medieval mind the poem became endowed with prophetic import. In a time of stress the *Aeneid* was opened at random. On whatever verse the eye fell, an omen, favorable or otherwise, was deduced. The story goes that Charles I of England, just before his execution, opened the *Aeneid* at Book IV, lines 615–621, a passage that foretells the death of Aeneas.

## 11.            THE STORY OF THE *AENEID* IN BRIEF

Book I. Under Aeneas the Trojans sail toward Italy. Juno contrives a storm, and the Trojans are shipwrecked on the coast of Libya. They are welcomed by Queen Dido in her palace at Carthage. At a banquet Aeneas recounts his adventures.

Book II. Aeneas tells about the destruction of Troy and his escape with his father Anchises, his son Ascanius, and a few Trojan followers.

Book III. After unsuccessful attempts to settle in Thrace and Crete, the Trojans land in Western Sicily, where Anchises dies. After sailing from Sicily, the Trojans are driven by a storm to the coast of Libya.

Book IV. Dido falls madly in love with Aeneas. Mercury warns Aeneas of his divine mission to seek a home in Italy. Aeneas leaves Carthage, and Dido in despair kills herself.

Book V. Aeneas lands in Sicily on the anniversary of his father's death. Funeral games are held to mark the occasion. Aeneas then sails for Italy.

Book VI. Landing at Cumae, Aeneas meets the Sibyl. He visits the underworld to consult Anchises, who prophesies the future greatness of Rome.

Book VII. Aeneas lands on the left bank of the Tiber and is welcomed by envoys from King Latinus, who offers Aeneas his daughter Lavinia in marriage. Juno stirs up strife between the Trojans and the Italians.

Book VIII. Aeneas sails up the river to Palanteum, later the Palatine Hill, and makes an alliance with King Evander. Vulcan at Venus's request forges weapons for Aeneas.

Book IX. Turnus in Aeneas's absence attacks the Trojan camp. Ascanius with bow and arrow kills Numanus, brother-in-law of Turnus. Turnus enters the Trojan camp and slays many Trojans.

Book X. Aeneas returns with Etrurian allies and Pallas, son of King Evander. Turnus slays Pallas and Aeneas slays Mezentius, an exiled Etrurian king.

Book XI. After a twelve days' truce for the burial of the dead, the Trojans advance on Laurentum. Camilla, warrior maiden and ally of Turnus, is slain by a Trojan.

Book XII. Turnus agrees to single combat with Aeneas. King Latinus and Aeneas meet at an altar in the plain to arrange for the combat. Juturna, Turnus's sister, incites the Latins to violate the truce and attack the Trojans. Aeneas is wounded, but is miraculously cured with the help of Venus. Aeneas and Turnus finally meet, and Aeneas slays Turnus.

**12.**          A  SELECTED  BIBLIOGRAPHY  ON  VERGIL

### 1. *Vergil's Life*

Conway, R. S.  *The Youth of Vergil.*  Manchester, 1915.
Frank, Tenney.  *Vergil: a Biography.*  Henry Holt & Co., 1922.
Glover, T. R.  *Virgil.*  The Macmillan Co., 1912.
Nardi, Bruno.  *The Youth of Vergil.*  Harvard University Press, 1930.
Nettleship, Henry.  *Ancient Lives of Vergil.*  Oxford University Press, 1879.

### 2. *Vergilian Studies and Criticism*

Boissier, G.  *The Country of Horace and Vergil.*  Stechert, 1923.
Comparetti, Domenico.  *Vergil in the Middle Ages.*  Stechert, 1929.
Conway, R. S.  *Harvard Lectures on the Vergilian Age.*  Harvard University Press, 1928.
Drew, D. L.  *Allegory of the Aeneid.*  B. H. Blackwell, 1927.
Fowler, W. W.  *Aeneas at the Site of Rome.*  Oxford University Press, 1917.
————. - *The Death of Turnus.*  B. H. Blackwell, 1919.
Glover, T. R.  *Vergil.*  The Macmillan Co., 1924.
Mackail, J. W.  *Virgil and His Meaning to the World Today.*  Boston: Marshall Jones Co., 1922.
Nitchie, Elizabeth.  *Master Vergil.*  D. C. Heath & Co., 1930.
Prescott, H. W.  *Development of Virgil's Art.*  The University of Chicago Press, 1927.
Rand, E. K.  *In Quest of Virgil's Birthplace.*  Harvard University Press, 1930.
Saunders, Catharine, *Vergil's Primitive Italy.*  Oxford University Press, 1930.
Sellar, W. Y.  *Roman Poets of the Augustan Age: Virgil.*  Oxford University Press, 1908.
Showerman, Grant.  *Monuments and Men of Ancient Rome.*  Appleton-Century Co., 1935.
Slaughter, M. S.  *Roman Portraits.*  Yale University Press, 1925.
Waterman, Florence.  "Studies and Tests on Vergil's *Aeneid," Harvard Bulletins in Education.*  Harvard University Press, 1930.

### 3. *Translations*

Ballard, H. W.  *Aeneid.*  Charles Scribner's Sons, 1908.
Conington, J. P.  *Virgil: Works.*  (Home Library).  Longmans, Green & Co., 1892.
Dryden, John.  *Virgil: Works.*  London: Milford, 1925.
Fairclough, H. R.  *Virgil.*  2 Vols.  G. P. Putman's Sons, 1929.
Jackson, John.  *Virgil.*  Oxford Junior Series, 1920.
Mackail, J. W.  *Aeneid.*  The Macmillan Co., 1908.
Williams, T. C.  *Aeneid.*  Houghton Mifflin Co., 1908.

### 4. *Critical Editions*

Conington, J. P., Nettleship, H., and Haverfield, F.  *P. Vergili Maronis Opera.*  London: George Bell & Sons, 1898.
Mackail, J. W.  *Aeneid.*  Oxford University Press, 1930.

### 5. *Fiction*

Atherton, Gertrude.  *Dido, Queen of Hearts.*  Horace Liveright, 1929.
White, E. L.  *Helen.*  Doubleday, Doran & Co., 1925.

## A BRIEF SURVEY OF LATIN POETRY

**13.** Latin poetry is to a great extent imitative, in its meter and its material, of Greek poetry, although there were in Italy early indigenous forms, mostly hymns, prayers, and chants, associated with religious ceremonials. The first known Roman poet was Livius Andronicus. He was a Greek who had been taken prisoner and brought to Rome. He wrote plays in Latin, the first of which was acted in 240 B.C. He also translated the *Odyssey* into the native Italian meter called Saturnian.

**14.** After Livius Andronicus came the epic poet Naevius, who wrote (also in Saturnian verse) the *Bellum Punicum*, an epic poem on the First Punic War. He produced his first play in 235 B.C. Next came Ennius, who wrote an epic poem, the *Annales*, on the history of Rome. Ennius was the first Roman poet to employ dactylic hexameter, a verse form which had long been used by Greek writers and which Vergil was later to bring to so high a degree of perfection that Tennyson called it the "stateliest measure ever moulded by the lips of man." Other poets followed Ennius, mostly imitators or adapters of Greek writers, most important of whom were Plautus and Terence, who produced Latin comedies written chiefly in iambic or trochaic meters.

**15.** It is not until early in the first century before Christ that a significant original Roman poet appears. He is a brooding, rather mysterious figure, Titus Lucretius Carus (*ca.* 95–*ca.* 52 B.C.), author of a poem on natural phenomena called *De Rerum Natura*. Lucretius hammers out in throbbing, pulsating, clangorous hexameters his scientific beliefs, and wrests into rhythm discussions on the origin of human speech, on the evolution of society, on the atom, and on the physical foundation of the world. His is a strange, absorbing poem, crammed with startlingly modern views.

**16.** A little later in the century comes a period enormously rich in poets. There was a group of energetic, scholarly, modernistic writers, who in their search for novelty and literary preciseness ransacked mythological obscurities and studded their poems with subtle classical allusions. The best known of these poets is Gaius Valerius Catullus (*ca.* 87–*ca.* 54 B.C.), a lyric poet of great power and passion. His were universal themes: love, friendship, hate. His lyrics, epigrams, and wedding hymns give him kinship with poets like Burns and Heine.

**17.** Next comes what is known as the Augustan Age, the Golden Age of Latin literature, remarkable for the patronage of literary men and for the brilliance of its poets, orators, and historians. The poet par excellence of this period was Vergil, author of the great national epic, the *Aeneid*. With Vergil may be linked Quintus Horatius Flaccus, genial satirist of himself and his fellow-countrymen and the greatest Roman writer of lyric poetry. Horace was born at Venusia in 65 B.C., his father being a poor freedman. Under the guidance of his father, however, he studied in Rome, and later in Athens. Although he fought against Octavian at Philippi, he later became, through his friendship with Vergil and Maecenas, a beloved and honored member of the court circle, and spent the rest of his life as "poet laureate" of the Empire. He died in 8 B.C. His *Odes* in particular have served as a model for perfection of phrase and elegance of style. To this period belongs also Publius Ovidius Naso (43 B.C.–A.D. 18), who in his *Metamorphoses* shaped the mythology of the ancient world into smooth and fascinating stories in verse which have been the source book on classical mythology for Italian, French, German, and English writers. To this period belongs also Manilius, who wrote an astronomical poem entitled *Aetna;* Phaedrus, a freedman of Augustus, who produced a collection of *Fables* in iambic meter, five books of which are extant; and others, both named and nameless, whose works have come down to us either in minute fragments or by reputation.

**18.** The Golden Age was followed by the Silver Age, a period that synchronized with the stabilization of the Roman Empire and the extension of Latin culture throughout Western Europe and Northern Africa. Prose writers were most numerous and most prominent in this age. Poets were fewer, less imaginative, less varied in their subjects, less personal in their treatment. Persius inveighs against conditions of his days in six tortuous satires. Columella, imitating Vergil, wrote on agriculture. Statius was the author of two epics, the *Thebais* and the *Achilleis*, the latter unfinished. In addition Statius wrote shorter, occasional pieces collected under the title *Silvae*.

**19.** Martial, the epigrammatist, is a kind of poetic journalist, a Roman versifying columnist. He puts down in verse the varied happenings of the day: an invitation, a lament on his poverty, a hit at some notorious Roman, praise of the Emperor Domitian, an epitaph on a little child, mottoes to accompany presents. All the trivial common incidents of everyday life are grist to his poetic mill. He is witty and observant, laughs at the weaknesses of his fellows and himself, and, despite his complaints, takes huge relish in living. Born in Spain about A.D. 40, he came to Rome in 66, where he lived for some thirty-five years, returning to Spain shortly before his death about A.D. 102. Fifteen books of his poems survive, twelve of which are published under the head of *Epigrams*. His other three books were, respectively, *Liber Spectaculōrum, Xenia,* and *Apophoreta*.

**20.** Juvenal also is a satirist, but different from the genial Horace. He rants and roars, lashing the vices of his day with harsh invective. In sweeping denunciations he fulminates against the corruption of Roman society, and presents a dark but absorbing picture of his time. Sixteen of his *Satires* survive. Far beyond the Silver Age there is a succession of Roman poets and poems of varying degrees of excellence. There is, first, the stirring poem *Pervigilium Veneris* (The Vigil of Venus), an anonymous rhapsody on Spring and the Resurgence of Life, swaying and swinging in melodious verse.

**21.** In the fourth century A.D. the poets Ausonius and Claudian appear. The later centuries are crowded with names but they become more and more the names of poets who were not Roman in the national sense, but provincials who used the language of Rome as their literary instrument and the classical Latin authors as their models.

## FIGURES OF SPEECH

**22.** The following figures of speech and other literary devices are common in the *Aeneid* and other Latin poetry.

1. *Alliteration:* the repetition of the same letter at the beginning of two or more adjacent words or syllables; e.g., **magnō cum murmure montis** (*Aen.* I, 55); **magnō miscērī murmure** (*Aen.* I, 124).
2. *Anaphora:* the repetition, for emphasis, of a word at the beginning of each of a series of phrases; e.g., **Tū ... tū ... tū** (*Aen.* I, 78–79); **nunc ... nunc ... nunc** (*Aen.* IV, 376–377).
3. *Anastrophe:* the placing of a preposition after, instead of before, the word that it governs; e.g., **Ītaliam contrā** (*Aen.* I, 13).
4. *Aposiopesis:* a sudden break in a sentence, making the sentence incomplete but the meaning clear; e.g., **Quōs ego —** (*Aen.* I, 135).
5. *Apostrophe:* a pretended turning from one's audience to address directly an absent person or thing; e.g., **Trōjaque nunc stāret, Priamīque arx alta manērēs** (*Aen.* II, 56).
6. *Asyndeton:* the omission of the conjunction; e.g., **urbe, domō sociās** (*Aen.* I, 600).
7. *Chiasmus:* a crisscross arrangement of words; e.g., **Īlionēa petit dextrā laevāque Serestum** (*Aen.* I, 611).
8. *Ellipsis:* omission of a word or words grammatically necessary to complete a sentence or clause; e.g., **advectī (sumus)** (*Aen.* I, 558); **Aeolus haec contrā (ait)** (*Aen.* I, 76).
9. *Hendiadys:* the expression of one idea by the use of two nouns joined by **et** instead of by one noun modified by an adjective or by another noun in the genitive; e.g., **vinclīs et carcere** (*Aen.* I, 54); **molemque et montīs imposuit** (*Aen.* I. 61–62).
10. *Hysteron proteron:* a reversal of the logical sequence of ideas; e.g., **moriāmur et in media arma ruāmus** (*Aen.* II, 353).
11. *Litotes:* an understatement, usually in the form of a negative statement implying a positive statement; e.g., **nōn similī poenā** (*Aen.* I, 136); **nōn indēbita rēgna** (*Aen.* VI, 66–67).
12. *Metaphor:* an implied comparison; e.g., **sedet custōs** (*Aen.* IV, 186).

13. *Metonymy:* the substitution of one word for another related to the first word; e.g., **Bacchī** ( = **vīnī**) (*Aen.* I, 215); **Vulcānō** ( = **ignī**) (*Aen.* II, 311).

14. *Onomatopeia:* an adaptation of the sound of words to the sense; e.g., **magnō cum murmure montis** (*Aen.* I. 55); **īnsequitur clamorque virum strīdorque rudentum** (*Aen.* I. 87).

15. *Oxymoron:* an apparent contradiction of terms: e.g., **via invia** (*Aen.* III, 383).

16. *Personification:* the endowing of inanimate things with human characteristics; e.g., **ultrīcēs posuēre cubīlia Cūrae** (*Aen.* VI, 274); **pallentēsque habitant Morbī** (*Aen.* VI, 275).

17. *Polysyndeton:* the repetition of a conjunction with each of a series of words or clauses; e.g., **Thessandrus Sthenelusque ducēs et dīrus Ulixēs** (*Aen.* II, 261).

18. *Prolepsis:* the use of an epithet by which the result of the act of the verb is anticipated; e.g., **ut furentem incendat rēgīnam** (*Aen.* I, 658–660).

19. *Simile:* an expressed comparison; e.g., **quālis opēs . . . fūcōs . . . arcent** (*Aen.* I, 430–435); **quāle per incertam lūnam sub lūce malignā est iter in silvīs** (*Aen.* VI, 270–271).

20. *Synchysis:* an interlocking order of words; e.g., **saevae memorem Jūnōnis ob īram** (*Aen.*, I, 4).

21. *Synecdoche:* the use of a part of a unit to represent the entire unit; e.g., **Natat carīna** (*Aen.* IV, 398); **caeruleam advertit puppim** (*Aen.* VI, 410).

22. *Tmesis:* the separation of two parts of a compound word by an intervening word or phrase; e.g., **quae mē cumque vocant terrae** (*Aen.* I, 610).

23. *Zeugma:* the use of a verb with two expressions, for only one of which the verb is appropriate; e.g., **jūra magistrātūsque legunt** (*Aen.* I, 426); **Massylīque ruunt equitēs et odōra canum vīs** (*Aen.* IV, 132).

## LATIN VERSIFICATION

**23.** Rhythm in Latin poetry depends largely on a regularized succession of long and short syllables. Quantity [1] rather than stress accent is the important element in Latin poetry. At any rate, this is true of poetry in the classical period with which we are here concerned.

### DACTYLIC HEXAMETER

**24.** Vergil's *Aeneid* and most of the other selections in this book are written in dactylic hexameter, that is, in a meter in which each line consists of six feet, each of which contains one long and two short syllables or the metrical equivalent of two long syllables, i.e., a spondee. A dactyl may be represented thus: − ∪ ∪ or ♩♪♪ and a spondee may be represented thus: − − or ♩♩. The sixth foot in a dactylic hexameter always consists of two syllables, the second of which may

---

[1] On the quantity of syllables in Latin see section 45 of this Appendix.

be long or short (*syllaba anceps*).  The fifth foot is regularly (although not always) a dactyl.  Any of the first four feet may be a dactyl or a spondee.  The regular metrical scheme of a dactylic hexameter may, therefore, be represented thus:

| _ ∪ ∪ | _ ∪ ∪ | _ ∪ ∪ | _ ∪ ∪ | _ ∪ ∪ | _ ∪ |
| or | or | or | or | rarely or | |
| _ _ | _ _ | _ _ | _ _ | _ _ | |

Take for example the first line of the *Aeneid:*

Ar - ma vi-rum-que ca-nō, Trō-jae quī prī-mus ab  ō-rīs
_ ∪ ∪ | _ ∪ ∪ |_  _ | _ _ | _ ∪ ∪ |_ _

In musical notation the rhythm of the above line could be represented thus:

♩ ♫♫ | ♩ ♫♫ | ♩ ♩ | ♩ ♩ | ♩ ♫♫ | ♩ ♩

The rhythm of a dactylic hexameter is that of the march (4–4 time) and not that of the waltz (3–4 time).  That is to say, a foot or measure in dactylic hexameter is a sound-group consisting of *four* units, one long syllable counting as two units and each short syllable counting as one unit.  On the first syllable of each foot (which is always long) there is a slight metrical accent, as in march-time music.

### SCANSION

**25.** As an aid to the metrical reading of a line of Latin poetry, it is often desirable to indicate the "scansion" of the line.  A good way to do this is to copy the line, indicate below each syllable the quantity of that syllable (as was done in section 24 above), and then divide these syllables into feet (as was also done in section 24 above).

**26.** Another device which will serve as a preparation for the metrical reading of a line of Latin poetry is to "scan" the line orally, that is, designate the quantity of each syllable in order by saying "long" or "short."  For example, the line

Ar-ma vi-rum-que ca-nō, Trō-jae quī prī-mus ab ōrīs (*Aen.* I, 1)

would be scanned orally thus:  "Long, short, short; long, short, short; long, long; long, long; long, short, short; long, long."  If the pupil is careful to hold the word "long" and hurry the word "short" he will easily fall into the appropriate four-four rhythm.  In written or oral scansion the pupil will soon discover that a set of two, four, six, eight, or ten long syllables in succession is always immediately followed (in dactylic hexameter) by another long syllable, and that a short syllable (except at the end of the line) is always immediately followed by another short syllable and then by a long one.

**27.** A preponderance of long syllables gives a line a slow, stately movement; a preponderance of short syllables gives it a light, rapid, graceful movement.  A line with a spondee in the fifth foot is called *spondaic*. Such verses are rare in the *Aeneid*. An example is:

Cōnstitit atque oculīs Phrygia agmina circumspexit (*Aen.* II, 68)

**28.** There is frequently a slight metrical pause somewhere near the middle of the line, especially if there is a break in the thought. This pause is called *caesura* (Latin for "a cutting"). The commonest place for a caesura is in the third foot; e.g.,

Arma virumque canō, || Trōjae quī prīmus ab ōrīs (*Aen.* I, 1)
Urbs antīqua fuit || (Tyriī tenuēre colōnī) (*Aen.* I, 12)

### POETIC LICENSES

**29.** There are certain poetic licenses, employed by Vergil and other Latin poets, which complicate the problem of reading metrically. The greatest difficulty arises from what is called *elision*, the slurring of a final vowel or diphthong (or a final *–m* and its preceding vowel) with the first syllable of the following word if it begins with a vowel or *h*; for example, the line

lītora multum ille et terrīs jactātus et altō (*Aen.* I, 3)

is, for all practical purposes, scanned or read as if written

lī-to-ra mul-t' il-l' et ter-rīs jac-tā-tus et al-tō.

A good way to indicate the presence of an elision is to place a curved line below the letters to be run together in reading, thus:

lītora multum ille et terrīs jactātus et altō (*Aen.* I, 3)

mōnstrum horrendum, īnfōrme, īngēns, cui lūmen adēmptum (*Aen.* III, 658)

**30.** Occasionally Latin poets fail to elide and this failure is called *hiátus* (Latin for "gaping," or "yawning"). Hiatus usually occurs at a marked pause in the line; e.g.,

posthabitā coluisse Samō; hīc illius arma (*Aen.* I, 16)
et vēra incessū patuit dea. Ille ubi mātrem (*Aen.* I, 405)

**a.** In a very few instances a long vowel or diphthong at the end of a word loses half of its quantity before an initial vowel in the next word and is treated as if it were short but not elided. This is called *semi-hiatus*. An example is:

victor apud rapidum Simoënta sub Īliŏ altō (*Aen.* V, 261)

**31.** Sometimes the last syllable of a line is elided with the first syllable of the line following. Such a linking together is called *synapheia* (Greek for "junction"), and the first of two such lines is said to be *hyper-metric*. An example is:

jactēmur doceās; ignārī hominumque locōrumque
errāmus, ventō hūc vāstīs et flūctibus āctī; (*Aen.* I, 332–333)

**32.** The slurring of two vowels within a word so as to form one syllable is called *synizesis* (Greek for "a sitting together"); e.g.,

> Ītaliam, fātō profugus, Lavīniạque vēnit (*Aen.* I, 2)
> ūnius ob noxam et furiās Ājācis Oīleī (*Aen.* I, 41)

**33** Sometimes a syllable that is ordinarily short is lengthened for metrical reasons. This lengthening is called *diastole*. An example is:

> lītora jactētūr, odiīs Jūnōnis inīquae (*Aen.* I, 668)

**34.** Sometimes a syllable that is ordinarily long is shortened for metrical reasons. This shortening is called *systole*. An example is:

> Obstipuī stetĕruntque comae, et vōx faucibus haesit (*Aen.* II, 774)

### LYRIC METERS

**35.** In addition to dactylic hexameter the Greek poets developed a large variety of meters especially for songs to be sung to the accompaniment of the lyre; hence the name *lyric* meter. Roman poets, such as Horace and Catullus, adapted these meters to Latin. Selections in Part II of this book illustrate the following meters in addition to dactylic hexameter discussed in sections 23 and 24:

1. *Elegiac Couplet:* a dactylic hexameter followed by a line which is dactylic hexameter, except that the *third* and *sixth* feet each consists of a single long syllable, followed by a pause.

   The metrical arrangement of the second line in the Elegiac Couplet is:

   $$ \_\,\overline{\cup\cup}\mid\_\,\overline{\cup\cup}\mid\_\,\wedge\mid\_\,\cup\,\cup\mid\_\,\cup\,\cup\mid\_\,\wedge\,{}^1 $$

   In Part II of this book, Selection IV from Catullus and all the selections from Martial, Ausonius, and Claudian employ this couplet.

2. *Sapphic Strophe:* a metrical arrangement of four lines (three Lesser Sapphics and one Adonic) as follows:

   $$ \_\,\cup\mid\_\,\_\mid\_\,\|\,\cup\,\cup\mid\_\,\cup\mid\_\,\breve{} $$
   $$ \_\,\cup\mid\_\,\_\mid\_\,\|\,\cup\,\cup\mid\_\,\cup\mid\_\,\breve{} $$
   $$ \_\,\cup\mid\_\,\_\mid\_\,\|\,\cup\,\cup\mid\_\,\cup\mid\_\,\breve{} $$
   $$ \_\,\cup\,\cup\mid\_\,\breve{} $$

   Selections II and V from Horace employ this strophe.

3. *Glyconic-Pherecratic Strophe:* a metrical arrangement of four lines (three Glyconics and one Pherecratic) as follows:

---

¹ In the first half of this line a spondee may be used in place of a dactyl; in the second half only a dactyl is allowed.

$$\_ \_ \mid \_ \cup \cup \mid \_ \cup \mid \overset{\cup}{\smile}$$
$$\_ \_ \mid \_ \cup \cup \mid \_ \cup \mid \overset{\cup}{\smile}$$
$$\_ \_ \mid \_ \cup \cup \mid \_ \cup \mid \overset{\cup}{\smile}$$
$$\_ \_ \mid \_ \cup \cup \mid \_ \mid \_$$

Substitution of a short syllable for a long first or second syllable is allowed. Selection I from Catullus employs this strophe.

4. *Phalaecean or Hendecasyllabic Meter:* a line consisting of eleven syllables arranged as follows:
$$\_ \_ \mid \_ \cup \cup \mid \_ \cup \mid \_ \cup \mid \_ \overset{\cup}{\smile}$$

Selections II and III from Catullus employ this meter.

5. *Lesser Asclepiad Meter:* a line consisting of twelve syllables arranged as follows
$$\_ \_ \mid \_ \cup \cup \mid \_ \wedge \mid \_ \cup \cup \mid \_ \cup \mid \_$$

Selection IV from Horace employs this meter.

6. *First Asclepiad Strophe:* a metrical arrangement of two lines (a Glyconic coupled with a Lesser Asclepiad) as follows:
$$\_ \_ \mid \_ \cup \cup \mid \_ \cup \mid \overset{\cup}{\smile}$$
$$\_ \_ \mid \_ \cup \cup \mid \_ \wedge \mid \_ \cup \cup \mid \_ \cup \mid \overset{\cup}{\smile}$$

Selection I from Horace employs this strophe.

7. *Third Asclepiad Strophe:* a metrical arrangement of four lines (two Lesser Asclepiads, a Pherecratic, and a Glyconic) as follows:
$$\_ \_ \mid \_ \cup \cup \mid \_ \wedge \mid \_ \cup \cup \mid \_ \cup \mid \overset{\cup}{\smile}$$
$$\_ \_ \mid \_ \cup \cup \mid \_ \wedge \mid \_ \cup \cup \mid \_ \cup \mid \overset{\cup}{\smile}$$
$$\_ \_ \mid \_ \cup \cup \mid \_ \mid \overset{\cup}{\smile}$$
$$\_ \_ \mid \_ \cup \cup \mid \_ \cup \mid \overset{\cup}{\smile}$$

Selection III from Horace employs this strophe.

8. *Iambic Strophe:* an Iambic Trimeter coupled with an Iambic Dimeter, as follows:
$$\cup \_ \mid \cup \_ \mid \cup \_ \mid \cup \_ \mid \cup \_ \mid \cup \overset{\cup}{\smile}$$
$$\cup \_ \mid \cup \_ \mid \cup \_ \mid \cup \overset{\cup}{\smile}$$

Substitutions and resolutions are somewhat freely allowed except in the last foot. Selection VI from Horace employs this strophe.

9. *Iambic Trimeter:* a metrical arrangement consisting normally of six iambic feet as follows:
$$\cup \_ \mid \cup \_ \mid \cup \_ \mid \cup \_ \mid \cup \_ \mid \cup \overset{\cup}{\smile}$$

Substitutions and resolutions are freely allowed except in the last foot. Selections I–IV from Phaedrus employ this meter.

# LATIN GRAMMAR

## PRONUNCIATION

**36.** In Latin a vowel may be long or short. A long vowel should be sounded approximately twice as long as a short vowel. In this book each long vowel has a *macron* above it. A vowel without a *macron* is to be understood as short. The following general rules in regard to the quantity of Latin vowels will be found useful:

(1) A vowel before **ns** or **nf** is always long.

(2) A vowel before another vowel is regularly short.

(3) A vowel before final **m**, final **r**, final **t**, or before **nt** anywhere is regularly short.

**37.** Latin vowels differ not only in *quantity* (the time it takes to pronounce them properly) but also in *quality*. Scholars are pretty well agreed that the Romans pronounced their vowels as follows:

> Long **ā** as in **Mārcus** (or as in English *father*)
> Short **a** as in **tabula** (or as in English *ah*)
> Long **ē** as in **mēnsa** (or as in English *they*)
> Short **e** as in **sella** (or as in English *seller*)
> Long **ī** as in **prīma** (or as in English *machine*)
> Short **i** as in **quid** (or as in English *hid*)
> Long **ō** as in **nōn** (or as in English *fore*)
> Short **o** as in **bonus** (or as in English *obey*)
> Long **ū** as in **Brūtus** (or as in English *brute*)
> Short **u** as in **sum** (or as in English *full*)

**38.** Always after **q** and sometimes after **g** and **s** Latin **u** has the sound of Latin **v** or English *w*; e.g., in **quid, lingua, persuādeō.**

**39.** Five Latin *diphthongs* (double sounds) are used in this book: **ae** [1] as in **saepe, au** [1] as in **laudō, oe** [1] as in **proelium, eu** [1] as in **neu,** and **ui** [1] as in **cui.**

**40.** In general, consonants have the same sound in Latin as in English. The following exceptions should be noted:

Latin **b** before **s** or **t** has the sound of **p**; e.g., in **urbs, obtineō.**

Latin **c** is always *hard* as in English *cat*, never *soft* as in English *city*.

Latin **g** is always *hard* as in English *get*, never *soft* as in English *germ*.

Latin **j** (sometimes called i-consonant) has the sound of English *y* in *yet*.

Latin **s** always has the sound of *s* as in English *son*, never the sound of *z* as in English *rose*.

Latin **t** always has the sound of *t* as in English *ten*, never the sound of *sh* as in English *nation*.

Latin **v** always has the sound of English *w*.

Latin **ch, ph,** and **th** are pronounced as Latin **c, p,** and **t.**

**41.** Latin double consonants are always pronounced separately; e.g., **sel-la, an-nus.**

**42.** A Latin word has as many syllables as it has vowels or diphthongs. Apparent

---

[1] The first three sounds are like those represented in English *aisle, loud,* and *oil;* eu is pronounced *eh-oo* and ui is pronounced *oo-ee*.

exceptions are such words as **quid, lin–gua**, and **per–suā–de–ō**, in which the **u** has the sound of English *w* as is explained in section 38.

**43.** In separating a Latin word into syllables a single consonant is pronounced with the vowel (or diphthong) following it; if there are two or more consonants between vowels, as many consonants are pronounced with the vowel following as can be easily and distinctly pronounced with that vowel.

**44.** The last syllable of a word is called the *ultima*, the next to the last the *penult*, and the second from the last the *antepenult*.

**45.** A syllable is long if it contains a long vowel or a diphthong or if it ends in a consonant; e.g., the first syllable in **ā–cer, ae–ger, ag–ger**.

*a.* In words like **patris** the poets often use a division **pat–ris**, which makes the first syllable long.

**46.** In a Latin word of two syllables the accent is placed on the penult (**ter'–ra, a'–gō**); in a word of three or more syllables the accent is placed on the penult if that syllable is long (**a–mī'–cus, ā–mit'–tō**); otherwise the accent is placed on the antepenult (**a'–di–tus, Sē'–qua–na**).[1]

## DECLENSIONS

### *NOUNS*

**47.**                          **FIRST DECLENSION**

|        | SINGULAR | PLURAL |
|--------|----------|--------|
| *Nom.* | puella   | puellae |
| *Gen.* | puellae  | puellārum |
| *Dat.* | puellae  | puellīs |
| *Acc.* | puellam  | puellās |
| *Abl.* | puellā   | puellīs |

*a.* For certain nouns of the first declension there is also a locative singular form which is identical with the genitive; e.g., **Rōmae**, *at Rome*.

*b.* In poetry certain peculiarities may be found; e.g., –āī for –ae in the genitive singular: **aulāī** (*Aen.* III, 354); **aurāī** (*Aen.* VI, 747); –um for –ārum in the genitive plural: **Aeneadum** (*Aen.* I, 565); **Dardanidum** (*Aen.* II, 242).

*c.* Certain first declension nouns have a dative-ablative plural form ending in –ābus; e.g., **deābus, fīliābus.**

**48.**                          **SECOND DECLENSION**

|        | SINGULAR | PLURAL | SINGULAR | PLURAL | SINGULAR | PLURAL |
|--------|----------|--------|----------|--------|----------|--------|
| *Nom.* | servus   | servī    | puer   | puerī    | proelium    | proelia |
| *Gen.* | servī    | servōrum | puerī  | puerōrum | proeliī (ī) | proeliōrum |
| *Dat.* | servō    | servīs   | puerō  | puerīs   | proeliō     | proeliīs |
| *Acc.* | servum   | servōs   | puerum | puerōs   | proelium    | proelia |
| *Abl.* | servō    | servīs   | puerō  | puerīs   | proeliō     | proeliīs |

[1] An apparent exception to the second part of this rule for accent is the vocative form of certain nouns and adjectives ending in –ius (**Pa–tri'–cī, Ver–gi'–lī, ē–gre'–gī**) which results from contraction.

*a.* The vocative singular of a noun like **servus** ends in **e**; the vocative singular of a noun like **Antōnius** or **fīlius** ends in **ī**; otherwise the vocative form is the same as the nominative.

*b.* For certain nouns of the second declension there is also a locative singular form which is identical with the genitive; e.g., **Saguntī,** *at Saguntum;* **domī,** *at home.*

*c.* In poetry certain peculiarities may be found; e.g., **-um** for **-ōrum** in the genitive plural; **deum** (*Aen.* I, 9); **Argīvum** (*Aen.* I, 40).

**49.**                                    **THIRD DECLENSION**

*a.* CONSONANT-STEMS

|  | SINGULAR | PLURAL | SINGULAR | PLURAL | SINGULAR | PLURAL |
|---|---|---|---|---|---|---|
| *Nom.* | mīles | mīlitēs | rēx | rēgēs | corpus | corpora |
| *Gen.* | mīlitis | mīlitum | rēgis | rēgum | corporis | corporum |
| *Dat.* | mīlitī | mīlitibus | rēgī | rēgibus | corporī | corporibus |
| *Acc.* | mīlitem | mīlitēs | rēgem | rēgēs | corpus | corpora |
| *Abl.* | mīlite | mīlitibus | rēge | rēgibus | corpore | corporibus |

*b.* i-STEMS

|  | SINGULAR | PLURAL | SINGULAR | PLURAL | SINGULAR | PLURAL |
|---|---|---|---|---|---|---|
| *Nom.* | cīvis | cīvēs | mōns | montēs | mare | maria |
| *Gen.* | cīvis | cīvium | montis | montium | maris | marium |
| *Dat.* | cīvī | cīvibus | montī | montibus | marī | maribus |
| *Acc.* | cīvem | cīvēs (īs) | montem | montēs (īs) | mare | maria |
| *Abl.* | cīve | cīvibus | monte | montibus | marī | maribus |

*a.* In poetry certain peculiarities may be found; e.g., the Greek accusative singular in **-a**; **āera** (*Aen.* I, 300); **aethera** (*Aen.* I, 379).

**50.**                                    **FOURTH DECLENSION**

|  | SINGULAR | PLURAL | SINGULAR | PLURAL |
|---|---|---|---|---|
| *Nom.* | exercitus | exercitūs | cornū | cornua |
| *Gen.* | exercitūs | exercituum | cornūs | cornuum |
| *Dat.* | exercituī | exercitibus | cornū | cornibus |
| *Acc.* | exercitum | exercitūs | cornū | cornua |
| *Abl.* | exercitū | exercitibus | cornū | cornibus |

*a.* In poetry certain irregularities may be found; e.g., **-ū** for **-uī** in the dative singular: **metū** (*Aen.* I, 257); **portū** (*Aen.* III, 292); **-um** for **-uum** in the genitive plural; e.g., **currum** (*Aen.* VI, 653).

**51.**                                    **FIFTH DECLENSION**

|  | SINGULAR | PLURAL | SINGULAR | PLURAL |
|---|---|---|---|---|
| *Nom.* | diēs (*m. or f.*) | diēs | rēs (*f.*) | rēs |
| *Gen.* | diēī | diērum | reī | rērum |
| *Dat.* | diēī | diēbus | reī | rēbus |
| *Acc.* | diem | diēs | rem | rēs |
| *Abl.* | diē | diēbus | rē | rēbus |

**52.** **NOUNS OF IRREGULAR OR DEFECTIVE DECLENSION**

| | SINGULAR | SINGULAR | PLURAL | SINGULAR | PLURAL |
|---|---|---|---|---|---|
| *Nom.* | nēmō | vīs | vīrēs | domus | domūs |
| *Gen.* | (nūllīus) | —— | vīrium | domūs (ī) | domuum (ōrum) |
| *Dat.* | nēminī | —— | vīribus | domuī (ō) | domibus |
| *Acc.* | nēminem | vim | vīrēs (īs) | domum | domōs (ūs) |
| *Abl.* | (nūllō) | vī | vīribus | domō (ū) | domibus |

**53.** **DECLENSION OF GREEK NOUNS**

FIRST DECLENSION

| | | | |
|---|---|---|---|
| *Nom.* | Pēnelopē | Aenēās | Anchīsēs |
| *Gen.* | Pēnelopēs | Aenēae | Anchīsae |
| *Dat.* | Pēnelopae | Aenēae | Anchīsae |
| *Acc.* | Pēnelopēn | Aenēam (ān) | Anchīsēn (am) |
| *Voc.* | Pēnelopē | Aenēā | Anchīsē (ā, a) |
| *Abl.* | Pēnelopā | Aenēā | Anchīsā |

SECOND DECLENSION

| | | | | |
|---|---|---|---|---|
| *Nom.* | Dēlos (us) | Īlion (um) | Panthūs | Androgeōs (us) |
| *Gen.* | Dēlī | Īliī | Panthī | Androgeī (eō) |
| *Dat.* | Dēlō | Īliō | Panthō | Androgeō |
| *Acc.* | Dēlon (um) | Īlion (um) | Panthūn | Androgeōn (ō, ōna) |
| *Voc.* | Dēle | Īlion (um) | Panthū | Androgeōs |
| *Abl.* | Dēlō | Īliō | Panthō | Androgeō |

THIRD DECLENSION

| | | | | |
|---|---|---|---|---|
| *Nom.* | Solōn (Solō) | āēr, *air* | Xenophōn | Atlās |
| *Gen.* | Solōnis | āeris | Xenophōntis | Atlantis |
| *Dat.* | Solōnī | āerī | Xenophōntī | Atlantī |
| *Acc.* | Solōna (em) | āera (em) | Xenophōnta (em) | Atlanta |
| *Voc.* | Solōn | āēr | Xenophōn | Atlā |
| *Abl.* | Solōne | āere | Xenophōnte | Atlante |

| | | | |
|---|---|---|---|
| *Nom.* | Thalēs | Paris | hērōs |
| *Gen.* | Thal–ētis (is) | Paridis (os) | hērōis |
| *Dat.* | Thal–ētī (ī) | Paridī (ī) | hērōī |
| *Acc.* | Thal–ēta (ēn, em) | Par–ida (im, in) | hērōa (em) |
| *Voc.* | Thalē | Pari (Paris) | hērōs |
| *Abl.* | Thalē | Paride | hērōe |

SECOND AND THIRD DECLENSIONS

| | | | |
|---|---|---|---|
| *Nom.* | Orpheus | Athōs | Oedipūs |
| *Gen.* | Orpheī (ēī) | Athō (ōnis) | Oedip–odis (ī) |
| *Dat.* | Orpheō (eī) | Athō | Oedipidī |
| *Acc.* | Orpheum (ea) | Athō (ōn, ōnem) | Oedip–um (oda) |
| *Voc.* | Orpheu | Athōs | Oedipe |
| *Abl.* | Orpheō | Athōne | Oedip–ide (ō) |

| Nom. | Achillēs (eus) | Sōcratēs | Dīdō |
|------|----------------|----------|------|
| Gen. | Achillis (e)ī, eos | Sōcratis (ī) | Dīdūs (ōnis) |
| Dat. | Achillī | Sōcratī | Dīdō (ōnī) |
| Acc. | Achillem (ea, ēn) | Sōcratēn (em) | Dīdō (ōnem) |
| Voc. | Achillēs (ē, eu, e) | Sōcratē (es) | Dīdō |
| Abl. | Achille (ī) | Sōcrate | Dīdō (ōne) |

## ADJECTIVES[1]

### 54.  FIRST AND SECOND DECLENSIONS

| | SINGULAR | | | PLURAL | | |
|------|------------|------------|-------------|----------|----------|----------|
| Nom. | magnus (m.) | magna (f.) | magnum (n.) | magnī | magnae | magna |
| Gen. | magnī | magnae | magnī | magnōrum | magnārum | magnōrum |
| Dat. | magnō | magnae | magnō | magnīs | magnīs | magnīs |
| Acc. | magnum | magnam | magnum | magnōs | magnās | magna |
| Abl. | magnō | magnā | magnō | magnīs | magnīs | magnīs |
| | | | | | | |
| Nom. | līber (m.) | lībera (f.) | līberum (n.) | līberī | līberae | lībera |
| Gen. | līberī | līberae | līberī | etc. | etc. | etc. |
| | etc. | etc. | etc. | | | |
| | | | | | | |
| Nom. | meus (m.) | mea (f.) | meum (n.) | meī | meae | mea |
| Gen. | meī | meae | meī | etc. | etc. | etc. |
| | etc. | etc. | etc. | | | |
| | | | | | | |
| Nom. | noster (m.) | nostra (f.) | nostrum (n.) | nostrī | nostrae | nostra |
| Gen. | nostrī | nostrae | nostrī | etc. | etc. | etc. |
| Dat. | nostrō | nostrae | nostrō | | | |
| Acc. | nostrum | nostram | nostrum | | | |
| Abl. | nostrō | nostrā | nostrō | | | |

### 55.  THIRD DECLENSION

#### a. THREE TERMINATIONS

| | SINGULAR | | | PLURAL | | |
|------|-----------|-----------|-----------|-----------|-----------|-----------|
| Nom. | ācer (m.) | ācris (f.) | ācre (n.) | ācrēs | ācrēs | ācria |
| Gen. | ācris | ācris | ācris | ācrium | ācrium | ācrium |
| Dat. | ācrī | ācrī | ācrī | ācribus | ācribus | ācribus |
| Acc. | ācrem | ācrem | ācre | ācrēs (īs) | ācrēs (īs) | ācria |
| Abl. | ācrī | ācrī | ācrī | ācribus | ācribus | ācribus |

#### b. TWO TERMINATIONS

| | SINGULAR | | PLURAL | |
|------|---------------|-----------|-------------|----------|
| Nom. | omnis (m., f.) | omne (n.) | omnēs | omnia |
| Gen. | omnis | omnis | omnium | omnium |
| Dat. | omnī | omnī | omnibus | omnibus |
| Acc. | omnem | omne | omnēs (īs) | omnia |
| Abl. | omnī | omnī | omnibus | omnibus |

[1] The vocative singular of an adjective like **magnus** ends in –e; the vocative singular of an adjective like **ēgregius** ends in –ī; the vocative singular masculine of **meus** is **mī**; otherwise the vocative form is the same as the nominative.

### c. ONE TERMINATION

| | SINGULAR | | PLURAL | |
|---|---|---|---|---|
| *Nom.* | pār (*m., f.*) | pār (*n.*) | parēs | paria |
| *Gen.* | paris | paris | parium | parium |
| *Dat.* | parī | parī | paribus | paribus |
| *Acc.* | parem | pār | parēs (īs) | paria |
| *Abl.* | parī | parī | paribus | paribus |

### 56. PRESENT PARTICIPLE

| | | | | |
|---|---|---|---|---|
| *Nom.* | portāns (*m., f.*) | portāns (*n.*) | portantēs | portantia |
| *Gen.* | portantis | portantis | portantium | portantium |
| *Dat.* | portantī | portantī | portantibus | portantibus |
| *Acc.* | portantem | portāns | portantēs (īs) | portantia |
| *Abl.* | portante (ī) | portante (ī) | portantibus | portantibus |

### 57. NUMERALS

| | SINGULAR | | | PLURAL | |
|---|---|---|---|---|---|
| *Nom.* | ūnus (*m.*) | ūna (*f.*) | ūnum (*n.*) | trēs (*m., f.*) | tria (*n.*) |
| *Gen.* | ūnīus | ūnīus | ūnīus | trium | trium |
| *Dat.* | ūnī | ūnī | ūnī | tribus | tribus |
| *Acc.* | ūnum | ūnam | ūnum | trēs (trīs) | tria |
| *Abl.* | ūnō | ūnā | ūnō | tribus | tribus |

| | PLURAL | | | SINGULAR | PLURAL |
|---|---|---|---|---|---|
| *Nom.* | duo (*m.*) | duae (*f.*) | duo (*n.*) | mīlle (*m., f., n.*) | mīlia (*n.*) |
| *Gen.* | duōrum | duārum | duōrum | mīlle | mīlium |
| *Dat.* | duōbus | duābus | duōbus | mīlle | mīlibus |
| *Acc.* | duōs (duo) | duās | duo | mīlle | mīlia |
| *Abl.* | duōbus | duābus | duōbus | mīlle | mīlibus |

### 58. PRONOMINALS [1]

| | SINGULAR | | | SINGULAR | | |
|---|---|---|---|---|---|---|
| *Nom.* | sōlus (*m.*) | sōla (*f.*) | sōlum (*n.*) | alter (*m.*) | altera (*f.*) | alterum (*n.*) |
| *Gen.* | sōlīus | sōlīus | sōlīus | alterīus | alterīus | alterīus |
| *Dat.* | sōlī | sōlī | sōlī | alterī | alterī | alterī |
| *Acc.* | sōlum | sōlam | sōlum | alterum | alteram | alterum |
| *Abl.* | sōlō | sōlā | sōlō | alterō | alterā | alterō |

The plurals are like those of **magnus** and **līber.**

### 59. DEMONSTRATIVES

| | SINGULAR | | | PLURAL | | |
|---|---|---|---|---|---|---|
| *Nom.* | hic (*m.*) | haec (*f.*) | hoc (*n.*) | hī | hae | haec |
| *Gen.* | hujus | hujus | hujus | hōrum | hārum | hōrum |
| *Dat.* | huic | huic | huic | hīs | hīs | hīs |
| *Acc.* | hunc | hanc | hoc | hōs | hās | haec |
| *Abl.* | hōc | hāc | hōc | hīs | hīs | hīs |

[1] These are **alius, alter, neuter, nūllus, sōlus, tōtus, ūllus, uter,** and **uterque. Alius** has **aliud** in the nominative and accusative singular neuter.

|  | SINGULAR | | | PLURAL | | |
|------|----------|----------|----------|---------|----------|----------|
| *Nom.* | īdem (*m.*) | eadem (*f.*) | idem (*n.*) | eīdem | eaedem | eadem |
| *Gen.* | ejusdem | ejusdem | ejusdem | eōrundem | eārundem | eōrundem |
| *Dat.* | eīdem | eīdem | eīdem | eīsdem | eīsdem | eīsdem |
| *Acc.* | eundem | eandem | idem | eōsdem | eāsdem | eadem |
| *Abl.* | eōdem | eādem | eōdem | eīsdem | eīsdem | eīsdem |

SINGULAR

|  |  |  |  |
|------|------|------|------|
| *Nom.* | ille (*m.*) | illa (*f.*) | illud (*n.*) |
| *Gen.* | illīus | illīus | illīus |
| *Dat.* | illī | illī | illī |
| *Acc.* | illum | illam | illud |
| *Abl.* | illō | illā | illō |

The plural is regular.

*a.* The demonstrative **iste** is declined like **ille**.

**60.** INTENSIVE

SINGULAR

|  |  |  |  |
|------|------|------|------|
| *Nom.* | ipse (*m.*) | ipsa (*f.*) | ipsum (*n.*) |
| *Gen.* | ipsīus | ipsīus | ipsīus |
| *Dat.* | ipsī | ipsī | ipsī |
| *Acc.* | ipsum | ipsam | ipsum |
| *Abl.* | ipsō | ipsā | ipsō |

The plural is regular.

**61.** DECLENSION OF COMPARATIVES

|  | SINGULAR | | PLURAL | |
|------|----------|--------------|----------|----------|
| *Nom.* | altior (*m., f.*) | altius (*n.*) | altiōrēs | altiōra |
| *Gen.* | altiōris | altiōris | altiōrum | altiōrum |
| *Dat.* | altiōrī | altiōrī | altiōribus | altiōribus |
| *Acc.* | altiōrem | altius | altiōrēs | altiōra |
| *Abl.* | altiōre | altiōre | altiōribus | altiōribus |

|  | SINGULAR | PLURAL | |
|------|----------|----------|----------|
| *Nom.* | plūs (*n.*) [1] | plūrēs (*m., f.*) | plūra (*n.*) |
| *Gen.* | plūris | plūrium | plūrium |
| *Dat.* | —— | plūribus | plūribus |
| *Acc.* | plūs | plūrēs | plūra |
| *Abl.* | plūre | plūribus | plūribus |

[1] Masculine and feminine forms of **plūs** are lacking in the singular.

## PRONOUNS

**62.**                              **PERSONAL**

|  | SINGULAR | PLURAL |  | SINGULAR | PLURAL |
|---|---|---|---|---|---|
| *Nom.* | ego | nōs |  | tū | vōs |
| *Gen.* | meī [1] | nostrum (nostrī) |  | tuī [1] | vestrum (vestrī) |
| *Dat.* | mihi | nōbīs |  | tibi | vōbīs |
| *Acc.* | mē | nōs |  | tē | vōs |
| *Abl.* | mē | nōbīs |  | tē | vōbīs |

|  | SINGULAR |  |  | PLURAL |  |  |
|---|---|---|---|---|---|---|
| *Nom.* | is (*m.*) | ea (*f.*) | id (*n.*) | eī | eae | ea |
| *Gen.* | ejus | ejus | ejus | eōrum | eārum | eōrum |
| *Dat.* | eī | eī | eī | eīs | eīs | eīs |
| *Acc.* | eum | eam | id | eōs | eās | ea |
| *Abl.* | eō | eā | eō | eīs | eīs | eīs |

**63.**               **REFLEXIVE THIRD PERSON**

|  | SINGULAR | PLURAL |
|---|---|---|
| *Nom.* | —— [2] | —— [2] |
| *Gen.* | suī | suī |
| *Dat.* | sibi | sibi |
| *Acc.* | sē | sē |
| *Abl.* | sē | sē |

**64.**                        **RELATIVE**

|  | SINGULAR |  |  | PLURAL |  |  |
|---|---|---|---|---|---|---|
| *Nom.* | quī (*m.*) | quae (*f.*) | quod (*n.*) | quī | quae | quae |
| *Gen.* | cujus | cujus | cujus | quōrum | quārum | quōrum |
| *Dat.* | cui | cui | cui | quibus | quibus | quibus |
| *Acc.* | quem | quam | quod | quōs | quās | quae |
| *Abl.* | quō | quā | quō | quibus | quibus | quibus |

**65.**                    **INTERROGATIVE [3]**

|  | SINGULAR |  |
|---|---|---|
| *Nom.* | quis (*m., f.*) | quid (*n.*) |
| *Gen.* | cujus | cujus |
| *Dat.* | cui | cui |
| *Acc.* | quem | quid |
| *Abl.* | quō | quō |

The plural is like that of the relative pronoun **quī**.

[1] Any form of **ego** or **tū** except a nominative may be used as a reflexive as well as a personal pronoun.
[2] The nominative of a reflexive pronoun is lacking.
[3] The corresponding interrogative adjective (**quī, quae, quod**) is declined like the relative pronoun

## 66.                                    DISTRIBUTIVE [1]

### SINGULAR

| | | |
|---|---|---|
| *Nom.* | quisque (*m., f.*) | quidque (*n.*) |
| *Gen.* | cujusque | cujusque |
| *Dat.* | cuique | cuique |
| *Acc.* | quemque | quidque |
| *Abl.* | quōque | quōque |

The plural is rare.

## 67.                                    INDEFINITE

| | | |
|---|---|---|
| *Nom.* | quisquam (*m., f.*) | quidquam (*n.*) |
| *Gen.* | cujusquam | cujusquam |
| *Dat.* | cuiquam | cuiquam |
| *Acc.* | quemquam | quidquam |
| *Abl.* | quōquam | quōquam |

The plural is lacking.

| | SINGULAR | | | PLURAL | |
|---|---|---|---|---|---|
| *Nom.* | quīdam (*m.*) [2] | quaedam (*f.*) | quiddam (*n.*) | quīdam | quaedam | quaedam |
| *Gen.* | cujusdam | cujusdam | cujusdam | quōrundam | quārundam | quōrundam |
| *Dat.* | cuidam | cuidam | cuidam | quibusdam | quibusdam | quibusdam |
| *Acc.* | quendam | quandam | quiddam | quōsdam | quāsdam | quaedam |
| *Abl.* | quōdam | quādam | quōdam | quibusdam | quibusdam | quibusdam |

| | SINGULAR | | | PLURAL | |
|---|---|---|---|---|---|
| *Nom.* | aliquis (*m.*) | aliqua (*f.*) | aliquid (*n.*) | aliquī | aliquae | aliqua |
| *Gen.* | alicujus | alicujus | alicujus | aliquōrum | aliquārum | aliquōrum |
| *Dat.* | alicui | alicui | alicui | aliquibus | aliquibus | aliquibus |
| *Acc.* | aliquem | aliquam | aliquid | aliquōs | aliquās | aliqua |
| *Abl.* | aliquō | aliquā | aliquō | aliquibus | aliquibus | aliquibus |

## 68.                        COMPARISON OF ADJECTIVES

### a. REGULAR

| POSITIVE | COMPARATIVE | SUPERLATIVE |
|---|---|---|
| altus, –a, –um | altior, –ius | altissimus, –a, –um |
| fortis, forte | fortior, –ius | fortissimus, –a, –um |
| līber, –a, –um | līberior, –ius | līberrimus, –a, –um |
| ācer, ācris, ācre | ācrior, –ius | ācerrimus, –a, –um |
| vetus, veteris (*gen.*) | veterior, –ius | veterrimus, –a, –um |
| facilis, facile | facilior, –ius | facillimus, –a, –um |
| humilis, humile | humilior, –ius | humillimus, –a, –um |
| similis, simile | similior, –ius | simillimus, –a, –um |

[1] The distributive adjective (**quīque, quaeque, quodque**) follows the declension of the relative pronoun.

[2] The indefinite adjective (**quīdam, quaedam, quoddam**) follows the declension of the relative pronoun.

### b. Irregular

| POSITIVE | COMPARATIVE | SUPERLATIVE |
|---|---|---|
| bonus, –a, –um | melior, –ius | optimus, –a, –um |
| malus, –a, –um | pejor, –us | pessimus, –a, –um |
| magnus, –a, –um | major, –us | maximus, –a, –um |
| parvus, –a, –um | minor, –us | minimus, –a, –um |
| multus, –a, –um | ——, plūs | plūrimus, –a, –um |
| īnferus, –a, –um | īnferior, –ius | īnfimus or īmus, –a, –um |
| superus, –a, –um | superior, –ius | suprēmus or summus, –a, –um |
| —— | prior, –ius | prīmus, –a, –um |
| —— | propior, –ius | proximus, –a, –um |
| —— | ulterior, –ius | ultimus, –a, –um |

**69.** ## COMPARISON OF ADVERBS

#### a. Regular

| POSITIVE | COMPARATIVE | SUPERLATIVE |
|---|---|---|
| lātē | lātius | lātissimē |
| fortiter | fortius | fortissimē |
| ācriter | ācrius | ācerrimē |
| facile | facilius | facillimē |

#### b. Irregular

| POSITIVE | COMPARATIVE | SUPERLATIVE |
|---|---|---|
| bene | melius | optimē |
| male | pejus | pessimē |
| magnopere | magis | maximē |
| multum | plūs | plūrimum |
| parum | minus | minimē |
| prope | propius | proximē |
| saepe | saepius | saepissimē |
| diū | diūtius | diūtissimē |

## CONJUGATIONS

### REGULAR VERBS

**70.** ## FIRST CONJUGATION

*Principal Parts:* **portō, portāre, portāvī, portātus**
*Stems:* **portā–, portāv–, portāt–**

#### ACTIVE VOICE
#### PASSIVE VOICE
##### INDICATIVE

| PRESENT | | PRESENT | |
|---|---|---|---|
| portō | portāmus | portor | portāmur |
| portās | portātis | portāris | portāminī |
| portat | portant | portātur | portantur |

## ACTIVE VOICE        PASSIVE VOICE

### Indicative

**IMPERFECT**      **IMPERFECT**

| | | | |
|---|---|---|---|
| portābam | portābāmus | portābar | portābāmur |
| portābās | portābātis | portābāris | portābāminī |
| portābat | portābant | portābātur | portābantur |

**FUTURE**      **FUTURE**

| | | | |
|---|---|---|---|
| portābō | portābimus | portābor | portābimur |
| portābis | portābitis | portāberis | portābiminī |
| portābit | portābunt | portābitur | portābuntur |

**PERFECT**      **PERFECT**

| | | | |
|---|---|---|---|
| portāvī | portāvimus | portātus sum | portātī sumus |
| portāvistī | portāvistis | portātus es | portātī estis |
| portāvit | portāvērunt | portātus est | portātī sunt |

**PLUPERFECT**      **PLUPERFECT**

| | | | |
|---|---|---|---|
| portāveram | portāverāmus | portātus eram | portātī erāmus |
| portāverās | portāverātis | portātus erās | portātī erātis |
| portāverat | portāverant | portātus erat | portātī erant |

**FUTURE PERFECT**      **FUTURE PERFECT**

| | | | |
|---|---|---|---|
| portāverō | portāverimus | portātus erō | portātī erimus |
| portāveris | portāveritis | portātus eris | portātī eritis |
| portāverit | portāverint | portātus erit | portātī erunt |

### Subjunctive

**PRESENT**      **PRESENT**

| | | | |
|---|---|---|---|
| portem | portēmus | porter | portēmur |
| portēs | portētis | portēris | portēminī |
| portet | portent | portētur | portentur |

**IMPERFECT**      **IMPERFECT**

| | | | |
|---|---|---|---|
| portārem | portārēmus | portārer | portārēmur |
| portārēs | portārētis | portārēris | portārēminī |
| portāret | portārent | portārētur | portārentur |

**PERFECT**      **PERFECT**

| | | | |
|---|---|---|---|
| portāverim | portāverīmus | portātus sim | portātī sīmus |
| portāverīs | portāverītis | portātus sīs | portātī sītis |
| portāverit | portāverint | portātus sit | portātī sint |

**PLUPERFECT**      **PLUPERFECT**

| | | | |
|---|---|---|---|
| portāvissem | portāvissēmus | portātus essem | portātī essēmus |
| portāvissēs | portāvissētis | portātus essēs | portātī essētis |
| portāvisset | portāvissent | portātus esset | portātī essent |

IMPERATIVE

| | | | | |
|---|---|---|---|---|
| *Present* | portā | portāte | portāre | portāminī |
| *Future* | portātō | portātōte | portātor | |
| | portātō | portantō | portātor | portantor |

INFINITIVES

| | | |
|---|---|---|
| *Present* | portāre | portārī |
| *Perfect* | portāvisse | portātus esse |
| *Future* | portātūrus esse | portātum īrī |

PARTICIPLES

| | | |
|---|---|---|
| *Present* | portāns, –antis | |
| *Perfect* | ———— | portātus, –a, –um |
| *Future* | portātūrus, –a, –um | portandus, –a, –um |

GERUND

| | |
|---|---|
| *Nom.* | ———— |
| *Gen.* | portandī |
| *Dat.* | portandō |
| *Acc.* | portandum |
| *Abl.* | portandō |

GERUNDIVE

| | | | |
|---|---|---|---|
| *Nom.* | ———— | ———— | ———— |
| *Gen.* | portandī | portandae | portandī |
| *Dat.* | portandō | portandae | portandō |
| *Acc.* | portandum | portandam | portandum |
| *Abl.* | portandō | portandā | portandō |
| | etc. | etc. | etc. |

SUPINE

| | |
|---|---|
| *Acc.* | portātum |
| *Abl.* | portātū |

**71.**                     SECOND CONJUGATION

*Principal Parts:* **moneō, monēre, monuī, monitus**
*Stems:* **monē–, monu–, monit–**

ACTIVE VOICE                    PASSIVE VOICE

INDICATIVE

PRESENT / PRESENT

| | | | |
|---|---|---|---|
| moneō | monēmus | moneor | monēmur |
| monēs | monētis | monēris | monēminī |
| monet | monent | monētur | monentur |

IMPERFECT / IMPERFECT

| | | | |
|---|---|---|---|
| monēbam | monēbāmus | monēbar | monēbāmur |
| monēbās | monēbātis | monēbāris | monēbāminī |
| monēbat | monēbant | monēbātur | monēbantur |

FUTURE / FUTURE

| | | | |
|---|---|---|---|
| monēbō | monēbimus | monēbor | monēbimur |
| monēbis | monēbitis | monēberis | monēbiminī |
| monēbit | monēbunt | monēbitur | monēbuntur |

|                ACTIVE  VOICE                |                PASSIVE  VOICE               |
| :------------------------------------------ | :------------------------------------------ |

INDICATIVE

| PERFECT | | PERFECT | |
| :--- | :--- | :--- | :--- |
| monuī | monuimus | monitus sum | monitī sumus |
| monuistī | monuistis | monitus es | monitī estis |
| monuit | monuērunt | monitus est | monitī sunt |

| PLUPERFECT | | PLUPERFECT | |
| :--- | :--- | :--- | :--- |
| monueram | monuerāmus | monitus eram | monitī erāmus |
| monuerās | monuerātis | monitus erās | monitī erātis |
| monuerat | monuerant | monitus erat | monitī erant |

| FUTURE  PERFECT | | FUTURE  PERFECT | |
| :--- | :--- | :--- | :--- |
| monuerō | monuerimus | monitus erō | monitī erimus |
| monueris | monueritis | monitus eris | monitī eritis |
| monuerit | monuerint | monitus erit | monitī erunt |

SUBJUNCTIVE

| PRESENT | | PRESENT | |
| :--- | :--- | :--- | :--- |
| moneam | moneāmus | monear | moneāmur |
| moneās | moneātis | moneāris | moneāminī |
| moneat | moneant | moneātur | moneantur |

| IMPERFECT | | IMPERFECT | |
| :--- | :--- | :--- | :--- |
| monērem | monērēmus | monērer | monērēmur |
| monērēs | monērētis | monērēris | monērēminī |
| monēret | monērent | monērētur | monērentur |

| PERFECT | | PERFECT | |
| :--- | :--- | :--- | :--- |
| monuerim | monuerīmus | monitus sim | monitī sīmus |
| monuerīs | monuerītis | monitus sīs | monitī sītis |
| monuerit | monuerint | monitus sit | monitī sint |

| PLUPERFECT | | PLUPERFECT | |
| :--- | :--- | :--- | :--- |
| monuissem | monuissēmus | monitus essem | monitī essēmus |
| monuissēs | monuissētis | monitus essēs | monitī essētis |
| monuisset | monuissent | monitus esset | monitī essent |

IMPERATIVE

| | | | | |
| :--- | :--- | :--- | :--- | :--- |
| *Present* | monē | monēte | monēre | monēminī |
| *Future* | monētō | monētōte | monētor | ——— |
| | monētō | monentō | monētor | monentor |

INFINITIVES

| | | |
| :--- | :--- | :--- |
| *Present* | monēre | monērī |
| *Perfect* | monuisse | monitus esse |
| *Future* | monitūrus esse | monitum īrī |

## Participles

| | | |
|---|---|---|
| *Present* | monēns, –entis | |
| *Perfect* | ———— | monitus, –a, –um |
| *Future* | monitūrus, –a, –um | monendus, –a, –um |

### Gerund

| | |
|---|---|
| *Nom.* | ———— |
| *Gen.* | monendī |
| *Dat.* | monendō |
| *Acc.* | monendum |
| *Abl.* | monendō |

### Gerundive

| | | | |
|---|---|---|---|
| *Nom.* | ———— | ———— | ———— |
| *Gen.* | monendī | monendae | monendī |
| *Dat.* | monendō | monendae | monendō |
| *Acc.* | monendum | monendam | monendum |
| *Abl.* | monendō | monendā | monendō |
| | etc. | etc. | etc. |

### Supine

| | |
|---|---|
| *Acc.* | monitum |
| *Abl.* | monitū |

## 72. THIRD CONJUGATION

*Principal Parts:* **dūcō, dūcere, dūxī, ductus**

*Stems:* **dūce–, dūx–, duct–**

### ACTIVE VOICE  ·  PASSIVE VOICE

#### Indicative

**PRESENT**

| dūcō | dūcimus | dūcor | dūcimur |
|---|---|---|---|
| dūcis | dūcitis | dūceris | dūciminī |
| dūcit | dūcunt | dūcitur | dūcuntur |

**IMPERFECT**

| dūcēbam | dūcēbāmus | dūcēbar | dūcēbāmur |
|---|---|---|---|
| dūcēbās | dūcēbātis | dūcēbāris | dūcēbāminī |
| dūcēbat | dūcēbant | dūcēbātur | dūcēbantur |

**FUTURE**

| dūcam | dūcēmus | dūcar | dūcēmur |
|---|---|---|---|
| dūcēs | dūcētis | dūcēris | dūcēminī |
| dūcet | dūcent | dūcētur | dūcentur |

**PERFECT**

| dūxī | dūximus | ductus sum | ductī sumus |
|---|---|---|---|
| dūxistī | dūxistis | ductus es | ductī estis |
| dūxit | dūxērunt | ductus est | ductī sunt |

**PLUPERFECT**

| dūxeram | dūxerāmus | ductus eram | ductī erāmus |
|---|---|---|---|
| dūxerās | dūxerātis | ductus erās | ductī erātis |
| dūxerat | dūxerant | ductus erat | ductī erant |

| ACTIVE VOICE | | PASSIVE VOICE | |
|---|---|---|---|

INDICATIVE

| FUTURE PERFECT | | FUTURE PERFECT | |
|---|---|---|---|
| dūxerō | dūxerimus | ductus erō | ductī erimus |
| dūxeris | dūxeritis | ductus eris | ductī eritis |
| dūxerit | dūxerint | ductus erit | ductī erunt |

SUBJUNCTIVE

| PRESENT | | PRESENT | |
|---|---|---|---|
| dūcam | dūcāmus | dūcar | dūcāmur |
| dūcās | dūcātis | dūcāris | dūcāminī |
| dūcat | dūcant | dūcātur | dūcantur |

| IMPERFECT | | IMPERFECT | |
|---|---|---|---|
| dūcerem | dūcerēmus | dūcerer | dūcerēmur |
| dūcerēs | dūcerētis | dūcerēris | dūcerēminī |
| dūceret | dūcerent | dūcerētur | dūcerentur |

| PERFECT | | PERFECT | |
|---|---|---|---|
| dūxerim | dūxerīmus | ductus sim | ductī sīmus |
| dūxerīs | dūxerītis | ductus sīs | ductī sītis |
| dūxerit | dūxerint | ductus sit | ductī sint |

| PLUPERFECT | | PLUPERFECT | |
|---|---|---|---|
| dūxissem | dūxissēmus | ductus essem | ductī essēmus |
| dūxissēs | dūxissētis | ductus essēs | ductī essētis |
| dūxisset | dūxissent | ductus esset | ductī essent |

IMPERATIVE

| | | | | |
|---|---|---|---|---|
| *Present* | dūc [1] | dūcite | dūcere | dūciminī |
| *Future* | dūcitō | dūcitōte | dūcitor | ————— |
| | dūcitō | dūcuntō | dūcitor | dūcuntor |

INFINITIVES

| | | |
|---|---|---|
| *Present* | dūcere | dūcī |
| *Perfect* | dūxisse | ductus esse |
| *Future* | ductūrus esse | ductum īrī |

PARTICIPLES

| | | |
|---|---|---|
| *Present* | dūcēns, −entis | ————— |
| *Perfect* | ————— | ductus, −a, −um |
| *Future* | ductūrus, −a, −um | dūcendus, −a, −um |

[1] **Dūc, dīc, fac,** and **fer** are the singular imperative active forms of **dūcō, dīcō, faciō,** and **ferō.** The singular imperative active form of all other third conjugation verbs ends in −e.

|        | GERUND    |        | GERUNDIVE |          |          |
|--------|-----------|--------|-----------|----------|----------|
| *Nom.* | ———       | *Nom.* | ———       | ———      | ———      |
| *Gen.* | dūcendī   | *Gen.* | dūcendī   | dūcendae | dūcendī  |
| *Dat.* | dūcendō   | *Dat.* | dūcendō   | dūcendae | dūcendō  |
| *Acc.* | dūcendum  | *Acc.* | dūcendum  | dūcendam | dūcendum |
| *Abl.* | dūcendō   | *Abl.* | dūcendō   | dūcendā  | dūcendō  |
|        |           |        | etc.      | etc.     | etc.     |

SUPINE

*Acc.*  ductum
*Abl.*  ductū

**73.**                  THIRD CONJUGATION IN –*IŌ*

*Principal Parts:* **capiō, capere, cēpī, captus**
*Stems:* **cape–, cēp–, capt–**

ACTIVE VOICE                        PASSIVE VOICE

INDICATIVE

PRESENT

| capiō  | capimus | capior   | capimur   |
| capis  | capitis | caperis  | capiminī  |
| capit  | capiunt | capitur  | capiuntur |

IMPERFECT

| capiēbam | capiēbāmus | capiēbar   | capiēbāmur   |
| capiēbās | capiēbātis | capiēbāris | capiēbāminī  |
| capiēbat | capiēbant  | capiēbātur | capiēbantur  |

FUTURE

| capiam | capiēmus | capiar   | capiēmur   |
| capiēs | capiētis | capiēris | capiēminī  |
| capiet | capient  | capiētur | capientur  |

PERFECT

| cēpī    | cēpimus  | captus sum | captī sumus |
| cēpistī | cēpistis | captus es  | captī estis |
| cēpit   | cēpērunt | captus est | captī sunt  |

PLUPERFECT

| cēperam | cēperāmus | captus eram | captī erāmus |
| cēperās | cēperātis | captus erās | captī erātis |
| cēperat | cēperant  | captus erat | captī erant  |

FUTURE PERFECT

| cēperō  | cēperimus | captus erō  | captī erimus |
| cēperis | cēperitis | captus eris | captī eritis |
| cēperit | cēperint  | captus erit | captī erunt  |

| ACTIVE VOICE | | PASSIVE VOICE | |
|---|---|---|---|

SUBJUNCTIVE

| PRESENT | | PRESENT | |
|---|---|---|---|
| capiam | capiāmus | capiar | capiāmur |
| capiās | capiātis | capiāris | capiāminī |
| capiat | capiant | capiātur | capiantur |

| IMPERFECT | | IMPERFECT | |
|---|---|---|---|
| caperem | caperēmus | caperer | caperēmur |
| caperēs | caperētis | caperēris | caperēminī |
| caperet | caperent | caperētur | caperentur |

| PERFECT | | PERFECT | |
|---|---|---|---|
| cēperim | cēperīmus | captus sim | captī sīmus |
| cēperīs | cēperītis | captus sīs | captī sītis |
| cēperit | cēperint | captus sit | captī sint |

| PLUPERFECT | | PLUPERFECT | |
|---|---|---|---|
| cēpissem | cēpissēmus | captus essem | captī essēmus |
| cēpissēs | cēpissētis | captus essēs | captī essētis |
| cēpisset | cēpissent | captus esset | captī essent |

IMPERATIVE

| Present | cape | capite | capere | capìminī |
|---|---|---|---|---|
| Future | capitō | capitōte | capitor | ———— |
|  | capitō | capiuntō | capitor | capiuntor |

INFINITIVES

| Present | capere | capī |
|---|---|---|
| Perfect | cēpisse | captus esse |
| Future | captūrus esse | captum īrī |

PARTICIPLES

| Present | capiēns, –ientis | ———— |
|---|---|---|
| Perfect | ———— | captus, –a, –um |
| Future | captūrus, –a, –um | capiendus, –a, –um |

| GERUND | | GERUNDIVE | | |
|---|---|---|---|---|
| Nom. | ———— | Nom | ———— | ———— |
| Gen. | capiendī | Gen. | capiendī | capiendae | capiendī |
| Dat. | capiendō | Dat. | capiendō | capiendae | capiendō |
| Acc. | capiendum | Acc. | capiendum | capiendam | capiendum |
| Abl. | capiendō | Abl. | capiendō | capiendā | capiendō |
|  |  |  | etc. | etc. | etc. |

SUPINE

| Acc. | captum |
|---|---|
| Abl. | captū |

**74.** FOURTH CONJUGATION

*Principal Parts:* **audiō, audīre, audīvī, audītus**

*Stems:* **audī–, audīv–, audīt–**

ACTIVE VOICE  PASSIVE VOICE

INDICATIVE

PRESENT | | PRESENT
--- | --- | --- | ---
audiō | audīmus | audior | audīmur
audīs | audītis | audīris | audīminī
audit | audiunt | audītur | audiuntur

IMPERFECT | | IMPERFECT
--- | --- | --- | ---
audiēbam | audiēbāmus | audiēbar | audiēbāmur
audiēbās | audiēbātis | audiēbāris | audiēbāminī
audiēbat | audiēbant | audiēbātur | audiēbantur

FUTURE | | FUTURE
--- | --- | --- | ---
audiam | audiēmus | audiar | audiēmur
audiēs | audiētis | audiēris | audiēminī
audiet | audient | audiētur | audientur

PERFECT | | PERFECT
--- | --- | --- | ---
audīvī | audīvimus | audītus sum | audītī sumus
audīvistī | audīvistis | audītus es | audītī estis
audīvit | audīvērunt | audītus est | audītī sunt

PLUPERFECT | | PLUPERFECT
--- | --- | --- | ---
audīveram | audīverāmus | audītus eram | audītī erāmus
audīverās | audīverātis | audītus erās | audītī erātis
audīverat | audīverant | audītus erat | audītī erant

FUTURE PERFECT | | FUTURE PERFECT
--- | --- | --- | ---
audīverō | audīverimus | audītus erō | audītī erimus
audīveris | audīveritis | audītus eris | audītī eritis
audīverit | audīverint | audītus erit | audītī erunt

SUBJUNCTIVE

PRESENT | | PRESENT
--- | --- | --- | ---
audiam | audiāmus | audiar | audiāmur
audiās | audiātis | audiāris | audiāminī
audiat | audiant | audiātur | audiantur

IMPERFECT | | IMPERFECT
--- | --- | --- | ---
audīrem | audīrēmus | audīrer | audīrēmur
audīrēs | audīrētis | audīrēris | audīrēminī
audīret | audīrent | audīrētur | audīrentur

| ACTIVE VOICE | | PASSIVE VOICE | |
|---|---|---|---|
| | SUBJUNCTIVE | | |

| PERFECT | | PERFECT | |
|---|---|---|---|
| audīverim | audīverīmus | audītus sim | audītī sīmus |
| audīverīs | audīverītis | audītus sīs | audītī sītis |
| audīverit | audīverint | audītus sit | audītī sint |

| PLUPERFECT | | PLUPERFECT | |
|---|---|---|---|
| audīvissem | audīvissēmus | audītus essem | audītī essēmus |
| audīvissēs | audīvissētis | audītus essēs | audītī essētis |
| audīvisset | audīvissent | audītus esset | audītī essent |

### IMPERATIVE

| | | | | |
|---|---|---|---|---|
| *Present* | audī | audīte | audīre | audīminī |
| *Future* | audītō | audītōte | audītor | ———— |
| | audītō | audiuntō | audītor | audiuntor |

### INFINITIVES

| | | |
|---|---|---|
| *Present* | audīre | audīrī |
| *Perfect* | audīvisse | audītus esse |
| *Future* | audītūrus esse | audītum īrī |

### PARTICIPLES

| | | |
|---|---|---|
| *Present* | audiēns, –ientis | ———— |
| *Perfect* | ———— | audītus, –a, –um |
| *Future* | audītūrus, –a, –um | audiendus, –a, –um |

| GERUND | | GERUNDIVE | | |
|---|---|---|---|---|
| *Nom.* | ———— | *Nom.* | ———— | ———— |
| *Gen.* | audiendī | *Gen.* | audiendī | audiendae | audiendī |
| *Dat.* | audiendō | *Dat.* | audiendō | audiendae | audiendō |
| *Acc.* | audiendum | *Acc.* | audiendum | audiendam | audiendum |
| *Abl.* | audiendō | *Abl.* | audiendō | audiendā | audiendō |
| | | | etc. | etc. | etc. |

| SUPINE | |
|---|---|
| *Acc.* | audītum |
| *Abl.* | audītū |

**75.**                     **DEPONENT VERBS** [1]

      I. cōnor, cōnārī, cōnātus sum
     II. polliceor, pollicērī, pollicitus sum
   III. sequor, sequī, secūtus sum
   IV. potior, potīrī, potītus sum

[1] The following verbs are semi-deponent; i.e., the present system is active and the perfect system is passive: **audeō, audēre, ausus sum,** *dare;* **gaudeō, gaudēre, gavīsus sum,** *rejoice;* **soleō, solēre, solitus sum,** *be accustomed;* **fīdō, fīdere, fīsus sum,** *trust.*

## INDICATIVE

### PRESENT

| | | | |
|---|---|---|---|
| cōnor | polliceor | sequor | potior |
| cōnāris | pollicēris | sequeris | potīris |
| cōnātur | pollicētur | sequitur | potītur |
| etc. | etc. | etc. | etc. |

### IMPERFECT

| | | | |
|---|---|---|---|
| cōnābar | pollicēbar | sequēbar | potiēbar |

### FUTURE

| | | | |
|---|---|---|---|
| cōnābor | pollicēbor | sequar | potiar |

### PERFECT

| | | | |
|---|---|---|---|
| cōnātus sum | pollicitus sum | secūtus sum | potītus sum |

### PLUPERFECT

| | | | |
|---|---|---|---|
| cōnātus eram | pollicitus eram | secūtus eram | potītus eram |

### FUTURE PERFECT

| | | | |
|---|---|---|---|
| cōnātus erō | pollicitus erō | secūtus erō | potītus erō |

## SUBJUNCTIVE

### PRESENT

| | | | |
|---|---|---|---|
| cōner | pollicear | sequar | potiar |

### IMPERFECT

| | | | |
|---|---|---|---|
| cōnārer | pollicērer | sequerer | potīrer |

### PERFECT

| | | | |
|---|---|---|---|
| cōnātus sim | pollicitus sim | secūtus sim | potītus sim |

### PLUPERFECT

| | | | |
|---|---|---|---|
| cōnātus essem | pollicitus essem | secūtus essem | potītus essem |

## IMPERATIVES

### PRESENT

| | | | |
|---|---|---|---|
| cōnāre | pollicēre | sequere | potīre |
| etc. | etc. | etc. | etc. |

## Infinitives

### PRESENT

| | | | |
|---|---|---|---|
| cōnārī | pollicērī | sequī | potīrī |

### PERFECT

| | | | |
|---|---|---|---|
| cōnātus esse | pollicitus esse | secūtus esse | potītus esse |

### FUTURE

| | | | |
|---|---|---|---|
| cōnātūrus esse | pollicitūrus esse | secūtūrus esse | potītūrus esse |

## Participles

### PRESENT

| | | | |
|---|---|---|---|
| cōnāns | pollicēns | sequēns | potiēns |

### PERFECT

| | | | |
|---|---|---|---|
| cōnātus | pollicitus | secūtus | potītus |

### FUTURE ACTIVE

| | | | |
|---|---|---|---|
| cōnātūrus | pollicitūrus | secūtūrus | potītūrus |

### FUTURE PASSIVE

| | | | |
|---|---|---|---|
| cōnandus | pollicendus | sequendus | potiendus |

## Gerund

| | | | |
|---|---|---|---|
| cōnandī | pollicendī | sequendī | potiendī |

## Gerundive

| | | |
|---|---|---|
| *Gen.* cōnandī, –ae, –ī | | *Gen.* sequendī, –ae, –ī |
| *Gen.* pollicendī, –ae, –ī | | *Gen.* potiendī, –ae, –ī |

## Supine

| | | | |
|---|---|---|---|
| cōnātum | pollicitum | secūtum | potītum |
| cōnātū | pollicitū | secūtū | potītū |

## *IRREGULAR VERBS*

**76.**                                 **SUM**

*Principal Parts:* **sum, esse, fuī, futūrus**

### INDICATIVE

| PRESENT | | PERFECT | |
|---|---|---|---|
| sum | sumus | fuī | fuimus |
| es | estis | fuistī | fuistis |
| est | sunt | fuit | fuērunt |

| IMPERFECT | | PLUPERFECT | |
|---|---|---|---|
| eram | erāmus | fueram | fuerāmus |
| erās | erātis | fuerās | fuerātis |
| erat | erant | fuerat | fuerant |

| FUTURE | | FUTURE PERFECT | |
|---|---|---|---|
| erō | erimus | fuerō | fuerimus |
| eris | eritis | fueris | fueritis |
| erit | erunt | fuerit | fuerint |

### SUBJUNCTIVE

| PRESENT | | IMPERFECT | |
|---|---|---|---|
| sim | sīmus | essem [1] | essēmus |
| sīs | sītis | essēs | essētis |
| sit | sint | esset | essent |

| PERFECT | | PLUPERFECT | |
|---|---|---|---|
| fuerim | fuerīmus | fuissem | fuissēmus |
| fuerīs | fuerītis | fuissēs | fuissētis |
| fuerit | fuerint | fuisset | fuissent |

### IMPERATIVE

| *Present* | es | este |
|---|---|---|
| *Future* | estō | estōte |
| | estō | suntō |

### INFINITIVES

*Present*  esse          *Perfect*  fuisse          *Future*  futūrus esse [2]

### PARTICIPLE

*Future*  futūrus, −a, −um

[1] Alternate forms of the imperfect subjunctive are: **forem, forēs, foret,** etc.
[2] An alternate form of the future active infinitive is **fore.**

**77.**

## POSSUM

*Principal Parts:* **possum, posse, potuī**

### INDICATIVE

<table>
<tr><th colspan="2">PRESENT</th><th colspan="2">PERFECT</th></tr>
<tr><td>possum</td><td>possumus</td><td>potuī</td><td>potuimus</td></tr>
<tr><td>potes</td><td>potestis</td><td>potuistī</td><td>potuistis</td></tr>
<tr><td>potest</td><td>possunt</td><td>potuit</td><td>potuērunt</td></tr>
</table>

<table>
<tr><th colspan="2">IMPERFECT</th><th colspan="2">PLUPERFECT</th></tr>
<tr><td>poteram</td><td>poterāmus</td><td>potueram</td><td>potuerāmus</td></tr>
<tr><td>poterās</td><td>poterātis</td><td>potuerās</td><td>potuerātis</td></tr>
<tr><td>poterat</td><td>poterant</td><td>potuerat</td><td>potuerant</td></tr>
</table>

<table>
<tr><th colspan="2">FUTURE</th><th colspan="2">FUTURE PERFECT</th></tr>
<tr><td>poterō</td><td>poterimus</td><td>potuerō</td><td>potuerimus</td></tr>
<tr><td>poteris</td><td>poteritis</td><td>potueris</td><td>potueritis</td></tr>
<tr><td>poterit</td><td>poterunt</td><td>potuerit</td><td>potuerint</td></tr>
</table>

### SUBJUNCTIVE

<table>
<tr><th colspan="2">PRESENT</th><th colspan="2">PERFECT</th></tr>
<tr><td>possim</td><td>possīmus</td><td>potuerim</td><td>potuerīmus</td></tr>
<tr><td>possīs</td><td>possītis</td><td>potuerīs</td><td>potuerītis</td></tr>
<tr><td>possit</td><td>possint</td><td>potuerit</td><td>potuerint</td></tr>
</table>

<table>
<tr><th colspan="2">IMPERFECT</th><th colspan="2">PLUPERFECT</th></tr>
<tr><td>possem</td><td>possēmus</td><td>potuissem</td><td>potuissēmus</td></tr>
<tr><td>possēs</td><td>possētis</td><td>potuissēs</td><td>potuissētis</td></tr>
<tr><td>posset</td><td>possent</td><td>potuisset</td><td>potuissent</td></tr>
</table>

### INFINITIVES

*Present*  posse                          *Perfect*  potuisse

### PARTICIPLE

*Present*  potēns, –entis

**78.** VOLŌ, NŌLŌ, MĂLŌ

*Principal Parts:* **volō, velle, voluī**
**nōlō, nōlle, nōluī**
**mālō, mālle, māluī**

INDICATIVE

PRESENT

| volō | volumus | nōlō | nōlumus | mālō | mālumus |
| vīs | vultis | nōn vīs | nōn vultis | māvīs | māvultis |
| vult | volunt | nōn vult | nōlunt | māvult | mālunt |

IMPERFECT

| volēbam | nōlēbam | mālēbam |
| volēbās | nōlēbās | mālēbās |
| etc. | etc. | etc. |

FUTURE

| volam | nōlam | mālam |
| volēs | nōlēs | mālēs |
| etc. | etc. | etc. |

PERFECT

| voluī | nōluī | māluī |
| voluistī | nōluistī | māluistī |
| etc. | etc. | etc. |

PLUPERFECT

| volueram | nōlueram | mālueram |
| voluerās | nōluerās | māluerās |
| etc. | etc. | etc. |

FUTURE PERFECT

| voluerō | nōluerō | māluerō |
| volueris | nōlueris | mālueris |
| etc. | etc. | etc. |

SUBJUNCTIVE

PRESENT

| velim | nōlim | mālim |
| velīs | nōlīs | mālīs |
| etc. | etc. | etc. |

| | | |
|---|---|---|
| vellem | nōllem | māllem |
| vellēs | nōllēs | māllēs |
| etc. | etc. | etc. |

PERFECT

| | | |
|---|---|---|
| voluerim | nōluerim | māluerim |
| voluerīs | nōluerīs | māluerīs |
| etc. | etc. | etc. |

PLUPERFECT

| | | |
|---|---|---|
| voluissem | nōluissem | māluissem |
| voluissēs | nōluissēs | māluissēs |
| etc. | etc. | etc. |

IMPERATIVE

| | | |
|---|---|---|
| *Present* —— | nōlī    nōlīte | —— |

INFINITIVES

| | | |
|---|---|---|
| *Present* velle | nōlle | mālle |
| *Perfect* voluisse | nōluisse | māluisse |

PARTICIPLES

| | | |
|---|---|---|
| *Present* volēns, –entis | nōlēns, –entis | —— |

**79.** **FERŌ**

*Principal Parts:* **ferō, ferre, tulī, lātus**

| ACTIVE VOICE | PASSIVE VOICE |
|---|---|

INDICATIVE

PRESENT

| | | | |
|---|---|---|---|
| ferō | ferimus | feror | ferimur |
| fers | fertis | ferris | feriminī |
| fert | ferunt | fertur | feruntur |

IMPERFECT

| | |
|---|---|
| ferēbam | ferēbar |
| ferēbās | ferēbāris |
| etc. | etc. |

### FUTURE

| | |
|---|---|
| feram | ferar |
| ferēs | ferēris |
| etc. | etc. |

### PERFECT

| | |
|---|---|
| tulī | lātus sum |
| tulistī | lātus es |
| etc. | etc. |

### PLUPERFECT

| | |
|---|---|
| tuleram | lātus eram |
| tulerās | lātus erās |
| etc. | etc. |

### FUTURE PERFECT

| | |
|---|---|
| tulerō | lātus erō |
| tuleris | lātus eris |
| etc. | etc. |

## SUBJUNCTIVE

### PRESENT

| | |
|---|---|
| feram | ferar |
| ferās | ferāris |
| etc. | etc. |

### IMPERFECT

| | |
|---|---|
| ferrem | ferrer |
| ferrēs | ferrēris |
| etc. | etc. |

### PERFECT

| | |
|---|---|
| tulerim | lātus sim |
| tulerīs | lātus sīs |
| etc. | etc. |

### PLUPERFECT

| | |
|---|---|
| tulissem | lātus essem |
| tulissēs | lātus essēs |
| etc. | etc. |

## IMPERATIVE

| | | | | |
|---|---|---|---|---|
| *Present* | fer | ferte | ferre | feriminī |
| *Future* | fertō | fertōte | fertor | ———— |
| | fertō | feruntō | fertor | feruntor |

| ACTIVE VOICE | PASSIVE VOICE |
|---|---|

### INFINITIVES

| | | |
|---|---|---|
| *Present* | ferre | ferrī |
| *Perfect* | tulisse | lātus esse |
| *Future* | lātūrus esse | lātum īrī |

### PARTICIPLES

| | | |
|---|---|---|
| *Present* | ferēns, −entis | —— |
| *Perfect* | —— | lātus |
| *Future* | lātūrus | ferendus |

| GERUND | | GERUNDIVE | |
|---|---|---|---|
| *Nom.* | —— | *Nom.* | —————— |
| *Gen.* | ferendī | *Gen.* | ferendī, −ae, −ī |
| | etc. | | etc. |

### SUPINE

| | |
|---|---|
| *Acc.* | lātum |
| *Abl.* | lātū |

**80.**

## EŌ

*Principal Parts:* **eō, īre, īvī (iī), itūrus**

### INDICATIVE

| PRESENT | | PERFECT |
|---|---|---|
| eō | īmus | īvī (iī) |
| īs | ītis | īvistī (iistī) |
| it | eunt | etc. |

| IMPERFECT | PLUPERFECT |
|---|---|
| ībam | īveram (ieram) |
| ībās | īverās (ierās) |
| etc. | etc. |

| FUTURE | FUTURE PERFECT |
|---|---|
| ībō | īverō (ierō) |
| ībis | īveris (ieris) |
| etc. | etc. |

### SUBJUNCTIVE

| PRESENT | PERFECT |
|---|---|
| eam | īverim (ierim) |
| eās | īverīs (ierīs) |
| etc. | etc. |

| | IMPERFECT | PLUPERFECT |
|---|---|---|
| | īrem | īvissem (īssem) |
| | īrēs | īvissēs (īssēs) |
| | etc. | etc. |

| | IMPERATIVE | | INFINITIVES | | PARTICIPLES | |
|---|---|---|---|---|---|---|
| *Present* | ī | īte | *Present* | īre | *Present* | iēns (*gen.* euntis) |
| *Future* | ītō | ītōte | *Perfect* | iisse *or* īsse | *Perfect* | —— |
| | ītō | euntō | *Future* | itūrus esse | *Future* | itūrus |

GERUND

*Nom.* ——
*Gen.* eundī
etc.

**81.** FĪŌ [1]

*Principal Parts:* **fīō, fierī, factus sum**

INDICATIVE

| PRESENT | | PERFECT |
|---|---|---|
| fīō | —— | factus sum |
| fīs | —— | factus es |
| fit | fīunt | etc. |

| IMPERFECT | PLUPERFECT |
|---|---|
| fīēbam | factus eram |
| fīēbās | factus erās |
| etc. | etc. |

| FUTURE | FUTURE PERFECT |
|---|---|
| fīam | factus erō |
| fīēs | factus eris |
| etc. | etc. |

SUBJUNCTIVE

| PRESENT | | PERFECT |
|---|---|---|
| fīam | fīāmus | factus sim |
| fīās | fīātis | factus sīs |
| fīat | fīant | etc. |

| IMPERFECT | PLUPERFECT |
|---|---|
| fierem | factus essem |
| fierēs | factus essēs |
| etc. | etc. |

| IMPERATIVE | | INFINITIVES | | PARTICIPLES | |
|---|---|---|---|---|---|
| fī | fīte | *Present* | fierī | *Present* | —— |
| | | *Perfect* | factus esse | *Perfect* | factus |
| | | *Future* | factum īrī | *Future* | faciendus |

[1] In all forms of **fīō** the **i** is long except when it is followed by **er**.

## DEFECTIVE VERBS

**82.** COEPĪ, MEMINĪ

*Principal Parts:* **coepī, coepisse** [1]

**meminī, meminisse** [2]

### INDICATIVE

#### PERFECT

| | |
|---|---|
| coepī | meminī [2] |
| coepistī | meministī |
| etc. | etc. |

#### PLUPERFECT

| | |
|---|---|
| coeperam | memineram |
| coeperās | meminerās |
| etc. | etc. |

#### FUTURE PERFECT

| | |
|---|---|
| coeperō | meminerō |
| coeperis | memineris |
| etc. | etc. |

### SUBJUNCTIVE

#### PERFECT

| | |
|---|---|
| coeperim | meminerim |
| coeperīs | meminerīs |
| etc. | etc. |

#### PLUPERFECT

| | |
|---|---|
| coepissem | meminissem |
| coepissēs | meminissēs |
| etc. | etc. |

### IMPERATIVE

| | |
|---|---|
| —— | mementō |
| —— | mementōte |

### INFINITIVES

| | |
|---|---|
| *Perfect*  coepisse | meminisse |

[1] **Coepī** is found only in the perfect, pluperfect, and future perfect in classical Latin. The present tenses are supplied by forms of **incipiō**.

[2] A perfect tense form of **meminī** has the force of a present, a pluperfect form the force of an imperfect, and a future perfect tense form the force of a future.

# RULES OF SYNTAX

## *AGREEMENT*

**83.** A predicate noun agrees with its subject in case:
1. With forms of the verb **sum;** e.g., **Celtae sunt** *Gallī.*
2. With the passive of verbs of making, calling, or choosing; e.g., **Celtae** *Gallī* **appellantur.**

**84.** An adjective agrees with its noun in gender, number, and case:
1. An attributive adjective; e.g., *Fortēs* **Gallī fortiter pugnāvērunt.**
2. A predicate adjective; e.g., **Gallī erant** *fortēs.*

    *a.* An adjective belonging to one or more nouns may agree with the nearest of them; e.g., **Nostrī nōn** *eādem* **alacritāte et studiō ūtēbantur.**

**85.** A finite verb agrees with its subject in person and number; e.g., **Nōs** *stāmus* **et magister** *stat.*

    *a.* A verb belonging to two or more subjects may agree with the nearest; e.g., **Orgetorīgis fīlia et fīlius** *captus est.*
    *b.* A verb may agree with its subject in sense; e.g., **Pars Gallōrum** *captī sunt.*

**86.** A noun in apposition with another noun agrees with it in case; e.g., **Caesar Ariovistum,** *rēgem* **Germānōrum, vīcit.**

**87.** A pronoun agrees with its antecedent in gender and number, but not necessarily in case; e.g., **Ariovistus erat rēx Germānōrum, sed Caesar** *eum* **vīcit; Ariovistus,** *quem* **Caesar vīcit, erat rēx Germānōrum.**

    *a.* A pronoun also agrees with its antecedent in person; e.g., **Vōs,** *quī* **adestis, bonī discipulī estis.**

## USES OF THE CASES

### THE NOMINATIVE

**88. As Subject.** The subject of a finite verb is in the nominative case; e.g., *Caesar* **Ariovistum vīcit.**

    *a.* The subject of a historical infinitive is in the nominative case; e.g., *Caesar* **cotīdiē frūmentum postulāre.**

### THE GENITIVE

**89.** When one noun is used to limit or qualify another noun not meaning the same person or thing, it is regularly in the genitive.

**90. Possession or Connection.** The genitive may be used to express possession or connection; e.g., *Caesaris* **mīlitēs erant fortēs; Tigurīnī avum** *Pisōnis* **interfēcerant.**

**91. Genitive of the Whole (Partitive Genitive).** The genitive may be used to express the whole of which a part is mentioned; e.g., **Pars** *arcis* **capta est; Omnium** *Gallōrum* **fortissimī erant Belgae.**

    *a.* This use of the genitive is sometimes extended to include such expressions as **aliquid** *perīculī, some(thing of) danger.*

**92. Genitive of Quality or Description.** A noun in the genitive modified by an adjective may be used to describe another noun; e.g., **Nerviī erant hominēs magnae** *virtūtis.*

- a. A genitive so used may express measure; e.g., *Diērum* **quīndecim supplicātiō dē-crēta est.**
- b. The genitive of certain adjectives of quantity may be used to express indefinite value; e.g., **Commiī auctōritās** *magnī* **habēbātur** (*Commius's influence was considered of great value*). In such a use the noun **pretiī** is to be understood with the adjective.

**93. Objective Genitive.** The genitive may be used to indicate the object or application of the verbal idea in a noun; e.g., **Orgetorīx cupiditāte** *rēgnī* **adductus est.**

- a. The objective genitive may be used with a few adjectives; e.g., **Orgetorīx erat cupidus** *rēgnī.*
- b. This use of the genitive is also extended to a few verbs; e.g., **Caesar veteris** *injūriae* **oblīviscī** (*to forget*) **nōlēbat.**
- c. The genitive is used with certain verbs of feeling; e.g., **miserēre** *animī* (*Aen.* II, 144).

**94. Genitive of Specification.** In poetry a genitive of specification is sometimes found with adjectives; e.g., **dīves** *opum* (*Aen.* I, 14); **fessī** *rērum* (*Aen.* I, 178).

**95. Genitive of Definition.** In poetry a genitive of definition is sometimes found; e.g., **urbem** *Patavī* (*Aen.* I, 247). In prose the phrase would be **urbem Patavium.**

**96. Genitive with Verbs of Plenty.** In poetry a genitive is found with verbs denoting plenty; e.g., **implentur veteris** *Bacchī* (*Aen.* I, 215); **animum explēsse** *flammae* (*Aen.* II, 586–587).

## THE DATIVE

**97. As Indirect Object.** The dative is used as indirect object; e.g., **Orgetorīx** *Dumnorīgī* **fīliam suam dat.**

**98. Dative with Special Verbs.** The dative is used with certain verbs [1]; e.g., **Caesar** *Commiō* **cōnfīdēbat.**

- a. In poetry **misceō** and **commisceō** sometimes take the dative; e.g., **miscetque** *virīs* (*Aen.* I, 440).

**99. Dative with Adjectives.** The dative is used with certain adjectives of quality, attitude, or relation [2]; e.g., **Belgae sunt proximī** *Germānīs.*

**100. Dative of Reference.** The dative may be used with almost any verb to express the person to whom the action refers or whom it concerns; e.g., **Belgae** *sibi* **magnam auctōritātem in rē mīlitārī sūmunt.**

- a. The dative of reference used with certain verbs of taking away sometimes has the force of an ablative; e.g., **Caesar** *mīlitī* **scūtum dētrāxit** (*Caesar snatched a shield from a soldier*). This use is sometimes called the dative of separation.
- b. The dative of reference is sometimes used instead of a genitive; e.g., **Helvētiī sē ad pedēs** *Caesarī* (= Caesaris) **prōjēcērunt.**

[1] Among the verbs taking the dative are: cōnfīdō, crēdō, faveō, ignōscō, imperō, licet, noceō, parcō, pāreō, persuādeō, placeō, resistō, satisfaciō, studeō, suādeō.
[2] Among the adjectives taking the dative are: adversus, amīcus, cōnsimilis, fidēlis, fīnitimus, grātus, incognitus, inimīcus, inūsitātus, necessārius, nōtus, pār, perīculōsus, proximus, secundus, similis, ūtilis.

**101. Dative of Purpose.** The dative of a few nouns may be used to express purpose, tendency, or result [1]; e.g., **Caesar funditōrēs** *subsidiō* **oppidānīs mittit.**

  a. The dative of purpose and the dative of reference are frequently used in combination and are therefore sometimes referred to as the "double dative." In such a combination the dative of purpose regularly tells *for what* a thing is or is done and the dative of reference tells *for whom*.

**102. Dative with Compound Verbs.** The dative is used with certain verbs compounded with **ad–, ante–, circum–, com–, in–, inter–, ob–, post–, prae–, pro–, sub–,** or **super–** [2]; e.g., **Helvētiī cēterīs** *Gallīs* **virtūte praestant** (*stand ahead for;* i.e., *excel*).

  a. If the verb so compounded is itself transitive, it may take a direct object as well as a dative; e.g., **Helvētiī** *Germānīs* **bellum** **īnferunt**; **Caesar** *mūnītiōnī* **Labiēnum praeficit.**

**103. Dative of Direction.** In poetry a dative may be used to express direction. The prose construction would regularly be the accusative with **ad**; e.g., **īnferretque deōs Latiō** (*Aen.* I, 6); **dēmittimus Orcō** (*Aen.* II, 398).

**104. Dative of Possession.** The dative may be used with any form of the verb **sum** to express possession, the subject of the verb being the person or thing possessed; e.g., **Allobrogēs dēmōnstrant** *sibi* **esse nihil** (i.e., *sē* **habēre nihil**).

**105. Dative of Agent.** The dative is regularly used with the passive periphrastic verb phrase to express the person or persons by whom the action called for is to be performed; e.g., **Caesarī omnia ūnō tempore erant agenda** (*for Caesar everything was to be done at the same time;* i.e., *everything had to be done by Caesar at the same time*); **Caesar nōn exspectandum esse** *sibi* **statuit** (*Caesar decided that he ought not to wait*).

  a. This construction is frequent in poetry with any passive verb form; e.g., **vetor Fātīs** (*Aen.* I, 39); **neque cernitur ūllī** (*Aen.* I, 440).

## THE ACCUSATIVE

**106. As Direct Object.** The accusative may be used as the direct object of a transitive verb; e.g., **Caesar duās** *legiōnēs* **cōnscrīpsit.**

  a. Certain verbs of inquiring, requesting, or teaching may take a secondary object in addition to the direct object; e.g., **Id tē ōrō.**
  b. Certain transitive verbs compounded with **trāns–** or **circúm–** may take a secondary object depending in thought upon the preposition; e.g., **Caesar cōpiās suās** *flūmen* **trādūxit** (i.e., **Caesar cōpiās suās trāns flūmen trādūxit**).
  c. The accusative object is retained with the passive of a verb which in the active takes a secondary object; e.g., **circum terga datī** (*Aen.* II, 218–219).

**107. As Predicate Accusative.** An active [3] verb of making, calling, or choosing may take a second accusative in predicate agreement with the direct object; e.g., **Rōmānī Celtās** *Gallōs* **appellant.**

---

[1] Nouns most commonly used in this way are: **auxilium, cūra, impedīmentum, praesidium, salūs, subsidium, ūsus.**
[2] Among the compound verbs taking the dative are: **accidō, adaequō, adfīgō, adjungō, antepōnō, appropinquō, circumjiciō, contingō, impōnō, īnferō, injiciō, īnsistō, interdīcō, intersum, obveniō, occurrō, praecipiō, praeferō, praeficiō, praestō, praesum, prōspiciō, subjiciō.**
[3] For the case with passive verbs of this sort see App. 83, 2.

**108. As Subject of an Infinitive.** An accusative may be used as the subject of an infinitive; e.g., **Caesar jubet** *pontem* **rescindī; Caesar cognōvit** *Helvētiōs* **per Prōvinciam iter facere cōnārī.**

  *a.* For the case of the subject of a historical infinitive see App. 88, *a.*

**109. Place Whither.** An accusative may be used with the preposition **ad, in,** or **sub** to express place whither; e.g., **Caesar** *in Prōvinciam* **contendit.**

  *a.* The accusative without a preposition is regularly used to express place whither with names of towns and a few other words; e.g., **Hannibal** *Carthāginem* **rediit; Trēverī** *domum* **contendērunt.**

  *b.* In poetry the accusative of a wide variety of words may be used without a preposition to express place whither; e.g., *Ītaliam* **vēnit** (*Aen.* I, 2); **aliās āvexerat** *ōrās* (*Aen.* I, 512).

  *c.* An accusative with the preposition **ad** may be used to express the idea of *to the vicinity of* a town; e.g., **Caesar** *ad Genavam* **pervēnit.**

**110. Duration of Time.** An accusative may be used without a preposition to express duration of time; e.g., **Casticī pater rēgnum in Sēquanīs multōs** *annōs* **obtinuerat.**

**111. Extent of Space.** An accusative may be used without a preposition to express extent of space; e.g., *Mīlia* **passuum ūndēvīgintī Caesar mūrum et fossam perdūcit.**

**112. With Various Prepositions.** The accusative may be used with various prepositions [1] to express various relations; e.g., **Helvētiī** *per fīnēs* **Sēquanōrum cōpiās suās trādūxerant.**

**113. Accusative of Respect.** The accusative of respect, a Greek construction, is frequent in poetry; e.g., **nūda** *genū, bare-kneed* (*Aen.* I, 320); **nigrantīs** *terga* **juvencōs,** *black-backed oxen* (*Aen.* VI, 243).

**114. Accusative with Middle Voice.** A Greek construction, the accusative used with a perfect passive participle, with reflexive force, is often found in Latin poetry; e.g., **lacrimīs** *oculōs* **suffūsa** (*Aen.* I, 228); **tūnsae** *pectora* (*Aen.* I, 481).

  See also App. 188.

**115. Cognate Accusative.** An intransitive verb may take an accusative noun with a meaning kindred to its own; e.g., **longam īre** *viam* (*Aen.* IV, 467–468); **nec vōx** *hominem* **sonat** (*Aen.* I, 328); *mortāle* **sonāns** (*Aen.* VI, 50).

**116. Adverbial Accusative.** In poetry a neuter accusative of an adjective, in the singular or plural, may be used in an adverbial sense; e.g., *aeternum* **lātrāns** (*Aen.* VI, 401); *torva* **tuentem** (*Aen.* VI, 467).

## THE ABLATIVE

**117. Place Whence.** The ablative with the preposition **ab, dē,** or **ex** may be used to express place whence; e.g., **Caesar** *ab urbe* **proficīscitur.**

  *a.* The ablative without a preposition is regularly used to express place whence with names of towns and a few other words; e.g., **Caesar** *Rōmā* **proficīscitur; Helvētiī** *domō* **proficīscuntur.**

  *b.* In poetry the ablative of a wide variety of words is used without a preposition to express place whence; e.g., *Ītaliā* **āvertere** (*Aen.* I, 38); **exspīrantem** *pectore* (*Aen.* I, 44).

---

[1] Among the prepositions taking the accusative are: **ad, ante, apud, circā, circiter, circum, citrā, contrā, extrā, īnfrā, inter, intrā, juxtā, ob, per, post, praeter, prope, propter, secundum, suprā, trāns, ultrā.**

c. The ablative with the preposition **ab** may be used to express distance from a town or the idea of *from the vicinity of* a town; e.g., **Caesar** *ā* **Bibracte nōn longē aberat; Labiēnus** *ā* **Genavā proficīscitur.**

d. The ablative of a few nouns with the preposition **ab** or **ex** may be used to express point of view from which, where the English conception is generally that of place where; e.g., **Nerviī impetum in Rōmānōs** *ā fronte* **et** *ab utrōque latere* **faciunt; Helvētiī** *ūnā ex parte* **flūmine Rhēnō continentur.**

e. The idea of source is expressed by the ablative, generally without a preposition; e.g., **nāte** *deā* (*Aen.* I, 582).

f. In poetry the ablative without a preposition is sometimes used to express the material from which something is made; e.g., *rōboribus* **textīs** (*Aen.* II, 186).

**118. Ablative of Separation.** The ablative with the preposition **ab, dē,** or **ex** may be used to express separation; e.g., **Tempestātēs hostēs** *ā pugnā* **prohibuērunt; Haeduī sē** *ab hostibus* **dēfendere nōn potuērunt.**

a. The ablative without a preposition may be used with certain verbs of separation [1]; e.g., **Hostēs** *itinere* **exercitum nostrum prohibēre cōnantur; Dumnorīx dīxit Galliam omnī** *nōbilitāte* **spoliārī.**

**119. Ablative of Agent.** The ablative with the preposition **ab** may be used with a passive verb to express the personal agency; e.g., **Gallī** *ab Caesare* **superātī sunt.**

**120. Ablative of Cause.** The ablative without a preposition may be used to express cause; e.g., **Dumnorīx** *grātiā* (*because of his personal popularity*) **apud Sēquanōs plūrimum poterat.**

a. The ablative with the preposition **ex** or **dē** is sometimes used to express cause; e.g., **Quā** *dē causā* **Helvētiī reliquōs Gallōs virtūte praecēdunt.**

b. The ablative of certain nouns with or without the preposition **dē** or **ex** may be used to express the cause or the standard in accordance with which an act is performed; e.g., **Mōribus suīs Helvētiī Orgetorīgem ex vinculīs causam dīcere coēgērunt; ūna legiō** *ex cōnsuētūdine* **frūmentātum missa est.**

**121. Ablative of Comparison.** The ablative without a preposition may be used with a comparative; e.g., **Castra hostium amplius** *mīlibus* **passuum octō in lātitūdinem patēbant.**

a. Comparison is more commonly expressed by the use of **quam**; e.g., **Pejus Sēquanīs** *quam* **Haeduīs acciderat** (*A worse thing had happened to the Sequanians than to the Haeduans*).

**122. Ablative of Accompaniment.** The ablative with the preposition **cum** may be used to express accompaniment; e.g., **Helvētiī** *cum* **omnibus** *cōpiīs* **proficīscuntur; Caesar Crassum** *cum legiōne* **ūnā ad Venetōs mittit.**

a. The ablative without a preposition may be used in certain military expressions [2] to express accompaniment; e.g., **Caesar omnibus** *cōpiīs* **sequitur.**

**123. Ablative of Means.** The ablative without a preposition may be used to express the means or instrument of an action; e.g., **Rōmānī** *pīlīs* **et** *gladiīs* **pugnāvērunt.**

a. The ablative of means or instrument is usually a noun referring to a thing, but persons may also be thought of as a means; e.g., **Eā** *legiōne,* **quam sēcum habēbat, et** *mīlitibus* **quī ex Prōvinciā convēnerant, Caesar mūrum et fossam perdūcit.**

---

[1] Among these verbs of separation are: **abstineō, arceō, careō, dēsistō, līberō, prohibeō, spoliō.**

[2] This use of the ablative without a preposition is limited to military expressions in which the ablative noun is modified by an adjective other than a numeral.

**124. Ablative of Manner.** The ablative of certain abstract nouns with the preposition cum may be used to express manner; e.g., Cicerō *cum* summā *dīligentiā* mīlitēs in castrīs continuerat.

 a. The ablative without a preposition may be used to express manner, if the noun is modified by an adjective; e.g., Nōn eādem *dīligentiā* castra hostium ab decumānā portā mūnīta erant.
 b. The ablative of certain nouns without a preposition may be used to express manner; e.g., cāsū, dolō, jūre, injūriā, meritō, sponte, vī.
 c. In poetry the use of the ablative without a preposition is extended to include other nouns besides those listed under *b*; e.g., cumulō (*Aen.* I, 105); nōdō (*Aen.* I, 320).

**125. Ablative of Degree of Difference.** The ablative without a preposition may be used with a comparative idea to express degree of difference; e.g., Post mortem Orgetorīgis *nihilō* minus (*less by nothing*) Helvētiī ē fīnibus exīre cōnantur; Paucīs ante *diēbus* (*before by a few days*) equitēs fūgerant.

**126. Ablative of Respect or Specification.** The ablative without a preposition may be used to specify in what respect a noun, verb, or adjective is to be taken; e.g., Helvētiī reliquōs Gallōs *virtūte* praecēdunt.

 a. The ablative is used with dignus, indignus, and dignor; e.g., haud talī mē dignor honōre (*Aen.* I, 335).

**127. Ablative of the Way By Which.** The ablative of certain words may be used to express the way or route by which; e.g., Erant itinera duo, *quibus* Helvētiī domō exīre possent.

 a. This usage is common in poetry; e.g., pelagō (*Aen.* I, 364); caelō (*Aen.* I, 395).

**128. Ablative with Certain Deponents.** The ablative is used with the deponent verbs ūtor, fruor, fungor, potior, vēscor, and their compounds; e.g., Britannī ūtuntur *nummō* aureō; Rōmānī *castrīs* Helvētiōrum potītī sunt.

**129. Ablative of Quality or Description.** The ablative modified by an adjective may be used to describe a person or thing; e.g., Bellovacī erant *magnā auctōritāte.*

**130. Ablative of Attendant Circumstance.** The ablative modified by an adjective or a genitive may be used to express attendant circumstance; e.g., Gallī concilium *voluntāte* Caesaris (*with Caesar's consent*) indīcunt.

**131. Ablative Absolute Phrase.** The ablative of a noun or pronoun with a participle, adjective, or noun in agreement may be used to express an attendant circumstance of an action; e.g., Omnibus *rēbus comparātīs,* Helvētiī diem dīcunt.

 a. An ablative absolute phrase containing the name of the consul or consuls of a given year is often used to indicate that year; e.g., Orgetorīx, *M. Messālā et M. Pisōne cōnsulibus* (i.e., in 61 B.C.), conjūrātiōnem fēcit.
 b. An ablative absolute phrase is often used in Latin where a more exact expression would be used in English:
   (1) To express time or temporal circumstance; e.g., Hōc *proeliō factō* (*When* or *after this battle had been fought*), Caesar pontem in Ararī facit.
   (2) To express cause; e.g., *Prōspectū* tenebrīs *adēmptō* (*Since the view was cut off by the darkness*), multa vulnera accipiuntur.
   (3) To express concession; e.g., Id oppidum, *paucīs dēfendentibus* (*although there were few defending it*), Caesar expugnāre nōn potuit.

(4) To express condition; e.g., **Sēquanīs invītīs** (*If the Sequanians should be unwilling*), **Helvētiī per angustiās īre nōn poterant.**

c. In poetry a participle is sometimes used impersonally; e.g., **lībātō,** *a libation having been made* (*Aen.* I, 737).

**132. Place Where.**[1] The ablative with the preposition **in** or **sub** may be used to express place where; e.g., **Erat omninō in Galliā Ulteriōre legiō ūna; Ceutronēs sub imperiō Nerviōrum sunt.**

a. The ablative **locō, locīs, parte,** or **partibus** is regularly used without a preposition when accompanied by an adjective.

b. In poetry the ablative of a wide variety of words is used without a preposition to express place where; e.g., **terrīs et altō** (*Aen.* I, 3); **vāstō antrō** (*Aen.* I, 52).

**133. Time When.** The ablative without a preposition may be used to express time when or within which; e.g., **Eō diē Caesar hostēs cōnsequitur; Caesar ūnō diē pontem in flūmine facit.**

**134. Ablative with Various Prepositions.** The ablative is used with various prepositions to express various relations [2]; e.g., **Dīviciācus prō Gallīs locūtus est.**

## THE LOCATIVE

**135.** The locative is used to express place where with the names of towns and a few other words; e.g., **Rōmae** (*at Rome*) **supplicātiō redditur; Helvētiī domī** (*at home*) **nihil habēbant, quō famem tolerārent.**

a. This usage is extended in poetry; e.g., **fīdēns animī** (*Aen.* II, 61); **āmēns animī** (*Aen.* IV, 203).

## THE VOCATIVE

**136.** The vocative is used in direct address; e.g., **Dēsilīte, commīlitōnēs; Mūsa, mihī causās memorā** (*Aen.* I, 8).

## USES OF TENSES

**137.**                            **TENSES IN THE INDICATIVE**

1. The present indicative represents an act as going on or a situation as true at the time of speaking; e.g., **Mīlitēs pugnant** (*The soldiers fight* or *are fighting*).

a. The present tense is often used in narration to refer vividly to action in the past. The present tense so used is commonly called a *historical present*; e.g., **Ad eās rēs cōnficiendās Orgetorīx dēligitur** (*was chosen*).

b. **Dum** (in the sense of *while* or *during the time that*) takes the present tense even to represent an act as going on in the past; e.g., **Dum in hīs locīs Caesar morātur** (*was delaying*), **lēgātī ad eum vēnērunt.**

2. The imperfect indicative represents an act as going on in past time or a situation as continuing in past time; e.g., **Mīlitēs pugnābant** (*The soldiers were fighting*).

a. The imperfect tense may also be used to express habitual action or attempted action. In the latter use it is called the *conative* imperfect.

---

[1] For the use of the locative to express place where, see App. 135.
[2] Among the prepositions taking the ablative are: **ab, cōram, cum, dē, ex, palam, prae, prō, sine, sub.**

3. The future indicative represents an act as about to take place in the future; e.g., **Mīlitēs** *pugnābunt* (*The soldiers will fight*).
4. The perfect indicative represents an act as having been completed at the time of speaking; e.g., **Caesar** *vēnit* (*Caesar came* or *has come*).
5. The pluperfect indicative represents an act as having been completed at some time in the past; e.g., **Caesar** *vēnerat* (*Caesar had come*).
6. The future perfect represents an act as about to be completed at some future time; e.g., **Caesar** *vēnerit* (*Caesar will have come*).

**138.**                    TENSES IN THE SUBJUNCTIVE

1. In an independent use a present subjunctive represents an act as wanted, possible, or wished for at a future time; an imperfect subjunctive represents an act as possible or wished for at the present time; the pluperfect subjunctive represents an act as possible or wished for at a past time. See examples under App. 149, *a*.
2. In a subordinate clause a present or imperfect subjunctive represents time contemporaneous with or future to the time of the verb of the clause on which the subjunctive clause depends; a perfect or pluperfect subjunctive regularly represents time past in relation to the time of the verb of the clause on which the subjunctive clause depends.

   *a.* In accordance with the so-called rule for the *sequence of tenses* a present or perfect tense is usually found in a subjunctive clause subordinate to a clause the verb of which is a "primary" tense (i.e., a present, a future, or a perfect) and an imperfect or pluperfect tense is usually found in a subjunctive clause subordinate to a clause the verb of which is a "secondary" tense (i.e., an imperfect, a historical perfect,[1] or a pluperfect); thus:

   |         |                                      |                                 |
   |---------|--------------------------------------|---------------------------------|
   | PRIMARY | Caesar quaerit (*asks*)              | ubi hostēs sint (*are*)         |
   |         | Caesar quaeret (*will ask*)          | or **fuerint** (*have*          |
   |         | Caesar quaesīvit) (*has asked*)      | *been*).                        |
   | SECONDARY | Caesar quaerēbat (*was asking*)    | ubi hostēs **essent**           |
   |         | Caesar quaesīvit (*asked*)           | (*were*) or **fuissent**        |
   |         | Caesar quaesīverat (*had asked*)     | (*had been*).                   |

   *b.* Exceptions to the above statements are:
   (1) a pluperfect subjunctive in a past-future clause; see App. 156, *a*.
   (2) an imperfect subjunctive in a present condition contrary to fact or a pluperfect subjunctive in a past condition contrary to fact; see App. 157, 2.

**139.**                    TENSES IN THE INFINITIVE

The tense of the infinitive denotes time relative to that of the verb on which it depends:
1. A present infinitive represents an act as going on at the same time as that indicated by the verb on which it depends.
2. A perfect infinitive represents an act as already completed at the time indicated by the verb on which it depends.
3. A future infinitive represents an act as yet to come at a time later than that indicated by the verb on which it depends.

[1] A historical present (see App. 137, 1, *a*) is also commonly considered a "secondary" tense.

## VOICE

**140.** The active voice represents the subject of the verb (or verb phrase) as acting; the passive voice represents the subject of the verb (or verb phrase) as being acted upon.

   *a.* Certain intransitive verbs are sometimes used in the impersonal passive (i.e., in the third person singular); e.g., Ācriter *pugnātur* (*There is a fierce battle* or, *I, you, he, she, we, they fight fiercely*); Diū *pugnātum est* (*There was a long battle* or *I, you, he, she, we, they fought for a long time*).

   *b.* In poetry the passive voice is sometimes used in a reflexive sense to represent an act as done by the actor for or to himself; e.g., **galeam** *induitur, he puts on the helmet* (*Aen.* II, 392–393).

## USES OF THE INDICATIVE

**141. The Indicative in Independent Clauses.** The indicative is used to make a statement of fact or to ask a question of fact.

**142. The Indicative in Dependent Clauses.** In general an indicative in a dependent clause is used to make a statement of fact.

**143. Temporal Clause.** The indicative is used in a temporal clause of fact introduced by **antequam, cum, postquam, priusquam, simul atque,** or **ubi**; e.g., **Cum Caesar in Galliam** *vēnit,* **erant duae factiōnēs; Ubi dē Caesaris adventū Helvētiī certiōrēs** *factī sunt,* **lēgātōs ad eum mīsērunt.**

**144. Parenthetical** *Ut*-**Clause.** The indicative is used in a parenthetical clause introduced by **ut** (in the sense of *as*); e.g., **Hujus Commiī operā, ut anteā** *dēmōnstrāvimus,* **superiōribus annīs Caesar ūsus erat.**

**145. Clause of Reason.** The indicative is used in clauses of cause or reason introduced by **quia, quod,** or **quoniam** when the reason is given on the authority of the writer or speaker; e.g., **Hōrum omnium fortissimī sunt Belgae, quod ā Prōvinciā longissimē** *absunt.*

**146.** *Quod*-**Clause of Fact.** The indicative is used in a substantive **quod**-clause of fact; e.g., **Accēdēbat quod līberōs suōs ab sē abstractōs esse obsidum nōmine** *dolēbant.*

**147. Conditions of Fact.** The indicative is used in conditions of fact; e.g., **Sī populus Rōmānus pācem nōbīscum** *faciet,* **in eam partem ībimus, ubi cōnstitueris; sī pietāte** *merēmur,* **dā deinde augurium** (*Aen.* II, 690–691).

   *a.* For the use of the subjunctive in past-future conditions see App. 156, *a.*

## USES OF THE SUBJUNCTIVE

### THE SUBJUNCTIVE IN INDEPENDENT CLAUSES

**148. Independent Volitive Subjunctive.** The subjunctive may be used in an independent clause to express the will of the speaker or writer; e.g., **Ad cēnam nūptiālem** *prōgrediāmur* (*Let us proceed to the wedding banquet*); **Venus hoc mātrimōnium** *probet* (*Let Venus approve this marriage*).

   *a.* This use of the subjunctive in the first person plural is commonly called the *hortatory* subjunctive; its use in the second or third person is commonly called the *jussive* subjunctive.

   *b.* The negative adverb used with a hortatory or jussive subjunctive is **nē**; e.g., **Nunc diūtius** *nē* **morēmur** (*Let us now no longer delay*).

   *c.* The volitive subjunctive may be used in a question of deliberation or perplexity; e.g., *Ēloquar* **an** *sileam* (*Shall I speak or be silent*)?

**149. The Optative Subjunctive.** The subjunctive may be used in an independent clause to express a wish.[1] The negative is regularly **nē**.

a. In such a use the present subjunctive expresses a wish with reference to the future, the imperfect subjunctive expresses an unfulfilled wish with reference to the present, and the pluperfect subjunctive expresses an unfulfilled wish with reference to the past; e.g., **Utinam Caesar** *veniat* (*May Caesar come*)! **Utinam Caesar** *venīret* (*I wish that Caesar were coming*)! **Utinam Caesar** *vēnisset* (*I wish that Caesar had come*)!

**150. The Potential Subjunctive.** The subjunctive may be used to express possibility; e.g., **Aliquis** *dīcat* (*Someone may say*).

a. The potential subjunctive is used in the conclusion (i.e., the principal clause) of certain types of conditional sentences:

(1) Referring to the future; e.g., ***Veniat*** (*He would come*), **sī invītētur** (*if he should be invited*).

(2) Referring to the present; e.g., **Hanc sententiam ego** *probārem* (*I should approve this idea*), **sī nūllam praeterquam vītae nostrae jactūram fierī vidērem** (*if I saw that no loss would result except of our own lives*).

(3) Referring to the past; e.g., **Hannibal novissimum agmen** *perturbāvisset* (*Hannibal would have thrown the rear line into confusion*), **nisi Numidae in vacua Rōmāna castra iter āvertissent** (*if the Numidians had not diverted their course to the empty Roman camp*).

## THE SUBJUNCTIVE IN DEPENDENT CLAUSES

### A. In Non-Fact Clauses

**151. Substantive Volitive Clause.**[2] The subjunctive may be used in a substantive volitive clause [3] introduced by **ut** or **nē**; e.g., **Orgetorīx Helvētiīs persuāsit ut dē fīnibus** *exīrent*; **Gallī petīvērunt nē ea** *ēnūntiārentur*.

a. The subjunctive may be used in an indirect question of deliberation or perplexity introduced by an interrogative word; e.g., **Nōn satis Brūtō cōnstābat quid** *ageret* (*It was not very clear to Brutus what he should do*).

**152. Substantive Clause of Hindrance.** The subjunctive may be used in a substantive clause of hindrance, prevention, or check [4] introduced by **nē**; e.g., **Dumnorīx vulgus prohibēbat nē frūmentum** *cōnferrent* (*Dumnorix was keeping the people from bringing the grain*).

a. An infinitive with its subject in the accusative may be used in a positive statement with **prohibeō**; e.g., **Barbarī nostrōs ē nāvibus** *ēgredī* **prohibēbant.**

b. With a negative expression of hindrance, prevention, or check the subjunctive clause is introduced by **quīn** or **quōminus**; e.g., **Remī Suessiōnēs nōn dēterrēre potuerant**

---

[1] Wishes are generally introduced by the adverb **utinam**, which has no exact English equivalent.
[2] This sort of clause is sometimes called a substantive clause of purpose.
[3] The substantive volitive clause is most commonly used as the object of a verb of will or endeavor or mental urgency; e.g., **cōgō, hortor, imperō, mandō, moneō, prōnūntiō, persuādeō, petō, postulō, statuō, suādeō, volō.**
[4] Some commonly used verbs of hindrance, prevention, or check are: **dēterreō, obstō, prohibeō, recūsō, teneō.**

*quīn* cum aliīs Belgīs *cōnsentīrent* (*The Remi had not been able to keep the Suessiones from siding with the other Belgians*); Duodēvīgintī nāvēs ventō tenēbantur, *quōminus* in eundem portum venīre *possent* (*Eighteen ships were held back by the wind from being able to come to the same port*).

**153. Clause of Fearing.** The subjunctive may be used in a substantive clause of fearing introduced by nē [1]; e.g., Mīlitēs nōn jam timēbant nē ab hoste *circumvenīrentur* (*The soldiers no longer feared that (lest) they should be surrounded by the enemy*).

**154. Clause of Purpose.** The subjunctive may be used in an adverbial clause introduced by ut or nē to express purpose; e.g., Helvētiī oppida sua incendunt, ut spem reditiōnis *tollerent;* Caesar Helvētiōs domum revertī jussit, nē Germānī in fīnēs Helvētiōrum *trānsīrent.*

*a.* When the clause of purpose contains a comparative it is regularly introduced by quō; e.g., Caesar praesidia dispōnit, *quō* facilius Helvētiōs flūmen trānsīre prohibēre possit.

**155. Relative Clause of Purpose.** The subjunctive may be used in a clause introduced by a relative pronoun or adverb to express purpose; e.g., Caesar equitātum mīsit, *quī* impetum hostium *sustinēret.*

**156. Clause of Anticipation.** The subjunctive may be used in a clause introduced by dum, antequam, or priusquam to represent an act as anticipated; e.g., Caesar nōn exspectāre statuit, dum Helvētiī omnēs fortūnās sociōrum *cōnsūmerent.*

*a.* The imperfect or pluperfect subjunctive may be used in any clause dependent on a past main verb to represent an act as future to the time of the main verb; e.g., Omnīnō bīduum supererat, cum exercituī frūmentum metīrī *oportēret* (*Only a two-day period was left, when it would be necessary to deal out grain to the army*); dēlituī, dum vēla darent, sī forte *dēdissent* (*I hid, until they should set sail, if haply they should set sail*). Such a clause may be called a past-future clause.

**157. Conditional Clauses.** The subjunctive may be used in conditional clauses as follows:

1. In the present or perfect tense to express a future less vivid condition.
2. In the imperfect or pluperfect tense to express a condition contrary to fact.

For examples see under App. 150, *a.*

**158. Relative Clause of Possibility.** The subjunctive may be used in a relative clause to express possibility; e.g., Erat iter ūnum inter montem et flūmen, quō vix singulī carrī *dūcerentur* (*There was one route between the mountain and the river, by which carts could with difficulty be drawn one at a time*).

### B. IN FACT CLAUSES

**159. Substantive *Ut*-Clause of Fact.**[2] The subjunctive may be used in a substantive clause introduced by ut to express a fact[3]; e.g., Eā nocte accidit ut *esset* lūna plēna (*that there was a full moon*); Caesar effēcit ut nāvigāre *posset* (*that he was able to sail*).

---

[1] A clause of fearing may be introduced by ut as an equivalent of nē nōn; e.g., Mīlitēs timēbant *ut* Caesar *venīret* (*The soldiers feared that Caesar would not come*).

[2] A clause of this sort is sometimes called a substantive clause of result.

[3] Substantive ut-clauses of fact are found especially with accidit, contingit, efficiō, ēvenit, and faciō.

**160. Substantive Clauses of Doubt.** The subjunctive may be used in a substantive clause introduced by **quīn** with a negative expression of doubt; e.g., **Nōn est dubium *quīn* Helvētiī plūrimum *possint*** (*that the Helvetians are very powerful*).

**161. Clauses of Result.** The subjunctive may be used in a clause introduced by ut to express result [1]; e.g., **Tanta commūtātiō facta est, ut nostrī proelium *redintegrārent*** (*that our men renewed the fight*).

**162. Relative Clause of Description.**[2] The subjunctive may be used in a relative clause of fact to describe the antecedent of the relative [3]; e.g., **Erant omnīnō itinera duo, quibus Helvētiī exīre *possent*** (*were able*)**; Sunt nōn nūllī, quī prīvātim plūs *possint*** (*are more powerful*) **quam ipsī magistrātūs.**

    *a.* A relative clause of description sometimes contains an accessory idea of *cause;* e.g., **Caesar arbitrātus est Dumnorīgem nihil prō sānō factūrum esse, quī imperium *neglēxisset*** (*since he had disregarded his command*).

**163. *Cum*-Clause of Temporal Circumstance.** The subjunctive may be used in a clause introduced by **cum** to express the temporal circumstance under which an act took place [4]; e.g., **Cum *esset* Caesar in Citeriōre Galliā** (*When Caesar was in Nearer Gaul*), **crēbrī rumōrēs ad eum adferēbantur; Cum Caesar ad silvārum initium *pervēnisset*** (*When Caesar had come to the edge of the forests*), **hostēs subitō in nostrōs impetum fēcērunt.**

**164. *Cum*-Clause of Cause.** The subjunctive may be used in a clause introduced by **cum** to express cause; e.g., **Cum Helvētiī suā sponte Sēquanīs persuādēre nōn *possent*** (*Since the Helvetians were not able on their own account to persuade the Sequanians*), **lēgātōs ad Dumnorīgem mittunt.**

**165. *Cum*-Clause of Concession.** The subjunctive may be used in a clause introduced by **cum** to express concession or an adversative idea; e.g., **Cum haec ita *sint*** (*Although these things are so*), **tamen** (*nevertheless*) **vōbīscum pācem faciam.**

**166. Indirect Question.** The subjunctive may be used in a substantive clause introduced by an interrogative word to express an indirect question of fact [5]; e.g., **Caesar quaesīvit cūr** (*why*) **Ariovistus proeliō nōn *dēcertāret*.**

**167. Subordinate Clause in Indirect Discourse.** The subjunctive may be used in any subordinate clause of fact in indirect discourse to indicate that the subordinate clause is to be considered an integral part of the indirect discourse; e.g., **Rēmī dīxērunt Germānōs, quī trāns Rhēnum *incolerent*, cum Belgīs sē conjūnxisse.**

**168. *Quod*-Clause of Quoted Reason.** The subjunctive may be used in a clause of reason introduced by **quod, quia,** or **quoniam** to show that the reason is given on the authority of someone other than the writer or speaker; e.g., **Haeduī vēnērunt ad Caesarem questum** (*to complain*), **quod Germanī fīnēs eōrum *populārentur*.**

    *a.* The subjunctive may be used in a clause introduced by **nōn quod** or **nōn quia** to show that the reason given is repudiated; e.g., **Posterō diē Hannibal interiōrem Galliae regiōnem petit, nōn quia celerior ad Alpēs via *esset*, sed quod crēdēbat minus obviōs futūrōs esse Rōmānōs.**

---

[1] The clause on which a clause of result depends usually contains some such word as **ita** (*so*), **tam** (*so*), or **tantus** (*so much*).

[2] A clause of this sort is sometimes called a relative clause of characteristic.

[3] Relative clauses of description are especially common after negative or indefinite expressions.

[4] This use of the subjunctive is limited to the imperfect and pluperfect tenses.

[5] An indirect question is commonly used as the object of a verb of asking, saying, knowing, or perceiving.

**169. Subjunctive by Attraction.** The subjunctive may be used in a clause of fact subordinate to a subjunctive clause or to an infinitive phrase to indicate that the clause is to be considered an integral part of the clause or phrase on which it depends; e.g., **Tanta commūtātiō facta est ut eī mīlitēs, quī** *cecidissent* (*who had fallen down*), **proelium redintegrārent.**

## USE OF THE IMPERATIVE

**170.** The imperative is used in direct command; e.g., **Dēsilīte, commīlitōnēs.**

*a.* In poetry **nē** may be used with the imperative to express a negative command. The construction in prose would regularly be **nōlī** with the infinitive; e.g., **equō** *nē crēdite* (*Aen.* II, 48); **Nē saevī** (*Aen.* VI, 544).

## USES OF THE INFINITIVE

**171. Complementary Infinitive.** The infinitive may be used to complete the meaning of certain verbs [1]; e.g., **Helvētiī cum fīnitimīs pācem** *facere* **cōnstituērunt** (*decided to make peace*).

*a.* The complementary infinitive has no subject of its own.

**172. Indirect Statement.** The infinitive with an accusative subject may be used to express an indirect statement depending on a word of saying, thinking, knowing, or perceiving; e.g., **Rēmī dīxērunt reliquōs omnēs Belgās** *esse* (*were*) **in armīs et Germānōs cum Belgīs sē** *conjūnxisse* (*had united*).

*a.* For the force of the tense of an infinitive see App. 139.

**173. Substantive Infinitive.** The infinitive with or without an accusative subject may be used as the subject or object of a verb.

1. As subject; e.g., **Frūmentum exercituī** *mētīrī* **oportēbat** (*It was necessary to deal out grain to the army*).
2. As object; e.g., **Caesar pontem** *rescindī* **jussit** (*Caesar ordered the bridge to be torn down*).

**174. Infinitive of Purpose.** In poetry an infinitive may be used to express purpose. The prose construction would regularly be the subjunctive with **ut** or the gerund or gerundive with **ad** or **causā**; e.g., **Nōn nōs** *populāre* **vēnimus** (*Aen.* I, 527–528); **dederat comam** *diffundere* **ventīs** (*Aen.* I, 319).

**175. Infinitive Used instead of Substantive Clause.** In poetry an infinitive may be used instead of a substantive clause with **ut** and the subjunctive; e.g., *celerāre* **fugam suādet** (*Aen.* I, 357); *festīnāre* **fugam stimulat** (*Aen.* IV, 575–576).

**176. Infinitive Used with Noun.** In poetry an infinitive may be used with a noun. The prose construction would be a genitive of the gerund or the gerundive; e.g., **amor cāsūs** *cognōscere* **nostrōs** (*Aen.* II, 10); **cupīdō Stygiōs** *innāre* **lacūs** (*Aen.* VI, 133–134).

**177. Infinitive Used with Adjective.** In poetry an infinitive may be used with an adjective; e.g., **certa** *morī* (*Aen.* IV, 564); **praestantior** *ciēre* **virōs** (*Aen.* VI, 164–165).

---

[1] Among the verbs which commonly take the complementary infinitive are: **audeō, coepī, cōnor, cōnstituō, contendō, cupiō, dēbeō, dēsistō, dubitō** (*hesitate*), **incipiō, īnstituō, mālō, nōlō, parō, persevērō, possum, recūsō, s.atuō, studeō, timeō, videor** (*seem*), **volō.**

**178. Historical Infinitive.** The present infinitive may be used in the sense of the imperfect indicative with its subject in the nominative case; e.g., **Ulixēs** *terrēre* (*Aen.* II, 97–98); **perfidus ille tē** *colere* (*Aen.* IV, 421–422). This infinitive is called the historical infinitive.

**179. Infinitive of Exclamation.** The infinitive may be used in an exclamatory sense; e.g., **Mēne inceptō** *dēsistere?* (*Aen.* I, 37); **mēne occumbere nōn** *potuisse* (*Aen.* I, 97–98).

## USES OF THE PARTICIPLE

**180. Dependent Participial Phrase.** A participle in agreement with the subject or with some other noun or pronoun in a clause and itself modified by one or more words may be used to express the attendant circumstance of an action; e.g., **Hīs rēbus** *adductī*, **Helvētiī cum fīnitimīs pācem cōnfirmāre cōnstituērunt.**

**181. Ablative Absolute Phrase.** The ablative of a noun or pronoun with participle in agreement may be used to express the attendant circumstance of an action; e.g., **Omnibus rēbus ad profectiōnem** *comparātīs,* **Helvētiī diem cōnstituunt.** For additional examples see App. 131, *a* and *b*.

**182. Active Periphrastic Verb Phrase.** The future active participle may be used with any form of the verb **sum** to express an action as intended or as going to take place; e.g., **Frūmentum omne praeter id, quod sēcum** *portātūrī* **erant, dēlent** (*They destroyed all the grain except that which they were going to carry with them*).

**183. Passive Periphrastic Verb Phrase.** The future passive participle may be used with any form of the verb **sum** to express an action as necessary or obligatory; e.g., **Omnia ūnō tempore erant** *agenda* (*Everything was* or *had to be done at the same time*).

**184. Gerundive Phrase.** A future passive participle (gerundive) of a transitive verb may be used in agreement with a noun or pronoun as the equivalent of a gerund with that noun or pronoun as its object [1]; e.g., **Helvētiī erant cupidī** *bellī gerendī* (*The Helvetians were desirous of war being carried on;* i.e., *of carrying on war*).

a. A future passive participle (gerundive) modifying **suī** agrees with it in form (i.e., is in the genitive singular) even when the **suī** has a plural meaning; e.g., **Rōmānī hostibus nūllam facultātem suī** *colligendī* **relinquunt** (*The Romans leave the enemy no chance of collecting themselves*).

**185. Future Passive Participle (Gerundive) Agreeing with the Direct Object.** The future passive participle (gerundive) may be used in agreement with the object of **cūrō** or **dō**; e.g., **Caesar pontem** *faciendum* **cūrat** (*Caesar has a bridge made); Caesar reliquum exercitum Sabīnō et Cottae in Morinōs** *dūcendum* **dat** (*Caesar gives the rest of the army to Sabinus and Cotta to be led against the Morini*).

**186. Deponent Participle Used as a Passive.** In poetry the perfect participle of a deponent verb may be used as a passive; e.g., *comitātus* **Achātē** (*Aen.* I, 312); **pelagō** *remēnsō* (*Aen.* II, 181).

**187. Perfect Participle Used with Present Force.** In poetry a perfect participle may be used in a present sense; e.g., **tūnsae,** *beating* (*Aen.* I, 481).

**188.** In poetry a passive participle is sometimes used in a reflexive sense to represent an act as done by the actor to or for himself; e.g., **sinūs** *collēcta* **fluentīs** (*Aen.* I, 320). See also App. 114.

---

[1] In the dative or with a preposition a gerundive phrase must be used instead of a gerund with a direct object; e.g., **Ad eās rēs cōnficiendās** (not **ad eās rēs cōnficiendum**) **Orgetorīx dēligitur.**

## USES OF THE GERUND

**189.** The gerund of an intransitive verb may be used in any case except in the nominative or in the accusative without a preposition; the gerund of a transitive verb may be used only in the genitive or in the ablative without a preposition.

*a.* For the use of the gerundive phrase see App. 184.

**190. The Gerund with *ad*.** The gerund of an intransitive verb may be used in the accusative with **ad** to express purpose; e.g., **Mīlitēs erant alacrēs *ad pugnandum*** (*for fighting*).

**191. The Gerund with *causā* or *grātiā*.** The gerund may be used in the genitive followed by **causā** or **grātiā** to express purpose; e.g., **Nostrī in locum inīquiōrem *pugnandī causā*** (*for the sake of fighting*) **nōn prōgressī sunt.**

## USES OF THE SUPINE

**192. The Supine in *-um*.** The accusative form of the supine ending in **-um** may be used with verbs of motion to express purpose; e.g., **Haeduī vēnērunt *questum*** (*to complain*).

**193. The Supine in *-ū*.** The ablative form of the supine ending in **-ū** may be used with a few adjectives to express respect [1]; e.g., **Id erat facile *factū*** (*This was easy to do*).

## SUMMARY OF MOOD USES IN INDIRECT DISCOURSE

**194.** The moods used in indirect discourse may be summarized as follows:

1. With a verb of saying, thinking, knowing, or perceiving (or an equivalent expression) the infinitive with an accusative subject is used to express an indirect statement of fact. The negative is **nōn**.
2. With a verb of asking, saying, knowing, or perceiving (or an equivalent expression) a clause introduced by an interrogative word and with its verb in the subjunctive may be used to express an indirect question of fact. The negative is **nōn**.
3. With a verb of commanding (or an equivalent expression) a clause with its verb in the subjunctive may be used to express an indirect command.[2] The negative is **nē**.
4. A subordinate clause of fact in indirect discourse may have its verb in the subjunctive to show that the clause is to be considered an integral part of what is said or asked or commanded.

## POETIC USES

**195.** In poetry certain unusual forms and constructions are found:

1. A change of conjugation from 2nd to 3rd; e.g., **fervĕre** (*Aen.* IV, 409); **fulgĕre** (*Aen.* VI, 826).

---

[1] The adjectives with which the supine in **-ū** is most frequently used are: **facilis, difficilis, horribilis, mīrābilis,** and **optimus.**

[2] The subjunctive in an indirect command has a volitive force like that of a subjunctive in a substantive volitive clause (see App. 151) or of a subjunctive in independent use (see App. 148).

2. Archaic forms:

    *a.* -ībat for -iēbat; -ībant for -iēbant; lēnībat (*Aen.* VI, 468).

    *b.* Ollī for illī (*Aen.* I, 254); ollīs for illīs (*Aen.* VI, 730); quīs for quibus (*Aen.* I, 95); mī for mihi (*Aen.* VI, 104).

    *c.* A present infinitive passive ending in –ier for –ī; e.g., accingier (*Aen.* IV, 493).

    *d.* Third person plural perfect indicative active ending in –ēre for –ērunt; e.g., tenuēre (*Aen.* I, 12); latuēre (*Aen.* I, 130).

3. The use of dare with a noun instead of a verb: e.g., gemitum dedēre for gemuērunt (*Aen.* II, 53); dedit ruīnam for ruit (*Aen.* II, 310); lacrimās dedit for lacrimāvit (*Aen.* IV, 370).

4. A plural noun form may be used with the force of a singular; e.g., scēptra (*Aen.* I, 78); silentia (*Aen.* I, 730).

# GENERAL VOCABULARY

# GENERAL VOCABULARY

Words included in the College Entrance Examination Board's *Latin Word List* are indicated by an asterisk (*). Words included in the New York Syllabus list, but not included in the College Board list, are indicated by a dagger (†). Regular verbs of the first conjugation are indicated by the numeral 1; verbs of the second conjugation with *-uī* and *-itus* are indicated by the numeral 2; verbs of the fourth conjugation with *-īvī* or *(-iī)* and *-ītus* are indicated by the numeral 4.

## A

Ā! ah! alas!

*ā, ab *prep. with abl.* from, away from; *agt. with passive verbs,* by; *of time,* from, after, since

Abās, –antis *m. name of* 1) *an Argive king;* 2) *a comrade of Aeneas*

*abdō, –dere, –didī, –ditus put away; hide; shut up; plunge

abdūcō, –dūcere, –dūxī, –ductus lead away; draw back

abeō, –īre –īvī (–iī), –itūrus go away, depart, withdraw; deviate

*abhorreō, –ēre, –uī shrink from; shudder at

abiēs, –ietis *f.* spruce, fir

ablātus *see* auferō

abluō, –ere, –luī, –lūtus wash off; purify, cleanse

abnegō 1 deny, refuse

abnuō, –ere, –uī, –nūtus refuse (*by nod*); decline, reject

aboleō, –ēre, –ēvi, –itus blot out, remove, destroy

abripiō, –ere, –uī, –reptus snatch away; snatch, seize

abrumpō, –ere, –rūpī, –ruptus break off; break, rive; destroy; violate

abruptum, –ī *n.* precipice, abyss

abscindō, –ere, –scidī, –scissus tear away; tear; rend, cleave

abscondō, –ere, –condī (–condidī), –conditus put away, conceal, hide; lose sight of

absēns, –sentis absent; distant; left behind

absistō, –ere, –stitī withdraw *or* depart from; cease, desist; forbear

abstineō, –ēre, –tinuī, –tentus hold back; refrain; restrain (*oneself*)

abstrūdō, –ere, –ūsī, –ūsus thrust away; hide

abstulī *see* auferō

†absum, abesse, āfuī (abfuī), āfutūrus be absent *or* away from; be distant; be wanting

absūmō, –ere, –sūmpsī, –sūmptus take away; consume, devour; destroy

*ac *see* atque

Acamās, –antis *m. one of the Greeks before Troy*

acanthus, –ī *m.* acanthus, bear's-foot, *a flowering plant*

Acarnān, –ānis of Acarnania (*a country of Greece*), Acarnanian

*accēdō, –ere, –cessī, –cessūrus come *or* go to; draw near, approach

accelerō 1 hasten

*accendō, –ere, –cendī, –cēnsus set on fire, kindle; inflame, excite, arouse; enrage; inspire

accessus, –ūs *m.* approach

accīdō, –ere, –cīdī, –cīsus cut into, hew

accingō, –ere, –cīnxī, –cīnctus gird; *with a reflexive or the passive used as a middle,* gird oneself; equip, make ready; resort to

*accipiō, –ere, –cēpī, –ceptus take to oneself; admit, let in, receive, accept; welcome; hear, learn; conceive

accītus, –ūs *m.* summons

acclīvis, –e sloping, ascending

accommodō 1 fit, adjust; gird on

accubō, –āre, –cubuī, –cubitūrus lie, recline near

accumbō, –ere, –cubuī, –cubitūrus recline at (*a table*); take one's place at the table

accumulō 1 heap up; heap high, load; honor

accurrō, –ere, –currī (–cucurrī), cursūrus run *or* hasten to

*ācer, ācris, ācre sharp, keen; fierce, violent, stern, severe; ardent, zealous; spirited, valiant

*acerbus, –a, –um sour, bitter; harsh, implacable, cruel, savage; untimely

acernus, -a, -um of maple wood, maple

acerra, -ae f. incense box, censer

acervus, -ī m. pointed pile; heap, pile

Acesta, -ae f. a town in Sicily

Acestēs, -ae m. a king in Sicily

Achaemenidēs, -ae m. a comrade of Ulysses

Achāicus, -a, -um of Achaea (a district in Northern Peloponnesus), Achaean; Grecian

Achātēs, -ae m. a faithful companion of Aeneas

Acherōn, -ontis m. a river of the underworld; the underworld

Achillēs, -is (ī) m. the greatest of the Greek heroes before Troy

Achillēus, -a, -um of Achilles

Achīvī, -ōrum m. pl. inhabitants of Achaea, Achaeans; Greeks

Achīvus, -a, -um Achaean; Greek

Acīdalius, -a, -um of Acidalia (a spring in Boeotia sacred to Venus), Acidalian; Acīdalia, -ae f. Venus

*aciēs, -ēī f. sharp edge, edge; keen vision, sight, eye; battle line, battle array

Acragās, -antis m. Agrigentum, a city in Sicily

Acroceraunia, -ōrum n. pl. a dangerous promontory forming the northwestern extremity of Epirus.

acta, -ae f. shore, beach, strand

Actius, -a, -um of Actium, a promontory on the coast of Epirus

*acuō, -ere, -uī, -ūtus sharpen

*acūtus, -a, -um sharpened, sharp; pointed, jagged

*ad prep. with acc. to, toward; near; among; at; by

adamās, -antis m. adamant, a very hard metal

Adamastus, -ī m. father of Achaemenides

addīcō, -ere, -dīxī, -dictus assent to; yield, resign oneself

addō, -ere, -didī, -ditus give in addition, put to, put on, add, lend

adductus, -a, -um drawn, drawn tight; strained, contracted

*adeō adv. to that point or degree, so; in fact, actually, precisely; just; even

†adeō, -īre, -īvī (-iī), -itus go to, approach, reach; visit; encounter, meet; aspire to

adfātus, -ūs m. speech

adfectō 1 make for, seize

†adferō, -ferre, attulī, adlātus bring

adfīgō, -ere, -fīxī, -fixus fasten, attach to

*adflīgō, -ere, -flīxī, -flīctus shatter, cast down

adflō 1 breathe upon, inspire

adfluō, -ere, -flūxī flow to; come (to)

adfor, -fārī, -fātus address, speak to

adfore, adforem see adsum

adglomerō 1 gather at (with dat.)

*adgredior, -gredī, -gressus go to, attack; address; attempt

adhaereō, -ēre, -haesī, -haesūrus cling

*adhibeō 2 have present, invite

*adhūc adv. hitherto, till now, as yet

*adigō, -ere, -ēgī, -āctus drive to; drive, hurl; force

*adimō, -ere, -ēmī, -ēmptus take to oneself, take away; pluck out; snatch away

*aditus, -ūs m. a going to, approach; audience; means of access, entrance

†adjiciō (adiciō), -ere, -jēcī, -jectus throw at, add

adjuvō, -āre, -jūvī, -jūtus aid, assist

adlābor, -ī, -lāpsus glide to

adligō 1 hold (to), bind

adloquor, -ī, -locūtus address, speak to

†admīror, -ārī, -ātus wonder at, be surprised at

*admittō, -ere, -mīsī, -missus admit

*admoneō 2 warn, admonish, remind

admoveō, -ēre, -mōvī, -mōtus move or bring to, waft to; offer

adnītor, -ī, -nīxus strive; strain every nerve, lean on

adnō 1 swim to, float to

adnuō, -ere, -nuī, -nūtus nod assent, promise

adoleō, -ēre, -oluī (-olēvī), -ultus magnify; honor, worship; offer

adoperiō, -īre, -operuī, -opertus cover

*adorior, -īrī, -ortus attempt

adōrō 1 pray to; worship, adore

adparō 1 prepare

adquīrō, -ere, -quīsīvī, -quīsītus acquire, gain

Adrastus, -ī m. an Argive king

adsentiō, -īre, -sēnsī, -sēnsus assent, agree

adservō 1 guard, watch

adsiduē unceasingly

*adsiduus, -a, -um constant, unceasing

adsimilis, -e like

adspīrō 1 breathe or blow upon; favor, smile upon

adstringō, -ere, -strīnxī, -strictus contract; congeal

adsuēscō, -ere, -suēvī, -suētus make familiar to

adsultus, -ūs m. attack, assault

*adsum, adesse, adfuī, adfutūrus be at hand, be present, be near, be at; appear; assist, be propitious

adsurgō, -ere, -surrēxī, -surrēctūrus rise

adulterium, -ī n. adultery

adultus, -a, -um adult, full-grown

adūrō, -ere, -ussī, -ustus burn
advehō, -ere, -vexī, -vectus carry to; *passive used as a middle*, sail to
advēlō 1 veil, wreathe
advena, -ae *m. or f.* stranger, foreigner
adveniō, -īre, -vēnī, -ventūrus come to, come
adventō 1 come *or* draw near, approach
†adventus, -ūs *m.* coming, approach, arrival
adversor, -ārī, -ātus oppose, resist
*adversus, -a, -um turned toward, fronting, facing, opposing, face to face; adverse
†advertō, -ere, -vertī, -versus turn to *or* toward; turn (*the mind*) to, give heed, note, notice
advocō 1 call (*to oneself*), summon
advolvō, -ere, -volvī, -volūtus roll to *or* toward
adytum, -ī *n.* sanctuary, shrine; tomb
Aeacidēs, -ae *m.* descendant of Aeacus; *i.e., Achilles*
Aeaeus, -a, -um of Aeaea, *the fabled abode of Circe*
*aedēs, -is *f.* hearth; *pl.* apartments; house, dwelling
aedificō 1 build, construct
Aegaeus, -a, -um of the Aegean Sea, Aegean
*aeger, -gra, -grum sick, sickly, diseased; weary, weak, suffering, wretched; anxious, distressed, heartsick, pining
aemulus, -a, -um rivalling, competing; envious, jealous
Aeneadae, -ārum *m. pl.* followers of Aeneas; Trojans
Aeneās, -ae (*acc.* -ān) *m.* a Trojan, *hero of the Aeneid*
*aēnus, -a, -um of bronze, brazen; *as noun,* aēnum, -ī *n.* kettle, cauldron
Aeolia, -ae *f. an island near Sicily, the fabled abode of Aeolus*
Aeolidēs, -ae *m.* son *or* descendant of Aeolus
Aeolius, -a, -um of Aeolus, *god of the winds*
Aeolius, -a, -um Aeolian *or* Lesbian; *i.e., lyric; the lyric poetess Sappho was a native of Lesbos*
Aeolus, -ī *m. god of the winds*
aequaevus, -a, -um of the same *or* equal age
aequālis, -e equal, like; *as noun,* aequālis, -is *m.* companion, comrade
*aequō 1 make equal, adjust, equal, match, do justice to; requite; *partic.* aequātus, -a, -um made even, regular, abreast
*aequor, -oris *n.* a level surface; surface of the sea, sea, waters; wave, billow
aequoreus, -a, -um of the sea
*aequus, -a, -um even, level; just, fair; equal;

requited; kindly, propitious; *as noun,* aequum, -ī *n.* justice
*āēr, āeris *m.* air; breeze; mist, cloud
aerātus, -a, -um made of *or* covered with bronze; brazen
aereus, -a, -um made of *or* plated with bronze; brazen
aeripēs, -edis bronze-footed, bronze-hoofed
āerius, -a, -um airy, high, lofty, towering
*aes, aeris *n.* copper, bronze; *anything made from these materials, as a shield, arms, cymbals, trumpet, cauldron, chariot, or beak of a ship*
aesculētum, -ī *n.* oak forest
*aestās, -ātis *f.* summer, summer air
aestīvus, -a, -um of summer
aestuō 1 boil, burn; seethe, surge
aestuōsus, -a, -um summerlike, sweltering
*aestus, -ūs *m.* heat, flame; tide; sea, strait; flood, waters
*aetās, -ātis *f.* age; old age; years, time
aeternum *adv.* forever, unceasingly, eternally
*aeternus, -a, -um everlasting, eternal, undying, endless
*aethēr, -eris *m.* upper air, ether; air; vault of heaven, sky, heaven; upper world
aetherius, -a, -um of the ether, of heaven; heavenly, celestial
Aethiops, -opis *m.* an Ethiopian
Aethōn, -ontis *m. one of the horses of the sun*
aethra, -ae *f.* sky, firmament
Aetna, -ae *f. a volcano in Sicily*
Aetnaeus, -a, -um of Aetna
*aevum, -ī *n.* age, time; old age
Āfer, Āfrī *m.* an African
affābilis, -e easily addressed
Āfrica, -ae *f. Northern Africa*
Āfricus, -ī *m.* the southwest wind
Agamemnonius, -a, -um of *or* belonging to Agamemnon, *leader of the Greeks in the Trojan War*
Agathyrsī, -ōrum *m. pl. a people of Scythia*
Agēnor, -oris *m. a king of Phoenicia and ancestor of Dido*
*ager, agrī *m.* field, land
*agger, -eris *m.* heap, mound; elevation, embankment; dike; rampart
aggerō, -ere, -gessī, -gestus bear to; heap upon
aggerō 1 heap up, increase
agitātor, -ōris *m.* driver, charioteer
*agitō 1 drive with violence; chase, torment, harass, persecute; speed, hasten
*agmen, -inis *n.* army (*on the march*), column, train; orderly array, formation; rank, line;

phalanx, band, company, troops; mass, herd, flock; course, motion, sweep

**agna,** –ae f. a ewe lamb

*****agnōscō,** –ere, –nōvī, –nitus recognize

**agnus,** –ī m. lamb

*****agō,** –ere, ēgī, āctus drive, pursue; conduct, steer, bring; do, execute; lead, impel, compel, force; spend, pass; treat; **age** come!

*****agrestis,** –e of the country, country, rustic

†**agricola,** –ae m. farmer, peasant

**ait** see ajō

**Ājāx,** –ācis m. name of two Greek heroes before Troy: 1) the son of Telamon; 2) the son of Oïleus

*****ajō** defective say, assert, affirm

**ajunt** see ajō

*****āla,** –ae f. wing, pinion

*****alacer (alacris),** –cris, –e active; eager, joyful

**ālātus,** –a, –um winged

**Alba, Alba Longa,** –ae f. an ancient city of Latium

**Albānus,** –a, –um of Alba, Alban; as noun, **Albānī,** –ōrum, m. pl. the Albans

**albēscō,** –ere grow white, dawn

*****albus,** –a, –um white

**Alcīdēs,** –ae m. descendant of Alcaeus; i.e., Hercules

*****āles, ālitis** winged; as noun, **āles, ālitis** m. or f. winged creature, bird

**Alētēs,** –is m. a comrade of Aeneas

**Alfius,** –ī m. a man's name

*****aliēnus,** –a, –um of another, another's, foreign

**āliger,** –gera, –gerum winged

**alimenta,** –ōrum n. pl. food

**ālipēs,** –pedis wing-footed

**aliquī (aliquis),** –qua, –quod indef. adj. some, any

*****aliquis,** –quid indef. pron. someone, anyone

*****aliter** adv. otherwise

*****alius,** –a, –ud another, other, else; **alius** ... **alius** one ... another; **aliī** ... **aliī** some ... others

*****almus,** –a, –um nourishing, fostering; propitious, benign, benignant, kindly, gracious; genial

*****alō,** –ere, aluī, altus (alitus) nourish, feed, sustain, support; encourage, strengthen; rear, cherish

**Alōīdēs,** –ae m. descendant of Aloeus; in pl., the giants Otus and Ephialtes

**Alphēus,** –ī m. a river in Elis

**Alpīnus,** –a, –um of the Alps, Alpine

*****altāria,** –ium n. pl. altar

**altē** adv. high, on high, aloft

*****alter,** –tera, –terum one of the two, the other, another; second; **alter** ... **alter,** the one ... the other

**alternō** 1 do by turns; waver, hesitate

*****alternus,** –a, –um one after the other; in turn, by turns; alternate

**altrīx,** –īcis f. nurse

*****altus,** –a, –um high, on high, lofty, aloft; deep, profound; noble, exalted; as noun, **altum,** –ī n. heaven; sea, the deep

**alumnus,** –ī m. nursling, foster-child; child, son

**alveus,** –ī m. hollow, cavity; hold (of a ship); boat

**alvus,** –ī f. belly, body

**amāns,** –antis loving, fond; as noun, m. or f. lover

**amāracus,** –ī m. or f. marjoram

**amārus,** –a, –um bitter, unpleasant, unwelcome

**Amaryllis,** –idis (acc. **Amaryllida**) f. name of a shepherdess

**Amāzōn,** –onis f. one of a fabled race of female warriors

**Amāzonis,** –idis f. an Amazon

**Amāzonius,** –a, –um of the Amazons

**ambāgēs,** –is f. turning, winding, intricacy; riddle, mystery; details

**ambedō,** –ere, –ēdī, –ēsus gnaw around, eat; devour; char

**ambiguus,** –a, –um wavering, vacillating; uncertain, undecided; twofold, double; treacherous; insinuating; obscure

**ambiō,** –īre, –īvī (–iī), –ītus go around, surround, encircle; approach

*****ambō,** –ae, –ō both; two

**ambrosius,** –a, –um ambrosial, divine; immortal; lovely

*****āmēns,** –entis senseless; frantic, distracted; amazed

**ames,** –itis m. net pole

**amiciō,** –īre, –icuī (–ixī), –ictus throw around; wrap, envelop, veil

*****amictus,** –ūs m. outer garment; mantle, robe; veil

**amīcus,** –a, –um friendly

*****amīcus,** –ī m. friend

**āmittō,** –ere, –mīsī, –missus send away; let go; lose

*****amnis,** –is m. river, stream; torrent

*****amō** 1 love, cherish; hug

**amoenus,** –a, –um lovely, charming, delightful

**amor,** –ōris m. love, affection, fondness; passion, longing, yearning, eagerness, desire, lust; object of love; love charm; personified, Love, Cupid

āmoveō, –ēre, –mōvī, –mōtus take away, remove

amphora, –ae f. a large storage jar

Amphrȳsius, –a, –um of the Amphrysus, a river in Thessaly near which Apollo fed the flocks of Admetus; vātēs Amphrȳsia the Cumaean Sibyl, so called because she was inspired of Apollo

*amplector, –tī, –plexus twine about, wind about, encircle, enfold, embrace

amplexus, –ūs m. embrace

*amplius comp. adv. more, longer

amplus, –a, –um grand, roomy, spacious; splendid, glorious

amputō 1 cut off

Amycus, –i, m. name of 1) a king of the Bebrycians; 2) a comrade of Aeneas

*an, anne interrog. conj., introducing the second member of a double question, or

anceps, –cipitis double, twofold; doubtful, dubious; perplexing; wavering

Anchīsēs, –ae m. father of Aeneas

Anchīsēus, –a, –um of Anchises

Anchīsiadēs, –ae m. descendant of Anchises, especially his son Aeneas

*ancora, –ae f. anchor

Ancus, –ī m. Ancus Marcius, fourth king of Rome

Androgēōs, –ō (ī) m. name of 1) a son of Minos, slain by the Athenians; 2) a Greek hero slain in the sack of Troy

Andromachē, –ēs (–ae) f. a Trojan woman, wife of Hector

*anguis, –is m. or f. serpent, snake

*angustus, –a, –um narrow; as noun, angustum, –ī n. narrow place

anhēlitus, –ūs m. panting, heaving

anhēlō 1 breathe with difficulty, pant

anhēlus, –a, –um panting, heaving

anīlis, –e old woman's, old-womanish

*anima, –ae f. breath, breath of life; life, existence; soul, shade, spirit

animal, –ālis n. living being, animal

animō 1 become alive

animōsus, –a, –um spirited; proud

animula, –ae f. soul, spirit

*animus, –ī m. soul, spirit; heart; disposition, affection, temper; courage, daring; passion, anger, wrath; pride; mind, sense, feeling, thought, conviction, attention; impulse, will, purpose

Anius, –ī m. king of Delos and priest of Apollo

Anna, –ae f. sister of Dido

annālis, –e yearly, annual; as noun, annālēs, –ium m. pl. annals, recital, account, story

anne see an

*annus, –ī m. year; season; circuit (of a year)

annuus, –a, –um annual, yearly

ānser, –eris m. gander

Antandros, –ī f. a town in Mysia

*ante adv. and prep.: 1) as adv., before, beforehand, previously, hitherto, sooner; 2) as prep. with acc., before, in front of; above, beyond

anteferō, –ferre, –tulī, –lātus carry before; put before, prefer

antemna, –ae f. sail yard

Antēnor, –oris m. a Trojan leader, founder of Patavium (modern Padua)

Antēnoridēs, –ae m. descendant of Antenor

*antequam conj., sometimes written separately, ante . . . quam sooner . . . than, i.e., before

Antheus, –ī m. a comrade of Aeneas

antīquē adv. of old

*antīquus, –a, –um of olden times, of old, ancient; old, aged; former; time-honored, long-standing

*antrum, –ī n. cave, cavern, grotto

anus, –ūs f. old woman

Āoniī, –ōrum m. pl. the Boeotians

Āornos, –ī m. the Greek name of Lake Avernus

aper, –prī m. wild boar

*aperiō, –īre, –peruī, –pertus uncover, lay bare; show, disclose, reveal; open, divide, make a way through

†apertus, –a, –um open, clear

apex, –icis m. tip, point, summit

apis, –is f. bee

Apollō, –inis m. god of music and prophecy

*appāreō, –ēre, –uī, –itūrus appear, become visible; be disclosed, be seen

*appellō 1 call, name; declare, proclaim

appellō, –ere, –pulī, –pulsus drive to, bring to

*appetō, –ere, –īvī (–iī), –ītus seek

applicō 1 drive to, direct to

aprīcus, –a, –um exposed to the sun, sunny; sun-loving

*aptō 1 fit, adjust; fit out, equip, prepare

*aptus, –a, –um fitted, studded with

*apud prep. with acc. with, near by; among

Āpulus, –ī m. an Apulian, a native of a district in Southeastern Italy

*aqua, –ae f. water

Aquilō, –ōnis m. the north wind; wind

aquōsus, –a, –um watery, rainy, rain-bearing

*āra, –ae f. altar; Ārae, –ārum f. pl. the Altars, a name given to a reef in the Mediterranean Sea off the coast of Africa

arānea, –ae f. spider web, cobweb

arātor, –ōris m. plowman

arātrum, –ī n. plow
arbiter, –trī m. judge, ruler, lord
arbitrium, –ī n. choice, will
*arbor (arbōs), –oris f. tree; trunk, shoot
arboreus, –a, –um treelike, branching
arbuteus, –a, –um of the arbutus or strawberry tree
Arcadius, –a, –um of Arcadia, a district in the Peloponnesus
arcānus, –a, –um secret, hidden; as noun, arcānum, –ī n. a secret
*arceō, –ēre, –cuī bind, confine; keep off, debar
*accessō, –ere, –sīvī, –sītus cause to come, call, summon
arcitenēns, –entis bow-bearing; as noun, m. archer; used especially to refer to the archer god Apollo
Arctos, –ī f. the constellations of the Great and Little Bear; the North
Arctūrus, –ī m. a star in the constellation Boötes
*arcus, –ūs m. bow; rainbow; curve; bend
ārdēns, –entis burning, blazing, fiery, flashing; spirited, ardent, eager, earnest; in hot haste
*ārdeō, –ēre, ārsī, ārsūrus be on fire, blaze, burn; flash, sparkle, glitter, glow; be fiery; be resplendent, be conspicuous; be eager
ārdēscō, –ere, ārsī take fire, become inflamed
ārdor, –ōris m. burning; ardor, eagerness
*arduus, –a, –um steep; high, lofty, towering; on high, aloft; erect; as noun, arduum, –ī n. high place, height
āreō, –ēre, –uī be dry, dry up, wither
Arethūsa, –ae f. a fountain in Sicily
argenteus, –a, –um of silver
*argentum, –ī n. silver; silver plate
Argī, –ōrum m. pl. Argos, a city in Greece
Argīvus, –a, –um of Argos, Argive; Greek; as noun, Argīvī, –ōrum m. pl. Argives, Greeks
Argolicus, –a, –um of Argolis, Argolic; Argive, Greek
*argūmentum, –ī n. argument; evidence
arguō, –ere, –uī, –ūtus prove, reveal, betray
āridus, –a, –um dry, parched
ariēs, –etis m. ram; battering-ram
arista, –ae f. ear or head of grain
*arma, –ōrum n. pl. tools, implements, utensils; arms, weapons; armor; equipment; tackle, rigging, rudder; deeds of arms, warfare, war; warriors, troops
armātus, –a, –um equipped; armed; as noun, armātus, –ī m. armed man, warrior
Armeniī, –ōrum m. pl. a remote tribe of Asia
*armentum, –ī n. cattle for plowing; herd, drove
armiger, –erī m. armor-bearer

armipotēns, –entis powerful in arms, valiant
armisonus, –a, –um resounding with arms
†armō 1 equip, arm
armus, –ī m. shoulder; flank (of an animal)
*arō 1 plow, till; inhabit; sail over
*arrigō, –ere, –rēxī, –rēctus direct to; raise, uplift; partic. arrēctus, –a, –um erect; attentive, keen, eager, excited
arripiō, –ere, –ripuī, –reptus seize; hasten to
*ars, artis f. skill, dexterity; art; practice, profession; work of art, workmanship; artifice, craft, deception, cunning
artifex, –icis m. artist, artisan; contriver, schemer, plotter
*artus, –ūs m. joint; limb; frame, body
artus, –a, –um close, tight, closely fitting
*arvum, –ī n. plowed land, cultivated field, field; land, region; shore
*arx, arcis f. citadel, fortress, stronghold; height; hill; peak, pinnacle, tower
as, assis m. a small Roman coin
Ascanius, –ī m. son of Aeneas
ascendō, –ere, –scendī, –scēnsus climb, mount, ascend
ascēnsus, –ūs m. climbing, ascent
Asia, –ae f. Asia Minor
aspargō, –inis f. sprinkling, spray
aspectō 1 look at, gaze at; look upon, face
aspectus, –ūs m. sight, view, appearance
*asper, –era, –erum rough; thorny, jagged; embossed; harsh, cruel, fierce, relentless; bitter, tempestuous
asperō 1 roughen, ruffle
aspersus, –a, –um sprinkled, spattered
aspiciō, –ere, –spexī, –spectus look at, look upon, see, behold; regard, consider
Assaracus, –ī m. a king of Troy and grandfather of Anchises
ast see at
*astō, –āre, astitī stand near, stand by, stand; hang over; settle upon, alight
Astraea, –ae f. goddess of Justice
*astrum, –ī n. star; pl. heaven
Astyanax, –actis m. son of Hector and Andromache
asȳlum, –ī n. place of refuge; sanctuary
*at, ast conj. but; yet, at least
Atalanta, –ae f. beautiful daughter of Schoenaeus of Boeotia
*āter, ātra, ātrum black, dark, sable, dusky; gloomy, dismal; deadly
Atiī, –ōrum m. pl. a Roman gens
Atlantiadēs, –dae m. descendant of Atlas, i.e., Mercury

**Atlās, –antis** *m. a mountain in Northern Africa; personified as a giant supporting the sky on his shoulders*

***atque, ac** conj.* and, and also; *with comparatives and words of likeness or difference,* as, than

**Atrīdēs, –ae** *m.* descendant of Atreus, *especially Agamemnon or Menelaus*

**ātrium, –ī** *n.* court, hall, room

***ātrōx, –ōcis** harsh, relentless, savage

**Atticus, –a, –um** Attic, of Athens

***attingō, –ere, attigī, attāctus** touch, find, reach, arrive at

**attollō, –ere** lift up, raise up, throw up; rear, erect, build; arouse; *with a reflexive, or the passive used as a middle,* lift oneself, rise

***attonō, –āre, –uī, –itus** thunder at, stun; strike with awe

**†attonitus, –a, –um** thunderstruck; awed, amazed, astounded, dazed

**attrectō 1** touch, handle

**Atys, –yos** *m. a comrade of Ascanius*

***auctor, –ōris** *m.* originator; counsellor; founder, builder; backer, voucher, sponsor; progenitor

***audāx, –ācis** bold, daring; dauntless, resolute; confident

**audēns, –entis** bold; daring

***audeō, –ēre, ausus** *semi-dep.* dare, venture, make bold

***audiō 4** hear, hear of; listen to, heed

***auferō, auferre, abstulī, ablātus** take away, carry off, remove; hide

**Aufidus, –ī** *m. a river in Apulia near Horace's birthplace*

**†augeō, –ēre, auxī, auctus** augment, increase, add to

**augur, –uris** *m. or f.* prophet, seer

***augurium, –ī** *n.* art of divination, augury; omen, portent, token; foreboding

**Augustus, –ī** *m. title conferred on Octavian as emperor*

**aula, –ae (–āī)** *f.* court, hall, palace

**aulaea, –ōrum** *n. pl.* tapestry, drapery, curtains

**Aulis, –idis** *f. a town on the coast of Boeotia*

***aura, –ae (–āī)** *f.* air (*in motion*), breeze; breath of air, breath; light of day, light; gleam, radiance; upper world; ether, ethereal nature; popular favor, applause

**aurātus, –a, –um** overlaid *or* ornamented with gold, gilded, interwoven with gold

**†aureus, –a, –um** of gold, golden; ornamented with gold, gilded; gleaming, glittering

**auricomus, –a, –um** golden-haired; golden-leafed, with golden foliage

**aurīga, –ae** *m.* charioteer, driver

***auris, –is** *f.* ear

***aurōra, –ae** *f.* morning, dawn; *personified,* Aurora, *goddess of morning*

***aurum, –ī** *n.* gold; money; gold plate; gold thread

**Ausonia, –ae** *f. a region in Southern Italy;* Italy

**Ausonius, –a, –um** Ausonian, Italian

**auspex, –icis** *m. or f.* seer; guide, leader, protector

***auspicium, –ī** *n.* divination (*from the flight of birds*); *pl.* auspices; token, will, inclination; power, authority

**Auster, –trī** *m.* south wind, wind

**ausum, –ī** *n.* daring deed

***aut** *conj.* or. **†aut . . . aut** either . . . or

***autem** *conj.* on the other hand, however, but; furthermore

**Automedōn, –ontis** *m. a Greek charioteer of Achilles and later armor-bearer of Pyrrhus*

**autumnālis, –e** of autumn

**autumnus, –ī** *m.* autumn

**auxiliāris, –e** strengthening

***auxilium, –ī** *n.* help, aid, assistance

***avāritia, –ae** *f.* greediness

**avārus, –a, –um** greedy, grasping, covetous

**āvehō, –ere, –vexī, –vectus** carry away, bear away; *passive used as a middle,* sail away

**āvellō, –ere, –vellī, –vulsus** tear off, pull away; carry off

**avēna, –ae** *f.* reed pipe

**aveō, avēre** be well; **avē** hail, *a form of salutation*

**Avernus, –ī** *m. a lake in Campania near the fabled entrance to the underworld;* the underworld

**Avernus, –a, –um** of Avernus; *as noun,* **Averna, –ōrum** *n. pl. the region around Lake Avernus,* the underworld

**āversus, –a, –um** turned away; askance; averse, hostile, estranged

**āvertō, –ere, –vertī, –versus** turn away; remove, carry off; avert, debar; turn aside

**aviditās, –ātis** *f.* greediness

***avidus, –a, –um** eager

***avis, –is** *f.* bird

**āvius, –a, –um** out of the way, pathless; *as noun,* **āvia, –ōrum** *n. pl.* out-of-the-way places, by-ways

**avunculus, –ī** *m.* a mother's brother, uncle

***avus, –ī** *m.* grandfather, grandsire; ancestor

***axis, –is** *m.* axletree; chariot; pole; sky, firmament, heavens; dome, vault

## B

Babylōnius, –a, –um Babylonian, of Babylon, *an ancient city on the Euphrates River*
bāca, –ae *f.* berry
bācātus, –a, –um set with pearls, of pearls
bacchor, –ārī, –ātus celebrate the rites of Bacchus; revel, rush wildly, run madly, rave
Bacchus, –ī *m. god of wine;* wine
baculum, –ī *n.* staff, walking stick
balteus, –ī *m.* belt, strap
barathrum, –ī *n.* abyss
barba, –ae *f.* beard
barbaricus, –a, –um barbaric
*barbarus, –a, –um barbarous, savage
Barcaeī, –ōrum *m. pl. inhabitants of Barce, a town in Libya*
Barcē, –ēs *f. nurse of Sychaeus*
Baucis, Baucidis *f. wife of Philemon*
*beātus, –a, –um happy, blessed
Bebrycius, –a, –um of Bebrycia, *a country in Asia Minor*
Bēlīdēs, –ae *m.* descendant of Belus
bellātrīx, –īcis *f.* female warrior
†bellō 1 wage war, war
*bellum, –ī *n.* war; conflict; *personified,* War
bellus, –a, –um handsome, agreeable
bēlua, –ae *f.* beast, monster
Bēlus, –ī *m. name of* 1) *an ancestor of Palamedes;* 2) *the father of Dido;* 3) *an ancestor of Dido*
*bene *adv.* well
benignitās, –ātis *f.* kindness
benignus, –a, –um kindly, friendly, gracious
Berecyntius, –a, –um of Berecyntus, *a mountain in Phrygia sacred to Cybele*
Beroē, –ēs *f. wife of Doryclus, a comrade of Aeneas*
*bibō, –ere, bibī drink, quaff
bibulus, –a, –um thirsty, dry
bicolor, –ōris of two colors; piebald, dappled
bidēns, –entis having two teeth; *as noun, f.* sheep (*suitable for sacrifice*)
biforis, –e double
bifōrmis, –e two-formed, having two shapes
bīgae, –ārum *f. pl.* team of two horses; two-horse chariot
bijugus, –a, –um of two yoked together; of two-horse chariots
bilinguis, –e double-tongued, treacherous
*bīnī, –ae, –a two each; two
bipatēns, –entis open on both sides; wide open
bipennis, –is *f.* two-edged axe; battle-axe
birēmis, –is *f.* galley (*with two banks of oars*); bireme

*bis *adv.* twice
Bitiās, –ae *m. a Carthaginian nobleman*
blaesus, –a, –um lisping
blanditiae, –ārum *f. pl.* endearments
blandulus, –a, –um charming
blandus, –a, –um caressing, flattering, alluring; enticing; tranquil, quiet
Bōla, –ae *f. a town in Latium*
*bonus, –a, –um good, kind, kindly, kindhearted
Boreās, –ae *m.* north wind
*bōs, bovis *m. or f.* ox, bullock, cow; *pl.* cattle
*bracchium, –ī *n.* forearm, arm; branch; sail yard
brattea, –ae *f.* thin plate *or* leaf of metal; metal
*brevis, –e short, shallow; *as noun,* brevia, –ium *n. pl.* shoals, shallows
breviter *adv.* briefly
Briareus, –eī *m. a hundred-armed giant*
Britannī, –ōrum *m. pl.* the Britons
brūma, –ae *f.* the winter solstice; winter
brūmālis, –e of winter, wintry
Brūtus, –ī *m. L. Junius Brutus, liberator of Rome*
būbō, –ōnis *m. or f.* owl
bustum, –ī *n.* funeral pile
Būtēs, –ae *m. a Bebrycian boxer*
Būthrōtum, –ī *n. a city on the coast of Epirus*
Byrsa, –ae *f. the citadel of Carthage*

## C

cachinnus, –ī *m.* laughter
cacūmen, –inis *n.* summit, peak
Cadmēis, –idis Cadmean, of Cadmus
Cadmus, –ī *m. founder of Thebes*
*cadō, –ere, cecidī, cāsūrus fall, be lowered; sink, set, wane; subside; fall dead, be slain, perish
cādūcifer, –era, –erum caduceus-bearing
cadūcus, –a, –um fallen, slain
cadus, –ī *m.* jar; urn
Caeciliānus, –ī *m. a man's name*
*caecus, –a, –um blind; blinded; blinding; reckless; uncertain, indiscriminate; hidden, secret, unknown; obscure, dark, murky, dismal; meaningless; ineffectual
*caedēs, –is *f.* killing, murder, slaughter; blood, gore
*caedō, –ere, cecīdī, caesus cut; cut down, kill, slay; sacrifice
caelestis, –e heavenly, celestial; of the gods; *as noun,* caelestēs, –ium *m. or f. pl.* gods
caelicola, –ae *m. or f.* dweller in heaven, god
caelifer, –era, –erum sky-bearing; heaven-upholding

caelō 1 emboss, engrave, chase
*caelum, -ī n. sky, welkin; air; weather; heaven; upper world
Caeneus, -ī m. *a mythical character, originally a girl named Caenis, changed by Neptune into a boy, but later, according to Vergil, restored to her proper sex*
caenum, -ī n. mud, mire, filth
*caeruleus (caerulus), -a, -um deep blue, sky-blue, dark blue; sea-colored, sea-green; dark; as *noun*, caerula, -ōrum n. *pl.* the sea; dark blue sea
Caesar, -aris m. *C. Octavius Thurinus, who through adoption by Julius Caesar became C. Julius Caesar Octavianus, with the later title of Augustus, the first emperor of Rome*
caesariēs, -ēī f. hair, locks
caespes, -itis m. turf, sod
caestus, -ūs m. a boxing glove *(weighted with balls of lead or iron)*
Caīcus, -ī m. *a comrade of Aeneas*
Cājēta, -ae f. *a town on the coast of Latium*
calamus, -ī m. reed, reed pipe
calcar, -āris n. spur
Calchās, -antis m. *a famous seer with the Greeks before Troy*
calcō 1 tread, tread out
*caleō, -ēre, -uī, calitūrus be hot, glow
calidus, -a, -um warm, hot
cālīgō, -āre reek with mist; be gloomy
cālīgō, -inis f. fog, mist; darkness
callidus, -a, -um clever, cunning
callis, -is m. path, walk
calor, -ōris m. warmth, heat
calx, calcis f. heel; foot
Calymnē, -nēs f. *a small island off the coast of Asia Minor*
Camarīna, -ae f. *a town on the southern coast of Sicily*
Camillus, -ī m. *M. Furius Camillus, conqueror of Veii and savior of Rome from the Gauls*
camīnus, -ī m. furnace, forge; chimney; crater
*campus, -ī m. plain, field; level surface; race-course
*candeō, -ēre, -uī be white, shine
candidus, -a, -um white, fair, beautiful
candor, -ōris m. whiteness
cāneō, -ēre, -uī be white *or* gray
*canis, -is m. *or* f. dog
canistrum, -ī n. basket
canna, -ae f. reed
*canō, -ere, cecinī, cantus sing, chant; sing of, celebrate; tell of, recount; proclaim; reveal, foretell, predict

canōrus, -a, -um tuneful, melodious
cantō 1 sing of
cantus, -ūs m. singing, song, strain; cry; peal; trumpet-blowing
*cānus, -a, -um white-haired, hoary; venerable, time-honored
capella, -ae f. she-goat
capessō, -ere, -sīvī, -sītus seize; strive to reach; do, execute, perform, carry out
*capillus, -ī m. hair
*capiō, -ere, cēpī, captus take, seize, capture, take possession of, occupy, settle upon; catch, deceive, delude, ensnare; captivate
Capitōlium, -ī n. the Capitol *at Rome*
capra, -ae f. she-goat
caprigenus, -a, -um of the goat kind, of goats
*captīvus, -a, -um captured, plundered; as *noun*, captīvus, -ī m. captive
captō 1 strive to seize, catch at; listen to
capulus, -ī m. hilt
*caput, -itis n. head; peak, summit; life; person, creature
Capys, -yos m. *name of* 1) *a comrade of Aeneas;* 2) *a king of Alba*
carbasus, -ī f. canvas; sail
*carcer, -eris m. prison, prison house; barrier, starting place
carchēsium, -ī n. drinking cup, beaker
cardō, -inis m. pivot; socket, turning point, hinge; crisis
*careō, -ēre, -uī, -itūrus be without, be free from, be deprived of; forego, relinquish
Cārica, -ae f. Carian fig
*carīna, -ae f. keel; hull; boat, skiff, ship
*carmen, -inis n. song, hymn, lay; note, strain; incantation; verse, inscription; prophecy, prediction
carō, carnis f. meat
Carpathius, -a, -um of Carpathus, *an island in the Aegean Sea;* Carpathian
*carpō, -ere, -psī, -ptus pluck, catch; feed on, enjoy; consume, waste; pursue, hasten
Carthāgō, -inis f. Carthage, *a city in Northern Africa*
*cārus, -a, -um dear, precious, beloved; fond, loving
casa, -ae f. cottage
cāseus, -ī m. cheese
Caspius, -a, -um of the Caspian Sea; Caspian
Cassandra, -ae f. *a daughter of Priam and priestess of Apollo*
cassus, -a, -um deprived of
castanea, -ae f. chestnut
*castellum, -ī n. fortress, stronghold, fastness

castīgō 1 punish, flog; chide, rebuke

*castra, –ōrum n. pl. camp, encampment

Castrum Inuī n. a town on the coast of Latium

*castus, –a, –um pure, chaste, guiltless, righteous, holy

*cāsus, –ūs m. fall, downfall; chance, fortune; calamity, disaster; misfortune; hazard, vicissitude; fate; crisis

catēna, –ae f. chain

*caterva, –ae f. crowd, troop, throng

Catō, –ōnis m. M. Porcius Cato, an early Roman statesman

Catullus, –ī m. a Roman poet

catulus, –ī m. whelp

Caucasus, –ī m. a chain of mountains between the Black and Caspian seas

cauda, –ae f. tail

Caulōn, –ōnis m. a town on the southern coast of Italy

Caurus, –ī m. northwest wind

*causa, –ae f. cause, reason; occasion, pretext; lawsuit

cautēs, –is f. pointed rock; crag, cliff

cautus, –a, –um careful

cavea, –ae f. hollow place; theatre, amphitheatre

*caveō, –ēre, cāvī, cautūrus beware, take care

caverna, –ae f. hollow, cavity; cavern, grotto

cavō 1 hollow out, scoop out; partic. cavātus, –a, –um vaulted

*cavus, –a, –um hollow; vaulted; enfolding, enveloping

Cecropidēs, –ae m. descendant of Cecrops, fabled founder of Athens; as noun, m. pl. Athenians

*cēdō, –ere, cessī, cessūrus withdraw, depart, recede, give way; be behind; yield, submit; fall to

Celaenō, –ūs f. one of the Harpies

*celeber, –bris, –bre frequented, surrounded; distinguished

*celebrō 1 throng, frequent, attend in numbers; honor, celebrate, solemnize

*celer, –eris, –ere swift, speedy, fleet, rapid

celeriter adv. quickly

*celerō 1 quicken, hasten, speed

cella, –ae f. storehouse, cell

cēlō 1 hide, conceal

*celsus, –a, –um high, lofty

cēna, –ae f. dinner

cēnō 1 dine

Centaurus, –ī m. a Centaur; as noun, f. the name of a ship

*centum indecl. adj. hundred

centumgeminus, –a, –um hundredfold; hundred-armed (an epithet of Briareus)

cēra, –ae f. wax

Ceraunia, –ōrum n. pl. a mountain range in Epirus

Cerberus, –ī m. the fabled three-headed watchdog at the entrance to the underworld

Cereālis, –e of Ceres; with arma, utensils (for preparing flour or bread)

cerebrum, –ī n. brain

Cerēs, –eris f. the goddess of agriculture; corn, grain; bread

*cernō, –ere, crēvī, crētus (certus) see, behold, perceive; discern, descry

*certāmen, –inis n. contest, struggle, strife; emulation, rivalry; energy

certātim adv. emulously, eagerly

†certē adv. certainly, surely; at least, at any rate

*certō 1 contend, strive, struggle, fight; engage in; vie with

*certus, –a, –um fixed, definite, settled; unchanging, unswerving, resolute; unerring; trusty, faithful; resolved, determined; certain, inevitable; certum facere inform

cerva, –ae f. hind, deer

*cervīx, –īcis f. neck, shoulder

*cervus, –ī m. stag, deer

*cessō 1 cease, stop; loiter, be slow, be idle; hesitate

*cēterī, –ae, –a (rare in the singular) rest of, remaining, other

cētus, –ī m. (nom. pl. cētē n.) sea monster, whale

*ceu adv. as, like, just as, just like; as when; as if

Chalcidicus, –a, –um of Chalcis; of Cumae, a colony of the Euboean city Chalcis

Chāōn, –onis m. a Trojan, brother of Helenus

Chāonia, –ae f. a country in Northwestern Epirus

Chāonius, –a, –um of Chaonia

chaos, –ī n. chaos, confusion; personified by Vergil as the god of the underworld; the underworld

Charōn, –ontis m. the fabled ferryman of the dead over the river Styx

Charybdis, –is f. a whirlpool in the strait of Messina between Italy and Sicily

Chimaera, –ae f. a fabulous fire-breathing monster which had the head of a lion, the body of a goat, and the tail of a dragon; the name of a ship

chlamys, –ydis f. a woollen upper garment worn in Greece; a mantle

Chloē, –ēs f. a woman's name

chorēa, –ae f. dance (in a circle)

*chorus, –ī m. choral dance, a dance; chorus, choir; band, troop

*cibus, –ī m. food

Cicones, –um m. pl. a Thracian people living near the river Hebrus

*cieō, ciēre, cīvī, citus stir up, agitate; arouse, stimulate; make, cause, produce, call forth; call, call upon

*cingō, –ere, cīnxī, cīnctus surround, encircle, circle about; invest, beset; gird, bind

cingulum, –ī n. girdle, belt

*cinis, –eris m. ashes, embers; tomb

circā adv. and prep. with acc. around, about

Circē, –ēs f. a famous sorceress, daughter of the sun

circuitus, –ūs m. a going around, circuit

circulus, –ī m. circlet, circle, band

*circum 1) adv. around, about; 2) prep. with acc. around, about, at, near

*circumdō, –dare, –dedī, –datus put or place around; surround, encircle, enclose; overlay

circumferō, –ferre, –tulī, –lātus carry around, bear around, cast around, encircle; lustrate, purify

circumflectō, –ere, –flexī, –flexus turn about, bend around

circumfundō, –ere, –fūdī, –fūsus pour around, surround, wrap, envelop; passive used as a middle, surround, crowd around, encompass

circumspiciō, –ere, –spexī, –spectus look about, survey, examine

circumstō, –āre, –stetī stand around or about; surround, beset

circumtextus, –a, –um woven around

†circumveniō, –īre, –vēnī, –ventus come around, surround, encircle

circumvolō 1 fly around; hover over; envelop

circumvolvō, –ere, –volvī, –volūtus roll around, revolve

circus, –ī m. circle; racecourse

Cisseus, –eī m. a king of Thrace, the father of Hecuba

Cithaerōn, –ōnis m. a mountain in Boeotia sacred to Bacchus

cithara, –ae f. cithern, lute, harp, lyre

citō adv. quickly, speedily, swiftly, soon

citrā prep. with acc. this side of, less than

*citus, –a, –um quick, speedy, swift, rapid

*cīvīlis, –e of a citizen; civil, civic

*cīvis, –is m. or f. citizen, fellow citizen, fellow countryman or fellow countrywoman

clādēs, –is f. disaster, calamity; havoc; scourge

*clam adv. secretly, stealthily

*clāmō 1 cry out, call upon

†clāmor, –ōris m. shout, shouting, cry, outcry; cheering, applause; threat; protest; wail, shriek, scream; noise, roar, din

clangor, –ōris m. noise, din, flapping; blare

clārēscō, –ere, clāruī become clear, grow loud

Clarius, –a, –um of Claros, a town in Ionia, and the seat of a temple and oracle of Apollo

*clārus, –a, –um clear, bright, brilliant; manifest; loud, distinct, clear-toned; renowned, famed, distinguished; illustrious, glorious

classicum, –ī n. battle signal (on the trumpet)

*classis, –is f. fleet; ship

*claudō, –ere, clausī, clausus shut, close; shut in, enclose

claudus, –a, –um lame; maimed, disabled

claustrum, –ī n. bar, bolt; barrier, barricade; headland

clāvus, –ī m. nail; tiller, rudder, helm

*cliēns, –entis m. client, dependent

*clipeus, –ī m. shield, buckler

clīvus, –ī m. slope, hillside

Cloanthus, –ī m. a comrade of Aeneas

Cluentius, –ī m. a Roman gentile name

Clymenē, –ēs f. an Ethiopian queen, mother of Phaëthon

Clymenēius, –a, –um of Clymene, the mother of Phaëthon

coctilis, –e baked; of brick

Cōcȳtus, –ī m. a river of the underworld

coeō, –īre, –īvī (–iī), –itūrus come together, meet; curdle, congeal, unite

*coepī, –isse, coeptus begin, commence

coeptum, –ī n. attempt; undertaking; design

coërceō, –ēre, –uī, –itus confine, restrain, hold fast, hold back

coetus, –ūs m. meeting; assembly, company; flock

Coeus, –ī m. one of the Titans

cognātus, –a, –um related by blood, kindred

*cognōmen, –inis n. family name, surname; name, appellation

*cognōscō, –ere, cognōvī, cognitus learn, ascertain; recognize; know

*cōgō, –ere, coēgī, coāctus drive together, collect, assemble; condense, force, compel

cohibeō, –ēre, –uī, –itus confine, restrain

*cohors, –tis f. company (of soldiers); line (of ships), fleet

Collātīnus, –a, –um of Collatia, a Sabine town

*colligō, –ere, –lēgī, –lēctus gather, collect, assemble; reef (sails)

*collis, –is m. hill

*collum, –ī n. neck

*colō, –ere, –uī, cultus till, cultivate; dwell in, inhabit; regard, esteem, cherish, honor

*colōnus, –ī m. tiller of the soil; settler, emigrant, colonist

color, –ōris m. color, complexion, tint, hue

coluber, –brī m. serpent, snake

columba, –ae f. dove, pigeon

columna, –ae f. pillar, column

*coma, –ae f. hair, locks, tresses; foliage

comāns, –antis hairy; plumed, crested

comedō, –ēsse (–edere), –ēdī, –ēsus eat

*comes, –itis m. or f. companion, comrade, follower; attendant

†comitātus, –ūs m. escort, suite, retinue, train

comitō 1 or *comitor, –ārī, –ātus accompany, escort; follow; attend

*commendō 1 commit, entrust; command

commisceō, –ēre, –miscuī, –mixtus mix with, intermingle with, blend with

commissum, –ī n. misdeed, fault, offense, crime

*committō, –ere, –mīsī, –missus join, unite; begin, engage in; commit; commit offense

†commoveō, –ēre, –mōvī, –mōtus move, stir; rouse, shake; disturb, alarm, excite, agitate

*commūnis, –e common; in common

commūtō 1 change

cōmō, –ere, cōmpsī, cōmptus arrange, dress

compāgēs, –is f. joint, seam; bar, fastening; framework, structure

†comparō 1 make ready, prepare

*compellō 1 address, accost, speak to

†compellō, –ere, –pulī, –pulsus drive together; drive

compescō, –ere, –pescuī restrain, quench

*complector, –ī, –plexus embrace, clasp; enfold, envelop; hold

†compleō, –ēre, –ēvī, –ētus fill up, fill; crowd, throng; complete

complexus, –ūs m. embrace

†compōnō, –ere, –posuī, –positus put together; found, build; lay, place; put to rest; quiet, calm, allay; settle, arrange

compositō adv. according to agreement

comprecor, –ārī, –ātus pray

†comprehendō (comprēndō), –ere, –endī, –ēnsus seize, grasp; recount, enumerate

comprimō, –ere, –pressī, –pressus check, curb, quell, restrain, stay, hold back, press together

concavus, –a, –um hollow

*concēdō, –ere, –cessī, –cessus withdraw, depart, go or come away; grant; permit

concha, –ae f. conch shell, shell

conchȳlium, –ī n. shellfish, oyster

†concidō, –ere, –cidī fall, collapse

*conciliō 1 win, secure, win the favor of

*concilium, –ī n. gathering, assembly; council

concipiō, –ere, –cēpī, –ceptus take hold of; conceive; imagine; comprehend; begin

*concitō 1 stir up

concitus, –a, –um aroused; roughened with

conclāmō 1 shout, cry out

conclūdō, –ere, –clūsī, –clūsus shut in; surround, enclose

*concordia, –ae f. harmony

concors, –dis of one heart, in concord, harmonious; friendly, peaceful

concrēscō, –ere, –crēvī, –crētus grow together; partic. concrētus, –a, –um ingrown, ingrained; stiffened, matted

concurrō, –ere, –currī (–cucurrī), –cursūrus run together; encounter, fight; run, rush

concursus, –ūs m. throng, concourse, crowd

†concutiō, –ere, –cussī, –cussus shake violently, shake; agitate, alarm; stun, overwhelm

condēnsus, –a, –um crowded together, huddled together

*condiciō, –ōnis f. terms of agreement

*condō, –ere, –didī, –ditus put together, found, establish; lay to rest; consign; store up, treasure up; hide, conceal

†cōnferō, –ferre, contulī, conlātus bring together, match, contend; with gradūs as object, walk side by side, keep pace with

*cōnfertus, –a, –um crowded together, in close array

*cōnficiō, –ere, –fēcī, –fectus do thoroughly; finish, complete, accomplish; waste, spend, exhaust

*cōnfīdō, –ere, –fīsus trust, rely upon, have faith in

cōnfigō, –ere, –fīxī, –fīxus pierce through, transfix

cōnfīō, –fierī, –fectus be done

†cōnfiteor, –ērī, –fessus confess, acknowledge, avow, reveal

*cōnflīgō, –ere, –flīxī, –flīctūrus strike together; contend

cōnfugiō, –ere, –fūgī flee for help, flee for refuge

cōnfundō, –ere, –fūdī, –fūsus pour together; mix, mingle, blend; confuse, disturb, bewilder; break, violate

congemō, –ere, –uī groan or sigh deeply

congerō, –ere, –gessī, –gestus bring together, collect; heap up; erect

†congredior, –ī, –gressus come together, meet, encounter; engage in battle

congressus, -ūs *m.* meeting; interview; encounter, match

cōnifer, -era, -erum cone-bearing

cōnitor, -nītī, -nīxus (-nīsus) exert oneself, strain every nerve

†conjiciō (coniciō), -ere, -jēcī, -jectus throw, cast, hurl, shoot; *with reflexive,* dash, hasten

†conjugium, -ī *n.* marriage, wedlock; husband, wife

†conjungō, -ere, -jūnxī, -jūnctus join together, unite, clasp; attach

*conjūnx, conjugis *m. or f.* spouse, consort; husband, wife; bride, betrothed

conlābor, -ī, -lāpsus fall, sink, faint, swoon

conlūceō, -ēre shine, gleam

conlūstrō 1 survey

*cōnor, -ārī, -ātus try, attempt, endeavor

cōnsanguineus, -ī *m.* kinsman, relative, brother

cōnsanguinitās, -ātis *f.* blood-relationship

cōnscendō, -ere, -scendī, -scēnsus mount, climb, ascend, embark upon

*cōnscientia, -ae *f.* consciousness

*cōnscius, -a, -um aware, aware of, having knowledge of, knowing, conscious (*of guilt*); witnessing, confederate

cōnsenēscō, -ere, -senuī grow old together

*cōnsequor, -ī, -secūtus follow, pursue

cōnserō, -ere, -sēvī, -satus sow, plant

cōnsessus, -ūs *m.* sitting together, assembly

*cōnsīdō, -ere, -sēdī, -sessūrus sit down; alight, perch; settle; anchor; sink down

*cōnsilium, -ī *n.* deliberation; counsel, advice; measure; plan, purpose

*cōnsistō, -ere, -stitī, -stitūrus place oneself, post oneself; stand, pause, halt; rest

cōnsonō, -āre, -uī sound together; resound

cōnsors, -sortis *m. or f.* sharer, partner

†cōnspectus, -ūs *m.* sight, view; presence

*cōnspiciō, -ere, -spexī, -spectus catch sight of, espy; see, behold; find

cōnsternō 1 strike with terror

cōnsternō, -ere, -strāvī, -strātus bestrew, cover; lay on the ground

*cōnstituō, -ere, -uī, -ūtus place, put, set; build, erect; resolve, determine

†cōnstō, -āre, -stitī, -stātūrus stand together; be fixed, be settled; cōnstat it is evident

*cōnsul, -ulis *m.* consul, *one of the two chief Roman magistrates*

*cōnsulō, -ere, -uī, -tus consult; *with dat.* have regard for

*cōnsultum, -ī *n.* advice, counsel, response

*cōnsūmō, -ere, -sūmpsī, -sūmptus use up, consume, spend

cōnsurgō, -ere, -surrēxī, -surrēctūrus rise, arise, leap to one's feet

contāctus, -ūs *m.* touch

contāgium, -ī *n.* infection

*contemnō, -ere, -tempsī, -temptus despise, defy

contemptrīx, -īcis *f.* despiser, scorner; *as adj.,* scornful

*contendō, -ere, -tendī, -tentus draw together, stretch, strain; labor, strive; hasten; aim, direct; contend, fight

*1. contentus, -a, -um content, contented, satisfied

2. contentus, -a, -um tight-drawn

conterminus, -a, -um close (*to*)

conterreō, -ēre, -uī, -itus frighten greatly, terrify, alarm

contexō, -ere, -texuī, -textus weave together; construct, build

conticēscō, -ere, -ticuī become silent, cease speaking, be silent

contiguus, -a, -um adjoining

*contineō, -ēre, -tinuī, -tentus hold together; restrain, check, stay, stop

†contingō, -ere, -tigī, -tāctus touch; gain, reach, hit; stain, defile; befall, fall to, be one's lot; *contingit it happens, it befalls

continuō *adv.* forthwith, straightway, immediately

contorqueō, -ēre, -torsī, -tortus turn quickly, whirl around; hurl, discharge, shoot

*contrā 1) *adv.* opposite, on the other side; in opposition, against; in reply; 2) *prep. with acc.* opposite, over against; against; facing, fronting; in reply to

contrahō, -ere, -trāxī, -tractus gather, assemble, muster, draw together; lessen

contrārius, -a, -um opposite, contrary, adverse, opposing, hostile

contremīscō, -ere, -tremuī tremble, quake

contundō, -ere, -tudī, -tūsus (-tūnsus) bruise; subdue, crush

contus, -ī *m.* pole, pike

*cōnūbium, -ī *n.* wedlock, marriage

cōnus, -ī *m.* cone; peak

convallis, -is *f.* valley, vale, glen

convectō 1 bring together, collect

convellō, -ere, -vellī, -vulsus tear up, tear away, rend asunder, shatter, uproot, wrench, batter

†conveniō, -īre, -vēnī, -ventūrus come together, assemble, gather

conventus, -ūs *m.* assembly, throng

†convertō, -ere, -vertī, -versus turn, invert; change

convexum, -ī n. hollow, cavity, recess; arch, vault; upper world

*convīvium, -ī n. feast, banquet

convolvō, -ere, -volvī, -volūtus roll up; coil

convulsus see convellō

coörior, -īrī, -ortus arise, break forth, break out

*cōpia, -ae f. abundance, plenty; store, means; forces; opportunity, permission

*cor, cordis n. heart; soul; feeling, emotion

Cora, -ae f. a town in Latium

cōram adv. in one's presence, before one's eyes, with one's own eyes, in person

Corinthus, -ī f. a city in Greece

1. corneus, -a, -um of horn

2. corneus, -a, -um of cornel wood

cornipēs, -edis horn-footed, hoofed

*cornū, -ūs n. horn, antler; end (of a yardarm)

cornum, -ī n. cornel cherry

Coroebus, -ī m. a Phrygian ally of the Trojans

*corōna, -ae f. crown; garland, wreath, chaplet

corōnō 1 crown, wreathe

corporeus, -a, -um of the body, corporeal, fleshly

*corpus, -oris n. body; corpse, carcass; person; frame, framework; form, figure, beauty

corrigō, -ere, -rēxī, -rēctus straighten, remedy

†corripiō, -ere, -ripuī, -reptus snatch, snatch up, catch up, seize; speed on or along, dash over

*corrumpō, -ere, -rūpī, -ruptus spoil, damage, injure; taint, infect

cortex, -icis m. bark

cortīna, -ae f. cauldron, kettle; tripod (of Apollo); oracle

coruscō, -āre wave to and fro; brandish

*coruscus, -a, -um waving; gleaming, flashing, glittering

corvus, -ī m. crow

Corybantius, -a, -um of the Corybantes, priests of Cybele

Cōrycis, -idis Corycian, of Corycium, a cave on Mt. Parnassus

Corynaeus, -ī m. a comrade of Aeneas

Corythus, -ī m. a town in Etruria

Cossus, -ī m. A. Cornelius Cossus, consul 428 B.C.

costa, -ae f. rib, side

cothurnus, -ī m. buskin; hunting boot

crās adv. tomorrow

crassus, -a, -um thick, clotted

crāstinus, -a, -um of tomorrow, tomorrow's

*crātēr, -ēris m. mixing bowl; bowl, jar

crātis, -is f. wickerwork

creātrīx, -īcis f. mother

*crēber, -bra, -brum frequent, repeated, numerous, incessant; abounding in; fresh

crēbrēscō, -ere, crēbruī become frequent; increase in strength; freshen

*crēdō, -ere, -didī, -ditus believe, suppose; trust, confide in; entrust

cremō 1 burn, consume

*creō 1 make, create, bring forth

crepitō, -āre rattle, rustle, crackle

*crepō, -āre, -uī, -itūrus rattle, crash

Crēs, -ētis m. a Cretan

*crēscō, -ere, crēvī, crētus grow; spring, be born

Crēsius, -a, -um of Crete, Cretan

Crēssa, -ae f. Cretan woman

Crēta, -ae f. Crete, an island in the Mediterranean Sea

Crētaeus, -a, -um of Crete, Cretan

crētus, -a, -um born, descended, sprung

Creūsa, -ae f. daughter of Priam and wife of Aeneas

*crīmen, -inis n. charge, accusation, reproach; sin, guilt, guilty act, crime

*crīnis, -is, m. hair; lock of hair; trail of light

Crīnīsus, -ī m. a river in Southwestern Sicily; a river-god

crīnītus, -a, -um long-haired

crīspō 1 curl; wave, brandish, wield

*crista, -ae f. crest, plume

cristātus, -a, -um crested, plumed

croceus, -a, -um saffron-colored, ruddy

*crūdēlis, -e cruel; fierce, deadly, bitter, unnatural; merciless, ruthless; relentless

crūdēliter adv. cruelly, barbarously, ruthlessly

crūdus, -a, -um bloody, raw; of rawhide; sturdy, lusty, vigorous

cruentō 1 make bloody

*cruentus, -a, -um bloody, bloodstained; blood-thirsty

*cruor, -ōris m. blood, gore

cubīle, -is n. bed, couch

cubitum, -ī n. elbow

*culmen, -inis n. roof; top, summit

*culpa, -ae f. fault, offense, weakness

culpātus, -a, -um blamed, blameworthy

culter, -trī m. knife

cultor, -ōris m. worshiper

cultrīx, -īcis f. inhabitant, dweller on

cultus, -ūs m. cultivation; mode of life; dress; plight

*cum prep. with abl. with

*cum conj., temporal, when, while; causative, since; adversative, though, although

Cūmae, –ārum f. pl. a town on the coast of Campania

Cūmaeus, –a, –um of Cumae

Cūmānus, –a, –um Cumaean, of Cumae

cumba, –ae f. boat, skiff

*–cumbō, –ere, –cubuī, –cubitūrus lie

cumulō 1 heap up; load, load down; increase, augment

cumulus, –ī m. heap, mass, pile

cūnābula, –ōrum n. pl. cradle; birthplace

*cūnctor, –ārī, –ātus delay, linger; hesitate; be reluctant, resist

*cūnctus, –a, –um whole, entire, all together

cuneus, –ī m. wedge; wedge-shaped division of a theater

*cupīdō, –inis f. desire, longing, eagerness, passion; personified, Cupīdō, –inis m. Cupid, Love, the son of Venus; god of love

†cupiō, –ere, –īvī (–iī), –ītus long, long for, desire

cupressus, –ī f. cypress

*cūr adv. why? wherefore?

*cūra, –ae f. care; anxiety, solicitude, distress, trouble; concern, duty, charge, business; affection, love, pangs of love; object of love, darling; personified, Care

Curēs, –ium m. pl. a town of the Sabines

Cūrētes, –um m. pl. the primitive inhabitants of Crete; Cretans

*cūrō 1 care for, trouble oneself about; refresh; heed; care

*currō, –ere, cucurrī, cursūrus run, scud, skim over, speed

*currus, –ūs m. chariot, car

*cursus, –ūs m. running; race, chase; haste; passage, voyage; course; flight; charge; evolution

curvāmen, –inis n. curve

curvātūra, –ae f. curve

curvō 1 bend, curve; hollow out, arch

*curvus, –a, –um curved, curving, winding

*cuspis, –idis f. point; spear, lance

†custōdia, –ae f. guarding; watch, guard, sentinel

*custōs, –ōdis m. or f. guard; watchman, guardian; keeper, protector

*–cutiō, –ere, –cussī, –cussus shake; strike

cutis, –is f. skin

Cybelus, –ī m. a mountain in Phrygia

Cyclades, –um f. pl. a cluster of islands in the Aegean Sea

Cyclōpius, –a, –um of the Cyclops

Cyclōps, –ōpis m. a one-eyed giant

cycnus, –ī m. swan

Cyllēnius, –a, –um of Cyllene, a mountain in Arcadia, the birthplace of Mercury; as noun, Cyllēnius, –ī m. Mercury

cymbium, –ī n. cup, bowl (shaped like a boat)

Cȳmodocē, –ēs f. a sea nymph

Cȳmothoē, –ēs f. a sea nymph

Cynthus, –ī m. a mountain in Delos, the birthplace of Diana and Apollo

cyparissus, –ī f. cypress

Cyprius, –a, –um of Cyprus

Cyprus, –ī f. an island in the eastern part of the Mediterranean Sea

Cythēra, –ōrum n. pl. an island in the Aegean Sea, near which Venus is fabled to have risen from the foam of the sea

Cythorēus, –a, –um of Cythera; as noun, Cytherēa, –ae f. Venus

cytisus, –ī m. snail-clover, clover

D

Daedalus, –ī m. a fabled Athenian artisan, the father of Icarus

*damnō 1 condemn, sentence; doom, consign

damnōsus, –a, –um causing loss, destructive

damnum, –ī n. loss, destruction

Danaüs, –a, –um of Danaüs, a fabled king of Greece who settled in Argos; Greek, Grecian; as noun, Danaī, –ōrum m. pl. the Greeks

*daps, dapis f. feast, banquet; food, viands; sacrificial feast

Dardania, –ae f. Troy

Dardanidēs, –ae m. descendant of Dardanus, i.e., a Trojan

Dardanis, –idis f. daughter of Dardanus, i.e., a Trojan woman

Dardanius, –a, –um of Dardanus, descendant of Dardanus, i.e., Trojan

Dardanus, –ī m. one of the founders of the Trojan dynasty

Dardanus, –a, –um of Dardanus; Trojan

Darēs, –ētis m. a Trojan boxer, comrade of Aeneas

dator, –ōris m. giver

Daunias, –adis f. Daunus's land, i.e., Apulia

Daunus, –ī m. early king of Apulia

*dē prep. with abl. from, away from, down from; out of, of; according to

dea, –ae f. goddess

dēbellō 1 subdue, quell, vanquish

*dēbeō 2 owe; pass. be due, be destined

dēbilis, –e weak, disabled

†dēcēdō, –ere, –cessī, –cessūrus withdraw, retire, depart

*decem *indecl. adj.* ten
*dēcernō, –ere, –crēvī, –crētus resolve, determine
dēcerpō, –ere, –cerpsī, –cerptus pluck
*dēcertō 1 struggle
*decet, –ēre, –uit it is fitting, it is proper
dēcidō, –ere, –cidī fall down, fall
dēcipiō, –ere, –cēpī, –ceptus deceive, betray
Decius, –ī *m. a Roman gentile name*
*dēclārō 1 proclaim, pronounce
dēclīnō 1 bend down, turn aside
*dēclīvis, –e downward
decor, –ōris *m.* grace, beauty
decorō 1 adorn, decorate
*decōrus, –a, –um comely, becoming, beautiful, adorned
dēcrēscō, –ere, –crēvī grow less, decrease
dēcurrō, –ere, –currī (–cucurrī), –cursūrus run down; hasten, speed
*decus, –oris *n.* grace, beauty; honor, glory; pride; ornament, decoration
*dēdecus, –oris *n.* disgrace; blemish
dēdignor, –ārī, –ātus disdain, scorn; reject
†dēdūcō, –ere, –dūxī, –ductus lead down, drag down, launch; drag away; lead, conduct
*dēfendō, –ere, –fendī, –fēnsus ward off, protect, defend
†dēfēnsor, –ōris *m.* protector, defender
*dēferō, –ferre, –tulī, –lātus bear, carry, convey; bring word, report; *passive used as a middle,* sail
*dēfessus, –a, –um wearied, exhausted, spent
*dēficiō, –ere, –fēcī, –fectus fail, be wanting; desert; faint; sink
dēfīgō, –ere, –fīxī, –fīxus fix, fasten; cast down
dēfleō, –ēre, –ēvī, –ētus weep for, bewail, lament
dēfluō, –ere, –flūxī, –flūxūrus flow down; fall down
dēfōrmis, –e unsightly, ugly
dēfrēnātus, –a, –um unbridled, unrestrained
dēfungor, –ī, –fūnctus finish, have done with, go through with
dēgener, –eris degenerate; ignoble
dēgō, –ere, dēgī pass, spend
dehinc *adv.* hence, henceforth; then, thereupon
dehīscō, –ere yawn, gape, open, gape open
*deinde *adv.* from this *or* that time, hereafter, thereafter; then, next, afterwards; thereupon; now
Dēiopēa, –ae *f. a nymph*
Dēiphobē, –ēs *f. a priestess of Apollo and Diana*
Dēiphobus, –ī *m. a son of Priam*
dējiciō (dēiciō), –ere, –jēcī, –jectus hurl down,

cast down; drive down, dislodge; bring down; cast; deprive of, bereave of
dēlābor, –ī, –lāpsus glide down, fall down, swoop down; descend, fall
dēliciae, –ārum *f. pl.* pet
*dēligō, –ere, –lēgī, –lēctus choose, select
dēlitēscō, –ere, –lituī hide, lie hid
Dēlius, –a, –um of Delos; of Apollo, *who was born on Delos*
Dēlos, –ī *f. an island in the Aegean Sea, the birthplace of Apollo*
Delphicus, –a, –um Delphic, of Delphi, *a shrine sacred to Apollo*
delphīn, –īnis *m.* dolphin
*dēlūbrum, –ī *n.* shrine, temple, sanctuary
dēlūdō, –ere, –sī, –sus deceive, delude
*dēmēns, –entis out of one's mind; mad, crazy, frantic, foolish
dēmentia, –ae *f.* folly, madness
†dēmittō, –ere, –mīsī, –missus send down, let fall, shed; consign; admit; *partic.* dēmissus, –a, –um hanging, lowered; downcast, subdued; descended, derived
dēmō, –ere, dēmpsī, dēmptus take away, remove; dispel
Dēmoleos, –ī *m. a Greek chieftain*
dēmoror, –ārī, –ātus delay, detain
*dēmum *adv.* at last, at length, only
dēnī, –ae, –a ten each, ten
*dēnique *adv.* finally, at length, at last; in short
*dēns, dentis *m.* tooth; fluke (*of an anchor*)
*dēnsus, –a, –um thick; close, crowded, compact, serried; thick and fast, incessant
*dēnūntiō 1 announce, foretell
dēpāscō, –ere, –pāvī, –pāstus *or dep.* dēpāscor, –ī, –pāstus feed upon, consume, devour
dēpellō, –ere, –pulī, –pulsus drive away, ward off
dēpendeō, –ēre hang down
†dēpōnō, –ere, –posuī, –positus lay down, lay aside, put away; set apart
*dēprecor, –ārī, –ātus beg off, pray to be delivered from; avert by prayer
dēprēnsus, –a, –um caught, overtaken
dēprōmō, –ere, –prōmpsī, –prōmptus draw out
dērigēscō, –ere, –riguī become stiff, swoon; curdle, congeal
dēripiō, –ere, –ripuī, –reptus tear away, strip off, tear off; launch
dēsaeviō, –īre, –iī vent one's rage
dēscendō, –ere, –scendī, –scēnsūrus climb down, go down, descend; fall; stoop to; penetrate

dēscēnsus, –ūs *m.* descent
dēscrībō, –ere, –scrīpsī, –scrīptus write down, write; map out, sketch
*dēserō, –ere, –seruī, –sertus leave behind, abandon, forsake
dēserta, –ōrum *n. pl.* waste lands, wilderness
dēsertus, –a, –um abandoned, deserted; lonely; unpeopled, unfrequented
dēsīderium, –ī *n.* heart's desire
dēsīdō, –ere, –sēdī settle down, sink
*dēsignō 1 mark out, designate, describe
*dēsinō, –ere, –sīvī (–siī), –sitūrus leave off, cease
*dēsistō, –ere, –stitī, –stitūrus leave off, desist from, abandon
dēspectō 1 look down upon
*dēspiciō, –ere, –spexī, –spectus look down upon; scorn, reject
dēstinō 1 make fast; destine, doom
dēstruō, –ere, –strūxī, –strūctus tear down, destroy
dēsuētus, –a, –um unaccustomed, unused, disused; dormant
*dēsum, –esse, –fuī be wanting, be missing
dēsuper *adv.* from above, above
dēterior, –ius worse, less good
dēterreō 2 frighten away, deter
dētineō, –ēre, –tinuī, –tentus keep back, detain, hold
dētorqueō, –ēre, –torsī, –tortus turn away, turn from
dētrahō, –ere, –trāxī, –tractus drag away; take from
dētrūdō, –ere, –trūsī, –trūsus thrust down, push off
dēturbō 1 hurl down; drive away, dislodge
Deucaliōn, –ōnis *m. a man's name*
*deus, –ī *m.* god, deity
dēveniō, –īre, –vēnī, –ventūrus come down; come to, arrive at
dēvolō 1 fly down
dēvolvō, –ere, –volvī, –volūtus roll down, hurl down
dēvōtus, –a, –um devoted, doomed
dēvoveō, –ēre, –vōvī, –vōtus curse
*dexter, –tra, –trum right, to *or* on the right; favorable, propitious; as *noun*, dextra (–tera), –ae *f.* right hand; pledge, faith
Diāna, –ae *f. daughter of Jupiter and Latona and sister of Apollo*
Diaulus, –ī *m. a man's name*
diciō, –ōnis (*nom. sing. not in use*) *f.* power, dominion, sway
dicō 1 proclaim, appoint, set apart, assign, consecrate

*dīcō, –ere, dīxī, dictus say, speak, utter; sing, chant; speak of, tell, describe; call, name
Dictaeus, –a, –um of Dicte, *a mountain in Crete;* of Crete, Cretan
dictum, –ī *n.* word, command, mandate
Dīdō, –ūs (–ōnis) *f. the fabled founder and queen of Carthage*
dīdūcō, –ere, –dūxī, –ductus draw apart, separate, divide, rend asunder; distract
Didymāōn, –onis *m. a skillful artificer*
*diēs, –ēī (diī) *m. or f.* day, daylight; time, appointed time
*differō, differre, distulī, dīlātus put off, postpone, defer
*difficilis, –e not easy, difficult; hard, painful, dangerous
diffīdō, –ere, –fīsus *semi-dep.* distrust, have no confidence in
diffugiō, –ere, –fūgī flee in different directions, disperse, scatter
diffundō, –ere, –fūdī, –fūsus pour (*in different directions*); scatter, spread abroad
dīgerō, –ere, –gessī, –gestus set in order, arrange; explain, interpret
*digitus, –ī *m.* finger, toe
*dignor, –ārī, –ātus count worthy, deem worthy; deign
*dignus, –a, –um worthy, deserved, fitting, suitable, proper
dīgredior, –gredī, –gressus go away, depart
dīgressus, –ūs *m.* departure, parting
dīlābor, –ī, –lāpsus glide away, vanish
*dīligō, –ere, –lēxī, –lēctus love, cherish; *perf. partic.* beloved
dīmidium, –ī *n.* half
†dīmittō, –ere, –mīsī, –missus send away, send forth; let go, dismiss, send
dīmoveō, –ēre, –mōvī, –mōtus part, cleave; drive away, dissipate
dīnumerō 1 count, reckon, compute
Diomēdēs, –is *m. son of Tydeus and one of the bravest of the Greeks before Troy*
Diōnaeus, –a, –um of Dione, *the mother of Venus*
Diōrēs, –is *m. a comrade of Aeneas*
Dīrae, –ārum *f. pl.* the Furies
*dīrigō, –ere, –rēxī, –rēctus direct
dirimō, –ere, –ēmī, –ēmptus take apart; break off, end
*dīripiō, –ere, –ripuī, –reptus tear in pieces; plunder, ravage, pillage
dīruō, –ere, –ruī, –rutus destroy
*dīrus, –a, –um dreadful, awful, fearful, dire, fell, grim; ill-omened, portentous
dīs *see* dīves

Dīs, Dītis *m.* Pluto, *god of the underworld*

†discēdō, –ere, –cessī, –cessūrus go apart; depart, withdraw

discernō, –ere, –crēvī, –crētus separate; distinguish; embroider

discerpō, –ere, –cerpsī, –cerptus tear in pieces

discessus, –ūs *m.* departure

*discō, –ere, didicī learn, learn how, learn about

discolor, –ōris of different color

discordia, –ae *f.* discord, strife; *personified,* Discord

discors, –cordis discordant, different

*discrīmen, –inis *n.* difference, distinction, discrimination; distance, interval; note; crisis, hazard, peril, vicissitude

discumbō, –ere, –cubuī, –cubitūrus recline

discurrō, –ere, –currī (–cucurrī), –cursūrus run in different directions, separate

disjiciō (disiciō), –ere, –jēcī, –jectus scatter, disperse; shatter, demolish

disjungō, –ere, –jūnxī, –jūnctus separate, keep away from

dispellō, –ere, –pulī, –pulsus drive apart, scatter, disperse; dissipate

dispendium, –ī *n.* cost, expenditure

dispēnsō 1 distribute

*dispergō, –ere, –persī, –persus scatter, disperse

dispiciō, –ere, –spexī, –spectus see through; discern

dispōnō, –ere, –posuī, –positus set in order, arrange, distribute

dissiliō, –īre, –uī leap apart; be rent asunder

*dissimulō 1 make unlike; repress one's feelings, dissemble; disguise, conceal

dissociābilis, –e irreconcilable, incompatible

dissuādeō, –ēre, –suāsī, –suāsūrus dissuade

distendō, –ere, –tendī, –tentus stretch out; fill, distend, pack

distentus, –a, –um distended, full

distō, –āre stand apart, be distant; differ

distringō, –ere, –strīnxī, –strictus bind apart; stretch out

dītissimus *see* dīves

*diū *adv.* long, for a long time

dīva, –ae *f.* goddess

dīvellō, –ere, –vellī, –vulsus rend asunder, tear in pieces; tear apart, tear away; separate

dīverberō 1 strike asunder; cut asunder, cleave

*dīversus, –a, –um diverse, different, various, divers; in different directions; distant, remote

*dīves, dīvitis *or* dīs, dītis rich, wealthy, abounding in

*dīvidō, –ere, –vīsī, –vīsus divide, part, separate; distribute, turn in different directions

*dīvīnus, –a, –um divine, sacred, heavenly; inspired, prophetic

*dīvitiae, –ārum *f. pl.* riches, wealth

*dīvus, –a, –um divine; *as noun,* dīvus, –ī, *m.* god

*dō, dare, dedī, datus give, bestow, assign, offer, appoint, expose; grant, permit, vouchsafe; put, place, throw, fling; make, spread, shed; produce, emit, utter; *with* vēla *or* lintea, spread *or* make sail, set sail

*doceō, –ēre, –uī, doctus teach; show, tell, explain

doctus, –a, –um learned, wise, lettered

Dōdōnaeus, –a, –um of Dodona, *a town in Epirus*

*doleō 2 be pained, suffer, smart; grieve

dōlium, –ī *n.* jar

Dolopes, –um *m. pl. a people of Thessaly*

†dolor, –ōris *m.* pain, pang, suffering, anguish; grief, sorrow; indignation, resentment

dolōsus, –a, –um tricky

*dolus, –ī *m.* deceit, guile, craft, wile; plot, treachery, fraud, crime

domina, –ae *f.* mistress, wife, queen

†dominor, –ārī, –ātus be lord, rule, reign

*dominus, –ī *m.* lord, master, tyrant; husband

domitor, –ōris *m.* tamer, ruler

*domō, –āre, –uī, –itus tame, master, subdue, vanquish

*domus, –ūs *f.* house, palace; habitation, home, abode; household; race, line

*dōnec *conj.* until

*dōnō 1 present, give, reward, bestow

*dōnum, –ī *n.* gift, offering; prize, reward

Donȳsa, –ae *f. a small island in the Aegean Sea*

Dōricus, –a, –um Doric; Grecian

dormiō 4 sleep, spend in sleep

dorsum, –ī *n.* back; ridge, reef, ledge

Doryclus, –ī *m. a comrade of Aeneas*

dōs, dōtis *f.* dowry, endowment

dōtālis, –e belonging to a dowry; as a dowry

dracō, –ōnis *m.* serpent; dragon

Drepanum, –ī *n. a town on the western coast of Sicily*

Drūsus, –ī *m. a Roman family name*

Dryopes, –um *m. pl. a people of Epirus*

*dubitō 1 be in doubt, doubt, question; hesitate

*dubius, –a, –um doubtful, uncertain, hesitating; wavering, vacillating, irresolute; critical, perilous, hazardous

*dūcō, –ere, dūxī, ductus lead, lead away,

guide, conduct, bring; trace, build; draw
out, choose, derive; prolong, spend, waste;
think; *pass.* be sprung from
**ductor,** –ōris *m.* leader
**\*dūdum** *adv.* long ago; formerly; lately, re-
cently, but now
**\*dulcis,** –e sweet, fragrant; fresh; dear, be-
loved; pleasant, delightful, charming
**Dūlichium,** –ī *n. an island near Ithaca*
**\*dum** *conj.* while, as long as, so long as; until
**dūmōsus,** –a, –um full of thorn bushes, bushy
**dūmus,** –ī *m.* bramble, brier, thicket
**\*duo,** –ae, –o two
**\*duplex,** –icis two, twofold, double; both
**duplicō** 1 bend double
**dūritiēs,** –ēī *f.* hardness
**dūrō** 1 make hard; be firm, endure, persevere
**\*dūrus,** –a, –um hard, unyielding; rough,
dangerous, raw, bitter, cruel, unfeeling, stern;
long-suffering, patient, toilworn; sturdy,
hardy
**\*dux, ducis** *m.* leader, guide; chieftain, king
**Dymās,** –antis *m. a Trojan warrior*

# E

**\*ē** *see* **ex**
**\*ebur,** –oris *n.* ivory
**eburnus,** –a, –um of ivory
**\*ecce** *interj.* lo! behold!
**\*ecquī, ecqua, ecquod** *indef. interrog. adj.* any?
**ecquid** *adv.* anything at all? any at all?
**edāx,** –ācis eating, consuming, devouring,
greedy
**ēdīcō,** –ere, –dīxī, –dictus proclaim; order,
command, bid
**ēdisserō,** –ere, –uī, –tus set forth, explain, re-
late, tell
**\*edō, ēsse (edere),** ēdī, ēsus eat, consume, de-
vour
**ēdoceō,** –ēre, –uī, -doctus teach, inform
(*in detail*)
**ēdūcō,** –ere, –dūxī, –ductus lead forth *or* out;
bring forth, bear; raise up, build up; erect;
forge
**\*efferō, efferre, extulī, ēlātus** carry out *or* away,
bring out, take out; draw; put forth, dis-
play; lift up, raise, elevate; *with* **pedem** *or*
**gressum,** go forth, depart
**efferus,** –a, –um wild, frenzied, furious, savage
**effētus,** –a, –um worn out, exhausted
**\*efficiō,** –ere, –fēcī, –fectus make, form
**effigiēs,** –ēī *f.* effigy, image, statue; copy,
likeness

**effingō,** –ere, –fīnxī, –fictus form, fashion; por-
tray, represent
**efflō** 1 blow forth, breathe out
**effodiō,** –ere, –fōdī, –fossus dig out, excavate,
dredge; dig up; gouge out, bore out
**effor,** –ārī, –ātus speak out, say, speak, utter;
tell
**effringō,** –ere, -frēgī, –frāctus break out, dash out
**†effugiō,** –ere, –fūgī flee, escape; speed along;
shun
**effugium,** –ī *n.* flight, escape
**effulgeō,** –ēre, –sī shine forth, glitter, gleam
**effundō,** –ere, –fūdī, –fūsus pour out, pour
forth; shed; lose, waste; utter; let loose,
slacken
**effūsus,** –a, –um poured out; spread out; scat-
tered, disheveled, dissolved; headlong, in
headlong haste
**egēns,** –entis in want, needy; wanting, desirous
of; *as noun, m.* beggar
**egēnus,** –a, –um needy, destitute, poor
**\*egeō,** –ēre, –uī be in need; need, require
**egestās,** –ātis *f.* poverty, want
**\*ego, meī** I
**ēgredior,** –ī, –gressus step forth, go *or* come
out; disembark, land
**\*ēgregius,** –a, –um excellent, distinguished;
noble, illustrious
**ei** *interj.* ah! alas!
**ējectō** 1 cast forth
**ējectus,** –a, –um outcast, wrecked
**ējiciō (ēiciō),** –ere, –jēcī, –jectus cast out; ship-
wreck
**ēlābor,** –ī, –lāpsus glide out *or* away, slip by;
dodge, escape
**ēlegāns,** –antis fine, elegant
**elephantus,** –ī *m.* elephant; ivory
**ēlīdō,** –ere, –līsī, –līsus dash out, dash up
**Ēlis,** –idis *f. a district in the western part of the
Peloponnesus*
**Elissa,** –ae *f. another name of Dido*
**ēloquor,** –loquī, –locūtus speak out; speak, tell
**ēlūdō,** –ere, –lūsī, –lūsus elude, evade
**ēluō,** –ere, –uī, –ūtus wash out; wash away,
cleanse
**Ēlysium,** –ī *n. the abode of the blessed in the
underworld*
**ēmētior,** –īrī, –mēnsus measure out; pass by,
traverse
**ēmicō,** –āre, –micuī spring out, leap forth,
bound forward, dash forward, leap up
**ēmittō,** –ere, –mīsī, –missus send forth; dis-
miss, let loose
**\*emō,** –ere, ēmī, ēmptus buy

ēmoveō, –ēre, –mōvī, –mōtus remove; displace, dispel; upheave

*ēn *interj.* lo! see! behold!

Enceladus, –ī *m.* *a giant*

*enim *postpositive conj.* for; indeed, in truth

ēniteō, –ēre, –uī shine forth, beam

ēnītor, –ī, –nīsus (–nīxus) bring forth, bear, farrow; struggle up

Ennius, –ī *m.* *an early Latin poet*

ēnō 1 swim out; float *or* fly away

*ēnsis, –is *m.* sword, blade; knife

Entellus, –ī *m.* *a Sicilian boxer*

ēnumerō 1 count out; count up, recount, enumerate

*eō, īre, īvī (iī), itūrus go, go forth, come, proceed; rush; resort to, have recourse to

Ēŏus, –a, –um of Dawn; eastern, oriental; *as noun,* Ēŏus, –ī *m.* Dawn, Morning; *one of the horses of the sun-god*

Epēos, –ī *m.* *one of the Greeks before Troy*

Epimēthis, –idis *f.* daughter of Epimetheus, *i.e.,* *Pyrrha*

Ēpīrus, –ī *f.* *a district in the northwestern part of Greece*

*epulae, –ārum *f. pl.* feast, feasting, banquet; food, viands

epulor, –ārī, –ātus feast, banquet

Ēpytidēs, –ae *m.* descendant *or* son of Epytus

Ēpytus, –ī *m.* *a Trojan*

*eques, –itis *m.* horseman, rider, knight

†equester (equestris), –tris, –tre of horsemen

*equidem *adv.* *regularly used with a first person singular verb* indeed, in fact; at least

*equus, –ī *m.* horse, steed

Erebus, –ī *m.* *the god of Darkness;* the underworld

*ergō 1) *adv.* therefore, accordingly, consequently, then; 2) *prep. with gen.* on account of

Ēridanus, –ī *m.* *the Greek name of the River Po*

*ērigō, –ere, –rēxī, –rēctus raise up, cast up; build, erect, raise

Erīnys, –yos *f.* *a Fury;* curse, scourge

Eriphȳlē, –ēs *f.* *the wife of Amphiaraus*

†ēripiō, –ere, –ripuī, –reptus snatch from, tear away; snatch, take away, remove; save, rescue, preserve; hasten

Erōtion, –ī *n.* *a girl's name meaning in Greek "Little Love"*

*errō 1 wander, roam, stray; hover about, linger; go *or* run hither and thither

error, –ōris *m.* wandering; mistake, error; delusion, deception; maze, puzzle

ērubēscō, –ere, –buī blush; blush at, respect

ēructō, –āre belch forth; vomit, cast up

*ērudiō 4 train, teach

ērumpō, –ere, –rūpī, –ruptus burst forth, break through

†ēruō, –ere, ēruī, ērutus tear up, uproot; overthrow, destroy

erus, –ī *m.* lord, master

Erycīnus, –a, –um of Eryx

Erymanthus, –ī *m.* *a mountain in Arcadia*

Eryx, –ycis *m.* *name of* 1) *a mountain in Western Sicily;* 2) *a son of Venus*

esca, –ae *f.* food, bait

*et 1) *adv.* also, too; 2) *conj.* and; †et . . . et *or* –que, both . . . and

*etiam *adv.* also, too, even, likewise; still

*etsī *conj.* even if, though, although

Euadnē, –ēs *f.* *wife of Capaneus, who threw herself upon the funeral pyre of her husband*

Euboïcus, –a, –um of Euboea, *an island in the western part of the Aegean Sea*

euhāns, –antis *partic.* crying "Euan," *a name of Bacchus*

Eumēlus, –ī *m.* *a comrade of Aeneas*

Eumenides, –um *f. pl.* kindly goddesses, *a euphemistic name of the Furies*

Eurōpa, –ae *f.* Europe

Eurōtās, –ae *m.* *a river in Laconia*

Eurōus, –a, –um of Eurus; eastern

Eurus, –ī *m.* the southeast *or* east wind; wind

Euryalus, –ī *m.* *a comrade of Aeneas*

Eurydicē, –ēs *f.* *wife of Orpheus, who died of the bite of a serpent and whom he tried to bring back from the underworld*

Eurypylus, –ī *m.* *one of the Greeks before Troy*

Eurytiōn, –ōnis *m.* *a comrade of Aeneas*

*ēvādō, –ere, –vāsī, –vāsus go forth, come out; pass over, pass by, escape; mount, ascend

ēvānēscō, –ere, –nuī vanish away; vanish, disappear

ēvehō, –ere, –vexī, –vectus carry out; lift up, raise, exalt

ēveniō, –īre, –vēnī, –ventūrus come out; come to pass, happen

†ēventus, –ūs *m.* event, occurrence; fortune

*ēvertō, –ere, –vertī, –versus overturn, upturn; overthrow, destroy, ruin

ēvinciō, –īre, –vīnxī, –vinctus bind; wind around, wreathe

ēvincō, –ere, –vīcī, –victus conquer, overcome, vanquish

ēvocō 1 call forth, summon

ēvolō 1 fly forth

ēvolvō, –ere, –volvī, –volūtus roll forth; unroll, unfold; recount; *with reflexive pronoun,* flow

*ex, ē *prep. with abl.* out of, from; of; since, after; according to; in, on

exaestuō 1 boil, boil up, seethe

exanimātus, –a, –um breathless, terrified

†exanimus, –a, –um *also* exanimis, –e lifeless, breathless; terrified

exārdēscō, –ere, –ārsī, –ārsūrus take fire, be kindled; blaze forth, blaze up

†exaudiō 4 hear, heed

†excēdō, –ere, –cessī, –cessūrus go out, withdraw, depart; leave, disappear

excidium, –ī *n.* destruction, overthrow

excidō, –ere, –cidī fall from; slip away, escape, vanish

excīdō, –ere, –cīdī, –cīsus cut out; hew out, quarry; hollow out, destroy

exciō, –īre, –īvī (–iī), –ītus (–itus) call forth; stir up, arouse, excite

*excipiō, –ere, –cēpī, –ceptus take up, take under one's care; receive, welcome; catch, surprise; foresee, detect; overtake, befall; reply, rejoin

excitō 1 arouse, excite, stir up, call forth; startle

exclāmō 1 cry out, shout

excolō, –ere, –coluī, –cultus cultivate; improve, refine

excubiae, –ārum *f. pl.* watch, guard, sentry, sentinel; watchfire

excūdō, –ere, –cūdī, –cūsus beat out, forge; strike from

†excutiō, –ere, –cussī, –cussus shake from, shake out; dash from; drive out, dislodge; rouse from; beat out; deprive of

exedō, –ere, –ēdī, –ēsus eat out; consume, destroy

*exemplum, –ī *n.* example

exeō, –īre, –iī (–īvī), –itūrus go forth *or* out; elude, avoid

*exerceō, –ēre, –uī, –itus employ, busy, keep busy; occupy; engage in, practice, train; consummate; pursue, harass, torment

*exercitus, –ūs *m.* army; host, band

exhālō 1 breathe out

exhauriō, –īre, –hausī, –haustus drain (*to the dregs*), exhaust; endure, undergo, suffer

exhibeō 2 display

*exigō, –ere, –ēgī, –āctus drive forth, drive out, drive; pass, spend; complete, finish; weigh, ponder, deliberate; investigate, ascertain

*exiguus, –a, –um little, small, scanty, feeble; few

eximō, –ere, –ēmī, –ēmptus take away, remove, banish

exin *or* exinde *adv.* then, next, afterwards

exitiālis, –e deadly, fatal, baneful

*exitium, –ī *n.* destruction, ruin

*exitus, –ūs *m.* egress, outlet; end, termination; result, event, issue

exōdī, –isse, –ōsus hate utterly, detest

exoptō 1 choose out; earnestly desire, long for

exōrdium, –ī *n.* beginning, introduction

exorior, –īrī, –ortus rise, arise

exōrō 1 earnestly entreat, beseech, implore

expallēscō, –ere, –palluī turn pale

*expediō 4 disentangle, extricate; bring forth, fetch out; set forth, explain

expellō, –ere, –pulī, –pulsus drive out, banish; deprive of

expendō, –ere, –pendī, –pēnsus weigh out, pay for; atone for, expiate

*experior, –īrī, –pertus try, make trial of, experience

expers, –tis having no part in

expleō, –ēre, –ēvī, –ētus fill out, fill up, complete; gorge, satisfy

explicō 1 unfold; set forth, describe

*explōrō 1 find out, search out, examine thoroughly, explore, investigate

*expōnō, –ere, –posuī, –positus put forth; set ashore, land

exposcō, –ere, –poposcī entreat, implore

exprōmō, –prōmere, –prōmpsī, –prōmptus bring forth, utter

exquīrō, –ere, –sīvī, –sītus seek out, search for; pray for

exsanguis, –e bloodless, lifeless; pale, wan

exsaturābilis, –e satiable

exscidium, –ī *n.* destruction, ruin; overthrow, downfall

exscindō, –ere, –scidī, –scissus tear out, tear down, tear to pieces; extirpate, destroy

exsecror, –ārī, –ātus curse

†exsequor, –ī, –secūtus follow out; execute, perform

exserō, –ere, –uī, –sertus expose

exsertō, –āre stretch out; thrust forth

exsertus, –a, –um projecting; bare, uncovered

*exsilium, –ī *n.* exile, banishment

*exsistō, –ere, –stitī stand out, arise

exsolvō, –ere, –solvī, –solūtus unbind; release, deliver, free

exsomnis, –e sleepless

exsors, –tis unallotted, special, distinguished; without lot in, deprived of

exspatior, –ārī, –ātus stray aimlessly, spread out, swerve from the track

exspectātus, –a, –um expected, long looked for

*exspectō 1 await, wait for, expect; delay; dally, linger

exspīrō 1 breathe out

*exstinguō, –ere, –stīnxī, –stīnctus put out, blot out, destroy

exstō, –āre stand forth; tower above, overtop

*exstruō, –ere, –strūxī, –strūctus build up, elevate; build, erect

exsul, –ulis m. or f. exile

*exsultō 1 leap up, boil up; throb; exult

exsuperō 1 rise above, rise high, mount above, overtop; pass by

exsurgō, –ere, –surrēxī rise, arise

exta, –ōrum n. pl. entrails, vitals

*extemplō adv. at once, forthwith, immediately

extendō, –ere, –tendī, –tentus stretch out, stretch; prolong, increase

*exterus (exter), –era, –erum outside, outer, foreign; extrēmus, –a, –um furthest, remotest; uttermost, utmost; last, final, extreme

*externus, –a, –um foreign, alien, strange; as noun, externus, –ī m. foreigner, stranger

exterreō 2 affright, terrify, appall; amaze

extorris, –e exiled, banished

*extrā prep. with acc. outside of, without, beyond

*extrēmus, –a, –um see exterus

*exuō, –ere, –uī, –ūtus put off, lay aside; strip, lay bare; free from

exūrō, –ere, –ussī, –ustus burn up, consume; burn out

*exuviae, –ārum f. pl. spoils; relics; skin

## F

Fabius, –ī m. a Roman gentile name

fabricātor, –ōris m. maker, contriver

Fabricius, –ī m. a Roman gentile name

fabricō 1 fashion, build

Fabullus, –ī m. a friend of Catullus

fābulōsus, –a, –um fabulous, celebrated in story

facessō, –ere, –cessīvī (–cessī), –cessītus perform, execute, do with zeal

*faciēs, –ēī f. appearance, aspect; face, countenance, features; sight; shape, form, image, kind

*facilis, –e easy, ready; pleasant, prosperous

*faciō, –ere, fēcī, factus make, do, form, build; execute, perform, fulfill; offer, suppose

†factum, –ī n. deed, act, action; enterprise, transaction

faenerātor, –ōris m. moneylender

faenus, –oris n. interest (on money), money-lending

faex, faecis f. brine (for pickling)

fāgus, –ī f. beech tree

fallāx, –ācis deceitful, treacherous

*fallō, –ere, fefellī, falsus deceive, disappoint; escape the notice of; beguile; violate; counterfeit

†falsus, –a, –um false, groundless, pretended; delusive, deceptive, spurious

falx, falcis f. sickle, pruning knife

*fāma, –ae f. report, rumor, story; good name, reputation; fame, renown; personified, Rumor, Gossip

*famēs, –is f. hunger, famine; thirst, greed; personified, Famine

famula, –ae f. female slave, servant, or attendant

*famulus, –ī m. slave, servant, attendant

fandum, –ī n. that which may be uttered; right

far, farris n. spelt, meal

*fās indecl. n. divine law, divine will, destiny; right, principle of right, obligation; with est, be right, lawful, destined, proper

fascis, –is m. bundle of rods; in pl., fascēs the emblem of authority among the Romans

fastīgium, –ī n. top, summit; roof, battlement; point

fastus, –ūs m. arrogance, disdain

†fātālis, –e fated, destined, appointed; fateful, fatal, destructive

*fateor, –ērī, fassus confess, acknowledge, admit; declare

*fatīgō 1 weary, tire out; worry, trouble, vex, plague; pursue; chide

fatīscō, –ere yawn; gape open

*fātum, –ī n. oracle, decree; fate, destiny; doom, disaster, death

*faux, –cis f. throat, jaws; mouth, entrance

*faveō, –ēre, fāvī, fautūrus be favorable, favor, be kindly; with ōre, speak words of good omen, refrain from words of ill omen, preserve a holy silence

favīlla, –ae f. ashes, embers, cinders

favor, –ōris m. favor, good will

favus, –ī m. honeycomb

*fax, facis f. torch, firebrand; flame, fiery train

fēcundus, –a, –um fertile, fruitful

*fēlīx, –īcis fruitful; happy, blessed, fortunate; gracious, propitious, auspicious

*fēmina, –ae f. woman, female

fēmineus, –a, –um of a woman or women, women's

fenestra, –ae f. window, opening; breach

fera, –ae *f.* wild beast, wild creature

fērālis, –e funereal, dismal, mournful

*ferē *adv.* about, nearly, almost; generally

feretrum, –ī *n.* bier

ferīna, –ae *f.* flesh of a wild animal; venison, game

*feriō, –īre strike, lash, beat; cut, slay

*ferō, ferre, tulī, lātus bear, carry, bring, wear; bear along, waft; endure; give birth to; tend, turn; offer, present, grant; destroy; be favorable, exalt; extol; bring word, report, say, boast, interpret; *with a reflexive, or the passive used as a middle,* advance, proceed; arise; rush; ride, sail

*ferōx, –ōcis bold, warlike, fierce, savage; haughty; fiery; spirited

ferrātus, –a, –um iron-shod

†ferreus, –a, –um of iron, iron

ferrūgineus, –a, –um iron-colored; dusky, rusty, dingy

*ferrum, –ī *n.* iron, steel; sword; arrow; ax

*ferus, –a, –um wild, savage, cruel; *as noun,* ferus, –ī *m.* wild beast, wild creature; horse

*ferveō, –ēre, –vī (–buī) (*also* fervō, –ere, fervī) boil, be hot; seethe, teem; be aglow, be alive

fervor, –ōris *m.* heat

†fessus, –a, –um weary, tired, worn, spent; storm-tossed, shattered

festīnō 1 make haste, hasten, quicken; hasten to perform

fēstus, –a, –um festal, festive

fētus, –a, –um pregnant, big with, teeming with; ovis fēta ewe, mother sheep

fētus, –ūs *m.* offspring, young, progeny; brood, litter; branch, growth

fibra, –ae *f.* fibre; *any vital organ*

fībula, –ae *f.* buckle, clasp, brooch

fictus, –a, –um false, feigned; *as noun,* fictum, –ī *n.* falsehood

Fidēna, –ae *f. a town of Latium*

fīdēns, –entis confident, bold

*fidēs, –eī *f.* faith, confidence, trust; belief, assurance; honor, honesty; pledge; *personified,* Good Faith, Honor

fidēs, –ium *f. pl.* lute, lyre, harp

fīdō, –ere, fīsus *semi-dep.* trust, have confidence in; dare, venture

*fīdūcia, –ae *f.* confidence, reliance

*fīdus, –a, –um faithful, loyal, devoted, trusty, trustworthy; safe, assuring

*fīgō, –ere, fixī, fixus fix, fasten, hang up; imprint, plant; pierce, transfix; set up, make

figūra, –ae *f.* form, figure

†filia, –ae *f.* daughter

*fīlius, –ī *m.* son

filum, –ī *n.* thread

fimus, –ī *m.* dung; mud, mire, filth

findō, –ere, fidī, fissus cleave, split; divide

*fingō, –ere, finxī, fictus form, fashion, make up, make; mould, shape; train, arrange; subdue, control; devise, invent; imagine

*fīnis, –is *m. (occasionally f.)* end, limit, termination; boundary, border, frontier, territory; starting point, goal

*fīnitimus, –a, –um bordering upon, neighboring; *as noun,* fīnitimus, –ī *m.* neighbor

*fīō, fierī, factus *used as pass. of* faciō, be made, become

firmō 1 make firm; support, steady; confirm, ratify; encourage, reassure

*firmus, –a, –um firm, strong; lasting; steadfast, resolute

fissilis, –e easily split, fissile

fīxus, –a, –um *see* fīgō

Flaccilla, –ae *f. Martial's mother*

flagellum, –ī *n.* whip, lash, scourge

*flāgitō 1 ask insistently, demand

*flagrō 1 burn, blaze; beam, glow

flāmen, –inis *n.* blast, gale, breeze

*flamma, –ae *f.* flame, blaze, fire; firebrand, torch; lightning; passion, love

flammifer, –era, –erum flame-bearing

flammō 1 set on fire, inflame, enkindle; excite

flātus, –ūs *m.* blowing, blast

flāvēns, –entis yellow, golden

*flāvus, –a, –um yellow, golden, auburn; yellowish-green

*flectō, –ere, flexī, flexus bend, turn, guide; move, influence, prevail upon, change

*fleō, –ēre, –ēvī, –ētus weep; lament, bewail

†flētus, –ūs *m.* weeping, tears; wailing, lamentation

flexilis, –e flexible, pliant

*flō 1 blow

*flōreō, –ēre, –uī blossom, bloom

flōreus, –a, –um flowery, blooming

*flōs, –ōris *m.* flower, blossom

flūctuō 1 ebb and flow; toss, surge, seethe

*flūctus, –ūs *m.* wave, billow, surge; water, sea

fluentum, –ī *n.* stream, flood

fluidus, –a, –um fluid, flowing

fluitō 1 flow; float, drift

*flūmen, –inis *n.* river, stream, flood

*fluō, –ere, flūxī, flūxūrus flow, stream; drip; ebb, pass away

fluviālis, –e of a river, river (*as adj.*)

*fluvius, –ī *m.* river, stream

focus, –ī *m.* hearth; altar; fireside, home

*fodiō, –ere, fōdī, fossus dig; prick, goad

foedē adv. foully, basely

foedō 1 befoul, pollute, defile; disfigure, mutilate, wound

*foedus, –a, –um foul, filthy; loathsome, dreadful

*foedus, –eris n. league, alliance, compact, treaty; truce; plan, principle

*folium, –ī n. leaf

fōmes, –itis m. tinder, kindling wood

*fōns, fontis m. spring, fountain; lake, river; water; source

*for, fārī, fātus say, speak, tell, utter

fore, forem see sum

*foris, –is f. door, gate; pl. doors, entrance

*fōrma, –ae f. form, shape, figure; appearance, beauty; kind

formīca, –ae f. ant

formīdō 1 dread

*formīdō, –inis f. fear, terror, dread

fōrmōsus, –a, –um beautiful, comely, handsome

fornix, –icis m. arch, vault

*fors (fortis) f. chance; abl. forte as adv., by chance, perchance, perhaps, haply

forsan, forsitan adv. perhaps, perchance, mayhap

*fortis, –e brave, valiant, stouthearted, gallant, dauntless; sturdy, stalwart

fortiter adv. boldly, manfully

*fortūna, –ae f. fortune, chance, fate, luck; good fortune; ill fortune, misfortune

fortūnātus, –a, –um fortunate, happy, blessed

*forum, –ī n. forum; court of justice

forus, –ī m. hatch, gangway (of a ship)

*fossa, –ae f. ditch

*foveō, –ēre, fōvī, fōtus cherish, foster, worship; fondle, caress; cherish a hope or purpose

frāctus, –a, –um broken, crushed, shattered

frāga, –ōrum n. pl. strawberries

fragilis, –e frail

fragor, –ōris m. crash, din, roar, uproar; applause

fragrāns, –antis sweet-scented, fragrant

*frangō, –ere, frēgī, frāctus break, dash to pieces; crush, bruise; baffle

*frāter, frātris m. brother

frāternus, –a, –um of a brother, brother's; brotherly, fraternal; friendly

fraudō 1 cheat, defraud

*fraus, fraudis f. deceit, deception, treachery

fraxineus, –a, –um of ash wood, ashen

fremitus, –ūs m. din, uproar; turmoil

*fremō, –ere, –uī roar, shriek, howl; resound, reëcho; applaud, shout (assent); be clamorous, bewail

frēnō 1 bridle; curb, check, restrain; govern

*frēnum, –ī n. bridle, bit, rein

*frequēns, –entis in large numbers, in throngs

frequentō 1 throng, haunt, frequent

*fretum, –ī n. strait; sea, waters

*frētus, –a, –um (with abl.) supported by; relying upon, depending upon

frīgeō, –ēre be cold; be stiff in death; be torpid

frīgidus, –a, –um cold, chill, frosty, wintry

*frīgus, –oris n. cold, frost, chill

frondātor, –ōris m. pruner of trees; foliage gatherer

frondēns, –entis leafy

frondeō, –ēre put forth leaves

frondēscō, –ere put forth leaves

frondeus, –a, –um leafy

frondōsus, –a, –um leafy

*frōns, frondis f. leaf, foliage; wreath, garland, chaplet

*frōns, frontis f. forehead, brow; countenance; prow, front

Frontō, –ōnis m. Martial's father

*frūctus, –ūs m. enjoyment; produce

*frūmentum, –ī n. grain, kernel of grain

*fruor, –ī, frūctus enjoy

*frūstrā adv. in vain, to no purpose, uselessly

frūstror, –ārī, –ātus disappoint; fail

frūstum, –ī n. bit, piece

frutex, –icis m. shrub, bush

frūx, frūgis f. fruit, grain; meal; cake

fūcus, –ī m. drone

*fuga, –ae f. flight, departure; exile; swift course, speed

*fugiō, –ere, fūgī, fugitūrus flee, flee from, hasten away, fly; recede; shun, avoid, escape

fugō 1 put to flight, drive away, banish

fulciō, –īre, fulsī, fultus prop up, sustain, support

fulcrum, –ī n. prop, support; leg of a couch

*fulgeō, –ēre, fulsī (also fūlgō, –ere, –sī) gleam, glitter, flash

fulgor, –ōris m. gleam, glitter, brightness, splendor

*fulmen, –inis n. lightning, thunderbolt

fulmineus, –a, –um like lightning, flashing

*fulvus, –a, –um yellow, tawny

fūmeus, –a, –um smoky

fūmō, –āre smoke, reek

*fūmus, –ī m. smoke

fūnāle, –is n. taper, torch

fundāmentum, –ī n. foundation

funditus adv. from the bottom, entirely, completely

fundō 1 found; organize; hold fast, secure

*fundō, –ere, fūdī, fūsus pour, pour out, pour forth; put to flight, rout; lay low, bring down, slay

fundus, –ī m. bottom, depth

fūnereus, –a, –um funeral, deadly, fatal

fungor, fungī, fūnctus perform, discharge

*fūnis, –is m. rope, cord, cable, hawser

*fūnus, –eris n. funeral rites, obsequies, funeral; murder, death; disaster; corpse

fūr, fūris m. or f. thief

furca, –ae f. fork, forked pole

*furiae, –ārum f. pl. madness, frenzy; remorse; personified, the Furies

furibundus, –a, –um mad, frantic, frenzied

furiō 1 madden, infuriate

*furō, –ere, –uī rave, rage, be mad, wild or frantic; seethe; roam wildly; be inspired

†furor, –ōris m. madness, frenzy, rage; passion; hatred, feud; personified, Rage

fūror, –ārī, –ātus steal away, withdraw

fūrtim adv. by stealth, secretly

fūrtīvus, –a, –um secret, stolen, hidden

*fūrtum, –ī n. theft; stealth, artifice, deceit

Fuscus, –ī m. a friend of Horace

fūsus, –a, –um poured out; extended, stretched out

futūrus, –a, –um coming, future, to be; as noun, futūrum, –ī n. future

## G

Gabiī, –ōrum m. pl. an ancient town in Latium

Gaetūlus, –a, –um of the Gaetuli, a tribe in Northern Africa

*galea, –ae f. helmet

Gallus, –a, –um of Gaul; as noun, Gallus, –ī m. a Gaul

Ganymēdēs, –is m. a Trojan prince, carried away by an eagle and made Jupiter's cup-bearer

Garamantes, –um m. pl. a tribe in the interior of Africa

Garamantis, –idis of the Garamantes

Gargiliānus, –ī m. a man's name

garriō 4 chatter

*gaudeō, –ēre, gāvīsus semi-dep. rejoice, delight in

†gaudium, –ī n. joy, gladness, delight

gaza, –ae f. wealth, riches, treasure

Gelā, –ae f. a town on the southern coast of Sicily

*gelidus, –a, –um cold, icy, chilly; clammy; torpid, sluggish

Gelōus, –a, –um of Gela

*geminus, –a, –um twin; twofold, double; both; two

†gemitus, –ūs m. groan, sigh, moan; lamentation, wailing; roar, howl of rage

gemma, –ae f. gem, jewel, precious stone

*gemō, –ere, –uī, –itus groan, sigh, wail; lament, sigh over, bewail; croak

gena, –ae f. cheek

*gener, –erī m. son-in-law

generātor, –ōris m. breeder

generō 1 beget

genetrīx, –īcis f. mother

geniālis, –e agreeable to one's Genius; cheerful, joyous, festive

*genitor, –ōris m. father, sire

genitus, –a, –um born of; descended from

genius, –ī m. tutelary divinity, divine guardian

*gēns, gentis f. clan, race, tribe; brood, swarm; people, nation

*genū, –ūs n. knee

*genus, –eris n. origin, descent, lineage; race, stock, family, nation, people; offspring, descendant; kind, species

germāna, –ae f. sister

germānus, –ī m. brother

*germānus, –a, –um having the same parents or parent

*gerō, –ere, gessī, gestus carry, bear, wear, possess; carry on, wage

gestāmen, –inis n. something borne; equipment, weapon

gestō 1 bear, wear, carry; possess

Geticus, –a, –um of the Getae, a tribe in Thrace

Gigās, –antis m. giant, son of Tartarus and Earth

*gignō, –ere, genuī, genitus bear, bring forth, beget

glaciālis, –e icy

glaciēs, –ēī f. ice

glaeba, –ae f. clod, soil

glaucus, –a, –um bluish-green, gray

Glaucus, –ī m. name of 1) a Boeotian fisherman who was changed into a sea-god; 2) a Lycian ally of the Trojans

globus, –ī m. ball, sphere

*glomerō 1 roll into a ball; roll up, gather, collect

*glōria, –ae f. fame, renown, glory; pride, ambition

glōrior, –ārī, –ātus boast of, take pride in (with abl.)

gnātus, –ī m. son

Gnōsius, –a, –um of Gnosus, a city in Crete; Cretan

Gorgō, –onis f. a Gorgon

**Gracchus, –ī** m. a Roman family name
**\*gradior, –ī, gressus** walk, step forward, stride forward, advance, proceed
**Gradīvus, –ī** m. another name for Mars
**\*gradus, –ūs** m. step, stride; pace; step (of a ladder or stairs)
**Grajus, –a, –um** Greek, Grecian; as noun, **Grajus, –ī** m. a Greek
**Grajugena, –ae** m. a Greek by birth; a Greek
**\*grāmen, –inis** n. grass, herb, herbage
**grāmineus, –a, –um** grassy
**grandaevus, –a, –um** aged
**grandis, –e** large, huge
**grandō, –inis** f. hail
**grātēs, –ium** f. pl. thanks; requital
**\*grātia, –ae** f. grace, charm; pleasure in, fondness for; thanks, gratitude
**grātor, –ārī, –ātus** congratulate, rejoice with
**\*grātus, –a, –um** pleasing, pleasant, agreeable; welcome
**gravidus, –a, –um** heavy, big with; teeming with, loaded
**\*gravis, –e** heavy, firm, ponderous; heavy with, pregnant; weighty, distinguished, venerable, revered; burdened, feeble, enfeebled; ill; severe, grievous, violent
**†gravitās, –ātis** f. weight
**graviter** adv. heavily, violently; deeply, mightily
**gravō 1** make heavy; burden, oppress, weigh down
**\*gremium, –ī** n. lap, bosom
**†gressus, –ūs** m. walking; step, gait; course, way
**\*grex, gregis** m. flock, herd
**grus, gruis** f. crane
**Grȳnēus, –a, –um** of Grynia, a city in Aeolis, and the site of a temple sacred to Apollo
**gubernāc(u)lum, –ī** n. helm, tiller
**gubernātor, –ōris** m. helmsman, pilot
**\*gurges, –itis** m. whirlpool; abyss, gulf; seething waters, billow, flood; sea, the deep
**gustō 1** taste
**gutta, –ae** f. drop
**guttur, –uris** n. throat, mouth
**Gyaros, –ī** f. an island in the Aegean Sea
**Gyās, –ae** m. a comrade of Aeneas
**gȳrus, –ī** m. circle, fold, coil

# H

**\*habēna, –ae** f. rein
**\*habeō 2** have, hold, possess; regard, consider; treat

**habilis, –e** easily held, light, handy
**\*habitō 1** occupy, inhabit, dwell
**habitus, –ūs** m. appearance, bearing; garb, dress
**hāc** adv. this way; **hāc ... hāc**, here ... there
**hāctenus** adv. thus far, to this point
**Hadria, –ae** f. the Adriatic Sea
**haedus, –ī** m. young goat, kid
**\*haereō, –ēre, haesī, haesūrus** stick, stick fast; cling, be rooted, be fastened, cleave; be fixed, be motionless; pause, linger
**hālitus, –ūs** m. breath, exhalation
**hālō 1** breathe; be fragrant
**Hammōn, –ōnis** m. a Libyan god identified with Jupiter
**hāmus, –ī** m. hook, link
**Hannibal, –alis** m. famous Carthaginian enemy of Rome in the third century B.C.
**\*harēna, –ae** f. sand, sandy shore, strand, beach; earth; arena
**harēnōsus, –a, –um** sandy
**Harpalycē, –ēs** f. a Thracian princess noted as a huntress and a warrior
**Harpyia, –ae** f. a Harpy
**\*harundō, –inis** f. reed; arrow
**\*hasta, –ae** f. spear, lance
**hastīle, –is** n. spear-shaft, spear; shaft, shoot
**\*haud** adv. not, not at all, by no means
**\*hauriō, –īre, hausī, haustus** drink, drain; exhaust; suffer; of sight or sound, drink in
**hebeō, –ēre** be dull, be sluggish
**hebetō 1** blunt, dull; dim, impair
**Hebrus, –ī** m. a river in Thrace
**Hecatē, –ēs** f. a goddess of the underworld, identified not only with Proserpina, but also with Luna in heaven and Diana on earth
**Hector, –oris** m. son of Priam and the greatest champion of Troy
**Hectoreus, –a, –um** of Hector
**Hecuba, –ae** f. wife of Priam
**heia** interj. come! away!
**Helena, –ae** f. the daughter of Jupiter and Leda and the wife of Menelaus
**Helenus, –ī** m. a son of Priam
**Helōrus, –ī** m. a river in Sicily
**Helymus, –ī** m. a Sicilian
**\*herba, –ae** f. grass, herb; herbage, vegetation; turf, sward
**Herculēs, –is** m. a son of Jupiter and Alcmena, renowned for his strength
**Herculeus, –a, –um** of Hercules; founded by Hercules
**hērēs, –ēdis** m. heir
**heri** adv. yesterday

**Hermionē, –ēs** *f. the daughter of Menelaus and Helen*

***hērōs, –ōis** m.* hero

**Hesperiă, –ae** *f.* Western Land; *i.e., Italy*

**Hesperides, –um** *f. pl.* daughters of Hesperus, *keepers of the garden of golden apples*

**Hesperius, –a, –um** western, Hesperian; Italian

***hesternus, –a, –um** of yesterday

***heu** *interj.* alas!

**heus** *interj.* ho!

**hiātus, –ūs** *m.* gaping; opening, yawning mouth

***hīberna, –ōrum** *n. pl.* winter quarters; winter

**hībernus, –a, –um** of winter, wintry, winter's; stormy, tempestuous

***hic, haec, hoc** this, this of mine; **hic . . . hic** this . . . that, the one . . . the other

***hīc** *adv.* here, at this time *or* place; hereupon

***hiems, hiemis** *f.* winter; winter storm, storm, tempest; *personified,* Storm-god

***hinc** *adv.* hence, from this time *or* place, from this source, henceforth; hereupon; **hinc . . . hinc,** on this side . . . on that

**hinnītus, –ūs** *m.* neighing

***hiō** 1 gape, open the mouth

**Hippocoōn, –ontis** *m. a comrade of Aeneas*

**Hippomenēs, –is** *m. suitor of Atalanta*

**hirsūtus, –a, –um** rough, shaggy

**hīscō, –ere** open one's mouth; gasp; falter

**Hispānus, –a, –um** Spanish

***hodiē** *adv.* today

**holus, holeris** *n.* vegetable, *e.g., cabbage*

***homō, –inis** *m. or f.* man, mankind; human being

***honor (honōs), –ōris** *m.* honor, homage, glory; prize, reward; charm, grace; offering, sacrifice, libation; institution, observance

**honōrātus, –a, –um** honored, observed, reserved

***hōra, –ae** *f.* hour; time, moment

**hornus, –a, –um** this year's

**horrendus, –a, –um** dreadful, awful, frightful

**horrēns, –entis** bristling, bristly; rough, shaggy

***horreō, –ēre, horruī** bristle, quiver, shudder; shudder at, dread

**horrēscō, –ere, horruī** shiver, shudder; dread; be thrilled

†**horridus, –a, –um** bristling, shaggy; grim, grisly, awful, dreadful; frightful

**horrificō** 1 terrify, appall

**horrificus, –a, –um** dreadful, frightful

**horrisonus, –a, –um** dread-sounding; of frightful sound; harsh-sounding

**horror, –ōris** *m.* bristling; shudder; horror, dread; frightful din, clash

**hortāmen, –inis** *n.* appeal, plea

**hortātor, –ōris** *m.* encourager; inciter, instigator

***hortor, –ārī, –ātus** encourage, urge, incite

**hortus, –ī** *m.* garden

***hospes, –itis** *m. or f.* guest-friend, host, guest, stranger

**hospita, –ae** *f.* stranger

†**hospitium, –ī** *n.* guest-friendship, friendship; guest-land; hospitality, shelter

**hospitus, –a, –um** strange, foreign

**hostia, –ae** *f.* victim, sacrifice; sacrificial victim

**hostīlis, –e** of an enemy, enemy's

***hostis, –is** *m. or f.* enemy, foe, foeman

***hūc** *adv.* hither, to this place, here; **hūc illūc** hither and thither

***hūmānus, –a, –um** human, of man *or* mankind

***humilis, –e** low, low-lying

**humō** 1 bury, inter

***humus, –ī** *f.* ground, earth

**Hyades, –um** *f. pl. a group of seven stars in the constellation Taurus*

**Hyblaeus, –a, –um** Hyblaean, of Mt. Hybla *in Sicily*

**Hydaspes, –is** *m. a river in India*

**hydra, –ae** *f.* a water serpent; *a monster in the underworld*

***Hymenaeus, –ī** *m.* the god of Marriage; marriage, wedlock, nuptials

**Hypanis, –is** *m. a Trojan*

**Hyperboreus, –a, –um** northern

**Hyrcānus, –a, –um** of the Hyrcani, *a people near the Caspian Sea*

**Hyrtacidēs, –ae** *m.* descendant of Hyrtacus; son of Hyrtacus

## I

**Iāpyx, –gis** *m. (acc. –ga) a west wind*

**Iarbās, –ae** *m. king of the Gaetuli*

**Iasidēs, –ae** *m.* descendant of Iāsius

**Iasius, –ī** *m. a son of Jupiter and Electra and brother of Dardanus*

**iaspis, –idis** *f.* jasper

***ibī** *adv.* in that place, there; thereupon

**ibīdem** *adv.* in the same place

**Īcarus, –ī** *m. a son of Daedalus, who, in the flight from Crete, fell into the sea*

**īcō, –ere, īcī, ictus** strike, smite

***ictus, –ūs** *m.* blow, stroke, thrust

**Īda, –ae** *f. name of a mountain,* 1) *in Crete;* 2) *near Troy*

**Īdaeus, –a, –um** of Ida

Īdaeus, –ī m. a charioteer of Priam

Īdalia, –ae f. and Īdalium, –ī n. a town and grove in Cyprus, sacred to Venus

Īdalius, –a, –um of Idalia

*idcircō adv. for that reason, therefore

*īdem, eadem, idem the same; likewise, also

ideō adv. for that reason

Īdomeneus, –eī m. a king of Crete and leader of the Cretans in the Trojan War

*Īdūs, Īduum f. pl. Ides, mid-month day for settling accounts

*igitur conj. therefore, then

*ignārus, –a, –um not knowing, ignorant, unaware; unacquainted, inexperienced

ignāvus, –a, –um lazy, slothful, idle

igneus, –a, –um fiery; glowing, gleaming

*ignis, –is m. fire, flame, light; firebrand; lightning; star; love, passion, fury, wrath

ignōbilis, –e common, mean, low-born, base

*ignōrō 1 be ignorant of, not know

*ignōscō, –ere, –nōvī, –nōtus pardon, forgive

*ignōtus, –a, –um unknown, strange; as noun, ignōtus, –ī m. a stranger

*īlex, –icis f. holm oak; oak

Īlia, –ae f. another name for Rhea Silvia, mother of Romulus and Remus

īlia, –ium n. pl. loins

Īliacus, –a, –um of Ilium, Trojan

Īlias, –adis f. a Trojan woman

īlicet adv. at once, straightway, forthwith

Īlionē, –ēs f. eldest daughter of Priam

Īlioneus, –eī m. a comrade of Aeneas

Īlium, –ī n. another name for Troy

Īlius, –a, –um of Ilium; Trojan

illāc adv. (by) that way

*ille, –a, –ud that yonder; he, she, it; that famous; the following

illīc adv. there, in that place

illinc adv. from that side, on that side

illūc adv. thither, in that direction

Īllyricus, –a, –um of Illyria, a region east of the Adriatic Sea

Īlus, –ī m. name 1) of an early king of Troy; 2) of Ascanius before the fall of Troy

*imāgō, –inis f. likeness, image; appearance, semblance; picture, conception; shade, phantom; form, shape

imbellis, –e unwarlike, feeble

*imber, –bris m. rain, rain cloud, storm; water, flood

imbuō, –ere, –uī, –ūtus tinge, stain

imitābilis, –e that may be imitated, imitable

imitor, –ārī, –ātus imitate, counterfeit

immadēscō, –ere, –duī become wet

*immānis, –e monstrous, dreadful, savage, cruel, atrocious; huge, vast, mighty

immemor, –oris unmindful, forgetful; heedless

†immēnsus, –a, –um unmeasured, boundless; huge, mighty, prodigious

immergō, –ere, –mersī, –mersus plunge into, drown

immeritus, –a, –um undeserving, unoffending

*immineō, –ēre overhang; threaten

immisceō, –ēre, –miscuī, –mixtus mix in, mingle with; with reflexive or the passive used as a middle, vanish into

immītis, –e cruel, merciless, fierce, ruthless, harsh, relentless

*immittō, –ere, –mīsī, –missus send into; drive to, bring upon; let go, let fly; let grow; with a reflexive or the passive used as a middle, rush into, dash in

*immō adv. nay rather, nay more

immorior, –ī, –mortuus die upon (with dat.)

†immortālis, –e undying

immōtus, –a, –um unmoved, unshaken, motionless, undisturbed, fixed, steadfast, unchangeable

immūgiō, –īre, –īvī (–iī) bellow within, roar, resound

immundus, –a, –um unclean, foul, filthy

immūnis, –e free from, exempt from (with gen.)

impār, –aris unequal, ill-matched

*impediō 4 entangle, obstruct; involve, interweave

†impellō, –ere, –pulī, –pulsus strike against, strike, smite; hurl upon, urge on, drive forward; set in motion; ply; compel, impel, drive

imperiōsus, –a, –um imperious, domineering

*imperium, –ī n. order, command, behest, mandate; power, sway, dominion, authority, mastery; empire, realms

*imperō 1 order, command

*impetus, –ūs m. attack, assault; violence, momentum

impiger, –gra, –grum quick, eager, nothing loath

impingō, –ere, –pēgī, –pāctus dash against, hurl against

impius, –a, –um unnatural, undutiful, wicked, godless; accursed, impious

implācātus, –a, –um unappeased, insatiate

implectō, –ere, –plexī, –plexus entwine, twist into

impleō, –ēre, –plēvī, –plētus fill, satisfy; passive used as a middle, take one's fill

*implicō, –āre, –āvī (–uī), –ātus (–itus) enfold;

entwine; infuse; *with reflexive,* cling to, clasp, grasp

implōrō 1 beseech, entreat

implūmis, –e without feathers, unfledged

†impōnō, –ere, –posuī, –positus place upon, lay upon; put; set over, impose

impotēns, –entis unbridled, unrestrained

imprecor, –ārī, –ātus pray (*against*)

imprimō, –ere, –pressī, –pressus press upon *or* into; stamp, engrave, chase

*improbus, –a, –um wicked, malicious, shameless, wanton, mischievous; ravenous

imprōvidus, –a, –um unforeseeing, heedless

imprōvīsus, –a, –um unforeseen, unexpected

impūbēs, –is beardless, youthful

impūne *adv.* without punishment, with impunity

*īmus *see* īnferus

*in *prep.:* 1) *with acc.,* into, to; upon, on; against, toward; for; among; 2) *with abl.,* in, on, upon, among; in case of

inaequālis, –e unequal, changeable

inamābilis, –e unlovely, hateful

*inānis, –e empty, vacant; vain, useless, fruitless, meaningless; unsubstantial, ghostly, phantom

inarātus, –a, –um unplowed

incalēscō, –ere, –caluī grow hot

incānus, –a, –um gray, hoary

incassum *adv.* in vain

incautus, –a, –um careless, off one's guard

†incēdō, –ere, –cessī, –cessūrus move on, proceed, walk along, advance; walk (*with dignity*); *sometimes nearly equivalent to* sum

†incendium, –ī *n.* fire, flame

*incendō, –ere, –cendī, –cēnsus cause to shine, make bright; set fire to, kindle; inflame, excite, enrage

inceptum, –ī *n.* beginning, undertaking, attempt; resolution, purpose

incertus, –a, –um uncertain, doubtful; indistinct, dim; fickle; ill-aimed

incessus, –ūs *m.* stately walk, gait, carriage

incestō 1 defile, pollute

*incidō, –ere, –cidī fall upon

incīdō, –ere, –cīdī, –cīsus cut into, cut

*incipiō, –ere, –cēpī, –ceptus begin, attempt

inclēmentia, –ae *f.* severity, cruelty

inclūdō, –ere, –clūsī, –clūsus shut up *or* in, enclose, confine

inclutus, –a, –um famous, renowned, illustrious

incognitus, –a, –um unknown

incohō 1 begin; build, erect

*incolō, –ere, –coluī dwell in, inhabit

*incolumis, –e unharmed, uninjured, safe, unscathed

incomitātus, –a, –um unaccompanied, unattended

inconcessus, –a, –um unpermitted, unlawful

incōnsultus, –a, –um unadvised, without advice

†incrēdibilis, –e incredible, past belief

increpitō 1 rail at, taunt, challenge; chide

increpō, –āre, –uī, –itus rattle; rebuke, challenge

incrēscō, –ere, –ēvī grow upon; shoot up

incubō, –āre, –uī, –itūrus lie upon, rest upon; brood over, hover over; gloat over

incultum, –ī *n.* waste land, wilderness

incultus, –a, –um untilled, uncultivated; uncared for, neglected, unkempt

†incumbō, –ere, –cubuī, –cubitūrus lie upon, rest upon; lean upon, lean over, overhang; fall upon, urge on; bend to, ply; exert oneself

incurrō, –ere, –currī (–cucurrī), –cursūrus run into, charge

incursō 1 run into *or* against

incurvō 1 bend

incūsō 1 blame; chide, reproach, upbraid

incutiō, –ere, –cussī, –cussus strike into, put into

indāgō, –inis *f.* circle (*of hunters or beaters*); toils

*inde *adv.* from that time *or* place, thence; then, next

indēbitus, –a, –um not due, unpromised

indēprēnsus, –a, –um undiscovered, undetected

Indī, –ōrum *m. pl.* people of India, Indians

indicium, –ī *n.* information; testimony, evidence

*indīcō, –ere, –dīxī, –dictus declare, proclaim; appoint, order

indigena, –ae *m. or f.* native

indignor, –ārī, –ātus deem unworthy, deem a disgrace; be indignant, be enraged; fret, chafe

indignus, –a, –um unworthy, undeserved; cruel

indomitus, –a, –um untamed, invincible; fierce, savage

†indūcō, –ere, –dūxī, –ductus lead in, lead on; draw on, put on; induce

indulgeō, –ēre, –dulsī favor, indulge in, give way to, yield to

*induō, –ere, –duī, –dūtus put on, assume; adorn; *passive as middle,* array oneself; *partic.* indūtus, –a, –um clad in, arrayed in

inēluctābilis, –e inevitable

inēmptus, –a, –um unbought

*ineō, –īre, –īvī (–iī), –itus go into, enter; be-gin, undertake

*inermis, –e unarmed, defenseless

iners, –ertis unskilled; lazy, timid, spiritless; lifeless

*inertia, –ae *f.* inactivity

inexpertus, –a, –um untried

inextrīcābilis, –e inextricable

īnfabricātus, –a, –um unwrought, unshaped, rough

īnfāmis, –e of ill report, notorious

īnfandus, –a, –um unutterable, unspeakable; dreadful, detestable, horrible, abominable, iniquitous

īnfāns, –fantis *m. or f.* infant

īnfaustus, –a, –um ill-omened, ill-fated

īnfectus, –a, –um not done, false

īnfectus, –a, –um stained; dyed; ingrained

īnfēlīx, –īcis unhappy, wretched; luckless, un-fortunate, ill-fated, ill-omened

īnfēnsus, –a, –um hostile, unfriendly

īnferiae, –ārum *f. pl.* a sacrifice in honor of the dead, funeral rites

īnfernus, –a, –um of the underworld

†īnferō, –ferre, –tulī, –lātus bring into, carry to; bring against, wage; offer, sacrifice; *with a reflexive or the passive used as a middle,* thread one's way, advance, proceed, follow

†īnferus, –a, –um low, below; *comp.* *īnferior, –ius lower, inferior, humbler; *superl.* *īmus, –a, –um lowest, deepest, inmost; lowest part of, bottom

*īnfestus, –a, –um hostile; threatening, deadly

īnficiō, –ere, –fēcī, –fectus put in, cast upon; make, cast

īnfīgō, –ere, –fīxī, –fīxus fix in *or* upon, impale; implant; fix

īnfindō, –ere, –fidī, –fissus cleave

īnfirmus, –a, –um weak, feeble; docile

infit *defective* begins

īnfitior, –ārī, –ātus deny, repudiate

inflammō 1 set on fire, inflame

īnflectō, –ere, –flexī, –flexus bend; influence, sway, touch

īnflō 1 blow into; fill, swell

īnfōrmis, –e shapeless, misshapen, unsightly, hideous, horrid

īnfrāctus, –a, –um broken, subdued

īnfrendeō, –ēre gnash

īnfrēnus, –a, –um unbridled

īnfula, –ae *f.* headband, fillet

īnfundō, –ere, –fūdī, –fūsus pour on, pour into *or* upon; spread over, permeate; *pass. as middle,* pour into

†ingeminō 1 redouble, repeat; be redoubled, increase

ingemō, –ere, –uī groan, sigh

*ingenium, –ī *n.* nature, character

*ingēns, –tis enormous, huge, vast, massive, mighty, stalwart, great

ingrātus, –a, –um unpleasant, disagreeable; ungrateful, unheeding

†ingredior, –ī, –gressus enter, go, walk, pro-ceed; enter upon, begin; *sometimes nearly equivalent to* sum

ingruō, –ere, –uī rush upon, burst upon, as-sail

inhibeō 2 check, hold back

inhiō 1 gape at; scan, scrutinize, pore over

inhonestus, –a, –um dishonorable, shameful, hideous

inhorreō, –ēre, –uī bristle; grow rough, roughen

inhospitālis, –e inhospitable

inhospitus, –a, –um inhospitable, dangerous

inhumātus, –a, –um unburied

*inimīcus, –a, –um unfriendly, hostile

*inīquus, –a, –um uneven; unfriendly, adverse, hostile, unjust; unhappy; dangerous; bitter

injiciō (iniciō), –ere, –jēcī, –jectus throw upon, hurl against

*injūria, –ae *f.* injustice, wrong, story of wrong; outrage, insult, affront

injussus, –a, –um unbidden

inlābor, –ī, –lāpsus glide into

inlaetābilis, –e joyless, mournful, dismal

inlīdō, –ere, –sī, –sus dash upon

inlūdō, –ere, –sī, –sus make sport of, jeer at, mock (*with dat.*)

*inlūstris, –e famous, illustrious, bright

inluviēs, –ēī *f.* filth, squalor

innectō, –ere, –nexuī, –nexus bind, fasten; in-vent, devise

innō 1 swim in, float upon, sail upon

innocuus, –a, –um harmless, innocent

innoxius, –a, –um harmless

innubus, –a, –um unwed, unmarried

innumerābilis, –e unnumbered, endless

innumerus, –a, –um numberless, countless

innūptus, –a, –um unwed, unmarried, virgin

inolēscō, –ere, –olēvī, –olitūrus grow in, be in-grained; become ingrained in

inopīnus, –a, –um unexpected

inops, –opis without resources, poor; helpless, bereft of

Īnōus, –a, –um descended from Ino, *who threw herself into the sea and was made a sea-goddess*

*inquam, inquit *defective* say

inquīrō, –ere, –quīsīvī, –quīsītus seek, inquire

inremeābilis, −e irretraceable, allowing no return

inrīdeō, −ēre, −rīsi, −rīsus laugh at, mock

inrigō 1 water, bedew; diffuse

inrītāmentum, −ī n. incitement, inducement

inrītō 1 vex, provoke

inritus, −a, −um useless, unavailing

inrumpō, −ere, −rūpī, −ruptus break in, burst in

inruō, −ere, −uī rush into, rush upon, attack

īnsānia, −ae f. madness, folly

īnsānus, −a, −um insane, mad, frantic, foolish; inspired

†īnscius, −a, −um not knowing, unaware, unwitting, ignorant; bewildered

īnscrībō, −ere, −scrīpsī, −scrīptus write upon, mark, inscribe

†īnsequor, −ī, −secūtus follow, pursue; ensue, harass; attempt

īnserō, −ere, −seruī, −sertus put into, insert, plant into, graft

īnsertō 1 thrust into, insert

īnsideō, −ēre, −sēdī sit down upon, take possession of, occupy

*īnsidiae, −ārum f. pl. ambush; snare, wile, deceit, artifice

īnsīdō, −ere, −sēdī, −sessus sit upon, sit down on, rest upon; settle upon; take possession of

*īnsigne, −is n. badge, ornament, adornment, decoration, device, mark

*īnsignis, −e notable, distinguished, conspicuous, renowned, eminent, marked; splendid, brilliant

īnsinuō 1 wind in, steal in

īnsistō, −ere, −stitī set foot upon, tread upon; enter upon, begin, press on

īnsitīvus, −a, −um grafted

īnsomnium, −ī n. dream

īnsonō, −āre, −uī sound, resound; crack

†īnsōns, −ontis guiltless, innocent, unoffending

īnspērātus, −a, −um unhoped for

īnspiciō, −ere, −spexī, −spectus look into or upon

īnspīrō 1 breathe into, inspire; kindle

īnstabilis, −e unstable, unsteady

īnstar n. indecl. equality, model, likeness, ideal, majesty; as adj., as large as (with gen.)

īnstaurō 1 renew, begin anew, restore; repeat, requite, repay

īnsternō, −ere, −strāvī, −strātus spread over, cover

īnstīgō 1 spur on, urge on, incite

*īnstituō, −ere, −uī, −ūtus build, found; establish, ordain

*īnstō, −āre, −stitī, −stātūrus stand on; press on, pursue; persist; be eager; be one's purpose

*īnstruō, −ere, −strūxī, −strūctus build; furnish, equip, bedeck, fit out; train; draw up, arrange, array

īnsuētus, −a, −um unaccustomed, unwonted, strange, unfamiliar

*īnsula, −ae f. isle, island

īnsultō 1 leap upon, dance upon; be insolent, insult, revile

īnsum, inesse, īnfuī, īnfutūrus be in or on, be present

īnsuō, −ere, −suī, −sūtus sew in

īnsuper adv. above, over; in addition, moreover

īnsuperābilis, −e invincible, unconquerable

īnsurgō, −ere, −surrēxī, −surrēctūrus rise upon, rise; with rēmīs, ply vigorously

intāctus, −a, −um untouched, unyoked; chaste, virgin; unwed

*integer, −gra, −grum untouched, unimpaired

integrō 1 begin anew, renew

intemerātus, −a, −um unsullied, inviolate, pure

intempestus, −a, −um unseasonable; gloomy, murky

intemptātus, −a, −um untried

*intendō, −ere, −tendī, −tentus stretch upon, stretch, swell; spread, cover, hang; partic. intentus, −a, −um stretched; attentive, eager

intentō 1 stretch out, hold out; threaten

*inter prep. with acc. between, among, amid, betwixt

*interclūdō, −ere, −clūsī, −clūsus shut off, cut off, prevent

*interdum adv. sometimes, at times, occasionally

*intereā adv. in the meantime, meanwhile

*intereō, −īre, −īvī (−iī), −itūrus perish

interfor, −ārī, −ātus interrupt

interfundō, −ere, −fūdī, −fūsus pour between, flow between

*interim adv. meantime

*interior, −ius inner, inside, on the inside; interior of; superl. intimus, −a, −um inmost, furthest

interluō, −ere flow between, wash

interpres, −pretis m. or f. intermediary, interpreter, representative; author, cause

interritus, −a, −um unterrified, fearless, undaunted, unafraid

†interrogō 1 ask

interruptus, −a, −um broken off, discontinued, interrupted

*intervāllum, -ī *n.* distance, interval

intexō, -ere, -texuī, -textus weave in, interlace, embroider, intertwine, interweave

intibum, -ī *n.* endive

intimus, -a, -um (*superl. of* interior) inmost, innermost

intonō, -āre, -tonuī thunder

intorqueō, -ēre, -torsī, -tortus twist upon; hurl against

*intrā *prep. with acc.* within

intractābilis, -e unmanageable, invincible

intremō, -ere, -uī tremble, shake, quake, quiver

*intrō 1 go into, enter

intrōgredior, -ī, -gressus step into, enter

*intus *adv.* on the inside, within

inultus, -a, -um unavenged

inūtilis, -e useless

Inuus, -ī *m. another name for Faunus;* Castrum Inuī, *see* Castrum

†invādō, -ere, -vāsī, -vāsus go into, enter, rush into, attack; enter upon, invade; accost, assail

invalidus, -a, -um weak, feeble, infirm, powerless

invehō, -ere, -vexī, -vectus bear, carry; *pass.* be borne, ride, sail

*inveniō, -īre, -vēnī, -ventus come upon, find, find out, discover

inventor, -ōris *m.* finder, contriver, deviser

invergō, -ere pour upon

invertō, -ere, -ī, -sus invert; turn end for end

invictus, -a, -um unconquered, unconquerable, resistless

*invideō, -ēre, -vīdī, -vīsus envy, grudge, begrudge, look askance at

*invidia, -ae *f.* envy, jealousy; grudge, hatred

invidiōsus, -a, -um envied

invidus, -a, -um envious, grudging

invīsō, -ere, -vīsī, -vīsus go to see, visit

invīsus, -a, -um hated, detested, hateful

invītō 1 invite, summon; tempt, incite

*invītus, -a, -um unwilling, reluctant; unfriendly

invius, -a, -um pathless, impassable, inaccessible

invocō 1 call upon

involvō, -ere, -volvī, -volūtus roll upon; wrap, envelop, involve; overwhelm

Īonius, -a, -um Ionian; *as noun,* Īonium, -ī *n.* the Ionian Sea, *south and east of lower Italy*

Īopās, -ae *m. a Carthaginian minstrel*

Īphitus, -ī *m. a Trojan*

*ipse, -a, -um self, one's own, very; himself, herself, itself; *pl.* themselves

*īra, -ae *f.* wrath, anger, rage, passion, resentment; object of wrath *or* hatred

†īrāscor, -ī, īrātus become angry

īrātus, -a, -um angry

Īris, -idis *f. goddess of the rainbow and messenger of the gods.*

*is, ea, id that, this; he, she, it

*iste, -a, -ud that, that of yours; yonder, yon

istīc *adv.* there (*where you are*)

istinc *adv.* from there (*where you are*)

*ita *adv.* so, thus, in that way, as follows

Ītalia, -ae *f.* Italy

Ītalus, -ī *m.* an Italian

Ītalus, -a, -um of Italy, Italian

*iter, itineris *n.* way, course, path; journey, voyage, passage

*iterum *adv.* a second time, again, once more, anew

Ithaca, -ae *f. an island in the Ionian Sea, the home of Ulysses*

Ithacus, -a, -um of Ithaca, Ithacan; *as noun,* Ithacus, -ī *m.* the Ithacan, *i.e., Ulysses*

Iūlus, -ī *m. another name for Ascanius*

Ixīōn, -onis *m. a king of the Lapithae and father of Pirithoüs*

Ixīonius, -a, -um of Ixion

## J

*jaceō, -ēre, -uī, -itūrus lie, lie dead; lie low, be outspread, be level; be situated

*jaciō, -ere, jēcī, jactus cast, hurl, fling; scatter, strew; heap up, construct

jactāns, -antis boastful

†jactō 1 hurl, cast, fling, throw, toss; pour forth, utter; drive, pursue; ponder, revolve; vaunt, boast, glory, display

jactūra, -ae *f.* throwing away, loss

jactus, -ūs *m.* throw

jaculor, -ārī, -ātus hurl a javelin; hurl, throw

*jaculum, -ī *n.* javelin, dart

*jam *adv.* now, already; at once, forthwith, straightway; presently, at length; actually, even; *with a neg.,* longer, more

jānitor, -ōris *m.* doorkeeper

jānua, -ae *f.* door, doorway; entrance, way

jecur, jecoris *n.* liver

jocus, -ī *m.* jest, joke

juba, -ae *f.* mane, crest

Juba, -ae *m. king of Numidia*

jubar, -aris *n.* ray of light, sunlight

*jubeō, -ēre, jussī, jussus command, order, bid, enjoin; urge

*jūcundus, -a, -um pleasant, delightful

*jūdex, –icis *m.* judge
†jūdicium, –ī *n.* judgment, verdict, decision
jugālis, –e of wedlock, conjugal, nuptial, matrimonial, of marriage
jūgerum, –ī *n. a measure of land, covering somewhat more than half an acre*
jugō 1 yoke; unite (*in marriage*)
*jugum, –ī *n.* yoke; team; ridge; thwart
Jūlius, –ī *m. a Roman gentile name*
jūnctūra, –ae *f.* joining, joint, fastening
juncus, –ī *m.* rush, *a marsh plant*
*jungō, –ere, jūnxī, jūnctus yoke, join, unite; clasp, fasten together
Jūnō, –ōnis *f. sister and wife of Jupiter and queen of the gods*
Jūnōnius, –a, –um of Juno; Junonian
Juppiter, Jovis *m.* Jupiter, Jove, *king of the gods*
*jūrō 1 take oath, swear; swear by
*jūs, jūris *n.* law, justice, right; claim, oath
†jussū (*abl. of obsolete* jussus) at the order, by the command
jussum, –ī *n.* command, order, mandate, bidding, injunction
jūstitia, –ae *f.* justice, righteousness
*jūstus, –a, –um just, righteous; fair, equitable
juvenālis, –e of youth, youthful
juvenāliter with youthful strength
*juvencus, –ī *m.* bullock
*juvenis, –e young (*of persons between the ages of seventeen and forty-five*); *as noun,* juvenis, –is *m. or f.* young man *or* woman
*juventa, –ae *f.* youth
juventās, –tātis *f.* youth, youthful vigor
*juventūs, –tūtis *f.* youth; the young, young men
*juvō, –āre, jūvī, jūtus help, aid; profit, avail; please, gratify
*jūxtā 1) *adv.* near, close by, hard by; 2) *prep. with acc.* near, next to, close to

## K

*Kalendae, –ārum *f. pl.* Kalends, *first day of the month*
Karthāgō, –inis *f.* Carthage, *an ancient city in Northern Africa*

## L

labefaciō, –ere, –fēcī, –factus cause to totter shake, agitate
lābēs, –is *f.* slip, fall; downward step; beginning; taint, stain

labō 1 totter, stagger, give away; waver, falter
*lābor, –ī, lāpsus glide, slip; descend; swoop; swoon, fall; fly, flow, float, pass
*labor (labōs), –ōris *m.* toil, labor, task, occupation; effort, struggle; trial, hardship, suffering, distress, disaster; eclipse; *personified,* Toil
*labōrō 1 work, fashion, elaborate
Labyrinthus, –ī *m.* the Labyrinth
lac, lactis *n.* milk; milky juice, sap
Lacaenus, –a, –um Lacedaemonian, Spartan
Lacedaemonius, –a, –um Lacedaemonian, Spartan
lacer, –era, –erum torn, mangled, mutilated
lacerō 1 rend, tear, mangle
*lacertus, –ī *m.* arm
*lacessō, –ere, –īvī, –ītus provoke, arouse, challenge
Lacīnius, –a, –um of Lacinium, *a promontory on the southern coast of Italy*
*lacrima, –ae *f.* tear
lacrimābilis, –e tearful; piteous
†lacrimō 1 weep, shed tears
*lacus, –ūs *m.* lake, pool, swamp, fen; river, stream
*laedō, –ere, laesī, laesus strike, smite, injure; thwart
laena, –ae *f.* cloak, mantle
Lāertius, –a, –um of Laërtes, *the father of Ulysses*
†laetitia, –ae *f.* joy, gladness, delight
*laetor 1 rejoice, exult, be glad
*laetus, –a, –um joyful, joyous, happy, gay, glad; rejoicing, exulting; gladsome, bounteous, fruitful, plenteous; sleek; auspicious, prosperous
*laevus, –a, –um left, on the left; clumsy; misguided; infatuated; *as noun,* laeva, –ae *f.* the left, the left hand
Lalagē, –es *f. a girl's name*
lambō, –ere lick, lap, touch, wash
lāmentum, –ī *n.* wailing, lamentation
lāmentābilis, –e deplorable, pitiable, sad
lampas, –adis *f.* lamp, torch; firebrand
languidus, –a, –um weak, languid
lāniger, –era, –erum wool-bearing, fleecy
laniō 1 tear, mangle, mutilate
Lāocoōn, –ontis *m. a Trojan, priest of Apollo*
Lāodamïa, –ae *f. the wife of the Grecian hero Protesilaüs, who killed herself because of his death at Troy*
Lāomedontēus, –a, –um of Laömedon, *father of Priam and king of Troy, notorious for his perfidy*

Lāomedontiadēs, –ae m. descendant of Laömedon, *i.e.*, *a Trojan*

lapidōsus, –a, –um stony; hard as stone

*lapis, –idis m. stone, marble

Lapithae, –ārum m. *pl. a mountain tribe of Thessaly who fought the Centaurs*

lāpsō, –āre slip

lāpsus, –ūs m. gliding motion; swoop; flight; descent

laquear, –āris n. panel, panelled ceiling

laqueus, –ī m. noose, snare

Lār, Laris m. *a household god, a tutelar divinity*

*largior, –īrī, –ītus be lavish

largus, –a, –um ample, spacious; copious, abundant, plentiful

Lārissaeus, –a, –um of Larissa, *a town in Thessaly, the home of Achilles*

lascīvus, –a, –um playful, frolicsome

lassus, –a, –um weary, tired

lātē *adv.* broadly, widely, far and wide

*latebra, –ae f. (*usually pl.*) hiding place, covert, retreat

latebrōsus, –a, –um full of hiding places, cavernous, crannied

*lateō, –ēre, –uī lie hidden, be concealed, be covered; lurk, skulk; escape the notice of

latex, –icis m. liquid, fluid; water, wine

Latīnus, –a, –um of Latium; *as noun*, Latīnī, –ōrum, m. *pl.* the Latins

Latīnus, –ī m. *king of Latium, father of Lavinia*

Latium, –ī n. *a district south of the Tiber in central Italy*

Lātōna, –ae f. *the mother of Apollo and Diana*

Lātōnia, –ae f. daughter of Latona, *i.e.*, *Diana*

Lātōus, –a, –um of Latona

lātrātus, –ūs m. barking, baying

lātrō 1 bark, bay

*lātus, –a, –um broad, wide, widespread

*latus, –eris n. side, flank

*laudō 1 praise, commend, extol

Laurēns, –entis of Laurentum, *a town in Latium;* Laurentian

*laurus, –ī f. laurel, bay; laurel wreath

*laus, laudis f. praise, glory, renown, honor; distinction; prowess, merit

Lāvīnia, –ae f. *the daughter of King Latinus*

Lavīnium, –ī n. *a town in Latium built by Aeneas*

Lāvīnius, –a, –um of Lavinium, Lavinian

lavō, –āre (–ere), lāvī, lautus (lōtus) lave, wash, bathe; moisten, sprinkle; drench

*laxō 1 loosen, let go, release; free, clear; relax, refresh, relieve

laxus, –a, –um loose, open, free

leaena, –ae f. lioness

lebēs, –ētis m. kettle, cauldron

Lebinthus, –ī f. *a small island off the coast of Asia Minor*

lectus, –ī m. bed, couch

Lēda, –ae f. *mother of Helen*

Lēdaeus, –a, –um of Leda, descended from Leda

lēgifer, –era, –erum law-bringing, lawgiving

*legō, –ere, lēgī, lēctus gather, collect, catch, furl; choose, pick, select; scan, survey; skim over, coast along, skirt, traverse

Lēnaeus, –a, –um of *or* to Bacchus; of wine

lēniō 4 soothe, appease, assuage, calm

*lēnis, –e soft, gentle

lentō 1 bend

*lentus, –a, –um pliant, flexible; tough; slow, lingering, lazy

*leō, –ōnis m. lion

lepus, –oris m. hare

Lerna, –ae f. *a marsh near Argos, the haunt of the Hydra*

Lesbia, –ae f. *a woman's name*

lētālis, –e deadly, fatal

Lēthaeus, –a, –um of Lethe, *a river in the underworld whose waters produced forgetfulness*

lētifer, –era, –erum death-dealing, deadly

*lētum, –ī n. death, destruction, ruin

Leucaspis, –is m. *a comrade of Aeneas*

Leucātē, –ēs (–ae) f. *a promontory at the southern extremity of the island of Leucadia*

levāmen, –inis n. solace, consolation

*levis, –e light, gentle; fleet, swift

*lēvis, –e smooth, polished; slippery

leviter lightly

*levō 1 lighten; lift; raise; take off, remove; relieve, mitigate, alleviate

lēvō 1 polish

*lēx, lēgis f. statute, law; term, condition

lībāmen, –inis n. libation, offering, sacrifice

libellus, –ī m. book

libēns, –entis willing, glad, cheerful

Līber, –erī m. *an Italian deity identified with Bacchus*

†līberālis, –e generous, liberal

*līberī, –ōrum m. *pl.* children

†lībertās, –tātis f. liberty, freedom

libet, –ēre, libuit (–itum est) *impers.* it is pleasing

Libitīna, –ae f. *goddess of burial; hence,* funeral pyre

*lībō 1 pour, pour a libation; offer, sacrifice; sip, taste, touch, lightly kiss; skim over

lībrō 1 swing, brandish; plant; poise, balance

Liburnī, –ōrum m. *pl. a people of Northern Illyria*

**Libya,** –ae *f. a region of Northern Africa;* Africa
**Libycus,** –a, –um of Libya, Libyan, African
**Libystis,** –idis Libyan, African
*\*licet,* –ēre, –uit (–itum est) *impers.* it is permitted; it is allowed; it is lawful; *as conj.,* although, though
**Licinius,** –ī *m. a friend of Horace*
**lignum,** –ī *n.* wood, wooden structure
**ligō** 1 bind
**līlium,** –ī *n.* lily
**Lilybēius,** –a, –um of Lilybaeum, *a promontory on the western coast of Sicily*
**limbus,** –ī *m.* border, fringe
*\*līmen,* –inis *n.* threshold, portal, door, entrance; palace, shrine, temple; abode; starting point
**līmes,** –itis *m.* path, track, trail, cross-path, boundary
**limōsus,** –a, –um muddy, slimy
**līmus,** –ī *m.* mud, slime
**līneus,** –a, –um of flax, linen
*\*lingua,* –ae *f.* tongue; note, cry
†**linquō,** –ere, līquī leave, quit; forsake, abandon, leave behind, desert; renounce, give up
**linteum,** –ī *n.* linen cloth, canvas, sail
**līnum,** –ī *n.* thread
**liquefaciō,** –ere, –fēcī, –factus melt
**līquēns,** –entis liquid, clear, limpid; flowing
*\*liquidus,* –a, –um liquid, fluid, limpid
**līquor,** –ī flow, melt, dissolve
**litō** 1 sacrifice; appease, propitiate
**lītoreus,** –a, –um of the seashore; on the bank
*\*lītus,* –oris *n.* seashore, coast, beach, strand
**lituus,** –ī *m.* curved horn; trumpet, clarion
**līvēns,** –entis dark, livid
**līvidus,** –a, –um dark, leaden, dusky
†**locō** 1 place, plant, set, set up; lay, found, build
**Locrī,** –ōrum *m. pl.* Locrians
*\*locus,* –ī *m. (generally neuter in the plural)* place, spot, region; site, position; situation, condition; chance, opportunity
†**longaevus,** –a, –um aged, venerable
**longē** *adv.* far, far off, afar; from *or* at a distance, from afar; long; *comp.* further, at greater length
*\*longinquus,* –a, –um remote; long, long-continued
*\*longus,* –a, –um long, deep; prolonged, long-continued, lasting, lingering; tedious, devious; distant, remote
**loquēla,** –ae *f.* speech, word
*\*loquor,* –ī, locūtus speak, say

*\*lōrīca,* –ae *f.* coat of mail, cuirass, corselet
**lōrum,** –ī *n.* thong, rein
**lūbricus,** –a, –um slippery, slimy
*\*lūceō,* –ēre, lūxī shine, gleam, be resplendent
**lūcidus,** –a, –um shining, gleaming, glittering, bright
**Lūcifer,** –erī *m.* morning star
**Lucrīnus,** –a, –um Lucrine, of Lake Lucrinus
**lucrum,** –ī *n.* gain
*\*luctor,* –ārī, –ātus wrestle, struggle
†**lūctus,** –ūs *m.* grief, mourning, sorrow, suffering, distress; *personified,* Grief
*\*lūcus,* –ī *m.* sacred grove, wood
**lūdibrium,** –ī *n.* sport, plaything
*\*lūdō,* –ere, lūsī, lūsus sport, play; make sport of, mock, deceive
*\*lūdus,* –ī *m.* sport, game, play
**luēs,** –is *f.* plague, pestilence; blight
*\*lūgeō,* –ēre, lūxī mourn, lament, bewail
*\*lūmen,* –inis *n.* light, glare; glow; eye; life; day; air
*\*lūna,* –ae *f.* moon, moonlight
**lūnātus,** –a, –um moon-shaped, crescent
**luō,** –ere, luī wash away, atone for, pay
**lupa,** –ae *f.* she-wolf
*\*lupus,* –ī *m.* wolf
*\*lūstrō* 1 illuminate; examine, survey, review; run over, traverse, double; purify; *pass. used as middle,* perform an expiatory sacrifice
**lūstrum,** –ī *n. an expiatory sacrifice, made every five years;* hence, a period of five years
**lustrum,** –ī *n.* haunt of wild beasts; den, lair
**lūsus,** –ūs *m.* sport, play
*\*lūx,* lūcis *f.* light, daylight, day, dawn; life; glory, defense
*\*lūxuria,* –ae *f.* extravagance
**lūxus,** –ūs *m.* luxury, dalliance; splendor, magnificence
**Lyaeus,** –ī *m. a Greek name for Bacchus; as adj.,* of Bacchus
**lychnus,** –ī *m.* lamp
**Lycia,** –ae *f. a district in Southwestern Asia Minor*
**Lycius,** –a, –um of Lycia, Lycian; *as noun,* Lyciī, –ōrum *m. pl.* the Lycians
**Lyctius,** –a, –um of Lyctus, *a town in Crete;* Cretan
**Lycurgus,** –ī *m. a king of Thrace, who forbade the worship of Bacchus*
**Lycus,** –ī *m. a comrade of Aeneas*
**Lȳdius,** –a, –um of Lydia, Lydian
**lympha,** –ae *f.* water
**lynx,** lyncis *m. or f.* lynx

# M

**Machāōn, -onis** *m. one of the Greeks before Troy*
**māchina, -ae** *f.* engine, contrivance
**maciēs, -ēī** *f.* leanness, emaciation
*****mactō** 1 sacrifice, offer; slaughter, slay
*****macula, -ae** *f.* spot
**maculō** 1 spot, stain
**maculōsus, -a, -um** spotted, mottled, dappled
**madefaciō, -ere, -fēcī, -factus** wet, soak, drench
*****madeō, -ēre, -uī** be wet, drip; *partic.* **madēns, -entis,** dripping, wet
**madēscō, -ere, maduī** become wet, be soaked, be drenched
**madidus, -a, -um** wet, dripping, drenched
**maeander, -drī** *m.* a winding *or* wavy line; *so named from the River Maeander in Asia Minor*
**Maeonius, -a, -um** of Maeonia, *a province of Lydia;* Lydian
**Maeōtius, -a, -um** of the Maeotians, *a people of Scythia*
**maereō, -ēre** mourn, grieve, sorrow
*****maeror, -ōris** *m.* sorrow
*****maestus, -a, -um** sad, unhappy, anxious, sorrowful, doleful, gloomy
**māgālia, -ium** *n. pl.* huts
**magicus, -a, -um** magic
*****magis** *adv.* more, rather
*****magister, -trī** *m.* master, leader, captain; pilot, helmsman; teacher, trainer; tutor, guardian
*****magistrātus, -ūs** *m.* magistracy; magistrate
†**magnanimus, -a, -um** great-souled; high-spirited
†**magnitūdō, -inis** *f.* size
*****magnus, -a, -um** great, large, huge, vast; powerful, mighty; noble, illustrious; important; **maximus (nātū)** eldest
**Māja, -ae** *f. daughter of Atlas and mother of Mercury*
**māla, -ae** *f.* jaw; cheekbone
**male** *adv.* badly, ill; hardly, scarcely; *with an adjective, sometimes equivalent to a negative*
**Malea, -ae** *f. a promontory on the southern coast of the Peloponnesus*
**malesuādus, -a, -um** persuading to evil
**malignus, -a, -um** ill-disposed, malicious, envious; scanty
*****mālō, mālle, māluī** wish rather, prefer
**malum, -ī** *n.* evil; sin, crime; ill, woe, misfortune, adversity, calamity; pest
**mālum, -ī** *n.* apple

*****malus, -a, -um** evil, bad, wicked; hostile; noxious, poisonous
**mālus, -ī** *m.* mast
**mamma, -ae** *f.* breast
†**mandātum, -ī** *n.* command, injunction, instruction
*****mandō** 1 consign, commit, entrust; command, enjoin
**mandō, -ere, mandī, mānsus** chew; *of a horse,* champ
**māne** in the morning
*****maneō, -ēre, mānsī, mānsūrus** stay, remain, abide, linger; abide by; await, wait for
*****Mānēs, -ium** *m. pl.* the spirits of the dead; soul, shade; underworld
**manicae, -ārum** *f. pl.* manacles
*****manifestus, -a, -um** clear, evident; conspicuous
**mānō** 1 drip, trickle, drop, be wet
**mānsuēscō, -ere, -suēvī, -suētus** grow soft, soften
*****mānsuētūdō, -inis** *f.* mildness
**mantēle, -is** *n.* towel, napkin
*****manus, -ūs** *f.* hand, fist; band, troop; prowess, handiwork
**Mārcellus, -ī** *m. a Roman name; especially the son of Octavia*
*****mare, -is** *n.* sea
**marītō** 1 wed
**marītus, -ī** *m.* husband; suitor
*****marmor, -oris** *n.* marble
**marmoreus, -a, -um** of marble; marble-like, like marble, glassy
**Marpēsius, -a, -um** of Marpesus, *a mountain in Paros;* Parian
**Mārs, Mārtis** *m. the god of war;* war, battle, conflict
**Mārtius, -a, -um** of Mars
**massa, -ae** *f.* mass; curd
**Massȳlus, -a, -um** of the Massyli, *a people of Northern Africa; as noun,* **Massȳlī, -ōrum** *m. pl.* Massylians
*****māter, mātris** *f.* mother, dam; native land
**māteria, -ae** *f.* material
**māternus, -a, -um** of one's mother, mother's, maternal
**mātūrō** 1 hasten, speed
*****mātūrus, -a, -um** ripe, mature; advanced
**Maurus, -a, -um** Moorish
**Maurūsius, -a, -um** of the Mauri, *a nation in Northern Africa;* Moorish, African
**Māvors, -ortis** *another name for Mars*
**Māvortius, -a, -um** of Mars; descended from Mars; warlike

maximus, –a, –um *superl. of* magnus
Maximus, –ī *m. a Roman name*
meātus, –ūs *m.* course, motion, movement
medicāmen, –inis *n.* drug, ointment
medicō 1 medicate, drug
medicus, –ī *m.* physician
mediocritās, –ātis *f.* mean, middle ground
meditor, –ārī, –ātus meditate, reflect upon; purpose, design
medium, –ī *n.* middle, midst
*medius, –a, –um middle, middle of, midst of, heart of; intervening, between
Medōn, –ontis *m. a Trojan*
medulla, –ae *f.* marrow
Megarēius, –a, –um of Megareus
Megareus, –ī, *m. father of Hippomenes*
Megarus, –a, –um of Megara, *a city in Sicily*
mel, mellis *n.* honey
Meliboeus, –a, –um of Meliboea, *a town in Thessaly;* Meliboean
Meliboeus, –ī *m. name of a shepherd*
melior (*comp. of* bonus) better
Melitē, –ēs *f. a sea nymph*
melius *adv. comp. of* bene
Melpomenē, –ēs *f. muse of lyric poetry*
*membrum, –ī *n.* limb; body, frame
*meminī, –isse *defective* remember
Memmius, –ī *m. a Roman gentile name*
Memnōn, –onis *m. son of Tithonus and Aurora, and king of the Ethiopians*
*memor, –oris remembering, mindful; relentless
memorābilis, –e memorable; glorious
†memorō 1 call to mind, mention; recount, relate, tell; say, speak; call
mendāx, –ācis false, lying, untruthful
Menelāus, –ī *m. king of Sparta and husband of Helen*
Menoetēs, –ae *m. a comrade of Aeneas*
*mēns, mentis *f.* mind, intellect; memory; heart; feeling, disposition; intention, purpose
*mēnsa, –ae *f.* table, board; food, viands, feast
*mēnsis, –is *m.* month
mēnsor, –ōris *m.* measurer, surveyor
mēnstruus, –a, –um monthly
mentior, –īrī, –ītus lie, pretend
mentītus, –a, –um deceitful, lying
mentum, –ī *n.* chin; beard
mercor, –ārī, –ātus buy; pay for
Mercurius, –ī *m. the son of Jupiter and Maia; messenger of the gods*
*mereō 2 *and* *mereor, –ērī, –itus deserve, be worthy of, merit, earn

*mergō, –ere, mersī, mersus plunge, sink, overwhelm; hide, conceal
mergus, –ī *m.* diver, gull
meritō *adv.* deservedly
meritum, –ī *n.* service, merit
meritus, –a, –um deserving; deserved, due
mersō 1 overwhelm
merus, –a, –um pure, unmixed; true; sheer; *as noun,* merum, –ī *n.* unmixed wine
*–met *intensive suffix used with pronouns*
*mēta, –ae *f.* turning place; bound, limit; end; point, promontory
metallum, –ī *n.* metal
*mētior, –īrī, mēnsus measure
metō, –ere, messuī, messus reap, cut
metuō, –ere, metuī fear, be afraid of, dread
*metus, –ūs *m.* fear, dread, alarm; *personified,* Fear
*meus, –a, –um my, mine
mī: *contraction of* mihi
*micō, –āre, –uī quiver, dart; gleam, flash
migrō 1 go away, depart
*mīles, –itis *m.* soldier, soldiery
†mīlitāris, –e martial, soldier-producing
*mīlle *indecl. adj.* a thousand; *as noun,* mīlia, –ium *n. pl.* thousands
*mīnae, –ārum *f. pl.* threats, menaces; perils
mināx, –ācis menacing, threatening
Minerva, –ae *f. the goddess of the liberal and the household arts, more or less closely identified with Pallas Athena of the Greeks*
minimē *adv.* (*superl. of* parum) least
minister, –trī *m.* servant, attendant; tool, accomplice
ministerium, –ī *n.* service; office, duty
ministrō 1 serve; manage; provide; lend, furnish
Minōius, –a, –um of Minos, *king of Crete*
*minor, –ārī, –ātus threaten, menace; portend; rise threateningly, tower aloft, tower; totter
minor, –us (*comp. of* parvus) less; *as noun,* minōrēs, –um *m. pl.* descendants, posterity
Mīnōs, –ōis *m. a king of Crete who after death was made a judge in the underworld*
Mīnōtaurus, –ī *m. a Cretan monster, partly man and partly bull*
minuō, –ere, –uī, –ūtus lessen, break into pieces
minus *adv.* (*comp. of* parum) less
†mīrābilis, –e wonderful, marvellous
mīrandus, –a, –um to be wondered at; wondrous, marvellous
*mīror, –ārī, –ātus wonder at, marvel at, admire; wonder
*mīrus, –a, –um wonderful, marvellous

*misceō, -ēre, miscuī, mixtus mix, mingle; unite, blend; confuse, throw into confusion; drive in confusion, rout, scatter; agitate; stir up; spread

Mīsēnus, -ī m. a Trojan trumpeter, comrade of Aeneas

*miser, -era, -erum wretched, unhappy; hapless, ill-fated; unfortunate, pitiable

miserābilis, -e wretched, pitiable, pitiful, deplorable

miserandus, -a, -um to be pitied, piteous, wretched, hapless

*misereor, -ērī, -itus pity, take pity on, have compassion on

miserēscō, -ere take pity on

miseret, -ēre, -uit impers. it causes (one) to feel pity; mē miseret, I pity

*miseror, -ārī, -ātus pity, take pity on, have compassion on

mītēscō, -ere become mild, grow mild, become gentle, grow peaceful

mītigō 1 make gentle, soften, appease

*mītis, -e mild; gentle, merciful; mellow, ripe

mitra, -ae f. a Phrygian cap

*mittō, -ere, mīsī, missus let go, send, dispatch; cause to go, consign, hurl; dismiss, banish, dispel, end, finish; offer, pay

Mnēstheus, -eī (-eos) m. a comrade of Aeneas

mōbilitās, -ātis f. ease of motion; motion, movement

moderāmen, -inis n. control, guidance

*modo adv. only, merely, but; just now, but now, lately

*modus, -ī m. measure; limit, bound; way, wise, manner; plan, method

*moenia, -ium n. pl. walls, ramparts, fortifications; city; structures, buildings

mola, -ae f. meal

*mōlēs, -is f. mass, burden, weight; bulk, size; massive structure; engine of war; dike; toil, task, effort; turmoil, tumult, disturbance

*mōlior, -īrī, -ītus strive, devise, contrive; plan, essay, attempt, undertake; toil along, pursue; build, rear; prepare, produce, cause

molliō 4 soften, soothe, assuage

*mollis, -e soft; tender, gentle; delicate; easy, favorable; subtle

molliter adv. softly, delicately

*moneō 2 remind; warn, admonish; advise; predict

monīle, -is n. necklace

monitum, -ī n. admonition, warning, command

monitus, -ūs m. admonition, warning; prediction; advice, behest

Monoecus, -ī m. a town with a temple of Hercules on the coast of Liguria

*mōns, montis m. mountain, hill; cliff

†mōnstrō 1 show, point out, indicate; direct, enjoin, appoint, prescribe

*mōnstrum, -ī n. warning; omen, portent; prodigy, monster, portentous object

montānus, -a, -um of a mountain, mountain (as adj.)

*monumentum, -ī n. reminder, token, memento; relic; record, tradition

*mora, -ae f. delay, hindrance, obstruction; respite

*morbus, -ī m. sickness, disease; personified, Disease

moribundus, -a, -um dying; mortal

*morior, -ī, mortuus die, be slain

*moror, -ārī, -ātus delay, pause, linger, tarry; cause delay, detain; care for, regard

*mors, -tis f. death

*morsus, -ūs m. biting, bite; eating; fluke; teeth, fangs

mortālis, -e mortal, human; as noun, mortālis, -is m. a mortal man

mortifer, -era, -erum death-bringing, death-dealing, deadly

mōrus, -ī f. mulberry tree

*mōs, mōris m. custom, practice, habit, usage; institution; manner, way; precedent

*mōtus, -ūs m. motion, movement, swiftness; tumult, disturbance

*moveō, -ēre, mōvī, mōtus move, remove; shake; sway, quake; arouse, excite, agitate, trouble, disturb; influence, affect, impress; revolve, ponder, meditate; with fāta as object, disclose

*mox adv. soon, presently, afterwards

*mūcrō, -ōnis m. sharp point; blade, sword

*mūgiō 4 low, bellow; rumble, roar

mūgītus, -ūs m. bellowing

*mulceō, -ēre, mulsī, mulsus soothe, quiet, calm, appease

Mulciber, -eris (-berī) m. Vulcan

multifidus, -a, -um finely split

multiplex, -icis having many folds; manifold

multum adv. much, greatly, abundantly

*multus, -a, -um much; dense, heavy; great, high, abundant; many a; pl. many

mundus, -ī m. world

mūnificus, -a, -um benevolent, generous

*mūniō 4 fortify; build

*mūnus, -eris n. duty, function, service, trib-

*multō, abl. to adv.; much*

ute; offering, sacrifice; gift, present, prize, reward; boon, favor

mūrex, -icis *m.* purple shellfish; purple dye, purple; jagged rock *or* reef

†murmur, -uris *n.* murmur, murmuring; roaring, rumbling; uproar

*mūrus, -ī *m.* wall

Mūsa, -ae *f.* Muse, *one of the nine goddesses of poetry and music*

Mūsaeus, -ī *m. a Greek bard of the Heroic Age*

mūtābilis, -e changeable, inconstant

*mūtō 1 change, alter, turn; exchange

mūtus, -a, -um silent

mūtuus, -a, -um mutual, in exchange

Mycēnae, -ārum (*also* Mycēna, -ae) *f. a city of Argolis, the seat of Agamemnon's rule*

Myconus, -ī *f. one of the Cyclades, a group of islands in the Aegean Sea*

Mygdonidēs, -ae *m. the son of Mygdon*

Myrmidones, -um *m. pl.* Myrmidons, *a Thessalian tribe*

myrteus, -a, -um of myrtle, myrtle (*as adj.*)

myrtus, -ī (-ūs) *f.* myrtle

# N

Nāis, Nāidos (-is) *f.* Naïd, *a water nymph*

*nam for (*to introduce an explanatory statement*)

*namque for; *cf.* nam

nāris, -is *f.* nostril; *pl.* nostrils; nose

nārrō 1 tell, relate, report

Nārycius, -a, -um Narycian; of Naryx, *a Locrian town*

*nāscor, -ī, nātus be born; spring up, arise; *partic.* nātus, -a, -um born, sprung

nāsus, -ī *m.* nose

nāta, -ae *f.* daughter

nātālis, -e native

natō 1 swim, float

*nātūra, -ae *f.* nature

nātus, -ī *m.* son; *pl.* children, offspring, young

nātus, -ūs *m.* (*used only in abl. sing.*) nātū by birth, by age; *see* magnus

*nauta, -ae *m.* sailor, boatman, mariner

Nautēs, -is *m. a Trojan soothsayer*

nauticus, -a, -um of the sailors

†nāvālis, -e pertaining to ships, naval; *as noun,* nāvālia, -um *n. pl.* dock, dockyard

nāvifragus, -a, -um ship-destroying

nāvigium, -ī *n.* ship, boat, vessel

*nāvigō 1 sail, sail upon

*nāvis, -is *f.* ship, vessel

nāvita, -ae *m.* boatman

Naxos, -ī *f. one of the Cyclades, a group of islands in the Aegean Sea*

nē *adv.* not; †nē . . . quidem not even

*nē *neg. adv. and conj.* not; that . . . not, in order that . . . not, lest; *after words of fearing,* lest, that

*-ne *enclitic interrogative particle; in an indirect question,* whether

-ne *intensive particle sometimes appended to the exclamatory infinitive*

nebula, -ae *f.* mist, cloud

*nec *see* neque

necdum nor yet, and not yet

*necesse *indecl. adj.* necessary, inevitable; destined, fated

nectar, -aris *n.* nectar

*nectō, -ere, nexuī (nexī), nexus bind, fasten, join, tie; sheathe; nexus, -a, -um close-knit

†nefandus, -a, -um unspeakable; wicked, impious, accursed, abominable; *as noun,* nefandum, -ī *n.* wrong

*nefās *n. indecl. that which is wrong in the sight of the gods;* impiety, guilt, sin, wickedness, abomination; *as indecl. adj.,* abominable, wicked, impious, wrong

*negō 1 say no, refuse, say . . . not, deny

*nēmō, *dat.* nēminī, *acc.* nēminem *m.* no one, nobody

nemorōsus, -a, -um woody, well-wooded

*nemus, -oris *n.* grove, glade, wood

Neoptolemus, -ī *m. son of Achilles and also called Pyrrhus*

*nepōs, -ōtis *m.* grandson; *pl.* grandchildren, descendants, posterity

Neptūnius, -a, -um Neptunian, of Neptune

Neptūnus, -ī *m.* Neptune, *god of the sea*

*neque *or* *nec *conj.* nor, and . . . not; †neque (nec) . . . neque (nec) neither . . . nor

nequeō, -īre, -īvī (-iī) not be able, be unable, cannot, could not

*nēquīquam *adv.* in vain, to no purpose

Nēreis, -idis *f.* daughter of Nereus, Nereid, *a sea nymph*

Nēreus, -eī (-eōs) *m. a god of the sea*

Nēritos, -ī *f. an island near Ithaca*

*nervus, -ī *m.* sinew, gut; bowstring

*nesciō, -īre, -īvī (-iī) not know, be ignorant; nesciō quis some

nescius, -a, -um not knowing, ignorant, unconscious, unaware

Nestor, -oris *m. an aged Greek*

*nēve *or* *neu *conj.* and not, nor, or not, or lest

*nex, necis *f.* killing, murder, slaughter, death

nexus, *see* nectō

*nī (nisi) if not, unless

nī (nē) that not, not

nīdus, -ī *m.* nest; *pl.* nestlings

*niger, -gra, -grum black, swarthy, swart, sable, dusky, dark

nigrāns, -antis black, dusky

nigrēscō, -ere, nigruī grow black, grow dark

*nihil (nīl) *n. indecl.* nothing, naught; *as adv.,* not at all, not

Nīlus, -ī *m.* Nile, *a river in Egypt*

nimbōsus, -a, -um stormy, cloud-capped

*nimbus, -ī *m.* rain cloud, cloud, storm, tempest, rain

nīmīrum *adv.* without doubt, verily, of a truth

*nimius, -a, -um too great, excessive; nimium *adv.* too, too much

Ninus, -ī *m.* an ancient king of Babylon

Niobē, -bae (-bēs) *f. daughter of Tantalus, wife of King Amphion, and proud mother of seven sons and seven daughters*

Nīsaeē, -ēs *f. a sea nymph*

*nisi if not, unless

nīsus, -ūs *m.* effort, striving, exertion; posture

Nīsus, -ī *m. a Trojan*

*niteō, -ēre, -uī gleam, shine; *partic.* nitēns, -entis gleaming, bright, shining, sparkling, starry, beaming; glossy, sleek

nitēscō, -ere, nituī become bright, glisten, shine

nitidus, -a, -um shining

*nītor, -ī, nīsus (nīxus) lean upon, rest upon, support oneself by, tread upon; climb, mount, force one's way

nitor, -ōris *m.* brightness, sheen

nivālis, -e snowy, snow-white

niveus, -a, -um snowy, snow-white

*nix, nivis *f.* snow

nīxor, -ārī, -ātus struggle

*nō, nāre, nāvī swim, float, sail

*noceō, -ēre, -uī, -itūrus injure, harm, do mischief

†nocturnus, -a, -um at night, by night, nocturnal

nōdō 1 tie *or* fasten in a knot

*nōdus, -ī *m.* knot, fastening; bond, fetter; fold, coil

Nomas, -adis *m.* Numidian

*nōmen, -inis *n.* name, fame

Nōmentum, -ī *n. a Sabine town*

†nōminō 1 call by name

*nōn not, no

*nōndum not yet

*nōnus, -a, -um ninth

*nōscō, -ere, nōvī, nōtus become acquainted with; recognize; *in perfect system,* know

*noster, -tra, -trum our, our own, ours, of us

nota, -ae *f.* mark, sign

nōtitia, -ae *f.* knowledge, acquaintance

*notō 1 mark, observe, note, notice

†nōtus, -a, -um known, well-known, familiar, wanted

Notus, -ī *m.* south wind; wind (*in general*)

novāle, -is *n.* fallow land

*novem *indecl. adj.* nine

noviēns *adv.* nine times

novitās, -ātis *f.* newness, strangeness

novō 1 make new, renew, repair; change

*novus, -a, -um new, fresh, early; strange; *superl.* novissimus, -a, -um last

*nox, noctis *f.* night; darkness

noxa, -ae *f.* hurt, harm; fault, crime

noxius, -a, -um harmful, baneful

*nūbēs, -is *f.* cloud, mist

*nūbila, -ōrum *n. pl.* clouds

†nūbilus, -a, -um cloudy

nūbō, -ere, nūpsī, nūptus marry

*nūdō 1 bare, strip, lay bare, reveal, expose

nūdulus, -a, -um naked

nūdus, -a, -um naked, bare, open; unburied

*nūllus, -a, -um none, no

*num *interrog. particle implying a negative answer; in indirect questions,* whether

*nūmen, -inis *n.* nod, divine will, divine purpose, divine power, divine influence, divine help; will; sanction, favor, permission; power, might; deity, divinity; presence (*of the god or goddess*)

numerō 1 number, reckon

*numerus, -ī *m.* number, company, order

Numidae, -ārum *m. pl.* Numidians

Numitor, -ōris *m. a king of Alba and the grandfather of Romulus*

*numquam *adv.* never

numquid *adv.* at all (*sign of a question implying a negative answer*)

*nunc *adv.* now

nūntia, -ae *f.* messenger

*nūntiō 1 announce, report

*nūntius, -ī *m.* messenger; tidings, message

*nūper *adv.* recently, lately

nurus, -ūs *f.* daughter-in-law

*nusquam *adv.* nowhere, never

nūtō 1 nod, sway, totter

nūtrīmentum, -ī *n.* nourishment; fuel

nūtriō 1 nurse, feed

nūtrīx, -īcis *f.* nurse

*nūtus, -ūs *m.* nod

*nympha, -ae *f.* nymph

Nȳsa, -ae *f. a mountain and city of India*

## O

Ō *interjection* O! oh!

Oaxes, –is *m. a river in Crete*

*ob *prep. with acc.* on account of, for

obdūcō, –ere, –dūxī, –ductus draw before, draw over, overspread

*obeō, –īre, –īvī (–iī), –itus go to meet; envelop, encircle, surround; traverse, visit; engage in

obitus, –ūs *m.* a meeting (*of death*); *hence,* death, destruction

objectō 1 expose

objectus, –a, –um *see* objiciō

objectus, –ūs *m.* projection; shelter, barrier

*objiciō (obiciō), –ere, –jēcī, –jectus throw before, cast before; present, offer; expose; *partic.* objectus, –a, –um thrown before; projecting

oblinō, –ere, –lēvī, –litus smear

oblīquō 1 turn obliquely, slant, set slanting

oblīquus, –a, –um turned sideways, lying across

*oblivīscor, –ī, oblītus forget, be forgetful; *partic.* oblītus, –a, –um forgetful, forgetting

oblīvium, –ī *n.* forgetfulness

obloquor, –ī, –locūtus talk *or* sing in response to

oblūctor, –ārī, –ātus wrestle against, brace oneself against

obmūtēscō, –ere, –mūtuī become dumb, be struck dumb

obnītor, –ī, –nīsus (–nīxus) press against; struggle, wrestle

oborior, –īrī, –ortus arise, spring up, well up, flow; *partic.* obortus, –a, –um rising, starting

†obruō, –ere, –ruī, –rutus overwhelm, crush, sink

obscēnus, –a, –um filthy, foul, horrible, loathsome; ill-omened

*obscūrus, –a, –um dark, dim, murky; unseen; shrouded in darkness

observō 1 note, observe, watch

*obsideō, –ēre, –sēdī, –sessus besiege, block; occupy

†obsidiō, –ōnis *f.* siege, blockade

obsolētus, –a, –um old, run-down

†obstipēscō, –ere, –stipuī become senseless, be dazed, be amazed, be astonished, stand aghast

obstō, –āre, –stitī, –stātūrus stand in the way of, oppose, block, withstand, hinder; check, thwart; resist

obstrepō, –ere, –uī, –itūrus roar, resound, murmur

obstringō, –ere, –strīnxī, –strictus bind up, confine

obstruō, –ere, –strūxī, –strūctus stop, close up

obtegō, –ere, –tēxī, –tēctus cover over, hide

obtorqueō, –ēre, –torsī, –tortus twist

obtruncō 1 lop off; cut down, slay, slaughter

obtundō, –ere, –tudī, –tūsus (–tūnsus) beat against, blunt; *partic.* obtūsus (obtūnsus), –a, –um blunted, unfeeling

obtūtus, –ūs *m.* gaze, look

obuncus, –a, –um hooked

obvertō, –ere, –tī, –versus turn toward, turn

†obvius, –a, –um in the way of, in the path of; meeting; exposed to

*occāsus, –ūs *m.* fall

*occidō, –ere, occidī, occāsūrus fall, perish; set, sink

occubō, –āre lie, lie dead

occulō, –ere, –culuī, –cultus hide; *partic.* occultus, –a, –um hidden, secret

*occultō 1 hide, conceal

occumbō, –ere, –cubuī, –cubitūrus fall, fall upon, fall a victim to, succumb, die, be slain

*occupō 1 seize, take possession of; cover

*occurrō, –ere, –currī (–cucurrī), –cursūrus run to meet, meet; meet the gaze of, appear, present itself; intervene

Ōceanus, –ī *m.* the ocean

*ōcior, –us *comp. adj.* fleeter, swifter

†ōcius *comp. adv.* more fleetly, more speedily, more swiftly

*oculus, –ī *m.* eye

*ōdī, ōdisse hate, detest

†odium, –ī *n.* hate, hatred

odor, –ōris *m.* odor; perfume, fragrance; stench

odōrātus, –a, –um fragrant

odōrus, –a, –um keen-scented

Oeagrius, –a, –um Oeagrian, of Oeagrus, *father of Orpheus*

Oenōtrus, –a, –um Oenotrian, of Oenotria, *i.e., Southern Italy*

Oetaeus, –a, –um of Oeta, *a mountain in Southern Thessaly*

offa, –ae *f.* cake

*offerō, –ferre, obtulī, oblātus offer, present; sē offerre meet; *pass. as middle,* meet

*officium, –ī *n.* service, kindness; obligation, duty

Oīleus, –eī, (–ī, –eōs) *m. a Locrian chieftain, father of Ajax*

Ōlearos, –ī *f. one of the Cyclades, a group of islands in the Aegean Sea*

oleō, –ēre, –uī smell; *partic.* olēns, –entis smelling

cleum, -ī n. olive oil, oil
olfaciō, -ere, -fēcī, -factus smell
*ōlim adv. once, once upon a time, formerly, sometime, one day, hereafter; at times, sometimes
olīva, -ae f. olive, olive wreath
olīvum, -ī n. olive oil, oil
ollī, ollīs archaic for illī, illīs
Olympus, -ī m. Mt. Olympus, the home of the gods
*ōmen, -inis n. omen, portent, sign; bridal auspices, marriage rites
*omnīnō adv. altogether, wholly, entirely
omniparēns, -entis adj. all-producing; as noun, f. mother of all things
omnipotēns, -entis omnipotent, almighty, all-powerful
*omnis, -e all, every, whole, universal
Onchestius, -a, -um of Onchestus, a city in Boeotia
†onerō 1 load, lade, freight; stow, put, heap
onerōsus, -a, -um heavy; laden, loaded
*onus, -eris n. load, burden
onustus, -a, -um laden
opācō 1 shade
*opācus, -a, -um shady, shadowy, gloomy, dark, obscure
operiō, -īre, -uī, -pertus hide, cover; partic. opertus, -a, -um secret, hidden
operor, -ārī, -ātus be busy, be employed
opertum, -ī n. secret place; secret
opifex, -ficis m. artisan
opīmus, -a, -um rich, fertile, sumptuous
opperior, -īrī, -pertus (-perītus) await
oppetō, -ere, -īvī (-iī), -ītus meet, encounter; especially encounter death, die, fall
*oppidum, -ī n. town
oppōnō, -ere, -posuī, -positus place before, expose; set against, place against, put in the way of; partic. oppositus, -a, -um opposing
*opprimō, -ere, -pressī, -pressus crush; partic. oppressus, -a, -um overpowered, overwhelmed
*oppugnō 1 assault, lay siege to
*ops, opis f. power, ability, might; help; pl. opēs resources, wealth, means; assistance, aid, help; dominion, power
*optō 1 long for, choose, desire, wish for, wish, hope
opulentus, -a, -um rich
*opus, -eris n. work, task, labor; opus est (with abl.) there is need of
*ōra, -ae f. shore, coast, region
ōrāculum (ōrāclum), -ī n. oracle
*orbis, -is m. circle, circuit, orbit, cycle, course;

coil, fold; orbis (terrārum) the world, the earth
orbus, -a, -um bereaved, childless
Orcus, -ī m. god of the underworld; the underworld
*ōrdior, -īrī, ōrsus begin
*ōrdō, -inis m. row, series, line, train; order, succession; class; bank (of oars); ōrdine in order, duly; ex ōrdine in succession
Orēas, -adis f. Oread, a mountain nymph
Orestēs, -ae (-is) m. son of Agamemnon and Clytemnestra
orgia, -ōrum n. pl. orgies, rites of Bacchus, revels
Oriēns, -entis m. dawn; east, the Orient
*orīgō, -inis f. origin, beginning, source; descent; stock, race
Oriōn, -ōnis m. a constellation
*orior, -īrī, ortus arise, be born, spring
ōrnātus, -ūs m. adornment, decoration, ornament; garment
*ōrnō 1 adorn
ornus, -ī f. ash tree
*ōrō 1 beg, pray, beseech, entreat
Orontēs, -is (-ī, -ae) m. a Lycian chief, follower of Aeneas
Orpheus, -eī (-eōs) m. a celebrated Thracian bard of the Heroic Age
ōrsus partic. of ōrdior
ortus partic. of orior
ortus, -ūs m. rising, origin
Ortygia, -ae f. an ancient designation of Delos; also the name of an island near Syracuse
*ōs, ōris n. mouth, lips; face, countenance, features
*os, ossis n. bone, inmost part; pl. ossa frame
*ōsculum, -ī n. little mouth; lips; kiss
Ossa, -ae f. a mountain in Thessaly
*ostendō, -ere, -endī, -entus stretch before, hold forth; show, point out, reveal, disclose
†ostentō 1 show, display, exhibit
ōstium, -ī n. mouth; entrance
ostrum, -ī n. blood of the sea snail; purple
Othryadēs, -ae m. son of Othrys
*ōtium, -ī n. leisure, ease; idleness; peace, repose
ovīle, -is n. sheepfold
ovis, -is f. sheep
*ovō 1 rejoice, exult
ōvum, -ī n. egg

## P

*pābulum, -ī n. fodder, forage
Pachȳnum, -ī n. a promontory of Sicily

pacīscor, -ī, pactus barter; stipulate, agree upon

*pācō 1 subdue, make peaceful

*pactum, -ī n. agreement

pactus partic. of pacīscor

paeān, -ānis (acc. paeāna) m. paean, hymn (to Apollo)

paenitentia, -ae f. repentance

*paenitet, -ēre, -ituit impers. it repents, causes regret; mē paenitet I repent, I regret

Palaemōn, -onis m. a sea divinity

palaestra, -ae f. wrestling ground; wrestling

Palamēdēs, -is m. a Greek

Palinūrus, -ī m. pilot of Aeneas; also the name of a promontory

palla, -ae f. robe, mantle

Palladium, -ī n. a statue of Pallas

Pallas, -adis f. a Greek goddess, more or less closely identified with Minerva

†pallēns, -entis pale, wan

*palleō, -ēre, -uī be pale

pallēscō, -ere, palluī turn pale

pallidulus, -a, -um pale

pallidus, -a, -um pale, wan, pallid

pallor, -ōris m. pallor, paleness

*palma, -ae f. palm (of the hand), hand; palm branch; palm, prize; victory

palmōsus, -a, -um palmy, abounding in palms

palmula, -ae f. oar blade

pālor, -ārī, -ātus fly in panic

palumbēs, -is f. wood pigeon

*palūs, -ūdis f. marsh, pool; marsh water

palūstris, -e of the marsh or swamp

pampineus, -a, -um of vine leaves; wreathed with vines

Pandarus, -ī m. a Mysian chieftain

*pandō, -ere, pandī, passus (pānsus) spread out, stretch out, extend; throw open, open; unfold, unfurl; disclose, reveal; partic. passus, -a, um unbound, dishevelled

pānis, -is m. bread

Panopēa, -ae f. a Nereid, a sea nymph

Panopēs, -is m. a Sicilian

Pantagiās, -ae m. a Sicilian stream

Panthūs, -ī m. a Trojan priest

papāver, -eris n. poppy

Paphos, -ī f. a city in Cyprus

*pār, paris equal, even; alike, like; well-balanced

parātus, -a, -um ready

parātus, -ūs m. preparation

Parcae, -ārum f. pl. the Fates

*parcō, -ere, pepercī (parsī), parsūrus spare; restrain; forbear, refrain from

parcus, -a, -um frugal

*parēns, -entis m. or f. parent; father, mother; ancestor

*pāreō, -ēre, -uī, pāritūrus obey

*pariēs, -etis m. wall of a building

parilis, -e equal

*pariō, -ere, peperī, partus give birth to, bring forth, bear; win, secure, obtain; bring upon

Paris, -idis m. son of Priam, who carried off Helen and thus caused the Trojan War

pariter adv. equally, in like manner, on equal terms; together; side by side; in even line

Parius, -a, -um Parian, of Paros

parma, -ae f. buckler, shield

Parnāsus (-os), -ī m. Parnassus, a mountain in Phocis

†parō 1 prepare, get ready, make ready

Paros, -ī f. one of the Cyclades, a group of islands in the Aegean Sea

*pars, partis f. part, share, portion; quarter, side

Parthenopaeus, -ī m. one of the Seven against Thebes

Parthī, -ōrum m. pl. a remote tribe in Asia

partior, -īrī, -ītus share, divide, distribute

partus, -a, -um partic. of pariō

partus, -ūs m. birth; offspring

*parum adv. too little, (but) little

parumper adv. for a little while

parvulus, -a, -um little, very small

*parvus, -a, -um little, small

*pāscō, -ere, pāvī, pāstus feed, nourish, pasture; feast; pass. as middle, graze, feed; feed on

pāscuum, -ī n. pasture

Pāsiphaē, -ēs f. wife of Minos and mother of the Minotaur

*passim adv. here and there, everywhere

passus, -a, -um partic. of pandō

passus, -a, -um partic. of patior

*passus, -ūs m. step

*pāstor, -ōris m. herdsman, shepherd

Patavium, -ī n. a city of the Veneti; the modern Padua

*patefaciō, -ere, -fēcī, -factus open, throw open, lay open

patēns partic. of pateō

*pateō, -ēre, -uī lie open, stand open; extend, stretch; appear, be manifest; partic. patēns, -entis open

*pater, patris m. father, sire; forefather, ancestor; pl. parents, elders; senators

*patera, -ae f. bowl, cup

paternus, -a, -um of one's father, paternal

patēscō, –ere, patuī open to the view; lie open, be disclosed, be revealed; become disclosed

*patior, –ī, passus suffer, endure; permit, allow; partic. patiēns, –entis submitting to, enduring, submissive

*patria, –ae f. (one's own) country, native country, fatherland; land, country

†patrius, –a, –um of one's father or ancestors; of one's country, native; paternal, ancestral

Patrōn, –ōnis m. a comrade of Aeneas

patrōnus, –ī m. protector, patron

patruus, –ī m. uncle (on the father's side)

patulus, –a, –um spreading

*paucī, –ae, –a few, a few

*paulātim adv. little by little, gradually

*paulisper adv. for a little while

*paulum adv. a little, a little while

pauper, –eris poor, needy

pauperiēs, –ēī f. poverty, humble circumstances

paupertās, –ātis f. poverty, humble circumstances

*paveō, –ēre, pāvī be afraid; tremble with fear

pavidus, –a, –um affrighted, dismayed, trembling, timid

pavitō 1 be in terror, be terrified, quake with fear

pavor, –ōris m. terror, fear, trembling

*pāx, pācis f. peace; favor, grace, indulgence

pecten, –inis m. comb; pick (for playing the lyre)

*pectus, –oris n. breast, bosom; heart

*pecus, –oris n. cattle; animal; herd, flock, throng

*pecus, –udis f. beast, animal; sheep, goat, cow

*pedes, –itis m. foot soldier; as adj., on foot

*pelagus, –ī n. sea; flood

Pelasgus, –a, –um Pelasgian, Greek; as noun, Pelasgī, –ōrum m. pl. Pelasgians, regarded by the ancients as the primitive inhabitants of Greece; Greeks

Peliās, –ae m. a Trojan

Pēlīdēs, –ae m. son of Peleus; i.e., Achilles

Pēlion, –ī n. a mountain in Thessaly

pellāx, –ācis wily, artful, deceitful

*pellis, –is f. skin, hide

*pellō, –ere, pepulī, pulsus beat, drive; drive out, drive away, expel, banish

Pelopēus, –a, –um of Pelops; Grecian

Pelōrus, –ī m. or Pelōrum, –ī n. a promontory of Northeastern Sicily

pelta, –ae f. shield

Penātēs, –ium m. pl. gods of the storeroom, household gods; gods of the state

*pendeō, –ēre, pependī hang, be suspended; linger; partic. pendēns, –entis pendent

*pendō, –ere, pependī, pēnsus weigh out; pay

Pēneleus, –ī m. a Greek

penetrālia, –ium n. pl. interior; innermost apartments, innermost sanctuary

*penetrālis, –e innermost, inner

penetrō 1 penetrate, enter, reach; make one's way into; thread

*penitus inwardly, within; far away; deeply, thoroughly, carefully

Penthesilēa, –ae f. queen of the Amazons

Pentheus, –eī (–eōs) m. king of Thebes

penus, –ūs f. food, stores, provisions, viands

peplum, –ī n. robe, mantle; especially the mantle used to drape the statue of Minerva

*per prep. with acc. through, over, along, across, amid; throughout, during; by, by means of; because of

†peragō, –ere, –ēgī, –āctus go through with, finish, consummate, achieve, accomplish; pursue, continue

peragrō 1 wander over, wander through

percellō, –ere, –culī, –culsus strike down

†percipiō, –ere, –cēpī, –ceptus catch

percurrō, –ere, –currī (–cucurrī), –cursus run over, run through, enumerate

percussus, –a, –um partic. of percutiō

percutiō, –ere, –cussī, –cussus smite, strike, beat; partic. percussus, –a, –um stricken, struck

*perdō, –ere, –didī, –ditus lose, destroy; partic. perditus, –a, –um lost, ruined, undone, forlorn, wretched

peredō, –ere, –ēdī, –ēsus eat up, consume

peregrīnus, –a, –um foreign

perēmptus, –a, –um partic. of perimō

perennis, –e everlasting

*pereō, –īre, –iī, –itūrus perish, die

pererrō 1 wander over; reconnoitre; scan, survey

†perferō, –ferre, –tulī, –lātus bear, endure; convey, carry; report; sē perferre, betake oneself

*perficiō, –ere, –fēcī, –fectus complete, accomplish, finish; work; partic. perfectus, –a, –um wrought

perfidus, –a, –um faithless

perflō 1 blow over

perfringō, –ere, –frēgī, –frāctus crash through

perfundō, –ere, –fūdī, –fūsus pour over, drench; wet, bedew, moisten, anoint; dip; dye; bathe, wash

Pergama, –ōrum n. pl. the citadel of Troy; Troy

Pergameus, -a, -um of Pergamum, *the citadel of Troy*

†pergō, -ere, perrēxī, perrēctūrus proceed

perhibeō 2 present; say

*perīculum (perīclum), -ī *n.* danger, hazard, peril, jeopardy

perimō, -ere, -ēmī, -ēmptus take away, annihilate, destroy, kill; *partic.* perēmptus, -a, -um ruined, destroyed

Periphās, -antis *m.* *a Greek*

*perītus, -a, -um experienced, wise

perjūrium, -ī *n.* perjury

perjūrus, -a, -um false, perjured

perlābor, -ī, -lāpsus glide over

perlegō, -ere, -lēgī, -lēctus scan, survey, examine

permātūrēscō, -ere, -mātūruī ripen

permētior, -īrī, -mēnsus measure over, traverse

permisceō, -ēre, -miscuī, -mixtus mix, mingle

*permittō, -ere, -mīsī, -missus entrust, consign, commit, give over; suffer, allow, permit

permixtus *partic. of* permisceō

permulceō, -ēre, -mulsī, -mulsus soothe

pernīx, -īcis nimble, swift, fleet

perōdī, -ōdisse, -ōsus hate

perōsus, -a, -um hating, detesting, loathing

*perpetuus, -a, -um continuous, unbroken; all

perrumpō, -ere, -rūpī, -ruptus break through, burst through

persentiō, -īre, -sēnsī, -sēnsus feel deeply; feel; perceive

†persequor, -ī, -secūtus follow

persolvō, -ere, -solvī, -solūtus render, pay

personō, -āre, -uī, -itus sound through; cause to resound *or* reëcho

perstō, -āre, -stitī, -stātūrus continue standing; continue fixed; persist

pertaedet, -ēre, -taesum est *impers.* it wearies; mē pertaedet I am weary, I loathe

pertemptō 1 try; fill, pervade

perustus, -a, -um sunburned, tanned

†perveniō, -īre, -vēnī, -ventūrus come, arrive, make one's way

pervius, -a, -um giving passage through, communicating

*pēs, pedis *m.* foot; sheet

*pestis, -is *f.* pestilence, plague; affliction, ruin, destruction

Petēlia, -ae *f.* *a town of Southern Italy*

*petō, -ere, -īvī, -ītus seek, make for, steer for; ask, aim, aim at; attack; scan

Phaeāces, -um *m. pl.* Phaeacians, *inhabitants of Corcyra*

Phaedra, -ae *f.* *queen of Theseus*

Phaëthōn, -ontis *m.* *son of Phoebus and Clymene, an Ethiopian queen; also a name of the sun-god*

phalānx, -angis *f.* phalanx, host; fleet

phalerae, -ārum *f. pl.* trappings (*of horses*)

*pharetra, -ae *f.* quiver

Phēgeus, -eī (-eōs) *m.* *a Trojan*

Philēmōn, -onis *m.* *husband of Baucis*

Philoctētēs, -ae *m.* *a Greek chieftain*

philomēla, -ae *f.* nightingale

Phīnēius, -a, -um of Phineus, *a Thracian king*

Phlegethōn, -ontis *m.* *a river of the underworld*

Phlegōn, -ontis *m.* *one of the horses of the sun*

Phlegyās, -ae *m.* *father of Ixion*

Phōcis, -idis *f.* *a mountainous country between Boeotia and Thessaly*

Phoebē, -ēs (-ae) *f.* Diana, *sister of Phoebus Apollo*

Phoebēus, -a, -um of Phoebus

Phoebus, -ī *m.* *another name for Apollo*

Phoenīces, -um *m. pl.* Phoenicians

Phoenīssa, -ae *f.* Phoenician woman, *especially* Dido

Phoenīx, -īcis *m.* *a Greek chieftain*

Pholoē, -ēs *f.* *a Cretan slave-woman*

Phorbās, -antis *m.* *a Trojan*

Phorcus, -ī *m.* *a sea divinity*

Phryges, -um *m. pl.* Phrygians, Trojans

Phrygius, -a, -um Phrygian, Trojan

Phthīa, -ae *f.* *a district of Thessaly*

piāculum, -ī *n.* expiation; expiatory offering *or* sacrifice

picea, -ae *f.* pitch pine, pine

piceus, -a, -um pitchy, pitch black

pictūra, -ae *f.* picture, painting

pictūrātus, -a, -um embroidered

pictus, -a, -um *partic. of* pingō

Pīerius, -a, -um Pierian, of Pieria, *a region in Macedonia sacred to the Muses*

†pietās, -ātis *f.* duty, dutifulness, affection; devotion, loyalty; goodness, righteousness, piety; virtue, character

piger, -gra, -grum lazy, sluggish; barren

piget, -ēre, -uit *impers.* it displeases, it irks; mē piget, I am annoyed; I regret

*pignus, -oris *n.* pledge, token

pīneus, -a, -um of pine

*pingō, -ere, pīnxī, pictus paint, embroider, tattoo

*pinguis, -e fat, rich, fertile

pīnifer, -era, -erum pine-bearing, pine-clad, pine-covered

*pinna, -ae *f.* feather, wing, pinion

*pīnus, -ūs (-ī) *f.* pine, pine tree

piō 1 expiate, atone for; appease, propitiate

Pīrithoüs, –ī m. *king of the Lapithae*

pirum, –ī n. pear

pirus, –ī f. pear tree

piscis, –is m. fish

piscōsus, –a, –um abounding in fish, fish-haunted

pistrix, –icis f. *any strange sea monster*

*pius, –a, –um devoted, dutiful, loyal; right-eous, good, holy

*placeō 2 please; placet it pleases; it is ordained, it is decreed

placidē gently, softly, quietly

†placidus, –a, –um gentle, quiet, tranquil, peaceful, serene, calm; gracious; propitious

placitus, –a, –um, pleasing, agreeable

*plācō 1 appease, assuage, calm; soothe

1. plaga, –ae f. region, district, tract

2. plaga, –ae f. net, toils, snare

plangor, –ōris m. wailing, lamentation; *properly a beating of the breast or face in token of grief*

planta, –ae f. sole of the foot; foot

*plānus, –a, –um level

plaudō, –ere, plausī, plausus beat, beat time to; flap, flutter; applaud

*plausus, –ūs m. applause, clapping; fluttering, flapping

Plēïades, –um f. pl. *the seven daughters of Atlas who were changed into a constellation*

Plēmyrium, –ī n. *a promontory near Syracuse in Sicily*

*plēnus, –a, –um full, filled, stocked

plicō, –āre, –āvī (–uī), –itus fold, coil

plūma, –ae f. feather

plumbum, –ī n. lead

plūrimus, –a, –um (*superl. of* multus) most, very many, abundant, abounding

plūs, plūris (*comp. of* multus) more

pluvius, –a, –um rainy, rain-bringing

pōculum, –ī n. drinking vessel, cup, goblet

*poena, –ae f. penalty, punishment, satisfac-tion; vengeance

Poenus, –ī m. a Carthaginian

Polītēs, –ae m. *a son of Priam*

pollex, –icis m. thumb

*polliceor, –ērī, –itus promise

polluō, –ere, –uī, –ūtus defile, pollute; outrage, wrong, violate

Pollūx, –ūcis m. *son of Jupiter and Leda and half brother of Castor*

*polus, –ī m. pole; sky, heaven

Polyboetēs, –ae m. *a Trojan priest*

Polydōrus, –ī m. *a son of Priam*

Polyphēmus, –ī m. *a Cyclops*

Pōmetiī, –ōrum m. pl. *Vergil's name for Suessa Pometia, a Volscian town*

pompa, –ae f. procession, ceremonial

pōmum, –ī n. fruit; apple

*pondus, –eris n. weight, burden

pōne adv. behind, after

*pōnō, –ere, posuī, positus place, put, set, lay; set up, erect, found, build; institute, es-tablish, appoint; lay down, lay aside

Ponticus, –a, –um Pontic, of Pontus, *a district in Asia Minor famous for its pines*

pontifex, –ficis, m. high priest

Pontilliānus, –ī m. *a man's name*

*pontus, –ī m. deep sea, sea, deep

populāris, –e of the people; popular

pōpuleus, –a, –um of poplar

populō (*dep.* *populor) 1 *originally*, go on a tribal raid; *hence*, ravage, lay waste, rob, plunder; bereave

*populus, –ī m. tribe, nation, people

*porrigō, –ere, –rēxī, –rēctus reach out, stretch forth, extend

porrō adv. farther on, afar, at a distance

*porta, –ae f. gate, portal, outlet

portendō, –ere, –tendī, –tentus portend, presage, foretell

portentum, –ī n. omen, sign; monstrosity

porticus, –ūs f. portico, colonnade

portitor, –ōris m. ferryman

*portō 1 bear, carry

Portūnus, –ī m. god of harbors

*portus, –ūs m. harbor, port, haven

*poscō, –ere, poposcī demand, ask; request, beg, entreat, supplicate

*possideō, –ēre, –sēdī, –sessus hold, possess

*possum, posse, potuī be able, can; avail, have power, have influence

*post prep. with acc. after, behind; *as adv.*, afterwards, hereafter

*posterus, –a, –um next, following

posthabeō, –ēre, –uī, –itus place after, esteem less

posthāc adv. hereafter, henceforth

*postis, –is m. doorpost, door; beam

postpōnō, –ere, –posuī, –positus place after

*postquam conj. after

postrēmus, –a, –um (*superl. of* posterus) last, lowest, hindmost

postumus, –a, –um (*superl. of* posterus) last, latest-born

Postumus, –ī m. *a friend of Martial*

*potēns, –entis powerful, mighty; having power over, ruling

potentia, –ae f. might, power, strength

*potestās, –ātis f. power, authority

\*potior, –īrī, –ītus gain possession of, secure, win, obtain

potior, –ius (*comp. of* potis) preferable, better

potis, –e able

\*potius *adv.* preferably, rather

pōtō 1 drink

\*prae *prep. with abl.* before

praecelsus, –a, –um very high, lofty

\*praeceps, –cipitis headlong, swift, in haste; *as noun*, praeceps, –cipitis *n.* steep edge, verge, precipice; in praeceps downwards

praeceptum, –ī *n.* warning, bidding, injunction

\*praecipiō, –ere, –cēpī, –ceptus take in advance, anticipate; advise, teach

praecipitō 1 *trans.*, cast *or* drive headlong, throw, hurl; *intrans.*, fall headlong, rush down, fall, plunge, descend; hasten

praecipuē *adv.* especially

\*praecipuus, –a, –um particular, especial, chief

\*praeclārus, –a, –um illustrious, glorious, distinguished

praeclūdō, –ere, –sī, –sus shut up, stop

praecō, –ōnis *m.* herald

praecordia, –ōrum *n. pl.* breast, bosom, heart

\*praeda, –ae *f.* booty, spoil, plunder, prey

praedīcō, –ere, –dīxī, –dictus foretell

praedictum, –ī *n.* prediction, prophecy

praeeō, –īre, praeiī, praeitūrus go before; lead

†praeferō, –ferre, –tulī, –lātus put before, rank before, prefer

\*praeficiō, –ere, –fēcī, –fectus place in charge, set over

praefīgō, –ere, –fīxī, –fīxus fasten on the front of, tip; praefīxus, –a, –um, tipped, pointed

praefīxus, –a, –um *partic. of* praefīgō

praemetuō, –ere, –uī fear in anticipation, dread

\*praemittō, –ere, –mīsī, –missus send ahead, send forward

\*praemium, –ī *n.* reward, prize

praenatō, –āre flow past, glide by

praeparō 1 prepare, make ready beforehand

praepes, –etis flying, fleet, swift

praepinguis, –e exceeding fat, exceeding rich

praepōnō, –ere, –posuī, –positus place before, prefer

praeripiō, –ere, –ripuī, –reptus snatch away, tear away

praeruptus, –a, –um precipitous, steep

praesaepe, –is *n.* enclosure; hive

praesāgus, –a, –um foreboding

praescius, –a, –um foreknowing, prescient, having foreknowledge

\*praesēns, –entis at hand, present; instant; ready

praesentiō, –īre, –sēnsī, –sēnsus perceive beforehand

praesideō, –ēre, –sēdī preside over

praestāns, –antis surpassing, preëminent, excellent, distinguished

\*praestō, –āre, –stitī, –stitus surpass, be better; praestat *impers.* it is better

praetendō, –ere, –tendī, –tentus hold out, stretch out; proffer, extend to; praetentus, –a, –um stretched before, lying in front of

\*praeter *prep. with acc.* by, beyond; before

\*praetereā *adv.* besides, moreover; after that

\*praetereō, –īre, –iī (–īvī), –itus pass by, pass, outstrip

praeterlābor, –ī, –lāpsus glide by, sail by, flow by

praetervehō, –ere, –vexī, –vectus carry past; *pass. as middle*, be borne past, sail by

praetexō, –ere, –texuī, –textus fringe, border; cover, cloak, conceal, hide

praevertō, –ere, –vertī, –versus surprise; surpass; occupy

praevideō, –ēre, –vīdī, –vīsus foresee

prātum, –ī *n.* meadow, mead

prāvus, –a, –um crooked; wrong, false

\*precor, –ārī, –ātus pray to, pray, beseech, entreat, supplicate, beg for

\*prehendō, –ere, –hendī, –hēnsus seize, grasp

\*premō, –ere, pressī, pressus press; press upon, be close upon, pursue closely; tread upon; overpower, overwhelm; bury, keep buried; hide, cover, conceal; restrain, repress, curb, check, keep down, keep back, confine, bind; rule

prēndō (*for* prehendō), –ere, prēndī, prēnsus seize, grasp, catch

prēnsō 1 grasp at, lay hold of, seize

pressō 1 press, squeeze

pretiōsus, –a, –um of great value, valuable

\*pretium, –ī *n.* price; prize; reward

\*prex, precis *f.* prayer, entreaty

Priamēius, –a, –um of Priam

Priamidēs, –ae *m.* son of Priam

Priamus, –ī *m.* Priam, *king of Troy*

\*prīdem *adv.* long ago, long since

prīmaevus, –a, –um in the first period of life, youthful

†prīmō *adv.* at first

†prīmum *adv.* first, soon; ut prīmum, cum prīmum, as soon as

\*prīmus, –a, –um (*superl. of* prior) first, first part of; in prīmīs especially

\*prīnceps, –cipis foremost, first; *as noun, m.* chief, chieftain, leader, founder

\*prīncipium, –ī n. beginning; prīncipiō (abl. sing. as adv.) in the beginning, first, in the first place

\*prior, –us former, first; as noun, priōrēs, –um m. pl. ancestors

prīscus, –a, –um old, ancient

\*prīstinus, –a, –um old, former

Pristis, –is f. name of a ship

prius adv. before, sooner

\*priusquam conj. (often prius . . . quam) sooner . . . than, before; with negative, until

\*prō prep. with abl. for, in return for; before; on account of; instead, instead of, in place of

prō interjection ah! oh! O!

proavus, –ī m. great-grandfather; ancestor, forefather

\*probō 1 prove good; test; approve

Procās, –ae m. an Alban king

procāx, –ācis boisterous

†prōcēdō, –ere, –cessī, –cessūrus go or come forward, advance, proceed; pass by

procella, –ae f. gust, blast, storm

procerēs, –um m. pl. chiefs, chieftains, nobles, princes

prōclāmō 1 cry out, make outcry

Procris, –is f. a Grecian heroine

\*procul adv. far off, at a distance, far away, far; from afar; at a little distance

†prōcumbō, –ere, –cubuī, –cubitūrus fall; bend forward; sink down

prōcurrō, –ere, –currī (–cucurrī), cursūrus run forward; run out, jut out, project

prōcurvus, –a, –um curving, winding

procus, –ī m. suitor

prōdeō, –īre, –iī (–īvī), –itūrus go forward, advance, move on; come forward

prōdigiōsus, –a, –um marvellous, prodigious

prōdigium, –ī n. prodigy, omen, portent

prōditiō, –ōnis f. betrayal, treason, treachery; accusation

\*prōdō, –ere, –didī, –ditus betray, give over; prove false to; hand down, transmit

†prōdūcō, –ere, –dūxī, –ductus lead forth, prolong, protract

\*proelium, –ī n. battle

profānus, –a, –um uninitiated, unholy

prōferō, –ferre, –tulī, –lātus carry forward, bear forth, extend

\*proficīscor, –ī, profectus set out, set forth

\*profiteor, –ērī, –fessus avow, profess

profor, –fārī, –fātus speak

profugus, –a, –um fugitive; exiled, outcast

profundus, –a, –um deep, profound; high

\*prōgeniēs, –ēī f. offspring, children, progeny; race

prōgignō, –ere, –genuī, –genitus bring forth, bear

†prōgredior, –ī, –gressus step forth, advance, proceed

\*prohibeō 2 keep off, keep away; ward off, avert; prevent; forbid

\*prōjiciō (prōiciō), –ere, –jēcī, –jectus hurl forward; fling down; throw, cast; fling aside, throw away; partic. projectus, –a, –um projecting

prōlābor, –ī, –lāpsus slip; fall in ruin

\*prōlēs, –is f. offspring, progeny; race; line, lineage

prōluō, –ere, –luī, –lūtus wash; drench; fill

prōluviēs, –ēī f. overflow; discharge

prōmereor, –ērī, –itus deserve

Promēthīdēs, –ae m. son of Prometheus, i.e., Deucalion

prōmissum, –ī n. promise

†prōmittō, –ere, –mīsī, –missus promise, pledge

prōmō, –ere, prōmpsī, prōmptus bring forth

prōmptus, –a, –um ready, inclined

(prōmptus, –ūs) m. only in the phrase in prōmptū easy

pronepōs, –ōtis m. great-grandson

prōnuba, –ae f. bride's attendant, bridewoman

\*prōnus, –a, –um bending forward; headlong; prone

propāgō, –inis f. offspring, race, progeny; shoot, slip

\*prope adv. and prep. with acc. near

properē adv. swiftly, hastily

\*properō 1 hasten, haste, make haste

propinquō 1 approach, draw near

\*propinquus, –a, –um near, kindred, related

propior, –ius nearer

propius adv. nearer, more closely; favorably

†prōpōnō, –ere, –posuī, –positus propose, set up, offer

prōpositum, –ī n. purpose

\*proprius, –a, –um one's very own, belonging to, peculiar; permanent, lasting

\*propter prep. with acc. near to; on account of

prōpugnāculum, –ī n. defense, bulwark

\*prōra, –ae f. prow, bow

prōripiō, –ere, –ripuī, –reptus drag forth; hurry

prōrumpō, –ere, –rūpī, –ruptus belch forth, pour forth; partic. prōruptus, –a, –um dashing, rushing, raging

†prōsequor, –ī, –secūtus accompany, escort, attend, follow; continue, proceed

Prōserpina, –ae f. wife of Pluto and queen of the underworld

prōsiliō, –īre, –uī (–iī) leap forth, dart forward

prōspectō 1 gaze upon

prōspectus, –ūs m. prospect, view

prōsper or prōsperus, –a, –um propitious, auspicious, favorable

prōspiciō, –ere, –spexī, –spectus look forth, look out, gaze out upon; see before one; descry

*prōsum, prōdesse, prōfuī, prōfutūrus avail, be useful

prōtēctus, –a, –um partic. of prōtegō

prōtegō, –ere, –tēxī, –tēctus protect, shelter

prōtendō, –ere, –tendī, –tentus (–tēnsus) stretch forth

*prōtinus adv. forward; continuously; straightway, forthwith

prōtrahō, –ere, –trāxī, –tractus drag forth

prōvectus, –a, –um advanced (in years)

prōvehō, –ere, –vexī, –vectus bear, carry, carry forward; pass. as middle, sail on, go, proceed

proximus, –a, –um (superl. of propior) nearest, next, neighboring

*prūdēns, –entis foreseeing, wise

†prūdentia, –ae f. foresight; wisdom

pruīna, –ae f. frost

prūna, –ae f. live coal

pūbēns, –entis full-grown, full of sap

*pūbēs, –is f. group of young men, youthful band; groin, waist; brood

pūbēscō, –ere, pūbuī grow up

*pūblicus, –a, –um common

pudeō, –ēre be ashamed; usually impers., *pudet, –ēre, puduit (puditum est) it causes shame; mē pudet I am ashamed

pudīcus, –a, –um modest, virtuous

*pudor, –ōris m. shame; modesty, honor, sense of shame

†puella, –ae f. girl

puellāris, –e girlish, maidenly

*puer, –ī m. boy

puerīlis, –e of a boy, youthful

*pugna, –ae f. fight, battle, combat, contest, struggle, conflict

†pugnō 1 fight, battle, struggle, contend; fight against, resist

pugnus, –ī m. fist, clenched hand

*pulcher, –chra, –chrum fair, beautiful, comely

pullus, –a, –um dark, dark-colored

*pulsō 1 beat, lash, strike

pulsus, –a, –um partic. of pellō

pulsus, –ūs m. beat; trampling

pulverulentus, –a, –um dusty

*pulvis, –eris m. dust

pūmex, –icis m. pumice stone; porous or hollow rock

pūniceus, –a, –um scarlet, red, crimson, purple

Pūnicus, –a, –um Punic, Carthaginian

*puppis, –is f. stern; ship; ā puppī from behind, astern

pūrgō 1 make clean; sē purgāre vanish, dissolve

*purpura, –ae f. purple

purpureus, –a, –um purple, crimson, ruddy, rosy, lustrous, bright-colored, gay, bright

pūrus, –a, –um pure, clear; hasta pūra a headless spear

*putō 1 clear up; think, suppose, consider, believe

Pygmaliōn, –ōnis m. brother of Dido

pyra, –ae f. funeral pile, pyre

pȳramis, –idis f. pyramid

Pȳramus, –ī m. a Babylonian youth, lover of Thisbe

Pyrgō, –ūs f. a Trojan woman

Pyroīs, –entis m. one of the horses of the sun

Pyrrha, –ae f. wife of Deucalion

Pyrrhus, –ī m. son of Achilles; also known as Neoptolemus

## Q

*quā interrog., rel., and indefinite adv.: 1) interrog., where? how? in what way? 2) rel., where; 3) indefinite, in any way

quadrīgae, –ārum f. pl. four-horse chariot

quadrijugī, –ōrum m. pl. four-horse team

quadrupēs, –edis m. or f. four-footed animal, quadruped; especially courser, steed

*quaerō, –ere, quaesīvī (–iī), –ītus seek, be in quest of, look for; inquire, ask

quaesītor, –ōris m. judge, examiner

*quaesō defective entreat, beseech

*quālis, –e interrog. and rel. adj.: 1) interrog., what sort? of what sort? of what nature? 2) rel., (such) as

*quam interrog. and rel. adv.: 1) interrog., how? 2) rel., as much as, as; with comparatives, than; with superlatives, as . . . as possible

*quamquam conj. and adv. although; and yet, however

*quamvīs conj. however much, though, although

*quandō conj. and adv.: 1) conj., when, since, because; 2) interrog. adv. when? 3) indef. adv., at any time, ever

*quantus, –a, –um interrog. and rel. adj.: 1) in-

*terrog.*, how great? how much? 2) *rel.*, *(as great)* as, *(as much)* as; **quantum** how much? how greatly? as far as

**quārē** *or* **quā rē** *interrog. and rel. adv.:* 1) *interrog.*, why? wherefore? on account of what? 2) *rel.*, for which reason, on which account, wherefore

*****quārtus, –a, –um** fourth

**qua**ssō 1 brandish, shake; shatter

**quater** *adv.* four times

*****quatiō, –ere, —, quassus** shake, shatter; flap; lash

*****quattuor** *indecl. adj.* four

*****–que** *and;* **–que et** both . . . and

**queō, quīre, quīvī (quiī)** be able, can

**quercus, –ūs** *f.* oak tree

*****querēla, –ae** *f.* complaint

*****queror, –ī, questus** complain, lament, bewail

**questus, –ūs** *f.* complaint, lament

*****quī, quae, quod** *rel. pron.* who, which, that; *as rel. adj.*, what

*****quī, quae, quod** *interrog. adj.* what? what sort of?

*****quia** *conj.* because

**quianam** *adv.* why? why, pray?

*****quīcumque, quaecumque, quodcumque** *indef. rel. pron.* whoever, whatever, whichever, whosoever; *as indef. rel. adj.* whatsoever

**quid** *adv.* why?

*****quidem** *adv.* indeed, truly, to be sure, at least; **nē** . . . **quidem** not even

*****quiēs, –ētis** *f.* rest, repose, sleep; pause, lull

*****quiēscō, –ere, –ēvī, –ētus** become quiet; rest, repose; cease

*****quiētus, –a, –um** quiet, tranquil, peaceful, calm

*****quīn** *conj. and adv.* by which not, that not, that; why not? nay, nay even, why!

**quīnī, –ae, –a** five each, five

**quīnquāgintā** *indecl. adj.* fifty

**quippe** *adv.* surely, verily, I suppose, to be sure, forsooth

**Quirīnus, –ī** *m. a name for Romulus after his deification*

*****quis, quid** *interrog. pron.* who? what? which?

*****quis (quī), qua (quae), quid (quod)** *indef. pron.* anyone, anything; *as indef. adj.*, any

*****quisnam (quīnam), quaenam, quidnam (quodnam)** *interrog. pron.* who, pray? what, pray? *as interrog. adj.*, what, pray?

*****quisquam, quicquam (quidquam)** *indef. pron.* anyone, anything; *as indef. adj.*, any

*****quisque, quaeque, quicque (quidque)** *and* **quodque** *indef. pron. or adj.* each

*****quisquis, quicquid (quidquid)** *indef. rel. pron.* whoever, whatever, whosoever, whatsoever

*****quīvīs, quaevīs, quodvīs** *indef. adj.* any (you wish)

*****quō** *interrog. and rel. adv.:* 1) *interrog.*, whither? to what place? 2) *rel.*, to which place, whither

**quō** *(abl. sing. of rel. pron.* **quī** *used as conj.)* whereby, in order that

**quōcircā** *conj.* for which reason, wherefore

**quōcumque** *conj. and adv.* whithersoever

*****quod** *conj.* that, in that, because, as to the fact that; wherefore; therefore; but

**quōmodō** *or* **quō modō** in what way? just as

**quōnam** *adv.* whither, pray?

*****quondam** *adv.* once, at one time, formerly; at times, sometimes

*****quoniam** *conj.* since, inasmuch as

*****quoque** *(emphasizing the word it follows)* also, too

*****quot** *indecl. interrog. adj.* how many? *as rel. adj.*, *(as many)* as

**quotannīs** *adv.* yearly, annually

*****quotiēns** *interrog. adv.* how often? *as rel. adv.*, *(as often)* as

**quousque** *adv.* how far? how long?

# R

**rabidus, –a, –um** raving, mad, frenzied

*****rabiēs, –ēī** *f.* madness, rage, fury, frenzy

**radiō** 1 shine, gleam

*****radius, –ī** *m.* rod, measuring rod; spoke *(of a wheel)*; ray, beam

*****rādīx, –īcis** *f.* root

**rādō, –ere, rāsī, rāsus** rub, graze, pass near, skim along

**rāmāle, –is** *n.* twig, chip

*****rāmus, –ī** *m.* branch, bough

**rāna, –ae** *f.* frog

†**rapidus, –a, –um** rushing, tearing, fierce, wild; rapid, swift, hurrying

*****rapiō, –ere, rapuī, raptus** seize, snatch, snatch away, carry away, take, plunder, steal, ravish; rescue; turn swiftly; scour; hurry

**raptō** 1 hurry along

**raptor, –ōris** *m.* plunderer; *as adj.*, ravening, prowling

**raptum, –ī** *n.* booty, plunder

**rārēscō, –ere** begin to open

**rārus, –a, –um** loose, wide apart; at intervals here and there, scattered; *of nets*, wide-meshed; *of words*, broken, inarticulate

**rāstrum, –ī** *n.* hoe, rake

*ratiō, –ōnis *f.* purpose; way, manner
*ratis, –is *f.* raft, bark, ship, boat, vessel
ratus, –a, –um *partic. of* reor
*raucus, –a, –um hoarse, noisy, ringing, deep-sounding
rebellis, –e insurgent, rebellious
recēdō, –ere, –cessī, –cessūrus withdraw, depart, retire, recede; vanish, stand back
*recēns, –entis fresh, recent, new
recēnseō, –ēre, –uī, –sus review
recidīvus, –a, –um falling back; restored, rising again
recidō, –ere, reccidī fall back (*upon*)
recingō, –ere, –cīnxī, –cīnctus ungird, loosen
†recipiō, –ere, –cēpī, –ceptus take back; regain, recover, rescue; take, receive, admit
reclūdō, –ere, –sī, –sus unclose; open, open up, reveal, disclose; unsheathe
recolō, –ere, –coluī, –cultus till again; think over, contemplate, reflect upon
recondō, –ere, –didī, –ditus conceal, hide; bury; put away
*recordor, –ārī, –ātus recall, recollect, remember
*rēctē *adv.* properly, suitably, rightly
rēctor, –ōris *m.* ruler; steersman, helmsman
rēctum, –ī *n.* right, virtue
rēctus, –a, –um straight, right, direct
recubō, –āre lie down, recline, lie
recursō, –āre run back; return, recur; keep returning
recursus, –ūs *m.* running back, retreat, return
*recūsō 1 refuse, object to, decline
recutiō, –ere, –cussī, –cussus shake violently, shake
*reddō, –ere, –didī, –ditus give back, return, restore; give up; reply, answer; make, render
*redeō, –īre, –īvī (–iī), –itūrus go back, come back, return
redimiō 4 bind, wreathe, encircle
†redimō, –ere, –ēmī, –ēmptus buy back, ransom
reditus, –ūs *m.* return
redoleō, –ēre, –uī be fragrant with, be redolent of, smell of
redūcō, –ere, –dūxī, –ductus lead back, bring back, draw back; bring anew; rescue; *partic.*
reductus, –a, –um withdrawn, retired
redux, –icis led back, restored, returned, safe
refellō, –ere, –fellī refute, contradict
†referō, –ferre, rettulī, relātus bear back, carry back, bring back; bear again; bear away, carry off; waft, convey; reproduce, revive, renew; resemble; recall; repeat; change;

relate, say, speak, utter; pay; sē referre return, go back
rēfert, –ferre, –tulit *impers.* it makes a difference
refīgō, –ere, –fīxī, –fīxus unfasten, loosen; take down
reflectō, –ere, –flexī, –flexus turn back, turn
refringō, –ere, –frēgī, –frāctus break off
refugiō, –ere, –fūgī, –fugitūrus flee back, speed away; recoil, shrink; face back
refulgeō, –ēre, –fulsī flash back, flash, be resplendent, be refulgent; glitter, glisten
refundō, –ere, –fūdī, –fūsus pour back; stir up, upheave; *pass.*, flow back; overflow
rēgālis, –e regal, princely, royal
rēgia, –ae *f.* royal palace
rēgificus, –a, –um regal, princely
*rēgīna, –ae *f.* queen, princess
*regiō, –ōnis *f.* direction, line; quarter, region, district, territory
†rēgius, –a, –um royal, kingly; queenly
rēgnātor, –ōris *m.* ruler, sovereign
*rēgnō 1 reign, rule; reign over
*rēgnum, –ī *n.* reign, rule, sway; sovereign power; ruling power; power, sovereignty; kingdom, realm, domain
*regō, –ere, rēxī, rēctus direct, guide; sway, rule, control; wield
rejiciō (reiciō), –ere, –jēcī, –jectus fling back, hurl back
relanguēscō, –ere, –languī collapse, grow faint
relaxō 1 unbar, loose
relegō, –ere, –lēgī, –lēctus coast along again
relevō 1 relieve, rest
*rēligiō, –ōnis *f.* reverence for what is divine; ceremonial, worship, observance; religious offering; religion
rēligiōsus, –a, –um sacred, holy
*relinquō, –ere, –līquī, –lictus leave, relinquish, abandon
†rēliquiae, –ārum *f. pl.* remains, relics, remnant; survivors
relūceō, –ēre, –lūxī shine back; flash, gleam, glow
remeō, –āre, –āvī return, go back
remētior, –īrī, –mēnsus measure again; retrace, traverse again; note again
rēmex, –igis *m.* oarsman, rower; band of rowers
rēmigium, –ī *n.* rowing; rowing movement, oarage; oars; oarsmen
*remittō, –ere, –mīsī, –missus send back, return; release; relinquish; resign; pay back
remollēscō, –ere soften

remordeō, –ēre, –mordī, –morsus bite again;
torment, distress, vex

remoror, –ārī, –ātus delay

†removeō, –ēre, –mōvī, –mōtus remove

remūgiō, –īre bellow back; resound, reëcho

*rēmus, –ī m. oar

Remus, –ī m. brother of Romulus

renārrō 1 tell again, recount again, recount

renāscor, –ī, –nātus be born again, grow again;
be renewed

renovō 1 renew; make new, repeat

*reor, rērī, ratus think, believe, suppose

repāgula, –ōrum n. pl. fastenings, bars

reparābilis, –e reparable, able to be repaired

reparō 1 refurnish, replace, repair, restore

repellō, –ere, reppulī, repulsus drive back,
repel, repulse; baffle; rebuff; reject

rependō, –ere, –pendī, –pēnsus pay back;
make requital; balance, weigh against

*repente adv. suddenly

*reperiō, –īre, repperī, repertus find out, find,
discover

*repetō, –ere, –īvī (–iī), –ītus seek again; recol-
lect, remember, recall; retrace; repeat; go
back to

repleō, –ēre, –ēvī, –ētus fill, refill

repōnō, –ere, –posuī, –positus put back, re-
store, replace; lay down; lay aside; place,
put; store away, store up; bury; partic.
repositus (repostus), –a, –um buried; re-
mote, distant

reportō 1 bring back

reposcō, –ere demand, ask for

repostus partic. of repōnō

†reprimō, –ere, –pressī, –pressus check

repugnō 1 fight against, oppose

repulsa, –ae f. refusal

requiēs, –ēī (–ētis) f. rest, repose, respite

requiēscō, –ere, –ēvī, –ētus come to rest, rest

*requīrō, –ere, –sīvī (–siī), –sītus search for,
seek; ask, ask for; miss; express regret for

*rēs, reī f. thing, affair, occurrence, incident,
circumstance, event, matter, issue, condi-
tion, situation; state, commonwealth; pl.
interests; achievements, exploits; fortunes,
misfortunes; power, empire; world

rescindō, –ere, –scidī, –scissus raze, tear down

reservō 1 reserve, keep back

reses, –idis inactive, dormant

†residō, –ere, –sēdī take one's seat, sit down;
settle; become quiet, grow calm, subside

resignō 1 unseal

†resistō, –ere, –stitī halt, stop; stand revealed,
stand forth; oppose, resist, withstand

†resolvō, –ere, –solvī, –solūtus unfasten, un-
bind, open, unseal; relax; break; unravel;
sever

resonō 1 resound, reverberate, reëcho

respectō, –āre regard

†respiciō, –ere, –spexī, –spectus gaze back,
look back, look behind; look back upon,
look back and see; consider, regard, heed,
be mindful of

*respondeō, –ēre, –spondī, –spōnsus answer,
reply; correspond

†respōnsum, –ī n. answer, reply, response

restinguō, –ere, –stīnxī, –stīnctus put out,
quench, extinguish

*restituō, –ere, –uī, –ūtus replace, restore

*restō, –āre, restitī remain; survive

resultō 1 rebound, reverberate, reëcho

resupīnus, –a, –um bending back, lying on
one's back; with head high, with head
thrown back, haughty

resurgō, –ere, –surrēxī, –surrēctūrus rise again,
revive

rēte, –is n. net

retegō, –ere, –tēxī, –tēctus uncover, unveil,
reveal, disclose

retentō 1 hold back

retināculum, –ī n. cable, mooring rope, hawser

retineō, –ēre, –tinuī, –tentus hold back

retrahō, –ere, –trāxī, –tractus draw again

*retrō adv. backwards, back

retrōrsus (retrōversus) backwards, back

*reus, –ī m. the accused, defendant (in a trial);
as adj., answerable to, bound to

revellō, –ere, –vellī, –vulsus tear off, pull off,
tear away, drag away; remove, disturb,
desecrate

*revertor, –ī, –versus return

revinciō, –īre, –vīnxī, –vīnctus bind back, bind
fast; bind; wreathe

revīsō, –ere revisit, visit again; visit; return
to

revocō 1 call back, recall; retrace; renew,
revive, repair, restore

revolvō, –ere, –volvī, –volūtus roll back, bring
back, unroll; revolve, ponder; rehearse; fall
back, sink back; transform

revomō, –ere, –uī belch forth, throw up

*rēx, rēgis m. king; as adj., dominant, ruling

Rhadamanthus, –ī m. a judge in the underworld

Rhēsus, –ī m. a Thracian chieftain

Rhoetēus or Rhoetēius, –a, –um Rhoetean, of
Rhoeteum, a promontory on the Hellespont
near Troy

rhombus, –ī m. flatfish, turbot

Semīramis, –idis *f. a mythical queen of Assyria and builder of the walls of Babylon*

sēmita, –ae *f.* footpath, path

sēmivir, –ī *adj.* half-man; unmanly, effeminate

\*semper *adv.* always, ever, continually

sēmūstus, –a, –um half-burned, half-consumed

\*senātus, –ūs *m.* senate

senecta, –ae *f.* old age, age

\*senectūs, –ūtis *f.* old age; *personified*, Age

\*senex, senis old; *as noun, m.* old man; *comp.* senior older, elderly; *as noun*, senior, –ōris *m.* aged man, venerable man

sēnī, –ae, –a six each; six

senīlis, –e old man's, aged

†sēnsus, –ūs *m.* feeling, emotion; soul, spirit

\*sententia, –ae *f.* opinion, view, judgment, thought; purpose

\*sentiō, –īre, sēnsī, sēnsus perceive, note; understand, know

sentis, –is *m.* brier, bramble

sentus, –a, –um thorny; rough

\*sepeliō, –īre, –īvī (–iī), sepultus bury

\*septem *indecl. adj.* seven

septemgeminus, –a, –um sevenfold; of seven months

septēnī, –ae, –a seven at a time, seven each; seven

\*septimus, –a, –um seventh

\*sepulcrum, –ī *n.* grave; tomb; pyre; burial

sepultus, –a, –um buried; overcome

sequāx, –ācis following, pursuing

\*sequor, –ī, secūtus follow, pursue; attend, accompany; seek

sera, –ae *f.* a bar (*for a door*)

serēnō 1 make clear, clear away, calm; manifest

\*serēnus, –a, –um clear, cloudless; calm; fair, placid

Serestus, –ī *m. a comrade of Aeneas*

Sergestus, –ī *m. a comrade of Aeneas*

Sergius, –a, –um *a Roman family name*

seriēs, –ēī *f.* row; succession, series

\*sermō, –ōnis *m.* conversation, talk, speech, discourse; rumor, gossip

serō, –ere, –uī, sertus weave; converse; discuss

\*serō, –ere, sēvī, satus sow; beget; *partic.* satus, –a, –um sown; begotten of, son (*or* daughter) of

sērō *adv.* late

serpēns, –entis *m.* snake, serpent

\*serpō, –ere, serpsī creep, crawl; creep *or* steal upon, creep in

Serrānus, –ī *m. C. Atilius Regulus Serranus, famous for his opposition to Carthage in the First Punic War*

\*sertum, –ī *n.* wreath, garland

\*sērus, –a, –um late; too late; tardy

serva, –ae *f.* female slave

\*serviō 4 be a slave, serve

servitium, –ī *n.* slavery, bondage

\*servō 1 save, rescue; preserve, reserve, guard, maintain; nurse; keep, hold, contain; watch, observe; *partic.* servāns, –antis observant

\*seu *see* sīve

\*sevērus, –a, –um stern, strict, cruel; gloomy, dismal

\*sī *conj.* if, in case; if only; whether

sībilus, –a, –um hissing

Sibylla, –ae *f.* Sibyl, prophetess

\*sīc *adv.* so, thus, in this manner

Sicānia, –ae *f.* Sicily

Sicānius, –a, –um of Sicily, Sicilian

Sicānus, –a, –um of Sicily, Sicilian; *as noun*, Sicānī, –ōrum *m. pl.* Sicilians

siccō 1 dry; stanch; milk dry

\*siccus, –a, –um dry; thirsty; parched

sīcubi *adv.* if anywhere; wherever

Siculus, –a, –um of Sicily, Sicilian

sīdereus, –a, –um starry

\*sīdō, –ere, sīdī sit down; alight upon, perch upon

Sīdōn, –ōnis *f. a city of Phoenicia*

Sīdŏnius, –a, –um of Sidon, Sidonian

\*sīdus, –eris *n.* constellation, star; meteor; heaven; season

Sīgēus, –a, –um of Sigeum, *a promontory near Troy*

\*signō 1 mark, note; mark out, indicate; fix one's eyes upon

\*signum, –ī *n.* mark, sign, clew, signal; token, indication; figure, design; standard, ensign

\*silentium, –ī *n.* silence, stillness

\*sileō, –ēre, –uī be silent; *partic.* silēns, –entis silent, noiseless, still

silex, –icis *m. or f.* flint; crag, cliff

\*silva, –ae *f.* forest, woodland; growth, shoots

silvestris, –e rustic, woodland (*as adj.*)

Silvius, –ī *m. name of* 1) *a son of Aeneas by Lavinia;* 2) *a descendant, Silvius Aeneas*

\*similis, –e like, similar

Simoīs, –entis *m. a river near Troy*

simplex, –icis simple, unmixed, unpolluted, pure; frank, honest

\*simul *adv.* at the same time, at once; at the same time with, together with; simul ac (*occasionally* ac *is omitted*) as soon as

\*simulācrum, –ī *n.* likeness, image; semblance, imitation; statue; shade, phantom

*simulō 1 make like, counterfeit; feign, pretend
*sīn *conj.* but if
sincērus, –a, –um pure, chaste
*sine *prep. with abl.* without
*singulī, –ae, –a one each; single, separate, each
*sinister, –tra, –trum left, on the left hand
sinistra, –ae *f.* left hand
*sinō, –ere, sīvī, situs place; let, permit, allow, suffer
Sinōn, –ōnis *m. a Greek whose story helped induce the Trojans to take the Wooden Horse within the walls*
sinuō 1 bend, curve; cause to wind *or* writhe
*sinus, –ūs *m.* bend, curve; winding course; bosom; fold; sail; hollow, nook; bay, gulf
Sīrēnes, –um *f. pl.* Sirens, *fabulous creatures, part maiden, part bird, who lived on rocky islands off the coast of Campania, and by their singing enticed sailors to shipwreck*
Sirius, –ī *m. the Dog Star*
*sistō, –ere, stitī, status cause to stand, place, set; bring; stop, stay; uphold; come to a stand, settle, abide
sitiō 4 be thirsty
sitis, –is *f.* thirst; drought
situs, –ūs *m.* place, position; structure; neglect
*sīve *or* *seu *conj.* or if; or; sīve (seu) . . . sīve (seu) if . . . or if, whether . . . or, either . . . or
smaragdus, –ī *m.* emerald
sōbrius, –a, –um sober, moderate
*socer, –ī *m.* father-in-law; *pl.* parents-in-law
*societās, –ātis *f.* fellowship
sociō 1 ally, associate, make sharer, make an associate in; bind, unite
*socius, –a, –um allied, friendly, confederate; *as noun,* socius, –ī *m.* ally, associate, mate, companion, comrade; follower, friend
*sōl, sōlis *m.* sun; sunlight, sunshine; day
sōlācium, –ī *n.* consolation, solace, comfort
sōlāmen, –inis *n.* consolation, solace, comfort
*soleō, –ēre, solitus *semi-dep.* be wont, be accustomed
*solidus, –a, –um firm, compact, unyielding; solid, massive; stanch; entire
solium, –ī *n.* seat; throne
sollemne, –is *n.* solemn rite, holy offering
sollemnis, –e wonted, accustomed; sacred, solemn
sollertia, –ae *f.* cleverness
*sollicitō 1 trouble, disturb
sollicitus, –a, –um troubled, anxious
*sōlor, –ārī, –ātus console oneself for; comfort, cheer; relieve

*solum, –ī *n.* ground, land, soil, earth; surface; sward
*sōlus, –a, –um alone, only; lonely, solitary
*solvō, –ere, solvī, solūtus loosen, release, set free; relax; unbind, unfurl; break up; cast off; palsy, benumb; dispel, dismiss, banish; pay, discharge
somnium, –ī *n.* dream
*somnus, –ī *m.* sleep, slumber; dream; *personified,* Sleep
sonipēs, –pedis *m.* prancing steed, charger
†sonitus, –ūs *m.* sound, din; clang, blare, scream, crash, thunder
*sonō, –āre, sonuī, sonātūrus sound, resound; roar, thunder, scream, ring, rattle, twang, buzz; echo
sonōrus, –a, –um noisy, sounding; howling, roaring
sōns, sontis guilty
sonus, –ī *m.* sound, tone
sōpītus, –a, –um lulled (*to sleep*); dormant
*sopor, –ōris *m.* deep sleep, slumber; *personified,* Sleep
sopōrātus, –a, –um drowsy; soporific
sopōrifer, –era, –erum sleep-bringing *or* sleep-inducing
sopōrus, –a, –um sleepy, drowsy
sorbeō, –ēre, –uī suck in, swallow
sordēs, –is *f.* filth, squalor
sordidus, –a, –um filthy, squalid, dirty, stained; base, vile
*soror, –ōris *f.* sister
*sors, sortis *f.* lot, allotment; portion, fortune; fate, doom, destiny; oracle
sortior, –īrī, –ītus draw lots; assign by lot; allot
sortītus, –ūs *m.* allotment
sospitō 1 protect, preserve
*spargō, –ere, sparsī, sparsus scatter, strew; spread, circulate; sprinkle, spatter; bathe
Sparta, –ae *f. the capital of Laconia*
Spartānus, –a, –um of Sparta, Spartan
spatior, –ārī, –ātus walk to and fro; walk, wander, wander about
*spatium, –ī *n.* space; interval, distance; course; place; time
*speciēs, –ēī *f.* sight, appearance; form, shape
spectāculum, –ī *n.* sight, spectacle; grandstand
spectātor, –ōris *m.* spectator
*spectō 1 gaze at, view
specula, –ae *f.* lookout, watchtower
speculor, –ārī, –ātus keep watch, observe; descry
speculum, –ī *n.* mirror

*spēlunca, –ae *f.* cave, cavern, grotto
*spernō, –ere, sprēvī, sprētus spurn, scorn, disdain; slight; reject
*spērō 1 hope, hope for, expect; apprehend; believe
*spēs, –eī *f.* hope, expectation; object of hope
spīceus, –a, –um of ears (*of grain*)
*spīculum, –ī *n.* dart, arrow
spīna, –ae *f.* thorn
Spīō, –ūs *f.* *one of the Nereids*
spīra, –ae *f.* coil, fold
spīrābilis, –e that may be breathed, breathable
*spīritus, –ūs *m.* breath, breath of life; air; spirit, soul
*spīrō 1 breathe; breathe forth, exhale; blow
spissus, –a, –um thick, dense; compact
splendidus, –a, –um brilliant, magnificent, resplendent
*splendor, –ōris *m.* brilliance
*spoliō 1 strip; plunder, despoil, rob; deprive
*spolium, –ī *n.* (*usually* spolia, –ōrum *n. pl.*) spoils, booty, plunder; trophy
sponda, –ae *f.* couch
spondeō, –ēre, spopondī, spōnsus pledge, promise
spōnsa, –ae *f.* betrothed, promised bride
*sponte (*abl. of obsolete* spōns) *f.* of one's own accord *or* will, voluntarily; in one's own way
sprētus, –a, –um *see* spernō
*spūma, –ae *f.* froth, foam, spray
spūmeus, –a, –um foamy, foaming; foam-covered
spūmō 1 froth, foam; be covered with foam
spūmōsus, –a, –um foamy, foaming
spurcus, –a, –um dirty, foul
squāleō, –ēre, –uī be filthy; be unkempt
squālor, –ōris *m.* filth, squalor
squāma, –ae *f.* scale
squāmeus, –a, –um scaly
*stabilis, –e firm, fixed; enduring, lasting
stabulō, –āre have one's stable, have a stable; dwell, be kept
*stabulum, –ī *n.* stable, stall; covert, haunt
stāgnō 1 be stagnant; be sluggish; be overflowed
*stāgnum, –ī *n.* standing water, pool; sluggish stream; water
*statiō, –ōnis *f.* standing; resting place, haunt; roadstead, anchorage
*statuō, –ere, statuī, –ūtus set, place; found, establish; raise, throw up, erect, build
*stella, –ae *f.* star; meteor

stellātus, –a, –um set with stars; studded, gleaming
sterilis, –e barren, sterile, unfruitful
*sternō, –ere, strāvī, strātus spread out, strew, stretch on the ground; lay low; overthrow, destroy; slay; make smooth, level, pave
Sthenelus, –ī *m.* *a Greek, the charioteer of Diomedes*
Stilichō, –ōnis *m.* *a famous Roman general who* A.D. 398 *defeated Gildo, leader of an insurrection in Africa*
stīllō 1 drop, drip
stimulō 1 prick; goad on, spur; arouse
*stimulus, –ī *m.* spur
stīpes, –itis *m.* trunk
stīpō 1 crowd, pack, stow away; crowd around, throng, attend
stipula, –ae *f.* stalk, straw
*stirps, –pis *f.* stem, trunk; stock, blood, lineage; race; scion, offspring
*stō, –āre, stetī, stātūrus stand; rise, stand on end, be erect; be erected, be built; rest, be moored; stand firm, be strong; be supported; linger, remain, continue; be centered in; be resolved; *sometimes nearly equivalent to* sum
strāgēs, –is *f.* slaughter, carnage
strātum, –ī *n.* spread, coverlet; bed, couch
strātus, –a, –um *see* sternō
*strepitus, –ūs *m.* noise, din, uproar; hum, bustling
strepō, –ere, –uī rattle; be noisy; hum, buzz
*strīdeō, –ēre (*in Vergil apparently always* strīdō, –ere), strīdī creak, grate; howl, roar; rustle; whistle, whir; hiss; twang; gurgle
strīdor, –ōris *m.* creaking, clanging; roaring; whistling
*stringō, –ere, strīnxī, strictus graze; strip, trim; *partic.* strictus, –a, –um drawn
Strophades, –um *f. pl.* *two islands west of the Peloponnesus*
*struō, –ere, strūxī, strūctus heap up; build, erect; prepare, arrange; aim at; contrive, accomplish
Strȳmōn, –onis *m.* *a river in Macedonia*
†studium, –ī *n.* zeal, eagerness, desire; fondness, eager pursuit; partisan feeling, cheers, applause; faction, party
*stultus, –a, –um dull, foolish
stupefaciō, –ere, –fēcī, –factus stupefy, daze, stun
*stupeō, –ēre, –uī be dazed, be amazed, marvel; marvel at
stupor, –ōris *m.* stupidity

**stuppa, –ae** *f.* tow, hemp, oakum

**stuppeus, –a, –um** of tow, hempen

**Stygius, –a, –um** of the Styx, Stygian; of the underworld, infernal

**Styx, Stygis** *f. a fabled river in the underworld*

*suādeō, –ēre, suāsī, suāsūrus** urge, advise, counsel, persuade

**suāvis, –e** pleasant, agreeable

*sub** *prep.* 1) *with abl.,* under, below, beneath; at the foot of; close after, behind; in, within; at; among; 2) *with acc.,* under, below, beneath; to, toward; before; down to; near; after

**subāctus, –a, –um** *see* **subigō**

**subdō, –ere, –didī, –ditus** subdue

**subdolus, –a, –um** deceitful

†**subdūcō, –ere, –dūxī, –ductus** draw up, haul on shore, beach; remove from under; remove secretly, filch away

**subeō, –īre, –iī, –itus** go under; take up, bear; carry, draw; go into, go within, enter; draw near, approach; come after, follow; take another's place, succeed; enter one's mind, occur to; come up to, reach, gain

**subigō, –ere, –ēgī, –āctus** drive under, drive on, propel; force, compel; subdue, vanquish

*subitō** *adv.* suddenly, unexpectedly

*subitus, –a, –um** sudden, unexpected

**subjectus, –a, –um** *see* **subjiciō**

†**subjiciō, –ere, –jēcī, –jectus** place under; vanquish, make bow; *partic.* **subjectus, –a, –um** set beneath, lying beneath; conquered

**sublābor, –ī, –lāpsus** slip away, fail

**sublātus, –a, –um** *see* **tollō** *or* **sufferō**

*sublīmis, –e** aloft, on high, uplifted

**submergō, –ere, –mersī, –mersus** sink, submerge; drown

†**submittō, –ere, –mīsī, –missus** send under *or* down; subject; bring up

**submoveō, –ēre, –mōvī, –mōtus** drive away, remove

**subnectō, –ere, –nexuī, –nexus** bind under, fasten beneath; bind, fasten

**subnīxus, –a, –um** leaning upon, resting on; supported by

**subolēs, –is** *f.* offspring; child

**subrīdeō, –ēre, –rīsī** smile

**subrigō, –ere, surrēxī, surrēctus** raise, lift

**subsīdō, –ere, –sēdī, –sessūrus** settle down; sink, subside; sink to the bottom, remain

**subsistō, –ere, –stitī** stay behind; stop, halt

**subtēmen, –inis** *n.* woof; thread

**subter** *adv. and prep. with the acc.* under, below, beneath

**subtexō, –ere, –uī, –textus** weave under; obscure, veil

**subtrahō, –ere, –trāxī, –tractus** draw from under; withdraw; *pass.,* be swept from under, fly beneath

**suburgeō, –ēre** force up to, drive close to

**subvectō 1** convey to; transport, carry

**subvehō, –ere, –vexī, –vectus** carry; *pass. as middle,* ride, drive

**subvolvō, –ere** roll up

*succēdō, –ere, –cessī, –cessūrus** go under, take up; draw; go within, enter; draw near, approach

**successus, –ūs** *m.* success

**succingō, –ere, –cīnxī, –cīnctus** bind under; gird; clothe; equip, furnish

**succrēscō, –ere, –crēvī, –crētūrus** grow, be replaced

**succumbō, –ere, –cubuī, –cubitūrus** fall under, yield to

†**succurrō, –ere, –currī, –cursūrus** run under; go to the aid of, succour, relieve; enter one's mind, occur

**sūdō 1** sweat; reek with, be drenched with

**sūdor, –ōris** *m.* sweat, perspiration

*suēscō, –ere, suēvī, suētus** become accustomed; *perf.,* be accustomed, be wont; be trained

**sufferō, –ferre, sustulī, sublātus** bear up; withstand

**sufficiō, –ere, –fēcī, –fectus** dip in; suffuse; supply; be able

**suffundō, –ere, –fūdī, –fūsus** pour in, fill; suffuse, bedew

*suī** *(gen.),* **sibi** *(dat.),* **sē** *(acc. or abl.) reflexive pron.* himself, herself, itself; themselves; him, her, it; them

**sulcō 1** plow a furrow, plow

*sulcus, –ī** *m.* furrow; trench; track, trail

**sulpur, –uris** *n.* sulphur

*sum, esse, fuī, futūrus** be

*summa, –ae** *f.* chief point, substance; decision

**summum, –ī** *n.* surface; **summō tenus** up to the surface; barely

*summus, –a, –um** *(superl. of* **superus***)* highest, greatest, supreme, most important, principal, utmost, chief; top of, summit of; tip of; crest of, crown of; surface of; end of; last, final

*sūmō, –ere, sūmpsī, sūmptus** take, take up; adopt; employ; *with* **poenās,** exact

*super** *adv.* above; besides; too, in addition; over and above, more, left, remaining; *prep.* 1) *with acc.,* over, above; on, upon, on the heights of; beyond; 2) *with abl.*, on, upon; in behalf of, for; about, concerning

superbia, –ae *f.* pride, insolence, arrogance

*superbus, –a, –um proud, haughty, insolent, arrogant; gorgeous, splendid, magnificent

superēmineō, –ēre rise above, tower above

*superī, –ōrum *m. pl.* the gods above

superimpōnō, –ere, –posuī, –positus place upon

superinjiciō (superiniciō), –ere, –jēcī, –jectus throw upon

supernē *adv.* above, in the upper world

*superō 1 be above; mount to, rise above, overtop, tower above; pass over; pass beyond; be left over, survive, remain; be superior to; overcome, overpower, vanquish; surmount; win over, conciliate; pass by, win; slay, destroy; exult, be triumphant

superstes, –itis surviving

*supersum, –esse, –fuī be left over, remain, survive

†superus, –a, –um upper, above, on high; *as noun,* superī, –ōrum *m. pl.* the gods above

supīnus, –a, –um lying on the back; *of the hands,* with the palms upward; suppliant

suppleō, –ēre, –ēvī, –ētus fill up

*supplex, –icis kneeling, suppliant, humble

suppliciter *adv.* in the manner of suppliants, suppliantly, humbly

*supplicium, –ī *n.* punishment, penalty

suppōnō, –ere, –posuī, –positus place under; apply

*suprā *prep. with acc.* above, over

suprēmus, –a, –um last, final; extremity of; *as noun,* suprēmum, –ī *n.* the last; *pl.* the last offices *or* rites

sūra, –ae *f.* calf (*of the leg*); leg, ankle

*surgō, –ere, surrēxī, surrēctus raise up, prick up; rise, arise

sūs, suis *m. or f.* swine, pig

*suscipiō, –ere, –cēpī, –ceptus take up, lift up; undertake, attempt; reply

suscitō 1 stir up; arouse, excite

suspectus, –a, –um suspected, mistrusted

suspectus, –ūs *m.* upward look; height

*suspendō, –ere, –pendī, –pēnsus hang up; sling, suspend; dedicate, consecrate

suspēnsus, –a, –um hung up, exposed; anxious, distracted; uncertain; inspired, entranced

*suspiciō, –ere, –spexī, –spectus look up at; observe; suspect, mistrust

suspīrium, –ī *n.* sigh

suspīrō 1 sigh

sustulī *see* tollō *or* sufferō

susurrus, –ī *m.* murmur, humming

sūtilis, –e sewed, stitched, seamy

*suus, –a, –um his, her, its, one's, their; his own, her own, *etc.;* suitable, appropriate; favorable, prospering

Sȳchaeus, –ī *m. the husband of Dido*

syrtis, –is *f.* sandy shoal; Syrtis, –is *f.* the Syrtis, *one of two sandy and shallow bays on the northern coast of Africa*

## T

tābeō, –ēre melt away; be drenched, be dripping

tābēs, –is *f.* wasting; pining

tābēscō, –ere, tābuī waste away, melt

tābidus, –a, –um wasting

*tabula, –ae *f.* board, plank

tabulātum, –ī *n.* floor, story

tābum, –ī *n.* matter; gore

*taceō, –ēre, –uī, –itus be silent, be still; *partic.* tacitus, –a, –um silent, noiseless; in silence, unmentioned; in secret; hidden

tāctus, –ūs *m.* touch

*taeda, –ae *f.* pine wood; torch; nuptial torch; marriage

taedet, –ēre, –uit *impers.* it disgusts, it wearies; mē taedet I am weary of, I loathe

taedium, –ī *n.* loathing, disgust

Taenarius, –a, –um of Taenarus, *a promontory in Greece on which was a grotto leading to the underworld*

taenia, –ae *f.* ribbon, head band, fillet

taeter, –tra, –trum disgusting, foul, loathsome

tālāria, –ium *n. pl.* winged sandals; hem of a robe (*the heel part*)

talentum, –ī *n.* talent, *a Greek weight*

*tālis, –e such, of such sort; the following, as follows

*tam *adv.* so, so very; *with following* quam, as

Tamasēus, –a, –um pertaining to Tamasus, *a town on the island of Cyprus*

*tamen *adv.* yet, nevertheless, still

*tamquam *adv.* as, just as

Tanais, –is *m. a river in Europe (now the Don)*

*tandem *adv.* at length, at last; *in questions,* pray

*tangō, –ere, tetigī, tāctus touch; reach; move, affect; encounter; come home to one

Tantalis, –idis *f.* daughter of Tantalus; *i.e., Niobe*

Tantalus, –ī *m. son of Jupiter, punished in the underworld for insulting the gods*

*tantum *adv.* only, merely

*tantus, –a, –um so great, so much; so far

tardē *adv.* slowly, tardily

*tardō 1 make slow; hamper, hinder
*tardus, –a, –um slow; slowly passing; sluggish; lingering
Tarentum, –ī n. a town in Calabria
Tarquinius, –ī m. Tarquin; especially Tarquinius Priscus and Tarquinius Superbus, respectively the fifth and seventh kings of Rome
Tartareus, –a, –um of Tartarus; infernal
Tartarus, –ī m. and Tartara, –ōrum n. pl. Tartarus, the abode of the lost in the underworld; the underworld
taurīnus, –a, –um of a bull, a bull's
*taurus, –ī m. bull
*tēctum, –ī n. roof; shelter, covert; building, dwelling, house, palace; abode, habitation
Tegeaeus, –a, –um of Tegea, a town in Arcadia
tegmen and tegumen, –inis n. covering; garment; skin
*tegō, –ere, tēxī, tēctus cover; cloak, hide, conceal; shelter; shield, protect
tēla, –ae f. warp, web
*tellūs, –ūris f. earth; land, soil; personified, Earth
*tēlum, –ī n. missile, weapon; spear, javelin, arrow, shaft; blow
temerārius, –a, –um rash
temerō 1 treat rashly; profane, desecrate
temnō, –ere scorn, despise, defy
tēmō, –ōnis m. pole (of a chariot)
*temperantia, –ae f. moderation
temperō 1 restrain, control, calm, quiet; temper; refrain, refrain from
*tempestās, –ātis f. weather; bad weather, storm, tempest; personified, Storm-god
*templum, –ī n. consecrated place; temple, shrine, sanctuary
*temptō 1 test, try; search, probe; search for, seek for; attempt, endeavor
*tempus, –oris n. time, period, season; moment, juncture; suitable time, opportunity; pl. the temples, head
tenāx, –ācis tenacious, persistent, holding fast; clinging
*tendō, –ere, tetendī, tentus stretch, stretch out; hold out, extend; bend, turn; aim, direct; struggle, strive; make one's way, hold one's way, push on, proceed; steer; go; pitch one's tent
*tenebrae, –ārum f. pl. darkness, shades, gloom; shades of the dead
tenebrōsus, –a, –um dark, gloomy
Tenedos, –ī f. an island near Troy
*teneō, –ēre, –uī hold, have, keep, hold possession of, possess; occupy, inhabit; bind;

retain, hold back, detain, cling to; grasp, seize; reach; make, gain, win; derive
tener, –era, –erum tender, delicate
tentōrium, –ī n. tent
*tenuis, –e thin; fine-drawn, slender; delicate, feeble; gentle; airy, unsubstantial
tenus postpositive prep. with abl. up to, as far as, to, just to
*tepeō, –ēre be warm, be lukewarm
tepidus, –a, –um warm, lukewarm
*ter adv. three times, thrice
terebrō 1 bore, bore into, pierce
teres, –etis smooth, polished; round
tergeminus, –a, –um threefold, triple
*tergum, –ī n. back; chine; rear; body; skin, hide; ā tergō from behind
tergus, –oris n. back (of an animal); skin, hide
terminō 1 bound, limit
*terminus, –ī m. boundary, limit; consummation, goal
ternī, –ae, –a three each; three
ternus, –a, –um triple
terō, –ere, trīvī, trītus rub; graze, touch; wear away, waste, beat
*terra, –ae f. earth, world; ground, soil; land, country, region; personified, Terra parēns Mother Earth
terrēnus, –a, –um of the earth, earthly, earthy
*terreō, –ēre, terruī, territus affright, frighten, terrify; spread terror
terribilis, –e frightful, dreadful, fearful
terrificō, –āre terrify
terrificus, –a, –um fear-inspiring
territō, –āre terrify, frighten
*tertius, –a, –um third
*testis, –is m. or f. witness
*testor, –ārī, –ātus invoke, call to witness; swear by, swear; bear witness, attest
testūdō, –inis f. tortoise, tortoise shell, lyre; testudo, a military formation of overlapping shields; vaulted roof, roof
Teucer (Teucrus), –crī m. name of 1) the father-in-law of Dardanus, and the first of the Trojan kings; 2) a son of Telamon and half brother of Ajax
Teucrī, –ōrum m. pl. followers of Teucer, Trojans
Teucria, –ae f. the land of Teucer, Troy
*texō, –ere, texuī, textus weave; interweave, intermingle; frame, build
textilis, –e woven
textum, –ī n. (woven) cloth
*thalamus, –ī m. chamber, bed chamber; marriage bed, marriage

Thalīa, –ae *f. a sea nymph, daughter of Nereus*
Thapsus, –ī *f. a town and peninsula on the eastern coast of Sicily*
theātrum, –ī *n.* theater
Thēbae, –ārum *f. pl.* Thebes, *a city in Boeotia*
Themis, –idis *f. goddess of law and of prophecy*
Thersilochus, –ī *m. a Trojan ally*
thēsaurus, –ī *m.* treasure, hoard
Thēseus, –eī (–eos) *m. a fabled king of Athens*
Thessandrus, –ī *m. one of the Grecian host before Troy*
Thetis, –idis *f. a daughter of Nereus and the mother of Achilles*
Thisbē, –ēs *f. a Babylonian maiden, in love with Pyramus*
Thoās, –antis *m. one of the Grecian host before Troy*
Thrācius, –a, –um *of Thrace, Thracian*
Thrāx, –ācis *m.* a Thracian
Thrēicius,' –a, –um *Thracian*
Thrēissa, –ae *f.* a Thracian woman
Thybris, –idis *m.* the Tiber River
Thyias, –ados *f.* Bacchante, Thyiad
Thymbraeus, –a, –um *of Thymbra, a city near Troy, and the seat of a temple of Apollo; as noun,* Thymbraeus, –ī *m. another name for Apollo*
Thymoetēs, –ae *m. a Trojan*
thymum, –ī *n.* thyme
Tiberīnus, –a, –um *of the Tiber*
tigris, –is *m. or f.* tiger, tigress
Timāvus, –ī *m. a river in Northeastern Italy*
*timeō, –ēre, –uī fear, be afraid of; be apprehensive
†timidus, –a, –um timid, shrinking
†timor, –ōris *m.* fear, dread, apprehension, anxiety
*ting(u)ō, –ere, tīnxī, tīnctus wet; dip, bathe; stain
Tisiphonē, –ēs *f. one of the Furies*
Tītān, –ānis *m. a name given* 1) *to each of the six sons of Caelus and Terra;* 2) *to the sun-god as a son of Hyperion, a Titan*
Tītānia, –ae *f.* daughter of a Titan, *e.g., Pyrrha*
Tītānis, –idis *f.* daughter of a Titan, *e.g., Latona*
Tītānius, –a, –um *of a Titan*
Tīthōnus, –ī *m. the husband of Aurora*
titubō 1 totter, reel, stagger
titulus, –ī *m.* title, fame
Titus, –ī *m. a friend of Martial*
Tityos, –ī *m. a giant who offered violence to Latona*
Tītyrus, –ī *m. name of a shepherd*

Tmarius, –a, –um *of Tmarus, a mountain in Epirus*
*togātus, –a, –um of the toga; wearing the toga
tolerābilis, –e endurable, tolerable
*tollō, –ere, sustulī, sublātus lift up, raise up, raise; exalt; upheave, stir up; take away, carry off
*tondeō, –ēre, totondī, tōnsus cut close, clip, trim; shear; feed upon, crop; graze
tonitrus, –ūs *m.* thunder
*tonō, –āre, tonuī thunder, roar, rumble; loudly invoke
Torquātus, –ī *m. a Roman family name*
*torqueō, –ēre, torsī, tortus turn, twist, whirl; cause to curl; hurl, drive
torrēns, –entis *m.* torrent
*torreō, –ēre, torruī, tostus burn; parch, roast; boil, surge
tortus, –ūs *m.* twisting; coil
*torus, –ī *m.* cushion; couch, bed
*torvus, –a, –um stern, grim, fierce, savage
*tot *indecl. adj.* so many
*totidem *indecl. adj.* just as many, as many, the same number
*totiēns *adv.* so often, so many times
*tōtus, –a, –um the whole, entire, all
*trabs, trabis *f.* beam, timber; doorpost; ship, bark
tractābilis, –e manageable; yielding, gracious; nōn tractābile violent, inclement
*tractō 1 handle
tractus, –ūs *m.* expanse; region, quarter
*trādō, –ere, trādidī, –ditus hand over, give over, surrender
*trahō, –ere, trāxī, tractus draw, drag; sweep along; carry away, lead, bring; draw in, absorb; drag out, spend, prolong
trājiciō (trāiciō), –ere, –jēcī, –jectus throw across, pass across, pass; pass through, pierce
trāmes, –itis *m.* cross-path; path; course
trānō 1 swim across; float over, sail over; fly over, fly through
tranquillus, –a, –um calm, tranquil; *as noun,* tranquillum, –ī *n.* calm weather
*trāns *prep. with acc.* across, over, beyond
trānscrībō, –ere, –scrīpsī, –scrīptus transcribe; transfer
trānscurrō, –ere, –currī (–cucurrī), –cursus run across, shoot across
†trānseō, –īre, –īvī (–iī), –itus go across, pass over; pass by, pass, elapse
trānsferō, –ferre, –tulī, –lātus carry across; transfer, remove

trānsfīgō, –ere, –fīxī, –fīxus thrust through; pierce, transfix

trānsiliō, –īre, –uī leap across

trānsitus, –ūs m. passage

†trānsmittō, –ere, –mīsī, –missus send across; hand over, transfer, assign; *with reflexive*, go across, cross

trānsportō 1 carry across, transport

trānstrum, –ī n. bench, thwart

trānsversus, –a, –um across one's course; across, athwart

tremefaciō, –ere, –fēcī, –factus cause to tremble; *pass.*, tremble, shake

tremendus, –a, –um dread, awful

tremēscō, –ere tremble, shake, quake; tremble at

tremibundus, –a, –um trembling

*tremō, –ere, –uī tremble, shake, quiver; tremble at, dread

tremor, –ōris m. trembling, shudder, shiver

trepidō 1 tremble, shake; be in fear; scurry about

*trepidus, –a, –um trembling, shaking, quaking; agitated, anxious

*trēs, tria three

tricorpor, –oris having three bodies, three-bodied

tridēns, –entis m. three-pointed spear; trident

trietēricus, –a, –um triennial (*really biennial by our system, which does not count both ends of a period of time*)

trifaux, –faucis having three throats

trifidus, –a, –um three-cleft, forked

trīgintā *indecl. adj.* thirty

trilīx, –īcis triply-woven, three-ply

Trīnacria, –ae f. Sicily

Trīnacrius, –a, –um of Sicily, Sicilian

Triōnēs, –um m. pl. the constellations of the Great and Little Bear

triplex, –icis threefold, triple

tripūs, –odis m. tripod, oracle

*trīstis, –e sad, mournful, sorrowful, unhappy; melancholy, gloomy, dreary, dismal; dread, grim, woeful, baleful

trisulcus, –a, –um three-furrowed, three-forked

Trītōn, –ōnis m. a sea-god, son of Neptune

Trītōnia, –ae f. an epithet or name of Minerva

Trītōnis, –idis f. an epithet or name of Minerva

†triumphō 1 celebrate a triumph; triumph over, conquer

*triumphus, –ī m. triumph, triumphal procession

Trivia, –ae f. an epithet or name of Diana

trivium, –ī n. crossroads, a place where three ways meet

Trōas, –adis f. a Trojan woman

Trōilus, –ī m. a son of Priam

Trōius, –a, –um of Troy, Trojan

Trōja, –ae f. Troy

Trōjānus, –a, –um of Troy, Trojan

Trōjugena, –ae m. or f. born at Troy, a Trojan

Trōs, –ōis m. a Trojan; as adj., Trojan

trucīdō 1 butcher, slay

trudis, –is f. pole, pike, boat hook

trūdō, –ere, trūsī, trūsus push, push along

truncō 1 cut off, strip

*truncus, –ī m. trunk (of a tree); headless body, trunk

truncus, –a, –um stripped, lopped; maimed, mutilated

trux, trucis wild, fierce, harsh

*tū, tuī thou, you

†tuba, –ae f. trumpet

*tueor, –ērī, tūtus watch over; guard, protect; look at, gaze upon, behold

Tullus, –ī m. Tullus Hostilius, the third king of Rome

*tum adv. then, at that time; thereupon; further, besides

*tumeō, –ēre swell, be swollen

†tumidus, –a, –um swelling, swollen; dashing, violent

tumulō 1 entomb, bury

*tumultus, –ūs m. uprising, upheaval; uproar, confusion, tumult

*tumulus, –ī m. mound, hill, hillock; grave, tomb

*tunc adv. then, at that time

*tundō, –ere, tutudī, tūnsus strike, beat; assail; importune

tunica, –ae f. tunic, an undergarment

*turba, –ae f. mob, crowd, throng; troop, band; herd, flock

†turbidus, –a, –um wild, disordered, troubled, agitated; dark, murky, turbid

†turbō 1 crowd, throng; throw into confusion, agitate, disturb; scatter; trouble, perplex; be troubled, be in a panic

*turbō, –inis m. whirling motion; whirlwind; storm, tempest; wind, blast

turdus, –ī m. thrush

tūreus, –a, –um of frankincense

turgidus, –a, –um distended, swollen

tūricremus, –a, –um incense-burning

turma, –ae f. troop of cavalry, squadron

*turpis, –e ugly; foul, filthy, loathsome; base, shameful, disgraceful

*turris, –is f. tower, turret

turrītus, –a, –um turreted; with turreted diadem; tower-like turtur, –ūris m. turtledove

tūs, tūris n. frankincense

tussiō, –īre cough

tussis, –is f. cough

tūtāmen, –inis n. defense, protection

tūtēla, –ae f. guardianship; guardian

tūtor, –ārī, –ātus guard, protect, defend; favor, support

*tūtus, –a, –um safe, protected; sheltered; secure, trustworthy; as noun, tūtum, –ī n. safety, shelter

*tuus, –a, –um thy, your; as noun, tuī, –ōrum m. pl. your comrades

Tȳdeus, –eī m. one of the Seven against Thebes, and the father of Diomedes

Tȳdīdēs, –ae m. son of Tydeus, i.e., Diomedes

Tyndaris, –idis f. daughter of Tyndareus, an appellation loosely used of Helen

Typhōius, –a, –um of Typhoeus, a giant destroyed by the thunderbolts of Jupiter

tyrannus, –ī m. king, ruler; tyrant, despot

Tyrius, –a, –um of Tyre, Tyrian; as noun, Tyriī, –ōrum m. pl. the Tyrians, the Carthaginians

Tyros, –ī f. Tyre, a famous city of Phoenicia

Tyrrhēnus, –a, –um Tyrrhenian, Tuscan

# U

*ūber, –eris n. udder, breast; bosom; richness, fertility, fruitfulness

ūber, –eris adj. rich, fertile, fruitful

*ubi interrog. adv. where? as rel. adv. where, when, as soon as

ubīque adv. anywhere, everywhere

Ūcalegōn, –ontis m. a Trojan

ūdus, –a, –um wet, moist, damp

*ulcīscor, –ī, ultus avenge

Ulixēs, –ī m. Ulysses

*ūllus, –a, –um any, any one

ulmus, –ī f. elm tree

*ulterior, –ius further, farther, remoter

*ultimus, –a, –um furthest, most distant, remotest; last, final; extreme, most exacting; as noun, ultima, –ōrum n. pl. the end, goal

*ultor, –ōris m. avenger

†ultrā 1) adv. further, more; 2) prep. with acc. beyond

ultrīx, –īcis avenging, vengeful; as noun, f. avenger

*ultrō adv. beyond; besides, moreover; actually; unexpectedly; without being accosted; of one's own will, voluntarily

ultus, –a, –um see ulcīscor

ululātus, –ūs m. howl; wail, shriek

*ululō 1 howl, wail, shriek, cry; invoke or address with shrieks

ulva, –ae f. sedge grass

umbō, –ōnis m. boss (of a shield); shield

*umbra, –ae f. shade, shadow, darkness, gloom; ghost, phantom

umbrifer, –era, –erum shade-giving, shady

umbrō 1 cover with shade, shade

ūmectō 1 wet, moisten, bedew

ūmēns, –entis damp, moist, dewy

*umerus, –ī m. shoulder

*ūmidus, –a, –um moist, damp, dewy; watery, liquid

*umquam adv. at any time, ever

*ūnā adv. together, at the same time, together with

ūnanimus, –a, –um of one mind, having the same feelings; sympathizing

ūnctus, –a, –um see unguō

*uncus, –a, –um crooked, hooked

*unda, –ae f. wave, billow; waters, sea, stream

*unde interrog. adv. whence? from whom or which? from which or what source? as rel. adv., whence, from which

*undique adv. from all sides, on all sides, everywhere

undō 1 rise or roll in waves, surge, swell; seethe, sway, flutter

undōsus, –a, –um full of waves, billowy, surging; wave-washed

unguentum, –ī n. ointment, perfume

*unguis, –is m. fingernail, claw

unguō, –ere, ūnxī, ūnctus anoint, smear

ūnicus, –a, –um one and only

*ūnus, –a, –um one; only one, only, alone; single; the same; common, unchanged; ad ūnum to the last one, to a man

*urbs, urbis f. town, city

*urgeō, –ēre, ursī push, press, urge on; press hard, pursue; press down upon; punish, torment

urna, –ae f. jar, urn, vase

*ūrō, –ere, ussī, ustus burn; destroy; worry, vex; pass., be consumed, burn with love

ursa, –ae f. she-bear

*usquam adv. anywhere

*usque adv. as far as; ever, constantly, continually

*ūsus, –ūs m. use, purpose

*ut or *utī adv. and conj.: 1) interrog. adv., how? 2) rel. adv., as, just as; where; 3) conj., when, as; that, in order that; so that; ut prīmum as soon as

**utcumque** *adv. and conj.* in whatever way, however

*****uterque, utraque, utrumque** either; each

**uterus, –ī** *m.* belly

*****utinam** *adv.* oh that, would that

*****ūtor, –ī, ūsus** use, employ, make use of; enjoy

**utrōque** *adv.* to either side, in either direction

**ūva, –ae** *f.* bunch of grapes, grapes

*****uxor, –ōris** *f.* wife

**uxōrius, –a, –um** excessively devoted to one's wife, overfond

## V

**vacca, –ae** *f.* cow, heifer

**vacō** 1 be empty, be free from; *impers.*, there is time, there is leisure

*****vacuus, –a, –um** empty, vacant, unoccupied, deserted; clear

*****vādō, –ere** go, walk, proceed, advance; make haste, rush

*****vadum, –ī** *n.* shoal, shallow place, shallow; bottom, depths; waters, sea

**vāgīna, –ae** *f.* sheath, scabbard

**vāgītus, –ūs** *m.* crying, wailing

*****vagor, –ārī, –ātus** stroll, rove, wander about, roam; spread abroad; ride to and fro

**vagulus, –a, –um** wandering

*****valeō, –ēre, –uī, –itūrus** be strong, be powerful; be able, can; **valē, valēte** farewell

**valide** *adv.* strongly

†**validus, –a, –um** strong, stout, stanch, sturdy; powerful, vigorous

*****vallēs** *or* **vallis, –is** *f.* valley, vale

**valva, –ae** *f.* door

*****vānus, –a, –um** empty, idle; groundless, fruitless; false, cheating, deceiving

**vapor, –ōris** *m.* steam; heat, fire

*****varius, –a, –um** various, manifold; different, chequered, varied, varying; variegated, diversified; changeable, inconstant, fluctuating

*****vāstō** 1 lay waste, ravage, pillage

*****vāstus, –a, –um** waste, wild, desolate; vast, huge, immense, enormous, mighty

*****vātēs, –is** *m. or f.* seer, prophet, prophetess, soothsayer; poet, bard

*****–ve** *enclitic conj.* or

**vectō** 1 carry, convey

*****vehō, –ere, vexī, vectus** bear, carry, convey; bring, usher in; *pass. as middle*, sail, ride

*****vel** *conj.* or; **vel ... vel** either ... or

**vēlāmen, –inis** *n.* covering; veil; garment, clothing

**Velīnus, –a, –um** of Velia, *a town on the coast of Lucania*

**vēlivolus, –a, –um** sail-winged, studded with sails

*****vellō, –ere, vellī (vulsī), vulsus** pluck, pull up, tear up

**vellus, –eris** *n.* fleece; wool; fillet

*****vēlō** 1 cover, veil, wrap; equip with sails; bind, wreathe, adorn

**vēlōciter** swiftly

*****vēlōx, –ōcis** swift, fleet, quick

*****vēlum, –ī** *n.* sail; awning, canvas; **vēla dare,** set sail

*****velut** *or* **velutī** *adv. and conj.* just as, even as

**vēna, –ae** *f.* vein; metal

**vēnābulum, –ī** *n.* hunting spear

**vēnātrīx, –īcis** *f.* huntress

*****vēndō, –ere, –didī, –ditus** put on sale, sell

**venēnō** 1 poison, make poisonous

*****venēnum, –ī** *n.* drug, love charm, potion; poison, venom

**venerābilis, –e** worthy of veneration, revered, venerable, holy

*****veneror, –ārī, –ātus** pray to, beseech; worship, adore

*****venia, –ae** *f.* favor, indulgence

*****veniō, –īre, vēnī, ventūrus** come, arrive; go

*****vēnor, –ārī, –ātus** hunt

**venter, –tris** *m.* belly; hunger

**ventōsus, –a, –um** windy; stormy, tempestuous

*****ventus, –ī** *m.* wind, breeze; blast; air

**Venus, –eris** *f. the goddess of Love*

**venustus, –a, –um** lovely, charming

**vēr, vēris** *n.* spring

*****verber, –eris** *n.* lash, blow

**verberō** 1 beat, lash; strike

*****verbum, –ī** *n.* word; utterance

**vērē** *adv.* truly

*****vereor, –ērī, –itus** respect; fear

**Vergilius, –ī** *m. famous Roman poet*

†**vērō** *adv.* in truth, in fact, indeed, really

**verrō, –ere, verrī, versus** sweep, sweep over; skim over, skim

**versō** 1 turn about, whirl; roll, toss; ply, execute; turn, direct; turn over, ponder, meditate

*****versus, –ūs** *m.* turning; row, tier

*****vertex, –icis** *m.* highest point, top, peak, summit; zenith; crown (*of the head*), head; whirlpool

*****vertō, –ere, vertī, versus** turn about, turn, change, alter; twist, ply; overturn, destroy; invert; drive away; *pass. as middle*, turn, revolve, march on

verū, –ūs n. spit

*vērum conj. but, but yet, but in truth

*vērus, –a, –um true, sincere, real, genuine; as noun, vērum, –ī n. truth

vēscor, –ī feed upon, eat, devour; enjoy

*Vesper, –eris (–erī) m. evening; personified, Vesper, the evening star; the West

vespillō, –ōnis m. undertaker

Vesta, –ae f. the goddess of the hearth

*vester, –tra, –trum your, yours

vēstibulum, –ī n. entrance, portal, fore-court

*vēstīgium, –ī n. footprint, footstep, track; trace, token

vēstīgō, –āre track; search, seek

vestiō 4 clothe, cover

*vestis, –is f. covering; clothing, dress; robe, garment; tapestry, drapery

*vetō, –āre, vetuī, vetitus forbid, prohibit; oppose

*vetus, –eris old, aged, ancient; former

†vetustās, –ātis f. length of time, lapse of time

vetustus, –a, –um old, ancient, well-seasoned

*vexō 1 shake; harass

*via, –ae f. way, road, street; course, path; journey, passage; entrance

viātor, –ōris m. wayfarer, traveller

vibrō 1 shake, brandish; dart, vibrate

vīburnum, –ī n. a low tree or shrub

vīcīnia, –ae f. vicinity, neighborhood; nearness

†vīcīnus, –a, –um near, near-by, neighboring, adjoining

*vicis (gen., no nom. being found), f. change, interchange; chance, fortune, fate; turn

vicissim adv. in turn

†victor, –ōris m. victor, winner, conqueror; as adj., victorious, triumphant

†victōria, –ae f. victory

victrīx, –īcis victorious, triumphant; as noun, f. victress

†vīctus, –ūs m. living, sustenance; food

*videō, –ēre, vīdī, vīsus see, behold, perceive, observe, witness; understand; pass., be seen; seem, appear; seem best

viduō 1 deprive

viduus, –a, –um bereft of wife or husband

vigeō, –ēre, –uī thrive, grow strong, flourish; be powerful

vigil, –ilis awake, wakeful, sleepless, watchful; perpetual, ever-burning; as noun, vigil, –ilis m. watchman, guard

*vigilō 1 be awake, watch; wake up, awake

*vīgintī indecl. adj. twenty

vigor, –ōris m. force, energy

*vīlla, –ae f. farmhouse

villus, –ī m. shaggy hair; nap (of cloth)

vīmen, –inis n. twig, stem; shoot

*vinciō, –īre, vīnxī, vīnctus bind; fetter, pinion; encircle

vinclum see vinculum

*vincō, –ere, vīcī, victus conquer, be victorious, prevail; overcome, overpower; defeat, subdue, vanquish; prevail over, beat; dispel, banish; win, achieve

*vinculum or vinclum, –ī n. fastening; chain, fetter; tie, bond, thong; rope, cord, cable; imprisonment, confinement

vindex, –icis m. or f. defender; avenger, punisher

*vindicō 1 claim; rescue, deliver, defend

*vīnum, –ī n. wine

violābilis, –e that may be profaned, violable

violēns, –entis impetuous, eager; gracious

violentus, –a, –um violent, boisterous, impetuous

*violō 1 injure, wrong, profane, violate

vīpereus, –a, –um of vipers, snaky, of snakes

*vir, virī m. man; hero; husband

virectum, –ī n. green place, grassy spot; greensward, glade

vireō, –ēre –uī be green

virga, –ae f. twig, shoot; wand

virgineus, –a, –um of a maiden, maiden's, virgin (as adj.)

*virgō, –inis f. maid, maiden, virgin; especially Virgō Astraea, goddess of justice

virgultum, –ī n. thicket, copse

viridāns, –antis green, verdant

*viridis, –e green, verdant; fresh, blooming; hale, vigorous

virīlis, –e manly

*virtūs, –ūtis f. manliness; bravery, courage; valor, heroism; prowess, heroic deed; merit

*vīs, vis f. strength, might, power, potency; force, violence; pack; pl. strength, power

viscum, –ī n. mistletoe

*vīscus, –eris n. flesh; vital organs, vitals

*vīsō, –ere, vīsī, vīsus visit, go to see; see, behold

vīsum, –ī n. sight, vision; apparition, portent

†vīsus, –ūs m. seeing; sight; vision

*vīta, –ae f. life; spirit

vītālis, –e vital, of life

vitiō 1 spoil, injure

vītis, –is f. vine, grapevine

*vitium, –ī n. flaw; crack

*vītō 1 shun, avoid

*vitta, –ae f. fillet; chaplet, headband

vitulus, –ī m. bullock

vīvidus, –a, –um lively, vigorous; ardent

*vīvō, -ere, vīxī, vīctūrus live, be alive; abide, linger
*vīvus, -a, -um alive, living; flowing, running; natural, lifelike
*vix adv. scarcely, barely, hardly; with difficulty
vōciferor, -ārī, -ātus cry out, exclaim, scream
*vocō 1 call, address; name; call by name, mention; invite, summon; call upon, invoke, challenge
volātilis, -e winged, flying
volātus, -ūs m. flight
volitō 1 fly, fly about, flit; float
*volō 1 fly; float, hover; speed, shoot; be hurled; as noun, volantēs, -tum m. or f. pl. flying creatures, birds
*volō, velle, voluī be willing, wish, desire; will; purpose, intend, mean; give out, represent
volūbilis, -e rolling
*volucer, -cris, -cre flying, winged; fleet, swift, fleeting; as noun, volucris, -is f. winged creature, flying creature, bird
volūmen, -inis n. roll; coil; fold
*voluntās, -ātis f. will, wish, desire; consent
*voluptās, -ātis f. pleasure, joy, delight
volūtō 1 turn over and over, roll; whirl; writhe; cause to resound, roll back, echo; revolve, ponder, meditate
*volvō, -ere, volvī, volūtus roll, turn, roll on, sweep along; hurl, toss; unroll; run the round of, undergo; order, ordain, decree; pass. as middle, roll, flow, glide; wallow, writhe, grovel

vōmer, -eris m. plowshare
vomō, -ere, -uī, -itus throw up, belch forth; pour forth, discharge
vorāgō, -inis f. abyss, chasm, depth, whirlpool
vorō 1 swallow, engulf
vōtum, -ī n. vow, votive offering; prayer, supplication
*voveō, -ēre, vōvī, vōtus vow, promise solemnly
*vōx, vōcis f. voice; utterance, speech; tone, note, cry, sound, word
Vulcānius, -a, -um of Vulcan
Vulcānus, -ī m. Vulcan, the god of fire; fire
vulgō 1 spread abroad, make known
vulgō adv. commonly, generally
*vulgus, -ī n. (rarely masculine) common people, crowd, throng; herd, mob, rabble
*vulnus, -eris n. wound, injury; pain, pang, resentment; stroke, blow; weapon
vulpēs, -is f. fox
vultur, -uris m. vulture
*vultus, -ūs m. countenance, face; expression, look; in pl., the features

### X

Xanthus, -ī m. the name of 1) a river near Troy; 2) a river in Epirus, named after that near Troy; 3) a river in Lycia

### Z

Zacynthos, -ī f. an island west of the Peloponnesus
Zephyrus, -ī m. west wind; wind

# Participles

|        | Active                  | Passive                  |
|--------|-------------------------|--------------------------|
| Pres.  | monēns, monentis        | ———                      |
| Perf.  | ———                     | monitus (esse)           |
| Fut.   | monitūrus (esse)        | monendus, -a, -um (esse) |

# Present System

## Active

### Present Tense

Present stem + person endings: o, s, t, et cetera

### Imperfect Tense

Present stem + ba + person endings: o, s, t, etc.

### Future Tense

1st & 2nd conj.: Present stem + bi + person endings: bo, bis, etc.

3rd & 4th: Present stem + ē + person endings: Ex. ducam, ducēs, etc.

## Passive

### Present Tense

Present stem + passive endings: r, ris, tur, etc.

### Imperfect Tense

Present stem + ba + passive person endings: r, ris, tur, etc.

### Future Tense

1st & 2nd: Present stem + bi + passive person endings: Ex. bor, beris, etc.

3rd & 4th: Present stem + ē + passive person endings: Ex. ducar, duceris, etc.

## Perfect System
### Active
#### Perfect Tense

Perfect stem + special person endings; ī, istī, etc.

#### Past Perfect Tense

Perfect stem + era + regular person endings: m, s, t, etc.

#### Future Perfect Tense

Perfect stem + eri + regular person endings: ero, eris, etc.


### Passive
#### Perfect Tense

Perfect passive participle with present tense of sum

#### Past Perfect Tense

Perfect passive participle with imperfect of sum

#### Future Perfect Tense

Perfect passive participle with future of sum